2005
FACTS & FIGURES

TABLES FOR THE CALCULATION OF DAMAGES

AUSTRALIA
Lawbook Co.
Sydney

CANADA and U.S.A.
Carswell
Toronto

HONG KONG
Sweet & Maxwell
Asia

NEW ZEALAND
Brookers
Auckland

SINGAPORE AND MALAYSIA
Sweet & Maxwell Asia
Singapore and Kuala Lumpur

2005
FACTS & FIGURES

TABLES FOR THE CALCULATION OF DAMAGES

Compiled and Edited by:

Members of the
Professional Negligence Bar Association

General Editor: Robin de Wilde Q.C.

LONDON
SWEET & MAXWELL
2005

Published in 2005 by
Sweet & Maxwell Limited of
100 Avenue Road, Swiss Cottage
London, NW3 3PF
www.sweetandmaxwell.co.uk

Designed and typeset by J&L Composition, Filey, North Yorkshire
Printed in Great Britain by Bath Press, Bath

No natural forests were destroyed to make this product:
only farmed timber was used and re-planted.

ISBN 0421 905 301

A CIP catalogue record for this book is available from the British Library.

ACKNOWLEDGEMENTS

The editors who prepared this edition were Robin de Wilde Q.C., Simon Levene, Peter Jennings, Harry Trusted, Tejina Mangat and Michael Jarvis (of Dixon Wilson Chartered Accountants).

We wish to acknowledge and appreciate the assistance we derived from the Family Law Bar Association and their permission to use these tables taken from At a Glance (and its electronic companion @ a Glance): Tables D1 (Interest Base Rates), H1 and H2 (Social Security Benefits), H4 (Foster Care Allowances) and H6 (Comparable Earnings).

We are grateful to Barclays Capital for the use of their table at F2 (Barclays Equity Index).

We are grateful to Gayle Siblock who kindly provided us with the BUPA hospital charges, Table I3.

Our thanks go to Robert Owen of Bacon & Woodrow for preparation of the Inflation Table at E2.

We are grateful to Adrian Gallop, Government Actuary for his assistance in preparing the second table in B3, in respect of projected changes of mortality into the future.

We are very grateful to Paul Stagg for his rewriting of the benefits material in Group H.

We are grateful to Rodney Nelson Jones of Field Fisher Waterhouse and Butterworths for allowing us to use and to develop his table for the calculation of special damage interest in D4.

Permission to use Table D9 (Judicial Rates of Interest) was given by W. Green.

We are grateful to Emap Consumer Media Limited, publishers of *Parker's Car Price Guide* on whose figures calculations in Table I8 are based.

Halifax plc gave us the up-to-date material for Tables E3 and E4 showing House Price Indices.

FTSE gave us permission to use the FTSE 100 Index and FTSE A All-share Index at Table F1.

Permission to use Table I5 (AA Technical Services Motoring Costs) was given by the AA Motoring Trust.

Our thanks go to Nicholas Leviseur for preparation of the notes on the Motability Scheme at I8.

We would like to thank Master Lush of the Court of Protection for his help.

We would like to thank Niall Baker and Ian Potter of Irwin Mitchell for the reworking of Table H5.

The historical information at Table I1 was provided by the British Nursing Association.

Permission to reproduce the Code of Best Practice on Rehabilitation at I10 was given to us by Bodily Injury Claims Management Association.

Table I13 (the Perpetual Calendar) is reproduced with permission from the International Management Diary published by Collins Debden Australia.

HMSO gave us kind permission to use Table B2 (Ogden Tables), Table B3 (Life Tables), Table D2 (the Table of Real and Nominal Interest Rates and Price Inflation), Table C3 (Average Earnings Index), Table C4 (Average Weekly Earnings), Table C5 (the Average Earnings Statistics) and the material from NHS leaflet HC13, NHS rates. The Inland Revenue and HMSO gave us permission to use the material in Table I7 (Taxation of Car and Fuel Benefits).

We are grateful to Peter Dickerson of Baker Tilly for helping us with Table F3 (Index-linked stock).

We are grateful to Keith Carter and Jenny Changreau of Keith Carter & Associates for the research undertaken in preparing the tables in C2 to C5.

Crown Copyright is reproduced with the permission of HMSO.

FOREWORD TO THE FIRST EDITION

by the Hon. Mr Justice Bell

The assessment of damages for personal injuries and consequential losses has become a matter of increasingly intricate calculation. Detailed schedules of damages and counter-schedules are vital to the proper portrayal of claim and defence to claim but they are arduous and time consuming to compile. Much the same building blocks of information and aids to calculation are required over and over again. This volume has gathered many of the most frequently used building blocks and aids together in a readily accessible form and those who prepare, argue and settle such cases should be grateful for it. Robin de Wilde and his committee have put a lot of work into what is in fact a manual of very practical assistance and they are to be congratulated on a new venture which should mature year by year with the help of your own suggestions.

May 1996

INTRODUCTION TO THE TENTH EDITION

"In the space of one hundred and seventy-six years the Lower Mississippi has shortened itself two hundred and forty-two miles. That is an average of a trifle over one mile and a third per year. Therefore, any calm person, who is not blind or idiotic, can see that in the Old Oolitic Silurian Period, just a million years ago next November, the Lower Mississippi River was upwards of one million three hundred thousand miles long, and stuck out over the Gulf of Mexico like a fishing-rod. And by the same token any person can see that seven hundred and forty-two years from now the Lower Mississippi will be only a mile and three-quarters long, and Cairo and New Orleans will have joined their streets together, and be plodding comfortably along under a single mayor and a mutual board of aldermen. There is something fascinating about science. One gets such wholesale returns of conjecture out of such a trifling investment of fact."

Mark Twain: "Life on the Mississippi".

This is the Tenth edition. It is hoped that we have returned to the normal timings, after the gross delays of last year. The editorial team remains constant, merely a year older and some of us a trifle wiser. The publication, perhaps through the delay and perhaps because of the insertion of the 5th edition of the Ogden Tables, sold more copies than ever before.

I begin to have sympathy with the Victorian High Court judge, who when told of a proposed reform said: "Reform, reform, aren't things bad enough as they are?" However, some things improve. The correspondence which I invite each year, and promptly reply to, has diminished. This is despite the occasional errors endemic in a publication which attempts to convey a vast quantity of factual and arithmetical material. Each year we go through an exhaustive proof reading process, which has attracted its own variety of psychiatric obsessional disorder, yet to be recognised in the textbooks. We look for ways to improve our search for errors. You, gentle reader, are asked, as always to help us in our search for perfection by telling us of any faults you find.

The Periodical Payments regime

On April 1, 2005, the new Periodical Payments regime came into effect, itself a product of the Courts Act 2003.

We have taken an editorial decision not to offer any help in *Facts & Figures* until a pattern of periodical payment orders have emerged and then, only if we are able to provide useful guidance to practitioners, to do so. This is not possible at present. One can only admire the zeal and determination of Lord Justice Dyson, who with his usual energy, has laid the foundation stones for this regime. The evolution of the practice and the creation of the first periodical payment orders will be interesting to watch.

The discount rate

This has been and will continue to be the focus of criticism particularly when our own chart (Table F3) indicates what has happened to the actual rates and the rolling three year index. There is also the complex question of indexation and the future upward costs of care—"wage cost inflation"—and how it is to be properly treated in the present lump sum regime. For those who cannot sleep at nights, there have been a series of articles in the Journal of Personal Injury Law by Mr Rowland Hogg, FCA, William Norris, QC and myself.

Clinical Negligence and publicly funded work

Focus No 47, April 2005, issued on behalf of the Legal Services Commission, has revealed that firstly, public funding for clinical negligence will not be curtailed as was anticipated and the costs benefit thresholds for Clinical Negligence cases will be raised to match those in the General Funding Code. Secondly, in respect of Personal Injury, the exclusion in Schedule 2 is to be widened to exclude all personal injury proceedings other than Clinical Negligence cases and cases covered by Directions.

Rehabilitation

In this edition we publish the 2004 Rehabilitation Code together with the updated Practitioner's Guide to Rehabilitation. The latter is a new feature for Facts & Figures and will be found at section 110. Rehabilitation is now mentioned in the revised Personal Injury Protocol, published in 2004. It also provides for an "Immediate Needs Assessment" that can be provided by an independent provider, so that the subsequent report is used wholly outside litigation. Parties that subscribe to the BICMA Agreement can find help with the implementation of proposed rehabilitation solutions. Avoidance can only take place if good reason is supplied in writing by either party. Treatment reports as a result of and post the Immediate Needs Assessment are discoverable in the same way as normal medical records. For more information on rehabilitation I refer you to: *www.bicma.org.uk*

Court of Protection matters

Master Denzil Lush, the present Master, could not have been more helpful, and it is through Master Lush's assistance that I have found Niall Baker and Ian Potter, partners in Irwin Mitchell in Sheffield, specialising in receivership and Court of Protection matters, who provide me with comments and practical advice on this area. Without that help, those pages would be less useful to those who need to understand some of the problems that arise. I am grateful to them.

Another feature which a degree of awareness will require in future years is the effect of the Mental Capacity Act 2005, passed into legislation in the dying days of the last Government. It is not likely to come into effect until 2007, but it will need to be appreciated for what it is, a transformation of the approach to the issue of mental capacity and what should be done if incapacity is suspected. Unlike much legislation, it has received considerable detailed revision including a Report from both Houses, and significant changes took place to the legislation, even the title of the Bill changing from that of the *"Mental Incapacity Bill"* to the *"Mental Capacity Bill"*. The next stage in this area is likely to be a revision of the Mental Health Act 1983.

New Material

There is little else that is new. There is an improvement to the Note on Bereavement Damages. There is an extended Note on DIY, Gardening and Housekeeping. There is a more detailed Note on Pension Losses, an area of some difficulty; there is no attempt to deal with the whole area comprehensively, but only an indication as to what the practitioner should be looking for. There are some figures from the Department of Employment about injuries in various industries. Also, where appropriate, tables have been updated. There will be some further revision to the Ogden Tables in late 2005 and early 2006, in an attempt to improve accuracy, particularly in life expectation.

Bernie Ecclestone

His activities, at age 74, continue to excite wonder and admiration. His control of Formula One Racing is being challenged by a rival group, a consortium of car makers, namely BMW, Daimler Chrysler, Fiat, Renault and Ferrari. He induced Ferrari to desert that rival group and signed them up until 2012. He has lost out in litigation to the Banks who took over the controlling interest which he previously sold to the German media company, Kirch, for $1.6 billion. Kirch later went into liquidation. His row with the owners of Silverstone has forced those owners to rethink their policy and approach to the concept of motor racing being held at the track. His position in the league of the richest men/women in Britain has been supplanted by the rise of the Mittal family. One newspaper has suggested that he now has a fortune in excess of £2.3 billion. Even at an annuity rate of 3.5 per cent, that would be worth something. He first came to my attention when he had an income of more than £33 million in one accounting year. Come what may, he still does not appear in Table C6: Comparable earnings.

A Plea

The success of Facts & Figures depends on you, the readers, telling us what we have rightly included and that which you require. We do need your feedback, to ensure that is continues to prosper. Nothing is taken for granted. We may include some quirky information, but the original purpose was and continues to be the provision of assistance to practitioners who have to create and consider the various constituents of a Schedule of Damages. Please tell me through either personal correspondence or through Sweet & Maxwell, where we have gone wrong, what we have missed and what is likely to be of assistance to you and others. We will only improve each edition with your help.

199, Strand
London WC2R 1DR
Email: julie.clarke@thomson.com
Chambers tel: 020 7520 4000
Direct: 020 7520 4051

Robin de Wilde, Q.C.
email: sweetandmaxwell.factsandfigures@thomson.com
May 2005

INTRODUCTION TO THE FIRST EDITION

Schedules of Damages have become more complex. These tables are intended as an assistance to those who have to check the details which support a Schedule. The Tables themselves come from a variety of primary sources. In one volume they should be easier to use.

The task of compiling this volume has proved more onerous than any of the members of the Committee assigned to the task would have imagined. The discussions as to what should be included or excluded became intense. When dealing with comparative and comparable earnings, should not Mr Bernie Ecclestone of Formula One Promotions and International Sports World receive a mention? He was paid in 1993 the sum of £30,750,109 and became easily the highest paid director by £8,000,000 or so. He is not included in the Table of Comparable Earnings.

We are also conscious that the application of each Table may or may not be easy depending on the contents. We do not intend to triple the size of the volume by setting out worked examples, but would refer the reader to the appropriate text books. It is intended as a source book, easily to hand, so that the practitioner may find what is needed quickly and easily in a single volume.

As this is our first foray into the world of tables, we appreciate that some matters will have been omitted that should be included and some of that which is included should not be present. We rely on our readers to tell us what is wanted and needed, so that the next annual update can be improved. The intention is that each edition is published in late January or early February of each year, incorporating the declarations announced in the Budget in November the previous year.

We have plundered shamelessly from a variety of sources. The final stimulus has been the Family Law Bar Association's "At A Glance" annual publication, but it is designed for practitioners in a different world, facing other demands and needs.

We are also grateful to Mr Justice Bell, who attended the final Advisory Committee Meeting and agreed to write a Foreword to this venture.

We conclude with the thought expressed by the historian Edward Gibbon in *The Decline and Fall of the Roman Empire*, when he states in a footnote about one Emperor that:

"Twenty-two acknowledged concubines and a library of sixty-two thousand volumes, attested the variety of his inclinations; and from the productions which he left behind him, it appears that the former as well as the latter were designed for use rather than ostentation."

These Tables, too, are designed for use rather than ostentation.

199 Strand
London WC2R 1DR
May 1996

Robin de Wilde, Q.C.

CONTENTS

Group F—Investment

Group G—Tax and National Insurance

Group H—Benefits, Allowances, Charges

Group I—Other Material

Group A
Life, Multiplier and Discount Tables

A

A1:   Ogden "At a Glance"

A2:   Loss of earnings multipliers adjusted for occupation and geography

A3:   Multipliers for fixed periods and at intervals

A4:   Combination Tables

A5:   Nil Discount Tables "At a Glance"

A6:   Tables of adjustments to multiplier for Fatal Accidents Acts dependency

A7:   Bereavement damages

A8:   Claims for losses of earnings and maintenance at public expense

A9:   Roberts v Johnstone Analysis

A10:   Auty Analysis

A11:   General Damages Table following *Heil v Rankin*

A1: Ogden "At a Glance"

The following two tables consist of the 2.5 per cent columns from Ogden Tables 1–26.

If it is accepted that 2.5 per cent is the appropriate discount factor, Ogden "At a Glance" contains all the appropriate multipliers.

Readers are reminded that the figures for loss of earnings must be adjusted in accordance with Section B of the Explanatory Notes to the Ogden Tables (Contingencies Other than Mortality) reproduced in Part B2. Multipliers already adjusted for these contingencies are set out in Table A2.

Ogden "At a Glance" – MALE (2.5%)

	Table 1 Pecuniary loss for life	Table 3 Loss of earnings to age 50	Table 5 Loss of earnings to age 55	Table 7 Loss of earnings to age 60	Table 9 Loss of earnings to age 65	Table 11 Loss of earnings to age 70	Table 13 Loss of earnings to age 75	Table 15 Loss of pension from age 50	Table 17 Loss of pension from age 55	Table 19 Loss of pension from age 60	Table 21 Loss of pension from age 65	Table 23 Loss of pension from age 70	Table 25 Loss of pension from age 75
0	34.76							6.38	5.07	3.94	2.96	2.13	1.44
1	34.79							6.57	5.22	4.05	3.05	2.19	1.48
2	34.65							6.73	5.35	4.15	3.12	2.24	1.52
3	34.51							6.90	5.48	4.25	3.19	2.30	1.56
4	34.36							7.06	5.61	4.35	3.27	2.35	1.59
5	34.20							7.24	5.75	4.46	3.35	2.41	1.63
6	34.04							7.41	5.89	4.57	3.43	2.46	1.67
7	33.87							7.59	6.03	4.68	3.51	2.52	1.71
8	33.70							7.78	6.18	4.79	3.59	2.58	1.75
9	33.52							7.96	6.32	4.90	3.68	2.64	1.79
10	33.34							8.16	6.48	5.02	3.77	2.70	1.83
11	33.16							8.35	6.63	5.14	3.85	2.77	1.87
12	32.96							8.55	6.79	5.26	3.94	2.83	1.91
13	32.77							8.76	6.95	5.38	4.04	2.90	1.95
14	32.57							8.97	7.12	5.51	4.13	2.96	2.00
15	32.36							9.19	7.29	5.64	4.23	3.03	2.04
16	32.15	22.74	24.69	26.38	27.82	29.05	30.06	9.41	7.47	5.78	4.33	3.10	2.09
17	31.94	22.30	24.30	26.03	27.51	28.77	29.80	9.64	7.64	5.91	4.43	3.18	2.14
18	31.73	21.86	23.90	25.67	27.19	28.48	29.54	9.87	7.83	6.06	4.54	3.25	2.19
19	31.52	21.40	23.50	25.31	26.87	28.19	29.28	10.11	8.02	6.20	4.64	3.33	2.24
20	31.30	20.94	23.09	24.95	26.55	27.90	29.01	10.36	8.22	6.35	4.75	3.40	2.29
21	31.08	20.46	22.66	24.57	26.21	27.60	28.74	10.62	8.42	6.51	4.87	3.48	2.34
22	30.85	19.97	22.23	24.19	25.87	27.29	28.46	10.88	8.62	6.66	4.98	3.56	2.40
23	30.62	19.47	21.79	23.79	25.52	26.97	28.17	11.14	8.83	6.82	5.10	3.65	2.45
24	30.38	18.96	21.33	23.39	25.16	26.64	27.87	11.42	9.04	6.99	5.22	3.73	2.51
25	30.13	18.43	20.87	22.98	24.79	26.31	27.57	11.70	9.26	7.15	5.35	3.82	2.56
26	29.88	17.90	20.39	22.55	24.41	25.97	27.26	11.98	9.49	7.33	5.47	3.91	2.62
27	29.62	17.34	19.90	22.12	24.02	25.62	26.94	12.28	9.72	7.50	5.60	4.00	2.68
28	29.36	16.78	19.40	21.68	23.63	25.27	26.62	12.58	9.96	7.68	5.73	4.09	2.74
29	29.09	16.20	18.89	21.22	23.22	24.90	26.29	12.89	10.20	7.87	5.87	4.19	2.80
30	28.81	15.61	18.37	20.76	22.81	24.53	25.95	13.21	10.45	8.05	6.01	4.28	2.86
31	28.53	15.00	17.83	20.28	22.38	24.15	25.60	13.53	10.70	8.25	6.15	4.38	2.93
32	28.24	14.37	17.28	19.79	21.94	23.75	25.24	13.86	10.96	8.44	6.29	4.48	2.99
33	27.94	13.73	16.71	19.29	21.50	23.35	24.88	14.20	11.22	8.65	6.44	4.58	3.06
34	27.63	13.08	16.13	18.78	21.04	22.94	24.50	14.55	11.50	8.85	6.59	4.69	3.13
35	27.31	12.41	15.54	18.25	20.57	22.52	24.12	14.91	11.78	9.06	6.74	4.79	3.20
36	26.99	11.72	14.93	17.71	20.09	22.09	23.73	15.27	12.06	9.28	6.90	4.90	3.27
37	26.66	11.01	14.31	17.16	19.60	21.65	23.32	15.65	12.35	9.50	7.06	5.01	3.34
38	26.32	10.28	13.67	16.59	19.09	21.19	22.91	16.03	12.65	9.73	7.23	5.13	3.41
39	25.97	9.54	13.01	16.01	18.58	20.73	22.49	16.43	12.96	9.96	7.39	5.24	3.48
40	25.61	8.78	12.34	15.42	18.05	20.25	22.06	16.83	13.27	10.19	7.57	5.36	3.56
41	25.25	8.00	11.65	14.81	17.51	19.77	21.61	17.25	13.60	10.44	7.74	5.48	3.64
42	24.88	7.20	10.95	14.19	16.95	19.27	21.16	17.68	13.93	10.69	7.92	5.61	3.71
43	24.50	6.38	10.23	13.55	16.39	18.77	20.70	18.12	14.27	10.94	8.11	5.73	3.79
44	24.11	5.54	9.49	12.90	15.81	18.25	20.24	18.58	14.62	11.21	8.30	5.86	3.88
45	23.72	4.67	8.73	12.24	15.22	17.72	19.76	19.05	14.99	11.48	8.50	6.00	3.96
46	23.32	3.79	7.96	11.56	14.62	17.19	19.28	19.54	15.36	11.76	8.70	6.13	4.05
47	22.92	2.88	7.17	10.86	14.01	16.64	18.78	20.04	15.75	12.05	8.91	6.28	4.14
48	22.51	1.95	6.35	10.15	13.38	16.08	18.28	20.56	16.15	12.35	9.12	6.42	4.23
49	22.08	0.99	5.52	9.42	12.74	15.51	17.76	21.10	16.57	12.66	9.34	6.57	4.32
50	21.65		4.66	8.67	12.08	14.93	17.24	21.65	16.99	12.98	9.57	6.72	4.41
51	21.21		3.78	7.91	11.41	14.33	16.70		17.43	13.31	9.80	6.88	4.51
52	20.76		2.87	7.12	10.72	13.72	16.15		17.89	13.64	10.04	7.04	4.61
53	20.30		1.94	6.31	10.01	13.09	15.59		18.36	13.99	10.29	7.21	4.71
54	19.84		0.99	5.48	9.29	12.46	15.02		18.85	14.36	10.55	7.38	4.82

Ogden "At a Glance" – MALE (2.5%) *continued*

	Table 1 Pecuniary loss for life	Table 3 Loss of earnings to age 50	Table 5 Loss of earnings to age 55	Table 7 Loss of earnings to age 60	Table 9 Loss of earnings to age 65	Table 11 Loss of earnings to age 70	Table 13 Loss of earnings to age 75	Table 15 Loss of pension from age 50	Table 17 Loss of pension from age 55	Table 19 Loss of pension from age 60	Table 21 Loss of pension from age 65	Table 24 Loss of pension from age 70	Table 25 Loss of pension from age 75
55	19.37			4.63	8.55	11.81	14.44		19.37	14.74	10.82	7.56	4.93
56	18.89			3.76	7.79	11.15	13.85			15.14	11.10	7.75	5.04
57	18.42			2.86	7.02	10.47	13.25			15.56	11.40	7.95	5.16
58	17.94			1.94	6.23	9.79	12.65			16.01	11.71	8.16	5.29
59	17.46			0.98	5.42	9.09	12.04			16.48	12.05	8.38	5.43
60	16.98				4.58	8.37	11.42			16.98	12.40	8.61	5.57
61	16.50				3.73	7.64	10.79				12.78	8.86	5.72
62	16.02				2.84	6.90	10.14				13.18	9.13	5.88
63	15.54				1.93	6.13	9.49				13.61	9.41	6.05
64	15.05				0.98	5.34	8.82				14.07	9.71	6.23
65	14.55					4.52	8.13				14.55	10.02	6.42
66	14.03					3.68	7.42					10.35	6.61
67	13.51					2.81	6.70					10.70	6.81
68	12.97					1.91	5.95					11.06	7.02
69	12.43					0.98	5.19					11.45	7.24
70	11.88						4.40					11.88	7.48
71	11.34						3.59						7.75
72	10.80						2.75						8.05
73	10.28						1.88						8.39
74	9.77						0.97						8.80
75	9.27												9.27
76	8.79												
77	8.33												
78	7.88												
79	7.45												
80	7.03												
81	6.61												
82	6.20												
83	5.81												
84	5.44												
85	5.09												
86	4.77												
87	4.47												
88	4.19												
89	3.94												
90	3.70												
91	3.47												
92	3.25												
93	3.07												
94	2.91												
95	2.76												
96	2.60												
97	2.45												
98	2.29												
99	2.14												
100	2.00												

Ogden "At a Glance" – FEMALE (2.5%)

	Table 2 Pecuniary loss for life	Table 4 Loss of earnings to age 50	Table 6 Loss of earnings to age 55	Table 8 Loss of earnings to age 60	Table 10 Loss of earnings to age 65	Table 12 Loss of earnings to age 70	Table 14 Loss of earnings to age 75	Table 16 Loss of pension from age 50	Table 18 Loss of pension from age 55	Table 20 Loss of pension from age 60	Table 22 Loss of pension from age 65	Table 24 Loss of pension from age 70	Table 26 Loss of pension from age 75
0	35.35							6.87	5.54	4.37	3.36	2.50	1.76
1	35.38							7.07	5.70	4.50	3.46	2.57	1.81
2	35.26							7.24	5.84	4.61	3.55	2.63	1.85
3	35.13							7.42	5.98	4.72	3.63	2.69	1.90
4	34.99							7.60	6.13	4.84	3.72	2.76	1.94
5	34.86							7.79	6.28	4.96	3.81	2.82	1.99
6	34.71							7.98	6.43	5.08	3.90	2.89	2.04
7	34.56							8.18	6.59	5.20	4.00	2.96	2.09
8	34.41							8.38	6.75	5.33	4.09	3.03	2.13
9	34.26							8.58	6.91	5.45	4.19	3.10	2.18
10	34.09							8.79	7.08	5.59	4.29	3.18	2.24
11	33.93							9.00	7.25	5.72	4.39	3.25	2.29
12	33.76							9.22	7.43	5.86	4.50	3.33	2.34
13	33.59							9.45	7.61	6.00	4.61	3.41	2.40
14	33.41							9.68	7.79	6.15	4.72	3.49	2.45
15	33.23							9.92	7.98	6.29	4.83	3.58	2.51
16	33.05	22.89	24.87	26.60	28.10	29.39	30.48	10.16	8.18	6.45	4.95	3.66	2.57
17	32.86	22.45	24.48	26.26	27.79	29.11	30.23	10.41	8.38	6.60	5.07	3.75	2.63
18	32.67	22.00	24.09	25.90	27.48	28.83	29.97	10.66	8.58	6.76	5.19	3.84	2.69
19	32.47	21.55	23.68	25.54	27.16	28.54	29.71	10.92	8.79	6.93	5.31	3.93	2.76
20	32.27	21.08	23.27	25.17	26.83	28.25	29.45	11.19	9.00	7.09	5.44	4.02	2.82
21	32.06	20.60	22.84	24.80	26.49	27.94	29.17	11.46	9.22	7.26	5.57	4.11	2.88
22	31.84	20.10	22.40	24.41	26.14	27.63	28.89	11.74	9.44	7.44	5.70	4.21	2.95
23	31.63	19.60	21.95	24.01	25.79	27.32	28.61	12.03	9.67	7.62	5.84	4.31	3.02
24	31.40	19.08	21.49	23.60	25.42	26.99	28.31	12.32	9.91	7.80	5.98	4.41	3.09
25	31.17	18.55	21.02	23.18	25.05	26.65	28.01	12.62	10.15	7.99	6.12	4.51	3.16
26	30.93	18.00	20.54	22.75	24.67	26.31	27.70	12.93	10.39	8.18	6.26	4.62	3.23
27	30.69	17.45	20.05	22.32	24.28	25.96	27.38	13.24	10.64	8.37	6.41	4.73	3.31
28	30.44	16.87	19.54	21.87	23.88	25.60	27.06	13.56	10.90	8.57	6.56	4.84	3.38
29	30.18	16.29	19.02	21.40	23.46	25.23	26.72	13.89	11.16	8.78	6.72	4.95	3.46
30	29.92	15.69	18.49	20.93	23.04	24.85	26.38	14.23	11.43	8.99	6.88	5.07	3.54
31	29.65	15.07	17.94	20.45	22.61	24.47	26.03	14.58	11.71	9.20	7.04	5.18	3.62
32	29.37	14.44	17.39	19.95	22.17	24.07	25.67	14.93	11.99	9.42	7.20	5.30	3.70
33	29.09	13.80	16.82	19.45	21.72	23.67	25.31	15.30	12.28	9.65	7.37	5.43	3.79
34	28.80	13.13	16.23	18.93	21.26	23.25	24.93	15.67	12.57	9.88	7.55	5.55	3.87
35	28.51	12.46	15.63	18.39	20.78	22.83	24.55	16.05	12.88	10.11	7.72	5.68	3.96
36	28.20	11.76	15.02	17.85	20.30	22.39	24.16	16.44	13.19	10.35	7.91	5.81	4.05
37	27.89	11.05	14.39	17.29	19.80	21.95	23.75	16.84	13.51	10.60	8.09	5.94	4.14
38	27.57	10.32	13.74	16.72	19.29	21.49	23.34	17.25	13.83	10.85	8.28	6.08	4.23
39	27.25	9.57	13.08	16.14	18.77	21.03	22.92	17.68	14.17	11.11	8.48	6.22	4.33
40	26.92	8.81	12.41	15.54	18.24	20.55	22.49	18.11	14.51	11.38	8.68	6.36	4.42
41	26.58	8.02	11.72	14.93	17.70	20.07	22.06	18.56	14.86	11.65	8.88	6.51	4.52
42	26.23	7.22	11.01	14.30	17.14	19.57	21.61	19.01	15.23	11.93	9.09	6.66	4.62
43	25.88	6.39	10.28	13.66	16.58	19.06	21.15	19.49	15.60	12.22	9.31	6.82	4.73
44	25.52	5.55	9.54	13.01	16.00	18.55	20.69	19.97	15.98	12.52	9.53	6.97	4.83
45	25.16	4.68	8.78	12.33	15.40	18.02	20.21	20.47	16.38	12.82	9.75	7.14	4.94
46	24.78	3.79	8.00	11.65	14.79	17.48	19.73	20.99	16.79	13.13	9.99	7.30	5.05
47	24.40	2.88	7.20	10.94	14.17	16.93	19.23	21.52	17.21	13.46	10.23	7.48	5.17
48	24.01	1.95	6.38	10.22	13.54	16.36	18.73	22.07	17.64	13.79	10.48	7.65	5.29
49	23.62	0.99	5.54	9.49	12.89	15.79	18.21	22.63	18.08	14.13	10.73	7.83	5.41
50	23.22		4.67	8.73	12.22	15.20	17.69	23.22	18.54	14.49	10.99	8.02	5.53
51	22.81		3.79	7.96	11.54	14.60	17.15		19.02	14.85	11.26	8.21	5.66
52	22.39		2.88	7.16	10.85	13.98	16.60		19.51	15.23	11.54	8.41	5.79
53	21.96		1.95	6.35	10.13	13.35	16.04		20.02	15.62	11.83	8.61	5.92
54	21.53		0.99	5.51	9.40	12.71	15.47		20.55	16.02	12.13	8.82	6.06

Ogden "At a Glance" – FEMALE (2.5%) *continued*

	Table 2 Pecuniary loss for life	Table 4 Loss of earnings to age 50	Table 6 Loss of earnings to age 55	Table 8 Loss of earnings to age 60	Table 10 Loss of earnings to age 65	Table 12 Loss of earnings to age 70	Table 14 Loss of earnings to age 75	Table 16 Loss of pension from age 50	Table 18 Loss of pension from age 55	Table 20 Loss of pension from age 60	Table 22 Loss of pension from age 65	Table 23 Loss of pension from age 70	Table 24 Loss of pension from age 75
55	21.10			4.65	8.65	12.05	14.89		21.10	16.44	12.44	9.04	6.21
56	20.66			3.77	7.89	11.39	14.30			16.88	12.77	9.27	6.36
57	20.21			2.87	7.11	10.70	13.70			17.34	13.10	9.51	6.51
58	19.76			1.94	6.30	10.00	13.08			17.82	13.46	9.75	6.67
59	19.30			0.99	5.48	9.29	12.46			18.31	13.82	10.01	6.84
60	18.84				4.63	8.55	11.82			18.84	14.21	10.28	7.02
61	18.37				3.76	7.80	11.17				14.61	10.57	7.20
62	17.89				2.86	7.03	10.50				15.03	10.86	7.39
63	17.41				1.94	6.24	9.82				15.47	11.17	7.59
64	16.91				0.98	5.43	9.12				15.93	11.48	7.80
65	16.40					4.59	8.40				16.40	11.81	8.01
66	15.88					3.73	7.66					12.15	8.22
67	15.33					2.84	6.90					12.49	8.43
68	14.77					1.93	6.13					12.84	8.65
69	14.20					0.98	5.33					13.21	8.87
70	13.61						4.51					13.61	9.10
71	13.02						3.67						9.35
72	12.43						2.80						9.62
73	11.84						1.91						9.94
74	11.27						0.98						10.29
75	10.71												10.71
76	10.17												
77	9.64												
78	9.12												
79	8.62												
80	8.13												
81	7.64												
82	7.17												
83	6.71												
84	6.26												
85	5.84												
86	5.44												
87	5.06												
88	4.71												
89	4.38												
90	4.07												
91	3.79												
92	3.53												
93	3.31												
94	3.10												
95	2.90												
96	2.72												
97	2.55												
98	2.38												
99	2.22												
100	2.06												

A2: Loss of earnings multipliers adjusted for occupation and geography

The Ogden tables dealing with loss of earnings (Ogden tables 21–28) are subject to adjustment for contingencies other than mortality (Ogden paragraphs 25 to 44). The tables which follow incorporate those factors without the need for further calculation.

The contingencies are the general level of economic activity (high, medium or low); the risks of illness and disability inherent in the occupation; and the part of the country where the claimant resides. At any rate for losses lasting more than a few years it will usually be appropriate to assume medium economic activity but the adjustment for that varies with age at trial, sex and intended retirement age. It is then subject to the further adjustments for occupation and geography which also vary with age.

Factors which increase the multiplier:

Less risky occupations: clerical or similar jobs such as civil servants, the professions and financial services industries. It is the particular job that matters rather than the industry.
Residence in the South East, East Anglia, South West and East Midlands.

Factors which decrease the multiplier:

More risky occupations: manual jobs such as construction, mining, quarrying and shipbuilding.
Residence in the North, North West, Wales and Scotland.

Neutral factors:

Occupations which are neither white collar nor heavy manual and other areas of the country are not listed in the explanatory notes to the Ogden tables but are presumably neutral.

There are six tables each for men and women, beginning with the table for two favourable factors—less risky occupation and favourable region—and ending with that for two unfavourable factors—more risky occupation and less favourable region. Each table has six columns corresponding to intended retirement age.

Thus if the claimant is a 32-year-old male solicitor, living in the South West and proposing to retire at 60, the first table on the next page gives the multiplier for loss of earnings to age 60 as 19.79. If he were a solicitor in the North West (one low risk and one high risk factor) the third table gives the multiplier as 19.29.

For ages not specifically identified in the notes to the Ogden tables the adjusted figures have been obtained by extrapolation and interpolation. Adjustments for different retirement ages have been made in accordance with paragraphs 38 and 39 of the notes to the Ogden tables. The tables assume a 2.5 per cent discount rate and a medium level of economic activity.

Male - 2.5% Loss of earnings in medium economic conditions in *both* low risk occupation *and* favourable geographical region

Age	To retiring age					
	50	55	60	65	70	75
16	22.74	24.69	26.38	27.82	28.90	29.91
17	22.30	24.30	26.03	27.51	28.63	29.65
18	21.86	23.90	25.67	27.19	28.34	29.39
19	21.40	23.50	25.31	26.87	28.05	29.13
20	20.94	23.09	24.95	26.55	27.73	28.84
21	20.46	22.66	24.57	26.21	27.41	28.54
22	19.97	22.23	24.19	25.87	27.07	28.23
23	19.47	21.79	23.79	25.52	26.73	27.92
24	18.96	21.33	23.39	25.16	26.37	27.59
25	18.43	20.87	22.98	24.74	26.02	27.27
26	17.90	20.39	22.55	24.31	25.66	26.93
27	17.34	19.90	22.12	23.88	25.29	26.59
28	16.78	19.40	21.68	23.44	24.92	26.25
29	16.20	18.89	21.22	22.99	24.53	25.90
30	15.61	18.37	20.76	22.54	24.14	25.53
31	15.00	17.83	20.28	22.07	23.74	25.16
32	14.37	17.28	19.79	21.59	23.32	24.79
33	13.73	16.71	19.29	21.11	22.91	24.41
34	13.08	16.13	18.78	20.62	22.48	24.01
35	12.40	15.52	18.21	20.16	22.05	23.61
36	11.70	14.90	17.64	19.69	21.60	23.21
37	10.98	14.27	17.06	19.21	21.15	22.78
38	10.24	13.62	16.46	18.71	20.68	22.36
39	9.49	12.94	15.85	18.21	20.21	21.93
40	8.74	12.29	15.28	17.70	19.76	21.52
41	7.97	11.61	14.68	17.25	19.30	21.10
42	7.18	10.92	14.08	16.65	18.83	20.67
43	6.37	10.21	13.45	16.11	18.35	20.24
44	5.53	9.47	12.81	15.55	17.86	19.80
45	4.66	8.70	12.14	14.95	17.31	19.31
46	3.77	7.93	11.45	14.34	16.77	18.81
47	2.86	7.13	10.74	13.72	16.21	18.30
48	1.94	6.31	10.03	13.09	15.65	17.79
49	0.98	5.47	9.29	12.44	15.07	17.26
50		4.62	8.56	11.76	14.47	16.71
51		3.75	7.81	11.07	13.86	16.15
52		2.85	7.04	10.36	13.23	15.58
53		1.93	6.24	9.64	12.60	15.00
54		0.99	5.43	8.92	11.96	14.42
55			4.58	8.21	11.28	13.79
56			3.72	7.48	10.65	13.23
57			2.83	6.74	10.00	12.65
58			1.92	5.98	9.35	12.08
59			0.97	5.20	8.68	11.50
60				4.40	7.99	10.91
61				3.58	7.30	10.29
62				2.73	6.59	9.68
63				1.85	5.85	9.06
64				0.94	5.10	8.42
65					4.32	7.76
66					3.51	7.09
67					2.68	6.40
68					1.82	5.68
69					0.94	4.96
70						4.20
71						3.43
72						2.63
73						1.80
74						0.93

Male - 2.5% Loss of earnings in medium economic conditions in *either* low risk occupation *or* favourable geographical region

Age	To retiring age					
	50	55	60	65	70	75
16	22.74	24.69	26.38	27.54	28.61	29.61
17	22.30	24.30	26.03	27.23	28.34	29.35
18	21.86	23.90	25.67	26.92	28.05	29.10
19	21.40	23.50	25.31	26.60	27.77	28.84
20	20.94	23.09	24.95	26.28	27.45	28.55
21	20.46	22.66	24.57	25.95	27.13	28.25
22	19.97	22.23	24.19	25.61	26.80	27.95
23	19.47	21.79	23.79	25.26	26.46	27.63
24	18.96	21.33	23.39	24.91	26.11	27.31
25	18.41	20.85	22.93	24.49	25.76	26.99
26	17.86	20.35	22.46	24.07	25.40	26.66
27	17.29	19.84	21.99	23.64	25.03	26.32
28	16.71	19.32	21.51	23.20	24.66	25.98
29	16.12	18.80	21.01	22.76	24.28	25.63
30	15.52	18.26	20.55	22.31	23.89	25.28
31	14.90	17.71	20.08	21.84	23.50	24.91
32	14.26	17.14	19.59	21.37	23.09	24.53
33	13.61	16.56	19.10	20.90	22.67	24.16
34	12.95	15.97	18.59	20.41	22.25	23.77
35	12.27	15.37	18.03	19.95	21.82	23.37
36	11.58	14.75	17.46	19.49	21.38	22.97
37	10.87	14.12	16.89	19.01	20.94	22.55
38	10.14	13.48	16.29	18.52	20.47	22.13
39	9.40	12.81	15.69	18.02	20.00	21.70
40	8.64	12.15	15.10	17.50	19.53	21.27
41	7.87	11.46	14.49	17.03	19.05	20.83
42	7.08	10.76	13.88	16.41	18.56	20.38
43	6.27	10.05	13.24	15.86	18.06	19.92
44	5.44	9.32	12.60	15.28	17.55	19.46
45	4.57	8.55	11.92	14.67	16.99	18.95
46	3.70	7.77	11.23	14.05	16.44	18.44
47	2.80	6.98	10.52	13.43	15.87	17.91
48	1.89	6.17	9.80	12.79	15.29	17.38
49	0.96	5.35	9.07	12.15	14.71	16.84
50		4.51	8.35	11.46	14.10	16.29
51		3.66	7.61	10.77	13.48	15.71
52		2.77	6.84	10.07	12.86	15.14
53		1.87	6.06	9.36	12.22	14.56
54		0.96	5.26	8.64	11.59	13.97
55			4.44	7.95	10.92	13.36
56			3.61	7.24	10.31	12.81
57			2.75	6.53	9.68	12.26
58			1.86	5.79	9.06	11.70
59			0.94	5.04	8.41	11.14
60				4.26	7.74	10.56
61				3.47	7.07	9.97
62				2.64	6.38	9.38
63				1.79	5.67	8.78
64				0.91	4.94	8.16
65					4.18	7.52
66					3.40	6.86
67					2.60	6.20
68					1.77	5.50
69					0.91	4.80
70						4.07
71						3.32
72						2.54
73						1.74
74						0.90

Male - 2.5% Loss of earnings in medium economic conditions in occupation and region with one low and one high risk factor

Age	To retiring age					
	50	55	60	65	70	75
16	22.63	24.57	26.25	27.40	28.47	29.46
17	22.19	24.18	25.90	27.10	28.19	29.20
18	21.75	23.78	25.54	26.78	27.91	28.95
19	21.29	23.38	25.18	26.47	27.63	28.69
20	20.81	22.95	24.80	26.13	27.29	28.37
21	20.32	22.50	24.40	25.76	26.94	28.05
22	19.81	22.05	24.00	25.40	26.58	27.72
23	19.29	21.59	23.58	25.04	26.21	27.38
24	18.77	21.12	23.16	24.66	25.84	27.03
25	18.22	20.63	22.69	24.23	25.48	26.70
26	17.66	20.12	22.20	23.79	25.10	26.35
27	17.08	19.60	21.72	23.35	24.72	26.00
28	16.50	19.08	21.23	22.91	24.34	25.64
29	15.90	18.54	20.73	22.45	23.95	25.28
30	15.30	18.00	20.26	21.99	23.55	24.91
31	14.68	17.44	19.78	21.51	23.14	24.53
32	14.03	16.88	19.29	21.03	22.72	24.15
33	13.39	16.29	18.79	20.55	22.30	23.76
34	12.73	15.70	18.28	20.06	21.87	23.36
35	12.06	15.10	17.71	19.60	21.43	22.95
36	11.37	14.48	17.14	19.13	20.99	22.54
37	10.66	13.86	16.56	18.65	20.53	22.11
38	9.94	13.21	15.97	18.15	20.06	21.69
39	9.21	12.55	15.37	17.65	19.59	21.25
40	8.45	11.88	14.76	17.10	19.08	20.79
41	7.68	11.18	14.14	16.61	18.58	20.31
42	6.89	10.48	13.51	15.97	18.06	19.83
43	6.09	9.76	12.86	15.40	17.54	19.34
44	5.27	9.03	12.21	14.81	17.00	18.86
45	4.42	8.27	11.53	14.19	16.43	18.32
46	3.57	7.50	10.84	13.56	15.86	17.78
47	2.70	6.72	10.13	12.93	15.27	17.23
48	1.82	5.92	9.42	12.28	14.68	16.69
49	0.92	5.12	8.70	11.64	14.09	16.13
50		4.31	7.98	10.95	13.48	15.56
51		3.49	7.26	10.27	12.85	14.98
52		2.64	6.52	9.58	12.23	14.39
53		1.78	5.76	8.88	11.59	13.81
54		0.91	4.99	8.18	10.96	13.22
55			4.21	7.52	10.33	12.64
56			3.42	6.86	9.76	12.12
57			2.60	6.18	9.16	11.59
58			1.77	5.48	8.57	11.07
59			0.89	4.77	7.95	10.54
60				4.03	7.32	9.99
61				3.28	6.69	9.43
62				2.50	6.04	8.87
63				1.70	5.36	8.30
64				0.86	4.67	7.72
65					3.96	7.11
66					3.22	6.49
67					2.46	5.86
68					1.67	5.21
69					0.86	4.54
70						3.85
71						3.14
72						2.41
73						1.65
74						0.85

Male - 2.5% Loss of earnings in medium economic conditions in *both* occupation with medium risk *and* medium geographical region

Age	To retiring age					
	50	55	60	65	70	75
16	22.63	24.57	26.12	27.26	28.32	29.31
17	22.19	24.18	25.77	26.96	28.05	29.06
18	21.75	23.78	25.41	26.65	27.77	28.80
19	21.29	23.38	25.06	26.33	27.49	28.55
20	20.81	22.95	24.70	26.02	27.17	28.26
21	20.32	22.50	24.32	25.69	26.85	27.96
22	19.81	22.05	23.95	25.35	26.53	27.66
23	19.29	21.59	23.55	25.01	26.19	27.35
24	18.77	21.12	23.16	24.66	25.84	27.03
25	18.23	20.64	22.70	24.24	25.49	26.72
26	17.69	20.15	22.23	23.82	25.14	26.39
27	17.11	19.64	21.77	23.40	24.77	26.05
28	16.55	19.13	21.29	22.97	24.41	25.71
29	15.96	18.61	20.80	22.52	24.03	25.37
30	15.36	18.08	20.34	22.08	23.65	25.02
31	14.75	17.53	19.87	21.62	23.26	24.65
32	14.11	16.97	19.39	21.15	22.85	24.28
33	13.47	16.39	18.90	20.68	22.44	23.91
34	12.82	15.81	18.40	20.20	22.02	23.52
35	12.15	15.21	17.85	19.75	21.60	23.13
36	11.46	14.60	17.28	19.29	21.16	22.73
37	10.76	13.98	16.71	18.82	20.72	22.32
38	10.03	13.34	16.13	18.33	20.26	21.90
39	9.30	12.68	15.53	17.84	19.80	21.48
40	8.54	12.01	14.93	17.29	19.30	21.02
41	7.77	11.31	14.31	16.81	18.80	20.55
42	6.98	10.61	13.68	16.17	18.29	20.08
43	6.17	9.89	13.04	15.60	17.78	19.60
44	5.35	9.16	12.38	15.02	17.25	19.13
45	4.49	8.39	11.70	14.40	16.67	18.59
46	3.63	7.62	11.01	13.77	16.11	18.07
47	2.74	6.83	10.30	13.14	15.53	17.52
48	1.85	6.03	9.58	12.50	14.94	16.98
49	0.94	5.22	8.85	11.85	14.35	16.43
50		4.39	8.13	11.16	13.74	15.86
51		3.56	7.40	10.47	13.11	15.28
52		2.69	6.65	9.78	12.49	14.70
53		1.82	5.88	9.07	11.85	14.11
54		0.93	5.10	8.36	11.21	13.52
55			4.31	7.70	10.57	12.92
56			3.50	7.01	9.98	12.40
57			2.66	6.32	9.37	11.86
58			1.80	5.61	8.76	11.32
59			0.91	4.88	8.14	10.78
60				4.12	7.49	10.22
61				3.36	6.84	9.65
62				2.56	6.18	9.08
63				1.74	5.49	8.49
64				0.88	4.78	7.89
65					4.05	7.28
66					3.29	6.64
67					2.51	6.00
68					1.71	5.33
69					0.88	4.65
70						3.94
71						3.21
72						2.46
73						1.68
74						0.87

Male - 2.5% Loss of earnings in medium economic conditions in *either* occupation with high risk *or* unfavourable geographical region

Age	To retiring age					
	50	55	60	65	70	75
16	22.51	24.44	25.98	27.12	28.18	29.16
17	22.08	24.06	25.64	26.82	27.91	28.91
18	21.64	23.66	25.28	26.51	27.63	28.65
19	21.19	23.27	24.93	26.20	27.34	28.40
20	20.69	22.81	24.55	25.86	27.01	28.08
21	20.17	22.34	24.15	25.50	26.66	27.76
22	19.65	21.87	23.75	25.15	26.31	27.44
23	19.12	21.40	23.34	24.78	25.95	27.10
24	18.58	20.90	22.92	24.41	25.57	26.76
25	18.03	20.42	22.46	23.98	25.21	26.42
26	17.48	19.91	21.98	23.55	24.84	26.08
27	16.91	19.40	21.50	23.11	24.47	25.73
28	16.33	18.88	21.02	22.67	24.09	25.38
29	15.74	18.36	20.51	22.21	23.70	25.02
30	15.14	17.82	20.05	21.76	23.30	24.65
31	14.53	17.27	19.58	21.29	22.90	24.28
32	13.89	16.70	19.09	20.81	22.48	23.89
33	13.25	16.12	18.60	20.34	22.07	23.51
34	12.60	15.54	18.09	19.85	21.64	23.11
35	11.93	14.94	17.53	19.39	21.21	22.71
36	11.25	14.33	16.97	18.92	20.76	22.31
37	10.55	13.71	16.39	18.45	20.31	21.88
38	9.83	13.08	15.80	17.96	19.85	21.46
39	9.11	12.42	15.21	17.47	19.38	21.03
40	8.35	11.74	14.59	16.89	18.85	20.54
41	7.58	11.03	13.95	16.38	18.33	20.03
42	6.79	10.33	13.31	15.73	17.79	19.53
43	5.99	9.61	12.66	15.14	17.25	19.02
44	5.18	8.87	12.00	14.55	16.70	18.52
45	4.34	8.11	11.31	13.91	16.11	17.96
46	3.50	7.35	10.61	13.27	15.52	17.41
47	2.64	6.57	9.90	12.64	14.93	16.85
48	1.78	5.78	9.20	11.99	14.33	16.29
49	0.90	5.00	8.48	11.34	13.73	15.72
50		4.20	7.77	10.65	13.11	15.14
51		3.39	7.06	9.97	12.48	14.55
52		2.56	6.32	9.28	11.85	13.95
53		1.72	5.58	8.59	11.22	13.36
54		0.88	4.82	7.90	10.59	12.77
55			4.07	7.27	9.98	12.20
56			3.31	6.62	9.42	11.70
57			2.52	5.97	8.85	11.20
58			1.71	5.30	8.27	10.69
59			0.86	4.61	7.68	10.17
60				3.89	7.07	9.65
61				3.17	6.46	9.11
62				2.41	5.83	8.57
63				1.64	5.18	8.02
64				0.83	4.51	7.45
65					3.82	6.87
66					3.11	6.27
67					2.37	5.66
68					1.61	5.03
69					0.83	4.39
70						3.72
71						3.03
72						2.32
73						1.59
74						0.82

Male - 2.5% Loss of earnings in medium economic conditions in *both* occupation with high risk *and* unfavourable geographical region

Age	To retiring age					
	50	55	60	65	70	75
16	22.40	24.32	25.85	26.99	28.03	29.01
17	21.97	23.94	25.51	26.68	27.76	28.76
18	21.53	23.54	25.16	26.37	27.48	28.51
19	21.08	23.15	24.80	26.06	27.20	28.26
20	20.56	22.67	24.40	25.70	26.84	27.91
21	20.03	22.18	23.98	25.32	26.47	27.56
22	19.49	21.70	23.56	24.94	26.09	27.21
23	18.94	21.20	23.12	24.55	25.70	26.85
24	18.39	20.69	22.69	24.15	25.31	26.48
25	17.83	20.20	22.21	23.72	24.93	26.13
26	17.28	19.68	21.72	23.27	24.55	25.77
27	16.70	19.16	21.24	22.82	24.16	25.41
28	16.12	18.64	20.74	22.37	23.77	25.04
29	15.53	18.10	20.23	21.91	23.37	24.67
30	14.92	17.56	19.76	21.44	22.96	24.29
31	14.31	17.00	19.28	20.96	22.55	23.90
32	13.67	16.44	18.79	20.48	22.12	23.51
33	13.03	15.86	18.29	19.99	21.69	23.11
34	12.38	15.27	17.78	19.50	21.26	22.70
35	11.72	14.67	17.21	19.03	20.81	22.29
36	11.04	14.06	16.65	18.56	20.37	21.88
37	10.35	13.45	16.07	18.08	19.91	21.45
38	9.64	12.81	15.48	17.59	19.44	21.02
39	8.92	12.16	14.89	17.09	18.97	20.58
40	8.16	11.46	14.25	16.50	18.41	20.05
41	7.38	10.75	13.60	15.96	17.85	19.51
42	6.60	10.04	12.94	15.29	17.29	18.98
43	5.81	9.32	12.28	14.69	16.72	18.44
44	5.01	8.59	11.61	14.07	16.15	17.91
45	4.19	7.83	10.92	13.42	15.54	17.33
46	3.37	7.08	10.22	12.78	14.94	16.75
47	2.54	6.32	9.51	12.13	14.33	16.17
48	1.70	5.54	8.81	11.48	13.72	15.59
49	0.86	4.77	8.10	10.83	13.11	15.01
50		4.00	7.40	10.15	12.48	14.41
51		3.22	6.71	9.47	11.85	13.81
52		2.43	6.00	8.79	11.22	13.21
53		1.63	5.28	8.11	10.59	12.61
54		0.83	4.55	7.43	9.97	12.02
55			3.84	6.84	9.39	11.48
56			3.12	6.23	8.86	11.01
57			2.37	5.62	8.32	10.53
58			1.61	4.98	7.78	10.06
59			0.81	4.34	7.23	9.57
60				3.66	6.65	9.08
61				2.98	6.07	8.57
62				2.27	5.49	8.06
63				1.54	4.87	7.54
64				0.78	4.25	7.01
65					3.59	6.46
66					2.93	5.90
67					2.23	5.33
68					1.52	4.73
69					0.78	4.13
70						3.50
71						2.85
72						2.19
73						1.49
74						0.77

Female - 2.5% Loss of earnings in medium economic conditions in *both* low risk occupation *and* favourable geographical region

Age	To retiring age					
	50	55	60	65	70	75
16	22.89	24.87	26.60	27.26	28.36	29.41
17	22.45	24.48	26.26	26.96	28.09	29.17
18	22.00	24.09	25.90	26.66	27.82	28.92
19	21.55	23.68	25.54	26.35	27.54	28.67
20	21.08	23.27	25.17	26.03	27.26	28.42
21	20.60	22.84	24.80	25.70	26.93	28.12
22	20.10	22.40	24.41	25.36	26.61	27.82
23	19.60	21.95	24.01	25.02	26.28	27.52
24	19.08	21.49	23.60	24.66	25.94	27.21
25	18.55	21.02	23.18	24.30	25.58	26.89
26	17.91	20.44	22.61	23.88	25.23	26.56
27	17.28	19.85	22.05	23.45	24.87	26.23
28	16.62	19.25	21.48	23.02	24.50	25.90
29	15.96	18.64	20.89	22.57	24.12	25.54
30	15.30	18.03	20.30	22.12	23.72	25.19
31	14.68	17.47	19.84	21.71	23.34	24.83
32	14.05	16.92	19.35	21.28	22.94	24.46
33	13.41	16.35	18.87	20.85	22.53	24.10
34	12.75	15.76	18.36	20.41	22.11	23.71
35	12.09	15.16	17.84	19.95	21.69	23.32
36	11.37	14.52	17.24	19.41	21.20	22.88
37	10.65	13.87	16.63	18.85	20.73	22.42
38	9.92	13.20	16.02	18.29	20.22	21.96
39	9.17	12.53	15.40	17.72	19.73	21.50
40	8.41	11.85	14.76	17.15	19.21	21.03
41	7.63	11.15	14.13	16.64	18.70	20.55
42	6.85	10.44	13.49	16.00	18.17	20.06
43	6.04	9.72	12.84	15.42	17.63	19.56
44	5.23	8.98	12.19	14.83	17.10	19.07
45	4.39	8.24	11.51	14.22	17.04	18.56
46	3.57	7.53	10.90	13.70	16.10	18.17
47	2.72	6.79	10.27	13.16	15.64	17.76
48	1.85	6.04	9.62	12.61	15.15	17.35
49	0.94	5.26	8.96	12.04	14.67	16.92
50		4.44	8.26	11.45	14.16	16.48
51		3.65	7.62	10.93	13.98	16.42
52		2.80	6.93	10.39	13.53	16.07
53		1.92	6.21	9.81	13.06	15.70
54		0.98	5.45	9.21	12.57	15.30
55			4.65	8.56	11.87	14.67
56			3.77	7.81	11.22	14.09
57			2.87	7.04	10.54	13.49
58			1.94	6.24	9.85	12.88
59			0.99	5.43	9.15	12.27
60				4.58	8.42	11.64
61				3.72	7.68	11.00
62				2.83	6.92	10.34
63				1.92	6.15	9.67
64				0.97	5.35	8.98
65					4.52	8.27
66					3.67	7.55
67					2.80	6.80
68					1.90	6.04
69					0.97	5.25
70						4.44
71						3.61
72						2.76
73						1.88
74						0.97

Female - 2.5% Loss of earnings in medium economic conditions in *either* low risk occupation *or* favourable geographical region

Age	To retiring age					
	50	55	60	65	70	75
16	22.32	24.25	25.80	26.98	28.07	29.11
17	21.89	23.87	25.47	26.68	27.80	28.87
18	21.45	23.49	25.12	26.38	27.53	28.62
19	21.01	23.09	24.77	26.07	27.26	28.37
20	20.55	22.69	24.41	25.76	26.98	28.12
21	20.06	22.25	24.06	25.43	26.65	27.83
22	19.56	21.80	23.68	25.09	26.33	27.53
23	19.05	21.34	23.29	24.76	26.01	27.24
24	18.53	20.87	22.89	24.40	25.67	26.92
25	17.99	20.39	22.48	24.05	25.32	26.61
26	17.44	19.90	22.02	23.63	24.97	26.29
27	16.89	19.41	21.56	23.21	24.61	25.96
28	16.31	18.90	21.08	22.78	24.24	25.63
29	15.74	18.37	20.59	22.33	23.87	25.28
30	15.14	17.84	20.09	21.89	23.47	24.93
31	14.53	17.29	19.63	21.48	23.10	24.57
32	13.91	16.75	19.15	21.06	22.70	24.21
33	13.28	16.18	18.67	20.63	22.30	23.84
34	12.62	15.60	18.17	20.20	21.88	23.46
35	11.96	15.00	17.65	19.74	21.46	23.08
36	11.25	14.37	17.06	19.20	20.98	22.64
37	10.54	13.73	16.46	18.65	20.51	22.18
38	9.81	13.07	15.85	18.09	20.01	21.73
39	9.07	12.40	15.24	17.53	19.52	21.27
40	8.33	11.73	14.61	16.96	19.01	20.80
41	7.54	11.02	13.96	16.44	18.47	20.30
42	6.76	10.30	13.31	15.78	17.92	19.79
43	5.95	9.57	12.65	15.19	17.36	19.27
44	5.14	8.84	11.99	14.58	16.81	18.75
45	4.31	8.09	11.30	13.96	16.73	18.22
46	3.50	7.38	10.69	13.43	15.78	17.82
47	2.66	6.66	10.06	12.89	15.31	17.39
48	1.81	5.91	9.41	12.33	14.82	16.96
49	0.92	5.14	8.75	11.76	14.32	16.52
50		4.34	8.06	11.16	13.81	16.07
51		3.55	7.42	10.65	13.62	15.99
52		2.73	6.74	10.11	13.17	15.64
53		1.86	6.04	9.54	12.70	15.26
54		0.96	5.29	8.94	12.21	14.86
55			4.51	8.30	11.51	14.22
56			3.66	7.57	10.88	13.66
57			2.78	6.83	10.22	13.08
58			1.88	6.05	9.55	12.49
59			0.96	5.26	8.87	11.90
60				4.44	8.17	11.29
61				3.61	7.45	10.67
62				2.75	6.71	10.03
63				1.86	5.96	9.38
64				0.94	5.19	8.71
65					4.38	8.02
66					3.56	7.32
67					2.71	6.59
68					1.84	5.85
69					0.94	5.09
70						4.31
71						3.50
72						2.67
73						1.82
74						0.94

	Female - 2.5% Loss of earnings in medium economic conditions in occupation and region with one low and one high risk factor							**Female - 2.5% Loss of earnings in medium economic conditions in *both* occupation with medium risk *and* medium geographical region**					

Age	50	55	60	65	70	75	Age	50	55	60	65	70	75
16	22.20	24.12	25.67	26.84	27.92	28.96	16	22.09	24.00	25.54	26.70	27.77	28.80
17	21.78	23.75	25.34	26.54	27.65	28.72	17	21.66	23.62	25.21	26.40	27.51	28.57
18	21.34	23.37	24.99	26.24	27.39	28.47	18	21.23	23.25	24.86	26.11	27.24	28.32
19	20.90	22.97	24.65	25.94	27.11	28.22	19	20.80	22.85	24.52	25.80	26.97	28.08
20	20.45	22.57	24.29	25.62	26.84	27.98	20	20.34	22.46	24.16	25.49	26.70	27.83
21	19.94	22.11	23.91	25.27	26.49	27.65	21	19.86	22.02	23.81	25.17	26.38	27.54
22	19.42	21.64	23.51	24.91	26.14	27.33	22	19.36	21.57	23.43	24.83	26.06	27.24
23	18.89	21.16	23.10	24.55	25.79	27.01	23	18.86	21.12	23.05	24.50	25.74	26.95
24	18.35	20.67	22.68	24.17	25.42	26.67	24	18.34	20.65	22.66	24.15	25.40	26.64
25	17.81	20.18	22.25	23.80	25.05	26.33	25	17.81	20.18	22.25	23.80	25.05	26.33
26	17.25	19.68	21.78	23.37	24.69	25.99	26	17.26	19.70	21.79	23.39	24.71	26.01
27	16.69	19.18	21.31	22.94	24.32	25.65	27	16.72	19.21	21.34	22.97	24.35	25.68
28	16.11	18.66	20.82	22.50	23.94	25.30	28	16.14	18.70	20.86	22.54	23.99	25.36
29	15.53	18.13	20.32	22.04	23.55	24.94	29	15.57	18.18	20.37	22.10	23.62	25.01
30	14.93	17.60	19.81	21.58	23.14	24.58	30	14.98	17.66	19.88	21.66	23.23	24.67
31	14.32	17.04	19.35	21.16	22.76	24.21	31	14.38	17.11	19.43	21.25	22.85	24.31
32	13.69	16.49	18.86	20.74	22.35	23.83	32	13.76	16.57	18.95	20.84	22.46	23.95
33	13.06	15.92	18.37	20.30	21.93	23.45	33	13.14	16.01	18.48	20.42	22.06	23.59
34	12.41	15.34	17.87	19.86	21.51	23.06	34	12.49	15.43	17.98	19.98	21.65	23.21
35	11.75	14.74	17.35	19.39	21.08	22.67	35	11.84	14.85	17.47	19.53	21.23	22.83
36	11.05	14.11	16.75	18.85	20.59	22.22	36	11.14	14.22	16.89	19.00	20.76	22.40
37	10.34	13.47	16.15	18.29	20.11	21.75	37	10.43	13.58	16.29	18.45	20.29	21.95
38	9.62	12.81	15.54	17.73	19.61	21.29	38	9.71	12.93	15.68	17.90	19.79	21.50
39	8.89	12.15	14.92	17.17	19.11	20.83	39	8.98	12.27	15.07	17.34	19.31	21.04
40	8.15	11.48	14.30	16.60	18.60	20.35	40	8.24	11.60	14.45	16.78	18.80	20.58
41	7.37	10.76	13.64	16.05	18.03	19.82	41	7.45	10.89	13.80	16.24	18.24	20.05
42	6.58	10.04	12.97	15.37	17.45	19.27	42	6.66	10.16	13.13	15.56	17.67	19.51
43	5.78	9.30	12.29	14.76	16.87	18.72	43	5.86	9.43	12.46	14.96	17.10	18.97
44	4.99	8.57	11.62	14.13	16.29	18.17	44	5.06	8.69	11.79	14.34	16.53	18.43
45	4.17	7.83	10.93	13.50	16.17	17.62	45	4.24	7.95	11.10	13.71	16.42	17.89
46	3.38	7.13	10.32	12.96	15.23	17.19	46	3.43	7.24	10.49	13.16	15.47	17.46
47	2.56	6.41	9.69	12.40	14.73	16.74	47	2.61	6.52	9.85	12.61	14.98	17.02
48	1.73	5.68	9.04	11.84	14.23	16.29	48	1.76	5.77	9.20	12.05	14.48	16.58
49	0.88	4.92	8.39	11.27	13.72	15.82	49	0.90	5.01	8.54	11.47	13.97	16.12
50		4.15	7.71	10.67	13.20	15.36	50		4.23	7.86	10.88	13.45	15.66
51		3.39	7.09	10.16	13.00	15.27	51		3.46	7.23	10.36	13.26	15.57
52		2.60	6.43	9.63	12.55	14.91	52		2.65	6.56	9.83	12.81	15.21
53		1.78	5.75	9.07	12.09	14.52	53		1.81	5.87	9.26	12.34	14.82
54		0.91	5.03	8.49	11.60	14.12	54		0.93	5.14	8.67	11.85	14.42
55			4.28	7.87	10.91	13.48	55			4.37	8.04	11.15	13.77
56			3.47	7.18	10.31	12.94	56			3.54	7.34	10.54	13.23
57			2.64	6.47	9.68	12.40	57			2.70	6.61	9.90	12.67
58			1.78	5.73	9.05	11.84	58			1.82	5.86	9.25	12.10
59			0.91	4.99	8.41	11.28	59			0.93	5.10	8.59	11.53
60				4.21	7.74	10.70	60				4.31	7.91	10.93
61				3.42	7.06	10.11	61				3.50	7.22	10.33
62				2.60	6.36	9.50	62				2.66	6.50	9.71
63				1.77	5.65	8.89	63				1.80	5.77	9.08
64				0.89	4.91	8.25	64				0.91	5.02	8.44
65					4.15	7.60	65					4.25	7.77
66					3.38	6.93	66					3.45	7.09
67					2.57	6.24	67					2.63	6.38
68					1.75	5.55	68					1.79	5.67
69					0.89	4.82	69					0.91	4.93
70						4.08	70						4.17
71						3.32	71						3.39
72						2.53	72						2.59
73						1.73	73						1.77
74						0.89	74						0.91

Female - 2.5% Loss of earnings in medium economic conditions in *either* occupation with high risk *or* unfavourable geographical region

Age	To retiring age					
	50	55	60	65	70	75
16	21.97	23.88	25.40	26.55	27.63	28.65
17	21.55	23.50	25.08	26.26	27.36	28.42
18	21.12	23.13	24.73	25.97	27.10	28.17
19	20.69	22.73	24.39	25.67	26.83	27.93
20	20.24	22.34	24.04	25.35	26.56	27.68
21	19.73	21.88	23.66	25.01	26.21	27.36
22	19.22	21.41	23.26	24.65	25.86	27.04
23	18.70	20.94	22.86	24.29	25.52	26.72
24	18.16	20.46	22.44	23.92	25.15	26.38
25	17.62	19.97	22.02	23.55	24.78	26.05
26	17.07	19.48	21.55	23.12	24.42	25.72
27	16.52	18.98	21.09	22.69	24.06	25.37
28	15.94	18.47	20.60	22.26	23.68	25.03
29	15.37	17.94	20.10	21.80	23.30	24.67
30	14.78	17.41	19.61	21.35	22.90	24.31
31	14.17	16.86	19.14	20.94	22.51	23.95
32	13.55	16.32	18.66	20.51	22.10	23.57
33	12.93	15.75	18.18	20.08	21.70	23.20
34	12.28	15.17	17.68	19.64	21.27	22.81
35	11.63	14.59	17.16	19.19	20.85	22.42
36	10.93	13.96	16.58	18.65	20.37	21.98
37	10.23	13.32	15.98	18.10	19.90	21.52
38	9.52	12.67	15.37	17.54	19.39	21.06
39	8.79	12.02	14.76	16.98	18.90	20.60
40	8.06	11.36	14.14	16.42	18.39	20.13
41	7.27	10.63	13.47	15.85	17.80	19.57
42	6.49	9.90	12.78	15.15	17.20	19.00
43	5.69	9.16	12.10	14.52	16.60	18.42
44	4.90	8.42	11.42	13.89	16.01	17.86
45	4.10	7.68	10.73	13.24	15.86	17.28
46	3.31	6.98	10.11	12.69	14.91	16.83
47	2.51	6.27	9.47	12.13	14.41	16.36
48	1.69	5.54	8.83	11.56	13.89	15.90
49	0.86	4.80	8.18	10.98	13.37	15.42
50		4.04	7.51	10.39	12.84	14.95
51		3.30	6.89	9.88	12.64	14.85
52		2.53	6.24	9.35	12.19	14.48
53		1.72	5.58	8.79	11.72	14.08
54		0.88	4.87	8.22	11.24	13.68
55			4.14	7.61	10.54	13.03
56			3.36	6.94	9.97	12.51
57			2.55	6.26	9.36	11.99
58			1.73	5.54	8.75	11.45
59			0.88	4.82	8.13	10.90
60				4.07	7.48	10.34
61				3.31	6.83	9.77
62				2.52	6.15	9.19
63				1.71	5.46	8.59
64				0.86	4.75	7.98
65					4.02	7.35
66					3.26	6.70
67					2.49	6.04
68					1.69	5.36
69					0.86	4.66
70						3.95
71						3.21
72						2.45
73						1.67
74						0.86

Female - 2.5% Loss of earnings in medium economic conditions in *both* occupation with high risk *and* unfavourable geographical region

Age	To retiring age					
	50	55	60	65	70	75
16	21.86	23.75	25.27	26.41	27.48	28.50
17	21.44	23.38	24.95	26.12	27.22	28.27
18	21.01	23.01	24.61	25.83	26.96	28.02
19	20.58	22.61	24.26	25.53	26.68	27.78
20	20.13	22.22	23.91	25.22	26.41	27.54
21	19.61	21.74	23.51	24.85	26.04	27.19
22	19.07	21.26	23.09	24.47	25.67	26.84
23	18.54	20.76	22.67	24.09	25.30	26.49
24	17.99	20.27	22.23	23.69	24.91	26.13
25	17.44	19.76	21.79	23.30	24.52	25.77
26	16.88	19.26	21.31	22.86	24.14	25.42
27	16.32	18.75	20.83	22.42	23.76	25.06
28	15.74	18.23	20.34	21.97	23.37	24.71
29	15.16	17.70	19.83	21.51	22.98	24.33
30	14.57	17.17	19.33	21.04	22.56	23.96
31	13.96	16.61	18.86	20.62	22.17	23.58
32	13.34	16.06	18.37	20.19	21.75	23.20
33	12.71	15.50	17.88	19.75	21.33	22.81
34	12.07	14.91	17.38	19.30	20.90	22.41
35	11.42	14.33	16.86	18.84	20.47	22.01
36	10.73	13.70	16.27	18.30	19.98	21.56
37	10.03	13.07	15.66	17.74	19.50	21.09
38	9.33	12.42	15.06	17.18	18.99	20.62
39	8.61	11.76	14.45	16.62	18.49	20.15
40	7.88	11.11	13.83	16.05	17.98	19.68
41	7.10	10.37	13.14	15.46	17.36	19.08
42	6.32	9.63	12.44	14.74	16.73	18.48
43	5.53	8.89	11.75	14.09	16.11	17.87
44	4.75	8.16	11.06	13.44	15.49	17.28
45	3.95	7.42	10.36	12.78	15.30	16.67
46	3.19	6.73	9.74	12.22	14.35	16.20
47	2.41	6.03	9.10	11.65	13.83	15.71
48	1.62	5.31	8.46	11.08	13.30	15.23
49	0.82	4.59	7.82	10.49	12.77	14.73
50		3.85	7.16	9.90	12.24	14.24
51		3.14	6.56	9.39	12.03	14.13
52		2.40	5.93	8.88	11.58	13.74
53		1.63	5.28	8.33	11.11	13.35
54		0.83	4.61	7.76	10.63	12.93
55			3.91	7.18	9.94	12.28
56			3.17	6.55	9.40	11.80
57			2.41	5.90	8.83	11.30
58			1.63	5.23	8.25	10.79
59			0.83	4.55	7.66	10.28
60				3.84	7.05	9.75
61				3.12	6.44	9.22
62				2.37	5.80	8.66
63				1.61	5.15	8.10
64				0.81	4.48	7.52
65					3.79	6.93
66					3.08	6.32
67					2.34	5.69
68					1.59	5.06
69					0.81	4.40
70						3.72
71						3.03
72						2.31
73						1.58
74						0.81

A3: Multipliers for fixed periods and at intervals

Introductory notes:

1. The purpose of the tables is to provide a means of calculating an appropriate multiplier which will produce the present day equivalent of a cost recurring, either continuously or at fixed intervals, over a given number of years. It does not allow for mortality or contingencies.

2. This table is based on a discount rate of 2.5 per cent per annum. The tables in B4 are based on rates of 1.5 per cent and 2 per cent. The Lord Chancellor has fixed the discount rate under the Damages Act 1996 (June 27, 2001) at 2.5 per cent, leaving open the possibility of a different rate in exceptional cases such as the effect of tax on large sums.

3. It is assumed that yearly loss is incurred at the *end* of each year in which the loss arises. (Continuous loss obviously accrues from day to day throughout the period. Weekly and monthly losses can in practice be treated as continuous.) For example:

    > For expenditure assumed to recur every 7 years the expenditure is shown as arising at the end of years 7, 14, and so on.

4. The table contains a number of columns: the number of years; the multiplier for a single payment in *n* years' time; that for a continuous loss over that period of *n* years; that for annual payments in the sense of a series of payments at intervals of 1 year; and those for payments at intervals of 2, 3, 4 and so on years.

5. The multiplier for a single payment in *n* years' time (second column) is the same as the discount factor for deferment for the next *n* years.

6. The table shows a multiplier appropriate to each year in which expenditure is to be incurred, and also cumulative multipliers for expenditure up to the end of that year. For example, at 2.5 per cent discount:

    > The multiplier for expenditure at the end of year 10 is 0.781. Thus the current lump sum required to provide £100 in 10 years' time is £78.10.

    And similarly:

    -   £100 a year continuously over the next 10 years has a present value of £886;

    -   £100 at the end of each of the next 10 years a present value of £875;

    -   £100 at the end of 2,4,6,8 and 10 years a present value of £432 (row 10, 2-yearly column);

    -   £100 at the end of 3,6 and 9 years a present value of £259 (row 9, 3-yearly column).

    The cumulative multipliers do not include an immediate payment: where one is needed in addition to the recurring payments add 1.00 to the multiplier.

7. The calculations have been rounded to 2 places of decimals.

Multipliers where there is evidence of life expectancy

8. In some cases there is medical evidence (agreed or not) of the particular claimant's life expectancy. As more distant losses have lower present value, the possibility of dying earlier than expected has more effect on the multiplier than that of dying later than expected. The multiplier for life of someone whose life expectancy is *n* years will therefore be lower than the multiplier for a fixed period of *n* years. The difference varies with sex and age. It is not large but at a discount rate of

2.5 per cent it is not negligible. Between the ages of 20 to 70 the difference, for both men and women, is normally within the range of 0.50 to 0.75.

Modifications

9. Multipliers for continuous loss for periods other than entire years can be obtained by interpolation:

   For continuous payments for 10 and 11 years the multipliers are 8.86 and 9.63.

   So for weekly payments for 10½ years the multiplier is approximately ½(8.86 + 9.63) = 9.25.

10. Multipliers for payments beginning after a deferred period can be derived by subtraction or by multiplying by a factor from the single payment column:

    Multipliers for 5-yearly payments for 15 and for 50 years are 2.36 and 5.40;

    So the multiplier for 5-yearly payments from years 20 to 50 inclusive is 5.40 − 2.36 = 3.14;

    Multiplier for one payment after 18 years is 0.641;

    So that for 5-yearly payments from years 23 to 68 inclusive is 5.40 × 0.641 = 3.46.

11. Multipliers for irregular payments can be found by adding individual figures from the single payment column.

Multipliers at 2.5 per cent discount

n	Single payment	Continuous loss	Frequency of payments in years											
			1	2	3	4	5	6	7	8	10	12	15	20
1	0.976	0.99	0.98											
2	0.952	1.95	1.93	0.95										
3	0.929	2.89	2.86		0.93									
4	0.906	3.81	3.76	1.86		0.91								
5	0.884	4.70	4.65				0.88							
6	0.862	5.58	5.51	2.72	1.79			0.86						
7	0.841	6.43	6.35						0.84					
8	0.821	7.26	7.17	3.54		1.73				0.82				
9	0.801	8.07	7.97		2.59									
10	0.781	8.86	8.75	4.32			1.67				0.78			
11	0.762	9.63	9.51											
12	0.744	10.39	10.26	5.07	3.34	2.47		1.61				0.74		
13	0.725	11.12	10.98											
14	0.708	11.84	11.69	5.77					1.55					
15	0.690	12.54	12.38		4.03		2.36						0.69	
16	0.674	13.22	13.06	6.45		3.14				1.49				
17	0.657	13.88	13.71											
18	0.641	14.53	14.35	7.09	4.67			2.25						
19	0.626	15.17	14.98											
20	0.610	15.78	15.59	7.70		3.75	2.97				1.39			0.61
21	0.595	16.39	16.18		5.26			2.14						
22	0.581	16.97	16.77	8.28										
23	0.567	17.55	17.33											
24	0.553	18.11	17.88	8.83	5.82	4.31		2.80		2.05		1.30		
25	0.539	18.65	18.42				3.51							
26	0.526	19.19	18.95	9.36										
27	0.513	19.71	19.46		6.33									
28	0.501	20.21	19.96	9.86		4.81				2.65				
29	0.489	20.71	20.45											
30	0.477	21.19	20.93	10.34	6.81		3.98	3.28			1.87		1.17	
31	0.465	21.66	21.40											
32	0.454	22.12	21.85	10.79		5.26				2.50				
33	0.443	22.57	22.29		7.25									
34	0.432	23.01	22.72	11.22										
35	0.421	23.43	23.15				4.40		3.07					
36	0.411	23.85	23.56	11.63	7.66	5.67		3.69				1.71		
37	0.401	24.26	23.96											
38	0.391	24.65	24.35	12.02										
39	0.382	25.04	24.73		8.04									
40	0.372	25.42	25.10	12.40		6.05	4.78			2.87	2.24			0.98
41	0.363	25.78	25.47											
42	0.354	26.14	25.82	12.75	8.40			4.04	3.42					
43	0.346	26.49	26.17											
44	0.337	26.84	26.50	13.09		6.38								
45	0.329	27.17	26.83		8.72		5.10						1.50	
46	0.321	27.49	27.15	13.41										
47	0.313	27.81	27.47											
48	0.306	28.12	27.77	13.72	9.03	6.69		4.35		3.18		2.01		
49	0.298	28.42	28.07						3.72					
50	0.291	28.72	28.36	14.01			5.40				2.53			
51	0.284	29.00	28.65		9.31									
52	0.277	29.28	28.92	14.28		6.97								
53	0.270	29.56	29.19											
54	0.264	29.83	29.46	14.55	9.58			4.61						
55	0.257	30.09	29.71				5.65							
56	0.251	30.34	29.96	14.80		7.22			3.97	3.43				
57	0.245	30.59	30.21		9.82									
58	0.239	30.83	30.45	15.04										
59	0.233	31.06	30.68											
60	0.227	31.30	30.91	15.26	10.05	7.44	5.88	4.84			2.76	2.24	1.72	1.21

n	Single payment	Continuous loss	Frequency of payments in years											
			1	2	3	4	5	6	7	8	10	12	15	20
61	0.222	31.52	31.13											
62	0.216	31.74	31.35	15.48										
63	0.211	31.95	31.56		10.26				4.18					
64	0.206	32.16	31.76	15.69		7.65				3.64				
65	0.201	32.36	31.96				6.08							
66	0.196	32.56	32.16	15.88	10.46			5.04						
67	0.191	32.76	32.35											
68	0.187	32.94	32.54	16.07		7.84								
69	0.182	33.13	32.72		10.64									
70	0.178	33.31	32.90	16.25			6.26		4.36		2.94			
71	0.173	33.48	33.07											
72	0.169	33.66	33.24	16.41	10.81	8.00		5.20		3.80		2.41		
73	0.165	33.82	33.40											
74	0.161	33.99	33.57	16.58										
75	0.157	34.14	33.72		10.96		6.42						1.88	
76	0.153	34.30	33.88	16.73		8.16								
77	0.149	34.45	34.03						4.51					
78	0.146	34.60	34.17	16.87	11.11			5.35						
79	0.142	34.74	34.31											
80	0.139	34.88	34.45	17.01		8.30	6.55			3.94	3.08			1.35
81	0.135	35.02	34.59		11.25									
82	0.132	35.15	34.72	17.15										
83	0.129	35.28	34.85											
84	0.126	35.41	34.97	17.27	11.37	8.42		5.48	4.63			2.54		
85	0.123	35.53	35.10				6.68							
86	0.120	35.66	35.22	17.39										
87	0.117	35.77	35.33		11.49									
88	0.114	35.89	35.45	17.50		8.54				4.06				
89	0.111	36.00	35.56											
90	0.108	36.11	35.67	17.61	11.60		6.79	5.58			3.18		1.99	
91	0.106	36.22	35.77						4.74					
92	0.103	36.32	35.87	17.72		8.64								
93	0.101	36.42	35.98		11.70									
94	0.098	36.52	36.07	17.81										
95	0.096	36.62	36.17				6.88							
96	0.093	36.72	36.26	17.91	11.79	8.73		5.68		4.15		2.63		
97	0.091	36.81	36.35											
98	0.089	36.90	36.44	18.00					4.83					
99	0.087	36.99	36.53		11.88									
100	0.085	37.07	36.61	18.08		8.82	6.97				3.27			1.43

1. The single payment column is the appropriate multiplier for one payment in n years' time.

2. The continuous loss column is for loss accruing from day to day: in practice it is appropriate for weekly and monthly losses as well.

3. The column headed "1" is for a series of payments at yearly intervals *at the end of each year* for n years. If you want an immediate payment as well, add 1.

4. The remaining columns similarly show the multiplier for a series of payments at intervals of 2, 3, 4 and so on years.

5. Thus at 2.5 per cent discount £100 paid after 10 years has a present value of £78.10;
    – £100 a year continuously over the next 10 years has a present value of £886;
    – £100 at the end of each of the next 10 years has a present value of £875;
    – £100 at the end of 2, 4, 6, 8 and 10 years has a present value of £432 (row 10, 2-yearly column);
    – £100 at the end of 3, 6 and 9 years has a present value of £259 (row 9, 3-yearly column);
    – £100 now and after 2, 4, 6 and 8 years (but not the 10th year) has a present value of £454 (row 8, 2-yearly column, plus 1).

A4: Combination Tables

Introductory notes:

1. The following table is a combination of Ogden Tables 27 and 28. This is intended for use when a claimant will suffer a loss over a known number of years, but that loss will not start to run immediately.

2. For example:

   a. The claimant is now thirty years old. He has a reduced life expectation, to the age of 60. For the last ten years of his life, he will need nursing care at a cost of £7,500 a year. His nursing needs will therefore start in twenty years.

   b. At 2.5 per cent discount, the multiplier for a period of ten years is 8.86 [Ogden Table 28].

   c. At 2.5 per cent discount, a loss that will not occur for a further twenty years must be discounted by multiplying it by 0.6103 [Ogden Table 27].

   d. The appropriate multiplier is therefore [8.86 × 0.6103] = 5.41 (to two decimal places).

3. The following points should also be remembered:

   a. When applying the multipliers to claims for loss of earnings, Ogden Tables 3–14 only take the ordinary risks of mortality into account. They do *not* take into account any other risks— *e.g.* that the claimant's job may be a risky one, or that unemployment in the claimant's area may be high. A further discount must be made for these risks: see Section B of the Introduction to the Ogden Tables (Contingencies other than Mortality).

   b. Ogden Table 27 (Discounting Factors for Term Certain) gives the discount factor for a period of *complete* years. So in the example above, where the date of trial is May 23, 2005 the need for nursing care will start on May 23, 2025.

   c. Ogden Table 28 (Multipliers for Pecuniary Loss for Term Certain) assumes that the loss will occur regularly throughout the year, *e.g.* a monthly nursing bill.

Combination grid (Discount rate 2.5%)

Years of loss	Years before loss starts to run															
	1	2	2.5	3	4	5	6	7.5	10	12.5	15	20	25	30	35	40
1	0.96	0.94	0.93	0.92	0.89	0.87	0.85	0.82	0.77	0.73	0.68	0.60	0.53	0.47	0.42	0.37
2	1.90	1.86	1.83	1.81	1.77	1.72	1.68	1.62	1.52	1.43	1.35	1.19	1.05	0.93	0.82	0.73
3	2.82	2.75	2.72	2.69	2.62	2.56	2.49	2.40	2.26	2.12	2.00	1.76	1.56	1.38	1.22	1.08
4	3.72	3.63	3.58	3.54	3.45	3.37	3.28	3.16	2.98	2.80	2.63	2.32	2.05	1.82	1.60	1.42
5	4.59	4.48	4.42	4.37	4.26	4.16	4.06	3.91	3.67	3.45	3.25	2.87	2.54	2.24	1.98	1.75
6	5.44	5.31	5.24	5.18	5.05	4.93	4.81	4.63	4.36	4.10	3.85	3.40	3.01	2.66	2.35	2.08
7	6.27	6.12	6.04	5.97	5.82	5.68	5.54	5.34	5.02	4.72	4.44	3.92	3.47	3.06	2.71	2.39
8	7.08	6.91	6.82	6.74	6.58	6.42	6.26	6.03	5.67	5.33	5.01	4.43	3.92	3.46	3.06	2.70
9	7.87	7.68	7.59	7.49	7.31	7.13	6.96	6.71	6.30	5.93	5.57	4.92	4.35	3.85	3.40	3.01
10	8.64	8.43	8.33	8.23	8.03	7.83	7.64	7.36	6.92	6.51	6.12	5.41	4.78	4.22	3.73	3.30
11	9.40	9.17	9.06	8.94	8.73	8.51	8.31	8.00	7.52	7.07	6.65	5.88	5.20	4.59	4.06	3.59
12	10.13	9.88	9.76	9.64	9.41	9.18	8.96	8.63	8.11	7.63	7.17	6.34	5.60	4.95	4.38	3.87
13	10.85	10.58	10.45	10.33	10.07	9.83	9.59	9.24	8.69	8.17	7.68	6.79	6.00	5.30	4.69	4.14
14	11.55	11.27	11.13	10.99	10.72	10.46	10.21	9.84	9.25	8.69	8.17	7.22	6.38	5.64	4.99	4.41
15	12.23	11.93	11.78	11.64	11.36	11.08	10.81	10.42	9.79	9.21	8.66	7.65	6.76	5.98	5.28	4.67
16	12.89	12.58	12.43	12.27	11.97	11.68	11.40	10.98	10.33	9.71	9.13	8.07	7.13	6.30	5.57	4.92
17	13.54	13.21	13.05	12.89	12.58	12.27	11.97	11.54	10.85	10.20	9.59	8.47	7.49	6.62	5.85	5.17
18	14.18	13.83	13.66	13.49	13.16	12.84	12.53	12.07	11.35	10.67	10.03	8.87	7.84	6.93	6.12	5.41
19	14.80	14.43	14.26	14.08	13.74	13.40	13.08	12.60	11.85	11.14	10.47	9.25	8.18	7.23	6.39	5.65
20	15.40	15.02	14.84	14.66	14.30	13.95	13.61	13.11	12.33	11.59	10.90	9.63	8.51	7.52	6.65	5.88
21	15.99	15.60	15.40	15.22	14.84	14.48	14.13	13.62	12.80	12.03	11.31	10.00	8.84	7.81	6.90	6.10
22	16.56	16.16	15.96	15.76	15.38	15.00	14.64	14.10	13.26	12.47	11.72	10.36	9.16	8.09	7.15	6.32
23	17.12	16.70	16.50	16.29	15.90	15.51	15.13	14.58	13.71	12.89	12.12	10.71	9.46	8.37	7.39	6.54
24	17.67	17.23	17.02	16.81	16.40	16.00	15.61	15.05	14.15	13.30	12.50	11.05	9.77	8.63	7.63	6.74
25	18.20	17.75	17.54	17.32	16.90	16.49	16.08	15.50	14.57	13.70	12.88	11.38	10.06	8.89	7.86	6.95
26	18.72	18.26	18.04	17.82	17.38	16.96	16.54	15.94	14.99	14.09	13.25	11.71	10.35	9.15	8.08	7.15
27	19.23	18.76	18.53	18.30	17.85	17.42	16.99	16.37	15.39	14.47	13.61	12.03	10.63	9.39	8.30	7.34
28	19.72	19.24	19.00	18.77	18.31	17.87	17.43	16.80	15.79	14.85	13.96	12.34	10.90	9.64	8.52	7.53
29	20.20	19.71	19.47	19.23	18.76	18.30	17.86	17.21	16.18	15.21	14.30	12.64	11.17	9.87	8.73	7.71
30	20.67	20.17	19.92	19.68	19.20	18.73	18.27	17.61	16.55	15.56	14.63	12.93	11.43	10.10	8.93	7.89
31	21.13	20.62	20.36	20.11	19.62	19.15	18.68	18.00	16.92	15.91	14.96	13.22	11.68	10.33	9.13	8.07
32	21.58	21.05	20.80	20.54	20.04	19.55	19.07	18.38	17.28	16.25	15.27	13.50	11.93	10.55	9.32	8.24
33	22.02	21.48	21.22	20.96	20.45	19.95	19.46	18.75	17.63	16.58	15.58	13.77	12.17	10.76	9.51	8.41
34	22.44	21.90	21.63	21.36	20.84	20.33	19.84	19.12	17.97	16.90	15.88	14.04	12.41	10.97	9.69	8.57
35	22.86	22.30	22.03	21.76	21.23	20.71	20.21	19.47	18.31	17.21	16.18	14.30	12.64	11.17	9.87	8.73
36	23.27	22.70	22.42	22.15	21.61	21.08	20.56	19.82	18.63	17.52	16.47	14.55	12.86	11.37	10.05	8.88
37	23.66	23.09	22.80	22.52	21.97	21.44	20.91	20.15	18.95	17.81	16.75	14.80	13.08	11.56	10.22	9.03
38	24.05	23.46	23.18	22.89	22.33	21.79	21.26	20.48	19.26	18.10	17.02	15.04	13.30	11.75	10.39	9.18
39	24.43	23.83	23.54	23.25	22.68	22.13	21.59	20.80	19.56	18.39	17.29	15.28	13.51	11.94	10.55	9.32
40	24.79	24.19	23.89	23.60	23.02	22.46	21.91	21.12	19.85	18.67	17.55	15.51	13.71	12.12	10.71	9.47
41	25.15	24.54	24.24	23.94	23.36	22.79	22.23	21.42	20.14	18.94	17.80	15.73	13.91	12.29	10.86	9.60
42	25.50	24.88	24.58	24.27	23.68	23.11	22.54	21.72	20.42	19.20	18.05	15.95	14.10	12.46	11.02	9.74
43	25.85	25.21	24.91	24.60	24.00	23.41	22.84	22.01	20.70	19.46	18.29	16.17	14.29	12.63	11.16	9.87
44	26.18	25.54	25.23	24.92	24.31	23.72	23.14	22.30	20.96	19.71	18.53	16.38	14.47	12.79	11.31	9.99
45	26.50	25.86	25.54	25.23	24.61	24.01	23.43	22.57	21.22	19.95	18.76	16.58	14.65	12.95	11.45	10.12
Years of loss	1	2	2.5	3	4	5	6	7.5	10	12.5	15	20	25	30	35	40

A5: Nil Discount Tables "At a Glance"

MALE (0%)

	Table 1 Pecuniary loss for life	Table 3 Loss of earnings to age 50	Table 5 Loss of earnings to age 55	Table 7 Loss of earnings to age 60	Table 9 Loss of earnings to age 65	Table 11 Loss of earnings to age 70	Table 13 Loss of earnings to age 75	Table 15 Loss of pension from age 50	Table 17 Loss of pension from age 55	Table 19 Loss of pension from age 60	Table 21 Loss of pension from age 65	Table 23 Loss of pension from age 70	Table 25 Loss of pension from age 75
0	83.24							33.97	29.19	24.49	19.92	15.54	11.43
1	82.62							34.11	29.31	24.59	20.00	15.59	11.47
2	81.62							34.09	29.29	24.57	19.98	15.58	11.45
3	80.60							34.07	29.27	24.55	19.96	15.56	11.43
4	79.58							34.04	29.24	24.52	19.93	15.53	11.41
5	78.55							34.01	29.21	24.49	19.91	15.51	11.39
6	77.52							33.98	29.18	24.47	19.88	15.49	11.37
7	76.48							33.94	29.15	24.44	19.85	15.46	11.35
8	75.45							33.91	29.12	24.40	19.82	15.43	11.33
9	74.41							33.88	29.08	24.37	19.79	15.41	11.30
10	73.38							33.84	29.05	24.34	19.76	15.38	11.28
11	72.34							33.80	29.01	24.31	19.73	15.35	11.25
12	71.30							33.77	28.98	24.27	19.70	15.32	11.23
13	70.26							33.73	28.94	24.24	19.67	15.29	11.20
14	69.22							33.69	28.90	24.20	19.63	15.26	11.18
15	68.18							33.65	28.87	24.16	19.60	15.23	11.15
16	67.15	33.53	38.32	43.02	47.58	51.94	56.02	33.61	28.83	24.13	19.57	15.20	11.12
17	66.11	32.54	37.32	42.02	46.58	50.94	55.02	33.58	28.79	24.09	19.53	15.17	11.10
18	65.09	31.55	36.33	41.03	45.59	49.95	54.02	33.54	28.76	24.06	19.50	15.14	11.07
19	64.08	30.57	35.35	40.05	44.61	48.97	53.04	33.52	28.73	24.04	19.48	15.12	11.05
20	63.08	29.58	34.37	39.07	43.63	47.99	52.06	33.49	28.71	24.01	19.45	15.09	11.02
21	62.07	28.60	33.39	38.09	42.65	47.01	51.07	33.47	28.68	23.98	19.42	15.06	11.00
22	61.06	27.62	32.41	37.11	41.67	46.02	50.09	33.44	28.65	23.95	19.39	15.03	10.97
23	60.05	26.63	31.42	36.13	40.69	45.04	49.10	33.41	28.62	23.92	19.36	15.00	10.95
24	59.03	25.65	30.44	35.15	39.71	44.06	48.12	33.39	28.59	23.89	19.33	14.97	10.92
25	58.02	24.67	29.46	34.17	38.73	43.08	47.13	33.36	28.56	23.86	19.30	14.94	10.89
26	57.01	23.68	28.48	33.19	37.75	42.10	46.15	33.33	28.53	23.83	19.27	14.91	10.86
27	56.00	22.70	27.50	32.21	36.77	41.12	45.17	33.30	28.50	23.80	19.24	14.88	10.83
28	54.99	21.72	26.52	31.23	35.79	40.14	44.19	33.27	28.47	23.76	19.20	14.85	10.80
29	53.98	20.73	25.54	30.25	34.81	39.16	43.21	33.25	28.44	23.73	19.17	14.82	10.77
30	52.97	19.75	24.56	29.27	33.83	38.18	42.23	33.22	28.41	23.70	19.14	14.79	10.74
31	51.96	18.77	23.58	28.29	32.86	37.20	41.24	33.19	28.38	23.66	19.10	14.75	10.71
32	50.94	17.78	22.60	27.31	31.88	36.23	40.26	33.16	28.34	23.63	19.06	14.72	10.68
33	49.93	16.80	21.62	26.34	30.90	35.25	39.28	33.13	28.31	23.59	19.03	14.68	10.65
34	48.91	15.82	20.64	25.36	29.92	34.27	38.30	33.10	28.28	23.56	18.99	14.64	10.61
35	47.90	14.83	19.66	24.38	28.95	33.29	37.32	33.07	28.24	23.52	18.95	14.61	10.58
36	46.88	13.85	18.67	23.40	27.97	32.31	36.34	33.03	28.21	23.48	18.91	14.57	10.54
37	45.86	12.86	17.69	22.42	26.99	31.34	35.36	33.00	28.17	23.44	18.87	14.53	10.50
38	44.85	11.88	16.71	21.44	26.01	30.36	34.38	32.97	28.14	23.40	18.83	14.49	10.47
39	43.83	10.89	15.73	20.46	25.04	29.38	33.40	32.94	28.10	23.36	18.79	14.45	10.43
40	42.81	9.90	14.75	19.49	24.06	28.41	32.42	32.91	28.06	23.32	18.75	14.41	10.39
41	41.80	8.92	13.77	18.51	23.09	27.43	31.44	32.88	28.03	23.29	18.71	14.36	10.35
42	40.78	7.93	12.79	17.54	22.12	26.46	30.47	32.86	28.00	23.25	18.67	14.32	10.31
43	39.78	6.94	11.81	16.56	21.15	25.49	29.50	32.83	27.97	23.21	18.63	14.28	10.27
44	38.77	5.95	10.83	15.59	20.18	24.53	28.53	32.82	27.94	23.18	18.59	14.25	10.24
45	37.77	4.97	9.85	14.62	19.21	23.56	27.57	32.80	27.92	23.15	18.56	14.21	10.20
46	36.78	3.98	8.87	13.65	18.25	22.60	26.61	32.80	27.91	23.13	18.53	14.17	10.16
47	35.79	2.99	7.89	12.68	17.29	21.65	25.66	32.80	27.89	23.11	18.50	14.14	10.13
48	34.80	1.99	6.91	11.71	16.33	20.70	24.71	32.81	27.89	23.09	18.47	14.10	10.09
49	33.82	1.00	5.93	10.75	15.37	19.75	23.76	32.82	27.88	23.07	18.44	14.07	10.06
50	32.84		4.95	9.78	14.42	18.79	22.81	32.84	27.88	23.06	18.42	14.04	10.02
51	31.85		3.97	8.81	13.46	17.84	21.87		27.89	23.04	18.39	14.01	9.99
52	30.87		2.98	7.84	12.50	16.89	20.92		27.89	23.03	18.37	13.98	9.95
53	29.90		1.99	6.87	11.54	15.95	19.98		27.90	23.03	18.35	13.95	9.92
54	28.93		1.00	5.89	10.58	15.00	19.04		27.93	23.03	18.34	13.93	9.89

MALE (0%) *continued*

	Table 1 Pecuniary loss for life	Table 3 Loss of earnings to age 50	Table 5 Loss of earnings to age 55	Table 7 Loss of earnings to age 60	Table 9 Loss of earnings to age 65	Table 11 Loss of earnings to age 70	Table 13 Loss of earnings to age 75	Table 15 Loss of pension from age 50	Table 17 Loss of pension from age 55	Table 19 Loss of pension from age 60	Table 21 Loss of pension from age 65	Table 23 Loss of pension from age 70	Table 25 Loss of pension from age 75
55	27.97			4.92	9.63	14.06	18.11		27.97	23.05	18.34	13.91	9.86
56	27.02			3.94	8.68	13.12	17.18			23.08	18.34	13.90	9.84
57	26.09			2.97	7.73	12.19	16.27			23.13	18.36	13.90	9.82
58	25.17			1.98	6.78	11.27	15.36			23.19	18.40	13.90	9.81
59	24.27			1.00	5.82	10.35	14.46			23.27	18.44	13.92	9.81
60	23.37				4.87	9.42	13.56			23.37	18.51	13.95	9.81
61	22.50				3.91	8.50	12.67				18.59	13.99	9.83
62	21.64				2.95	7.59	11.79				18.69	14.05	9.85
63	20.79				1.97	6.66	10.90				18.81	14.12	9.88
64	19.94				0.99	5.74	10.02				18.95	14.20	9.92
65	19.10					4.81	9.14				19.10	14.29	9.96
66	18.25					3.87	8.25					14.39	10.00
67	17.41					2.92	7.36					14.49	10.05
68	16.56					1.96	6.47					14.60	10.09
69	15.72					0.99	5.57					14.73	10.15
70	14.89						4.67					14.89	10.22
71	14.08						3.77						10.31
72	13.29						2.86						10.43
73	12.53						1.93						10.60
74	11.80						0.98						10.82
75	11.10												11.10
76	10.44												
77	9.81												
78	9.21												
79	8.64												
80	8.09												
81	7.56												
82	7.04												
83	6.55												
84	6.10												
85	5.67												
86	5.28												
87	4.92												
88	4.59												
89	4.29												
90	4.01												
91	3.75												
92	3.50												
93	3.29												
94	3.11												
95	2.93												
96	2.76												
97	2.59												
98	2.42												
99	2.25												
100	2.10												

FEMALE (0%)

	Table 2 Pecuniary loss for life	Table 4 Loss of earnings to age 50	Table 6 Loss of earnings to age 55	Table 8 Loss of earnings to age 60	Table 10 Loss of earnings to age 65	Table 12 Loss of earnings to age 70	Table 14 Loss of earnings to age 75	Table 16 Loss of pension from age 50	Table 18 Loss of pension from age 55	Table 20 Loss of pension from age 60	Table 22 Loss of pension from age 65	Table 24 Loss of pension from age 70	Table 26 Loss of pension from age 75
0	87.08							37.54	32.68	27.87	23.16	18.57	14.16
1	86.43							37.69	32.80	27.98	23.24	18.63	14.21
2	85.43							37.67	32.79	27.96	23.23	18.62	14.19
3	84.42							37.66	32.77	27.94	23.21	18.60	14.18
4	83.40							37.63	32.75	27.92	23.19	18.58	14.16
5	82.38							37.61	32.73	27.90	23.17	18.56	14.14
6	81.36							37.59	32.70	27.88	23.14	18.54	14.12
7	80.34							37.56	32.68	27.85	23.12	18.52	14.11
8	79.31							37.53	32.65	27.83	23.10	18.50	14.08
9	78.28							37.51	32.62	27.80	23.07	18.47	14.06
10	77.25							37.48	32.60	27.78	23.05	18.45	14.04
11	76.23							37.45	32.57	27.75	23.02	18.43	14.02
12	75.20							37.42	32.54	27.72	23.00	18.40	14.00
13	74.17							37.39	32.51	27.69	22.97	18.37	13.98
14	73.14							37.36	32.48	27.66	22.94	18.35	13.95
15	72.11							37.33	32.45	27.63	22.91	18.32	13.93
16	71.09	33.79	38.66	43.48	48.20	52.79	57.18	37.30	32.42	27.61	22.88	18.30	13.91
17	70.06	32.79	37.67	42.48	47.20	51.79	56.18	37.27	32.39	27.58	22.86	18.27	13.88
18	69.04	31.80	36.68	41.49	46.21	50.79	55.18	37.24	32.36	27.55	22.83	18.24	13.86
19	68.02	30.80	35.68	40.50	45.22	49.80	54.18	37.21	32.33	27.52	22.80	18.22	13.83
20	66.99	29.81	34.69	39.50	44.22	48.80	53.18	37.18	32.30	27.49	22.77	18.19	13.81
21	65.96	28.81	33.69	38.51	43.22	47.80	52.18	37.15	32.27	27.46	22.74	18.16	13.78
22	64.94	27.82	32.70	37.51	42.23	46.81	51.18	37.12	32.24	27.42	22.71	18.13	13.75
23	63.91	26.83	31.70	36.52	41.23	45.81	50.18	37.08	32.20	27.39	22.68	18.10	13.72
24	62.88	25.83	30.71	35.52	40.24	44.81	49.18	37.05	32.17	27.36	22.64	18.07	13.70
25	61.85	24.84	29.71	34.53	39.24	43.81	48.18	37.01	32.13	27.32	22.61	18.04	13.67
26	60.82	23.84	28.72	33.53	38.25	42.82	47.18	36.98	32.10	27.29	22.57	18.00	13.64
27	59.79	22.85	27.73	32.54	37.25	41.82	46.18	36.94	32.06	27.25	22.54	17.97	13.61
28	58.76	21.85	26.73	31.54	36.25	40.82	45.18	36.90	32.02	27.21	22.50	17.93	13.57
29	57.72	20.86	25.74	30.55	35.26	39.82	44.18	36.87	31.99	27.17	22.46	17.90	13.54
30	56.69	19.86	24.74	29.56	34.26	38.83	43.18	36.83	31.95	27.13	22.43	17.86	13.51
31	55.66	18.87	23.75	28.56	33.27	37.83	42.18	36.79	31.91	27.10	22.39	17.83	13.47
32	54.63	17.88	22.76	27.57	32.28	36.84	41.19	36.75	31.87	27.06	22.35	17.79	13.44
33	53.59	16.88	21.77	26.58	31.28	35.84	40.19	36.71	31.83	27.02	22.31	17.75	13.40
34	52.56	15.89	20.77	25.59	30.29	34.85	39.19	36.67	31.79	26.97	22.27	17.71	13.37
35	51.53	14.90	19.78	24.60	29.30	33.86	38.20	36.63	31.75	26.93	22.23	17.67	13.33
36	50.50	13.91	18.79	23.61	28.31	32.87	37.20	36.59	31.71	26.89	22.19	17.63	13.30
37	49.47	12.91	17.80	22.62	27.32	31.88	36.21	36.56	31.67	26.85	22.15	17.59	13.26
38	48.44	11.92	16.81	21.63	26.33	30.89	35.22	36.52	31.63	26.81	22.11	17.55	13.22
39	47.41	10.93	15.82	20.64	25.35	29.90	34.23	36.48	31.59	26.77	22.06	17.51	13.18
40	46.39	9.94	14.83	19.65	24.36	28.91	33.24	36.45	31.55	26.73	22.02	17.47	13.14
41	45.36	8.94	13.85	18.67	23.38	27.93	32.25	36.42	31.52	26.69	21.98	17.43	13.11
42	44.34	7.95	12.86	17.69	22.40	26.95	31.27	36.39	31.48	26.66	21.95	17.39	13.07
43	43.32	6.96	11.87	16.70	21.42	25.97	30.29	36.36	31.45	26.62	21.91	17.36	13.03
44	42.31	5.97	10.89	15.72	20.44	24.99	29.32	36.34	31.42	26.59	21.87	17.32	12.99
45	41.30	4.98	9.90	14.74	19.46	24.02	28.34	36.32	31.40	26.56	21.84	17.28	12.96
46	40.29	3.99	8.91	13.76	18.49	23.04	27.37	36.31	31.38	26.53	21.81	17.25	12.92
47	39.29	2.99	7.93	12.78	17.51	22.07	26.40	36.30	31.36	26.50	21.77	17.21	12.89
48	38.28	2.00	6.94	11.80	16.54	21.11	25.43	36.29	31.34	26.48	21.75	17.18	12.85
49	37.29	1.00	5.95	10.82	15.57	20.14	24.47	36.29	31.33	26.46	21.72	17.15	12.82
50	36.29		4.97	9.85	14.60	19.17	23.51	36.29	31.33	26.45	21.70	17.12	12.79
51	35.30		3.98	8.87	13.63	18.21	22.55		31.33	26.44	21.68	17.09	12.75
52	34.32		2.99	7.89	12.66	17.25	21.59		31.33	26.43	21.66	17.07	12.73
53	33.34		1.99	6.91	11.69	16.29	20.64		31.34	26.43	21.65	17.04	12.70
54	32.36		1.00	5.93	10.72	15.33	19.69		31.36	26.43	21.64	17.03	12.67

FEMALE (0%) *continued*

	Table 2 Pecuniary loss for life	Table 4 Loss of earnings to age 50	Table 6 Loss of earnings to age 55	Table 8 Loss of earnings to age 60	Table 10 Loss of earnings to age 65	Table 12 Loss of earnings to age 70	Table 14 Loss of earnings to age 75	Table 16 Loss of pension from age 50	Table 18 Loss of pension from age 55	Table 20 Loss of pension from age 60	Table 22 Loss of pension from age 65	Table 24 Loss of pension from age 70	Table 26 Loss of pension from age 75
55	31.39			4.95	9.76	14.38	18.74		31.39	26.45	21.64	17.01	12.65
56	30.44			3.96	8.79	13.43	17.80			26.47	21.65	17.01	12.63
57	29.49			2.98	7.82	12.48	16.87			26.51	21.66	17.01	12.62
58	28.54			1.99	6.86	11.53	15.93			26.56	21.69	17.01	12.61
59	27.61			1.00	5.89	10.58	15.00			26.61	21.72	17.03	12.61
60	26.69				4.92	9.64	14.08			26.69	21.77	17.05	12.61
61	25.77				3.94	8.69	13.15				21.82	17.08	12.62
62	24.86				2.97	7.74	12.23				21.89	17.11	12.63
63	23.95				1.98	6.79	11.31				21.96	17.16	12.64
64	23.04				1.00	5.84	10.38				22.04	17.20	12.66
65	22.12					4.88	9.45				22.12	17.24	12.67
66	21.20					3.92	8.52					17.28	12.68
67	20.27					2.95	7.59					17.32	12.68
68	19.33					1.98	6.66					17.36	12.67
69	18.39					0.99	5.73					17.40	12.66
70	17.45						4.79					17.45	12.66
71	16.52						3.85						12.67
72	15.62						2.91						12.71
73	14.74						1.95						12.78
74	13.88						0.99						12.90
75	13.07												13.07
76	12.29												
77	11.55												
78	10.83												
79	10.15												
80	9.49												
81	8.85												
82	8.23												
83	7.64												
84	7.09												
85	6.56												
86	6.07												
87	5.61												
88	5.18												
89	4.79												
90	4.44												
91	4.11												
92	3.81												
93	3.55												
94	3.32												
95	3.09												
96	2.88												
97	2.69												
98	2.51												
99	2.34												
100	2.16												

A6: Table of adjustments to multiplier for Fatal Accidents Acts dependency

These tables deal with the factors to be applied in fatal accident cases to allow for the possibility that the deceased would not have survived until trial. They derive from paras 45 to 66 of the explanatory notes to the Ogden tables and are set out here on one page for convenience. (The user will need to consider the current state of authority on the acceptability of this approach.)

PRE-TRIAL damages (factor to be applied to damages from date of accident to trial)

Age of deceased at date of accident	Period in years from accident to trial (or cessation of dependency if earlier)							
	Male	3	6	9	Female	3	6	9
10		1.00	1.00	1.00		1.00	1.00	1.00
20		1.00	1.00	1.00		1.00	1.00	1.00
30		1.00	1.00	1.00		1.00	1.00	1.00
40		1.00	0.99	0.99		1.00	1.00	0.99
50		0.99	0.99	0.98		1.00	0.99	0.99
60		0.98	0.97	0.95		0.99	0.98	0.97
70		0.96	0.92	0.87		0.98	0.95	0.92
80		0.89	0.79	0.69		0.93	0.84	0.76

POST-TRIAL damages (factor to be applied to damages from date of trial to retirement age)

Age of deceased at date of accident	Period in years from accident to trial							
	Male	3	6	9	Female	3	6	9
10		1.00	1.00	1.00		1.00	1.00	1.00
20		1.00	1.00	0.99		1.00	1.00	1.00
30		1.00	0.99	0.99		1.00	1.00	1.00
40		1.00	0.99	0.98		1.00	0.99	0.99
50		0.99	0.97	0.96		0.99	0.98	0.97
60		0.97	0.93	0.89		0.98	0.96	0.93
70		0.92	0.83	0.73		0.95	0.89	0.72
80		0.79	0.58	0.39		0.85	0.68	0.50

POST-RETIREMENT damages (for the period of dependency after retirement age)

1. First obtain the multiplier for the whole of life dependency by the following steps:

    (a) determine, from 0 per cent tables (Table A5), the expectation of life which the deceased would have had at the date of trial (or the shorter period for which the deceased would have provided the dependency);

    (b) determine the expected period for which the dependant would have been able to receive the dependency (for a widow, normally her life expectancy from 0 per cent tables; for a child, the period until it reaches adulthood);

    (c) take the lesser of the two periods;

    (d) treat the resulting period as a term certain and look up the multiplier for that period (Table A3, continuous loss column).

2. Obtain the multiplier for dependency from date of trial to retirement age (without the factors in the Post-Trial table above).

3. The post-retirement multiplier = [the whole life multiplier (stage 1) *minus* the multiplier for dependency to retirement age (stage 2)] × the factor in the Post-trial table above.

A7: Bereavement Damages

1. Pursuant to the Administration of Justice Act 1982, s.1A, bereavement damages can be claimed in Fatal Accident Act proceedings. This is a fixed sum, set by statute as amended (see below).

2. The claim for bereavement damages can only be brought by:

   (i)   A bereaved spouse, or

   (ii) Where the deceased was a minor who never married a claim may be brought by:
         (a) either of his parents if the deceased was legitimate.
         (b) The mother if the deceased was illegitimate.

3. Where there is a claim for damages for bereavement for the benefit of the parents of the deceased, the section 1A (4) of Fatal Accidents Act 1976 provides that:

   "The sum awarded shall be divided equally between them (subject to any deduction falling to be made in respect of costs not recovered from the defendant."

   Where the parents are divorced or separated and only one parent makes the claim, that parent will hold half of the bereavement damages on trust for the other parent.

4. The Administration of Justice Act 1982 contains a provision (at section 1A(5)) for the Lord Chancellor to vary the statutory sum. The original statute fixed the sum at £3,500, and that was raised by two subsequent statutory instruments (SI 1990/2575 and SI 2002/644). Hence the relevant dates and statutory sums are as follows:

   –   if the death was before January 1, 1983, the award is **nil**

   –   if the death was between January 1, 1983 and March 31, 1991, the award is **£3,500**

   –   if the death was between April 1, 1991 and March 31, 2002, the award is **£7,500**

   –   If the death was on or after April 1, 2002, the award is **£10,000**

5. The claimant is entitled to interest on bereavement damages from the date of death to the date of trial or settlement of the action – see *Prior v Hastie*.[1]

A8: Claims for Losses of Earnings and Maintenance at Public Expense

The Administration of Justice Act 1982, s.5 provides that where an injured claimant seeks to recover damages for losses of earnings, the defendant can set off against that claim any saving attributable to maintenance (either wholly or partly) at public expense in a hospital, nursing home or other institution.

This deduction is comparable to (but not the same as) the common law principle that where a claimant is in a private hospital or home (in respect of which damages are claimed from the defendant), credit must be giving for the domestic expenses thereby saved. This is the "domestic element" which was discussed in *Fairhurst v St. Helens and Knowsley Health Authority*.[2]

---

[1] [1987] C.L.Y. 1219.
[2] [1995] P.I.Q.R. Q1 at Q8 and Q9.

A9: Roberts v Johnstone Analysis

1. Seriously injured claimants will often need special accommodation which may need to be adapted for their particular needs. This will often mean that they have to move to a more expensive house. The applicable principles of law were set out by the Court of Appeal in *Roberts v Johnstone*.[1]

2. **Example:** A paraplegic claimant lives in an unsuitable house with a market value of £50,000. She wishes to buy a more suitable house for £90,000 and alter it (because of her disabilities) at a cost of £20,000. The alterations will not (in themselves) make any difference to the value of the adapted house. The claimant will continue to live in the adapted house for the rest of her life and the agreed life multiplier is 10. Following *Roberts v Johnstone*, the claim for accommodation costs is calculated as follows:

   (i) Costs of adaption: **£20,000**
   Recovered in full because wholly attributable to injuries and will not add value to the house.

   (ii) Costs of moving house: **£5,000**
   Recovered in full if the Claimant would not have moved house but for the accident.

   (iii) Loss of Use of Capital:
   As a result of the move, the Claimant is obliged to invest in the house, thereby foregoing the use of a part of her capital. The discount rate of 2.5 per cent is taken as the annual loss caused by this. Hence the claim is: -

   £40,000 (extra cost of the house) $\times$ 2.5% (discount rate) $\times$ 10 (agreed life multiplier) = **£10,000**

   Note that the Claimant does not recover the full additional capital cost of the house; if she did, the estate would derive a windfall benefit.

   (iv) Extra Annual Costs of Accommodation:
   If the costs of living in the more expensive house are higher, the Claimant can claim them. Items might include council tax, decorating costs and water charges. If these costs were £500 p.a., the claim would be: -

   £500 (extra annual costs) $\times$ 10 (agreed life multiplier) = **£5,000**

3. The total claim for accommodation in the example is therefore **£40,000**.

---

[1] [1989] Q.B. 878

A10: Auty Analysis

In *Wells v Wells*, the House of Lords made only passing reference to the calculation of future pension losses. The implication is that the multipliers for such losses are to be taken from the Ogden Tables, as are those for pecuniary losses for life and for loss of earnings. There is no justification for adopting a different approach. Since the mid-1980s, however, such claims have been based on the principles set out in *Auty v National Coal Board*.[1] This Analysis is a guide to those principles, but is included with the caution that it has almost certainly been superseded by *Wells v Wells*.

It is important to remember that the trial judge in *Auty* was not working from the Ogden Tables, but from a table of life expectation.

1. The net annual pension loss after tax: £433

2. The claimant and his wife were both aged 34 at the date of trial.

3. The life tables showed that the claimant's life expectation beyond the age of 65 was 6.68 years, and his wife's life expectation beyond the age of 65 was 10.4 years. She was therefore expected to survive him by 3.75 years.

4. **First discount**: the judge rounded 10.4 years down to 7. This is the equivalent of the discounting calculation (now 2.5 per cent) that has already been performed for one when one uses the Ogden Tables.

5. The basic pension loss at 65 was therefore [7 × £443] = £3,101

6. Loss of lump sum gratuity: £1,899

7. Total capital value of loss at retirement age [£3,101 + £1,899] = £5,000.

8. **Second discount**: Mr Auty was 34 years old. He was therefore being compensated for his pension loss 31 years prematurely. The judge discounted the sum of £5,000 at 5 per cent over 31 years, leaving £1,100. This discount would now be performed by Ogden Table 27 at 2.5 per cent.

9. **Third discount**: The Ogden Tables are based on mortality figures, discounted by 0.5–5 per cent. The Tables do not take the other contingencies of life—*e.g.* sickness, injury at work, redundancy—into account. Section B and C of the Explanatory Notes to the Tables shows how to adjust for "Contingencies other than Mortality". *These contingencies apply only to claims for loss of earnings, not to pension losses.* However, in *Auty* the judge discounted the pension claim by a further 27 per cent for contingencies. This brought the sum of £1,100 down to £800. Of this stage the Court of Appeal said[2]:

> "The discount for imponderables which the judge made in Auty's case was 27%. The judge said that the imponderables included voluntary wastage, redundancy, dismissal, supervening ill-health, disablement or death before 65, and said that death was the major discount."

10. Add value of loss of death in service benefit (£200).

11. Total value of award: **£1,000**.

Note: The three discounts bring the pension element alone (ignoring the lump sum and the death in service benefit) down to £500. If one simply applied Ogden Table 21 and a 2.5 per cent discount to the above pension loss the claimant would receive [6.59 × £433] = £2,853.

Employment tribunals have developed a different approach to the calculation of pension loss. Those interested are referred to the guidelines in Sneath, Sara, Daykin and Gallop, *Industrial Tribunals: Compensation for loss of pension rights* (2003, 3rd ed.) HMSO, approved by the Employment Appeal Tribunal in *Benson v Dairy Crest*.[3]

[1] [1985] 1 All E.R. 930.
[2] Waller L.J. in *Auty* at p.937.
[3] (EAT/192/89).

A11: General Damages Table following Heil v Rankin

General Introduction

On the following pages are two tables for use in updating awards of general damages in the light of the Court of Appeal's judgment in *Heil v Rankin*.[1] At Table E2 will be found an inflation table.

Notes to Tables

Annexed to the Court of Appeal's judgment in *Heil* was a rather smudged graph provided to show "very approximately" the scale of the increase.

1. The difficulty comes in applying the tapered increase in the graph. Putting a straight-edge along the top line of the court's graph (the "uplifted" line) shows the line to be a shallow curve. In discussion after judgment was given, their Lordships said that they had not intended to lay down a mathematical formula. We must therefore assume that the top line was intended to fit around what had actually been done in *Heil* (*i.e.* nothing) and the other seven cases.

2. Despite this, and with a little diffidence (though some confidence) we suggest the following formula. It is calculated on the following assumptions—

   a. The highest award of general damages at March 23, 2000 was around £150,000: awards of this amount or higher were increased by $33\frac{1}{3}$ per cent;

   b. There is no increase in awards that were worth up to £10,000 before that date;

   c. The uplift is 0 per cent at £10,000 and rises *in a straight line* to $33\frac{1}{3}$ per cent.

3. To find the value of an *old* award in *new* terms, that award must first be updated to March 23, 2000 using the Retail Price Index (reproduced below), in the usual way. Let us call this £A. The formula is:

$$\pounds A + [^{\pounds A-10,000}/_{420,000} \times \pounds A]$$

The part in square brackets is the uplift.

4. For example:

   a. On January 26, 1988, McNeill J. awarded the claimant in *Chan v Chan* general damages of £75,000.

   b. Updating £75,000 to March 23, 2000 in line with the Retail Price index gives £120,800.

   c. Subtract £10,000 from £120,800, and divide it by 420,000. This gives $^{110,800}/_{420,000} = 0.26$. This is the percentage uplift.

   d. Applying this uplift to the original award gives [0.26 × £120,800] = £31,400.

   e. The award in *Chan v Chan* was therefore worth [£120,800 + £31,400] = **£152,200** on March 23, 2000.

   f. Chan should then be updated from March 23, 2000 to present.

5. Because the degree of uplift varies with the size of the old award it is inaccurate to apply the *Heil v Rankin* uplift to a figure already adjusted for inflation to a date later than March 23, 2000. In March 2000 the RPI was 168.4.

---

[1] [2000] 2 W.L.R. 1173.

TABLES FOR UPDATING GENERAL DAMAGES

The table on this page shows the factor to allow for inflation from an earlier judgment date to March 23, 2000. The second table (overleaf) shows the appropriate new figure, following *Heil v Rankin* in relation to the conventional level of damages at £1,000 intervals up to £150,000.

Note that the uplift should be applied to the damages adjusted for inflation to March 23, 2000, thus:

(1) Damages awarded January 1990 × Inflation increase January 1, 1990–March 23, 2000
   (from first table)
   = Old award as at March 23, 2000
(2) Award uplifted under *Heil v Rankin* (from second table)
(3) Then multiply by an inflation uplift from March 23, 2000 onwards to the date of trial.

TABLE TO UPDATE FOR INFLATION TO MARCH 23, 2000

	J	F	M	A	M	J	J	A	S	O	N	D	
1980	2.708	2.670	2.634	2.547	2.424	2.500	2.480	2.474	2.459	2.443	2.424	2.411	1980
1981	2.396	2.374	2.339	2.274	2.259	2.246	2.236	2.220	2.207	2.188	2.165	2.151	1981
1982	2.139	2.138	2.120	2.078	2.063	2.057	2.057	2.056	2.057	2.047	2.037	2.041	1982
1983	2.038	2.030	2.026	1.998	1.990	1.985	1.974	1.965	1.957	1.950	1.943	1.938	1983
1984	1.939	1.931	1.925	1.900	1.893	1.888	1.890	1.872	1.869	1.857	1.852	1.853	1984
1985	1.846	1.832	1.815	1.777	1.769	1.765	1.768	1.764	1.764	1.762	1.756	1.753	1985
1986	1.750	1.743	1.741	1.724	1.721	1.722	1.727	1.722	1.713	1.711	1.696	1.690	1986
1987	1.684	1.677	1.674	1.654	1.653	1.653	1.650	1.649	1.645	1.637	1.629	1.630	1987
1988	1.630	1.624	1.618	1.592	1.586	1.580	1.578	1.561	1.554	1.538	1.531	1.527	1988
1989	1.517	1.506	1.500	1.473	1.464	1.459	1.458	1.454	1.444	1.433	1.421	1.418	1989
1990	1.409	1.401	1.387	1.346	1.334	1.329	1.328	1.315	1.302	1.292	1.295	1.296	1990
1991	1.293	1.286	1.282	1.265	1.261	1.256	1.259	1.256	1.251	1.246	1.242	1.241	1991
1992	1.242	1.236	1.232	1.213	1.209	1.209	1.213	1.212	1.208	1.204	1.205	1.210	1992
1993	1.221	1.213	1.209	1.198	1.193	1.194	1.197	1.192	1.187	1.188	1.189	1.187	1993
1994	1.192	1.185	1.182	1.168	1.164	1.164	1.169	1.164	1.161	1.160	1.159	1.153	1994
1995	1.153	1.146	1.142	1.130	1.126	1.124	1.129	1.123	1.118	1.124	1.124	1.117	1995
1996	1.121	1.116	1.112	1.104	1.101	1.101	1.105	1.100	1.095	1.095	1.094	1.091	1996
1997	1.091	1.086	1.084	1.077	1.073	1.069	1.069	1.062	1.057	1.056	1.055	1.053	1997
1998	1.056	1.051	1.047	1.036	1.030	1.031	1.033	1.029	1.024	1.024	1.024	1.024	1998
1999	1.031	1.029	1.029	1.019	1.017	1.017	1.020	1.018	1.013	1.011	1.010	1.007	1999
2000	1.010	1.005											2000
	J	F	M	A	M	J	J	A	S	O	N	D	

The Retail Price Index on March 23, 2000 was 168.4.

TABLE OF UPLIFTS FOLLOWING *HEIL v RANKIN*

Old	New	Old	New	Old	New
0–10,000	No change	57,000	63,378	104,000	127,276
11,000	11,026	58,000	64,628	105,000	128,745
12,000	12,057	59,000	65,883	106,000	130,229
13,000	13,092	60,000	67,142	107,000	131,712
14,000	14,133	61,000	68,407	108,000	133,200
15,000	15,178	62,000	69,676	109,000	134,693
16,000	16,228	63,000	70,949	110,000	136,190
17,000	17,283	64,000	72,228	111,000	137,693
18,000	18,342	65,000	73,511	112,000	139,200
19,000	19,407	66,000	74,799	113,000	140,712
20,000	20,476	67,000	76,092	114,000	142,229
21,000	21,549	68,000	77,390	115,000	143,750
22,000	22,628	69,000	78,692	116,000	142,276
23,000	23,711	70,000	79,999	117,000	146,807
24,000	24,799	71,000	81,311	118,000	148,343
25,000	25,892	72,000	82,628	119,000	149,883
26,000	26,990	73,000	83,950	120,000	151,428
27,000	28,092	74,000	85,276	121,000	152,979
28,000	29,199	75,000	86,607	122,000	154,533
29,000	30,311	76,000	87,942	123,000	156,093
30,000	31,428	77,000	89,283	124,000	157,657
31,000	32,550	78,000	90,629	125,000	159,226
32,000	33,676	79,000	91,979	126,000	160,800
33,000	34,807	80,000	93,333	127,000	162,379
34,000	35,942	81,000	94,693	128,000	163,962
35,000	37,083	82,000	96,057	129,000	165,549
36,000	38,228	83,000	97,426	130,000	167,143
37,000	39,378	84,000	98,800	131,000	168,740
38,000	40,533	85,000	100,179	132,000	170,343
39,000	41,692	86,000	101,562	133,000	171,950
40,000	42,857	87,000	102,945	134,000	173,562
41,000	44,026	88,000	104,343	135,000	175,179
42,000	45,199	89,000	105,740	136,000	176,800
43,000	46,378	90,000	107,142	137,000	178,426
44,000	47,561	91,000	108,549	138,000	180,057
45,000	48,750	92,000	109,961	139,000	181,692
46,000	49,942	93,000	111,378	140,000	183,333
47,000	51,140	94,000	112,800	141,000	184,978
48,000	52,342	95,000	114,226	142,000	186,628
49,000	53,549	96,000	115,657	143,000	188,283
50,000	54,761	97,000	117,092	144,000	189,942
51,000	55,978	98,000	118,533	145,000	191,607
52,000	57,200	99,000	119,978	146,000	193,276
53,000	58,426	100,000	121,428	147,000	194,949
54,000	59,657	101,000	122,883	148,000	196,628
55,000	60,892	102,000	124,342	149,000	198,311
56,000	62,133	103,000	125,807	150,000	200,000

Group B

The Ogden Tables and other material

B

B1: The Lord Chancellor's statement, July 27, 2001

THE LORD CHANCELLOR'S DEPARTMENT
Discount Rate
Setting the Discount Rate
Lord Chancellor's Reasons
27th July 2001

Introduction

On 25 June 2001 I made the Damages (Personal Injury) Order 2001 ("the 2001 Order") pursuant to section 1 of the Damages Act 1996. In setting a rate of 2.5% in the 2001 Order I had regard to what I believed to be the accurate figure for the average gross redemption yield on Index-Linked Government Stock for the 3 years leading up to 8 June 2001. Following my announcement of the discount rate, questions were raised as to the correctness of the 3-year average yield figure upon which I had relied.

These questions led me to have the information about the 3-year average yield figure checked thoroughly. Those checks revealed certain limited inaccuracies in the information underlying the average yield figure on which I had based my reasoning in making the 2001 Order. In the light of the correction of that average yield figure, I think it right that I should consider completely afresh, on the basis of the accurate average yield figure, what rate I should have set when I made the 2001 Order on 25 June 2001, in order to determine whether the 2001 Order should be withdrawn.

Decision

Having considered all the material available to me, including the accurate, corrected average yield figure, I have come to the conclusion that a discount rate of 2.5% was the appropriate rate to set. Therefore, I do not consider that the 2001 Order should be withdrawn. This statement sets out my reasons for coming to that conclusion.

Reasons

In determining the discount rate, I have applied the appropriate legal principle laid down authoritatively by the courts, and in particular by the House of Lords in *Wells v Wells* [1999] 1 AC 345.

I also consider that it is highly desirable to exercise my powers under the Act so as to produce a situation in which claimants and defendants may have a reasonably clear idea about the impact of the discount rate upon their cases, so as to facilitate negotiation of settlements and the presentation of cases in court. In order to promote this objective, I have concluded that I should:

a   set a single rate to cover all cases. This accords with the solution adopted by the House of Lords in *Wells v Wells*. It will eliminate scope for uncertainty and argument about the applicable rate. Similarly, I consider it is preferable to have a fixed rate, which promotes certainty and which avoids the complexity and extra costs that a formula would entail;

b   set a rate which is easy for all parties and their lawyers to apply in practice and which reflects the fact that the rate is bound to be applied in a range of different circumstances over a period of time. For this reason, I consider it appropriate to set the discount rate to the nearest half per cent, so as to ensure that the figure will be suitable for use in conjunction with the Ogden Tables, which are a ready means for parties to take into account actuarial factors in computing the quantum of damages;

c   set a rate which should obtain for the foreseeable future. I consider it would be very detrimental to the reasonable certainty which is necessary to promote the just and efficient resolution of disputes (by settlement as well as by hearing in court) to make frequent changes to the discount rate. Therefore, whilst I will remain ready to review the discount rate whenever I find there is a significant and established change in the relevant real rates of return to be expected, I do not propose to tinker with the rate frequently to take account of every transient shift in market conditions.

(I consider that the reasoning and conclusions in the above paragraph, which appeared in my original reasons for setting the discount rate in the 2001 Order, continue to apply.)

The principle which I must strive to apply is clear: ". . .the object of the award of damages for future expenditure is to place the injured party as nearly as possible in the same financial position he or she would have been in but for the accident. The aim is to award such a sum of money as will amount to no more, and at the same time no less, than the net loss." (*Wells v Wells* at 390A-B per Lord Hope of Craighead). I acknowledge that claimants who have suffered severe injuries are not in the position of ordinary investors. Such claimants have a pressing need for a dependable source of income to meet the costs of their future care. It is accordingly unrealistic to require severely injured claimants to take even moderate risks when they invest their damages awards.

Setting a single rate to cover all cases, whilst highly desirable for the reasons given above, has the effect that the discount rate has to cover a wide variety of different cases, and claimants with widely differing personal and financial characteristics. Moreover, as has become clear from the consultation exercise (including responses by expert financial analysts to questions which I posed them), the real rate of return on investments of any character (including investments in Index-Linked Government Securities) involves making assumptions for the future about a wide variety of factors affecting the economy as a whole, including for example the likely rate of inflation. In these circumstances, it is inevitable that any approach to setting the discount rate must be fairly broad-brush. Put shortly, there can be no single "right" answer as to what rate should be set. Since it is in the context of larger awards, intended to cover longer periods, that there is the greatest risk of serious discrepancies between the level of compensation and the actual losses incurred if the discount rate set is not appropriate, I have had this type of award particularly in mind when considering the level at which the discount rate should be set. (The above paragraphs also formed a part of my original reasons for setting the discount rate, and I consider that they continue to apply.)

The House of Lords in *Wells v Wells* determined the real rate of return obtainable by claimants through low-risk investment by reference to the gross redemption yields on Index-Linked Government Stock. Their Lordships assumed that a claimant would use his damages award to purchase the right portfolio of Index-Linked Government Stock to ensure that in future years the sums which he received from his portfolio by way of coupon payments and payments on redemption would be sufficient to meet his financial needs. The risk that an early sale of Index-Linked Government Stock might cause capital losses was removed by assuming that such a claimant would hold all his Index-Linked Government Stock until redemption.

The House of Lords thought it appropriate to set the discount rate by reference to the average yields on Index-Linked Government Stock. There is no single correct method by which this average yield may be calculated. Among other factors, the calculation will depend upon the length of the period under consideration, the stocks which are to be included within the average, the inflation assumption made and the form of average taken.

The majority of their Lordships considered it appropriate to set a discount rate by taking a 3-year average of Index-Linked Government Stock yields. I agree that, having regard to the benefits to be obtained in setting the discount rate for the foreseeable future, 3 years is an appropriate period over which to take an average. I note that Lord Lloyd of Berwick preferred a one year period; this confirms the need for judgements to be made in determining the appropriate average yield.

It appears from the speech of Lord Hope at 393E-F that his Lordship had regard to an average of gross redemption yields on Index-Linked Government Stock with lives of over 5 years. He did not give reasons for adopting that particular approach. I am aware that this approach has also been favoured by the Ogden Working Party. However, having regard to the basic reasoning of the House of Lords in *Wells v Wells*, I do not consider that I am obliged to follow it. As noted above, the House of Lords in *Wells v Wells* assumed that a claimant would generally hold all his Index-Linked Government Stock until redemption. Further, as was stated by Lord Clyde at 395H-396A, it was to be assumed that in each year of loss a proportion of the capital would have to be used. If these two assumptions are to be rendered consistent then it will be necessary for the claimant to purchase Index- Linked Government Stock which will mature in the short term, for otherwise the claimant would have to sell a proportion of his Index-Linked Government Stock prior to redemption in order to realise, in the short term, some of the capital value of his investments. Some claimants, whose losses extend over periods of about 5 years or so or less, would have to purchase all or most of their Index-Linked Government Stock (if that is what they chose to do with the damages paid to them) in this category of stock. I have therefore decided that it is proper to take an average over all Index-Linked Government Stock rather than to exclude Index-Linked Government Stock with less than 5 years to maturity.

Nevertheless, I consider that it would be inappropriate to include the gross redemption yields of such stock which is very near maturity ("near maturity ILGS" – which is stock for which the nominal value of the final coupon and redemption payments have become known with certainty). The gross redemption yield on such near maturity ILGS is a nominal yield rather than a real yield. Accordingly, I asked for a calculation of the size of the real yield element in the gross redemption yields of the near maturity ILGS and have included those real yields within my calculation of the average yield.

The average yield figure upon which Lord Hope relied at 393E-F in *Wells v Wells* was based on an inflation assumption of 5%. I consider that, given both the current rate of inflation and the Government's policy aim of maintaining that rate within an upper limit of 2.5%, an assumption of 3% is to be preferred for present purposes.

The House of Lords in *Wells v Wells* did not discuss what form of average should be taken of Index-Linked Government Stock yields. One method is to take an average which is weighted in accordance with the market value of each stock. To my mind, such a weighted average is not relevant to the present circumstances, as the choice of Index-Linked Government Stock portfolio which is necessary to ensure that the future financial needs of a claimant are adequately and promptly met does not depend upon the prevailing market values of Index-Linked Government Stock. I have therefore decided that it is appropriate to take a simple average of Index-Linked Government Stock yields.

A calculation of the simple average of the gross redemption yields of an Index-Linked Government Stock (with an appropriate adjustment for the yields of near maturity ILGS) at an assumed rate of inflation of 3% produces an average yield figure of 2.46%. Accordingly, I conclude that the net average yield on Index-Linked Government Stock, as adjusted to take account of tax, lies in the range between 2% and 2.5%. In my opinion, following *Wells v Wells*, the discount rate should be set within this range. Further, given that the rate is to be set to the nearest 0.5%, it is clear that the discount rate should either be 2% or 2.5%. I do not consider that the choice whether a rate of 2% or one of 2.5% is appropriate is a simple arithmetical matter, nor that *Wells v Wells* requires me to set one rate or the other. I must have regard to the basic principle to which I have referred above, and I have taken account of matters which I consider are relevant to the setting of a discount rate which is just as between claimants as a group and defendants as a group.

In the light of all the information now available to me, and considering the matter completely afresh, I have decided that on 25 June 2001 I should have set the discount rate at 2.5%.

In doing so, I have noted that the real rate of return to be expected from Index-Linked Government Securities tends to be higher the lower the rate of inflation is assumed to be (figures at assumed rates of inflation of 3% and 5% are readily available for comparison). The average gross redemption yield figure of 2.46% assumes an inflation figure of 3% extending into the future. But over recent years inflation has been kept close to or below the 2.5% target set by the Government, and Government policy and the function of the Bank of England remains firmly to maintain inflation according to that target. Although economists differ as to what inflation rates may be expected for the future, I note that the market's general expectation as to the rate of inflation for the future (as implied by market valuations of gilts) is well below 3%. I consider that it is reasonable to assume an inflation rate for the foreseeable future somewhere below 3%, and this in turn provides comfort that a discount rate set at 2.5% is reasonable. (The above paragraph and the larger part of the following four paragraphs were contained in my original reasons for setting the discount rate. They set out considerations which I consider continue to apply).

I am further supported in my conclusion that a discount rate of 2.5% is reasonable by indications that the rate of return in respect of Index-Linked Government Securities does not represent a pure and undistorted measure of the real rate of return which markets would afford in relation to investments with minimal risk which have emerged from the information which was provided in the responses to the consultation paper and the responses from expert financial analysts which I obtained, and by consideration of rates of return on other investments which are available at low risk to claimants. I have treated the following points as significant.

First, some responses to the consultation maintained that the market in Index-Linked Government Securities is at present distorted so that the prevailing yields are artificially low, and do not necessarily give a reliable indication of the real rate of return which markets would afford in relation to investments with minimal risk. The expert financial analysts whom I consulted concurred that the market is distorted at present. This appears to be a result of the minimum funding requirement introduced by the Pensions Act 1995 (which has, in effect, created additional demand for such securities on the part of pension funds) combined with a reduced supply of government securities generally, as the Government has reduced the national debt. The market in Index-Linked Government Securities has changed significantly since *Wells v Wells* was argued and decided. It is widely held that the continuing high demand for Index-Linked Government Stock and the scarcity of supply has led to yields being artificially low as compared with both past record and the yields presently available on similar investment instruments issued by other, comparable, national governments. I consider that the fact that yields in Index-Linked Government Stock appear to be artificially low at present militates against the suggestion that these yields over recent years should be taken as the sole indication of the rates of return that can be achieved through low risk investment in the market. Also, I consider that there is some reasonable prospect of a return to higher rates of return in respect of Index-Linked Government Stock when the Government's already announced plans to abolish the minimum funding requirement are carried into effect. Any distorting effect of the minimum funding requirement would be expected to be particularly pronounced in relation to the longer maturity stocks, whose yields have recently been lower than shorter maturity stocks.

Second, I have noted that the Court of Protection, even in the wake of *Wells v Wells*, has continued to invest, on the behalf of claimants, in multi-asset portfolios, including an equity element. Investment in this manner could be expected to produce real rates of return well in excess of 2.5%. The Court of

Protection has specific responsibility to ensure that the financial needs of those for whose benefit it acts will be met, ie its investment objectives are closely similar to those of the prudent claimant which the House of Lords identified in *Wells v Wells*. The Court of Protection takes competent financial advice as to the investment strategy which will best secure those objectives. Despite the decision of the House of Lords in *Wells v Wells* to set the discount rate by reference to yields on Index-Linked Government Securities, the Court of Protection has continued its former policy, with the agreement of the families concerned, of investing in portfolios comprising of a mixture of equities, gilts and cash. Master Lush of the Court of Protection has stated that none of the families of the Court's patients have chosen to invest in Index-Linked Government Stock since *Wells v Wells*, despite having been offered that option. Thus it appears that there are sensible, low risk investment strategies available to claimants which would enable them comfortably to achieve a real rate of return at 2.5% or above, without their being unduly exposed to risk in the equity markets. Although the House of Lords in *Wells v Wells* chose not to be guided by the practice of the Court of Protection, this was principally on the grounds that what the Court of Protection might do in the future was uncertain, and not on the grounds that its practice was irrelevant. I consider it is appropriate to take account of what has happened in the period since that decision.

Third, I consider that it is likely that real claimants with a large award of compensation, who sought investment advice and instructed their advisers as to the particular investment objectives which they needed to fulfil (as they could reasonably be expected to do) would not be advised to invest solely or even primarily in Index-Linked Government Securities, but rather in a mixed portfolio, in which any investment risk would be managed so as to be very low. This view is supported by the experience of the Court of Protection as to the independent financial advice they receive. It is also supported by the responses of the expert financial analysts whom I have consulted. No one responding to the consultation identified a single case in which the claimant had invested solely in Index-Linked Government Securities and doubts were expressed as to whether there was any such case. This suggests that setting the discount rate at 2.5% would not place an intolerable burden on claimants to take on excessive, i.e. moderate or above, risk in the equity markets, and would be a rate more likely to accord with real expectations of returns, particularly at the higher end of awards.

Finally, in deciding that a single rate of 2.5% should have been set by me on 25 June 2001, I have borne in mind that it will, of course, remain open for the Courts under section 1(2) of the Damages Act 1996 to adopt a different rate in any particular case if there are exceptional circumstances which justify it in doing so.

Irvine of Lairg
Lord Chancellor
July 27, 2001

B2: The Ogden Tables

Actuarial tables with explanatory notes for use in personal injury and fatal accident cases.

Prepared by an Inter-Professional Working Party of Actuaries, Lawyers, Accountants and other interested parties.

Fifth edition prepared by the Government Actuary's Department.

Members of the working party responsible for the fifth edition

Robin de Wilde Q.C.	*Chairman*
Chris Daykin C.B., FIA	*The Government Actuary*
Professor Andrew Burrows	*Formerly of The Law Commission*
Harvey McGregor Q.C.	*Invited by the Chairman*
Rowland Hogg, FCA	*Invited by the Chairman*
Anthony Carus, FIA	*Invited by the Chairman*
Alistair Kinley	*Association of British Insurers*
Dominic Claydon	*Association of British Insurers*
Grahame Codd, Solicitor	*Association of Personal Injuries Lawyers*
Chinu Patel, FIA	*Institute of Actuaries*
John Pollock, FFA	*Faculty of Actuaries*
James Campbell Q.C.	*Faculty of Advocates*
Nicholas Mostyn Q.C.	*Family Law Bar Association*
Richard Methuen Q.C.	*Personal Injuries Bar Association*
Simon Levene	*Professional Negligence Bar Association*
Martin Bruffell, Solicitor	*Forum of Insurance Lawyers*
Graeme Garrett, Solicitor	*The Law Society of Scotland*
John Meehan	*President, Law Society of Northern Ireland*
John Cushinan Q.C.	*General Council of the Bar of Northern Ireland*
Mary Menjou	*NHS Litigation Authority*
Michael Lyon	*Bank of England*
Harry Trusted, Barrister	*Secretary to the Working Party*

Contents

Tables 1 to 26

Introduction to the fifth edition

"When it comes to the explanatory notes we must make sure that they are readily comprehensible. We must assume the most stupid circuit judge in the country and before him are the two most stupid advocates. All three of them must be able to understand what we are saying".

Sir Michael Ogden, QC, on his explanatory notes to the First Edition of the Ogden Tables.[1]

Vale

1.   This is the first Edition to which neither Michael Ogden nor David Kemp has been a party.

2.   Michael Ogden believed that the task of chairing his Working Party would be one which, when completed, would be put away and forgotten. He never foresaw that it would produce an industry, all of its own, and not end with the classic decision of **Wells v Wells [1999] 1 A.C. 345**. When he passed on the Chairmanship to me, I said, when accepting, that he had passed a 19-year sentence upon me, for that was the period of his rôle in the post of Chairman. He laughed. It is not to everyone to become eponymous with a set of Tables, but when he spoke to the parliamentary draftsman about his mention in the Civil Evidence Act 1995, he was told that it was simpler to refer to his name and the Tables rather than use the full title of the Working Party.

3.   David Kemp started his work with his first wife, whom he commemorated by her photograph in Volume 1 of *Kemp & Kemp*, shortly after he came down from Cambridge. It was not his area of work as such, which was in the field of restrictive trade practice. He was due to go from Winchester College to Cambridge on a classics scholarship in 1939. World events intervened. When he did go to Corpus Christi, Cambridge, he elected to read law rather than classics, on the grounds that he had forgotten all his classics as a result of his war service. He obtained a First Class in Law. He regretted in retrospect, he said, not reading classics. He was skiing with his grandchildren in his 81st year.

4.   Each of them, in his own way, reformed the law of damages, put it on a more professional footing, and persuaded the courts that personal injury compensation was not a subject to be treated by merely wetting one's finger and holding it in the air to discern the direction of the wind. It is right that both should be remembered for what they did for those who have been and will be injured.

The purpose of the Ogden Tables

5.   The purpose of these Tables is to enable the simple calculation of full compensation for those victims who have suffered future loss as a result of wrongful injury. It is well established that such victims are entitled to full compensation.

6.   This is in accordance with the law. The rule was first stated by Lord Blackburn in those famous words to be found in **Livingstone v Rawyards Coal Company (1880) 5 App. Cas. 25** at **39.**

7.   Compensation should be both adequate and sufficient. The authority for that can be found in the speech of Lord Lloyd of Berwick in **Wells v Wells [1999] 1 A.C. 345** at **362** and following.

8.   The problem is to attain this worthy aim; whether it is currently attainable is debatable.

9.   In order to achieve that aim it is necessary for both the courts and society to look into the future. This is a perilous task and requires uncommon abilities. One Victorian judge described the quality necessary as demanding both the agility of an acrobat and the foresight of an Hebrew prophet.

10.   Money will always produce problems for the value today will not necessarily be the same in the future. Inflation is more likely to occur than deflation, but there have been periods in Britain, albeit usually short periods, where deflation has occurred.

1 Memoirs of Sir Michael Ogden Q.C., *Variety is the Spice of Legal Life*, p.182 (The Book Guild, 2002).

11. Any calculation of a rate of inflation must relate to some 'basket' of goods and services, and perhaps also of assets, whose prices are to be measured. There need be no unique definition or measured rate of inflation: different measures serve different purposes. For example, the retail prices index (RPI) gives a measure of inflation based on the cost of living appropriate to the expenditure patterns of typical households; its historic forbear was the price of corn. The RPI is also the measure used to uprate interest and principal on index-linked gilts. The average earnings index gives a measure of wage inflation, which has typically exceeded RPI inflation, on account of economy-wide productivity growth.

12. The present value of future monetary amounts must also depend on real interest returns, as well as inflation, over the intervening period, and therefore calculated amounts of damages require assumptions to be made for such returns, including what, if any, investment risks for which they compensate. In fact, the precedent set by **Wells v Wells [1999] 1 A.C. 345** was that the appropriate discount rate should be based on the 'risk free' rate.

13. The Ogden Tables were originally devised to enable future losses to be simply calculated through the application of a given discount rate defined in real terms, that is, after making allowance for the effects of future inflation. This was achieved by exploiting the properties of index-linked gilts to derive a market-related measure of prevailing real interest rates over an appropriate investment horizon. The use of index-linked gilts, being tradeable British Government securities, should, in general, be expected to yield discount rates close to risk-free returns.

14. The Ogden Tables also depend on the Expectation of Life figures, which are supplied by the Government Actuary. Those figures have been consistently rising as a result of better diet, care, housing and medical treatment. This means that the average length of life has risen dramatically. This is demonstrated by the figures issued by the Government Actuary on December 18, 2003, arising from the most recent census.

15. Apart from life expectancy the main factor in using the Ogden Tables is the appropriate choice of the discount rate, now fixed by the Lord Chancellor since June 25, 2001, and revisited on July 27, 2001, at $2\frac{1}{2}$%. The right choice of discount rate is vital if the proper aim of full and adequate compensation is to be achieved. It has never, since the Lord Chancellor made his first announcement, been within $\frac{1}{2}$% of the correct rate of return from Index Linked Gilts, after taking tax into account.

16. The Damages Act 1996 appreciated that the search for the most appropriate method would not necessarily be a single prescribed rate in all cases and at all times. Section 1(2) of the Damages Act 1996 therefore made provision for the Court to make variations to the discount rate if any party to the proceedings shows that it is more appropriate in the case in question. Unfortunately, in two separate cases,[2] the Court of Appeal has emasculated that provision in large and complex cases. It has ruled in each case that consistency and fairness and the use of the Lord Chancellor's chosen discount rate should be preferred. Neither decision is helpful in the desire to achieve full and proper compensation.

Other methods of calculating future pecuniary loss

17. It needs to be emphasised that the Ogden Tables are not the only way, or even the best way, of calculating and estimating future losses.

18. Actuaries, who are those chosen to value those most complex of entities, pension funds, calculate future claims and losses in a different and more subtle way than the methods used in the Ogden Tables. In the United States, professional economists are called to give evidence about future losses.

19. For that reason, the Government Actuary has written an Appendix on this issue. He explains how actuaries do value future claims and losses.

---

2 *Warriner v Warriner* [2002] 1 W.L.R. 1703; *Cooke & Others v United Bristol Health Care & Others* [2004] 1 W.L.R. 251.

20. I believe that it is essential that everyone understands the limits of the Ogden Tables. A failure to understand those limits could lead to the Ogden Tables being devalued. As with justice, the Tables need to be both fair and seen to be fair, as well as properly applied.

Removal of the previous Tables 1 to 18

21. This has been done as they relate to the past rather than the future. However, the fact that they are no longer published, saving valuable space, does not mean that in very particular circumstances, they may not be relevant to the calculations of damages.

Fatal Accident Act claims

22. The courts do not, at present, appear inclined to accept the guidance which we offered in the Fourth Edition of these Tables. The courts consider themselves bound by the speech of Lord Fraser in *Cookson v Knowles* **[1979] A.C. 556** at **574**. Nelson J. in *White v ESAB Group (UK) Limited* **[2002] P.I.Q.R. Q6** would have decided differently but for the words of Lord Fraser. In reality, in complex cases, the position is that financial experts often agree that the actual method we suggest is, in fact, the correct method.

23. These tables are designed for losses that occur after the date of trial. In the Explanatory Notes it is made clear that the purpose of the Tables is for the assessment of future pecuniary loss. The Tables use discount rates which are applicable to future losses. This is because it is assumed that once the claimant has received compensation he will invest it to produce an income. It is therefore fundamental that the discounted columns in the Tables should only be used for losses that arise after the date of trial or assessment.

24. If the guidance on multipliers in fatal accident cases given in section D of the Explanatory Notes is not followed, in order to select them from the date of death, it is essential that the 0% columns are used for the period prior to the trial (see paragraph 64).

Contingencies other than mortality

25. Certain inaccuracies have been noted in the figures used in Tables A, B and C for contingencies other than mortality. These inaccuracies were first revealed in the paper by Professors Lewis and McNabb.[3] They have since been confirmed by and acknowledged by the authors of the original paper, Haberman & Bloomfield,[4] as due to incomplete data. We have not been inclined to remove those Tables completely, for they do give an indication of the factors that should be considered. We are attempting to commission new work on this aspect for later editions of these Tables. Better figures may take some time to produce and a "health warning" exists on those presently produced.

Final matters

26. The core of the work which constitutes these Tables is produced by the Government Actuary and his team. The lawyers are merely an encumbrance, welcomed by him, so that the process can be refined and improved. He has to listen to arcane matters such as the "lost years" argument and other delights from the lawyers, but the Tables are intended as a mathematical tool to be used in the most simple way so that future pecuniary losses can be calculated without great stress and in the most accurate way that is easily available.

July 31, 2004   Robin de Wilde, Q.C.

3 (2002) 29 *Journal of Law and Society*.
4 Their paper is entitled: "Work Time Lost to Sickness, Unemployment and Stoppages: Measurement and Application"; (1990) *Journal of the Institute of Actuaries Volume* 117, 533.

Explanatory Notes:

Section A: General

Purpose of tables

1.   The tables have been prepared by the Government Actuary's Department. They provide an aid for those assessing the lump sum appropriate as compensation for a continuing future pecuniary loss or consequential expense or cost of care in personal injury and fatal accident cases.

Application of tables

2.   The tables set out multipliers. These multipliers enable the user to assess the present capital value of future annual loss (net of tax) or annual expense calculated on the basis of various assumptions which are explained below. Accordingly, to find the present capital value of a given annual loss or expense, it is necessary to select the appropriate table, find the appropriate multiplier and then multiply the amount of the annual loss or expense by that figure.

3.   Tables 1 to 26 deal with annual loss or annual expense extending over three different periods of time. In each case there are separate tables for men and women.

—   In Tables 1 and 2 the loss or expense is assumed to begin immediately and to continue for the whole of the rest of the claimant's life, allowing for different potential lifespans, including the possibility of early death or prolonged life. The tables apply to both the deceased and the dependants' lives in fatal accident cases.

—   In Tables 3 to 14 the loss or expense is assumed to begin immediately but to continue only until the claimant's retirement or earlier death. The age of retirement is assumed to be 50 in Tables 3 and 4, 55 in Tables 5 and 6, 60 in Tables 7 and 8, 65 in Tables 9 and 10, 70 in Tables 11 and 12, and 75 in Tables 13 and 14

—   In Tables 15 to 26 it is assumed that the annual loss or annual expense will not begin until the claimant reaches retirement but will then continue for the whole of the rest of his or her life.

4.   In Table 19 (males) and Table 20 (females) the age of retirement is assumed to be 60. In Table 21 (males) and Table 22 (females) the age of retirement is assumed to be 65 (and similarly for retirement ages 50, 55, 70 and 75). These tables all make due allowance for the chance that the claimant may not live to reach the age of retirement.

Mortality assumptions for Tables 1 to 18

5.   In previous editions of these tables, tables have been included based on the mortality rates experienced in England and Wales in a historical three-year period. Tables based on mortality experienced in the years 1990 to 1992, published by the Government Actuary's Department as English Life Tables No. 15 (ELT15), were set out in the Fourth Edition of the tables. The Working Party has decided that it is not necessary to publish these historic tables again in this edition and have correspondingly agreed that the tables to be published should be based on a reasonable estimate of the future mortality likely to be experienced by average members of the population alive today.

6.   On the basis of some reported cases, it appears that tables for pecuniary loss for life, e.g. cost of care, may have been misunderstood. The tables do not assume that the claimant dies after a period equating to the expectation of life, but take account of the possibilities that the claimant will live for different periods, e.g. die soon or live to be very old. The mortality assumptions relate to the general population of England and Wales. Unless there is clear evidence in an individual case to support the view that the individual is atypical and will enjoy longer or shorter expectation life, no further increase or reduction is required for mortality alone.

7.   For the purposes of preparing the official national population projections, the Government Actuary makes an estimate of the extent of future improvements in mortality. Tables 1 to 26 in this edition show the multipliers which result from the application of these projected mortality rates (derived from the 2002-based population projections for England and Wales, which were published in December 2003 on the GAD website *www.gad.gov.uk* . Details can also be found in the publication *National Population Projections 2002-based. PP2 No.24* from the Office of National Statistics). The actuaries on the Working Party consider that these alternative tables provide a more appropriate estimate of the value of future income streams than tables based on historic mortality which, given the rate at which mortality experience has improved, and continues to improve, are likely to underestimate future longevity to a significant extent. The Working Party therefore recommends the Courts to use Tables 1 to 26 contained in this latest edition of the tables.

Use of tables

8.   To find the appropriate figure for the present value of a particular loss or expense the user must first choose that table which relates to the period of loss or expense for which the individual claimant is to be compensated and to the sex of the claimant or, where appropriate, the claimant's dependants.

9.   If, for some reason the facts in a particular case do not correspond with the assumptions on which one of the tables is based, (*e.g.* it is known that the claimant will have a different retiring age from that assumed in the tables) then the tables can only be used if an appropriate allowance is made for this difference; for this purpose the assistance of an actuary should be sought, except for situations where specific guidance is given in these explanatory notes.

Rate of return

10.   The basis of the multipliers set out in the tables is that the lump sum will be invested and yield income (but that over the period in question the claimant will gradually reduce the capital sum, so that at the end of the period it is exhausted). Accordingly, an essential factor in arriving at the right figure is the choice of the appropriate rate of return.

11.   The annual rate of return currently to be applied is $2\frac{1}{2}$% (net of tax), as fixed by the Lord Chancellor on June 25, 2001, and reassessed on July 27, 2001, under the provisions of the Damages Act 1996, section 1. An annual rate of return of $2\frac{1}{2}$% has also been set for Scotland by the Scottish Ministers on February 8, 2002. The Lord Chancellor may make a fresh determination of this rate, after receiving advice from the Government Actuary and the Treasury. An annual rate of return of $2\frac{1}{2}$% has also been set for Scotland by (who was ultimately responsible for this?). Tables are accordingly shown for a range of possible annual rates of return ranging from $\frac{1}{2}$% to 5%, as in the previous edition. In addition, a 0% column has been included to show the multiplier without any discount for interest (*i.e.* expectations of life, or the equivalent for different periods). These are supplied to assist in the calculation of multipliers in Fatal Accident Act cases (see Section D).

12. Section 1(2) of the Damages Act 1996 makes provision for the Courts to make variations to the discount rate if any party to the proceedings shows that it is more appropriate in the case in question. Variations to the discount rate under this provision have, however, been rejected by the Court of Appeal in the cases of *Warriner v Warriner* [2002] 1 W.L.R. 1703 and *Cooke & Others v United Bristol Health Care & Others* [2004] 1 W.L.R. 251. A note by the Government Actuary in Appendix A of this edition describes how appropriate account could be taken by the Courts of different inflationary conditions. Use of such sound actuarial methodology would require tables at rates of return other than the rate set by the Lord Chancellor and for this reason also it has been deemed appropriate to continue to show a range of rates of return.

13. Previous editions of these tables explained how the current yields on index-linked government bonds could be used as an indicator of the appropriate real rate of return for valuing future income streams. Such considerations were endorsed by the House of Lords in *Wells v Wells* and the same argumentation was adopted by the Lord Chancellor when he set the rate on commencement of section 1 of the Damages Act 1996. In cases outwith the scope of these tables, the advice of an actuary should be sought.

Different retirement ages

14. In paragraph 9 above, reference was made to the problem that will arise when the claimant's retiring age is different from that assumed in the tables. Such a problem may arise in valuing a loss or expense beginning immediately but ending at retirement; or in valuing a loss or expense which will not begin until the claimant reaches retirement but will then continue until death. Tables are provided for retirement ages of 50, 55, 60, 65, 70 and 75. Where the claimant's actual retiring age would have been between two of these retirement ages for which tables are provided, the correct multiplier can be obtained by consideration of the tables for retirement age immediately above and below the actual retirement age, keeping the period to retirement age the same. Thus a woman of 42 who would have retired at 58 can be considered as being in between the cases of a woman of 39 with a retirement age of 55 and a woman of 44 with a retirement age of 60. The steps to take are as follows:

(1)   Determine between which retirement ages, for which tables are provided, the claimant's actual retirement age R lies. Let the lower of these ages be A and the higher be B.

(2)   Determine how many years must be subtracted from the claimant's actual retirement age to get to A and subtract that period from the claimant's age. If the claimant's age is X, the result of this calculation is $(X + A - R)$.

(3)   Look up this new reduced age in the Table corresponding to retirement age A at the appropriate rate of return. Let the resulting multiplier be M.

(4)   Determine how many years must be added to the claimant's actual retirement age to get to B and add that period to the claimant's age. The result of this calculation is $(X + B - R)$.

(5)   Look up this new increased age in the Table corresponding to retirement age B at the appropriate rate of return. Let the resulting multiplier be N.

(6)   Interpolate between M and N. In other words, calculate:

$(B - R) \times M + (R - A) \times N$

and divide the result by 5.

15. In the example given in paragraph 14, the steps would be as follows:

(1) A is 55 and B is 60.

(2)   Subtracting 3 years from the claimant's age gives 39.

(3) Looking up age 39 in Table 6 (for retirement age 55) gives 13.08 at a rate of return of $2\frac{1}{2}$%.

(4) Adding 2 years to the claimant's age gives 44.

(5) Looking up age 44 in Table 8 (for retirement age 60) gives 13.01 at a rate of return of $2\frac{1}{2}$%.

(6) Calculating $2 \times 13.08 + 3 \times 13.01$ and dividing by 5 gives 13.04 as the multiplier.

16. When the loss or expense to be valued is that from the date of retirement to death, and the claimant's date of retirement differs from that assumed in the tables, a different approach is necessary, involving the following three steps.

(1) Assume that there is a present loss which will continue for the rest of the claimant's life and from Table 1 or 2 establish the value of that loss or expense over the whole period from the date of assessment until the claimant's death.

(2) Establish the value of such loss or expense over the period from the date of assessment until the claimant's expected date of retirement following the procedure explained in paragraphs 14 and 15 above.

(3) Subtract the second figure from the first. The balance remaining represents the present value of the claimant's loss or expense between retirement and death.

17. If the claimant's actual retiring age would have been earlier than 50, or later than 75, the advice of an actuary should be sought.

Younger ages

18. Tables 1 and 2, which concern pecuniary loss for life, and Tables 15 to 26, which concern loss of pension from retirement age, have been extended down to age 0. In some circumstances the multiplier at age 0 is slightly lower than that at age 1; this arises because of the relatively high incidence of deaths immediately after birth.

19. Tables for multipliers for loss of earnings (Tables 3 to 14) have not been extended below age 16. In order to determine the multiplier for loss of earnings for someone who has not yet started work, it is first necessary to determine an assumed age at which the claimant would have commenced work and to find the appropriate multiplier for that age from Tables 3 to 14, according to the assumed retirement age. This multiplier should then be multiplied by the deferment factor from Table 27 which corresponds to the appropriate rate of return and the period from the date of the trial to the date on which it is assumed that the claimant would have started work. A similar approach can be used for determining a multiplier for pecuniary loss for life where the loss is assumed to commence a fixed period of years from the date of the trial. For simplicity the factors in Table 27 relate purely to the impact of compound interest and ignore mortality. At ages below 30 this is a reasonable approximation but at higher ages it would normally be appropriate to allow explicitly for mortality and the advice of an actuary should be sought.

Contingencies

20. Tables 1 to 26 make reasonable provision for the levels of mortality which members of the population of England and Wales alive today may expect to experience in future. The tables do not take account of the other risks and vicissitudes of life, such as the possibility that the claimant would for periods have ceased to earn due to ill-health or loss of employment. Nor do they take account of the fact that many people cease work for substantial periods to care for children or other dependants. Section B suggests ways in which allowance may be made to the multipliers for loss of earnings, to allow for certain risks other than mortality.

Impaired lives

21. In some cases, medical evidence may be available which asserts that a claimant's health impairments are equivalent to adding a certain number of years to their current age, or to treating the individual as having a specific age different from their actual age. In such cases, Tables 1 and 2 can be used with respect to the deemed higher age. For the other tables the adjustment is not so straightforward, as adjusting the age will also affect the assumed retirement age, but the procedures described in paragraphs 14 to 16 may be followed, or the advice of an actuary should be sought.

Fixed periods

22. In cases where pecuniary loss is to be valued for a fixed period, the multipliers in Table 28 may be used. These make no allowance for mortality or any other contingency but assume that regular frequent payments (*e.g.* weekly or monthly) will continue throughout the period. These figures should in principle be adjusted if the periodicity of payment is less frequent, especially if the payments in question are annually in advance or in arrears.

Variable loss or expense

23. The tables do not provide an immediate answer when the annual loss or expense to be valued is not assumed to be stable; where, for instance, the claimant's lost earnings were on a sliding scale or promotion was likely to be achieved. It may be possible to use the tables to deal with such situations by increasing the basic figure of annual loss or expenses; or it may be appropriate to split the overall multiplier into two or more parts and apply different multiplicands to each. In addition to contingent widows' pensions, cases such as *Singapore Bus v Lim Soon Yong* [1985] 1 W.L.R. 1075 at 1079 D-1080A, *Taylor v O'Connor* [1971] A.C. 115 at 127, 130, *Davies and others v Whiteways Cyder Co. Ltd and another* [1974] 3 All E.R. 168, etc., may necessitate actuarial advice with regard to other losses.

Spouses' pension benefits

24. If doubt exists whether the tables are appropriate to a particular case which appears to present significant difficulties of substance, it would be prudent to take actuarial advice. This might be appropriate in relation to the level of spouses' benefits, if these are to be assessed, since these are not readily valued using Tables 1 to 26. As a rough rule of thumb, if spouse's benefits are to be included when valuing pension loss from normal pension age, the multipliers in tables 15 to 26 should be increased by 5% for a female claimant (*i.e.* benefits to the male spouse) and by 15% for a male claimant if the spouse's pension would be half of the pension that the member was receiving at death. If the spouse's pension would be payable at a rate of two-thirds the member's pension at death the multipliers should be increased by 7% for a female claimant and by 20% for a male claimant.

Section B: Contingencies other than mortality

25. As stated in paragraph 20, the tables for loss of earnings (Tables 3 to 14) take no account of risks other than mortality. This section shows how the multipliers in these tables may be reduced to take account of risks other than mortality. This is based on work commissioned by the Institute of Actuaries and carried out by Professor S. Haberman and Mrs D. S. F. Bloomfield (*Work time lost to sickness, unemployment and stoppages: measurement and application* (1990), Journal of the Institute of Actuaries 117, 533–595). Although there was some debate within the actuarial profession about the details of this work, and in particular about the scope for developing it further, the findings were broadly accepted and were adopted by the Government Actuary and the other actuaries who were members of the Working Party when the Second Edition of the Tables was published.

26. Since the risk of mortality (including the risks of dying early or living longer) has already been taken into account in the tables, the principal contingencies in respect of which a further reduction is

to be made, particularly for earnings loss up to retirement age, are illness and unemployment. Even with the effective disappearance of the "job for life" there appears to be no scientific justification in the generality of cases for assuming significantly larger deductions than those given in this section. It should be noted that the authors of the 1990 paper (Professor Haberman and Mrs Bloomfield) wrote "All the results discussed in this paper should be further qualified by the caveat that the underlying models . . . assume that economic activity rates and labour force separation and accession rates do not vary in the future from the bases chosen. As mentioned already in the text, it is unlikely to be true that the future would be free from marked secular trends". The paper relied on Labour Force Surveys for 1973, 1977, 1981 and 1985 and English Life Tables No. 14 (1980–82). However, although it is now somewhat out of date, it is the best study presently available. Some related work has recently been published by Lewis, McNabb and Wass ("Methods of calculating damages for loss of future earnings" (2002) 2 J.P.I.L.). It is hoped that further research into the impact of contingencies other than mortality will be carried out in due course and the Ogden Working Party is in discussion with potential researchers in the hope of carrying this forward.

27.   Specific factors in individual cases may necessitate larger reductions. By contrast, there will also be cases where the standard multipliers should be increased, to take into account positive factors of lifestyle, employment prospects and life expectancy.

28.   The extent to which the multiplier needs to be reduced will reflect individual circumstances such as occupation and geographical region. In the short term, levels of economic activity and unemployment, including time lost through industrial action, are relevant. Reductions may be expected to be smaller for clerical workers than for manual workers, for those living in the South rather than the North, and for those in "secure" jobs and in occupations less affected by redundancy or industrial action.

29.   The factors described in subsequent paragraphs are for use in calculating loss of earnings up to retirement age. The research work did not investigate the impact of contingencies other than mortality on the value of future pension rights. Some reduction to the multiplier for loss of pension would often be appropriate when a reduction is being applied for loss of earnings. This may be less of a reduction than in the case of loss of earnings because of the ill-health contingency (as opposed to the unemployment contingency), particularly in cases where there are significant ill-health retirement pension rights. A bigger reduction may be necessary in cases where there is significant doubt whether pension rights would have continued to accrue (to the extent not already allowed for in the post-retirement multiplier) or in cases where there may be doubt over the ability of the pension fund to pay promised benefits. In the case of a defined contribution pension scheme, loss of pension rights may be able to be allowed for simply by increasing the future earnings loss (adjusted for contingencies other than mortality) by the percentage which the employer pays to the scheme in contributions.

30.   The suggestions which follow are intended only to provide a "ready reckoner" as opposed to precise figures.

The basic deduction for contingencies other than mortality

31.   Subject to the adjustments which may be made as described below, the multiplier which has been selected from the tables, *i.e.* in respect of risks of mortality only, should be reduced by *multiplying* it by a figure selected from the table below, under the heading "Medium".

Levels of economic activity and employment

32.   The medium set of reductions is appropriate if it is anticipated that economic activity is likely to correspond to that in the 1970s and 1980s (ignoring periods of high and low unemployment). The high set is appropriate if higher economic activity and lower unemployment rates are anticipated. The low set is appropriate if lower economic activity and higher unemployment rates are anticipated.

Table A
Loss of Earnings to Pension Age 65 (males)

Age at date of trial	High	Medium	Low
20	0.99	0.98	0.97
25	0.99	0.98	0.96
30	0.99	0.97	0.95
35	0.98	0.96	0.93
40	0.98	0.96	0.92
45	0.97	0.95	0.90
50	0.96	0.93	0.87
55	0.95	0.90	0.82
60	0.95	0.90	0.81

Lower pension ages (Males)

33. The figures will be higher for a lower pension age. For example, if pension age is 60, the figures should be as shown in Table B.

Table B
Loss of Earnings to Pension Age 60 (males)

Age at date of trial	High	Medium	Low
20	0.99	0.99	0.98
25	0.99	0.99	0.97
30	0.99	0.98	0.97
35	0.99	0.98	0.96
40	0.98	0.97	0.94
45	0.98	0.96	0.93
50	0.97	0.94	0.92
55	0.96	0.93	0.88

Female lives

34. As a rough guide, for female lives between ages 35 and 55 with a pension age of 60, the figures should be as shown in Table C. As for males, the factors will be lower if the pension age is higher (*e.g.* 65) and higher if the pension age is lower (*e.g.* 55).

Table C
Loss of Earnings to Pension Age 60 (females)

Age at date of trial	High	Medium	Low
35	0.95	0.95	0.94
40	0.93	0.93	0.92
45	0.90	0.90	0.88
50	0.91	0.90	0.88
55	0.95	0.94	0.93

Variations by occupation

35. The risks of illness, injury and disability are less for persons in clerical or similar jobs, *e.g.*, civil servants, the professions and financial services industries, and greater for those in manual jobs, *e.g.*, construction, mining, quarrying and ship-building. However, what matters is the precise nature of the work undertaken by the person in question, rather than the industry as such; for example, a secretary in the headquarters office of a large construction company may be at no greater risk than a secretary in a solicitor's office.

36. In less risky occupations the figures in Table A to C should be *increased* by a maximum of the order of 0.01 up to age 40, rising to 0.03 at age 55.

37. In more risky occupations the figures in Tables A to C should be *reduced* by a maximum of the order of 0.01 at age 25, 0.02 at age 40 and 0.05 at age 55.

Variations by geographical region

38. For persons resident in the South East, East Anglia, South West and East Midlands, the figures in Tables A to C should be *increased* by a maximum of the order of 0.01 up to age 40, rising to 0.03 at age 55.

39. For persons resident in the North, North West, Wales and Scotland, the figures in Tables A to C should be *reduced* by a maximum of the order of 0.01 at age 25, 0.02 at age 40 and 0.05 at age 55.

Section C: Summary of personal injury applications

40. To use the tables take the following steps:

(1) Choose the tables relating to the appropriate period of loss or expense.

(2) Choose the table, relating to that period, appropriate to the sex of the claimant (Tables 1 to 26).

(3) Choose the appropriate rate of return, as determined under section 1 of the Damages Act 1996, obtained from the lump sum.

(4) Find the figure under the column in the table chosen given against the age at trial of the claimant.

(5) Adjust the figure to take account of contingencies other than mortality, as specified in Section B above.

(6) Multiply the annual loss (net of tax) or expense by that figure.

41. In cases where the claimant's expected age of retirement differs from that assumed in the tables, the more complicated procedure explained in paragraphs 14 to 17 should be followed.

Example 1

42. The following is an example of the use of the tables in a personal injury case:
The claimant is female, aged 35 at the date of the trial. She lives in London and is an established civil servant who was working in an office at a salary of £25,000 net of tax. As a result of her injuries, she has lost her job. Her loss of earnings to retirement age of 60 is assessed as follows:

(1) Look up Table 8 for loss of earnings to pension age 60 for females.

(2) The appropriate rate of return is determined to be $2\frac{1}{2}$% (the rate set under section 1 of the Damages Act 1996).

(3) Table 8 shows that, on the basis of a $2\frac{1}{2}$% rate of return, the multiplier for a female aged 35 is 18.39.

(4) Now take account of risks other than mortality. On the assumption of high economic activity for the next few years Table C would require 18.39 to be multiplied by 0.95.

(5)   Based on Section B, further adjustment is necessary because the claimant (a) is in a secure non-manual job, and (b) lives in the South East.

(6)   The adjustments should be made as follows:

Basic adjustment to allow for short-term high economic activity (Table C)	0.95
Adjustment to allow for occupation, say	+0.01
	0.96
Adjustment for geographical region, say	+0.01
	0.97

(7)   The original multiplier taken from Table 8, namely 18.39, must therefore be multiplied by 0.97, resulting in a revised multiplier of 17.84.

(8)   The damages for loss of earnings are assessed as £466,000 (17.84 × 25,000).

Example 2

43.   The following is a second example of the use of the tables in a personal injury case:
The claimant is male, aged 48 at the date of the trial. He lives in Manchester and was working in a factory. His retirement age was 65 and his pre-retirement multiplicand has been determined as £20,000 a year net of tax. The multiplicand for costs of care is deemed to be £50,000 a year. As a result of his injuries, he has lost his job. His loss of earnings to retirement age of 65 is assessed as follows:

(1)   Look up Table 9 for loss of earnings to retirement age 65 for males.

(2)   The appropriate rate of return is determined to be $2\frac{1}{2}$% (the rate set under section 1 of the Damages Act 1996).

(3)   Table 9 shows that, on the basis of a $2\frac{1}{2}$% rate of return, the multiplier for a male aged 48 is 13.38.

(4)   Now take account of risks other than mortality. On the assumption of medium economic activity for the next few years, Table A would require 13.38 to be multiplied by 0.93.

(5)   Based on Section B, further adjustment is necessary because the claimant (a) is in a risky manual job, and (b) lives in the North West.

(6)   The adjustments should be made as follows:

Basic adjustment to allow for short-term medium economic activity (Table A)	0.93
Adjustment to allow for occupation, say	−0.02
	0.91
Adjustment for geographical region, say	−0.03
	0.88

(7)   The original multiplier taken from Table 9, namely 13.38, must therefore be multiplied by 0.88, resulting in a revised multiplier of 11.77.

(8)   The damages for loss of earnings are assessed as £235,400 (11.77 × 20,000).

44. The damages for cost of care are assessed as follows:

(1)   Look up Table 1 for the multiplier at age 48.

(2)   The appropriate rate of return is $2\frac{1}{2}$%.

(3)   Table 19 shows that, on the basis of a $2\frac{1}{2}$% rate of return, the multiplier at age 48 is 22.51.

(4)   No further adjustment is made for risks other than mortality.

(5)   The damages for cost of care are assessed at £1,125,500 (22.51 × 50,000).

Section D: Application of tables to fatal accident cases

45.   Whereas in personal injury cases the problem to be solved is that of setting a value on an income stream during the potential life of one person (the claimant), the situation is generally more complicated in fatal accident cases. Here the compensation is intended to reflect the value of an income stream during the lifetime of one or more dependants of the deceased (or the expected period for which the dependants would have expected to receive the dependency, if shorter) but limited according to the expectation of how long the deceased would have been able to provide the financial support, had he or she not been involved in the fatal accident.

46.   In principle, therefore, the compensation for post-trial dependency should be based on the present value at the date of the trial of the dependency during the expected future joint lifetime of the deceased and the dependant or claimant (had the deceased survived naturally to the date of the trial), subject to any limitations on the period of dependency and any expected future changes in the level of dependency, for example, on attaining retirement age. In addition there should be compensation for the period between the date of accident and the date of trial.

47.   A set of actuarial tables to make such calculations accurately would require tables similar to Tables 1 to 26 but for each combination of ages at the date of the trial of the deceased and the dependant to whom compensation is to be paid. The Working Party concluded that this would not meet the criterion of simplicity of application which was a central objective of these tables and recommend that, in complex cases, or cases where the accuracy of the multiplier is thought by the parties to be of critical importance and material to the resulting amount of compensation (for example in cases potentially involving very large claims where the level of the multiplicand is unambiguously established), the advice of a professionally qualified actuary should be sought. However, for the majority of cases, a certain amount of approximation will be appropriate, bearing in mind the need for a simple and streamlined process, and taking into consideration the other uncertainties in the determination of an appropriate level of compensation. The following paragraphs describe a methodology using Tables 1 to 26 which can be expected to yield satisfactory answers.

Damages for the period from the fatal accident to the date of trial

48.   The period of pre-trial dependency will normally be equal to the period between the date of the fatal accident and the date of the trial, substituting where appropriate the lower figure of the expected period for which the deceased would have provided the dependency, had he or she not been killed in the accident, or if the period of dependency would have been limited in some way, for example if the dependant is a child.

49.   A deduction may be made for the risk that the deceased might have died anyway, in the period between the date of the fatal accident and the date at which the trial takes place. In many cases this deduction will be small and could usually be regarded as de minimis. The need for a deduction

becomes more necessary the longer the period from the date of accident to the date of trial and the older the deceased at the date of death. As an illustration of the order of magnitude of the deduction, Table D shows some examples of factors by which the multiplier should be multiplied for different ages of the deceased and for different periods from the date of accident to the date of the trial.

Table D
Factor by which pre-trial damages should be multiplied to allow for the likelihood that the deceased would not in any case have survived to provide the dependency for the full period to the date of trial

| Age of deceased at date of accident | Period from date of accident to date of trial or date of cessation of dependency, if earlier (years) | | | | | |
| | Male deceased | | | Female deceased | | |
	3	6	9	3	6	9
10	1.00	1.00	1.00	1.00	1.00	1.00
20	1.00	1.00	1.00	1.00	1.00	1.00
30	1.00	1.00	1.00	1.00	1.00	1.00
40	1.00	0.99	0.99	1.00	1.00	0.99
50	0.99	0.99	0.98	1.00	0.99	0.99
60	0.98	0.97	0.95	0.99	0.98	0.97
65	0.98	0.95	0.92	0.99	0.97	0.95
70	0.96	0.92	0.87	0.98	0.95	0.92
75	0.93	0.86	0.79	0.96	0.91	0.85
80	0.89	0.79	0.69	0.93	0.84	0.76

Note: The factor for a period of zero years is clearly 1.00. Factors for other ages and periods not shown in the table may be obtained approximately by interpolation.

50. The resultant multiplier, after application of any discount for the possibility of early death of the deceased before the date of trial, even had the accident not taken place, is to be applied to the multiplicand, which is determined in the usual way. Interest will then be added up to the date of trial on the basis of special damages.

Damages from the date of trial to retirement age

51. The assessment of the multiplier involves the following steps:

(1) Determine the expected period for which the deceased would have been able to provide the dependency (see paragraph 52).

(2) Determine the expected period for which the dependant would have been able to receive the dependency (see paragraph 52).

(3) Take the lesser of the two periods.

(4) Treat the resulting period as a term certain for which the multiplier is to be determined and look up the figure in Table 28 for this period at the appropriate rate of interest.

(5) Apply any adjustment for contingencies other than mortality in accordance with Section B.

(6) If necessary, make an allowance for the risk that the deceased might have died anyway before the date of the trial (see paragraph 54)

52. The expected periods at (1) and (2) of paragraph 51 may be obtained from the 0% column of the appropriate table at the back of this booklet. For (1), Tables 3 to 14 will be relevant, according to the sex of the deceased and the expected age of retirement. The age at which the table should be entered is the age which the deceased would have been at the date of the trial. For (2) Tables 1 and 2 can be used, according to the sex of the dependant and looking up the table at the age of the dependant at the date of the trial.

53. If the period for which the dependency would have continued is a short fixed period, as in the case of a child, the figure at (2) would be the outstanding period at the date of the trial.

54. A deduction may be made for the risk that the deceased might have died anyway before the date of the trial. The need for such a deduction becomes more necessary the longer the period from the date of accident to the date of trial and the older the deceased at the date of death. As an illustration of the order of magnitude of the deduction, Table E shows some examples of the factor by which the multiplier, determined as above, should be multiplied for different ages of the deceased and for different periods from the date of accident to the date of the trial.

Table E
Factor by which post-trial damages should be multiplied to allow for the likelihood that the deceased would not in any case have survived to the date of trial in order to provide any post-trial dependency

Age of deceased at date of accident	Period from date of accident to date of trial (years)					
	Male deceased			Female deceased		
	3	6	9	3	6	9
10	1.00	1.00	1.00	1.00	1.00	1.00
20	1.00	1.00	0.99	1.00	1.00	1.00
30	1.00	0.99	0.99	1.00	1.00	1.00
40	1.00	0.99	0.98	1.00	0.99	0.99
50	0.99	0.97	0.96	0.99	0.98	0.97
60	0.97	0.93	0.89	0.98	0.96	0.93
65	0.95	0.90	0.83	0.97	0.94	0.89
70	0.92	0.83	0.73	0.95	0.89	0.82
75	0.87	0.72	0.58	0.91	0.81	0.68
80	0.79	0.58	0.39	0.85	0.68	0.50

Note: The factor for a period of zero years is clearly 1.00. Factors for other ages and periods not shown in the table may be obtained approximately by interpolation.

55. The resulting multiplier, after application of any discount for the possibility of early death of the deceased before the date of trial, even had the accident not taken place, is to be applied to the appropriate multiplicand, determined in relation to dependency as assessed for the period up to retirement age.

56. If there are several dependants, to whom damages are to be paid in respect of their own particular lifetime (or for a fixed period of dependency), separate multipliers should be determined for each and multiplied by the appropriate multiplicand using the procedure in paragraphs 51 to 55. The total amount of damages is then obtained by adding the separate components. If a single multiplicand is determined, but the damages are to be shared among two or more dependants so long as they are each alive, or during a period of common dependency, then the multiplier will be calculated using the procedure in paragraphs 51 to 55. However, at step (2) of paragraph 51 the expected period wil be the longest of the expected periods for which the dependency might last.

Damages for the period of dependency after retirement age

57. The method described in paragraphs 51 to 56 for pre-retirement age dependency cannot satisfactorily be applied directly to post-retirement age dependency with a sufficient degree of accuracy. We therefore propose a method which involves determining the multiplier by looking at dependency for the rest of life from the date of trial and then subtracting the multiplier for dependency up to retirement age.

58. The assessment of the multiplier for whole of life dependency involves the following steps:

(1) Determine the expectation of life which the deceased would have had at the date of trial, or such lesser period for which the deceased would have provided the dependency (see paragraph 59).

(2)   Determine the expected period for which the dependant would have been able to receive the dependency (see paragraph 59).

(3)   Take the lesser of the two periods.

(4)   Treat the resulting period as a term certain for which the multiplier is to be determined and look up the figure in Table 28 for this period at the appropriate rate of interest.

59.   The expected periods at (1) and (2) of paragraph 58 may be obtained from the 0% column of the appropriate table at the back of this booklet. For (1), Tables 1 or 2 will be relevant, according to the sex of the deceased. The age at which the table should be entered is the age which the deceased would have attained at the date of the trial. For (2) Tables 1 and 2 can be used, according to the sex of the dependant and looking up the table at the age of the dependant at the date of the trial.

60.   Deduct the corresponding multiplier for post-trial pre-retirement dependency, as determined in paragraphs 51 to 56, but without any adjustment for contingencies other than mortality, or that the deceased may have died anyway before the date of trial. The result is the multiplier for post-retirement dependency, which must then be applied to the appropriate multiplicand, assessed in relation to dependency after retirement age. The adjustment for contingencies other than mortality in respect of the damages for the period of dependency after retirement age will often be less than that required for pre-retirement age damages (see paragraph 29).

61.   A deduction may finally be made for the risk that the deceased might have died anyway before the date of trial. The need for such a deduction becomes more necessary the longer the period from the date of accident to the date of trial and the older the deceased at the date of death. As an illustration of the order of magnitude of the deduction, Table E shows some examples of the factor by which the multiplier, determined as above, should be multiplied for different ages of the deceased and for different periods from the date of accident to the date of the trial. The factors for this purpose are exactly the same deductions as used in the calculation at paragraphs 51 to 56.

Cases where dependency is not related to employment

62.   The layout of paragraphs 51 to 61 is based on the assumption that the dependency provided by the deceased would have changed at retirement age. This may not be appropriate in some cases, particularly in the important case of the deceased wife and mother whose contribution has been solely in the home or in the case of an adult child caring for an elderly parent or parents. In cases like this, where the deceased might have provided the dependency throughout their lifetime, paragraphs 57 to 61 should be ignored and paragraphs 51 to 56 used, with the difference that the expected period required at step (1) of paragraph 51 should be a whole of life expectancy, taken from Tables 1 and 2. This is also the approach to use when the deceased was already a pensioner.

Example 3

63.   The dependant is female, aged 38 at the date of the trial, which is taking place six years after the date of the fatal accident which killed the male deceased, at that time aged 37, on whom the dependant was financially dependent. The Court has determined a multiplicand, up to the deceased's normal retirement age of 65, of £30,000 and has decided that no post-retirement damages are payable. The damages are to be calculated as follows:

Pre-trial damages:

(1) Period between fatal accident and trial: 6 years

(2) Factor for possible early death (Table D for male aged 37 and 6 years): 0.99

(3) ∴ Pre-trial damages = 6 × 0.99 × £30,000
        = £178,200 (plus interest as special damages)

Post-trial damages:

(1) Expected period for which the deceased would have provided the dependency (Table 9 at 0% for male aged 43, the age as at the date of death): 21.15

(2) Expected period for which the dependant would have been able to receive the dependency (Table 2 at 0% for female aged 38): 48.44

(3) Lesser of two periods at (1) and (2) = 21.15

(4) Multiplier for term certain of 21.15 years at $2\frac{1}{2}$% rate of return (interpolating between the values for 21 and 22 years in Table 28).
        = (22 − 21.15) × 16.39 + (21.15 − 21) × 16.97
        = 16.48

(5) Adjustment factor for contingencies other than mortality (in accordance with Section B). Assume medium economic activity. Factor from Table A: 0.96

(6) Adjustment factor for the risk that the deceased might have died anyway before the date of trial (Table E for male aged 37 and 6 years): 0.99

(7) Post-trial damages = 16.48 × 0.96 × 0.99 × £30,000
        = £469,878

64. If the court wishes to select multipliers from the age at the date of death instead of following the guidance given above, it is essential to ensure that the period before the trial does not include a discount for early receipt. This could be achieved by selecting multipliers from the 0% columns of the appropriate tables and then applying the discount for early receipt to the period after the trial (using the discount rate set under section 1 of the Damages Act 1996). Thus, the calculations for example 3 above would then be:

(1) Expected period for which the deceased would have provided the dependency (Table 9 at 0% for male aged 37, the age as at the date of death): 26.99

(2) Deduct period between accidental death and date of trial of six years to give post-trial period: 20.99

(3) Expected post-trial period for which the dependant would have been able to receive the dependency (Table 2 at 0% for female aged 38): 48.44

(4) Lesser of two periods at (2) and (3) = 20.99

(5) Multiplier for term certain of 20.99 years at 2.5% rate of return (Table 28) = 16.38

(6) Adjustment factor for contingencies other than mortality (in accordance with Section B). Assume medium economic activity. Factor from Table A: 0.96

(7) Pre-trial damages $= 6 \times £30,000$
$= £180,000$ (plus interest as special damages)

(8) Post-trial damages $= 16.38 \times 0.96 \times £30,000$
$= £471,744$

This method can be extended to the following examples.

Example 4

65. The dependant is female, aged 50 at the date of the trial, which is taking place four years after the date of the fatal accident which killed the man, at that time aged 47, on whom she was financially dependent. The Court has determined a multiplicand, up to the deceased's normal retirement age of 60, of £50,000 and has decided that post-retirement damages should be payable based on a multiplicand of £30,000. The damages are to be calculated as follows:

Pre-trial damages:

(1) Period between fatal accident and trial: 4 years

(2) Factor for possible early death (Table D for male aged 47 and 4 years):   0.99

(3) ∴ Pre-trial damages $= 4 \times 0.99 \times £50,000$
$= £198,000$ (plus interest as special damages)

Post-trial pre-retirement damages:

(1) Expected period for which the deceased would have provided the dependency (Table 7 at 0% for male aged 51, the age as at the date of death): 8.81

(2) Expected period for which the dependant would have been able to receive the dependency (Table 2 at 0% for female aged 50): 36.29

(3) Lesser of the two periods at (1) and (2) = 8.81

(4) Multiplier for term certain of 8.81 years at $2\frac{1}{2}$% rate of return (interpolating between the values for 8 and 9 in Table 28)
$= (9 - 8.81) \times 7.26 + (8.81 - 8) \times 8.07$
$= 7.92$

(5) Adjustment factor for contingencies other than mortality (in accordance with Section B). Assume medium economic activity. Factor from Table B = 0.94.

(6) Adjustment factor for the risk that the deceased might have died anyway before the date of trial (Table E for male aged 47 and 4 years): 0.99.

(7) Post-trial pre-retirement damages $= 7.92 \times 0.94 \times 0.99 \times £50,000$
$= £368,518$

Post-retirement damages:

(1) Expectation of life of deceased at date of trial (Table 1 at 0% for male aged 51): 31.85

(2) Expected period for which the dependant would have been able to receive the dependency (Table 2 at 0% for female aged 50): 36.29

(3) Lesser of two periods at (1) and (2) = 31.85

(4) Multiplier for time certain of 31.85 years at 2½% rate of return (interpolating between the values for 31 and 32 in Tables 28)
= (32 − 31.85) × 21.66 + (31.85 − 30) × 22.12 = 22.05

(5) Deduct multiplier for post-trial pre-retirement damages before application of adjustment factors for contingencies other than mortality and for the risk that the deceased might have died anyway before the date of trial: 22.05 − 7.92 = 14.13

(6) Adjustment factor for the risk that the deceased might have died anyway before the date of trial (Table E for male aged 47 and 4 years): 0.99

(7) Post-retirement damages = 14.13 × 0.99 × £30,000
= £419,661

Example 5

66. There are two dependants, respectively a child aged 10 and a male aged 41 at the date of the trial, which is taking place three years after the date of the fatal accident which killed the woman, at that time aged 35, on whom both were financially dependent. She worked in London for a computer company and future economic activity is deemed by the Court to be high. The Court has determined a multiplicand, up to the deceased's normal retirement age of 62, of £50,000 for the male and £10,000 for the child, up to the age of 21, and has decided that post-retirement damages should be payable based on a multiplier of £20,000. The damages are to be calculated as follows:

Pre-trial damages:

(1) Period between fatal accident and trial: 3 years

(2) Factor for possible early death (Table D for female aged 35 and 3 years):   1.00

(3) ∴ Pre-trial damages = 3 × 1.00 × (£50,000 + £10,000)
= £180,000 (plus interest as special damages)

Post-trial pre-retirement damages:

(1) Expected period for which the deceased would have provided the dependency should be based on female aged 38 at the date of trial with retirement age of 62. First calculate as though deceased were aged 36 and had retirement age of 60 (Table 8 at 0% for female aged 36): 23.61

Then calculate as though deceased were aged 41 and had retirement age of 65 (Table 10 at 0% for female aged 41): 23.38

Interpolate for age 38 with retirement age of 62
= (3 × 23.61 + 2 × 23.38)/5 = 23.52

(2) Expected period for which the male dependant would have been able to receive the dependency (Table 1 at 0% for male aged 41): 41.80

Expected period for which child would have been able to receive the dependency = 11.00

(3) Lesser of two periods at (1) and (2) = 11.00 (in case of child)
23.52 (in case of man)

(4) Multiplier for term certain of 11 years at $2\frac{1}{2}$% (Table 28): 9.63

Multiplier for term certain of 23.52 years at $2\frac{1}{2}$% rate of return (interpolating between the values for 23 and 24 in Table 28)
$= (24 - 23.52) \times 17.55 + (23.52 - 23) \times 18.11$
$= 17.84$

(5) Adjustment factor for contingencies other than mortality (in accordance with Section B). Factor from Table C, allowing for occupation and geographical area: 0.96 (does not apply to child)

(6) Adjustment factor for the risk that the deceased might have died anyway before the date of trial (Table E for female aged 35 and 3 years): 1.00

(7) Pre-retirement damages $= 9.63 \times 1.00 \times £10,000 + 17.84 \times 0.96 \times 1.00 \times £50,000$
$= £96,300 + £856,320$
$= £952,620$

Post-retirement damages:

(1) Expectation of life of deceased at date of trial (Table 2 at 0% for female aged 38): 48.44

(2) Expected period for which the dependant would have been able to receive the dependency (Table 1 at 0% for male aged 41): 41.80 (no post retirement dependency for child)

(3) Lesser of two periods at (1) and (2) = 41.80.

(4) Multiplier for term certain of 41.80 years at $2\frac{1}{2}$% rate of return (interpolating between the values for 41 and 42 in Table 28)
$= (42 - 41.80) \times 25.78 + (41.80 - 41) \times 26.14 = 26.07$

(5) Deduct multiplier for post-trial pre-retirement damages before application of adjustment factors for contingencies other than mortality and for the risk that the deceased might have died anyway before the date of the trial: $26.07 - 17.84 = 8.23$

(6) Adjustment factor for the risk that the deceased might have died anyway before the date of trial (Table E for female aged 35 and 3 years) = 1.00

(7) Post-retirement damages $= 8.23 \times 1.00 \times £20,000$
$= £164,600.$

Section E: Concluding remarks

67. These tables are designed to assist the courts to arrive at suitable multipliers in a range of possible situations. However, they do not cover all possibilities and in more complex situations advice should be sought from a Fellow of the Institute of Actuaries or a Fellow of the Faculty of Actuaries.

68. In cases in which the award will be large, say, about £2 million or more at current prices, or where there are significant pension rights to be taken into consideration, more accurate calculations may be necessary. In such cases advice from an actuary will be desirable.

Christopher Daykin CB, MA, FIA
Government Actuary
London
June 2004

APPENDIX A

Allowing for different types of future inflation

1.   As discussed by Robin de Wilde Q.C. in the Introduction, the purpose of these Tables is to assist the Courts in making awards which will achieve their objective of fully compensating those victims who have suffered wrongful injury. Essentially what they are seeking to do is to place a single capital value on different streams of future payments, which have either been lost or forgone (*e.g.* loss of earnings) or will be incurred in addition to what otherwise might have been the case (*e.g.* costs of care).

2.   Setting a value on future cash-flows is exactly what many actuaries spend most of their time doing. The process requires assumptions about the amounts to be paid, the probabilities of their being paid and the investment returns which will be assumed to be obtained on any money invested to provide for the future payments.

3.   For the probability of the payments being made, we are mostly concerned in the Ogden Tables with whether the individual will survive to particular future ages. Inevitably one does not know this in advance and so the actuary will assume a model, based on statistical experience of what proportion of people live to each future age from any given age, and allowing for a reasonable assumption about how this experience might change in the future. In the 4th edition of the Ogden tables, Tables 19 to 36 made allowance for future improvement in prospects for life expectancy by using the mortality assumptions which had been used by the Government Actuary in the preparation of what were then the most up-to-date official national population projections for England and Wales. Tables 1 to 18 reflected a historic table of mortality experience from the period around the 1991 Census. It rapidly became clear that most people were in agreement that it made more sense to use the tables based on projected mortality, since this was a best estimate of how long on average people would live into the future, which is exactly what is needed for the purposes of the Tables. This edition of the Tables includes only figures based on projected mortality, now taken from the principal projection of the 2002 based official national population projections for England and Wales.

4.   The Tables are based on averages, but, in the absence of specific information to the contrary, it seems reasonable to assume that a claimant (or dependant) will live for an average future lifespan. In fact the Ogden Tables do not assume that the individual will live precisely for that period—no shorter and no longer. Effectively they look at what the future payments would be worth in each of the possible scenarios, in which he or she might live different future lifespans (from dying the next day to living to 120 or so). They then take an average based on the likelihood of each of the scenarios occurring. Allowance can be made for a claimant seeming to have higher or lower expectation of life than average, through assuming they are aged less or more than they actually are. The first column in Tables 1 and 2 (at a rate of return of 0.0%) shows what are usually referred to as the "expectations of life" (*i.e.* without any allowance for discount for the time value of money), so it can readily be seen how large an adjustment would be required to the actual age of the claimant in order to reduce or increase the expectation of life by the desired amount.

5.   Allowance can be made in other approximate ways for the probability that the stream of future payments will be worth less than would be the case on average for the population of England and Wales. For example, life expectancy is lower in Scotland than in England and Wales (about one year— or some 5%—lower for someone currently aged 65, on the basis of the projected mortality rates used in the official national population projections) and mortality in Wales, Northern Ireland and some regions of England would be between the Scottish level and the level for England and Wales as a whole. Correspondingly, the expectation of life in other regions of England and Wales is on average higher than for England and Wales as a whole. The proportionate impact on the discounted values which appear in the Tables would be a little lower than for expectation of life.

6. Actuaries would usually allow explicitly for the amount of the future payments they are seeking to value. If the payments are set as absolute amounts of money, this is straightforward. However, estimating the amount of future payments will often involve making an assumption about future price inflation, such as if the payments are related to the cost of living, either explicitly (for example, pension payments which go up each year in line with the movement in the Retail Price Index (RPI)) or implicitly (because the payments related to the amounts necessary to purchase a particular basket of goods and services). Allowance might be made in particular cases for the expected movements in particular price indices, which might differ from general retail price inflation. For example, it is common in assessing costs under medical insurance to allow for different indices of the costs of care or hospitalisation, which are often expected to go up faster than the RPI. In other cases the payments relate to future salary expectations, so the actuary will have to make allowance for the expected future growth of salaries, which may include a general component for the growth of earnings in the economy, as well as a specific component for the individual because of a reasonable expectation that their salary would increase relative to the average, because of career progression, seniority and other factors.

7. A simple way to think of how to model all these future payments is to break down the calculation into components. So the value of a future payment might be written as:

> Amount of future payment in today's money
> $\times$ Factor to allow for the relevant sort of inflation by the time of payment
> $\times$ Probability of the payment being made
> $\times$ Discount factor to allow for the time value of money

If looked at in this way, the payment amounts are explicitly increased to make allowance for future inflation (whether it be RPI inflation, medical inflation, salary growth or whatever) and the discount factor has to reflect the rate of return (in nominal terms) available on the assets held to provide for the future liability. In modern finance theory, it is generally thought inappropriate to base the discount factor on the assets actually held but to use something called the "risk-free rate of return", which in simple terms means the return on a very secure investment (such as a fixed interest security issued by the UK government) of term corresponding to the duration for which a discounting factor is needed.

8. Thus values could be obtained for future payments likely to be affected by different types of inflation, by allowing for those inflation rates explicitly and using a common risk-free rate of return, which would be based on the yields on government fixed interest securities (gilts).

9. Where the type of inflation with which we are concerned is the increase in the cost of living (as measured by the Retail Price Index), there is a shortcut available for this calculation, as the UK government has since 1981 been issuing index-linked government securities. These are also essentially risk-free investments (over their term), but the payments of interest and return of capital at the maturity date are not fixed in money terms but are increased in line with the movements in the UK RPI. So we can combine the factor for allowing for inflation in the formula in paragraph 7 above with the discount factor, replacing the rate of return on ordinary fixed interest securities by the real rate of return on index-linked gilts. This so-called 'real' rate of return is much lower than the rate of return on fixed interest securities, since it allows for the offsetting effect of inflation. The formula then becomes:

> Amount of future payment in today's money
> $\times$ Probability of the payment being made
> $\times$ *Real rate of return* discount factor to allow for the time value of money in respect of inflation linked payments

This is the basis on which the Ogden Tables are now prepared, and the rate of return, which is set by the Lord Chancellor in Regulations, is the real rate of return discount factor, derived from the returns on index-linked gilts, with an allowance for tax.

10. It is still possible to use this approach, and the rates of return on index-linked gilts, where the future payment streams are deemed to go up in line with earnings or with some other price index. This can be done in one of two ways. The first way would be to allow explicitly for the rate of increase of the future payments relative to prices, in other words to allow for the real rate of earnings growth or of costs of care (that is to say the growth in excess of price inflation). The formula at paragraph 7 would then become:

Amount of future payment in today's money
    × Factor to allow for the relevant sort of real inflation by the time of payment
       (*i.e.* the inflation in excess of future price inflation as measured by the RPI)
          × Probability of the payment being made
             × *Real rate of return* discount factor to allow for the time value of money in
               respect of inflation linked payments

11. Another way of doing it would be to allow implicitly for the relevant real rate of inflation by using a lower discount factor. This is equivalent to the formula in paragraph 9, but with the relevant type of inflation substituted for RPI inflation:

Amount of future payment in today's money
    × Probability of the payment being made
        × *Real rate of return* discount factor to allow for the time value of money in respect
          of inflation linked payments according to the relevant inflation index

12. Real earnings growth in the UK has averaged some $1\frac{1}{2}$ to 2% a year more than growth in the RPI. This is based on general earnings growth in the economy and does not allow for the growth of earnings which many individuals experience throughout their careers. It is, of course, uncertain what an appropriate assumption would be for the future, but actuaries commonly allow in their calculations for 2% real earnings growth (they might allow for somewhat less in the way of general earnings growth and include a specific allowance for the earnings progression of individuals). If we take 2% a year future real earnings growth as an example, the real rate of return discount factor which would allow properly for this type of inflation in the formula in paragraph 11 would be some two percentage points below the real rate of return based on RPI inflation in the formula in paragraph 9. Thus if the Lord Chancellor sets the rate for paragraph 9 at 0%, based on price inflation, the real rate of return to use in the Ogden Tables in order to allow properly for earnings inflation would be about $\frac{1}{2}$% (strictly, the pre-tax rate implicit in the 0% should be reduced by two percentage points and then a deduction made for tax, but it is unlikely that this would be very different, especially as the deduction for tax is an approximation). For a woman aged 40, this would increase the multiplier shown in Table 2 from 26.92 to 41.10, roughly a 53% increase in the amount of compensation due.

13. Future inflation in the costs of care is even more uncertain. To the extent that the care relates primarily to the services of carers or medical staff, then an earnings inflation assumption might be a reasonable proxy. Medical costs arising from medicines and hospitalisation are also generally expected to go up faster than ordinary retail price inflation, but perhaps not quite so much as earnings in the long term. If we were to make an assumption that costs of care would go up by 1% a year on average more than inflation as measured by the RPI, then the real rate of return to use in the Ogden Tables to allow for payments in respect of costs of care would be about $1\frac{1}{2}$% (*i.e.* $2\frac{1}{2}$% less 1%). For a woman aged 40, this would increase the multiplier shown in Table 2 from 26.92 to 32.87, roughly a 22% increase in the amount of compensation due.

14. An alternative way of approaching the problem, instead of amending the discount rate, would be to provide a supplementary table for increasing the multiplicand to allow for the fact that the payments are expected to increase faster than the rate of inflation implicit in the rate of discount set by the Lord Chancellor. A sample of such a table for use with the multipliers for loss of life in Tables 1 and 2 might be as follows:

Additional factors to be applied to the multiplicand to allow for the stream of payments to be valued going up by different percentages more than the RPI

Age at date of trial	Expected average yearly increase in excess of RPI increases				
	0.5%	1.0%	1.5%	2.0%	2.5%
Males					
20	1.13	1.29	1.48	1.72	2.02
30	1.11	1.25	1.41	1.60	1.84
40	1.10	1.21	1.34	1.49	1.67
50	1.08	1.17	1.27	1.38	1.52
60	1.06	1.13	1.20	1.28	1.38
Females					
20	1.13	1.30	1.50	1.76	2.08
30	1.12	1.26	1.43	1.64	1.89
40	1.10	1.22	1.36	1.53	1.72
50	1.08	1.18	1.29	1.42	1.56
60	1.07	1.14	1.22	1.31	1.42

Government Actuary's Department   July 2004

APPENDIX B

Comments by the Association of British Insurers and the NHS Litigation Authority

Introduction

1. The Association of British Insurers (ABI) is the trade association for the UK insurance industry and represents companies transacting over 95% of the domestic insurance in the United Kingdom. ABI representatives welcomed participating in the preparatory discussions leading to the preparation of this fifth edition of the tables. The NHS Litigation Authority is a Special Health Authority set up to handle all clinical negligence claims arising in England.

2. Representatives of both the ABI and the NHS Litigation Authority welcomed participating in the preparatory discussions leading to the preparation of this fifth edition of the tables.

3. At the time of writing this appendix, the law applicable to the valuation and payment of personal injury claims involving damages for future loss is on the cusp of significant change. Implementation of sections 100–101 of the Courts Act 2003 will for the first time lead to judicially ordered periodical payments in these claims. If these are assessed based on the claimant's annual needs—the "bottom up" approach—it is likely that the traditional multiplier & multiplicand approach, with which these tables assist, will become less relevant.

4. We recognise the refinements that this latest edition brings to the actuarial principles involved in assessing claims for future losses and expenses. First, the broadening of the range of retirement ages (as set out in tables 3–26 above) should enable insurers, legal representatives and the judiciary more readily to value and settle claims with these features. Second, the general updating of the multipliers to reflect recent improvements in projected mortality should be a positive development for those claims in which post-injury life expectancy remains on a par with that of the general population. Third, it is worth re-emphasising the reasons for removing what were tables 1–18 in the fourth edition: "*. . . the fact that they are no longer published . . . does not mean in very particular circumstances that they may not be relevant to the calculations of damages*".[1]

Reservations

5. However, certain aspects of the Introduction and Explanatory Notes to the present edition do give insurers and the NHS Litigation Authority cause for significant concern; some to the extent that we disagree with the points made.

6. The agreed purpose of the tables is to "*provide an aid for those assessing the lump sum appropriate as compensation . . .*"[2] in claims involving future losses. We do not accept that the tables or the accompanying text should seek to advocate reform of the legal basis on which compensation is assessed. In our view, so doing weakens the authority of the tables and undermines the consensus in the Working Party.

7. It is with some regret that we feel obliged to raise our concerns by way of this Appendix, but we judge it essential to respond to certain arguments and assertions which could, without further commentary or interpretation, be viewed as advocating approaches that we believe were not matters on which the various interests in the Working Party were agreed. We set out our main concerns below.

---

[1] See paragraph 21 of the Introduction to this edition.
[2] Paragraph 1 of the Explanatory Notes to this edition.

Multipliers in Fatal Accident Act Cases

8. In the fourth edition, we stated that: *". . . there is perhaps a danger that the use of overly scientific approaches in this area may bring a spurious accuracy to a calculation which, almost by definition, will prove wrong in the future."*[3]

9. The valuation of fatal accident claims is based on several informed judgments and assumptions (such as the period of dependency, its amount and any variation in it), which taken together are far more likely to affect the amount of the fatal accident claim than say preferring the methodology suggested in Section D of the current Explanatory Notes to that outlined by Lord Fraser in *Cookson v Knowles* [1979] A.C. 556. It is worth emphasising that Nelson J. in *White v ESAB* [2002] P.I.Q.R. Q76 considered himself bound by this authority.

Inflation and Appendix A

10. We do not accept the arguments or the table of factors in the latter part of Appendix A. The arguments are for an allowance to be made for different types of future inflation. It is our view that this is a matter reserved for the Lord Chancellor[4] to consider in prescribing any rate under the Damages Act 1996 (as amended). The Lord Chancellor specifically took inflation into account in setting the discount rate in 2001. He stated that setting the rate (emphasis added):

    *". . . **involves making assumptions for the future about a wide variety of factors affecting the economy as a whole, including for example the likely rate of inflation. In these circumstances, it is inevitable that any approach to setting the discount rate must be fairly broad-brush.** Put shortly, there can be no single 'right' answer as to what rate should be set. Since it is in the context of larger awards, intended to cover longer periods, that there is the greatest risk of serious discrepancies between the level of compensation and the actual losses incurred if the discount rate set is not appropriate, I have had this type of award particularly in mind when considering the level at which the discount rate should be set."*[5]

11. Since then, the Court of Appeal have been invited to examine the Lord Chancellor's decision and reasons for setting the discount rate at 2.5% on several occasions, most recently in *Cooke v United Bristol Health Care & others* [2004] 1 W.L.R. 251 (and earlier in *Warriner v Warriner* [2002] 1 W.L.R. 1703). In *Cooke* the argument was advanced that the multiplicand should be adjusted because care costs and earnings were asserted to rise at a rate faster than prices inflation.

12. Laws L.J. stated very clearly in *Cooke* that the effects of inflation were squarely within the factors considered by the Lord Chancellor in the reasons given in 2001 for setting the present discount rate. Therefore the Court of Appeal was bound by that rate. Laws L.J. said that:

    "The key rests in the fact, plain in my judgment beyond the possibility of sensible argument, that it is a premise of the Lord Chancellor's order that the effects of inflation in claims for future loss are to be catered for solely by means of the multiplier, conditioned as it is by the discount rate. Accordingly the multiplicand was necessarily treated as based on current costs at the date of trial."

13. We are firmly of the view that any arguments that seek to depart from the discount rate set by the Lord Chancellor—whether by way of applying a different discount rate in a particular case or arguing for an adjustment to the multiplicand, as advocated in Appendix A above—have been firmly rejected by the Court of Appeal for the time being. We are unable to support Appendix A and maintain that it is not the function of this Working Party to advocate an approach which would inevitably conflict with the current case law from the appeal courts.

---

[3] Ogden Tables, Fourth Edition - appendix C paragraph 10.
[4] And, as of June 2003, Secretary of State for Constitutional Affairs
[5] Setting the Discount Rate, Lord Chancellor's Reasons (July 27, 2001) http://www.dca.gov.uk/civil/discount.htm

14. In any event, it is apparent in any examination of compensation for future losses in personal injury claims that there is a notable lack of a credible body of evidence concerning how these awards are invested, managed and ultimately spent. We believe that proper research is required further to inform the debate in this important area.

Summary

15. We find ourselves unable to support the arguments advanced in the Explanatory Notes and Appendix A that challenge the current discount rate and the reasoning underlying its selection. These matters are reserved by statute to the Lord Chancellor and consequently the appellate Courts have refused to entertain them.

16. This present position reinforces the stability of the discount rate. The Lord Chancellor made this plain in setting the rate in 2001, when he envisaged: " . . . *a situation in which claimants and defendants may have a reasonably clear idea about the impact of the discount rate upon their cases, so as to facilitate negotiation of settlements and the presentation of cases in court.*"

Association of British Insurers and NHS Litigation Authority
September 2004

Table 1: Multipliers for pecuniary loss for life (males)

Age at date of trial	Multiplier calculated with allowance for projected mortality from the 2002-based population projections and rate of return of											Age at date of trial
	0.0%	0.5%	1.0%	1.5%	2.0%	2.5%	3.0%	3.5%	4.0%	4.5%	5.0%	
0	83.24	67.69	56.00	47.08	40.18	34.76	30.46	27.00	24.17	21.83	19.88	0
1	82.62	67.34	55.82	47.00	40.16	34.79	30.51	27.06	24.23	21.90	19.95	1
2	81.62	66.68	55.37	46.70	39.96	34.65	30.42	26.99	24.19	21.87	19.93	2
3	80.60	66.00	54.92	46.39	39.75	34.51	30.32	26.92	24.14	21.84	19.91	3
4	79.58	65.31	54.45	46.08	39.53	34.36	30.21	26.85	24.09	21.80	19.88	4
5	78.55	64.62	53.98	45.75	39.31	34.20	30.10	26.77	24.03	21.76	19.85	5
6	77.52	63.92	53.50	45.42	39.08	34.04	29.98	26.69	23.97	21.71	19.82	6
7	76.48	63.21	53.01	45.08	38.84	33.87	29.87	26.60	23.91	21.67	19.78	7
8	75.45	62.50	52.52	44.74	38.60	33.70	29.74	26.51	23.84	21.62	19.74	8
9	74.41	61.78	52.02	44.39	38.35	33.52	29.61	26.42	23.77	21.57	19.71	9
10	73.38	61.06	51.52	44.03	38.10	33.34	29.48	26.32	23.70	21.51	19.67	10
11	72.34	60.34	51.01	43.67	37.84	33.16	29.35	26.22	23.63	21.46	19.62	11
12	71.30	59.61	50.49	43.31	37.58	32.96	29.21	26.12	23.55	21.40	19.58	12
13	70.26	58.88	49.97	42.93	37.31	32.77	29.06	26.01	23.47	21.34	19.53	13
14	69.22	58.14	49.45	42.56	37.04	32.57	28.92	25.90	23.39	21.27	19.48	14
15	68.18	57.40	48.92	42.17	36.76	32.36	28.76	25.79	23.30	21.21	19.43	15
16	67.15	56.66	48.38	41.79	36.47	32.15	28.61	25.67	23.21	21.14	19.38	16
17	66.11	55.92	47.85	41.40	36.19	31.94	28.45	25.55	23.12	21.07	19.32	17
18	65.09	55.19	47.32	41.01	35.90	31.73	28.29	25.43	23.03	21.00	19.27	18
19	64.08	54.46	46.79	40.62	35.61	31.52	28.13	25.31	22.94	20.93	19.22	19
20	63.08	53.73	46.25	40.23	35.32	31.30	27.97	25.19	22.85	20.86	19.16	20
21	62.07	52.99	45.71	39.83	35.03	31.08	27.80	25.06	22.75	20.79	19.10	21
22	61.06	52.25	45.16	39.42	34.72	30.85	27.63	24.93	22.65	20.71	19.04	22
23	60.05	51.50	44.61	39.01	34.41	30.62	27.45	24.79	22.54	20.63	18.98	23
24	59.03	50.75	44.05	38.59	34.10	30.38	27.27	24.65	22.43	20.54	18.91	24
25	58.02	50.00	43.49	38.16	33.78	30.13	27.08	24.51	22.32	20.45	18.84	25
26	57.01	49.24	42.92	37.73	33.45	29.88	26.89	24.36	22.20	20.36	18.77	26
27	56.00	48.48	42.34	37.30	33.11	29.62	26.69	24.20	22.08	20.26	18.69	27
28	54.99	47.72	41.76	36.85	32.77	29.36	26.48	24.04	21.96	20.16	18.61	28
29	53.98	46.95	41.18	36.40	32.42	29.09	26.27	23.88	21.83	20.06	18.53	29
30	52.97	46.18	40.58	35.94	32.07	28.81	26.05	23.70	21.69	19.95	18.44	30
31	51.96	45.40	39.98	35.48	31.71	28.53	25.83	23.53	21.55	19.84	18.35	31
32	50.94	44.62	39.38	35.01	31.34	28.24	25.60	23.34	21.40	19.72	18.25	32
33	49.93	43.83	38.76	34.53	30.96	27.94	25.36	23.15	21.24	19.59	18.15	33
34	48.91	43.04	38.15	34.04	30.57	27.63	25.11	22.95	21.09	19.46	18.04	34
35	47.90	42.25	37.52	33.54	30.18	27.31	24.86	22.75	20.92	19.33	17.93	35
36	46.88	41.45	36.89	33.04	29.78	26.99	24.60	22.54	20.75	19.18	17.81	36
37	45.86	40.64	36.25	32.53	29.37	26.66	24.33	22.32	20.57	19.03	17.69	37
38	44.85	39.83	35.60	32.01	28.95	26.32	24.05	22.09	20.38	18.88	17.56	38
39	43.83	39.02	34.95	31.48	28.52	25.97	23.77	21.85	20.18	18.72	17.42	39
40	42.81	38.20	34.29	30.95	28.08	25.61	23.47	21.61	19.98	18.55	17.28	40
41	41.80	37.38	33.62	30.41	27.64	25.25	23.17	21.36	19.77	18.37	17.13	41
42	40.78	36.56	32.96	29.86	27.19	24.88	22.86	21.10	19.56	18.19	16.98	42
43	39.78	35.74	32.28	29.31	26.73	24.50	22.55	20.84	19.33	18.00	16.82	43
44	38.77	34.92	31.61	28.75	26.27	24.11	22.23	20.57	19.10	17.81	16.66	44
45	37.77	34.09	30.93	28.19	25.80	23.72	21.90	20.29	18.87	17.61	16.48	45
46	36.78	33.27	30.25	27.62	25.33	23.32	21.56	20.00	18.63	17.40	16.31	46
47	35.79	32.45	29.56	27.05	24.85	22.92	21.22	19.71	18.38	17.19	16.12	47
48	34.80	31.63	28.88	26.47	24.36	22.51	20.87	19.41	18.12	16.97	15.93	48
49	33.82	30.81	28.18	25.89	23.87	22.08	20.51	19.11	17.86	16.74	15.73	49
50	32.84	29.98	27.48	25.29	23.36	21.65	20.14	18.79	17.58	16.50	15.53	50
51	31.85	29.15	26.78	24.69	22.85	21.21	19.76	18.46	17.30	16.25	15.31	51
52	30.87	28.32	26.07	24.08	22.32	20.76	19.37	18.12	17.00	15.99	15.08	52
53	29.90	27.48	25.35	23.47	21.79	20.30	18.97	17.77	16.69	15.72	14.85	53
54	28.93	26.65	24.64	22.85	21.26	19.84	18.56	17.41	16.38	15.45	14.60	54

Table 1: Multipliers for pecuniary loss for life (males) *continued*

Age at date of trial	Multiplier calculated with allowance for projected mortality from the 2002-based population projections and rate of return of											Age at date of trial
	0.0%	*0.5%*	*1.0%*	*1.5%*	*2.0%*	*2.5%*	*3.0%*	*3.5%*	*4.0%*	*4.5%*	*5.0%*	
55	27.97	25.82	23.92	22.23	20.72	19.37	18.15	17.05	16.06	15.17	14.35	55
56	27.02	25.01	23.21	21.61	20.18	18.89	17.73	16.69	15.74	14.88	14.10	56
57	26.09	24.20	22.51	21.00	19.64	18.42	17.32	16.32	15.41	14.59	13.84	57
58	25.17	23.40	21.81	20.38	19.10	17.94	16.89	15.94	15.08	14.29	13.57	58
59	24.27	22.61	21.11	19.77	18.56	17.46	16.47	15.57	14.74	13.99	13.30	59
60	23.37	21.82	20.42	19.16	18.02	16.98	16.04	15.18	14.40	13.68	13.02	60
61	22.50	21.05	19.74	18.56	17.48	16.50	15.61	14.80	14.05	13.37	12.74	61
62	21.64	20.29	19.06	17.95	16.94	16.02	15.18	14.41	13.71	13.06	12.46	62
63	20.79	19.53	18.39	17.35	16.40	15.54	14.75	14.02	13.35	12.73	12.17	63
64	19.94	18.78	17.71	16.75	15.86	15.05	14.30	13.62	12.99	12.40	11.86	64
65	19.10	18.02	17.03	16.13	15.31	14.55	13.85	13.21	12.61	12.06	11.55	65
66	18.25	17.26	16.35	15.51	14.74	14.03	13.38	12.78	12.22	11.70	11.22	66
67	17.41	16.49	15.65	14.88	14.17	13.51	12.90	12.34	11.82	11.33	10.88	67
68	16.56	15.72	14.95	14.24	13.58	12.97	12.41	11.89	11.40	10.95	10.53	68
69	15.72	14.95	14.25	13.60	12.99	12.43	11.91	11.43	10.97	10.55	10.16	69
70	14.89	14.19	13.55	12.95	12.40	11.88	11.41	10.96	10.54	10.15	9.78	70
71	14.08	13.45	12.86	12.32	11.81	11.34	10.90	10.49	10.10	9.74	9.41	71
72	13.29	12.72	12.19	11.69	11.23	10.80	10.40	10.02	9.67	9.34	9.03	72
73	12.53	12.01	11.54	11.09	10.67	10.28	9.91	9.56	9.24	8.94	8.65	73
74	11.80	11.34	10.91	10.50	10.12	9.77	9.43	9.12	8.82	8.54	8.27	74
75	11.10	10.69	10.30	9.94	9.59	9.27	8.96	8.68	8.41	8.15	7.91	75
76	10.44	10.07	9.72	9.39	9.08	8.79	8.51	8.25	8.01	7.77	7.55	76
77	9.81	9.48	9.16	8.87	8.59	8.33	8.08	7.84	7.62	7.40	7.20	77
78	9.21	8.91	8.63	8.37	8.12	7.88	7.65	7.44	7.24	7.04	6.86	78
79	8.64	8.38	8.12	7.89	7.66	7.45	7.24	7.05	6.87	6.69	6.52	79
80	8.09	7.86	7.63	7.42	7.22	7.03	6.84	6.67	6.50	6.34	6.19	80
81	7.56	7.35	7.15	6.96	6.78	6.61	6.45	6.29	6.14	6.00	5.86	81
82	7.04	6.86	6.68	6.52	6.36	6.20	6.06	5.92	5.78	5.66	5.53	82
83	6.55	6.39	6.24	6.09	5.95	5.81	5.68	5.56	5.44	5.32	5.22	83
84	6.10	5.95	5.82	5.69	5.56	5.44	5.33	5.22	5.11	5.01	4.91	84
85	5.67	5.55	5.43	5.31	5.20	5.09	4.99	4.89	4.80	4.71	4.62	85
86	5.28	5.17	5.06	4.96	4.86	4.77	4.68	4.59	4.51	4.43	4.35	86
87	4.92	4.82	4.73	4.64	4.55	4.47	4.39	4.31	4.23	4.16	4.09	87
88	4.59	4.50	4.42	4.34	4.26	4.19	4.12	4.05	3.98	3.92	3.86	88
89	4.29	4.21	4.14	4.07	4.00	3.94	3.87	3.81	3.75	3.69	3.64	89
90	4.01	3.95	3.88	3.82	3.76	3.70	3.64	3.59	3.54	3.48	3.43	90
91	3.75	3.69	3.63	3.58	3.52	3.47	3.42	3.37	3.32	3.28	3.23	91
92	3.50	3.45	3.40	3.35	3.30	3.25	3.21	3.16	3.12	3.08	3.04	92
93	3.29	3.24	3.19	3.15	3.11	3.07	3.03	2.99	2.95	2.91	2.88	93
94	3.11	3.06	3.02	2.99	2.95	2.91	2.87	2.84	2.80	2.77	2.74	94
95	2.93	2.90	2.86	2.83	2.79	2.76	2.73	2.69	2.66	2.63	2.60	95
96	2.76	2.73	2.69	2.66	2.63	2.60	2.57	2.55	2.52	2.49	2.47	96
97	2.59	2.56	2.53	2.50	2.47	2.45	2.42	2.40	2.37	2.35	2.33	97
98	2.42	2.39	2.36	2.34	2.32	2.29	2.27	2.25	2.23	2.20	2.18	98
99	2.25	2.23	2.21	2.18	2.16	2.14	2.12	2.10	2.08	2.06	2.05	99
100	2.10	2.08	2.06	2.04	2.02	2.00	1.98	1.97	1.95	1.93	1.92	100

Table 2: Multipliers for pecuniary loss for life (females)

Age at date of trial	Multiplier calculated with allowance for projected mortality from the 2002-based population projections and rate of return of											Age at date of trial
	0.0%	0.5%	1.0%	1.5%	2.0%	2.5%	3.0%	3.5%	4.0%	4.5%	5.0%	
0	87.08	70.28	57.76	48.29	41.02	35.35	30.88	27.30	24.39	22.00	20.01	0
1	86.43	69.92	57.57	48.21	41.00	35.38	30.93	27.36	24.45	22.06	20.07	1
2	85.43	69.27	57.15	47.93	40.82	35.26	30.85	27.30	24.42	22.04	20.06	2
3	84.42	68.61	56.71	47.64	40.63	35.13	30.76	27.24	24.38	22.01	20.04	3
4	83.40	67.94	56.27	47.35	40.43	34.99	30.67	27.18	24.33	21.98	20.02	4
5	82.38	67.26	55.82	47.04	40.22	34.86	30.57	27.11	24.29	21.95	19.99	5
6	81.36	66.58	55.36	46.73	40.01	34.71	30.47	27.05	24.24	21.91	19.97	6
7	80.34	65.89	54.90	46.42	39.80	34.56	30.37	26.97	24.19	21.88	19.94	7
8	79.31	65.20	54.43	46.10	39.58	34.41	30.26	26.90	24.13	21.84	19.91	8
9	78.28	64.51	53.96	45.78	39.36	34.26	30.16	26.82	24.08	21.80	19.89	9
10	77.25	63.81	53.48	45.45	39.13	34.09	30.04	26.74	24.02	21.76	19.85	10
11	76.23	63.11	52.99	45.11	38.89	33.93	29.93	26.66	23.96	21.71	19.82	11
12	75.20	62.40	52.51	44.77	38.65	33.76	29.81	26.57	23.90	21.67	19.79	12
13	74.17	61.69	52.01	44.42	38.41	33.59	29.68	26.48	23.83	21.62	19.75	13
14	73.14	60.97	51.51	44.07	38.16	33.41	29.55	26.39	23.77	21.57	19.72	14
15	72.11	60.26	51.01	43.72	37.91	33.23	29.42	26.29	23.70	21.52	19.68	15
16	71.09	59.54	50.50	43.36	37.65	33.05	29.29	26.20	23.62	21.47	19.64	16
17	70.06	58.82	49.99	43.00	37.39	32.86	29.15	26.10	23.55	21.41	19.60	17
18	69.04	58.09	49.48	42.63	37.13	32.67	29.01	25.99	23.47	21.35	19.55	18
19	68.02	57.37	48.96	42.25	36.86	32.47	28.87	25.89	23.40	21.29	19.51	19
20	66.99	56.63	48.43	41.87	36.58	32.27	28.72	25.78	23.31	21.23	19.46	20
21	65.96	55.90	47.90	41.49	36.30	32.06	28.57	25.66	23.23	21.17	19.41	21
22	64.94	55.16	47.36	41.09	36.01	31.84	28.41	25.54	23.14	21.10	19.36	22
23	63.91	54.41	46.82	40.69	35.71	31.63	28.24	25.42	23.04	21.03	19.30	23
24	62.88	53.66	46.27	40.29	35.41	31.40	28.07	25.29	22.94	20.95	19.25	24
25	61.85	52.90	45.71	39.88	35.10	31.17	27.90	25.16	22.84	20.87	19.18	25
26	60.82	52.14	45.15	39.46	34.79	30.93	27.72	25.02	22.74	20.79	19.12	26
27	59.79	51.38	44.58	39.03	34.47	30.69	27.53	24.88	22.63	20.70	19.05	27
28	58.76	50.61	44.00	38.60	34.14	30.44	27.34	24.73	22.51	20.61	18.98	28
29	57.72	49.84	43.42	38.16	33.81	30.18	27.14	24.58	22.39	20.52	18.91	29
30	56.69	49.06	42.83	37.71	33.46	29.92	26.94	24.42	22.27	20.42	18.83	30
31	55.66	48.28	42.24	37.26	33.12	29.65	26.73	24.25	22.14	20.32	18.75	31
32	54.63	47.50	41.64	36.80	32.76	29.37	26.52	24.08	22.00	20.21	18.66	32
33	53.59	46.71	41.04	36.33	32.40	29.09	26.29	23.91	21.86	20.10	18.57	33
34	52.56	45.92	40.43	35.86	32.03	28.80	26.07	23.73	21.72	19.99	18.48	34
35	51.53	45.12	39.81	35.38	31.65	28.51	25.83	23.54	21.57	19.86	18.38	35
36	50.50	44.32	39.19	34.89	31.27	28.20	25.59	23.35	21.41	19.74	18.28	36
37	49.47	43.52	38.56	34.40	30.88	27.89	25.34	23.15	21.25	19.61	18.17	37
38	48.44	42.72	37.93	33.89	30.48	27.57	25.09	22.94	21.09	19.47	18.06	38
39	47.41	41.91	37.29	33.39	30.08	27.25	24.82	22.73	20.91	19.33	17.94	39
40	46.39	41.10	36.64	32.87	29.66	26.92	24.55	22.51	20.73	19.18	17.82	40
41	45.36	40.28	35.99	32.35	29.24	26.58	24.28	22.28	20.55	19.03	17.69	41
42	44.34	39.47	35.34	31.83	28.82	26.23	24.00	22.05	20.36	18.87	17.56	42
43	43.32	38.65	34.69	31.30	28.39	25.88	23.71	21.81	20.16	18.70	17.42	43
44	42.31	37.84	34.02	30.76	27.95	25.52	23.41	21.57	19.96	18.53	17.28	44
45	41.30	37.02	33.36	30.22	27.51	25.16	23.11	21.32	19.75	18.36	17.13	45
46	40.29	36.20	32.69	29.67	27.06	24.78	22.80	21.06	19.53	18.18	16.98	46
47	39.29	35.38	32.02	29.12	26.60	24.40	22.48	20.79	19.31	17.99	16.82	47
48	38.28	34.56	31.34	28.56	26.13	24.01	22.16	20.52	19.08	17.79	16.65	48
49	37.29	33.73	30.66	27.99	25.66	23.62	21.82	20.24	18.84	17.59	16.48	49
50	36.29	32.91	29.98	27.42	25.18	23.22	21.48	19.95	18.59	17.38	16.30	50
51	35.30	32.09	29.29	26.84	24.70	22.81	21.14	19.66	18.34	17.16	16.11	51
52	34.32	31.26	28.60	26.26	24.20	22.39	20.78	19.35	18.08	16.94	15.91	52
53	33.34	30.44	27.90	25.67	23.70	21.96	20.42	19.04	17.81	16.71	15.71	53
54	32.36	29.62	27.20	25.08	23.20	21.53	20.05	18.72	17.54	16.47	15.51	54

Table 2: Multipliers for pecuniary loss for life (females) *continued*

Age at date of trial	Multiplier calculated with allowance for projected mortality from the 2002-based population projections and rate of return of											Age at date of trial
	0.0%	0.5%	1.0%	1.5%	2.0%	2.5%	3.0%	3.5%	4.0%	4.5%	5.0%	
55	31.39	28.80	26.51	24.49	22.69	21.10	19.67	18.40	17.25	16.22	15.29	55
56	30.44	27.98	25.81	23.89	22.18	20.66	19.29	18.07	16.97	15.97	15.07	56
57	29.49	27.17	25.12	23.29	21.66	20.21	18.90	17.73	16.67	15.71	14.85	57
58	28.54	26.36	24.42	22.69	21.14	19.76	18.51	17.39	16.37	15.45	14.61	58
59	27.61	25.56	23.72	22.09	20.62	19.30	18.11	17.04	16.06	15.18	14.37	59
60	26.69	24.75	23.03	21.48	20.09	18.84	17.70	16.68	15.75	14.90	14.12	60
61	25.77	23.96	22.33	20.87	19.56	18.37	17.29	16.31	15.42	14.61	13.87	61
62	24.86	23.16	21.64	20.26	19.02	17.89	16.87	15.94	15.09	14.32	13.61	62
63	23.95	22.36	20.94	19.64	18.47	17.41	16.44	15.56	14.75	14.01	13.33	63
64	23.04	21.56	20.23	19.02	17.92	16.91	16.00	15.16	14.40	13.69	13.05	64
65	22.12	20.75	19.51	18.38	17.34	16.40	15.54	14.75	14.03	13.36	12.75	65
66	21.20	19.93	18.77	17.72	16.76	15.88	15.07	14.33	13.64	13.01	12.43	66
67	20.27	19.10	18.03	17.05	16.16	15.33	14.58	13.88	13.24	12.64	12.09	67
68	19.33	18.25	17.27	16.37	15.54	14.77	14.07	13.42	12.82	12.26	11.74	68
69	18.39	17.40	16.50	15.67	14.90	14.20	13.54	12.94	12.38	11.86	11.37	69
70	17.45	16.55	15.73	14.96	14.26	13.61	13.01	12.45	11.92	11.44	10.99	70
71	16.52	15.71	14.96	14.26	13.62	13.02	12.46	11.95	11.46	11.02	10.60	71
72	15.62	14.88	14.20	13.56	12.98	12.43	11.92	11.44	11.00	10.59	10.20	72
73	14.74	14.07	13.45	12.88	12.34	11.84	11.38	10.94	10.54	10.15	9.79	73
74	13.88	13.29	12.73	12.21	11.72	11.27	10.85	10.45	10.07	9.72	9.39	74
75	13.07	12.53	12.03	11.56	11.12	10.71	10.32	9.96	9.62	9.30	9.00	75
76	12.29	11.81	11.36	10.93	10.54	10.17	9.81	9.49	9.17	8.88	8.60	76
77	11.55	11.12	10.71	10.33	9.97	9.64	9.32	9.02	8.74	8.47	8.22	77
78	10.83	10.45	10.09	9.75	9.43	9.12	8.84	8.57	8.31	8.07	7.84	78
79	10.15	9.81	9.48	9.18	8.89	8.62	8.36	8.12	7.89	7.67	7.46	79
80	9.49	9.18	8.90	8.63	8.37	8.13	7.89	7.68	7.47	7.27	7.08	80
81	8.85	8.58	8.33	8.09	7.86	7.64	7.43	7.24	7.05	6.87	6.70	81
82	8.23	8.00	7.77	7.56	7.36	7.17	6.98	6.81	6.64	6.48	6.33	82
83	7.64	7.44	7.24	7.05	6.88	6.71	6.54	6.39	6.24	6.10	5.96	83
84	7.09	6.91	6.73	6.57	6.41	6.26	6.12	5.98	5.85	5.72	5.60	84
85	6.56	6.40	6.25	6.11	5.97	5.84	5.71	5.59	5.48	5.36	5.26	85
86	6.07	5.93	5.80	5.68	5.56	5.44	5.33	5.22	5.12	5.02	4.93	86
87	5.61	5.49	5.38	5.27	5.16	5.06	4.96	4.87	4.78	4.69	4.61	87
88	5.18	5.08	4.98	4.89	4.79	4.71	4.62	4.54	4.46	4.38	4.31	88
89	4.79	4.70	4.62	4.54	4.45	4.38	4.30	4.23	4.16	4.09	4.03	89
90	4.44	4.36	4.28	4.21	4.14	4.07	4.01	3.94	3.88	3.82	3.77	90
91	4.11	4.04	3.97	3.91	3.85	3.79	3.73	3.68	3.62	3.57	3.52	91
92	3.81	3.75	3.70	3.64	3.59	3.53	3.48	3.43	3.39	3.34	3.30	92
93	3.55	3.50	3.45	3.40	3.35	3.31	3.26	3.22	3.18	3.14	3.10	93
94	3.32	3.27	3.23	3.18	3.14	3.10	3.06	3.02	2.98	2.95	2.91	94
95	3.09	3.05	3.01	2.98	2.94	2.90	2.87	2.83	2.80	2.77	2.74	95
96	2.88	2.85	2.82	2.78	2.75	2.72	2.69	2.66	2.63	2.60	2.57	96
97	2.69	2.66	2.63	2.60	2.57	2.55	2.52	2.49	2.47	2.44	2.42	97
98	2.51	2.49	2.46	2.43	2.41	2.38	2.36	2.34	2.31	2.29	2.27	98
99	2.34	2.31	2.29	2.27	2.25	2.22	2.20	2.18	2.16	2.14	2.12	99
100	2.16	2.14	2.12	2.10	2.08	2.06	2.05	2.03	2.01	1.99	1.98	100

Table 3: Multipliers for loss of earnings to pension age 50 (males)

Age at date of trial	Multiplier calculated with allowance for projected mortality from the 2002-based population projections and rate of return of											Age at date of trial
	0.0%	0.5%	1.0%	1.5%	2.0%	2.5%	3.0%	3.5%	4.0%	4.5%	5.0%	
16	33.53	30.86	28.48	26.35	24.45	22.74	21.21	19.83	18.59	17.46	16.44	16
17	32.54	30.02	27.76	25.74	23.93	22.30	20.84	19.51	18.31	17.23	16.24	17
18	31.55	29.17	27.04	25.13	23.41	21.86	20.45	19.18	18.03	16.99	16.03	18
19	30.57	28.33	26.32	24.51	22.88	21.40	20.06	18.85	17.74	16.74	15.82	19
20	29.58	27.49	25.60	23.89	22.34	20.94	19.66	18.50	17.45	16.48	15.59	20
21	28.60	26.64	24.86	23.25	21.79	20.46	19.25	18.15	17.13	16.21	15.36	21
22	27.62	25.79	24.12	22.61	21.23	19.97	18.83	17.77	16.81	15.93	15.11	22
23	26.63	24.93	23.37	21.95	20.66	19.47	18.39	17.39	16.47	15.63	14.85	23
24	25.65	24.06	22.62	21.29	20.07	18.96	17.94	16.99	16.12	15.32	14.58	24
25	24.67	23.20	21.85	20.62	19.48	18.43	17.47	16.58	15.76	15.00	14.29	25
26	23.68	22.33	21.08	19.93	18.87	17.90	16.99	16.16	15.38	14.66	14.00	26
27	22.70	21.45	20.30	19.24	18.26	17.34	16.50	15.72	14.99	14.31	13.68	27
28	21.72	20.57	19.52	18.53	17.62	16.78	15.99	15.26	14.58	13.94	13.35	28
29	20.73	19.69	18.72	17.82	16.98	16.20	15.47	14.79	14.16	13.56	13.01	29
30	19.75	18.80	17.92	17.10	16.33	15.61	14.93	14.30	13.71	13.16	12.64	30
31	18.77	17.91	17.11	16.36	15.66	15.00	14.38	13.80	13.26	12.74	12.26	31
32	17.78	17.01	16.29	15.61	14.97	14.37	13.81	13.28	12.78	12.31	11.86	32
33	16.80	16.11	15.46	14.85	14.28	13.73	13.22	12.74	12.28	11.85	11.44	33
34	15.82	15.21	14.63	14.08	13.57	13.08	12.62	12.18	11.76	11.37	11.00	34
35	14.83	14.29	13.78	13.30	12.84	12.41	11.99	11.60	11.23	10.87	10.54	35
36	13.85	13.38	12.93	12.51	12.10	11.72	11.35	11.00	10.67	10.35	10.05	36
37	12.86	12.46	12.07	11.70	11.35	11.01	10.69	10.38	10.09	9.81	9.54	37
38	11.88	11.53	11.20	10.88	10.58	10.28	10.01	9.74	9.48	9.24	9.00	38
39	10.89	10.60	10.32	10.05	9.79	9.54	9.30	9.07	8.85	8.64	8.44	39
40	9.90	9.66	9.43	9.20	8.99	8.78	8.58	8.38	8.20	8.02	7.84	40
41	8.92	8.72	8.53	8.35	8.17	8.00	7.83	7.67	7.52	7.37	7.22	41
42	7.93	7.77	7.62	7.48	7.33	7.20	7.06	6.93	6.81	6.69	6.57	42
43	6.94	6.82	6.71	6.59	6.48	6.38	6.27	6.17	6.07	5.98	5.88	43
44	5.95	5.87	5.78	5.70	5.61	5.54	5.46	5.38	5.31	5.23	5.16	44
45	4.97	4.90	4.84	4.79	4.73	4.67	4.62	4.56	4.51	4.46	4.41	45
46	3.98	3.94	3.90	3.86	3.82	3.79	3.75	3.72	3.68	3.65	3.61	46
47	2.99	2.96	2.94	2.92	2.90	2.88	2.86	2.84	2.82	2.80	2.78	47
48	1.99	1.98	1.97	1.96	1.95	1.95	1.94	1.93	1.92	1.91	1.90	48
49	1.00	1.00	0.99	0.99	0.99	0.99	0.98	0.98	0.98	0.98	0.97	49

Table 4: Multipliers for loss of earnings to pension age 50 (females)

Age at date of trial	Multiplier calculated with allowance for projected mortality from the 2002-based population projections and rate of return of											Age at date of trial
	0.0%	0.5%	1.0%	1.5%	2.0%	2.5%	3.0%	3.5%	4.0%	4.5%	5.0%	
16	33.79	31.08	28.68	26.53	24.61	22.89	21.34	19.95	18.69	17.55	16.52	16
17	32.79	30.24	27.96	25.93	24.10	22.45	20.97	19.63	18.42	17.33	16.33	17
18	31.80	29.40	27.24	25.31	23.57	22.00	20.59	19.31	18.14	17.09	16.12	18
19	30.80	28.55	26.52	24.69	23.04	21.55	20.20	18.97	17.85	16.84	15.91	19
20	29.81	27.69	25.78	24.06	22.49	21.08	19.79	18.62	17.55	16.58	15.68	20
21	28.81	26.83	25.04	23.41	21.94	20.60	19.37	18.26	17.24	16.30	15.45	21
22	27.82	25.97	24.29	22.76	21.37	20.10	18.94	17.88	16.91	16.02	15.20	22
23	26.83	25.10	23.53	22.10	20.79	19.60	18.50	17.50	16.57	15.72	14.94	23
24	25.83	24.23	22.77	21.43	20.20	19.08	18.05	17.09	16.22	15.41	14.66	24
25	24.84	23.35	22.00	20.75	19.60	18.55	17.58	16.68	15.85	15.08	14.37	25
26	23.84	22.47	21.22	20.06	18.99	18.00	17.09	16.25	15.47	14.74	14.07	26
27	22.85	21.59	20.43	19.36	18.36	17.45	16.59	15.80	15.07	14.39	13.75	27
28	21.85	20.70	19.63	18.64	17.73	16.87	16.08	15.34	14.66	14.02	13.42	28
29	20.86	19.81	18.83	17.92	17.08	16.29	15.55	14.87	14.23	13.63	13.07	29
30	19.86	18.91	18.02	17.19	16.41	15.69	15.01	14.38	13.78	13.22	12.70	30
31	18.87	18.01	17.20	16.44	15.74	15.07	14.45	13.87	13.32	12.80	12.32	31
32	17.88	17.10	16.37	15.69	15.05	14.44	13.87	13.34	12.84	12.36	11.91	32
33	16.88	16.19	15.54	14.92	14.34	13.80	13.28	12.79	12.33	11.90	11.49	33
34	15.89	15.27	14.69	14.14	13.63	13.13	12.67	12.23	11.81	11.42	11.04	34
35	14.90	14.36	13.84	13.36	12.89	12.46	12.04	11.65	11.27	10.91	10.58	35
36	13.91	13.43	12.98	12.56	12.15	11.76	11.39	11.04	10.71	10.39	10.08	36
37	12.91	12.50	12.11	11.74	11.39	11.05	10.73	10.42	10.12	9.84	9.57	37
38	11.92	11.57	11.24	10.92	10.61	10.32	10.04	9.77	9.51	9.27	9.03	38
39	10.93	10.63	10.35	10.08	9.82	9.57	9.33	9.10	8.88	8.67	8.46	39
40	9.94	9.69	9.46	9.23	9.02	8.81	8.61	8.41	8.22	8.04	7.87	40
41	8.94	8.75	8.56	8.37	8.19	8.02	7.86	7.70	7.54	7.39	7.24	41
42	7.95	7.80	7.65	7.50	7.36	7.22	7.08	6.95	6.83	6.71	6.59	42
43	6.96	6.84	6.73	6.61	6.50	6.39	6.29	6.19	6.09	5.99	5.90	43
44	5.97	5.88	5.80	5.71	5.63	5.55	5.47	5.40	5.32	5.25	5.18	44
45	4.98	4.92	4.86	4.80	4.74	4.68	4.63	4.57	4.52	4.47	4.42	45
46	3.99	3.95	3.91	3.87	3.83	3.79	3.76	3.72	3.69	3.65	3.62	46
47	2.99	2.97	2.95	2.93	2.90	2.88	2.86	2.84	2.82	2.80	2.78	47
48	2.00	1.99	1.98	1.97	1.96	1.95	1.94	1.93	1.92	1.91	1.90	48
49	1.00	1.00	0.99	0.99	0.99	0.99	0.98	0.98	0.98	0.98	0.97	49

Table 5: Multipliers for loss of earnings to pension age 55 (males)

Age at date of trial	Multiplier calculated with allowance for projected mortality from the 2002-based population projections and rate of return of											Age at date of trial
	0.0%	*0.5%*	*1.0%*	*1.5%*	*2.0%*	*2.5%*	*3.0%*	*3.5%*	*4.0%*	*4.5%*	*5.0%*	
16	38.32	34.85	31.80	29.13	26.77	24.69	22.84	21.20	19.73	18.42	17.25	16
17	37.32	34.02	31.12	28.56	26.30	24.30	22.51	20.92	19.50	18.23	17.09	17
18	36.33	33.20	30.44	27.99	25.83	23.90	22.18	20.65	19.27	18.04	16.92	18
19	35.35	32.38	29.75	27.42	25.35	23.50	21.84	20.36	19.03	17.83	16.75	19
20	34.37	31.56	29.06	26.84	24.86	23.09	21.50	20.07	18.79	17.63	16.58	20
21	33.39	30.73	28.36	26.25	24.36	22.66	21.14	19.77	18.53	17.41	16.39	21
22	32.41	29.90	27.66	25.65	23.85	22.23	20.77	19.45	18.26	17.18	16.20	22
23	31.42	29.06	26.95	25.04	23.33	21.79	20.39	19.13	17.98	16.94	15.99	23
24	30.44	28.22	26.23	24.43	22.80	21.33	20.00	18.79	17.69	16.69	15.78	24
25	29.46	27.38	25.50	23.80	22.26	20.87	19.60	18.45	17.39	16.43	15.55	25
26	28.48	26.53	24.77	23.17	21.71	20.39	19.19	18.09	17.08	16.16	15.32	26
27	27.50	25.68	24.03	22.52	21.15	19.90	18.76	17.72	16.76	15.88	15.07	27
28	26.52	24.82	23.28	21.87	20.58	19.40	18.32	17.33	16.42	15.58	14.81	28
29	25.54	23.96	22.52	21.21	20.00	18.89	17.87	16.93	16.07	15.27	14.54	29
30	24.56	23.10	21.76	20.53	19.41	18.37	17.41	16.52	15.71	14.95	14.25	30
31	23.58	22.23	20.99	19.85	18.80	17.83	16.93	16.10	15.33	14.61	13.95	31
32	22.60	21.36	20.22	19.16	18.18	17.28	16.44	15.66	14.94	14.26	13.64	32
33	21.62	20.48	19.43	18.46	17.55	16.71	15.93	15.20	14.53	13.89	13.31	33
34	20.64	19.60	18.64	17.74	16.91	16.13	15.41	14.73	14.10	13.51	12.96	34
35	19.66	18.71	17.84	17.02	16.25	15.54	14.87	14.25	13.66	13.11	12.59	35
36	18.67	17.82	17.03	16.28	15.58	14.93	14.32	13.74	13.20	12.69	12.21	36
37	17.69	16.93	16.21	15.54	14.90	14.31	13.75	13.22	12.72	12.25	11.81	37
38	16.71	16.03	15.38	14.78	14.21	13.67	13.16	12.68	12.22	11.80	11.39	38
39	15.73	15.12	14.55	14.01	13.50	13.01	12.55	12.12	11.71	11.32	10.95	39
40	14.75	14.21	13.71	13.23	12.77	12.34	11.93	11.54	11.17	10.82	10.48	40
41	13.77	13.30	12.86	12.44	12.03	11.65	11.29	10.94	10.61	10.30	10.00	41
42	12.79	12.38	12.00	11.63	11.28	10.95	10.63	10.32	10.03	9.75	9.49	42
43	11.81	11.46	11.13	10.82	10.52	10.23	9.95	9.69	9.43	9.19	8.95	43
44	10.83	10.54	10.26	9.99	9.74	9.49	9.25	9.02	8.81	8.59	8.39	44
45	9.85	9.61	9.38	9.15	8.94	8.73	8.53	8.34	8.16	7.98	7.80	45
46	8.87	8.68	8.49	8.30	8.13	7.96	7.79	7.64	7.48	7.33	7.19	46
47	7.89	7.74	7.59	7.44	7.30	7.17	7.03	6.90	6.78	6.66	6.54	47
48	6.91	6.80	6.68	6.57	6.46	6.35	6.25	6.15	6.05	5.95	5.86	48
49	5.93	5.85	5.76	5.68	5.60	5.52	5.44	5.36	5.29	5.22	5.15	49
50	4.95	4.89	4.83	4.77	4.72	4.66	4.60	4.55	4.50	4.45	4.40	50
51	3.97	3.93	3.89	3.85	3.81	3.78	3.74	3.71	3.67	3.64	3.61	51
52	2.98	2.96	2.94	2.92	2.89	2.87	2.85	2.83	2.81	2.79	2.77	52
53	1.99	1.98	1.97	1.96	1.95	1.94	1.93	1.92	1.91	1.91	1.90	53
54	1.00	0.99	0.99	0.99	0.99	0.99	0.98	0.98	0.98	0.98	0.97	54

Table 6: Multipliers for loss of earnings to pension age 55 (females)

Age at date of trial	Multiplier calculated with allowance for projected mortality from the 2002-based population projections and rate of return of											Age at date of trial
	0.0%	0.5%	1.0%	1.5%	2.0%	2.5%	3.0%	3.5%	4.0%	4.5%	5.0%	
16	38.66	35.15	32.07	29.36	26.98	24.87	23.00	21.34	19.86	18.54	17.35	16
17	37.67	34.33	31.39	28.80	26.51	24.48	22.68	21.07	19.64	18.35	17.19	17
18	36.68	33.50	30.71	28.23	26.04	24.09	22.35	20.80	19.41	18.16	17.03	18
19	35.68	32.67	30.01	27.65	25.55	23.68	22.01	20.51	19.17	17.96	16.86	19
20	34.69	31.84	29.31	27.06	25.06	23.27	21.66	20.22	18.92	17.75	16.69	20
21	33.69	31.00	28.61	26.47	24.55	22.84	21.30	19.91	18.66	17.52	16.50	21
22	32.70	30.16	27.89	25.86	24.04	22.40	20.93	19.59	18.39	17.29	16.30	22
23	31.70	29.31	27.17	25.25	23.52	21.95	20.54	19.27	18.11	17.05	16.10	23
24	30.71	28.46	26.44	24.62	22.98	21.49	20.15	18.93	17.82	16.80	15.88	24
25	29.71	27.61	25.71	23.99	22.43	21.02	19.74	18.58	17.51	16.54	15.65	25
26	28.72	26.75	24.96	23.35	21.88	20.54	19.32	18.21	17.20	16.27	15.41	26
27	27.73	25.89	24.21	22.69	21.31	20.05	18.89	17.84	16.87	15.98	15.16	27
28	26.73	25.02	23.46	22.03	20.73	19.54	18.45	17.45	16.53	15.68	14.90	28
29	25.74	24.15	22.69	21.36	20.14	19.02	17.99	17.05	16.17	15.37	14.62	29
30	24.74	23.27	21.92	20.68	19.54	18.49	17.52	16.63	15.80	15.04	14.33	30
31	23.75	22.39	21.14	19.99	18.93	17.94	17.04	16.20	15.42	14.70	14.03	31
32	22.76	21.51	20.35	19.29	18.30	17.39	16.54	15.75	15.02	14.35	13.71	32
33	21.77	20.62	19.56	18.58	17.66	16.82	16.03	15.29	14.61	13.97	13.38	33
34	20.77	19.73	18.76	17.85	17.01	16.23	15.50	14.82	14.18	13.59	13.03	34
35	19.78	18.83	17.95	17.12	16.35	15.63	14.96	14.33	13.74	13.18	12.66	35
36	18.79	17.93	17.13	16.38	15.68	15.02	14.40	13.82	13.27	12.76	12.28	36
37	17.80	17.03	16.31	15.63	14.99	14.39	13.82	13.29	12.79	12.32	11.87	37
38	16.81	16.12	15.47	14.86	14.29	13.74	13.23	12.75	12.29	11.86	11.45	38
39	15.82	15.21	14.63	14.09	13.57	13.08	12.62	12.18	11.77	11.38	11.00	39
40	14.83	14.30	13.78	13.30	12.84	12.41	11.99	11.60	11.23	10.87	10.54	40
41	13.85	13.38	12.93	12.50	12.10	11.72	11.35	11.00	10.67	10.35	10.05	41
42	12.86	12.45	12.07	11.70	11.34	11.01	10.69	10.38	10.08	9.80	9.53	42
43	11.87	11.53	11.19	10.88	10.57	10.28	10.00	9.73	9.48	9.23	9.00	43
44	10.89	10.59	10.31	10.04	9.79	9.54	9.30	9.07	8.85	8.64	8.43	44
45	9.90	9.66	9.43	9.20	8.99	8.78	8.58	8.38	8.20	8.02	7.84	45
46	8.91	8.72	8.53	8.34	8.17	8.00	7.83	7.67	7.52	7.37	7.22	46
47	7.93	7.77	7.62	7.48	7.33	7.20	7.06	6.93	6.81	6.69	6.57	47
48	6.94	6.82	6.71	6.59	6.48	6.38	6.27	6.17	6.07	5.98	5.88	48
49	5.95	5.87	5.78	5.70	5.62	5.54	5.46	5.38	5.31	5.24	5.16	49
50	4.97	4.91	4.85	4.79	4.73	4.67	4.62	4.56	4.51	4.46	4.41	50
51	3.98	3.94	3.90	3.86	3.82	3.79	3.75	3.72	3.68	3.65	3.61	51
52	2.99	2.96	2.94	2.92	2.90	2.88	2.86	2.84	2.82	2.80	2.78	52
53	1.99	1.98	1.97	1.96	1.95	1.95	1.94	1.93	1.92	1.91	1.90	53
54	1.00	1.00	0.99	0.99	0.99	0.99	0.98	0.98	0.98	0.98	0.97	54

Table 7: Multipliers for loss of earnings to pension age 60 (males)

Age at date of trial	Multiplier calculated with allowance for projected mortality from the 2002-based population projections and rate of return of											Age at date of trial
	0.0%	0.5%	1.0%	1.5%	2.0%	2.5%	3.0%	3.5%	4.0%	4.5%	5.0%	
16	43.02	38.67	34.92	31.66	28.84	26.38	24.22	22.33	20.66	19.18	17.87	16
17	42.02	37.86	34.26	31.14	28.41	26.03	23.93	22.09	20.47	19.02	17.74	17
18	41.03	37.06	33.61	30.60	27.98	25.67	23.65	21.86	20.27	18.86	17.61	18
19	40.05	36.26	32.96	30.07	27.54	25.31	23.35	21.61	20.07	18.70	17.47	19
20	39.07	35.46	32.30	29.53	27.10	24.95	23.05	21.37	19.87	18.53	17.33	20
21	38.09	34.65	31.63	28.98	26.64	24.57	22.74	21.11	19.65	18.35	17.19	21
22	37.11	33.84	30.96	28.42	26.18	24.19	22.42	20.84	19.43	18.17	17.03	22
23	36.13	33.02	30.28	27.86	25.71	23.79	22.09	20.57	19.20	17.97	16.87	23
24	35.15	32.20	29.60	27.28	25.23	23.39	21.75	20.28	18.96	17.77	16.70	24
25	34.17	31.38	28.90	26.70	24.74	22.98	21.40	19.99	18.71	17.56	16.52	25
26	33.19	30.55	28.21	26.11	24.24	22.55	21.04	19.68	18.45	17.34	16.33	26
27	32.21	29.72	27.50	25.51	23.73	22.12	20.67	19.37	18.18	17.11	16.13	27
28	31.23	28.89	26.79	24.91	23.21	21.68	20.29	19.04	17.90	16.87	15.93	28
29	30.25	28.05	26.07	24.29	22.68	21.22	19.90	18.70	17.61	16.62	15.71	29
30	29.27	27.21	25.35	23.67	22.14	20.76	19.50	18.36	17.31	16.36	15.49	30
31	28.29	26.36	24.62	23.03	21.59	20.28	19.09	18.00	17.00	16.09	15.25	31
32	27.31	25.51	23.88	22.39	21.03	19.79	18.66	17.62	16.67	15.80	15.00	32
33	26.34	24.66	23.13	21.73	20.46	19.29	18.22	17.24	16.34	15.50	14.74	33
34	25.36	23.80	22.37	21.07	19.88	18.78	17.77	16.84	15.98	15.19	14.46	34
35	24.38	22.94	21.61	20.40	19.28	18.25	17.30	16.43	15.62	14.87	14.18	35
36	23.40	22.07	20.84	19.72	18.67	17.71	16.82	16.00	15.24	14.53	13.87	36
37	22.42	21.20	20.07	19.02	18.06	17.16	16.33	15.56	14.84	14.18	13.56	37
38	21.44	20.32	19.28	18.32	17.42	16.59	15.82	15.10	14.43	13.81	13.22	38
39	20.46	19.44	18.49	17.60	16.78	16.01	15.30	14.63	14.00	13.42	12.87	39
40	19.49	18.56	17.69	16.88	16.13	15.42	14.76	14.14	13.56	13.02	12.51	40
41	18.51	17.67	16.88	16.15	15.46	14.81	14.21	13.64	13.10	12.60	12.12	41
42	17.54	16.78	16.07	15.40	14.78	14.19	13.64	13.12	12.62	12.16	11.72	42
43	16.56	15.89	15.25	14.65	14.09	13.55	13.05	12.58	12.13	11.70	11.30	43
44	15.59	14.99	14.42	13.89	13.38	12.90	12.45	12.02	11.62	11.23	10.86	44
45	14.62	14.09	13.59	13.12	12.67	12.24	11.83	11.45	11.08	10.74	10.40	45
46	13.65	13.19	12.75	12.33	11.94	11.56	11.20	10.86	10.53	10.22	9.92	46
47	12.68	12.28	11.90	11.54	11.19	10.86	10.55	10.25	9.96	9.68	9.42	47
48	11.71	11.37	11.05	10.74	10.44	10.15	9.88	9.62	9.36	9.12	8.89	48
49	10.75	10.46	10.19	9.92	9.67	9.42	9.19	8.96	8.75	8.54	8.34	49
50	9.78	9.54	9.31	9.09	8.88	8.67	8.48	8.29	8.10	7.93	7.75	50
51	8.81	8.62	8.43	8.25	8.07	7.91	7.74	7.59	7.43	7.29	7.14	51
52	7.84	7.69	7.54	7.39	7.25	7.12	6.99	6.86	6.74	6.62	6.50	52
53	6.87	6.75	6.63	6.52	6.41	6.31	6.21	6.11	6.01	5.92	5.82	53
54	5.89	5.81	5.72	5.64	5.56	5.48	5.40	5.33	5.26	5.18	5.11	54
55	4.92	4.86	4.80	4.74	4.68	4.63	4.57	4.52	4.47	4.42	4.37	55
56	3.94	3.91	3.87	3.83	3.79	3.76	3.72	3.69	3.65	3.62	3.58	56
57	2.97	2.94	2.92	2.90	2.88	2.86	2.84	2.82	2.80	2.78	2.76	57
58	1.98	1.97	1.96	1.95	1.94	1.94	1.93	1.92	1.91	1.90	1.89	58
59	1.00	0.99	0.99	0.99	0.99	0.98	0.98	0.98	0.98	0.97	0.97	59

Table 8: Multipliers for loss of earnings to pension age 60 (females)

Age at date of trial	Multiplier calculated with allowance for projected mortality from the 2002-based population projections and rate of return of											Age at date of trial
	0.0%	0.5%	1.0%	1.5%	2.0%	2.5%	3.0%	3.5%	4.0%	4.5%	5.0%	
16	43.48	39.07	35.26	31.96	29.10	26.60	24.42	22.50	20.81	19.31	17.99	16
17	42.48	38.26	34.61	31.44	28.67	26.26	24.14	22.27	20.62	19.16	17.86	17
18	41.49	37.46	33.96	30.91	28.24	25.90	23.85	22.04	20.43	19.01	17.74	18
19	40.50	36.65	33.30	30.37	27.80	25.54	23.55	21.79	20.23	18.84	17.60	19
20	39.50	35.83	32.63	29.82	27.35	25.17	23.25	21.54	20.03	18.67	17.46	20
21	38.51	35.02	31.95	29.26	26.89	24.80	22.94	21.28	19.81	18.49	17.31	21
22	37.51	34.19	31.27	28.70	26.42	24.41	22.61	21.02	19.59	18.31	17.16	22
23	36.52	33.37	30.59	28.13	25.95	24.01	22.28	20.74	19.35	18.11	16.99	23
24	35.52	32.54	29.89	27.55	25.46	23.60	21.94	20.45	19.11	17.91	16.82	24
25	34.53	31.70	29.19	26.96	24.96	23.18	21.59	20.15	18.86	17.69	16.64	25
26	33.53	30.86	28.48	26.36	24.46	22.75	21.22	19.84	18.60	17.47	16.45	26
27	32.54	30.02	27.77	25.75	23.94	22.32	20.85	19.52	18.33	17.24	16.25	27
28	31.54	29.17	27.05	25.14	23.42	21.87	20.46	19.19	18.04	17.00	16.04	28
29	30.55	28.32	26.32	24.51	22.88	21.40	20.07	18.85	17.75	16.74	15.83	29
30	29.56	27.47	25.58	23.88	22.33	20.93	19.66	18.50	17.44	16.48	15.60	30
31	28.56	26.61	24.84	23.23	21.77	20.45	19.24	18.14	17.13	16.20	15.36	31
32	27.57	25.75	24.09	22.58	21.21	19.95	18.81	17.76	16.80	15.92	15.10	32
33	26.58	24.88	23.33	21.92	20.63	19.45	18.36	17.37	16.46	15.61	14.84	33
34	25.59	24.01	22.57	21.25	20.04	18.93	17.91	16.97	16.10	15.30	14.56	34
35	24.60	23.14	21.80	20.57	19.44	18.39	17.43	16.55	15.73	14.97	14.27	35
36	23.61	22.26	21.02	19.88	18.82	17.85	16.95	16.12	15.35	14.63	13.97	36
37	22.62	21.38	20.23	19.18	18.20	17.29	16.45	15.67	14.95	14.28	13.65	37
38	21.63	20.49	19.44	18.47	17.56	16.72	15.94	15.21	14.54	13.90	13.31	38
39	20.64	19.61	18.64	17.75	16.91	16.14	15.41	14.74	14.11	13.52	12.96	39
40	19.65	18.71	17.84	17.02	16.25	15.54	14.87	14.25	13.66	13.11	12.59	40
41	18.67	17.82	17.02	16.28	15.58	14.93	14.31	13.74	13.20	12.69	12.21	41
42	17.69	16.92	16.20	15.53	14.90	14.30	13.74	13.21	12.72	12.25	11.81	42
43	16.70	16.02	15.38	14.77	14.20	13.66	13.15	12.67	12.22	11.79	11.38	43
44	15.72	15.11	14.54	14.00	13.49	13.01	12.55	12.11	11.70	11.31	10.94	44
45	14.74	14.21	13.70	13.22	12.77	12.33	11.93	11.54	11.17	10.81	10.48	45
46	13.76	13.29	12.85	12.43	12.03	11.65	11.28	10.94	10.61	10.29	9.99	46
47	12.78	12.38	11.99	11.63	11.28	10.94	10.63	10.32	10.03	9.75	9.48	47
48	11.80	11.46	11.13	10.81	10.51	10.22	9.95	9.68	9.43	9.18	8.95	48
49	10.82	10.53	10.26	9.99	9.73	9.49	9.25	9.02	8.80	8.59	8.39	49
50	9.85	9.61	9.37	9.15	8.94	8.73	8.53	8.34	8.15	7.97	7.80	50
51	8.87	8.67	8.48	8.30	8.13	7.96	7.79	7.63	7.48	7.33	7.19	51
52	7.89	7.73	7.58	7.44	7.30	7.16	7.03	6.90	6.78	6.65	6.54	52
53	6.91	6.79	6.67	6.56	6.45	6.35	6.24	6.14	6.04	5.95	5.86	53
54	5.93	5.84	5.75	5.67	5.59	5.51	5.43	5.36	5.28	5.21	5.14	54
55	4.95	4.89	4.83	4.77	4.71	4.65	4.60	4.55	4.49	4.44	4.39	55
56	3.96	3.92	3.89	3.85	3.81	3.77	3.74	3.70	3.67	3.64	3.60	56
57	2.98	2.96	2.93	2.91	2.89	2.87	2.85	2.83	2.81	2.79	2.77	57
58	1.99	1.98	1.97	1.96	1.95	1.94	1.93	1.92	1.91	1.90	1.90	58
59	1.00	0.99	0.99	0.99	0.99	0.99	0.98	0.98	0.98	0.98	0.97	59

Table 9: Multipliers for loss of earnings to pension age 65 (males)

Age at date of trial	Multiplier calculated with allowance for projected mortality from the 2002-based population projections and rate of return of											Age at date of trial
	0.0%	0.5%	1.0%	1.5%	2.0%	2.5%	3.0%	3.5%	4.0%	4.5%	5.0%	
16	47.58	42.29	37.79	33.95	30.66	27.82	25.37	23.25	21.39	19.77	18.34	16
17	46.58	41.50	37.16	33.45	30.26	27.51	25.12	23.05	21.23	19.64	18.24	17
18	45.59	40.71	36.54	32.96	29.87	27.19	24.87	22.84	21.07	19.51	18.13	18
19	44.61	39.93	35.92	32.46	29.47	26.87	24.61	22.64	20.90	19.37	18.02	19
20	43.63	39.15	35.29	31.95	29.06	26.55	24.35	22.42	20.73	19.23	17.91	20
21	42.65	38.36	34.65	31.44	28.65	26.21	24.08	22.20	20.55	19.09	17.79	21
22	41.67	37.56	34.01	30.92	28.23	25.87	23.80	21.98	20.36	18.94	17.66	22
23	40.69	36.77	33.36	30.39	27.79	25.52	23.51	21.74	20.17	18.78	17.53	23
24	39.71	35.97	32.71	29.86	27.35	25.16	23.21	21.50	19.97	18.61	17.40	24
25	38.73	35.16	32.05	29.31	26.91	24.79	22.91	21.24	19.76	18.44	17.25	25
26	37.75	34.35	31.38	28.76	26.45	24.41	22.60	20.98	19.54	18.26	17.10	26
27	36.77	33.54	30.71	28.20	25.99	24.02	22.27	20.71	19.32	18.07	16.94	27
28	35.79	32.73	30.03	27.64	25.51	23.63	21.94	20.44	19.09	17.87	16.78	28
29	34.81	31.91	29.34	27.06	25.03	23.22	21.60	20.15	18.84	17.67	16.60	29
30	33.83	31.09	28.65	26.48	24.54	22.81	21.25	19.85	18.59	17.45	16.42	30
31	32.86	30.26	27.95	25.89	24.04	22.38	20.89	19.54	18.33	17.23	16.23	31
32	31.88	29.43	27.25	25.29	23.53	21.94	20.52	19.22	18.06	17.00	16.03	32
33	30.90	28.60	26.53	24.68	23.01	21.50	20.13	18.90	17.77	16.75	15.82	33
34	29.92	27.76	25.81	24.06	22.47	21.04	19.74	18.56	17.48	16.50	15.60	34
35	28.95	26.92	25.09	23.43	21.93	20.57	19.33	18.20	17.18	16.23	15.37	35
36	27.97	26.07	24.35	22.80	21.38	20.09	18.91	17.84	16.86	15.96	15.13	36
37	26.99	25.22	23.61	22.15	20.82	19.60	18.48	17.46	16.53	15.67	14.88	37
38	26.01	24.37	22.86	21.49	20.24	19.09	18.04	17.07	16.18	15.37	14.61	38
39	25.04	23.51	22.11	20.83	19.65	18.58	17.58	16.67	15.83	15.05	14.33	39
40	24.06	22.65	21.35	20.15	19.06	18.05	17.11	16.25	15.46	14.72	14.04	40
41	23.09	21.78	20.58	19.47	18.45	17.51	16.63	15.83	15.08	14.38	13.73	41
42	22.12	20.92	19.81	18.78	17.83	16.95	16.14	15.38	14.68	14.02	13.41	42
43	21.15	20.05	19.03	18.08	17.20	16.39	15.63	14.93	14.27	13.65	13.08	43
44	20.18	19.17	18.24	17.37	16.57	15.81	15.11	14.45	13.84	13.27	12.73	44
45	19.21	18.30	17.45	16.66	15.92	15.22	14.58	13.97	13.40	12.87	12.37	45
46	18.25	17.43	16.66	15.93	15.26	14.62	14.03	13.47	12.95	12.45	11.99	46
47	17.29	16.55	15.85	15.20	14.59	14.01	13.47	12.96	12.47	12.02	11.59	47
48	16.33	15.67	15.05	14.46	13.91	13.38	12.89	12.43	11.98	11.57	11.17	48
49	15.37	14.79	14.23	13.71	13.21	12.74	12.30	11.88	11.48	11.10	10.74	49
50	14.42	13.90	13.41	12.94	12.50	12.08	11.69	11.31	10.95	10.61	10.28	50
51	13.46	13.01	12.58	12.17	11.78	11.41	11.06	10.72	10.40	10.10	9.80	51
52	12.50	12.11	11.74	11.38	11.04	10.72	10.41	10.11	9.83	9.56	9.30	52
53	11.54	11.21	10.89	10.58	10.29	10.01	9.74	9.49	9.24	9.00	8.78	53
54	10.58	10.30	10.03	9.78	9.53	9.29	9.06	8.84	8.62	8.42	8.22	54
55	9.63	9.40	9.17	8.96	8.75	8.55	8.35	8.17	7.99	7.81	7.65	55
56	8.68	8.49	8.31	8.13	7.96	7.79	7.63	7.48	7.33	7.18	7.04	56
57	7.73	7.58	7.43	7.29	7.15	7.02	6.89	6.77	6.65	6.53	6.41	57
58	6.78	6.66	6.55	6.44	6.33	6.23	6.13	6.03	5.93	5.84	5.75	58
59	5.82	5.74	5.65	5.57	5.49	5.42	5.34	5.27	5.20	5.13	5.06	59
60	4.87	4.81	4.75	4.69	4.64	4.58	4.53	4.48	4.43	4.37	4.33	60
61	3.91	3.87	3.83	3.80	3.76	3.73	3.69	3.66	3.62	3.59	3.56	61
62	2.95	2.92	2.90	2.88	2.86	2.84	2.82	2.80	2.78	2.76	2.74	62
63	1.97	1.97	1.96	1.95	1.94	1.93	1.92	1.91	1.90	1.89	1.88	63
64	0.99	0.99	0.99	0.99	0.98	0.98	0.98	0.98	0.97	0.97	0.97	64

Table 10: Multipliers for loss of earnings to pension age 65 (females)

Age at date of trial	Multiplier calculated with allowance for projected mortality from the 2002-based population projections and rate of return of											Age at date of trial
	0.0%	0.5%	1.0%	1.5%	2.0%	2.5%	3.0%	3.5%	4.0%	4.5%	5.0%	
16	48.20	42.81	38.23	34.32	30.98	28.10	25.61	23.45	21.57	19.92	18.48	16
17	47.20	42.03	37.61	33.84	30.59	27.79	25.37	23.26	21.42	19.80	18.38	17
18	46.21	41.24	36.99	33.34	30.20	27.48	25.12	23.06	21.26	19.67	18.28	18
19	45.22	40.45	36.36	32.84	29.80	27.16	24.86	22.85	21.09	19.54	18.17	19
20	44.22	39.65	35.72	32.33	29.39	26.83	24.59	22.64	20.92	19.40	18.06	20
21	43.22	38.85	35.08	31.81	28.97	26.49	24.32	22.42	20.74	19.25	17.94	21
22	42.23	38.05	34.43	31.28	28.54	26.14	24.04	22.19	20.55	19.10	17.81	22
23	41.23	37.24	33.77	30.75	28.11	25.79	23.75	21.95	20.36	18.94	17.68	23
24	40.24	36.43	33.11	30.21	27.66	25.42	23.45	21.70	20.16	18.78	17.54	24
25	39.24	35.61	32.44	29.65	27.21	25.05	23.14	21.45	19.94	18.60	17.40	25
26	38.25	34.79	31.76	29.10	26.75	24.67	22.83	21.19	19.73	18.42	17.25	26
27	37.25	33.97	31.08	28.53	26.28	24.28	22.50	20.92	19.50	18.23	17.09	27
28	36.25	33.14	30.39	27.95	25.80	23.88	22.16	20.63	19.26	18.03	16.92	28
29	35.26	32.31	29.69	27.37	25.31	23.46	21.82	20.34	19.02	17.82	16.75	29
30	34.26	31.47	28.99	26.78	24.81	23.04	21.46	20.04	18.76	17.61	16.56	30
31	33.27	30.63	28.28	26.18	24.30	22.61	21.10	19.73	18.50	17.38	16.37	31
32	32.28	29.79	27.56	25.57	23.78	22.17	20.72	19.41	18.22	17.15	16.17	32
33	31.28	28.94	26.84	24.95	23.25	21.72	20.33	19.08	17.94	16.90	15.96	33
34	30.29	28.09	26.11	24.33	22.71	21.26	19.93	18.73	17.64	16.65	15.74	34
35	29.30	27.24	25.38	23.69	22.17	20.78	19.52	18.38	17.33	16.38	15.51	35
36	28.31	26.38	24.63	23.05	21.61	20.30	19.10	18.01	17.01	16.10	15.26	36
37	27.32	25.52	23.89	22.40	21.04	19.80	18.67	17.63	16.68	15.81	15.01	37
38	26.33	24.66	23.13	21.74	20.46	19.29	18.22	17.24	16.34	15.51	14.74	38
39	25.35	23.79	22.37	21.06	19.87	18.77	17.77	16.84	15.98	15.19	14.46	39
40	24.36	22.92	21.60	20.39	19.27	18.24	17.29	16.42	15.61	14.86	14.17	40
41	23.38	22.05	20.83	19.70	18.66	17.70	16.81	15.99	15.23	14.52	13.86	41
42	22.40	21.17	20.04	19.00	18.04	17.14	16.31	15.54	14.83	14.16	13.54	42
43	21.42	20.30	19.26	18.30	17.40	16.58	15.80	15.09	14.42	13.79	13.21	43
44	20.44	19.42	18.47	17.58	16.76	16.00	15.28	14.61	13.99	13.41	12.86	44
45	19.46	18.53	17.67	16.86	16.11	15.40	14.74	14.13	13.55	13.00	12.50	45
46	18.49	17.65	16.86	16.13	15.44	14.79	14.19	13.62	13.09	12.59	12.11	46
47	17.51	16.76	16.05	15.39	14.76	14.17	13.62	13.10	12.61	12.15	11.71	47
48	16.54	15.86	15.23	14.63	14.07	13.54	13.04	12.56	12.12	11.69	11.29	48
49	15.57	14.97	14.40	13.87	13.37	12.89	12.44	12.01	11.60	11.22	10.85	49
50	14.60	14.07	13.57	13.10	12.65	12.22	11.82	11.43	11.07	10.72	10.39	50
51	13.63	13.17	12.73	12.31	11.92	11.54	11.18	10.84	10.52	10.21	9.91	51
52	12.66	12.26	11.88	11.52	11.17	10.85	10.53	10.23	9.94	9.67	9.40	52
53	11.69	11.35	11.03	10.71	10.42	10.13	9.86	9.60	9.35	9.11	8.87	53
54	10.72	10.44	10.16	9.90	9.65	9.40	9.17	8.94	8.73	8.52	8.32	54
55	9.76	9.52	9.29	9.07	8.86	8.65	8.46	8.27	8.08	7.91	7.74	55
56	8.79	8.60	8.41	8.23	8.06	7.89	7.73	7.57	7.42	7.27	7.13	56
57	7.82	7.67	7.52	7.38	7.24	7.11	6.97	6.85	6.72	6.60	6.49	57
58	6.86	6.74	6.63	6.51	6.41	6.30	6.20	6.10	6.00	5.91	5.82	58
59	5.89	5.80	5.72	5.63	5.55	5.48	5.40	5.32	5.25	5.18	5.11	59
60	4.92	4.86	4.80	4.74	4.68	4.63	4.57	4.52	4.47	4.42	4.37	60
61	3.94	3.91	3.87	3.83	3.79	3.76	3.72	3.69	3.65	3.62	3.59	61
62	2.97	2.95	2.92	2.90	2.88	2.86	2.84	2.82	2.80	2.78	2.76	62
63	1.98	1.97	1.97	1.96	1.95	1.94	1.93	1.92	1.91	1.90	1.89	63
64	1.00	0.99	0.99	0.99	0.99	0.98	0.98	0.98	0.98	0.97	0.97	64

Table 11: Multipliers for loss of earnings to pension age 70 (males)

Age at date of trial	Multiplier calculated with allowance for projected mortality from the 2002-based population projections and rate of return of											Age at date of trial
	0.0%	0.5%	1.0%	1.5%	2.0%	2.5%	3.0%	3.5%	4.0%	4.5%	5.0%	
16	51.94	45.66	40.40	35.98	32.23	29.05	26.33	23.99	21.97	20.22	18.70	16
17	50.94	44.89	39.80	35.51	31.87	28.77	26.11	23.82	21.84	20.11	18.61	17
18	49.95	44.12	39.21	35.04	31.51	28.48	25.88	23.64	21.70	20.00	18.52	18
19	48.97	43.35	38.61	34.58	31.14	28.19	25.65	23.46	21.55	19.89	18.43	19
20	47.99	42.59	38.01	34.10	30.77	27.90	25.42	23.28	21.41	19.78	18.34	20
21	47.01	41.81	37.40	33.62	30.39	27.60	25.18	23.09	21.26	19.65	18.24	21
22	46.02	41.04	36.78	33.13	30.00	27.29	24.94	22.89	21.10	19.53	18.14	22
23	45.04	40.26	36.16	32.64	29.60	26.97	24.68	22.68	20.93	19.39	18.03	23
24	44.06	39.47	35.53	32.14	29.20	26.64	24.42	22.47	20.76	19.25	17.92	24
25	43.08	38.68	34.90	31.63	28.79	26.31	24.15	22.25	20.58	19.11	17.80	25
26	42.10	37.89	34.26	31.11	28.37	25.97	23.87	22.03	20.40	18.96	17.68	26
27	41.12	37.10	33.62	30.59	27.94	25.62	23.59	21.80	20.21	18.80	17.55	27
28	40.14	36.30	32.97	30.05	27.51	25.27	23.30	21.56	20.01	18.64	17.41	28
29	39.16	35.50	32.31	29.52	27.06	24.90	23.00	21.31	19.81	18.47	17.27	29
30	38.18	34.70	31.65	28.97	26.61	24.53	22.69	21.05	19.59	18.29	17.12	30
31	37.20	33.89	30.98	28.41	26.15	24.15	22.37	20.78	19.37	18.10	16.97	31
32	36.23	33.08	30.30	27.85	25.68	23.75	22.04	20.51	19.14	17.91	16.80	32
33	35.25	32.26	29.62	27.28	25.20	23.35	21.70	20.23	18.90	17.71	16.63	33
34	34.27	31.44	28.93	26.70	24.71	22.94	21.36	19.93	18.65	17.50	16.45	34
35	33.29	30.61	28.23	26.11	24.22	22.52	21.00	19.63	18.39	17.28	16.27	35
36	32.31	29.79	27.53	25.52	23.71	22.09	20.63	19.31	18.12	17.05	16.07	36
37	31.34	28.95	26.82	24.91	23.19	21.65	20.25	18.99	17.84	16.81	15.86	37
38	30.36	28.12	26.10	24.30	22.66	21.19	19.86	18.65	17.55	16.55	15.64	38
39	29.38	27.28	25.38	23.67	22.13	20.73	19.46	18.30	17.25	16.29	15.42	39
40	28.41	26.43	24.65	23.04	21.58	20.25	19.04	17.94	16.94	16.02	15.18	40
41	27.43	25.59	23.92	22.40	21.02	19.77	18.62	17.57	16.62	15.74	14.93	41
42	26.46	24.74	23.18	21.76	20.46	19.27	18.19	17.19	16.28	15.44	14.67	42
43	25.49	23.89	22.43	21.10	19.88	18.77	17.74	16.80	15.93	15.14	14.40	43
44	24.53	23.04	21.68	20.44	19.30	18.25	17.29	16.40	15.58	14.82	14.12	44
45	23.56	22.19	20.93	19.77	18.71	17.72	16.82	15.98	15.21	14.49	13.82	45
46	22.60	21.34	20.17	19.10	18.11	17.19	16.34	15.55	14.82	14.15	13.52	46
47	21.65	20.49	19.41	18.42	17.50	16.64	15.85	15.11	14.43	13.79	13.20	47
48	20.70	19.63	18.64	17.73	16.88	16.08	15.35	14.66	14.02	13.42	12.87	48
49	19.75	18.77	17.87	17.03	16.24	15.51	14.83	14.19	13.60	13.04	12.52	49
50	18.79	17.91	17.09	16.32	15.60	14.93	14.30	13.71	13.16	12.64	12.15	50
51	17.84	17.05	16.30	15.60	14.95	14.33	13.76	13.21	12.70	12.22	11.77	51
52	16.89	16.18	15.50	14.87	14.28	13.72	13.19	12.70	12.23	11.79	11.37	52
53	15.95	15.31	14.70	14.14	13.60	13.09	12.62	12.17	11.74	11.34	10.95	53
54	15.00	14.43	13.90	13.39	12.91	12.46	12.03	11.62	11.23	10.87	10.52	54
55	14.06	13.56	13.09	12.64	12.21	11.81	11.42	11.06	10.71	10.38	10.06	55
56	13.12	12.69	12.27	11.88	11.50	11.15	10.80	10.48	10.17	9.87	9.59	56
57	12.19	11.82	11.46	11.11	10.79	10.47	10.17	9.89	9.61	9.35	9.10	57
58	11.27	10.95	10.64	10.34	10.06	9.79	9.53	9.28	9.04	8.81	8.59	58
59	10.35	10.07	9.81	9.56	9.32	9.09	8.87	8.65	8.44	8.25	8.06	59
60	9.42	9.20	8.98	8.77	8.57	8.37	8.19	8.00	7.83	7.66	7.50	60
61	8.50	8.32	8.14	7.97	7.80	7.64	7.49	7.34	7.19	7.05	6.91	61
62	7.59	7.44	7.30	7.16	7.03	6.90	6.77	6.65	6.53	6.42	6.30	62
63	6.66	6.55	6.44	6.33	6.23	6.13	6.03	5.93	5.84	5.75	5.66	63
64	5.74	5.65	5.57	5.49	5.41	5.34	5.26	5.19	5.12	5.05	4.99	64
65	4.81	4.75	4.69	4.63	4.58	4.52	4.47	4.42	4.37	4.32	4.27	65
66	3.87	3.83	3.79	3.75	3.72	3.68	3.65	3.61	3.58	3.55	3.52	66
67	2.92	2.90	2.88	2.85	2.83	2.81	2.79	2.77	2.75	2.74	2.72	67
68	1.96	1.95	1.94	1.93	1.92	1.91	1.90	1.89	1.89	1.88	1.87	68
69	0.99	0.99	0.98	0.98	0.98	0.98	0.97	0.97	0.97	0.97	0.97	69

Table 12: Multipliers for loss of earnings to pension age 70 (females)

Age at date of trial	Multiplier calculated with allowance for projected mortality from the 2002-based population projections and rate of return of											Age at date of trial
	0.0%	**0.5%**	**1.0%**	**1.5%**	**2.0%**	**2.5%**	**3.0%**	**3.5%**	**4.0%**	**4.5%**	**5.0%**	
16	52.79	46.36	40.98	36.46	32.63	29.39	26.61	24.23	22.18	20.40	18.85	16
17	51.79	45.59	40.39	36.00	32.28	29.11	26.40	24.07	22.05	20.30	18.77	17
18	50.79	44.82	39.79	35.54	31.92	28.83	26.18	23.90	21.92	20.19	18.69	18
19	49.80	44.05	39.19	35.06	31.55	28.54	25.95	23.72	21.78	20.08	18.60	19
20	48.80	43.27	38.58	34.59	31.18	28.25	25.72	23.53	21.63	19.97	18.51	20
21	47.80	42.48	37.96	34.10	30.79	27.94	25.48	23.34	21.48	19.85	18.41	21
22	46.81	41.70	37.34	33.61	30.40	27.63	25.23	23.15	21.32	19.72	18.31	22
23	45.81	40.90	36.71	33.11	30.00	27.32	24.98	22.94	21.16	19.59	18.20	23
24	44.81	40.11	36.08	32.60	29.60	26.99	24.72	22.73	20.99	19.45	18.09	24
25	43.81	39.31	35.43	32.08	29.18	26.65	24.45	22.51	20.81	19.31	17.98	25
26	42.82	38.51	34.79	31.56	28.76	26.31	24.17	22.29	20.63	19.16	17.85	26
27	41.82	37.70	34.13	31.03	28.33	25.96	23.88	22.05	20.43	19.00	17.72	27
28	40.82	36.89	33.47	30.49	27.89	25.60	23.59	21.81	20.24	18.84	17.59	28
29	39.82	36.07	32.80	29.95	27.44	25.23	23.28	21.56	20.03	18.67	17.45	29
30	38.83	35.26	32.13	29.39	26.98	24.85	22.97	21.30	19.81	18.49	17.30	30
31	37.83	34.43	31.45	28.83	26.51	24.47	22.65	21.03	19.59	18.30	17.14	31
32	36.84	33.61	30.77	28.26	26.04	24.07	22.32	20.76	19.36	18.11	16.98	32
33	35.84	32.78	30.08	27.68	25.56	23.67	21.98	20.47	19.12	17.90	16.81	33
34	34.85	31.95	29.38	27.10	25.06	23.25	21.63	20.18	18.87	17.69	16.63	34
35	33.86	31.11	28.67	26.50	24.56	22.83	21.27	19.87	18.61	17.47	16.44	35
36	32.87	30.27	27.96	25.90	24.05	22.39	20.90	19.56	18.34	17.24	16.25	36
37	31.88	29.43	27.25	25.29	23.53	21.95	20.52	19.23	18.06	17.00	16.04	37
38	30.89	28.59	26.52	24.67	23.00	21.49	20.13	18.89	17.77	16.75	15.82	38
39	29.90	27.74	25.80	24.04	22.46	21.03	19.73	18.55	17.47	16.49	15.60	39
40	28.91	26.89	25.06	23.41	21.91	20.55	19.32	18.19	17.16	16.22	15.36	40
41	27.93	26.04	24.32	22.77	21.35	20.07	18.89	17.82	16.84	15.94	15.12	41
42	26.95	25.18	23.58	22.12	20.79	19.57	18.46	17.44	16.51	15.65	14.86	42
43	25.97	24.33	22.83	21.46	20.21	19.06	18.01	17.05	16.16	15.35	14.59	43
44	24.99	23.47	22.07	20.79	19.62	18.55	17.56	16.65	15.81	15.03	14.31	44
45	24.02	22.61	21.31	20.12	19.03	18.02	17.09	16.23	15.44	14.70	14.02	45
46	23.04	21.74	20.54	19.44	18.42	17.48	16.61	15.80	15.05	14.36	13.71	46
47	22.07	20.88	19.77	18.75	17.80	16.93	16.11	15.36	14.66	14.00	13.40	47
48	21.11	20.01	18.99	18.05	17.18	16.36	15.61	14.90	14.25	13.63	13.06	48
49	20.14	19.14	18.21	17.34	16.54	15.79	15.09	14.43	13.82	13.25	12.71	49
50	19.17	18.27	17.42	16.63	15.89	15.20	14.55	13.95	13.38	12.85	12.35	50
51	18.21	17.39	16.62	15.90	15.23	14.60	14.00	13.45	12.92	12.43	11.97	51
52	17.25	16.51	15.82	15.17	14.56	13.98	13.44	12.93	12.45	12.00	11.57	52
53	16.29	15.63	15.01	14.42	13.87	13.35	12.86	12.40	11.96	11.54	11.15	53
54	15.33	14.75	14.20	13.67	13.18	12.71	12.27	11.85	11.45	11.07	10.71	54
55	14.38	13.86	13.38	12.91	12.47	12.05	11.66	11.28	10.92	10.58	10.26	55
56	13.43	12.98	12.55	12.14	11.75	11.39	11.03	10.70	10.38	10.07	9.78	56
57	12.48	12.09	11.72	11.36	11.02	10.70	10.39	10.10	9.82	9.55	9.29	57
58	11.53	11.20	10.88	10.57	10.28	10.00	9.73	9.48	9.23	8.99	8.77	58
59	10.58	10.30	10.03	9.77	9.53	9.29	9.06	8.84	8.62	8.42	8.22	59
60	9.64	9.40	9.18	8.96	8.76	8.55	8.36	8.17	7.99	7.82	7.65	60
61	8.69	8.50	8.32	8.14	7.97	7.80	7.64	7.49	7.34	7.19	7.05	61
62	7.74	7.59	7.45	7.30	7.17	7.03	6.90	6.78	6.66	6.54	6.43	62
63	6.79	6.68	6.56	6.45	6.35	6.24	6.14	6.04	5.95	5.85	5.76	63
64	5.84	5.75	5.67	5.59	5.51	5.43	5.35	5.28	5.21	5.14	5.07	64
65	4.88	4.82	4.76	4.70	4.65	4.59	4.54	4.49	4.43	4.38	4.33	65
66	3.92	3.88	3.84	3.80	3.77	3.73	3.70	3.66	3.63	3.59	3.56	66
67	2.95	2.93	2.91	2.89	2.86	2.84	2.82	2.80	2.78	2.76	2.75	67
68	1.98	1.97	1.96	1.95	1.94	1.93	1.92	1.91	1.90	1.89	1.88	68
69	0.99	0.99	0.99	0.99	0.98	0.98	0.98	0.98	0.97	0.97	0.97	69

Table 13: Multipliers for loss of earnings to pension age 75 (males)

Age at date of trial	Multiplier calculated with allowance for projected mortality from the 2002-based population projections and rate of return of											Age at date of trial
	0.0%	0.5%	1.0%	1.5%	2.0%	2.5%	3.0%	3.5%	4.0%	4.5%	5.0%	
16	56.02	48.74	42.73	37.74	33.57	30.06	27.10	24.58	22.42	20.56	18.96	16
17	55.02	47.98	42.15	37.30	33.23	29.80	26.90	24.42	22.30	20.47	18.88	17
18	54.02	47.22	41.57	36.85	32.89	29.54	26.70	24.27	22.18	20.37	18.81	18
19	53.04	46.47	41.00	36.41	32.55	29.28	26.49	24.11	22.06	20.28	18.73	19
20	52.06	45.72	40.42	35.97	32.21	29.01	26.29	23.95	21.93	20.18	18.66	20
21	51.07	44.96	39.83	35.51	31.85	28.74	26.07	23.78	21.80	20.08	18.57	21
22	50.09	44.20	39.24	35.05	31.49	28.46	25.85	23.61	21.66	19.97	18.49	22
23	49.10	43.43	38.64	34.58	31.13	28.17	25.62	23.43	21.52	19.85	18.40	23
24	48.12	42.66	38.04	34.11	30.75	27.87	25.39	23.24	21.37	19.74	18.30	24
25	47.13	41.88	37.43	33.63	30.37	27.57	25.15	23.05	21.22	19.61	18.20	25
26	46.15	41.11	36.81	33.14	29.98	27.26	24.90	22.85	21.06	19.48	18.10	26
27	45.17	40.33	36.19	32.64	29.59	26.94	24.65	22.65	20.89	19.35	17.99	27
28	44.19	39.55	35.57	32.14	29.18	26.62	24.39	22.43	20.72	19.21	17.88	28
29	43.21	38.76	34.93	31.63	28.77	26.29	24.12	22.22	20.54	19.07	17.76	29
30	42.23	37.97	34.30	31.12	28.36	25.95	23.84	21.99	20.36	18.92	17.63	30
31	41.24	37.17	33.65	30.59	27.93	25.60	23.56	21.76	20.17	18.76	17.50	31
32	40.26	36.37	33.00	30.06	27.49	25.24	23.26	21.51	19.97	18.59	17.37	32
33	39.28	35.57	32.34	29.52	27.05	24.88	22.96	21.26	19.76	18.42	17.22	33
34	38.30	34.77	31.68	28.98	26.60	24.50	22.65	21.01	19.55	18.24	17.07	34
35	37.32	33.96	31.01	28.42	26.14	24.12	22.33	20.74	19.32	18.05	16.92	35
36	36.34	33.14	30.33	27.86	25.67	23.73	22.00	20.46	19.09	17.86	16.75	36
37	35.36	32.33	29.65	27.28	25.19	23.32	21.66	20.18	18.85	17.65	16.58	37
38	34.38	31.50	28.96	26.70	24.70	22.91	21.31	19.88	18.60	17.44	16.39	38
39	33.40	30.68	28.26	26.11	24.20	22.49	20.95	19.58	18.34	17.22	16.20	39
40	32.42	29.85	27.56	25.52	23.69	22.06	20.58	19.26	18.07	16.98	16.00	40
41	31.44	29.02	26.85	24.91	23.18	21.61	20.21	18.94	17.79	16.74	15.80	41
42	30.47	28.19	26.14	24.30	22.65	21.16	19.82	18.60	17.50	16.49	15.58	42
43	29.50	27.35	25.43	23.69	22.12	20.70	19.42	18.26	17.20	16.24	15.35	43
44	28.53	26.52	24.70	23.07	21.58	20.24	19.02	17.90	16.89	15.97	15.12	44
45	27.57	25.69	23.98	22.44	21.03	19.76	18.60	17.54	16.57	15.69	14.88	45
46	26.61	24.85	23.25	21.80	20.48	19.28	18.18	17.17	16.25	15.40	14.62	46
47	25.66	24.02	22.52	21.16	19.92	18.78	17.74	16.79	15.91	15.10	14.36	47
48	24.71	23.18	21.79	20.51	19.35	18.28	17.30	16.39	15.56	14.79	14.09	48
49	23.76	22.34	21.05	19.86	18.77	17.76	16.84	15.99	15.20	14.47	13.80	49
50	22.81	21.50	20.30	19.20	18.18	17.24	16.37	15.57	14.83	14.14	13.50	50
51	21.87	20.66	19.55	18.52	17.58	16.70	15.89	15.14	14.44	13.79	13.19	51
52	20.92	19.81	18.79	17.84	16.96	16.15	15.39	14.69	14.04	13.43	12.86	52
53	19.98	18.96	18.02	17.15	16.34	15.59	14.89	14.23	13.62	13.05	12.52	53
54	19.04	18.11	17.26	16.46	15.71	15.02	14.37	13.76	13.19	12.66	12.16	54
55	18.11	17.27	16.49	15.76	15.08	14.44	13.84	13.28	12.75	12.26	11.79	55
56	17.18	16.43	15.72	15.05	14.43	13.85	13.30	12.79	12.30	11.84	11.41	56
57	16.27	15.59	14.95	14.35	13.79	13.25	12.75	12.28	11.84	11.42	11.02	57
58	15.36	14.75	14.18	13.64	13.13	12.65	12.20	11.77	11.36	10.98	10.61	58
59	14.46	13.92	13.41	12.93	12.47	12.04	11.63	11.24	10.87	10.52	10.19	59
60	13.56	13.08	12.63	12.21	11.80	11.42	11.05	10.70	10.37	10.06	9.76	60
61	12.67	12.25	11.86	11.48	11.13	10.79	10.46	10.15	9.85	9.57	9.30	61
62	11.79	11.43	11.08	10.75	10.44	10.14	9.86	9.58	9.32	9.07	8.83	62
63	10.90	10.59	10.30	10.02	9.75	9.49	9.24	9.00	8.77	8.55	8.34	63
64	10.02	9.76	9.51	9.27	9.04	8.82	8.60	8.40	8.20	8.01	7.83	64
65	9.14	8.92	8.71	8.51	8.32	8.13	7.95	7.78	7.61	7.45	7.29	65
66	8.25	8.07	7.90	7.74	7.58	7.42	7.27	7.13	6.99	6.85	6.72	66
67	7.36	7.22	7.08	6.95	6.82	6.70	6.58	6.46	6.35	6.24	6.13	67
68	6.47	6.36	6.25	6.15	6.05	5.95	5.86	5.77	5.68	5.59	5.50	68
69	5.57	5.49	5.41	5.34	5.26	5.19	5.12	5.05	4.98	4.91	4.85	69
70	4.67	4.62	4.56	4.51	4.45	4.40	4.35	4.30	4.25	4.20	4.16	70
71	3.77	3.73	3.70	3.66	3.63	3.59	3.56	3.53	3.49	3.46	3.43	71
72	2.86	2.84	2.81	2.79	2.77	2.75	2.74	2.72	2.70	2.68	2.66	72
73	1.93	1.92	1.91	1.90	1.89	1.88	1.87	1.87	1.86	1.85	1.84	73
74	0.98	0.98	0.98	0.97	0.97	0.97	0.97	0.96	0.96	0.96	0.96	74

Table 14: Multipliers for loss of earnings to pension age 75 (females)

Age at date of trial	Multiplier calculated with allowance for projected mortality from the 2002-based population projections and rate of return of											Age at date of trial
	0.0%	**0.5%**	**1.0%**	**1.5%**	**2.0%**	**2.5%**	**3.0%**	**3.5%**	**4.0%**	**4.5%**	**5.0%**	
16	57.18	49.67	43.48	38.35	34.07	30.48	27.44	24.86	22.66	20.77	19.13	16
17	56.18	48.92	42.92	37.92	33.74	30.23	27.25	24.72	22.55	20.68	19.06	17
18	55.18	48.16	42.34	37.49	33.41	29.97	27.06	24.57	22.43	20.59	19.00	18
19	54.18	47.40	41.76	37.04	33.07	29.71	26.86	24.42	22.32	20.50	18.92	19
20	53.18	46.64	41.18	36.59	32.73	29.45	26.65	24.26	22.19	20.40	18.85	20
21	52.18	45.87	40.59	36.14	32.37	29.17	26.44	24.09	22.06	20.30	18.77	21
22	51.18	45.10	39.99	35.67	32.01	28.89	26.22	23.92	21.93	20.20	18.68	22
23	50.18	44.32	39.38	35.20	31.65	28.61	25.99	23.74	21.79	20.09	18.60	23
24	49.18	43.54	38.77	34.73	31.27	28.31	25.76	23.56	21.64	19.97	18.50	24
25	48.18	42.76	38.16	34.24	30.89	28.01	25.52	23.37	21.49	19.85	18.41	25
26	47.18	41.97	37.54	33.75	30.50	27.70	25.28	23.17	21.33	19.72	18.31	26
27	46.18	41.18	36.91	33.25	30.10	27.38	25.02	22.97	21.17	19.59	18.20	27
28	45.18	40.38	36.27	32.74	29.69	27.06	24.76	22.76	21.00	19.45	18.09	28
29	44.18	39.58	35.63	32.23	29.28	26.72	24.49	22.54	20.82	19.31	17.97	29
30	43.18	38.78	34.99	31.71	28.86	26.38	24.21	22.31	20.64	19.16	17.85	30
31	42.18	37.97	34.33	31.18	28.43	26.03	23.93	22.08	20.45	19.00	17.72	31
32	41.19	37.16	33.67	30.64	27.99	25.67	23.64	21.84	20.25	18.84	17.58	32
33	40.19	36.35	33.01	30.10	27.55	25.31	23.33	21.59	20.04	18.67	17.44	33
34	39.19	35.53	32.34	29.55	27.09	24.93	23.02	21.33	19.83	18.49	17.30	34
35	38.20	34.71	31.66	28.99	26.63	24.55	22.71	21.07	19.61	18.31	17.14	35
36	37.20	33.89	30.98	28.42	26.16	24.16	22.38	20.79	19.38	18.12	16.98	36
37	36.21	33.06	30.29	27.85	25.68	23.75	22.04	20.51	19.14	17.91	16.81	37
38	35.22	32.24	29.60	27.26	25.19	23.34	21.70	20.22	18.90	17.71	16.63	38
39	34.23	31.40	28.90	26.68	24.69	22.92	21.34	19.92	18.64	17.49	16.45	39
40	33.24	30.57	28.20	26.08	24.19	22.49	20.98	19.61	18.38	17.26	16.25	40
41	32.25	29.73	27.49	25.48	23.67	22.06	20.60	19.29	18.10	17.03	16.05	41
42	31.27	28.90	26.77	24.86	23.15	21.61	20.22	18.96	17.82	16.78	15.84	42
43	30.29	28.06	26.05	24.25	22.62	21.15	19.83	18.62	17.53	16.53	15.62	43
44	29.32	27.22	25.33	23.62	22.08	20.69	19.42	18.27	17.22	16.27	15.39	44
45	28.34	26.38	24.60	22.99	21.54	20.21	19.01	17.91	16.91	15.99	15.16	45
46	27.37	25.53	23.87	22.36	20.98	19.73	18.59	17.54	16.59	15.71	14.91	46
47	26.40	24.69	23.13	21.71	20.42	19.23	18.15	17.16	16.25	15.42	14.65	47
48	25.43	23.84	22.38	21.06	19.84	18.73	17.71	16.77	15.91	15.11	14.38	48
49	24.47	22.99	21.64	20.40	19.26	18.21	17.25	16.37	15.55	14.79	14.09	49
50	23.51	22.14	20.88	19.73	18.67	17.69	16.78	15.95	15.18	14.46	13.80	50
51	22.55	21.29	20.12	19.05	18.06	17.15	16.30	15.52	14.79	14.12	13.49	51
52	21.59	20.43	19.36	18.37	17.45	16.60	15.81	15.08	14.40	13.76	13.17	52
53	20.64	19.58	18.59	17.68	16.83	16.04	15.31	14.62	13.99	13.39	12.84	53
54	19.69	18.72	17.82	16.98	16.20	15.47	14.79	14.16	13.56	13.01	12.49	54
55	18.74	17.86	17.04	16.28	15.56	14.89	14.26	13.68	13.13	12.61	12.12	55
56	17.80	17.01	16.26	15.57	14.91	14.30	13.73	13.18	12.68	12.20	11.75	56
57	16.87	16.15	15.48	14.85	14.26	13.70	13.17	12.68	12.21	11.77	11.35	57
58	15.93	15.29	14.69	14.12	13.59	13.08	12.61	12.16	11.73	11.33	10.95	58
59	15.00	14.44	13.90	13.39	12.91	12.46	12.03	11.62	11.23	10.87	10.52	59
60	14.08	13.58	13.10	12.65	12.23	11.82	11.43	11.07	10.72	10.39	10.07	60
61	13.15	12.72	12.30	11.90	11.53	11.17	10.83	10.50	10.19	9.89	9.61	61
62	12.23	11.85	11.49	11.14	10.82	10.50	10.20	9.91	9.64	9.38	9.12	62
63	11.31	10.98	10.67	10.37	10.09	9.82	9.56	9.31	9.07	8.84	8.61	63
64	10.38	10.11	9.84	9.59	9.35	9.12	8.89	8.68	8.47	8.27	8.08	64
65	9.45	9.23	9.01	8.80	8.59	8.40	8.21	8.03	7.85	7.68	7.52	65
66	8.52	8.34	8.16	7.99	7.82	7.66	7.50	7.35	7.21	7.07	6.93	66
67	7.59	7.45	7.30	7.17	7.03	6.90	6.78	6.66	6.54	6.42	6.31	67
68	6.66	6.55	6.44	6.33	6.23	6.13	6.03	5.93	5.84	5.75	5.66	68
69	5.73	5.64	5.56	5.48	5.40	5.33	5.25	5.18	5.11	5.04	4.98	69
70	4.79	4.73	4.67	4.62	4.56	4.51	4.46	4.41	4.36	4.31	4.26	70
71	3.85	3.81	3.78	3.74	3.70	3.67	3.64	3.60	3.57	3.54	3.50	71
72	2.91	2.89	2.87	2.84	2.82	2.80	2.78	2.76	2.74	2.73	2.71	72
73	1.95	1.94	1.94	1.93	1.92	1.91	1.90	1.89	1.88	1.87	1.86	73
74	0.99	0.98	0.98	0.98	0.98	0.98	0.97	0.97	0.97	0.97	0.96	74

Table 15: Multipliers for loss of pension commencing age 50 (males)

Age at date of trial	Multiplier calculated with allowance for projected mortality from the 2002-based population projections and rate of return of											Age at date of trial
	0.0%	0.5%	1.0%	1.5%	2.0%	2.5%	3.0%	3.5%	4.0%	4.5%	5.0%	
0	33.97	24.05	17.13	12.26	8.82	6.38	4.64	3.39	2.48	1.83	1.35	0
1	34.11	24.27	17.37	12.50	9.04	6.57	4.80	3.52	2.59	1.92	1.43	1
2	34.09	24.38	17.54	12.68	9.22	6.73	4.94	3.64	2.70	2.00	1.50	2
3	34.07	24.49	17.70	12.86	9.40	6.90	5.09	3.77	2.80	2.09	1.57	3
4	34.04	24.59	17.87	13.05	9.58	7.06	5.23	3.90	2.91	2.19	1.65	4
5	34.01	24.70	18.03	13.23	9.76	7.24	5.39	4.03	3.03	2.28	1.73	5
6	33.98	24.80	18.20	13.42	9.95	7.41	5.55	4.17	3.15	2.39	1.82	6
7	33.94	24.90	18.36	13.61	10.14	7.59	5.71	4.31	3.27	2.49	1.91	7
8	33.91	25.00	18.53	13.80	10.34	7.78	5.88	4.46	3.40	2.60	2.00	8
9	33.88	25.10	18.70	14.00	10.53	7.96	6.05	4.61	3.53	2.72	2.10	9
10	33.84	25.20	18.87	14.20	10.73	8.16	6.22	4.77	3.67	2.84	2.20	10
11	33.80	25.30	19.04	14.40	10.94	8.35	6.41	4.93	3.82	2.96	2.31	11
12	33.77	25.40	19.21	14.60	11.15	8.55	6.59	5.10	3.97	3.09	2.42	12
13	33.73	25.50	19.38	14.80	11.36	8.76	6.78	5.28	4.12	3.23	2.54	13
14	33.69	25.60	19.55	15.01	11.58	8.97	6.98	5.46	4.28	3.37	2.67	14
15	33.65	25.70	19.73	15.22	11.80	9.19	7.19	5.64	4.45	3.52	2.80	15
16	33.61	25.80	19.91	15.43	12.02	9.41	7.40	5.84	4.63	3.68	2.94	16
17	33.58	25.90	20.09	15.65	12.25	9.64	7.61	6.04	4.81	3.84	3.08	17
18	33.54	26.01	20.27	15.88	12.49	9.87	7.84	6.25	5.00	4.01	3.24	18
19	33.52	26.12	20.46	16.10	12.73	10.11	8.07	6.46	5.20	4.19	3.40	19
20	33.49	26.24	20.65	16.34	12.98	10.36	8.31	6.69	5.40	4.38	3.57	20
21	33.47	26.35	20.85	16.57	13.24	10.62	8.55	6.92	5.62	4.58	3.74	21
22	33.44	26.46	21.04	16.81	13.49	10.88	8.81	7.16	5.84	4.78	3.93	22
23	33.41	26.57	21.24	17.05	13.76	11.14	9.07	7.40	6.07	5.00	4.13	23
24	33.39	26.69	21.44	17.30	14.02	11.42	9.33	7.66	6.31	5.22	4.33	24
25	33.36	26.80	21.64	17.55	14.30	11.70	9.61	7.93	6.56	5.45	4.55	25
26	33.33	26.91	21.84	17.80	14.57	11.98	9.89	8.20	6.82	5.70	4.77	26
27	33.30	27.03	22.04	18.06	14.86	12.28	10.19	8.49	7.09	5.95	5.01	27
28	33.27	27.14	22.25	18.32	15.15	12.58	10.49	8.78	7.38	6.22	5.26	28
29	33.25	27.26	22.45	18.58	15.44	12.89	10.80	9.08	7.67	6.50	5.52	29
30	33.22	27.37	22.66	18.85	15.74	13.21	11.12	9.40	7.97	6.79	5.80	30
31	33.19	27.49	22.87	19.12	16.05	13.53	11.45	9.73	8.29	7.09	6.09	31
32	33.16	27.60	23.09	19.40	16.36	13.86	11.79	10.06	8.62	7.41	6.39	32
33	33.13	27.72	23.30	19.67	16.68	14.20	12.14	10.41	8.96	7.74	6.71	33
34	33.10	27.84	23.52	19.96	17.01	14.55	12.50	10.77	9.32	8.09	7.04	34
35	33.07	27.95	23.74	20.24	17.34	14.91	12.87	11.15	9.69	8.45	7.40	35
36	33.03	28.07	23.96	20.54	17.68	15.27	13.25	11.54	10.08	8.83	7.77	36
37	33.00	28.19	24.18	20.83	18.02	15.65	13.64	11.94	10.48	9.23	8.15	37
38	32.97	28.30	24.40	21.13	18.37	16.03	14.05	12.35	10.90	9.64	8.56	38
39	32.94	28.42	24.63	21.43	18.73	16.43	14.46	12.78	11.33	10.08	8.99	39
40	32.91	28.54	24.86	21.74	19.10	16.83	14.90	13.23	11.78	10.53	9.44	40
41	32.88	28.66	25.09	22.06	19.47	17.25	15.34	13.69	12.25	11.01	9.91	41
42	32.86	28.79	25.33	22.38	19.86	17.68	15.80	14.17	12.75	11.50	10.41	42
43	32.83	28.92	25.58	22.71	20.25	18.12	16.28	14.67	13.26	12.03	10.94	43
44	32.82	29.05	25.83	23.05	20.66	18.58	16.77	15.19	13.80	12.57	11.49	44
45	32.80	29.19	26.08	23.40	21.07	19.05	17.28	15.73	14.36	13.15	12.08	45
46	32.80	29.34	26.35	23.76	21.50	19.54	17.81	16.29	14.94	13.75	12.69	46
47	32.80	29.49	26.62	24.13	21.95	20.04	18.36	16.88	15.56	14.39	13.34	47
48	32.81	29.65	26.90	24.51	22.41	20.56	18.93	17.49	16.20	15.06	14.03	48
49	32.82	29.81	27.19	24.89	22.88	21.10	19.52	18.12	16.88	15.76	14.76	49
50	32.84	29.98	27.48	25.29	23.36	21.65	20.14	18.79	17.58	16.50	15.53	50

Table 16: Multipliers for loss of pension commencing age 50 (females)

Age at date of trial	Multiplier calculated with allowance for projected mortality from the 2002-based population projections and rate of return of											Age at date of trial
	0.0%	0.5%	1.0%	1.5%	2.0%	2.5%	3.0%	3.5%	4.0%	4.5%	5.0%	
0	37.54	26.42	18.71	13.32	9.54	6.87	4.97	3.61	2.64	1.94	1.43	0
1	37.69	26.66	18.97	13.57	9.77	7.07	5.14	3.75	2.76	2.03	1.50	1
2	37.67	26.78	19.15	13.77	9.96	7.24	5.29	3.88	2.87	2.12	1.58	2
3	37.66	26.91	19.34	13.98	10.16	7.42	5.45	4.02	2.98	2.22	1.66	3
4	37.63	27.03	19.52	14.18	10.36	7.60	5.61	4.16	3.10	2.32	1.74	4
5	37.61	27.15	19.71	14.38	10.56	7.79	5.78	4.30	3.22	2.42	1.83	5
6	37.59	27.26	19.89	14.59	10.76	7.98	5.95	4.45	3.35	2.53	1.92	6
7	37.56	27.38	20.08	14.80	10.97	8.18	6.12	4.60	3.48	2.64	2.01	7
8	37.53	27.50	20.27	15.02	11.19	8.38	6.30	4.76	3.62	2.76	2.11	8
9	37.51	27.62	20.46	15.23	11.40	8.58	6.49	4.93	3.76	2.88	2.22	9
10	37.48	27.74	20.65	15.45	11.62	8.79	6.68	5.10	3.91	3.01	2.33	10
11	37.45	27.86	20.84	15.67	11.85	9.00	6.88	5.27	4.06	3.14	2.44	11
12	37.42	27.98	21.03	15.90	12.08	9.22	7.08	5.46	4.22	3.28	2.56	12
13	37.39	28.09	21.23	16.13	12.31	9.45	7.29	5.64	4.39	3.43	2.69	13
14	37.36	28.21	21.43	16.36	12.55	9.68	7.50	5.84	4.56	3.58	2.82	14
15	37.33	28.33	21.62	16.59	12.80	9.92	7.72	6.04	4.75	3.74	2.96	15
16	37.30	28.45	21.83	16.83	13.04	10.16	7.95	6.25	4.93	3.91	3.11	16
17	37.27	28.58	22.03	17.07	13.30	10.41	8.18	6.46	5.13	4.08	3.27	17
18	37.24	28.70	22.23	17.32	13.55	10.66	8.43	6.69	5.33	4.27	3.43	18
19	37.21	28.82	22.44	17.57	13.82	10.92	8.67	6.92	5.54	4.46	3.60	19
20	37.18	28.94	22.65	17.82	14.09	11.19	8.93	7.16	5.76	4.66	3.78	20
21	37.15	29.06	22.86	18.07	14.36	11.46	9.19	7.40	5.99	4.86	3.96	21
22	37.12	29.19	23.07	18.33	14.64	11.74	9.46	7.66	6.23	5.08	4.16	22
23	37.08	29.31	23.28	18.59	14.92	12.03	9.74	7.92	6.47	5.31	4.37	23
24	37.05	29.43	23.50	18.86	15.21	12.32	10.03	8.20	6.73	5.54	4.58	24
25	37.01	29.55	23.71	19.13	15.50	12.62	10.32	8.48	6.99	5.79	4.81	25
26	36.98	29.67	23.93	19.40	15.80	12.93	10.63	8.77	7.27	6.05	5.05	26
27	36.94	29.79	24.15	19.67	16.10	13.24	10.94	9.07	7.56	6.32	5.30	27
28	36.90	29.91	24.37	19.95	16.41	13.56	11.26	9.38	7.85	6.60	5.56	28
29	36.87	30.03	24.59	20.24	16.73	13.89	11.59	9.71	8.16	6.89	5.84	29
30	36.83	30.16	24.82	20.52	17.05	14.23	11.93	10.04	8.49	7.20	6.13	30
31	36.79	30.28	25.04	20.81	17.38	14.58	12.28	10.39	8.82	7.52	6.43	31
32	36.75	30.40	25.27	21.11	17.72	14.93	12.64	10.74	9.17	7.85	6.75	32
33	36.71	30.52	25.50	21.41	18.06	15.30	13.01	11.12	9.53	8.20	7.08	33
34	36.67	30.64	25.73	21.71	18.40	15.67	13.40	11.50	9.91	8.57	7.44	34
35	36.63	30.77	25.97	22.02	18.76	16.05	13.79	11.89	10.30	8.95	7.80	35
36	36.59	30.89	26.21	22.33	19.12	16.44	14.20	12.31	10.71	9.35	8.19	36
37	36.56	31.02	26.45	22.65	19.49	16.84	14.61	12.73	11.13	9.77	8.60	37
38	36.52	31.14	26.69	22.98	19.87	17.25	15.04	13.17	11.57	10.20	9.03	38
39	36.48	31.27	26.93	23.30	20.25	17.68	15.49	13.63	12.03	10.66	9.48	39
40	36.45	31.40	27.18	23.64	20.65	18.11	15.95	14.10	12.51	11.14	9.95	40
41	36.42	31.54	27.44	23.98	21.05	18.56	16.42	14.59	13.01	11.64	10.45	41
42	36.39	31.67	27.70	24.33	21.46	19.01	16.91	15.10	13.53	12.16	10.97	42
43	36.36	31.81	27.96	24.68	21.89	19.49	17.42	15.63	14.07	12.71	11.52	43
44	36.34	31.96	28.23	25.05	22.32	19.97	17.94	16.18	14.64	13.29	12.10	44
45	36.32	32.10	28.50	25.42	22.77	20.47	18.48	16.75	15.23	13.89	12.71	45
46	36.31	32.25	28.78	25.80	23.22	20.99	19.04	17.34	15.84	14.52	13.36	46
47	36.30	32.41	29.07	26.19	23.69	21.52	19.62	17.95	16.48	15.19	14.03	47
48	36.29	32.57	29.37	26.59	24.17	22.07	20.22	18.59	17.16	15.88	14.75	48
49	36.29	32.74	29.67	27.00	24.67	22.63	20.84	19.26	17.86	16.61	15.50	49
50	36.29	32.91	29.98	27.42	25.18	23.22	21.48	19.95	18.59	17.38	16.30	50

Table 17: Multipliers for loss of pension commencing age 55 (males)

Age at date of trial	Multiplier calculated with allowance for projected mortality from the 2002-based population projections and rate of return of											Age at date of trial
	0.0%	0.5%	1.0%	1.5%	2.0%	2.5%	3.0%	3.5%	4.0%	4.5%	5.0%	
0	29.19	20.38	14.29	10.08	7.13	5.07	3.62	2.60	1.87	1.35	0.98	0
1	29.31	20.56	14.50	10.27	7.31	5.22	3.75	2.70	1.96	1.42	1.04	1
2	29.29	20.65	14.63	10.42	7.45	5.35	3.86	2.80	2.03	1.48	1.09	2
3	29.27	20.74	14.77	10.57	7.59	5.48	3.97	2.89	2.11	1.55	1.14	3
4	29.24	20.83	14.90	10.72	7.74	5.61	4.09	2.99	2.20	1.62	1.20	4
5	29.21	20.91	15.04	10.87	7.89	5.75	4.21	3.09	2.28	1.69	1.26	5
6	29.18	20.99	15.18	11.02	8.04	5.89	4.33	3.20	2.37	1.76	1.32	6
7	29.15	21.08	15.31	11.18	8.19	6.03	4.46	3.31	2.46	1.84	1.38	7
8	29.12	21.16	15.45	11.33	8.35	6.18	4.59	3.42	2.56	1.92	1.45	8
9	29.08	21.24	15.59	11.49	8.51	6.32	4.72	3.54	2.66	2.01	1.52	9
10	29.05	21.33	15.73	11.65	8.67	6.48	4.86	3.66	2.77	2.10	1.60	10
11	29.01	21.41	15.87	11.81	8.83	6.63	5.00	3.78	2.87	2.19	1.68	11
12	28.98	21.49	16.01	11.98	9.00	6.79	5.14	3.91	2.99	2.29	1.76	12
13	28.94	21.57	16.15	12.14	9.17	6.95	5.29	4.05	3.10	2.39	1.84	13
14	28.90	21.65	16.29	12.31	9.34	7.12	5.45	4.18	3.22	2.49	1.93	14
15	28.87	21.73	16.43	12.48	9.52	7.29	5.61	4.33	3.35	2.60	2.03	15
16	28.83	21.81	16.58	12.66	9.70	7.47	5.77	4.47	3.48	2.72	2.13	16
17	28.79	21.90	16.73	12.83	9.88	7.64	5.94	4.63	3.62	2.84	2.23	17
18	28.76	21.98	16.88	13.01	10.07	7.83	6.11	4.78	3.76	2.96	2.34	18
19	28.73	22.07	17.03	13.20	10.27	8.02	6.29	4.95	3.91	3.10	2.46	19
20	28.71	22.17	17.19	13.39	10.47	8.22	6.47	5.12	4.06	3.23	2.58	20
21	28.68	22.26	17.35	13.58	10.67	8.42	6.66	5.30	4.22	3.38	2.71	21
22	28.65	22.35	17.51	13.77	10.87	8.62	6.86	5.48	4.39	3.53	2.85	22
23	28.62	22.44	17.67	13.96	11.08	8.83	7.06	5.67	4.56	3.69	2.99	23
24	28.59	22.53	17.83	14.16	11.30	9.04	7.27	5.86	4.74	3.85	3.13	24
25	28.56	22.62	17.99	14.36	11.51	9.26	7.48	6.06	4.93	4.02	3.29	25
26	28.53	22.71	18.15	14.57	11.74	9.49	7.70	6.27	5.12	4.20	3.45	26
27	28.50	22.80	18.32	14.77	11.96	9.72	7.93	6.49	5.33	4.39	3.62	27
28	28.47	22.89	18.48	14.98	12.19	9.96	8.16	6.71	5.54	4.58	3.80	28
29	28.44	22.99	18.65	15.19	12.43	10.20	8.40	6.94	5.75	4.79	3.99	29
30	28.41	23.08	18.82	15.41	12.66	10.45	8.65	7.18	5.98	5.00	4.19	30
31	28.38	23.17	18.99	15.63	12.91	10.70	8.90	7.43	6.22	5.22	4.40	31
32	28.34	23.26	19.16	15.85	13.15	10.96	9.16	7.68	6.46	5.45	4.62	32
33	28.31	23.35	19.33	16.07	13.41	11.22	9.43	7.95	6.72	5.70	4.84	33
34	28.28	23.44	19.51	16.30	13.66	11.50	9.71	8.22	6.98	5.95	5.08	34
35	28.24	23.53	19.68	16.53	13.93	11.78	9.99	8.50	7.26	6.22	5.34	35
36	28.21	23.62	19.86	16.76	14.19	12.06	10.28	8.80	7.55	6.49	5.60	36
37	28.17	23.71	20.04	16.99	14.46	12.35	10.58	9.10	7.84	6.78	5.88	37
38	28.14	23.80	20.22	17.23	14.74	12.65	10.89	9.41	8.15	7.08	6.17	38
39	28.10	23.90	20.40	17.47	15.02	12.96	11.21	9.73	8.47	7.40	6.48	39
40	28.06	23.99	20.58	17.72	15.31	13.27	11.54	10.07	8.81	7.73	6.80	40
41	28.03	24.08	20.77	17.97	15.61	13.60	11.88	10.42	9.16	8.07	7.14	41
42	28.00	24.18	20.96	18.23	15.91	13.93	12.23	10.78	9.52	8.44	7.49	42
43	27.97	24.28	21.15	18.49	16.22	14.27	12.60	11.15	9.90	8.82	7.87	43
44	27.94	24.38	21.35	18.76	16.54	14.62	12.97	11.54	10.30	9.21	8.26	44
45	27.92	24.49	21.55	19.03	16.86	14.99	13.36	11.95	10.71	9.63	8.68	45
46	27.91	24.60	21.76	19.31	17.20	15.36	13.77	12.37	11.14	10.07	9.12	46
47	27.89	24.71	21.97	19.60	17.55	15.75	14.18	12.81	11.60	10.53	9.58	47
48	27.89	24.84	22.20	19.90	17.90	16.15	14.62	13.27	12.07	11.01	10.07	48
49	27.88	24.96	22.42	20.21	18.27	16.57	15.07	13.74	12.57	11.52	10.59	49
50	27.88	25.09	22.65	20.52	18.65	16.99	15.53	14.24	13.08	12.05	11.13	50
51	27.89	25.22	22.89	20.84	19.03	17.43	16.01	14.75	13.62	12.61	11.70	51
52	27.89	25.36	23.13	21.17	19.43	17.89	16.51	15.29	14.19	13.20	12.31	52
53	27.90	25.50	23.38	21.51	19.84	18.36	17.03	15.85	14.78	13.82	12.95	53
54	27.93	25.66	23.64	21.86	20.27	18.85	17.58	16.43	15.40	14.47	13.63	54
55	27.97	25.82	23.92	22.23	20.72	19.37	18.15	17.05	16.06	15.17	14.35	55

Table 18: Multipliers for loss of pension commencing age 55 (females)

Age at date of trial	Multiplier calculated with allowance for projected mortality from the 2002-based population projections and rate of return of											Age at date of trial
	0.0%	0.5%	1.0%	1.5%	2.0%	2.5%	3.0%	3.5%	4.0%	4.5%	5.0%	
0	32.68	22.68	15.82	11.10	7.82	5.54	3.94	2.81	2.02	1.45	1.05	0
1	32.80	22.88	16.04	11.31	8.01	5.70	4.07	2.92	2.11	1.52	1.11	1
2	32.79	22.99	16.20	11.47	8.16	5.84	4.19	3.02	2.19	1.59	1.16	2
3	32.77	23.09	16.35	11.64	8.32	5.98	4.32	3.13	2.28	1.66	1.22	3
4	32.75	23.19	16.51	11.81	8.49	6.13	4.44	3.24	2.37	1.74	1.28	4
5	32.73	23.29	16.66	11.98	8.65	6.28	4.57	3.35	2.46	1.82	1.35	5
6	32.70	23.39	16.82	12.15	8.82	6.43	4.71	3.46	2.56	1.90	1.41	6
7	32.68	23.49	16.97	12.32	8.99	6.59	4.85	3.58	2.66	1.98	1.48	7
8	32.65	23.59	17.13	12.50	9.16	6.75	4.99	3.71	2.76	2.07	1.55	8
9	32.62	23.69	17.29	12.68	9.34	6.91	5.14	3.83	2.87	2.16	1.63	9
10	32.60	23.79	17.45	12.86	9.52	7.08	5.29	3.97	2.99	2.26	1.71	10
11	32.57	23.89	17.61	13.04	9.70	7.25	5.44	4.10	3.10	2.36	1.80	11
12	32.54	23.99	17.77	13.23	9.89	7.43	5.60	4.24	3.23	2.46	1.89	12
13	32.51	24.09	17.93	13.42	10.08	7.61	5.77	4.39	3.35	2.57	1.98	13
14	32.48	24.19	18.10	13.61	10.27	7.79	5.94	4.54	3.49	2.69	2.08	14
15	32.45	24.29	18.26	13.80	10.47	7.98	6.11	4.70	3.62	2.81	2.18	15
16	32.42	24.39	18.43	14.00	10.67	8.18	6.29	4.86	3.77	2.93	2.29	16
17	32.39	24.49	18.60	14.20	10.88	8.38	6.47	5.02	3.91	3.06	2.40	17
18	32.36	24.59	18.77	14.40	11.09	8.58	6.66	5.20	4.07	3.20	2.52	18
19	32.33	24.69	18.95	14.60	11.30	8.79	6.86	5.38	4.23	3.34	2.64	19
20	32.30	24.79	19.12	14.81	11.52	9.00	7.06	5.56	4.39	3.49	2.78	20
21	32.27	24.89	19.29	15.02	11.74	9.22	7.27	5.75	4.57	3.64	2.91	21
22	32.24	25.00	19.47	15.23	11.97	9.44	7.48	5.95	4.75	3.80	3.06	22
23	32.20	25.10	19.65	15.45	12.20	9.67	7.70	6.15	4.93	3.97	3.21	23
24	32.17	25.20	19.82	15.66	12.43	9.91	7.92	6.36	5.13	4.15	3.37	24
25	32.13	25.30	20.00	15.89	12.67	10.15	8.16	6.58	5.33	4.33	3.53	25
26	32.10	25.40	20.18	16.11	12.91	10.39	8.39	6.81	5.54	4.52	3.71	26
27	32.06	25.49	20.36	16.33	13.16	10.64	8.64	7.04	5.76	4.72	3.89	27
28	32.02	25.59	20.55	16.56	13.41	10.90	8.89	7.28	5.98	4.93	4.08	28
29	31.99	25.69	20.73	16.80	13.66	11.16	9.15	7.53	6.22	5.15	4.28	29
30	31.95	25.79	20.91	17.03	13.92	11.43	9.42	7.79	6.46	5.38	4.49	30
31	31.91	25.89	21.10	17.27	14.19	11.71	9.69	8.05	6.72	5.62	4.72	31
32	31.87	25.99	21.29	17.51	14.46	11.99	9.97	8.33	6.98	5.87	4.95	32
33	31.83	26.09	21.48	17.76	14.74	12.28	10.27	8.61	7.25	6.13	5.19	33
34	31.79	26.19	21.67	18.00	15.02	12.57	10.57	8.91	7.54	6.40	5.45	34
35	31.75	26.29	21.86	18.25	15.30	12.88	10.87	9.21	7.84	6.68	5.72	35
36	31.71	26.39	22.06	18.51	15.59	13.19	11.19	9.53	8.14	6.98	6.00	36
37	31.67	26.49	22.25	18.77	15.89	13.51	11.52	9.86	8.46	7.29	6.30	37
38	31.63	26.59	22.45	19.03	16.20	13.83	11.86	10.20	8.80	7.61	6.61	38
39	31.59	26.70	22.65	19.30	16.50	14.17	12.20	10.55	9.14	7.95	6.94	39
40	31.55	26.80	22.86	19.57	16.82	14.51	12.56	10.91	9.50	8.31	7.28	40
41	31.52	26.91	23.07	19.85	17.15	14.86	12.93	11.28	9.88	8.68	7.64	41
42	31.48	27.02	23.28	20.13	17.48	15.23	13.31	11.67	10.27	9.07	8.02	42
43	31.45	27.13	23.49	20.42	17.82	15.60	13.71	12.08	10.68	9.47	8.42	43
44	31.42	27.24	23.71	20.72	18.16	15.98	14.11	12.50	11.11	9.90	8.85	44
45	31.40	27.36	23.94	21.02	18.52	16.38	14.53	12.94	11.55	10.34	9.29	45
46	31.38	27.48	24.16	21.32	18.89	16.79	14.97	13.39	12.01	10.81	9.76	46
47	31.36	27.61	24.40	21.64	19.26	17.21	15.42	13.86	12.50	11.30	10.25	47
48	31.34	27.73	24.63	21.96	19.65	17.64	15.88	14.35	13.00	11.82	10.77	48
49	31.33	27.87	24.88	22.29	20.04	18.08	16.37	14.86	13.53	12.35	11.31	49
50	31.33	28.01	25.13	22.63	20.45	18.54	16.87	15.39	14.08	12.92	11.89	50
51	31.33	28.15	25.39	22.98	20.87	19.02	17.39	15.94	14.66	13.52	12.49	51
52	31.33	28.30	25.65	23.34	21.30	19.51	17.92	16.51	15.26	14.14	13.14	52
53	31.34	28.45	25.93	23.71	21.75	20.02	18.48	17.11	15.89	14.80	13.81	53
54	31.36	28.62	26.21	24.09	22.21	20.55	19.06	17.74	16.56	15.49	14.53	54
55	31.39	28.80	26.51	24.49	22.69	21.10	19.67	18.40	17.25	16.22	15.29	55

Table 19: Multipliers for loss of pension commencing age 60 (males)

Age at date of trial	Multiplier calculated with allowance for projected mortality from the 2002-based population projections and rate of return of											Age at date of trial
	0.0%	0.5%	1.0%	1.5%	2.0%	2.5%	3.0%	3.5%	4.0%	4.5%	5.0%	
0	24.49	16.85	11.64	8.08	5.63	3.94	2.76	1.95	1.38	0.98	0.70	0
1	24.59	17.00	11.81	8.23	5.76	4.05	2.86	2.03	1.44	1.03	0.73	1
2	24.57	17.07	11.92	8.35	5.88	4.15	2.94	2.09	1.50	1.07	0.77	2
3	24.55	17.14	12.03	8.47	5.99	4.25	3.03	2.17	1.56	1.12	0.81	3
4	24.52	17.21	12.13	8.59	6.10	4.35	3.12	2.24	1.62	1.17	0.85	4
5	24.49	17.28	12.24	8.71	6.22	4.46	3.21	2.32	1.68	1.22	0.89	5
6	24.47	17.35	12.35	8.83	6.34	4.57	3.30	2.40	1.74	1.28	0.93	6
7	24.44	17.41	12.46	8.95	6.46	4.68	3.40	2.48	1.81	1.33	0.98	7
8	24.40	17.48	12.57	9.08	6.58	4.79	3.50	2.56	1.88	1.39	1.03	8
9	24.37	17.54	12.68	9.20	6.70	4.90	3.60	2.65	1.96	1.45	1.08	9
10	24.34	17.61	12.79	9.33	6.83	5.02	3.70	2.74	2.03	1.51	1.13	10
11	24.31	17.67	12.90	9.46	6.96	5.14	3.81	2.83	2.11	1.58	1.19	11
12	24.27	17.74	13.01	9.59	7.09	5.26	3.92	2.93	2.19	1.65	1.25	12
13	24.24	17.80	13.13	9.72	7.22	5.38	4.03	3.03	2.28	1.72	1.31	13
14	24.20	17.87	13.24	9.85	7.36	5.51	4.15	3.13	2.37	1.80	1.37	14
15	24.16	17.93	13.35	9.98	7.49	5.64	4.27	3.23	2.46	1.88	1.44	15
16	24.13	17.99	13.47	10.12	7.63	5.78	4.39	3.34	2.56	1.96	1.51	16
17	24.09	18.06	13.59	10.26	7.78	5.91	4.51	3.46	2.66	2.05	1.58	17
18	24.06	18.13	13.71	10.40	7.92	6.06	4.65	3.57	2.76	2.14	1.66	18
19	24.04	18.20	13.83	10.55	8.07	6.20	4.78	3.70	2.87	2.23	1.74	19
20	24.01	18.27	13.95	10.70	8.23	6.35	4.92	3.82	2.98	2.33	1.83	20
21	23.98	18.34	14.08	10.85	8.39	6.51	5.06	3.95	3.10	2.43	1.92	21
22	23.95	18.41	14.20	11.00	8.55	6.66	5.21	4.09	3.22	2.54	2.01	22
23	23.92	18.48	14.33	11.15	8.71	6.82	5.36	4.23	3.34	2.65	2.11	23
24	23.89	18.55	14.46	11.31	8.87	6.99	5.52	4.37	3.48	2.77	2.21	24
25	23.86	18.62	14.58	11.46	9.04	7.15	5.68	4.52	3.61	2.89	2.32	25
26	23.83	18.69	14.71	11.62	9.21	7.33	5.84	4.68	3.75	3.02	2.44	26
27	23.80	18.76	14.84	11.78	9.39	7.50	6.01	4.84	3.90	3.15	2.56	27
28	23.76	18.83	14.97	11.95	9.56	7.68	6.19	5.00	4.05	3.29	2.68	28
29	23.73	18.90	15.10	12.11	9.74	7.87	6.37	5.17	4.21	3.44	2.82	29
30	23.70	18.97	15.24	12.28	9.93	8.05	6.55	5.35	4.38	3.59	2.95	30
31	23.66	19.04	15.37	12.45	10.12	8.25	6.74	5.53	4.55	3.75	3.10	31
32	23.63	19.11	15.50	12.62	10.31	8.44	6.94	5.72	4.72	3.92	3.25	32
33	23.59	19.17	15.64	12.79	10.50	8.65	7.14	5.91	4.91	4.09	3.41	33
34	23.56	19.24	15.77	12.97	10.70	8.85	7.35	6.11	5.10	4.27	3.58	34
35	23.52	19.31	15.91	13.15	10.90	9.06	7.56	6.32	5.30	4.46	3.76	35
36	23.48	19.38	16.04	13.33	11.10	9.28	7.78	6.54	5.51	4.65	3.94	36
37	23.44	19.44	16.18	13.51	11.31	9.50	8.00	6.76	5.72	4.86	4.13	37
38	23.40	19.51	16.32	13.69	11.52	9.73	8.23	6.99	5.95	5.07	4.34	38
39	23.36	19.58	16.46	13.88	11.74	9.96	8.47	7.22	6.18	5.30	4.55	39
40	23.32	19.64	16.60	14.07	11.96	10.19	8.71	7.47	6.42	5.53	4.77	40
41	23.29	19.71	16.74	14.26	12.18	10.44	8.97	7.72	6.67	5.77	5.01	41
42	23.25	19.78	16.88	14.46	12.41	10.69	9.23	7.99	6.93	6.03	5.26	42
43	23.21	19.85	17.03	14.66	12.65	10.94	9.50	8.26	7.20	6.30	5.52	43
44	23.18	19.93	17.18	14.86	12.89	11.21	9.77	8.54	7.49	6.58	5.79	44
45	23.15	20.00	17.34	15.07	13.14	11.48	10.06	8.84	7.78	6.87	6.08	45
46	23.13	20.09	17.50	15.29	13.39	11.76	10.36	9.15	8.09	7.18	6.38	46
47	23.11	20.17	17.66	15.51	13.65	12.05	10.67	9.47	8.42	7.50	6.70	47
48	23.09	20.26	17.83	15.73	13.92	12.35	10.99	9.80	8.76	7.84	7.04	48
49	23.07	20.35	18.00	15.96	14.20	12.66	11.32	10.14	9.11	8.20	7.40	49
50	23.06	20.44	18.17	16.20	14.48	12.98	11.66	10.50	9.48	8.57	7.77	50
51	23.04	20.53	18.35	16.44	14.77	13.31	12.01	10.87	9.86	8.97	8.17	51
52	23.03	20.63	18.53	16.69	15.07	13.64	12.38	11.26	10.26	9.38	8.58	52
53	23.03	20.73	18.72	16.95	15.38	13.99	12.76	11.66	10.68	9.81	9.02	53
54	23.03	20.84	18.92	17.21	15.70	14.36	13.16	12.09	11.13	10.26	9.49	54

Table 19: Multipliers for loss of pension commencing age 60 (males) *continued*

Age at date of trial	Multiplier calculated with allowance for projected mortality from the 2002-based population projections and rate of return of											Age at date of trial
	0.0%	*0.5%*	*1.0%*	*1.5%*	*2.0%*	*2.5%*	*3.0%*	*3.5%*	*4.0%*	*4.5%*	*5.0%*	
55	23.05	20.97	19.12	17.49	16.03	14.74	13.57	12.53	11.59	10.75	9.98	55
56	23.08	21.10	19.35	17.78	16.39	15.14	14.01	13.00	12.09	11.26	10.51	56
57	23.13	21.26	19.59	18.10	16.76	15.56	14.48	13.50	12.61	11.81	11.08	57
58	23.19	21.42	19.85	18.43	17.16	16.01	14.97	14.03	13.17	12.39	11.68	58
59	23.27	21.61	20.12	18.78	17.57	16.48	15.49	14.59	13.76	13.01	12.33	59
60	23.37	21.82	20.42	19.16	18.02	16.98	16.04	15.18	14.40	13.68	13.02	60

Table 20: Multipliers for loss of pension commencing age 60 (females)

Age at date of trial	Multiplier calculated with allowance for projected mortality from the 2002-based population projections and rate of return of											Age at date of trial
	0.0%	0.5%	1.0%	1.5%	2.0%	2.5%	3.0%	3.5%	4.0%	4.5%	5.0%	
0	27.87	19.07	13.11	9.05	6.28	4.37	3.06	2.15	1.51	1.07	0.76	0
1	27.98	19.24	13.29	9.22	6.43	4.50	3.16	2.23	1.58	1.12	0.80	1
2	27.96	19.33	13.42	9.36	6.55	4.61	3.25	2.31	1.64	1.17	0.84	2
3	27.94	19.41	13.55	9.49	6.68	4.72	3.35	2.39	1.71	1.22	0.88	3
4	27.92	19.50	13.67	9.63	6.81	4.84	3.45	2.47	1.77	1.28	0.93	4
5	27.90	19.58	13.80	9.77	6.94	4.96	3.55	2.55	1.84	1.34	0.97	5
6	27.88	19.66	13.93	9.91	7.08	5.08	3.66	2.64	1.92	1.40	1.02	6
7	27.85	19.74	14.05	10.05	7.21	5.20	3.76	2.73	1.99	1.46	1.07	7
8	27.83	19.82	14.18	10.19	7.35	5.33	3.87	2.83	2.07	1.52	1.12	8
9	27.80	19.90	14.31	10.33	7.49	5.45	3.99	2.92	2.15	1.59	1.18	9
10	27.78	19.99	14.44	10.48	7.64	5.59	4.10	3.02	2.24	1.66	1.24	10
11	27.75	20.07	14.57	10.63	7.78	5.72	4.22	3.13	2.32	1.73	1.30	11
12	27.72	20.15	14.71	10.78	7.93	5.86	4.35	3.23	2.42	1.81	1.36	12
13	27.69	20.23	14.84	10.93	8.08	6.00	4.47	3.34	2.51	1.89	1.43	13
14	27.66	20.31	14.97	11.08	8.24	6.15	4.60	3.46	2.61	1.97	1.50	14
15	27.63	20.39	15.11	11.24	8.40	6.29	4.74	3.58	2.71	2.06	1.57	15
16	27.61	20.47	15.25	11.40	8.56	6.45	4.88	3.70	2.82	2.15	1.65	16
17	27.58	20.55	15.38	11.56	8.72	6.60	5.02	3.83	2.93	2.25	1.73	17
18	27.55	20.64	15.52	11.72	8.89	6.76	5.16	3.96	3.04	2.35	1.82	18
19	27.52	20.72	15.66	11.89	9.06	6.93	5.31	4.09	3.16	2.45	1.91	19
20	27.49	20.80	15.80	12.05	9.23	7.09	5.47	4.23	3.29	2.56	2.00	20
21	27.46	20.88	15.94	12.22	9.40	7.26	5.63	4.38	3.42	2.67	2.10	21
22	27.42	20.96	16.09	12.39	9.58	7.44	5.79	4.53	3.55	2.79	2.20	22
23	27.39	21.04	16.23	12.57	9.77	7.62	5.96	4.68	3.69	2.91	2.31	23
24	27.36	21.12	16.37	12.74	9.95	7.80	6.13	4.84	3.83	3.04	2.42	24
25	27.32	21.20	16.52	12.92	10.14	7.99	6.31	5.01	3.98	3.18	2.54	25
26	27.29	21.28	16.66	13.10	10.33	8.18	6.50	5.18	4.14	3.32	2.67	26
27	27.25	21.36	16.81	13.28	10.53	8.37	6.68	5.35	4.30	3.46	2.80	27
28	27.21	21.44	16.96	13.46	10.72	8.57	6.88	5.53	4.47	3.62	2.94	28
29	27.17	21.52	17.11	13.65	10.93	8.78	7.08	5.72	4.64	3.78	3.08	29
30	27.13	21.60	17.25	13.83	11.13	8.99	7.28	5.92	4.82	3.94	3.23	30
31	27.10	21.68	17.40	14.02	11.34	9.20	7.49	6.12	5.01	4.12	3.39	31
32	27.06	21.75	17.55	14.22	11.55	9.42	7.71	6.33	5.21	4.30	3.56	32
33	27.02	21.83	17.71	14.41	11.77	9.65	7.93	6.54	5.41	4.49	3.73	33
34	26.97	21.91	17.86	14.61	11.99	9.88	8.16	6.76	5.62	4.69	3.92	34
35	26.93	21.99	18.01	14.81	12.22	10.11	8.40	6.99	5.84	4.89	4.11	35
36	26.89	22.07	18.17	15.01	12.45	10.35	8.64	7.23	6.07	5.11	4.31	36
37	26.85	22.14	18.33	15.22	12.68	10.60	8.89	7.47	6.30	5.33	4.52	37
38	26.81	22.22	18.48	15.43	12.92	10.85	9.15	7.73	6.55	5.57	4.74	38
39	26.77	22.30	18.64	15.64	13.16	11.11	9.41	7.99	6.81	5.81	4.98	39
40	26.73	22.38	18.81	15.86	13.41	11.38	9.68	8.26	7.07	6.07	5.22	40
41	26.69	22.46	18.97	16.07	13.66	11.65	9.96	8.55	7.35	6.34	5.48	41
42	26.66	22.55	19.14	16.30	13.92	11.93	10.25	8.84	7.64	6.62	5.75	42
43	26.62	22.63	19.31	16.53	14.19	12.22	10.55	9.14	7.94	6.91	6.04	43
44	26.59	22.72	19.48	16.76	14.46	12.52	10.86	9.46	8.25	7.22	6.34	44
45	26.56	22.81	19.66	17.00	14.74	12.82	11.18	9.78	8.58	7.54	6.65	45
46	26.53	22.90	19.84	17.24	15.03	13.13	11.51	10.12	8.92	7.88	6.98	46
47	26.50	23.00	20.02	17.49	15.32	13.46	11.86	10.47	9.28	8.24	7.33	47
48	26.48	23.10	20.21	17.74	15.62	13.79	12.21	10.84	9.65	8.61	7.70	48
49	26.46	23.20	20.40	18.00	15.93	14.13	12.57	11.22	10.03	9.00	8.09	49
50	26.45	23.31	20.60	18.27	16.24	14.49	12.95	11.61	10.44	9.40	8.49	50
51	26.44	23.41	20.80	18.54	16.57	14.85	13.35	12.02	10.86	9.83	8.92	51
52	26.43	23.53	21.01	18.82	16.91	15.23	13.75	12.45	11.30	10.28	9.38	52
53	26.43	23.65	21.23	19.11	17.25	15.62	14.17	12.90	11.77	10.76	9.86	53
54	26.43	23.78	21.45	19.41	17.61	16.02	14.61	13.36	12.25	11.26	10.36	54

Table 20: Multipliers for loss of pension commencing age 60 (females) *continued*

Age at date of trial	Multiplier calculated with allowance for projected mortality from the 2002-based population projections and rate of return of											Age at date of trial
	0.0%	*0.5%*	*1.0%*	*1.5%*	*2.0%*	*2.5%*	*3.0%*	*3.5%*	*4.0%*	*4.5%*	*5.0%*	
55	26.45	23.91	21.68	19.72	17.98	16.44	15.07	13.85	12.76	11.78	10.90	55
56	26.47	24.06	21.93	20.04	18.37	16.88	15.55	14.36	13.30	12.34	11.47	56
57	26.51	24.21	22.18	20.38	18.77	17.34	16.05	14.90	13.86	12.92	12.07	57
58	26.56	24.38	22.45	20.73	19.19	17.82	16.58	15.46	14.46	13.54	12.72	58
59	26.61	24.56	22.73	21.10	19.63	18.31	17.13	16.06	15.08	14.20	13.40	59
60	26.69	24.75	23.03	21.48	20.09	18.84	17.70	16.68	15.75	14.90	14.12	60

Table 21: Multipliers for loss of pension commencing age 65 (males)

Age at date of trial	Multiplier calculated with allowance for projected mortality from the 2002-based population projections and rate of return of											Age at date of trial
	0.0%	0.5%	1.0%	1.5%	2.0%	2.5%	3.0%	3.5%	4.0%	4.5%	5.0%	
0	19.92	13.50	9.19	6.28	4.30	2.96	2.04	1.42	0.98	0.69	0.48	0
1	20.00	13.62	9.32	6.39	4.41	3.05	2.11	1.47	1.03	0.72	0.51	1
2	19.98	13.68	9.40	6.48	4.49	3.12	2.17	1.52	1.07	0.75	0.53	2
3	19.96	13.73	9.49	6.58	4.58	3.19	2.24	1.57	1.11	0.78	0.56	3
4	19.93	13.78	9.57	6.67	4.66	3.27	2.30	1.63	1.15	0.82	0.58	4
5	19.91	13.84	9.65	6.76	4.75	3.35	2.37	1.68	1.20	0.86	0.61	5
6	19.88	13.89	9.74	6.85	4.84	3.43	2.44	1.74	1.24	0.89	0.64	6
7	19.85	13.94	9.82	6.95	4.93	3.51	2.51	1.80	1.29	0.93	0.67	7
8	19.82	13.99	9.91	7.04	5.02	3.59	2.58	1.86	1.34	0.97	0.71	8
9	19.79	14.04	9.99	7.14	5.11	3.68	2.65	1.92	1.39	1.02	0.74	9
10	19.76	14.09	10.08	7.23	5.21	3.77	2.73	1.99	1.45	1.06	0.78	10
11	19.73	14.14	10.16	7.33	5.31	3.85	2.81	2.05	1.50	1.11	0.82	11
12	19.70	14.18	10.25	7.43	5.40	3.94	2.89	2.12	1.56	1.15	0.86	12
13	19.67	14.23	10.33	7.53	5.50	4.04	2.97	2.19	1.62	1.20	0.90	13
14	19.63	14.28	10.42	7.63	5.61	4.13	3.06	2.27	1.69	1.26	0.94	14
15	19.60	14.33	10.51	7.73	5.71	4.23	3.14	2.34	1.75	1.31	0.99	15
16	19.57	14.37	10.60	7.84	5.82	4.33	3.23	2.42	1.82	1.37	1.03	16
17	19.53	14.42	10.68	7.94	5.92	4.43	3.32	2.50	1.89	1.43	1.08	17
18	19.50	14.47	10.78	8.05	6.03	4.54	3.42	2.59	1.96	1.49	1.14	18
19	19.48	14.53	10.87	8.16	6.15	4.64	3.52	2.67	2.04	1.56	1.19	19
20	19.45	14.58	10.96	8.27	6.26	4.75	3.62	2.76	2.12	1.63	1.25	20
21	19.42	14.63	11.06	8.39	6.38	4.87	3.72	2.86	2.20	1.70	1.31	21
22	19.39	14.68	11.15	8.50	6.50	4.98	3.83	2.95	2.28	1.77	1.38	22
23	19.36	14.73	11.25	8.62	6.62	5.10	3.94	3.05	2.37	1.85	1.44	23
24	19.33	14.79	11.35	8.73	6.74	5.22	4.06	3.16	2.47	1.93	1.52	24
25	19.30	14.84	11.44	8.85	6.87	5.35	4.17	3.26	2.56	2.01	1.59	25
26	19.27	14.89	11.54	8.97	7.00	5.47	4.29	3.37	2.66	2.10	1.67	26
27	19.24	14.94	11.64	9.09	7.13	5.60	4.41	3.49	2.76	2.20	1.75	27
28	19.20	14.99	11.74	9.22	7.26	5.73	4.54	3.61	2.87	2.29	1.83	28
29	19.17	15.04	11.83	9.34	7.39	5.87	4.67	3.73	2.98	2.39	1.92	29
30	19.14	15.09	11.93	9.47	7.53	6.01	4.80	3.85	3.10	2.50	2.02	30
31	19.10	15.14	12.03	9.59	7.67	6.15	4.94	3.98	3.22	2.61	2.12	31
32	19.06	15.19	12.13	9.72	7.81	6.29	5.08	4.12	3.34	2.72	2.22	32
33	19.03	15.23	12.23	9.85	7.95	6.44	5.23	4.25	3.47	2.84	2.33	33
34	18.99	15.28	12.33	9.98	8.10	6.59	5.38	4.40	3.60	2.96	2.44	34
35	18.95	15.33	12.43	10.11	8.25	6.74	5.53	4.54	3.74	3.09	2.56	35
36	18.91	15.37	12.53	10.25	8.40	6.90	5.69	4.70	3.89	3.23	2.68	36
37	18.87	15.42	12.63	10.38	8.55	7.06	5.85	4.85	4.04	3.37	2.81	37
38	18.83	15.46	12.74	10.52	8.71	7.23	6.01	5.02	4.19	3.51	2.95	38
39	18.79	15.51	12.84	10.65	8.86	7.39	6.18	5.18	4.35	3.67	3.09	39
40	18.75	15.55	12.94	10.79	9.03	7.57	6.36	5.36	4.52	3.83	3.24	40
41	18.71	15.60	13.04	10.93	9.19	7.74	6.54	5.53	4.70	3.99	3.40	41
42	18.67	15.65	13.15	11.08	9.36	7.92	6.72	5.72	4.88	4.17	3.57	42
43	18.63	15.69	13.26	11.22	9.53	8.11	6.92	5.91	5.07	4.35	3.74	43
44	18.59	15.74	13.36	11.37	9.70	8.30	7.11	6.11	5.26	4.54	3.92	44
45	18.56	15.79	13.48	11.53	9.88	8.50	7.32	6.32	5.47	4.74	4.12	45
46	18.53	15.85	13.59	11.68	10.07	8.70	7.53	6.53	5.68	4.95	4.32	46
47	18.50	15.90	13.71	11.85	10.26	8.91	7.75	6.76	5.90	5.17	4.53	47
48	18.47	15.96	13.83	12.01	10.45	9.12	7.98	6.99	6.14	5.40	4.76	48
49	18.44	16.02	13.95	12.18	10.65	9.34	8.21	7.23	6.38	5.64	4.99	49
50	18.42	16.08	14.08	12.35	10.86	9.57	8.45	7.48	6.63	5.89	5.24	50
51	18.39	16.14	14.20	12.52	11.07	9.80	8.70	7.74	6.89	6.15	5.50	51
52	18.37	16.21	14.33	12.70	11.28	10.04	8.96	8.01	7.17	6.43	5.78	52
53	18.35	16.27	14.46	12.88	11.50	10.29	9.22	8.28	7.46	6.72	6.07	53
54	18.34	16.35	14.60	13.07	11.73	10.55	9.50	8.58	7.76	7.03	6.38	54

Table 21: Multipliers for loss of pension commencing age 65 (males) *continued*

Age at date of trial	Multiplier calculated with allowance for projected mortality from the 2002-based population projections and rate of return of											Age at date of trial
	0.0%	*0.5%*	*1.0%*	*1.5%*	*2.0%*	*2.5%*	*3.0%*	*3.5%*	*4.0%*	*4.5%*	*5.0%*	
55	18.34	16.43	14.75	13.27	11.97	10.82	9.79	8.88	8.07	7.35	6.70	55
56	18.34	16.52	14.91	13.48	12.22	11.10	10.10	9.21	8.41	7.69	7.05	56
57	18.36	16.62	15.08	13.71	12.49	11.40	10.42	9.55	8.77	8.06	7.42	57
58	18.40	16.74	15.26	13.95	12.77	11.71	10.77	9.91	9.14	8.45	7.82	58
59	18.44	16.87	15.46	14.20	13.07	12.05	11.13	10.30	9.55	8.86	8.24	59
60	18.51	17.01	15.67	14.47	13.38	12.40	11.51	10.71	9.97	9.31	8.70	60
61	18.59	17.18	15.91	14.76	13.72	12.78	11.92	11.14	10.43	9.78	9.19	61
62	18.69	17.36	16.16	15.07	14.08	13.18	12.36	11.61	10.92	10.29	9.71	62
63	18.81	17.56	16.43	15.41	14.47	13.61	12.83	12.11	11.45	10.84	10.28	63
64	18.95	17.78	16.73	15.76	14.88	14.07	13.32	12.64	12.01	11.43	10.89	64
65	19.10	18.02	17.03	16.13	15.31	14.55	13.85	13.21	12.61	12.06	11.55	65

Table 22: Multipliers for loss of pension commencing age 65 (females)

Age at date of trial	Multiplier calculated with allowance for projected mortality from the 2002-based population projections and rate of return of											Age at date of trial
	0.0%	0.5%	1.0%	1.5%	2.0%	2.5%	3.0%	3.5%	4.0%	4.5%	5.0%	
0	23.16	15.62	10.58	7.19	4.91	3.36	2.31	1.60	1.11	0.77	0.54	0
1	23.24	15.75	10.72	7.33	5.03	3.46	2.39	1.66	1.15	0.81	0.56	1
2	23.23	15.82	10.82	7.43	5.12	3.55	2.46	1.72	1.20	0.84	0.59	2
3	23.21	15.89	10.92	7.54	5.22	3.63	2.53	1.77	1.25	0.88	0.62	3
4	23.19	15.96	11.03	7.65	5.32	3.72	2.61	1.84	1.30	0.92	0.65	4
5	23.17	16.02	11.13	7.76	5.43	3.81	2.68	1.90	1.35	0.96	0.68	5
6	23.14	16.09	11.23	7.86	5.53	3.90	2.76	1.96	1.40	1.00	0.72	6
7	23.12	16.15	11.33	7.98	5.64	4.00	2.84	2.03	1.45	1.05	0.75	7
8	23.10	16.22	11.43	8.09	5.74	4.09	2.93	2.10	1.51	1.09	0.79	8
9	23.07	16.28	11.53	8.20	5.85	4.19	3.01	2.17	1.57	1.14	0.83	9
10	23.05	16.35	11.64	8.32	5.96	4.29	3.10	2.25	1.63	1.19	0.87	10
11	23.02	16.41	11.74	8.43	6.08	4.39	3.19	2.32	1.70	1.24	0.91	11
12	23.00	16.47	11.85	8.55	6.19	4.50	3.28	2.40	1.76	1.30	0.96	12
13	22.97	16.54	11.95	8.67	6.31	4.61	3.38	2.48	1.83	1.35	1.00	13
14	22.94	16.60	12.06	8.79	6.43	4.72	3.47	2.57	1.90	1.41	1.05	14
15	22.91	16.66	12.16	8.91	6.55	4.83	3.58	2.65	1.98	1.48	1.11	15
16	22.88	16.73	12.27	9.04	6.67	4.95	3.68	2.74	2.05	1.54	1.16	16
17	22.86	16.79	12.38	9.16	6.80	5.07	3.79	2.84	2.13	1.61	1.22	17
18	22.83	16.86	12.49	9.29	6.93	5.19	3.90	2.93	2.22	1.68	1.28	18
19	22.80	16.92	12.60	9.42	7.06	5.31	4.01	3.03	2.30	1.75	1.34	19
20	22.77	16.98	12.71	9.55	7.19	5.44	4.12	3.14	2.39	1.83	1.41	20
21	22.74	17.05	12.82	9.68	7.33	5.57	4.24	3.24	2.49	1.91	1.47	21
22	22.71	17.11	12.93	9.81	7.47	5.70	4.37	3.35	2.58	2.00	1.55	22
23	22.68	17.17	13.05	9.95	7.61	5.84	4.49	3.47	2.68	2.08	1.62	23
24	22.64	17.23	13.16	10.08	7.75	5.98	4.62	3.59	2.79	2.18	1.70	24
25	22.61	17.29	13.27	10.22	7.89	6.12	4.75	3.71	2.90	2.27	1.79	25
26	22.57	17.35	13.39	10.36	8.04	6.26	4.89	3.83	3.01	2.37	1.87	26
27	22.54	17.41	13.50	10.50	8.19	6.41	5.03	3.96	3.13	2.47	1.96	27
28	22.50	17.47	13.62	10.64	8.34	6.56	5.18	4.09	3.25	2.58	2.06	28
29	22.46	17.53	13.73	10.79	8.50	6.72	5.32	4.23	3.37	2.70	2.16	29
30	22.43	17.59	13.85	10.93	8.66	6.88	5.48	4.38	3.50	2.81	2.27	30
31	22.39	17.65	13.96	11.08	8.82	7.04	5.63	4.52	3.64	2.94	2.38	31
32	22.35	17.71	14.08	11.23	8.98	7.20	5.79	4.67	3.78	3.07	2.49	32
33	22.31	17.77	14.20	11.38	9.15	7.37	5.96	4.83	3.93	3.20	2.61	33
34	22.27	17.83	14.32	11.53	9.31	7.55	6.13	4.99	4.08	3.34	2.74	34
35	22.23	17.88	14.43	11.68	9.49	7.72	6.31	5.16	4.24	3.49	2.87	35
36	22.19	17.94	14.55	11.84	9.66	7.91	6.49	5.34	4.40	3.64	3.01	36
37	22.15	18.00	14.68	12.00	9.84	8.09	6.67	5.51	4.57	3.80	3.16	37
38	22.11	18.06	14.80	12.16	10.02	8.28	6.86	5.70	4.75	3.96	3.32	38
39	22.06	18.12	14.92	12.32	10.21	8.48	7.06	5.89	4.93	4.14	3.48	39
40	22.02	18.18	15.04	12.49	10.39	8.68	7.26	6.09	5.12	4.32	3.65	40
41	21.98	18.23	15.17	12.65	10.59	8.88	7.47	6.30	5.32	4.51	3.83	41
42	21.95	18.30	15.30	12.83	10.78	9.09	7.68	6.51	5.53	4.70	4.01	42
43	21.91	18.36	15.43	13.00	10.98	9.31	7.90	6.73	5.74	4.91	4.21	43
44	21.87	18.42	15.56	13.18	11.19	9.53	8.13	6.96	5.97	5.13	4.42	44
45	21.84	18.49	15.69	13.36	11.40	9.75	8.37	7.19	6.20	5.35	4.63	45
46	21.81	18.55	15.83	13.54	11.62	9.99	8.61	7.44	6.44	5.59	4.86	46
47	21.77	18.62	15.97	13.73	11.84	10.23	8.86	7.69	6.70	5.84	5.10	47
48	21.75	18.69	16.11	13.92	12.06	10.48	9.12	7.96	6.96	6.10	5.36	48
49	21.72	18.77	16.26	14.12	12.29	10.73	9.39	8.23	7.23	6.37	5.62	49
50	21.70	18.84	16.40	14.32	12.53	10.99	9.67	8.52	7.52	6.66	5.90	50
51	21.68	18.92	16.56	14.53	12.78	11.26	9.95	8.81	7.82	6.96	6.20	51
52	21.66	19.00	16.71	14.74	13.03	11.54	10.25	9.12	8.14	7.27	6.51	52
53	21.65	19.09	16.88	14.96	13.29	11.83	10.56	9.44	8.46	7.60	6.84	53
54	21.64	19.18	17.04	15.18	13.56	12.13	10.88	9.78	8.81	7.95	7.19	54

Table 22: Multipliers for loss of pension commencing age 65 (females) *continued*

Age at date of trial	Multiplier calculated with allowance for projected mortality from the 2002-based population projections and rate of return of											Age at date of trial
	0.0%	*0.5%*	*1.0%*	*1.5%*	*2.0%*	*2.5%*	*3.0%*	*3.5%*	*4.0%*	*4.5%*	*5.0%*	
55	21.64	19.28	17.22	15.42	13.83	12.44	11.22	10.13	9.17	8.31	7.55	55
56	21.65	19.39	17.40	15.66	14.12	12.77	11.56	10.50	9.55	8.70	7.94	56
57	21.66	19.50	17.59	15.91	14.42	13.10	11.93	10.88	9.95	9.11	8.36	57
58	21.69	19.62	17.80	16.18	14.74	13.46	12.31	11.29	10.37	9.54	8.80	58
59	21.72	19.75	18.01	16.45	15.06	13.82	12.71	11.71	10.81	10.00	9.26	59
60	21.77	19.90	18.23	16.74	15.41	14.21	13.13	12.16	11.28	10.48	9.76	60
61	21.82	20.05	18.47	17.04	15.77	14.61	13.57	12.63	11.77	10.99	10.28	61
62	21.89	20.22	18.71	17.36	16.14	15.03	14.03	13.12	12.29	11.54	10.85	62
63	21.96	20.39	18.97	17.69	16.53	15.47	14.52	13.64	12.84	12.11	11.44	63
64	22.04	20.57	19.24	18.03	16.93	15.93	15.02	14.18	13.42	12.72	12.07	64
65	22.12	20.75	19.51	18.38	17.34	16.40	15.54	14.75	14.03	13.36	12.75	65

Table 23: Multipliers for loss of pension commencing age 70 (males)

Age at date of trial	Multiplier calculated with allowance for projected mortality from the 2002-based population projections and rate of return of											Age at date of trial
	0.0%	0.5%	1.0%	1.5%	2.0%	2.5%	3.0%	3.5%	4.0%	4.5%	5.0%	
0	15.54	10.37	6.95	4.67	3.15	2.13	1.45	0.98	0.67	0.46	0.32	0
1	15.59	10.46	7.04	4.76	3.22	2.19	1.50	1.02	0.70	0.48	0.33	1
2	15.58	10.50	7.11	4.82	3.29	2.24	1.54	1.06	0.73	0.50	0.35	2
3	15.56	10.54	7.17	4.89	3.35	2.30	1.58	1.09	0.76	0.53	0.37	3
4	15.53	10.58	7.23	4.96	3.41	2.35	1.63	1.13	0.79	0.55	0.38	4
5	15.51	10.62	7.29	5.02	3.47	2.41	1.67	1.17	0.82	0.57	0.40	5
6	15.49	10.65	7.35	5.09	3.54	2.46	1.72	1.21	0.85	0.60	0.42	6
7	15.46	10.69	7.42	5.16	3.60	2.52	1.77	1.25	0.88	0.62	0.44	7
8	15.43	10.73	7.48	5.23	3.67	2.58	1.82	1.29	0.92	0.65	0.47	8
9	15.41	10.76	7.54	5.30	3.74	2.64	1.87	1.33	0.95	0.68	0.49	9
10	15.38	10.80	7.60	5.37	3.80	2.70	1.93	1.38	0.99	0.71	0.51	10
11	15.35	10.83	7.66	5.44	3.87	2.77	1.98	1.42	1.03	0.74	0.54	11
12	15.32	10.86	7.73	5.51	3.95	2.83	2.04	1.47	1.06	0.77	0.56	12
13	15.29	10.90	7.79	5.59	4.02	2.90	2.10	1.52	1.11	0.81	0.59	13
14	15.26	10.93	7.85	5.66	4.09	2.96	2.15	1.57	1.15	0.84	0.62	14
15	15.23	10.96	7.92	5.73	4.16	3.03	2.22	1.62	1.19	0.88	0.65	15
16	15.20	11.00	7.98	5.81	4.24	3.10	2.28	1.68	1.24	0.92	0.68	16
17	15.17	11.03	8.04	5.88	4.32	3.18	2.34	1.73	1.28	0.95	0.71	17
18	15.14	11.07	8.11	5.96	4.40	3.25	2.41	1.79	1.33	1.00	0.75	18
19	15.12	11.10	8.18	6.04	4.48	3.33	2.48	1.85	1.39	1.04	0.78	19
20	15.09	11.14	8.25	6.12	4.56	3.40	2.55	1.91	1.44	1.09	0.82	20
21	15.06	11.17	8.31	6.20	4.64	3.48	2.62	1.98	1.49	1.13	0.86	21
22	15.03	11.21	8.38	6.29	4.73	3.56	2.69	2.04	1.55	1.18	0.90	22
23	15.00	11.25	8.45	6.37	4.81	3.65	2.77	2.11	1.61	1.23	0.95	23
24	14.97	11.28	8.52	6.45	4.90	3.73	2.85	2.18	1.67	1.29	0.99	24
25	14.94	11.31	8.59	6.54	4.99	3.82	2.93	2.25	1.74	1.34	1.04	25
26	14.91	11.35	8.66	6.62	5.08	3.91	3.01	2.33	1.80	1.40	1.09	26
27	14.88	11.38	8.73	6.71	5.17	4.00	3.10	2.41	1.87	1.46	1.14	27
28	14.85	11.42	8.80	6.80	5.27	4.09	3.19	2.49	1.94	1.52	1.20	28
29	14.82	11.45	8.87	6.89	5.36	4.19	3.27	2.57	2.02	1.59	1.26	29
30	14.79	11.48	8.94	6.98	5.46	4.28	3.37	2.65	2.10	1.66	1.32	30
31	14.75	11.51	9.01	7.07	5.56	4.38	3.46	2.74	2.18	1.73	1.38	31
32	14.72	11.54	9.08	7.16	5.66	4.48	3.56	2.83	2.26	1.81	1.45	32
33	14.68	11.57	9.15	7.25	5.76	4.58	3.66	2.93	2.34	1.88	1.52	33
34	14.64	11.60	9.22	7.34	5.86	4.69	3.76	3.02	2.43	1.96	1.59	34
35	14.61	11.63	9.29	7.43	5.96	4.79	3.86	3.12	2.53	2.05	1.67	35
36	14.57	11.66	9.36	7.53	6.07	4.90	3.97	3.22	2.62	2.14	1.75	36
37	14.53	11.69	9.43	7.62	6.17	5.01	4.08	3.33	2.72	2.23	1.83	37
38	14.49	11.71	9.50	7.71	6.28	5.13	4.19	3.44	2.82	2.32	1.92	38
39	14.45	11.74	9.56	7.81	6.39	5.24	4.31	3.55	2.93	2.42	2.01	39
40	14.41	11.77	9.63	7.91	6.50	5.36	4.43	3.67	3.04	2.53	2.10	40
41	14.36	11.79	9.71	8.00	6.62	5.48	4.55	3.79	3.16	2.64	2.20	41
42	14.32	11.82	9.78	8.10	6.73	5.61	4.68	3.91	3.27	2.75	2.31	42
43	14.28	11.85	9.85	8.21	6.85	5.73	4.81	4.04	3.40	2.87	2.42	43
44	14.25	11.88	9.92	8.31	6.97	5.86	4.94	4.17	3.53	2.99	2.54	44
45	14.21	11.90	10.00	8.41	7.10	6.00	5.08	4.31	3.66	3.12	2.66	45
46	14.17	11.94	10.07	8.52	7.22	6.13	5.22	4.45	3.80	3.25	2.79	46
47	14.14	11.97	10.15	8.63	7.35	6.28	5.37	4.60	3.95	3.39	2.92	47
48	14.10	12.00	10.23	8.74	7.49	6.42	5.52	4.75	4.10	3.54	3.07	48
49	14.07	12.03	10.31	8.86	7.62	6.57	5.68	4.91	4.26	3.70	3.21	49
50	14.04	12.07	10.40	8.97	7.76	6.72	5.84	5.08	4.42	3.86	3.37	50
51	14.01	12.10	10.48	9.09	7.90	6.88	6.00	5.25	4.59	4.03	3.54	51
52	13.98	12.14	10.56	9.21	8.05	7.04	6.17	5.42	4.77	4.20	3.71	52
53	13.95	12.18	10.65	9.33	8.19	7.21	6.35	5.60	4.95	4.39	3.89	53
54	13.93	12.22	10.74	9.46	8.35	7.38	6.53	5.80	5.15	4.58	4.08	54

Table 23: Multipliers for loss of pension commencing age 70 (males) *continued*

Age at date of trial	Multiplier calculated with allowance for projected mortality from the 2002-based population projections and rate of return of											Age at date of trial
	0.0%	*0.5%*	*1.0%*	*1.5%*	*2.0%*	*2.5%*	*3.0%*	*3.5%*	*4.0%*	*4.5%*	*5.0%*	
55	13.91	12.26	10.84	9.59	8.51	7.56	6.73	6.00	5.35	4.79	4.29	55
56	13.90	12.32	10.94	9.74	8.68	7.75	6.93	6.21	5.57	5.00	4.50	56
57	13.90	12.38	11.05	9.88	8.86	7.95	7.14	6.43	5.80	5.24	4.73	57
58	13.90	12.45	11.17	10.04	9.04	8.16	7.37	6.67	6.04	5.48	4.98	58
59	13.92	12.53	11.30	10.21	9.24	8.38	7.60	6.91	6.30	5.74	5.24	59
60	13.95	12.62	11.44	10.39	9.45	8.61	7.86	7.18	6.57	6.02	5.52	60
61	13.99	12.73	11.60	10.58	9.68	8.86	8.12	7.46	6.86	6.32	5.83	61
62	14.05	12.85	11.77	10.79	9.92	9.13	8.41	7.76	7.17	6.64	6.15	62
63	14.12	12.98	11.95	11.02	10.17	9.41	8.72	8.08	7.51	6.98	6.50	63
64	14.20	13.12	12.14	11.25	10.45	9.71	9.04	8.43	7.86	7.35	6.88	64
65	14.29	13.27	12.34	11.50	10.73	10.02	9.38	8.79	8.24	7.74	7.28	65
66	14.39	13.43	12.56	11.76	11.02	10.35	9.73	9.16	8.64	8.16	7.71	66
67	14.49	13.59	12.78	12.02	11.33	10.70	10.11	9.57	9.06	8.60	8.17	67
68	14.60	13.77	13.01	12.31	11.66	11.06	10.51	9.99	9.52	9.07	8.66	68
69	14.73	13.97	13.26	12.61	12.01	11.45	10.94	10.45	10.00	9.59	9.19	69
70	14.89	14.19	13.55	12.95	12.40	11.88	11.41	10.96	10.54	10.15	9.78	70

Table 24: Multipliers for loss of pension commencing age 70 (females)

Age at date of trial	Multiplier calculated with allowance for projected mortality from the 2002-based population projections and rate of return of											Age at date of trial
	0.0%	0.5%	1.0%	1.5%	2.0%	2.5%	3.0%	3.5%	4.0%	4.5%	5.0%	
0	18.57	12.34	8.23	5.51	3.70	2.50	1.69	1.15	0.78	0.53	0.36	0
1	18.63	12.45	8.34	5.61	3.79	2.57	1.74	1.19	0.81	0.56	0.38	1
2	18.62	12.50	8.42	5.69	3.86	2.63	1.80	1.23	0.85	0.58	0.40	2
3	18.60	12.55	8.50	5.77	3.94	2.69	1.85	1.27	0.88	0.61	0.42	3
4	18.58	12.60	8.58	5.86	4.01	2.76	1.90	1.32	0.91	0.64	0.44	4
5	18.56	12.65	8.65	5.94	4.09	2.82	1.96	1.36	0.95	0.66	0.47	5
6	18.54	12.70	8.73	6.02	4.17	2.89	2.01	1.41	0.99	0.69	0.49	6
7	18.52	12.75	8.81	6.10	4.25	2.96	2.07	1.45	1.02	0.72	0.51	7
8	18.50	12.80	8.89	6.19	4.33	3.03	2.13	1.50	1.06	0.76	0.54	8
9	18.47	12.85	8.96	6.27	4.41	3.10	2.19	1.56	1.11	0.79	0.56	9
10	18.45	12.89	9.04	6.36	4.49	3.18	2.26	1.61	1.15	0.82	0.59	10
11	18.43	12.94	9.12	6.45	4.57	3.25	2.32	1.66	1.19	0.86	0.62	11
12	18.40	12.99	9.20	6.54	4.66	3.33	2.39	1.72	1.24	0.90	0.65	12
13	18.37	13.04	9.28	6.63	4.75	3.41	2.46	1.78	1.29	0.94	0.68	13
14	18.35	13.08	9.36	6.72	4.84	3.49	2.53	1.84	1.34	0.98	0.72	14
15	18.32	13.13	9.44	6.81	4.93	3.58	2.60	1.90	1.39	1.02	0.75	15
16	18.30	13.18	9.52	6.90	5.02	3.66	2.68	1.96	1.44	1.06	0.79	16
17	18.27	13.23	9.61	7.00	5.11	3.75	2.75	2.03	1.50	1.11	0.83	17
18	18.24	13.27	9.69	7.09	5.21	3.84	2.83	2.10	1.56	1.16	0.87	18
19	18.22	13.32	9.77	7.19	5.31	3.93	2.91	2.17	1.62	1.21	0.91	19
20	18.19	13.37	9.86	7.29	5.40	4.02	3.00	2.24	1.68	1.26	0.95	20
21	18.16	13.41	9.94	7.39	5.50	4.11	3.08	2.32	1.75	1.32	1.00	21
22	18.13	13.46	10.02	7.49	5.61	4.21	3.17	2.40	1.81	1.38	1.05	22
23	18.10	13.50	10.11	7.59	5.71	4.31	3.26	2.48	1.88	1.44	1.10	23
24	18.07	13.55	10.19	7.69	5.82	4.41	3.36	2.56	1.96	1.50	1.15	24
25	18.04	13.59	10.28	7.79	5.92	4.51	3.45	2.64	2.03	1.57	1.21	25
26	18.00	13.64	10.36	7.89	6.03	4.62	3.55	2.73	2.11	1.63	1.27	26
27	17.97	13.68	10.45	8.00	6.14	4.73	3.65	2.82	2.19	1.70	1.33	27
28	17.93	13.72	10.53	8.10	6.25	4.84	3.75	2.92	2.28	1.78	1.39	28
29	17.90	13.77	10.62	8.21	6.37	4.95	3.86	3.02	2.36	1.86	1.46	29
30	17.86	13.81	10.70	8.32	6.48	5.07	3.97	3.12	2.45	1.94	1.53	30
31	17.83	13.85	10.79	8.43	6.60	5.18	4.08	3.22	2.55	2.02	1.61	31
32	17.79	13.89	10.88	8.54	6.72	5.30	4.20	3.33	2.64	2.11	1.68	32
33	17.75	13.93	10.96	8.65	6.84	5.43	4.31	3.44	2.75	2.20	1.76	33
34	17.71	13.97	11.05	8.76	6.97	5.55	4.44	3.55	2.85	2.29	1.85	34
35	17.67	14.01	11.14	8.88	7.09	5.68	4.56	3.67	2.96	2.39	1.94	35
36	17.63	14.05	11.22	8.99	7.22	5.81	4.69	3.79	3.07	2.50	2.03	36
37	17.59	14.09	11.31	9.11	7.35	5.94	4.82	3.92	3.19	2.60	2.13	37
38	17.55	14.13	11.40	9.22	7.48	6.08	4.96	4.05	3.31	2.72	2.23	38
39	17.51	14.17	11.49	9.34	7.62	6.22	5.09	4.18	3.44	2.83	2.34	39
40	17.47	14.21	11.58	9.46	7.75	6.36	5.24	4.32	3.57	2.96	2.45	40
41	17.43	14.25	11.67	9.59	7.89	6.51	5.39	4.46	3.71	3.09	2.57	41
42	17.39	14.29	11.76	9.71	8.03	6.66	5.54	4.61	3.85	3.22	2.70	42
43	17.36	14.33	11.86	9.84	8.18	6.82	5.69	4.77	4.00	3.36	2.83	43
44	17.32	14.37	11.95	9.97	8.33	6.97	5.85	4.92	4.15	3.50	2.97	44
45	17.28	14.41	12.05	10.10	8.48	7.14	6.02	5.09	4.31	3.66	3.11	45
46	17.25	14.46	12.15	10.23	8.64	7.30	6.19	5.26	4.48	3.82	3.26	46
47	17.21	14.50	12.25	10.37	8.79	7.48	6.37	5.44	4.65	3.98	3.42	47
48	17.18	14.55	12.35	10.50	8.96	7.65	6.55	5.62	4.83	4.16	3.59	48
49	17.15	14.60	12.45	10.65	9.12	7.83	6.74	5.81	5.02	4.34	3.76	49
50	17.12	14.65	12.56	10.79	9.29	8.02	6.93	6.01	5.21	4.53	3.95	50
51	17.09	14.70	12.67	10.94	9.47	8.21	7.13	6.21	5.42	4.73	4.14	51
52	17.07	14.75	12.78	11.09	9.65	8.41	7.34	6.42	5.63	4.94	4.35	52
53	17.04	14.81	12.89	11.25	9.83	8.61	7.56	6.64	5.85	5.16	4.56	53
54	17.03	14.87	13.01	11.41	10.02	8.82	7.78	6.88	6.09	5.40	4.79	54

Table 24: Multipliers for loss of pension commencing age 70 (females) *continued*

Age at date of trial	Multiplier calculated with allowance for projected mortality from the 2002-based population projections and rate of return of											Age at date of trial
	0.0%	*0.5%*	*1.0%*	*1.5%*	*2.0%*	*2.5%*	*3.0%*	*3.5%*	*4.0%*	*4.5%*	*5.0%*	
55	17.01	14.93	13.13	11.57	10.22	9.04	8.01	7.12	6.33	5.64	5.03	55
56	17.01	15.00	13.26	11.75	10.43	9.27	8.26	7.37	6.59	5.90	5.29	56
57	17.01	15.08	13.40	11.93	10.64	9.51	8.51	7.63	6.86	6.17	5.56	57
58	17.01	15.16	13.54	12.12	10.86	9.75	8.78	7.91	7.14	6.46	5.85	58
59	17.03	15.25	13.69	12.31	11.09	10.01	9.05	8.20	7.44	6.76	6.15	59
60	17.05	15.35	13.85	12.52	11.34	10.28	9.34	8.50	7.75	7.08	6.47	60
61	17.08	15.46	14.02	12.73	11.59	10.57	9.65	8.83	8.09	7.42	6.82	61
62	17.11	15.57	14.19	12.96	11.85	10.86	9.97	9.16	8.44	7.78	7.18	62
63	17.16	15.69	14.37	13.19	12.13	11.17	10.30	9.52	8.80	8.16	7.57	63
64	17.20	15.81	14.56	13.43	12.41	11.48	10.65	9.88	9.19	8.56	7.98	64
65	17.24	15.93	14.75	13.67	12.70	11.81	11.00	10.27	9.59	8.98	8.41	65
66	17.28	16.05	14.93	13.92	12.99	12.15	11.37	10.66	10.01	9.42	8.87	66
67	17.32	16.17	15.12	14.17	13.29	12.49	11.75	11.08	10.45	9.88	9.35	67
68	17.36	16.29	15.31	14.42	13.60	12.84	12.15	11.51	10.92	10.37	9.86	68
69	17.40	16.41	15.51	14.68	13.92	13.21	12.56	11.96	11.40	10.88	10.40	69
70	17.45	16.55	15.73	14.96	14.26	13.61	13.01	12.45	11.92	11.44	10.99	70

Table 25: Multipliers for loss of pension commencing age 75 (males)

Age at date of trial	Multiplier calculated with allowance for projected mortality from the 2002-based population projections and rate of return of											Age at date of trial
	0.0%	0.5%	1.0%	1.5%	2.0%	2.5%	3.0%	3.5%	4.0%	4.5%	5.0%	
0	11.43	7.51	4.95	3.27	2.17	1.44	0.96	0.64	0.43	0.29	0.20	0
1	11.47	7.57	5.02	3.33	2.22	1.48	1.00	0.67	0.45	0.31	0.21	1
2	11.45	7.60	5.06	3.38	2.26	1.52	1.02	0.69	0.47	0.32	0.22	2
3	11.43	7.63	5.10	3.42	2.30	1.56	1.05	0.72	0.49	0.33	0.23	3
4	11.41	7.65	5.14	3.47	2.35	1.59	1.08	0.74	0.51	0.35	0.24	4
5	11.39	7.68	5.19	3.52	2.39	1.63	1.11	0.76	0.52	0.36	0.25	5
6	11.37	7.70	5.23	3.56	2.43	1.67	1.15	0.79	0.54	0.38	0.26	6
7	11.35	7.72	5.27	3.61	2.48	1.71	1.18	0.82	0.57	0.39	0.27	7
8	11.33	7.75	5.31	3.66	2.52	1.75	1.21	0.84	0.59	0.41	0.29	8
9	11.30	7.77	5.36	3.70	2.57	1.79	1.24	0.87	0.61	0.43	0.30	9
10	11.28	7.79	5.40	3.75	2.61	1.83	1.28	0.90	0.63	0.45	0.32	10
11	11.25	7.81	5.44	3.80	2.66	1.87	1.32	0.93	0.66	0.47	0.33	11
12	11.23	7.84	5.48	3.85	2.71	1.91	1.35	0.96	0.68	0.49	0.35	12
13	11.20	7.86	5.53	3.90	2.76	1.95	1.39	0.99	0.71	0.51	0.36	13
14	11.18	7.88	5.57	3.95	2.81	2.00	1.43	1.02	0.73	0.53	0.38	14
15	11.15	7.90	5.61	4.00	2.86	2.04	1.47	1.06	0.76	0.55	0.40	15
16	11.12	7.92	5.65	4.05	2.91	2.09	1.51	1.09	0.79	0.57	0.42	16
17	11.10	7.94	5.70	4.10	2.96	2.14	1.55	1.13	0.82	0.60	0.44	17
18	11.07	7.96	5.74	4.15	3.01	2.19	1.59	1.16	0.85	0.63	0.46	18
19	11.05	7.99	5.79	4.21	3.06	2.24	1.64	1.20	0.88	0.65	0.48	19
20	11.02	8.01	5.83	4.26	3.12	2.29	1.68	1.24	0.92	0.68	0.51	20
21	11.00	8.03	5.88	4.31	3.18	2.34	1.73	1.28	0.95	0.71	0.53	21
22	10.97	8.05	5.92	4.37	3.23	2.40	1.78	1.33	0.99	0.74	0.56	22
23	10.95	8.07	5.97	4.43	3.29	2.45	1.83	1.37	1.03	0.77	0.58	23
24	10.92	8.09	6.01	4.48	3.35	2.51	1.88	1.41	1.07	0.81	0.61	24
25	10.89	8.11	6.06	4.54	3.41	2.56	1.93	1.46	1.11	0.84	0.64	25
26	10.86	8.13	6.11	4.59	3.47	2.62	1.99	1.51	1.15	0.88	0.67	26
27	10.83	8.15	6.15	4.65	3.53	2.68	2.04	1.56	1.19	0.91	0.70	27
28	10.80	8.17	6.20	4.71	3.59	2.74	2.10	1.61	1.24	0.95	0.73	28
29	10.77	8.19	6.24	4.77	3.65	2.80	2.15	1.66	1.28	0.99	0.77	29
30	10.74	8.21	6.29	4.83	3.71	2.86	2.21	1.71	1.33	1.03	0.81	30
31	10.71	8.23	6.33	4.89	3.78	2.93	2.27	1.77	1.38	1.08	0.84	31
32	10.68	8.24	6.38	4.94	3.84	2.99	2.34	1.83	1.43	1.12	0.88	32
33	10.65	8.26	6.42	5.00	3.91	3.06	2.40	1.89	1.48	1.17	0.93	33
34	10.61	8.27	6.47	5.06	3.98	3.13	2.46	1.95	1.54	1.22	0.97	34
35	10.58	8.29	6.51	5.12	4.04	3.20	2.53	2.01	1.60	1.27	1.02	35
36	10.54	8.30	6.55	5.18	4.11	3.27	2.60	2.07	1.66	1.33	1.06	36
37	10.50	8.32	6.60	5.25	4.18	3.34	2.67	2.14	1.72	1.38	1.11	37
38	10.47	8.33	6.64	5.31	4.25	3.41	2.74	2.21	1.78	1.44	1.17	38
39	10.43	8.34	6.68	5.37	4.32	3.48	2.81	2.28	1.85	1.50	1.22	39
40	10.39	8.35	6.73	5.43	4.39	3.56	2.89	2.35	1.91	1.56	1.28	40
41	10.35	8.36	6.77	5.49	4.46	3.64	2.97	2.42	1.98	1.63	1.34	41
42	10.31	8.37	6.81	5.55	4.54	3.71	3.04	2.50	2.06	1.70	1.40	42
43	10.27	8.39	6.86	5.62	4.61	3.79	3.13	2.58	2.13	1.77	1.47	43
44	10.24	8.40	6.90	5.68	4.69	3.88	3.21	2.66	2.21	1.84	1.54	44
45	10.20	8.41	6.95	5.75	4.77	3.96	3.30	2.75	2.29	1.92	1.61	45
46	10.16	8.42	6.99	5.82	4.85	4.05	3.38	2.84	2.38	2.00	1.68	46
47	10.13	8.44	7.04	5.88	4.93	4.14	3.48	2.93	2.47	2.08	1.76	47
48	10.09	8.45	7.09	5.95	5.01	4.23	3.57	3.02	2.56	2.17	1.85	48
49	10.06	8.46	7.13	6.02	5.10	4.32	3.67	3.12	2.65	2.26	1.93	49
50	10.02	8.48	7.18	6.10	5.18	4.41	3.77	3.22	2.75	2.36	2.03	50
51	9.99	8.49	7.23	6.17	5.27	4.51	3.87	3.32	2.86	2.46	2.12	51
52	9.95	8.50	7.28	6.24	5.36	4.61	3.97	3.43	2.96	2.56	2.22	52
53	9.92	8.52	7.33	6.32	5.45	4.71	4.08	3.54	3.07	2.67	2.33	53
54	9.89	8.54	7.38	6.39	5.55	4.82	4.19	3.65	3.19	2.79	2.44	54

Table 25: Multipliers for loss of pension commencing age 75 (males) *continued*

Age at date of trial	Multiplier calculated with allowance for projected mortality from the 2002-based population projections and rate of return of											Age at date of trial
	0.0%	*0.5%*	*1.0%*	*1.5%*	*2.0%*	*2.5%*	*3.0%*	*3.5%*	*4.0%*	*4.5%*	*5.0%*	
55	9.86	8.56	7.44	6.47	5.64	4.93	4.31	3.77	3.31	2.91	2.56	55
56	9.84	8.58	7.50	6.56	5.75	5.04	4.43	3.90	3.44	3.03	2.68	56
57	9.82	8.61	7.56	6.65	5.86	5.16	4.56	4.03	3.57	3.17	2.81	57
58	9.81	8.65	7.63	6.75	5.97	5.29	4.70	4.18	3.72	3.31	2.96	58
59	9.81	8.69	7.71	6.85	6.09	5.43	4.84	4.32	3.87	3.46	3.11	59
60	9.81	8.74	7.79	6.95	6.22	5.57	4.99	4.48	4.03	3.63	3.27	60
61	9.83	8.79	7.88	7.07	6.36	5.72	5.15	4.65	4.20	3.80	3.44	61
62	9.85	8.86	7.98	7.20	6.50	5.88	5.32	4.83	4.38	3.98	3.62	62
63	9.88	8.94	8.09	7.33	6.66	6.05	5.51	5.02	4.58	4.18	3.82	63
64	9.92	9.02	8.20	7.48	6.82	6.23	5.70	5.22	4.78	4.39	4.04	64
65	9.96	9.10	8.32	7.62	6.99	6.42	5.90	5.43	5.00	4.61	4.26	65
66	10.00	9.19	8.45	7.77	7.17	6.61	6.11	5.65	5.23	4.85	4.50	66
67	10.05	9.27	8.57	7.93	7.35	6.81	6.33	5.88	5.47	5.10	4.75	67
68	10.09	9.36	8.70	8.09	7.53	7.02	6.55	6.12	5.73	5.36	5.02	68
69	10.15	9.46	8.84	8.26	7.73	7.24	6.79	6.38	6.00	5.64	5.31	69
70	10.22	9.58	8.99	8.45	7.95	7.48	7.05	6.66	6.29	5.95	5.63	70
71	10.31	9.71	9.17	8.66	8.19	7.75	7.34	6.96	6.61	6.28	5.98	71
72	10.43	9.88	9.37	8.90	8.46	8.05	7.67	7.31	6.97	6.66	6.37	72
73	10.60	10.09	9.62	9.19	8.78	8.39	8.04	7.70	7.38	7.09	6.81	73
74	10.82	10.36	9.93	9.53	9.15	8.80	8.46	8.15	7.86	7.58	7.32	74
75	11.10	10.69	10.30	9.94	9.59	9.27	8.96	8.68	8.41	8.15	7.91	75

Table 26: Multipliers for loss of pension commencing age 75 (females)

Age at date of trial	Multiplier calculated with allowance for projected mortality from the 2002-based population projections and rate of return of											Age at date of trial
	0.0%	0.5%	1.0%	1.5%	2.0%	2.5%	3.0%	3.5%	4.0%	4.5%	5.0%	
0	14.16	9.27	6.09	4.01	2.65	1.76	1.17	0.78	0.52	0.35	0.24	0
1	14.21	9.35	6.17	4.09	2.72	1.81	1.21	0.81	0.55	0.37	0.25	1
2	14.19	9.39	6.23	4.15	2.77	1.85	1.24	0.84	0.57	0.38	0.26	2
3	14.18	9.42	6.28	4.20	2.82	1.90	1.28	0.87	0.59	0.40	0.27	3
4	14.16	9.46	6.34	4.26	2.87	1.94	1.32	0.90	0.61	0.42	0.29	4
5	14.14	9.50	6.39	4.32	2.93	1.99	1.36	0.93	0.64	0.44	0.30	5
6	14.12	9.53	6.45	4.38	2.98	2.04	1.39	0.96	0.66	0.46	0.32	6
7	14.11	9.57	6.51	4.44	3.04	2.09	1.44	0.99	0.69	0.48	0.33	7
8	14.08	9.60	6.56	4.50	3.09	2.13	1.48	1.02	0.71	0.50	0.35	8
9	14.06	9.63	6.62	4.56	3.15	2.18	1.52	1.06	0.74	0.52	0.36	9
10	14.04	9.67	6.68	4.62	3.21	2.24	1.56	1.09	0.77	0.54	0.38	10
11	14.02	9.70	6.73	4.69	3.27	2.29	1.61	1.13	0.80	0.56	0.40	11
12	14.00	9.73	6.79	4.75	3.33	2.34	1.65	1.17	0.83	0.59	0.42	12
13	13.98	9.77	6.85	4.81	3.39	2.40	1.70	1.21	0.86	0.61	0.44	13
14	13.95	9.80	6.90	4.88	3.46	2.45	1.75	1.25	0.89	0.64	0.46	14
15	13.93	9.83	6.96	4.94	3.52	2.51	1.80	1.29	0.93	0.67	0.48	15
16	13.91	9.87	7.02	5.01	3.58	2.57	1.85	1.33	0.96	0.70	0.51	16
17	13.88	9.90	7.08	5.08	3.65	2.63	1.90	1.38	1.00	0.73	0.53	17
18	13.86	9.93	7.14	5.14	3.72	2.69	1.96	1.42	1.04	0.76	0.56	18
19	13.83	9.96	7.20	5.21	3.78	2.76	2.01	1.47	1.08	0.79	0.58	19
20	13.81	9.99	7.25	5.28	3.85	2.82	2.07	1.52	1.12	0.83	0.61	20
21	13.78	10.03	7.31	5.35	3.92	2.88	2.13	1.57	1.16	0.86	0.64	21
22	13.75	10.06	7.37	5.42	3.99	2.95	2.19	1.62	1.21	0.90	0.67	22
23	13.72	10.09	7.43	5.49	4.07	3.02	2.25	1.68	1.25	0.94	0.71	23
24	13.70	10.12	7.49	5.56	4.14	3.09	2.31	1.73	1.30	0.98	0.74	24
25	13.67	10.15	7.55	5.63	4.22	3.16	2.38	1.79	1.35	1.02	0.78	25
26	13.64	10.17	7.61	5.71	4.29	3.23	2.44	1.85	1.40	1.07	0.81	26
27	13.61	10.20	7.67	5.78	4.37	3.31	2.51	1.91	1.46	1.11	0.85	27
28	13.57	10.23	7.73	5.85	4.45	3.38	2.58	1.97	1.51	1.16	0.89	28
29	13.54	10.26	7.79	5.93	4.52	3.46	2.65	2.04	1.57	1.21	0.94	29
30	13.51	10.28	7.85	6.00	4.60	3.54	2.73	2.11	1.63	1.26	0.98	30
31	13.47	10.31	7.91	6.08	4.69	3.62	2.80	2.17	1.69	1.32	1.03	31
32	13.44	10.34	7.97	6.16	4.77	3.70	2.88	2.25	1.75	1.37	1.08	32
33	13.40	10.36	8.03	6.23	4.85	3.79	2.96	2.32	1.82	1.43	1.13	33
34	13.37	10.39	8.09	6.31	4.94	3.87	3.04	2.39	1.89	1.49	1.18	34
35	13.33	10.41	8.15	6.39	5.02	3.96	3.13	2.47	1.96	1.56	1.24	35
36	13.30	10.43	8.21	6.47	5.11	4.05	3.21	2.55	2.03	1.62	1.30	36
37	13.26	10.46	8.27	6.55	5.20	4.14	3.30	2.64	2.11	1.69	1.36	37
38	13.22	10.48	8.33	6.63	5.29	4.23	3.39	2.72	2.19	1.77	1.43	38
39	13.18	10.50	8.39	6.71	5.38	4.33	3.48	2.81	2.27	1.84	1.49	39
40	13.14	10.53	8.45	6.79	5.48	4.42	3.58	2.90	2.36	1.92	1.56	40
41	13.11	10.55	8.51	6.88	5.57	4.52	3.68	3.00	2.45	2.00	1.64	41
42	13.07	10.57	8.57	6.96	5.67	4.62	3.78	3.09	2.54	2.09	1.72	42
43	13.03	10.60	8.63	7.05	5.77	4.73	3.88	3.19	2.63	2.17	1.80	43
44	12.99	10.62	8.70	7.14	5.87	4.83	3.99	3.30	2.73	2.27	1.88	44
45	12.96	10.64	8.76	7.22	5.97	4.94	4.10	3.41	2.84	2.36	1.98	45
46	12.92	10.67	8.82	7.31	6.07	5.05	4.21	3.52	2.94	2.47	2.07	46
47	12.89	10.69	8.89	7.41	6.18	5.17	4.33	3.63	3.05	2.57	2.17	47
48	12.85	10.72	8.96	7.50	6.29	5.29	4.45	3.75	3.17	2.68	2.27	48
49	12.82	10.75	9.02	7.59	6.40	5.41	4.57	3.88	3.29	2.80	2.38	49
50	12.79	10.77	9.09	7.69	6.52	5.53	4.70	4.00	3.42	2.92	2.50	50
51	12.75	10.80	9.16	7.79	6.63	5.66	4.83	4.14	3.55	3.04	2.62	51
52	12.73	10.83	9.24	7.89	6.75	5.79	4.97	4.27	3.68	3.18	2.74	52
53	12.70	10.86	9.31	7.99	6.87	5.92	5.11	4.42	3.82	3.31	2.88	53
54	12.67	10.90	9.39	8.10	7.00	6.06	5.26	4.57	3.97	3.46	3.02	54

Table 26: Multipliers for loss of pension commencing age 75 (females) *continued*

Age at date of trial	Multiplier calculated with allowance for projected mortality from the 2002-based population projections and rate of return of											Age at date of trial
	0.0%	*0.5%*	*1.0%*	*1.5%*	*2.0%*	*2.5%*	*3.0%*	*3.5%*	*4.0%*	*4.5%*	*5.0%*	
55	12.65	10.93	9.47	8.21	7.13	6.21	5.41	4.72	4.13	3.61	3.17	55
56	12.63	10.97	9.55	8.32	7.27	6.36	5.57	4.88	4.29	3.77	3.32	56
57	12.62	11.02	9.64	8.44	7.41	6.51	5.73	5.05	4.46	3.94	3.49	57
58	12.61	11.07	9.73	8.57	7.55	6.67	5.90	5.23	4.64	4.12	3.67	58
59	12.61	11.12	9.82	8.69	7.71	6.84	6.08	5.41	4.83	4.31	3.85	59
60	12.61	11.18	9.93	8.83	7.87	7.02	6.27	5.61	5.03	4.51	4.05	60
61	12.62	11.24	10.03	8.97	8.03	7.20	6.47	5.81	5.23	4.72	4.26	61
62	12.63	11.31	10.15	9.12	8.20	7.39	6.67	6.03	5.46	4.94	4.48	62
63	12.64	11.38	10.26	9.27	8.38	7.59	6.89	6.25	5.69	5.18	4.72	63
64	12.66	11.46	10.38	9.42	8.57	7.80	7.11	6.49	5.93	5.42	4.97	64
65	12.67	11.53	10.50	9.58	8.75	8.01	7.33	6.73	6.18	5.68	5.23	65
66	12.68	11.59	10.61	9.73	8.94	8.22	7.56	6.97	6.43	5.95	5.50	66
67	12.68	11.65	10.72	9.88	9.12	8.43	7.80	7.23	6.70	6.22	5.78	67
68	12.67	11.71	10.83	10.04	9.31	8.65	8.04	7.49	6.98	6.51	6.08	68
69	12.66	11.76	10.94	10.19	9.50	8.87	8.29	7.76	7.26	6.81	6.40	69
70	12.66	11.82	11.05	10.35	9.70	9.10	8.55	8.04	7.57	7.13	6.73	70
71	12.67	11.90	11.18	10.52	9.91	9.35	8.83	8.34	7.90	7.48	7.09	71
72	12.71	11.99	11.33	10.72	10.15	9.62	9.14	8.68	8.26	7.86	7.49	72
73	12.78	12.13	11.52	10.95	10.43	9.94	9.48	9.05	8.65	8.28	7.93	73
74	12.90	12.30	11.75	11.23	10.75	10.29	9.87	9.48	9.11	8.76	8.43	74
75	13.07	12.53	12.03	11.56	11.12	10.71	10.32	9.96	9.62	9.30	9.00	75

Table 27: Discounting factors for term certain

Term	0.5%	1.0%	1.5%	2.0%	2.5%	3.0%	3.5%	4.0%	4.5%	5.0%	Term
1	0.9950	0.9901	0.9852	0.9804	0.9756	0.9709	0.9662	0.9615	0.9569	0.9524	1
2	0.9901	0.9803	0.9707	0.9612	0.9518	0.9426	0.9335	0.9246	0.9157	0.9070	2
3	0.9851	0.9706	0.9563	0.9423	0.9286	0.9151	0.9019	0.8890	0.8763	0.8638	3
4	0.9802	0.9610	0.9422	0.9238	0.9060	0.8885	0.8714	0.8548	0.8386	0.8227	4
5	0.9754	0.9515	0.9283	0.9057	0.8839	0.8626	0.8420	0.8219	0.8025	0.7835	5
6	0.9705	0.9420	0.9145	0.8880	0.8623	0.8375	0.8135	0.7903	0.7679	0.7462	6
7	0.9657	0.9327	0.9010	0.8706	0.8413	0.8131	0.7860	0.7599	0.7348	0.7107	7
8	0.9609	0.9235	0.8877	0.8535	0.8207	0.7894	0.7594	0.7307	0.7032	0.6768	8
9	0.9561	0.9143	0.8746	0.8368	0.8007	0.7664	0.7337	0.7026	0.6729	0.6446	9
10	0.9513	0.9053	0.8617	0.8203	0.7812	0.7441	0.7089	0.6756	0.6439	0.6139	10
11	0.9466	0.8963	0.8489	0.8043	0.7621	0.7224	0.6849	0.6496	0.6162	0.5847	11
12	0.9419	0.8874	0.8364	0.7885	0.7436	0.7014	0.6618	0.6246	0.5897	0.5568	12
13	0.9372	0.8787	0.8240	0.7730	0.7254	0.6810	0.6394	0.6006	0.5643	0.5303	13
14	0.9326	0.8700	0.8118	0.7579	0.7077	0.6611	0.6178	0.5775	0.5400	0.5051	14
15	0.9279	0.8613	0.7999	0.7430	0.6905	0.6419	0.5969	0.5553	0.5167	0.4810	15
16	0.9233	0.8528	0.7880	0.7284	0.6736	0.6232	0.5767	0.5339	0.4945	0.4581	16
17	0.9187	0.8444	0.7764	0.7142	0.6572	0.6050	0.5572	0.5134	0.4732	0.4363	17
18	0.9141	0.8360	0.7649	0.7002	0.6412	0.5874	0.5384	0.4936	0.4528	0.4155	18
19	0.9096	0.8277	0.7536	0.6864	0.6255	0.5703	0.5202	0.4746	0.4333	0.3957	19
20	0.9051	0.8195	0.7425	0.6730	0.6103	0.5537	0.5026	0.4564	0.4146	0.3769	20
21	0.9006	0.8114	0.7315	0.6598	0.5954	0.5375	0.4856	0.4388	0.3968	0.3589	21
22	0.8961	0.8034	0.7207	0.6468	0.5809	0.5219	0.4692	0.4220	0.3797	0.3418	22
23	0.8916	0.7954	0.7100	0.6342	0.5667	0.5067	0.4533	0.4057	0.3634	0.3256	23
24	0.8872	0.7876	0.6995	0.6217	0.5529	0.4919	0.4380	0.3901	0.3477	0.3101	24
25	0.8828	0.7798	0.6892	0.6095	0.5394	0.4776	0.4231	0.3751	0.3327	0.2953	25
26	0.8784	0.7720	0.6790	0.5976	0.5262	0.4637	0.4088	0.3607	0.3184	0.2812	26
27	0.8740	0.7644	0.6690	0.5859	0.5134	0.4502	0.3950	0.3468	0.3047	0.2678	27
28	0.8697	0.7568	0.6591	0.5744	0.5009	0.4371	0.3817	0.3335	0.2916	0.2551	28
29	0.8653	0.7493	0.6494	0.5631	0.4887	0.4243	0.3687	0.3207	0.2790	0.2429	29
30	0.8610	0.7419	0.6398	0.5521	0.4767	0.4120	0.3563	0.3083	0.2670	0.2314	30
31	0.8567	0.7346	0.6303	0.5412	0.4651	0.4000	0.3442	0.2965	0.2555	0.2204	31
32	0.8525	0.7273	0.6210	0.5306	0.4538	0.3883	0.3326	0.2851	0.2445	0.2099	32
33	0.8482	0.7201	0.6118	0.5202	0.4427	0.3770	0.3213	0.2741	0.2340	0.1999	33
34	0.8440	0.7130	0.6028	0.5100	0.4319	0.3660	0.3105	0.2636	0.2239	0.1904	34
35	0.8398	0.7059	0.5939	0.5000	0.4214	0.3554	0.3000	0.2534	0.2143	0.1813	35
36	0.8356	0.6989	0.5851	0.4902	0.4111	0.3450	0.2898	0.2437	0.2050	0.1727	36
37	0.8315	0.6920	0.5764	0.4806	0.4011	0.3350	0.2800	0.2343	0.1962	0.1644	37
38	0.8274	0.6852	0.5679	0.4712	0.3913	0.3252	0.2706	0.2253	0.1878	0.1566	38
39	0.8232	0.6784	0.5595	0.4619	0.3817	0.3158	0.2614	0.2166	0.1797	0.1491	39
40	0.8191	0.6717	0.5513	0.4529	0.3724	0.3066	0.2526	0.2083	0.1719	0.1420	40
41	0.8151	0.6650	0.5431	0.4440	0.3633	0.2976	0.2440	0.2003	0.1645	0.1353	41
42	0.8110	0.6584	0.5351	0.4353	0.3545	0.2890	0.2358	0.1926	0.1574	0.1288	42
43	0.8070	0.6519	0.5272	0.4268	0.3458	0.2805	0.2278	0.1852	0.1507	0.1227	43
44	0.8030	0.6454	0.5194	0.4184	0.3374	0.2724	0.2201	0.1780	0.1442	0.1169	44
45	0.7990	0.6391	0.5117	0.4102	0.3292	0.2644	0.2127	0.1712	0.1380	0.1113	45
46	0.7950	0.6327	0.5042	0.4022	0.3211	0.2567	0.2055	0.1646	0.1320	0.1060	46
47	0.7910	0.6265	0.4967	0.3943	0.3133	0.2493	0.1985	0.1583	0.1263	0.1009	47
48	0.7871	0.6203	0.4894	0.3865	0.3057	0.2420	0.1918	0.1522	0.1209	0.0961	48
49	0.7832	0.6141	0.4821	0.3790	0.2982	0.2350	0.1853	0.1463	0.1157	0.0916	49
50	0.7793	0.6080	0.4750	0.3715	0.2909	0.2281	0.1791	0.1407	0.1107	0.0872	50
51	0.7754	0.6020	0.4680	0.3642	0.2838	0.2215	0.1730	0.1353	0.1059	0.0831	51
52	0.7716	0.5961	0.4611	0.3571	0.2769	0.2150	0.1671	0.1301	0.1014	0.0791	52
53	0.7677	0.5902	0.4543	0.3501	0.2702	0.2088	0.1615	0.1251	0.0970	0.0753	53
54	0.7639	0.5843	0.4475	0.3432	0.2636	0.2027	0.1560	0.1203	0.0928	0.0717	54
55	0.7601	0.5785	0.4409	0.3365	0.2572	0.1968	0.1508	0.1157	0.0888	0.0683	55

The column header reads: Factor to discount value of multiplier for a period of deferment

Table 27: Discounting factors for term certain *continued*

Term	Factor to discount value of multiplier for a period of deferment										Term
	0.5%	*1.0%*	*1.5%*	*2.0%*	*2.5%*	*3.0%*	*3.5%*	*4.0%*	*4.5%*	*5.0%*	
56	0.7563	0.5728	0.4344	0.3299	0.2509	0.1910	0.1457	0.1112	0.0850	0.0651	56
57	0.7525	0.5671	0.4280	0.3234	0.2448	0.1855	0.1407	0.1069	0.0814	0.0620	57
58	0.7488	0.5615	0.4217	0.3171	0.2388	0.1801	0.1360	0.1028	0.0778	0.0590	58
59	0.7451	0.5560	0.4154	0.3109	0.2330	0.1748	0.1314	0.0989	0.0745	0.0562	59
60	0.7414	0.5504	0.4093	0.3048	0.2273	0.1697	0.1269	0.0951	0.0713	0.0535	60
61	0.7377	0.5450	0.4032	0.2988	0.2217	0.1648	0.1226	0.0914	0.0682	0.0510	61
62	0.7340	0.5396	0.3973	0.2929	0.2163	0.1600	0.1185	0.0879	0.0653	0.0486	62
63	0.7304	0.5343	0.3914	0.2872	0.2111	0.1553	0.1145	0.0845	0.0625	0.0462	63
64	0.7267	0.5290	0.3856	0.2816	0.2059	0.1508	0.1106	0.0813	0.0598	0.0440	64
65	0.7231	0.5237	0.3799	0.2761	0.2009	0.1464	0.1069	0.0781	0.0572	0.0419	65
66	0.7195	0.5185	0.3743	0.2706	0.1960	0.1421	0.1033	0.0751	0.0547	0.0399	66
67	0.7159	0.5134	0.3688	0.2653	0.1912	0.1380	0.0998	0.0722	0.0524	0.0380	67
68	0.7124	0.5083	0.3633	0.2601	0.1865	0.1340	0.0964	0.0695	0.0501	0.0362	68
69	0.7088	0.5033	0.3580	0.2550	0.1820	0.1301	0.0931	0.0668	0.0480	0.0345	69
70	0.7053	0.4983	0.3527	0.2500	0.1776	0.1263	0.0900	0.0642	0.0459	0.0329	70
71	0.7018	0.4934	0.3475	0.2451	0.1732	0.1226	0.0869	0.0617	0.0439	0.0313	71
72	0.6983	0.4885	0.3423	0.2403	0.1690	0.1190	0.0840	0.0594	0.0420	0.0298	72
73	0.6948	0.4837	0.3373	0.2356	0.1649	0.1156	0.0812	0.0571	0.0402	0.0284	73
74	0.6914	0.4789	0.3323	0.2310	0.1609	0.1122	0.0784	0.0549	0.0385	0.0270	74
75	0.6879	0.4741	0.3274	0.2265	0.1569	0.1089	0.0758	0.0528	0.0368	0.0258	75
76	0.6845	0.4694	0.3225	0.2220	0.1531	0.1058	0.0732	0.0508	0.0353	0.0245	76
77	0.6811	0.4648	0.3178	0.2177	0.1494	0.1027	0.0707	0.0488	0.0337	0.0234	77
78	0.6777	0.4602	0.3131	0.2134	0.1457	0.0997	0.0683	0.0469	0.0323	0.0222	78
79	0.6743	0.4556	0.3084	0.2092	0.1422	0.0968	0.0660	0.0451	0.0309	0.0212	79
80	0.6710	0.4511	0.3039	0.2051	0.1387	0.0940	0.0638	0.0434	0.0296	0.0202	80

Table 28: Multipliers for pecuniary loss for term certain

Term	Multiplier for regular frequent payments for a term certain at rate of return of										Term
	0.5%	1.0%	1.5%	2.0%	2.5%	3.0%	3.5%	4.0%	4.5%	5.0%	
1	1.00	1.00	0.99	0.99	0.99	0.99	0.98	0.98	0.98	0.98	1
2	1.99	1.98	1.97	1.96	1.95	1.94	1.93	1.92	1.91	1.91	2
3	2.98	2.96	2.93	2.91	2.89	2.87	2.85	2.83	2.81	2.79	3
4	3.96	3.92	3.88	3.85	3.81	3.77	3.74	3.70	3.67	3.63	4
5	4.94	4.88	4.82	4.76	4.70	4.65	4.59	4.54	4.49	4.44	5
6	5.91	5.82	5.74	5.66	5.58	5.50	5.42	5.35	5.27	5.20	6
7	6.88	6.76	6.65	6.54	6.43	6.32	6.22	6.12	6.02	5.93	7
8	7.84	7.69	7.54	7.40	7.26	7.12	6.99	6.87	6.74	6.62	8
9	8.80	8.61	8.42	8.24	8.07	7.90	7.74	7.58	7.43	7.28	9
10	9.75	9.52	9.29	9.07	8.86	8.66	8.46	8.27	8.09	7.91	10
11	10.70	10.42	10.15	9.88	9.63	9.39	9.16	8.93	8.72	8.51	11
12	11.65	11.31	10.99	10.68	10.39	10.10	9.83	9.57	9.32	9.08	12
13	12.59	12.19	11.82	11.46	11.12	10.79	10.48	10.18	9.90	9.63	13
14	13.52	13.07	12.64	12.23	11.84	11.46	11.11	10.77	10.45	10.14	14
15	14.45	13.93	13.44	12.98	12.54	12.12	11.72	11.34	10.98	10.64	15
16	15.38	14.79	14.24	13.71	13.22	12.75	12.30	11.88	11.48	11.11	16
17	16.30	15.64	15.02	14.43	13.88	13.36	12.87	12.41	11.97	11.55	17
18	17.22	16.48	15.79	15.14	14.53	13.96	13.42	12.91	12.43	11.98	18
19	18.13	17.31	16.55	15.83	15.17	14.54	13.95	13.39	12.87	12.38	19
20	19.03	18.14	17.30	16.51	15.78	15.10	14.46	13.86	13.30	12.77	20
21	19.94	18.95	18.03	17.18	16.39	15.65	14.95	14.31	13.70	13.14	21
22	20.84	19.76	18.76	17.83	16.97	16.17	15.43	14.74	14.09	13.49	22
23	21.73	20.56	19.48	18.47	17.55	16.69	15.89	15.15	14.46	13.82	23
24	22.62	21.35	20.18	19.10	18.11	17.19	16.34	15.55	14.82	14.14	24
25	23.50	22.13	20.87	19.72	18.65	17.67	16.77	15.93	15.16	14.44	25
26	24.38	22.91	21.56	20.32	19.19	18.14	17.18	16.30	15.48	14.73	26
27	25.26	23.68	22.23	20.91	19.71	18.60	17.59	16.65	15.80	15.01	27
28	26.13	24.44	22.90	21.49	20.21	19.04	17.97	16.99	16.09	15.27	28
29	27.00	25.19	23.55	22.06	20.71	19.47	18.35	17.32	16.38	15.52	29
30	27.86	25.94	24.20	22.62	21.19	19.89	18.71	17.64	16.65	15.75	30
31	28.72	26.67	24.83	23.17	21.66	20.30	19.06	17.94	16.91	15.98	31
32	29.58	27.41	25.46	23.70	22.12	20.69	19.40	18.23	17.16	16.19	32
33	30.43	28.13	26.07	24.23	22.57	21.08	19.73	18.51	17.40	16.40	33
34	31.27	28.85	26.68	24.74	23.01	21.45	20.04	18.78	17.63	16.59	34
35	32.12	29.56	27.28	25.25	23.43	21.81	20.35	19.04	17.85	16.78	35
36	32.95	30.26	27.87	25.74	23.85	22.16	20.64	19.28	18.06	16.96	36
37	33.79	30.95	28.45	26.23	24.26	22.50	20.93	19.52	18.26	17.13	37
38	34.62	31.64	29.02	26.70	24.65	22.83	21.20	19.75	18.45	17.29	38
39	35.44	32.32	29.58	27.17	25.04	23.15	21.47	19.97	18.64	17.44	39
40	36.26	33.00	30.14	27.63	25.42	23.46	21.73	20.19	18.81	17.58	40
41	37.08	33.67	30.69	28.08	25.78	23.76	21.97	20.39	18.98	17.72	41
42	37.89	34.33	31.23	28.52	26.14	24.06	22.21	20.59	19.14	17.86	42
43	38.70	34.98	31.76	28.95	26.49	24.34	22.45	20.78	19.30	17.98	43
44	39.51	35.63	32.28	29.37	26.83	24.62	22.67	20.96	19.44	18.10	44
45	40.31	36.27	32.80	29.78	27.17	24.88	22.89	21.13	19.58	18.21	45
46	41.10	36.91	33.30	30.19	27.49	25.15	23.10	21.30	19.72	18.32	46
47	41.90	37.54	33.80	30.59	27.81	25.40	23.30	21.46	19.85	18.43	47
48	42.69	38.16	34.30	30.98	28.12	25.64	23.49	21.62	19.97	18.53	48
49	43.47	38.78	34.78	31.36	28.42	25.88	23.68	21.77	20.09	18.62	49
50	44.25	39.39	35.26	31.74	28.72	26.11	23.86	21.91	20.20	18.71	50
51	45.03	40.00	35.73	32.10	29.00	26.34	24.04	22.05	20.31	18.79	51
52	45.80	40.60	36.20	32.47	29.28	26.56	24.21	22.18	20.42	18.87	52
53	46.57	41.19	36.66	32.82	29.56	26.77	24.37	22.31	20.51	18.95	53
54	47.34	41.78	37.11	33.17	29.82	26.97	24.53	22.43	20.61	19.03	54
55	48.10	42.36	37.55	33.51	30.08	27.17	24.69	22.55	20.70	19.10	55

Table 28: Multipliers for pecuniary loss for term certain *continued*

Term	Multiplier for regular frequent payments for a term certain at rate of return of										Term
	0.5%	**1.0%**	**1.5%**	**2.0%**	**2.5%**	**3.0%**	**3.5%**	**4.0%**	**4.5%**	**5.0%**	
56	48.86	42.93	37.99	33.84	30.34	27.37	24.83	22.66	20.79	19.16	56
57	49.61	43.50	38.42	34.17	30.59	27.56	24.98	22.77	20.87	19.23	57
58	50.36	44.07	38.84	34.49	30.83	27.74	25.12	22.88	20.95	19.29	58
59	51.11	44.63	39.26	34.80	31.06	27.92	25.25	22.98	21.03	19.34	59
60	51.85	45.18	39.67	35.11	31.29	28.09	25.38	23.07	21.10	19.40	60
61	52.59	45.73	40.08	35.41	31.52	28.26	25.50	23.17	21.17	19.45	61
62	53.33	46.27	40.48	35.70	31.74	28.42	25.62	23.26	21.24	19.50	62
63	54.06	46.81	40.88	36.00	31.95	28.58	25.74	23.34	21.30	19.55	63
64	54.79	47.34	41.26	36.28	32.16	28.73	25.85	23.42	21.36	19.59	64
65	55.52	47.86	41.65	36.56	32.36	28.88	25.96	23.50	21.42	19.64	65
66	56.24	48.39	42.02	36.83	32.56	29.02	26.07	23.58	21.47	19.68	66
67	56.95	48.90	42.40	37.10	32.75	29.16	26.17	23.65	21.53	19.72	67
68	57.67	49.41	42.76	37.36	32.94	29.30	26.27	23.73	21.58	19.75	68
69	58.38	49.92	43.12	37.62	33.13	29.43	26.36	23.79	21.63	19.79	69
70	59.09	50.42	43.48	37.87	33.31	29.56	26.45	23.86	21.68	19.82	70
71	59.79	50.91	43.83	38.12	33.48	29.68	26.54	23.92	21.72	19.85	71
72	60.49	51.41	44.17	38.36	33.65	29.80	26.63	23.98	21.76	19.88	72
73	61.19	51.89	44.51	38.60	33.82	29.92	26.71	24.04	21.80	19.91	73
74	61.88	52.37	44.85	38.83	33.98	30.03	26.79	24.10	21.84	19.94	74
75	62.57	52.85	45.18	39.06	34.14	30.15	26.87	24.15	21.88	19.97	75
76	63.26	53.32	45.50	39.29	34.30	30.25	26.94	24.20	21.92	19.99	76
77	63.94	53.79	45.82	39.51	34.45	30.36	27.01	24.25	21.95	20.02	77
78	64.62	54.25	46.14	39.72	34.60	30.46	27.08	24.30	21.99	20.04	78
79	65.29	54.71	46.45	39.93	34.74	30.56	27.15	24.35	22.02	20.06	79
80	65.97	55.16	46.75	40.14	34.88	30.65	27.21	24.39	22.05	20.08	80

ACTUARIAL FORMULAE AND BASIS

The functions tabulated are:

Tables 1 and 2	$\bar{a}_x$
Tables 3 and 4	$\bar{a}_{x:\overline{55-x}}$
Tables 5 and 6	$\bar{a}_{x:\overline{60-x}}$
Tables 7 and 8	$\bar{a}_{x:\overline{65-x}}$
Tables 9 and 10	$\bar{a}_{x:\overline{70-x}}$
Tables 11 and 12	$(55-x)|\bar{a}_{55}$
Tables 13 and 14	$(60-x)|\bar{a}_{60}$
Tables 15 and 16	$(65-x)|\bar{a}_{65}$
Tables 17 and 18	$(70-x)|\bar{a}_{70}$
Table 19:	$1/(1+i)^n$
Table 20:	$\bar{a}_{\overline{n}}$

- Mortality assumptions for 2002-based official population projections for England and Wales

- Loadings: None

- Rate of return: As stated in the Tables

B3: Life tables and projected life tables

Tables based on 2001–2003 experience

| | United Kingdom | | | | England and Wales | | | |
| | Males | | Females | | Males | | Females | |
Age (x) in years	lx	ex	lx	ex	lx	ex	lx	ex
0	100000.0	75.92	100000.0	80.50	100000.0	76.17	100000.0	80.67
1	99411.7	75.37	99522.1	79.89	99412.6	75.62	99520.6	80.06
2	99370.7	74.40	99485.5	78.92	99370.9	74.66	99484.0	79.09
3	99345.0	73.42	99465.0	77.93	99345.1	73.68	99463.5	78.11
4	99327.1	72.43	99449.0	76.94	99328.0	72.69	99447.3	77.12
5	99310.4	71.44	99434.4	75.96	99312.1	71.70	99432.9	76.13
6	99297.1	70.45	99422.4	74.97	99299.2	70.71	99420.5	75.14
7	99284.3	69.46	99411.2	73.97	99286.3	69.72	99409.4	74.15
8	99272.9	68.47	99401.9	72.98	99275.2	68.73	99399.9	73.16
9	99262.6	67.47	99391.4	71.99	99264.9	67.73	99389.4	72.16
10	99251.4	66.48	99381.9	70.99	99254.2	66.74	99380.2	71.17
11	99240.6	65.49	99372.0	70.00	99244.1	65.75	99370.0	70.18
12	99227.6	64.50	99362.1	69.01	99231.5	64.75	99360.2	69.18
13	99213.2	63.51	99350.3	68.02	99217.7	63.76	99348.4	68.19
14	99194.3	62.52	99339.5	67.02	99198.8	62.78	99338.2	67.20
15	99171.9	61.53	99324.5	66.03	99177.0	61.79	99323.4	66.21
16	99146.4	60.55	99308.6	65.04	99152.7	60.80	99308.7	65.22
17	99109.5	59.57	99286.6	64.06	99117.3	59.83	99287.3	64.23
18	99056.1	58.60	99259.9	63.08	99066.6	58.86	99262.5	63.25
19	98980.5	57.65	99232.7	62.09	98995.1	57.90	99235.9	62.27
20	98907.9	56.69	99204.3	61.11	98925.9	56.94	99206.8	61.28
21	98825.4	55.74	99175.1	60.13	98844.9	55.98	99180.0	60.30
22	98745.7	54.78	99145.8	59.15	98770.4	55.03	99151.3	59.32
23	98658.7	53.83	99115.5	58.16	98689.1	54.07	99122.4	58.34
24	98577.6	52.87	99085.0	57.18	98611.0	53.11	99092.4	57.35
25	98493.7	51.92	99055.8	56.20	98531.9	52.16	99064.5	56.37
26	98408.5	50.96	99024.6	55.22	98450.5	51.20	99034.1	55.39
27	98325.5	50.00	98988.2	54.24	98371.2	50.24	98997.8	54.41
28	98237.9	49.05	98952.7	53.26	98291.0	49.28	98964.0	53.42
29	98147.4	48.09	98916.9	52.27	98205.5	48.32	98928.8	52.44
30	98050.4	47.14	98877.9	51.30	98112.8	47.37	98890.0	51.46
31	97951.5	46.19	98835.9	50.32	98018.4	46.41	98849.0	50.48
32	97849.5	45.24	98787.3	49.34	97919.8	45.46	98801.8	49.51
33	97742.0	44.28	98738.0	48.37	97817.7	44.51	98753.0	48.53
34	97630.8	43.33	98685.2	47.39	97710.3	43.55	98700.7	47.56
35	97514.6	42.39	98624.6	46.42	97599.4	42.60	98640.5	46.59
36	97398.2	41.44	98561.2	45.45	97489.1	41.65	98577.9	45.62
37	97275.5	40.49	98494.5	44.48	97371.2	40.70	98512.1	44.65
38	97142.8	39.54	98424.2	43.51	97243.7	39.75	98443.5	43.68
39	97007.4	38.60	98341.9	42.55	97114.9	38.81	98362.1	42.71
40	96854.8	37.66	98253.3	41.59	96968.3	37.86	98276.2	41.75
41	96689.8	36.72	98157.0	40.63	96807.9	36.93	98182.2	40.79
42	96513.1	35.79	98052.2	39.67	96640.0	35.99	98081.2	39.83
43	96325.6	34.85	97935.1	38.72	96459.5	35.06	97967.6	38.88
44	96115.9	33.93	97798.1	37.77	96256.8	34.13	97834.2	37.93
45	95905.5	33.00	97652.5	36.82	96052.8	33.20	97691.6	36.98
46	95669.7	32.08	97494.7	35.88	95823.5	32.28	97538.1	36.04
47	95403.0	31.17	97313.3	34.95	95563.4	31.36	97361.3	35.11
48	95101.9	30.27	97115.4	34.02	95270.3	30.46	97168.6	34.17
49	94783.6	29.37	96898.7	33.09	94961.8	29.56	96957.3	33.25
50	94427.1	28.48	96665.4	32.17	94617.0	28.66	96728.5	32.32
51	94042.5	27.59	96405.4	31.26	94242.2	27.77	96474.5	31.41
52	93633.1	26.71	96130.7	30.35	93843.7	26.89	96207.2	30.49
53	93187.2	25.84	95829.1	29.44	93410.4	26.01	95913.5	29.59
54	92706.7	24.97	95510.0	28.54	92946.2	25.14	95600.5	28.68
55	92186.2	24.10	95156.7	27.64	92441.2	24.27	95250.9	27.79

Tables based on 2001–2003 experience *continued*

| | United Kingdom | | | | England and Wales | | | |
| | Males | | Females | | Males | | Females | |
	lx	ex	lx	ex	lx	ex	lx	ex
Age (x) in years								
56	91609.7	23.25	94770.6	26.75	91880.3	23.42	94873.4	26.89
57	90981.8	22.41	94353.0	25.87	91269.2	22.57	94463.9	26.01
58	90272.7	21.58	93895.7	24.99	90577.7	21.74	94021.0	25.13
59	89498.0	20.77	93403.5	24.12	89827.6	20.92	93541.1	24.25
60	88654.7	19.96	92851.4	23.26	89008.5	20.11	93006.3	23.39
61	87697.6	19.17	92236.9	22.41	88087.1	19.31	92412.2	22.54
62	86672.1	18.39	91564.2	21.57	87094.2	18.53	91757.2	21.70
63	85541.0	17.63	90847.1	20.74	85996.4	17.76	91065.0	20.86
64	84327.1	16.87	90074.0	19.91	84823.8	17.00	90302.4	20.03
65	83019.2	16.13	89221.9	19.10	83547.1	16.25	89473.3	19.21
66	81611.6	15.40	88292.5	18.29	82174.1	15.51	88569.2	18.40
67	80091.0	14.68	87289.2	17.50	80688.5	14.79	87590.4	17.60
68	78415.1	13.99	86179.0	16.72	79048.4	14.08	86511.7	16.18
69	76620.8	13.30	84971.2	15.95	77273.5	13.40	85325.6	16.04
70	74647.2	12.64	83643.3	15.19	75336.5	12.73	84032.2	15.28
71	72562.7	11.99	82207.9	14.45	73277.9	12.07	82619.6	14.53
72	70260.6	11.37	80605.1	13.73	71002.0	11.44	81042.6	13.81
73	67804.1	10.76	78824.5	13.03	68571.7	10.83	79291.6	13.10
74	65162.8	10.18	76868.2	12.35	65964.8	10.24	77361.8	12.41
75	62313.8	9.62	74754.7	11.68	63138.6	9.67	75280.9	11.74
76	59297.8	9.08	72425.9	11.04	60123.4	9.13	72969.7	11.10
77	56128.7	8.57	69926.0	10.42	56947.0	8.61	70489.8	10.47
78	52814.9	8.07	67247.9	9.81	53623.4	8.12	67827.8	9.86
79	49414.1	7.60	64396.1	9.22	50219.8	7.63	64987.7	9.27
80	45842.8	7.15	61349.3	8.66	46626.4	7.18	61952.5	8.70
81	42230.4	6.72	58097.2	8.11	43001.0	6.75	58716.0	8.15
82	38591.4	6.30	54682.2	7.59	39326.9	6.33	55298.9	7.63
83	35029.8	5.89	51101.5	7.09	35709.8	5.92	51723.7	7.12
84	31463.1	5.51	47393.5	6.60	32100.9	5.53	48016.8	6.63
85	27992.8	5.13	43546.5	6.14	28607.4	5.15	44156.4	6.17
86	24368.4	4.81	39466.1	5.72	24927.6	4.83	40059.0	5.75
87	20989.6	4.51	35396.2	5.33	21495.7	4.52	35958.8	5.35
88	17815.1	4.22	31319.8	4.95	18263.4	4.23	31835.7	4.97
89	14877.0	3.96	27348.3	4.60	15259.5	3.97	27823.2	4.62
90	12173.0	3.72	23471.3	4.28	12495.4	3.74	23888.4	4.30
91	9857.3	3.48	19818.0	3.97	10120.7	3.50	20204.9	3.99
92	7848.9	3.25	16443.7	3.69	8066.3	3.26	16786.6	3.70
93	6079.5	3.04	13356.0	3.42	6249.6	3.06	13643.5	3.44
94	4591.8	2.87	10547.6	3.20	4729.3	2.89	10775.2	3.22
95	3420.4	2.68	8178.3	2.98	3528.2	2.70	8362.7	3.00
96	2461.3	2.53	6172.7	2.79	2540.2	2.55	6329.9	2.80
97	1737.1	2.38	4545.1	2.61	1802.1	2.39	4670.2	2.62
98	1179.1	2.27	3260.5	2.44	1228.5	2.28	3365.0	2.45
99	793.3	2.12	2271.3	2.29	828.9	2.14	2344.6	2.30
100	521.4	1.97	1545.2	2.13	546.4	1.98	1597.5	2.13

Tables based on 2001–2003 experience

	Scotland				Northern Ireland			
	Males		Females		Males		Females	
	lx	ex	lx	ex	lx	ex	lx	ex
Age (x) in years								
0	100000.0	73.50	100000.0	78.87	100000.0	75.56	100000.0	80.43
1	99412.8	72.93	99531.2	78.24	99384.2	75.02	99543.1	79.80
2	99378.0	71.96	99493.4	77.27	99345.9	74.05	99508.7	78.82
3	99356.2	70.97	99469.3	76.29	99314.4	73.08	99496.5	77.83
4	99331.7	69.99	99453.3	75.30	99292.1	72.09	99484.7	76.84
5	99304.6	69.01	99435.3	74.32	99278.5	71.10	99476.1	75.85
6	99287.9	68.02	99423.6	73.32	99262.5	70.11	99473.2	74.85
7	99274.7	67.03	99411.9	72.33	99254.6	69.12	99459.1	73.86
8	99263.8	66.04	99403.9	71.34	99233.3	68.13	99450.6	72.87
9	99255.3	65.04	99391.7	70.35	99217.5	67.14	99445.1	71.87
10	99240.9	64.05	99379.8	69.36	99199.3	66.16	99434.3	70.88
11	99226.8	63.06	99370.4	68.36	99181.7	65.17	99429.0	69.88
12	99207.8	62.07	99358.8	67.37	99171.8	64.17	99423.7	68.89
13	99188.7	61.09	99348.2	66.38	99152.1	63.19	99408.2	67.90
14	99168.6	60.10	99332.3	65.39	99135.0	62.20	99395.4	66.91
15	99147.7	59.11	99315.4	64.40	99096.6	61.22	99380.1	65.92
16	99117.1	58.13	99289.4	63.42	99053.8	60.25	99357.5	64.93
17	99065.6	57.16	99263.5	62.43	99011.0	59.27	99330.0	63.95
18	98989.1	56.20	99210.8	61.47	98946.2	58.31	99320.0	62.96
19	98880.4	55.26	99173.0	60.49	98847.6	57.37	99301.8	61.97
20	98776.9	54.32	99144.5	59.51	98763.3	56.42	99290.8	60.97
21	98683.7	53.37	99099.8	58.53	98672.9	55.47	99242.1	60.00
22	98562.4	52.44	99060.2	57.56	98565.4	54.53	99224.4	59.01
23	98424.4	51.51	99021.2	56.58	98466.4	53.58	99178.8	58.04
24	98318.1	50.57	98980.8	55.60	98369.8	52.64	99160.3	57.05
25	98188.2	49.63	98936.5	54.63	98270.7	51.69	99135.4	56.07
26	98064.7	48.69	98896.2	53.65	98177.5	50.74	99104.4	55.08
27	97945.2	47.75	98854.7	52.67	98079.1	49.79	99079.9	54.10
28	97784.0	46.83	98804.0	51.70	97962.7	48.85	99035.3	53.12
29	97634.4	45.90	98760.3	50.72	97875.9	47.89	99003.8	52.14
30	97484.6	44.97	98718.1	49.74	97787.4	46.93	98965.6	51.16
31	97325.3	44.04	98668.6	48.77	97715.3	45.97	98915.3	50.18
32	97184.1	43.11	98606.0	47.80	97612.2	45.01	98863.2	49.21
33	97008.9	42.18	98553.1	46.82	97531.4	44.05	98809.5	48.24
34	96852.7	41.25	98488.0	45.85	97430.4	43.10	98779.1	47.25
35	96681.0	40.32	98418.1	44.88	97307.3	42.15	98731.6	46.27
36	96496.5	39.40	98343.5	43.92	97198.6	41.20	98681.8	45.03
37	96325.6	38.47	98259.6	42.95	97066.7	40.25	98637.5	44.32
38	96133.9	37.54	98173.7	41.99	96947.1	39.30	98564.0	43.35
39	95932.4	36.62	98078.4	41.03	96802.1	38.36	98492.7	42.38
40	95716.4	35.70	97965.1	40.08	96656.1	37.42	98400.1	41.42
41	95510.7	34.78	97852.6	39.12	96475.1	36.49	98282.6	40.47
42	95242.1	33.88	97718.1	38.18	96312.2	35.55	98155.8	39.52
43	94990.8	32.96	97573.5	37.23	96108.2	34.62	98020.3	38.57
44	94701.0	32.06	97409.6	36.30	95938.3	33.68	97859.9	37.64
45	94421.5	31.16	97238.5	35.36	95746.9	32.75	97706.5	36.69
46	94113.7	30.26	97043.8	34.43	95547.9	31.82	97534.8	35.76
47	93781.3	29.36	96823.9	33.51	95291.2	30.90	97336.3	34.83
48	93405.7	28.48	96584.0	32.59	94986.2	30.00	97111.4	33.91
49	93000.8	27.60	96305.3	31.68	94642.8	29.10	96929.3	32.97
50	92528.7	26.74	96021.4	30.77	94290.8	28.21	96715.4	32.04
51	92053.0	25.87	95710.7	29.87	93893.6	27.33	96430.7	31.14
52	91532.3	25.02	95353.4	28.98	93502.2	26.44	96184.8	30.22
53	90958.8	24.17	94974.8	28.09	93069.0	25.56	95878.8	29.31
54	90325.7	23.34	94600.9	27.20	92554.2	24.70	95532.4	28.42
55	89663.8	22.51	94188.9	26.32	91983.0	23.85	95256.9	27.50

Tables based on 2001–2003 experience

| | Scotland | | | | Northern Ireland | | | |
| | Males | | Females | | Males | | Females | |
	lx	ex	lx	ex	lx	ex	lx	ex
Age (x) in years								
56	88927.9	21.69	93718.1	25.45	91408.4	23.00	94854.9	26.61
57	88115.0	20.89	93197.3	24.59	90826.2	22.14	94503.1	25.71
58	87223.0	20.09	92599.9	23.74	90118.4	21.31	94013.2	24.84
59	86192.3	19.33	91983.8	22.90	89363.6	20.49	93518.3	23.97
60	85128.9	18.56	91287.6	22.07	88463.9	19.69	92887.9	23.13
61	83843.8	17.84	90455.0	21.27	87459.1	18.91	92362.5	22.26
62	82518.8	17.12	89606.2	20.47	86408.6	18.14	91739.3	21.40
63	81069.4	16.42	88681.8	19.67	85302.5	17.36	90943.4	20.59
64	79474.3	15.74	87804.3	18.87	84072.1	16.61	90201.8	19.75
65	77871.3	15.05	86724.7	18.10	82771.9	15.86	89409.4	18.92
66	76171.4	14.37	85548.1	17.34	81254.2	15.15	88545.3	18.10
67	74369.5	13.71	84346.9	16.58	79585.6	14.46	87466.1	17.32
68	72377.2	13.07	82969.9	15.84	77890.3	13.76	86319.1	16.54
69	70402.1	12.43	81596.1	15.10	76137.8	13.07	85024.3	15.79
70	68130.3	11.82	79992.7	14.39	74056.2	12.42	83594.9	15.05
71	65847.1	11.22	78382.5	13.68	71843.9	11.79	82065.4	14.32
72	63325.5	10.64	76592.7	12.99	69484.8	11.17	80308.0	13.62
73	60669.1	10.09	74567.7	12.33	66896.9	10.58	78456.4	12.93
74	57773.3	9.57	72322.7	11.69	64034.1	10.03	76688.2	12.22
75	54726.5	9.07	69921.9	11.08	61161.6	9.48	74539.1	11.56
76	51718.4	8.57	67399.9	10.47	58120.8	8.95	72330.2	10.89
77	48602.5	8.09	64664.4	9.90	55052.7	8.42	70024.5	10.24
78	45342.9	7.64	61820.3	9.33	51933.2	7.90	67421.9	9.61
79	42020.4	7.20	58850.9	8.77	48336.8	7.45	64583.6	9.01
80	38654.7	6.78	55718.9	8.24	44777.2	7.00	61411.7	8.45
81	35169.5	6.41	52337.2	7.74	41098.4	6.58	58011.2	7.92
82	31862.7	6.02	48970.1	7.24	37455.7	6.18	54445.4	7.40
83	28784.1	5.61	45371.8	6.77	34070.3	5.74	50674.4	6.92
84	25559.6	5.25	41662.7	6.33	30728.0	5.31	46920.7	6.43
85	22371.3	4.93	37923.4	5.90	27004.3	4.97	43109.0	5.96
86	19244.1	4.65	34031.0	5.52	23506.8	4.64	38929.5	5.54
87	16371.0	4.38	30243.6	5.15	20133.3	4.33	34865.5	5.13
88	13730.4	4.12	26636.6	4.78	17037.9	4.03	30671.6	4.76
89	11410.6	3.86	23064.1	4.45	14144.7	3.75	26642.8	4.41
90	9274.0	3.63	19728.9	4.11	11458.2	3.51	22769.1	4.07
91	7508.6	3.37	16419.5	3.84	9182.2	3.26	18838.5	3.82
92	5948.9	3.12	13472.5	3.57	7126.7	3.05	15392.3	3.56
93	4602.0	2.89	10904.9	3.29	5472.3	2.83	12292.8	3.33
94	3387.7	2.75	8629.4	3.03	4165.1	2.56	9607.1	3.12
95	2499.2	2.55	6651.6	2.78	2977.7	2.38	7295.4	2.95
96	1801.3	2.35	4900.9	2.60			5296.8	2.87
97	1231.2	2.20	3550.3	2.40			3778.7	2.83
98	802.6	2.11	2424.6	2.28			2663.5	2.80
99	517.1	2.00	1672.2	2.08			1909.0	2.71
100	325.6	1.88	1090.6	1.92			1415.2	2.48

Expectation of life table

Expectations of life for age attained in 2004 allowing for the projected changes in mortality assumed in the 2003-based population projections produced by the Government Actuary's Department

		England and Wales			
Age	**Males**	**Females**	**Age**	**Males**	**Females**
0	83.2	87.1	51	31.8	35.2
1	82.6	86.4	52	30.8	34.3
2	81.6	85.4	53	29.8	33.3
3	80.6	84.4	54	28.8	32.3
4	79.6	83.4	55	27.9	31.3
5	78.5	82.4	56	26.9	30.4
6	77.5	81.3	57	26.0	29.4
7	76.5	80.3	58	25.1	28.5
8	75.4	79.3	59	24.2	27.5
9	74.4	78.3	60	23.3	26.6
10	73.3	77.2	61	22.4	25.7
11	72.3	76.2	62	21.6	24.8
12	71.3	75.2	63	20.7	23.9
13	70.2	74.1	64	19.8	23.0
14	69.2	73.1	65	19.0	22.0
15	68.1	72.1	66	18.1	21.1
16	67.1	71.1	67	17.3	20.1
17	66.1	70.0	68	16.4	19.2
18	65.1	69.0	69	15.6	18.2
19	64.0	68.0	70	14.7	17.3
20	63.0	67.0	71	13.9	16.3
21	62.0	65.9	72	13.1	15.4
22	61.0	64.9	73	12.4	14.6
23	60.0	63.9	74	11.6	13.7
24	59.0	62.8	75	11.0	12.9
25	58.0	61.8	76	10.3	12.2
26	57.0	60.8	77	9.7	11.4
27	56.0	59.8	78	9.1	10.7
28	54.9	58.7	79	8.5	10.1
29	53.9	57.7	80	8.0	9.4
30	52.9	56.7	81	7.5	8.8
31	51.9	55.6	82	6.9	8.2
32	50.9	54.6	83	6.5	7.6
33	49.9	53.6	84	6.0	7.0
34	48.9	52.5	85	5.6	6.5
35	47.8	51.5	86	5.2	6.0
36	46.8	50.5	87	4.9	5.6
37	45.8	49.4	88	4.5	5.2
38	44.8	48.4	89	4.3	4.8
39	43.8	47.4	90	4.0	4.4
40	42.7	46.3	91	3.7	4.1
41	41.7	45.3	92	3.5	3.8
42	40.7	44.3	93	3.3	3.6
43	39.7	43.3	94	3.1	3.3
44	38.7	42.3	95	2.9	3.1
45	37.7	41.2	96	2.8	2.9
46	36.7	40.2	97	2.6	2.7
47	35.7	39.2	98	2.4	2.5
48	34.7	38.2	99	2.3	2.4
49	33.7	37.2	100	2.1	2.2
50	32.8	36.2			

Notes:

1. There is a lack of material and easily available learning on this subject, apart from the explanation to be found in the Ogden Tables. What is written below is drawn, in part, from the Ogden Tables' Introduction.

2. The Government Actuary's Department has produced life tables of various kinds for a considerable period. The main life tables are the decennial Life Tables for England and Wales combined and for Scotland, which are based on data for the three years around a Census. Between Censuses, life tables known as Interim Life Tables are produced which are based on data for the numbers in the population and deaths by age and sex for the latest three-year period available. These interim life tables are produced for the United Kingdom as a whole, Great Britain, England and Wales and also each individual constituent country of the United Kingdom.

The Historic Tables

3. The latest published decennial Life Tables are the English Life Tables No. 15 and the Scottish Life Tables 1990–92. These are based on data on the numbers in the population and the numbers of deaths by age and sex for 1990 to 1992 (the three years around the 1991 Census).

4. The data from ELT No. 15 form the mortality assumptions underlying the calculation of the multipliers in Tables 1 to 18 of the Fourth Edition of the Ogden Tables. These Tables have not been reproduced in the Fifth Edition of the Ogden Tables.

5. The Ogden Tables take account of the possibilities that a claimant will live for different periods, e.g. die soon or live to be very old. The mortality assumptions relate to the general population of England and Wales. Unless there is clear evidence in an individual case to support the view that the individual concerned is atypical and will enjoy a shorter or longer than average life, no further increase or reduction is required for mortality alone. Examples of atypical individuals would be a lifelong smoker, someone suffering from a head injury or epilepsy, an immobile patient.

Projected Mortality

6. The life tables referred to above are based on historic data (and expectations of life which are calculated using this data), and effectively assume that the mortality rate for a given age and sex will remain constant in future years. However, there have been large improvements in mortality rates over the last hundred years or so. If improvements in mortality rates carry on into the future, awards of damages calculated on the basis of historic mortality rates are likely to under-compensate claimants.

7. At Appendix A to the Introduction to the Fourth Edition of the Ogden Tables there is an extract from ELT No. 15, which shows graphs indicating rates of mortality expressed in percentages of the 1911 rates on a logarithmic scale. They demonstrate in stark fashion the improvement in longevity which has taken place since 1911.

8. The sole exception is a small increase recently in the mortality of males in their late twenties and early thirties due to AIDS and increasing numbers of suicides, the same effect being present but to a lesser degree, for females. Even if this slight worsening of mortality were to continue, the effects on the tables of multipliers (in the Ogden Tables) would not be significant.

9. The Government Actuary's Department carries out official population projections for the United Kingdom and constituent countries usually every two years. In particular, these projections include assumptions of improving mortality rates at most ages in the years following the base year of the projections.

10. Tables 1–26 of the Fifth Edition of the Ogden tables give multipliers based on the projected mortality rates underlying the 2002-based population projections for England and Wales by the Government Actuary. These take as their base the estimated numbers in the population by sex and age in the constituent countries of the United Kingdom in mid-2002. The projections are made available in a series of reports covering each country entitled "Population Projections 2002–2042". Pages 1–15 of these reports describe the assumptions underlying the projections together with a comparison with the previous set of projections.

11. These are socially interesting because several factors are involved, these being errors in the original figures, net migration, fertility and mortality rates, which together with other revisions means that the general trend in the increase of expectation of life for the population as a whole has been seriously underestimated. This was the cause for the revision of the future projections of life expectation.

12. Table B3, "Expectation of Life Table", shows expectations of life in the year 2004 by age and sex allowing for future improvements based on the mortality assumptions underlying the interim 2003-based population projections for England and Wales combined, setting out the expectation of life to specific ages reached in the year 2004.

13. As mentioned earlier, the mortality rates used are for the population as a whole. In difficult cases, where the sums are large and the matter is in doubt, an actuary should be consulted. Expert medical evidence should be obtained in an atypical case.

14. It is intended to produce such a table for this each year.

B4: Multipliers for fixed periods and at intervals at 1.5 and 2 per cent

Multipliers at 1.5 per cent discount

n	Single payment	Continuous loss	1	2	3	4	5	6	7	8	10	12	15	20
											Frequency of payments in years			
1	0.985	0.99	0.99											
2	0.971	1.97	1.96	0.97										
3	0.956	2.93	2.91		0.96									
4	0.942	3.88	3.85	1.91		0.94								
5	0.928	4.82	4.78				0.93							
6	0.915	5.74	5.70	2.83	1.87			0.91						
7	0.901	6.65	6.60						0.90					
8	0.888	7.54	7.49	3.72		1.83				0.89				
9	0.875	8.42	8.36		2.75									
10	0.862	9.29	9.22	4.58			1.79				0.86			
11	0.849	10.15	10.07											
12	0.836	10.99	10.91	5.41	3.58	2.67		1.75				0.84		
13	0.824	11.82	11.73											
14	0.812	12.64	12.54	6.23					1.71					
15	0.800	13.44	13.34		4.38		2.59						0.80	
16	0.788	14.24	14.13	7.01		3.45				1.68				
17	0.776	15.02	14.91											
18	0.765	15.79	15.67	7.78	5.15			2.52						
19	0.754	16.55	16.43											
20	0.742	17.30	17.17	8.52		4.20	3.33				1.60			0.74
21	0.731	18.03	17.90		5.88				2.44					
22	0.721	18.76	18.62	9.24										
23	0.710	19.48	19.33											
24	0.700	20.18	20.03	9.94	6.58	4.90		3.22		2.38		1.54		
25	0.689	20.88	20.72				4.02							
26	0.679	21.56	21.40	10.62										
27	0.669	22.23	22.07		7.25									
28	0.659	22.90	22.73	11.28		5.56				3.10				
29	0.649	23.55	23.38											
30	0.640	24.20	24.02	11.92	7.89		4.66	3.86			2.24		1.44	
31	0.630	24.83	24.65											
32	0.621	25.46	25.27	12.54		6.18				3.00				
33	0.612	26.07	25.88		8.50									
34	0.603	26.68	26.48	13.14										
35	0.594	27.28	27.08				5.26		3.70					
36	0.585	27.87	27.66	13.73	9.08	6.76		4.44				2.12		
37	0.576	28.45	28.24											
38	0.568	29.02	28.81	14.30										
39	0.560	29.58	29.36		9.64									
40	0.551	30.14	29.92	14.85		7.31	5.81			3.55	2.80			1.29
41	0.543	30.69	30.46											
42	0.535	31.23	30.99	15.38	10.18			4.98	4.23					
43	0.527	31.76	31.52											
44	0.519	32.28	32.04	15.90		7.83								
45	0.512	32.80	32.55		10.69		6.32						1.95	
46	0.504	33.30	33.06	16.41										
47	0.497	33.80	33.55											
48	0.489	34.30	34.04	16.89	11.18	8.32		5.46		4.04		2.61		
49	0.482	34.78	34.52						4.71					
50	0.475	35.26	35.00	17.37			6.79				3.27			
51	0.468	35.73	35.47		11.65									
52	0.461	36.20	35.93	17.83		8.78								
53	0.454	36.66	36.38											
54	0.448	37.11	36.83	18.28	12.09			5.91						
55	0.441	37.55	37.27				7.23							
56	0.434	37.99	37.71	18.71		9.22		5.15	4.47					
57	0.428	38.42	38.13		12.52									
58	0.422	38.84	38.56	19.13										
59	0.415	39.26	38.97											
60	0.409	39.68	39.38	19.54	12.93	9.63	7.64	6.32			3.68	3.02	2.36	1.70

n	Single payment	Continuous loss	1	2	3	4	5	6	7	8	10	12	15	20
61	0.403	40.08	39.78											
62	0.397	40.48	40.18	19.94										
63	0.391	40.88	40.57		13.32				5.54					
64	0.386	41.27	40.96	20.33		10.01				4.86				
65	0.380	41.65	41.34				8.02							
66	0.374	42.02	41.71	20.70	13.70			6.70						
67	0.369	42.40	42.08											
68	0.363	42.76	42.44	21.06		10.38								
69	0.358	43.12	42.80		14.06									
70	0.353	43.48	43.15	21.42			8.38		5.89		4.03			
71	0.347	43.83	43.50											
72	0.342	44.17	43.84	21.76	14.4	10.72		7.04		5.20		3.36		
73	0.337	44.51	44.18											
74	0.332	44.85	44.51	22.09										
75	0.327	45.18	44.84		14.73		8.70						2.69	
76	0.323	45.50	45.16	22.41		11.04								
77	0.318	45.82	45.48						6.21					
78	0.313	46.14	45.79	22.73	15.04			7.35						
79	0.308	46.45	46.10											
80	0.304	46.76	46.41	23.03		11.34	9.01			5.50	4.34			2.01
81	0.299	47.06	46.71		15.34									
82	0.295	47.35	47.00	23.33										
83	0.291	47.65	47.29											
84	0.286	47.94	47.58	23.61	15.62	11.63		7.64	6.50			3.65		
85	0.282	48.22	47.86				9.29							
86	0.278	48.50	48.14	23.89										
87	0.274	48.78	48.51		15.90									
88	0.270	49.05	48.68	24.16		11.90				5.77				
89	0.266	49.32	48.95											
90	0.262	49.58	49.21	24.42	16.16		9.55	7.90			4.60		2.95	
91	0.258	49.84	49.47						6.76					
92	0.254	50.09	49.72	24.68		12.15								
93	0.250	50.35	49.97		16.41									
94	0.247	50.60	50.22	24.92										
95	0.243	50.84	50.46				9.79							
96	0.239	51.08	50.70	25.16	16.65	12.39		8.14		6.01		3.89		
97	0.236	51.32	50.94											
98	0.232	51.55	51.17	25.39					6.99					
99	0.229	51.78	51.40		16.88									
100	0.226	52.01	51.62	25.62		12.62	10.02				4.82			2.23

1. The single payment column is the appropriate multiplier for one payment in *n* years' time.

2. The continuous loss column is for loss accruing from day to day: in practice it is appropriate for weekly and monthly losses as well.

3. The column headed "1" is for a series of payments at yearly intervals at the *end of each year* for *n* years. If you want an immediate payment as well, add 1.

4. The remaining columns similarly show the multiplier for a series of payments at invervals of 2, 3, 4 and so on years.

5. Thus at 1.5 per cent discount £100 paid after 10 years has a present value of £86.20;
   – £100 a year continuously over the next 10 years has a present value of £929;
   – £100 at the end of each of the next 10 years has a present value of £922;
   – £100 at the end of 2, 4, 6, 8 and 10 years has a present value of £458 (row 10, 2-yearly column);
   – £100 at the end of 3, 6 and 9 years has a present value of £275 (row 9, 3-yearly column);
   – £100 now and after 2, 4, 6 and 8 years (but *not* the 10th year) has a present value of £472 (row 8, 2-yearly column, *plus* 1).

See further explanatory notes to table A3 at pages 15–16.

Multipliers at 2 per cent discount

n	Single payment	Continuous loss	1	2	3	4	5	6	7	8	10	12	15	20
			\<th colspan=13\>Frequency of payments in years											
1	0.980	0.99	0.98											
2	0.961	1.96	1.94	0.96										
3	0.942	2.91	2.88		0.94									
4	0.924	3.85	3.81	1.89		0.92								
5	0.906	4.76	4.71				0.91							
6	0.888	5.66	5.60	2.77	1.83			0.89						
7	0.871	6.54	6.47						0.87					
8	0.853	7.40	7.33	3.63		1.78				0.85				
9	0.837	8.24	8.16		2.67									
10	0.820	9.07	8.98	4.45			1.73				0.82			
11	0.804	9.88	9.79											
12	0.788	10.68	10.58	5.24	3.46	2.57		1.68				0.79		
13	0.773	11.46	11.35											
14	0.758	12.23	12.11	5.99					1.63					
15	0.743	12.98	12.85		4.20		2.47						0.74	
16	0.728	13.71	13.58	6.72		3.29				1.58				
17	0.714	14.43	14.29											
18	0.700	15.14	14.99	7.42	4.90				2.38					
19	0.686	15.84	15.68											
20	0.673	16.51	16.35	8.09		3.97	3.14				1.49			0.67
21	0.660	17.18	17.01		5.56				2.29					
22	0.647	17.83	17.66	8.74										
23	0.634	18.48	18.29											
24	0.622	19.10	18.91	9.36	6.18	4.59		3.00			2.20	1.41		
25	0.610	19.72	19.52				3.75							
26	0.598	20.32	20.12	9.96										
27	0.586	20.91	20.71		6.77									
28	0.574	21.49	21.28	10.54		5.16			2.86					
29	0.563	22.06	21.84											
30	0.552	22.62	22.40	11.09	7.32		4.30	3.55			2.05		1.30	
31	0.541	23.17	22.94											
32	0.531	23.70	23.47	11.62		5.69				2.73				
33	0.520	24.23	23.99		7.84									
34	0.510	24.74	24.50	12.13										
35	0.500	25.25	25.00				4.80		3.36					
36	0.490	25.74	25.49	12.62	8.33	6.18		4.04				1.90		
37	0.481	26.23	25.97											
38	0.471	26.71	26.44	13.09										
39	0.462	27.17	26.90		8.79									
40	0.453	27.63	27.36	13.54		6.64	5.26			3.19	2.50			1.13
41	0.444	28.08	27.80											
42	0.435	28.52	28.23	13.98	9.23			4.48	3.80					
43	0.427	28.95	28.66											
44	0.418	29.37	29.08	14.40		7.06								
45	0.410	29.79	29.49		9.64		5.67						1.71	
46	0.402	30.19	29.89	14.80										
47	0.394	30.59	30.29											
48	0.387	30.98	30.67	15.18	10.02	7.44		4.86		3.57		2.29		
49	0.379	31.36	31.05						4.18					
50	0.372	31.74	31.42	15.56			6.04				2.87			
51	0.364	32.11	31.79		10.39									
52	0.357	32.47	32.14	15.91		7.80								
53	0.350	32.82	32.50											
54	0.343	33.17	32.84	16.26	10.73			5.21						
55	0.337	33.51	33.17				6.37							
56	0.330	33.84	33.50	16.59		8.13		4.51		3.90				
57	0.323	34.17	33.83		11.06									
58	0.317	34.49	34.15	16.90										
59	0.311	34.80	34.46											
60	0.305	35.11	34.76	17.21	11.36	8.43	6.68	5.51			3.17	2.59	2.01	1.43

	Single payment	Continuous loss	Frequency of payments in years											
n			1	2	3	4	5	6	7	8	10	12	15	20
61	0.299	35.41	35.06											
62	0.293	35.71	35.35	17.50										
63	0.287	36.00	35.64		11.65				4.80					
64	0.282	36.28	35.92	17.78		8.72				4.19				
65	0.276	36.56	36.20				6.96							
66	0.271	36.83	36.47	18.05	11.92			5.78						
67	0.265	37.10	36.73											
68	0.260	37.36	36.99	18.31		8.98								
69	0.255	37.62	37.25		12.17									
70	0.250	37.87	37.50	18.56			7.21		5.04		3.42			
71	0.245	38.12	37.74											
72	0.240	38.36	37.98	18.80	12.41	9.22		6.02		4.43		2.83		
73	0.236	38.60	38.22											
74	0.231	38.84	38.45	19.03										
75	0.226	39.06	38.68		12.64		7.43						2.24	
76	0.222	39.29	38.90	19.26		9.44								
77	0.218	39.51	39.12						5.26					
78	0.213	39.72	39.33	19.47	12.85			6.23						
79	0.209	39.93	39.54											
80	0.205	40.14	39.74	19.68		9.64	7.64			4.63	3.63			1.64
81	0.201	40.35	39.95		13.05									
82	0.197	40.54	40.14	19.87										
83	0.193	40.74	40.34											
84	0.189	40.93	40.53	20.06	13.24	9.83		6.42	5.45			3.02		
85	0.186	41.12	40.71				7.82							
86	0.182	41.30	40.89	20.24										
87	0.179	41.48	41.07		13.42									
88	0.175	41.66	41.25	20.42		10.01				4.81				
89	0.172	41.83	41.42											
90	0.168	42.00	41.59	20.59	13.59		7.99	6.59			3.80		2.40	
91	0.165	42.17	41.75						5.62					
92	0.162	42.33	41.91	20.75		10.17								
93	0.159	42.49	42.07		13.75									
94	0.155	42.65	42.23	20.90										
95	0.152	42.80	42.38				8.14							
96	0.149	42.95	42.53	21.05	13.90	10.32		6.74		4.96		3.17		
97	0.146	43.10	42.68											
98	0.144	43.25	42.82	21.20					5.76					
99	0.141	43.39	42.96		14.04									
100	0.138	43.53	43.10	21.34		10.46	8.28				3.94			1.77

1. The single payment column is the appropriate multiplier for one payment in *n* years' time.

2. The continuous loss column is for loss accruing from day to day: in practice it is appropriate for weekly and monthly losses as well.

3. The column headed "1" is for a series of payments at yearly intervals at the *end of each year* for *n* years. If you want an immediate payment as well, add 1.

4. The remaining columns similarly show the multiplier for a series of payments at intervals of 2, 3, 4 and so on years.

5. Thus at 2 per cent discount £100 paid after 10 years has a present value of £82;
   - £100 a year continuously over the next 10 years has a present value of £907;
   - £100 at the end of each of the next 10 years has a present value of £898;
   - £100 at the end of 2, 4, 6, 8 and 10 years has a present value of £455 (row 10, 2-yearly column);
   - £100 at the end of 3, 6 and 9 years has a present value of £267 (row 9, 3-yearly column);
   - £100 now and after 2, 4, 6 and 8 years (but *not* the 10th year) has a present value of £463 (row 9, 2-yearly column, plus 1).

See further explanatory notes to table A3 at pages 15–16.

B5: Combination Tables at 1.5 and 2 per cent

See the explanatory note to table A4.

Combination grid (Discount rate 1.5%)

Years of loss	*Years before loss starts to run																Years of loss
	1	2	2.5	3	4	5	6	7.5	10	12.5	15	20	25	30	35	40	
1	0.98	0.96	0.96	0.95	0.94	0.92	0.91	0.89	0.86	0.82	0.79	0.74	0.68	0.64	0.59	0.55	1
2	1.94	1.91	1.90	1.88	1.86	1.83	1.80	1.76	1.70	1.64	1.58	1.46	1.36	1.26	1.17	1.09	2
3	2.89	2.85	2.83	2.81	2.76	2.72	2.68	2.62	2.53	2.44	2.35	2.18	2.02	1.88	1.74	1.62	3
4	3.83	3.77	3.74	3.71	3.66	3.60	3.55	3.47	3.35	3.22	3.11	2.88	2.68	2.48	2.31	2.14	4
5	4.75	4.68	4.64	4.61	4.54	4.47	4.41	4.31	4.15	4.00	3.85	3.58	3.32	3.08	2.86	2.66	5
6	5.65	5.57	5.53	5.49	5.41	5.33	5.25	5.13	4.95	4.77	4.59	4.26	3.96	3.67	3.41	3.16	6
7	6.55	6.45	6.40	6.36	6.26	6.17	6.08	5.95	5.73	5.52	5.32	4.94	4.58	4.25	3.95	3.66	7
8	7.43	7.32	7.27	7.21	7.11	7.00	6.90	6.75	6.50	6.26	6.03	5.60	5.20	4.82	4.48	4.16	8
9	8.30	8.18	8.12	8.06	7.94	7.82	7.70	7.53	7.26	6.99	6.74	6.25	5.81	5.39	5.00	4.64	9
10	9.15	9.02	8.95	8.89	8.75	8.62	8.50	8.31	8.01	7.71	7.43	6.90	6.40	5.94	5.52	5.12	10
11	10.00	9.85	9.78	9.70	9.56	9.42	9.28	9.07	8.74	8.42	8.12	7.53	6.99	6.49	6.03	5.59	11
12	10.83	10.67	10.59	10.51	10.35	10.20	10.05	9.83	9.47	9.12	8.79	8.16	7.57	7.03	6.53	6.06	12
13	11.64	11.47	11.39	11.30	11.14	10.97	10.81	10.57	10.18	9.81	9.45	8.78	8.15	7.56	7.02	6.52	13
14	12.45	12.27	12.18	12.09	11.91	11.73	11.56	11.30	10.89	10.49	10.11	9.38	8.71	8.08	7.50	6.97	14
15	13.24	13.05	12.95	12.86	12.67	12.48	12.29	12.02	11.58	11.16	10.75	9.98	9.26	8.60	7.98	7.41	15
16	14.03	13.82	13.72	13.61	13.41	13.22	13.02	12.73	12.27	11.82	11.39	10.57	9.81	9.11	8.45	7.85	16
17	14.80	14.58	14.47	14.36	14.15	13.94	13.74	13.43	12.94	12.47	12.01	11.15	10.35	9.61	8.92	8.28	17
18	15.56	15.33	15.21	15.10	14.88	14.66	14.44	14.12	13.61	13.11	12.63	11.72	10.88	10.10	9.38	8.70	18
19	16.30	16.06	15.94	15.83	15.59	15.36	15.13	14.80	14.26	13.74	13.24	12.29	11.41	10.59	9.83	9.12	19
20	17.04	16.79	16.66	16.54	16.30	16.06	15.82	15.47	14.90	14.36	13.83	12.84	11.92	11.07	10.27	9.54	20
21	17.77	17.50	17.37	17.25	16.99	16.74	16.49	16.13	15.54	14.97	14.42	13.39	12.43	11.54	10.71	9.94	21
22	18.48	18.21	18.07	17.94	17.68	17.41	17.16	16.78	16.16	15.57	15.01	13.93	12.93	12.00	11.14	10.34	22
23	19.19	18.90	18.76	18.62	18.35	18.08	17.81	17.42	16.78	16.17	15.58	14.46	13.42	12.46	11.57	10.74	23
24	19.88	19.59	19.44	19.30	19.01	18.73	18.46	18.05	17.39	16.75	16.14	14.98	13.91	12.91	11.98	11.12	24
25	20.57	20.26	20.11	19.96	19.67	19.38	19.09	18.67	17.99	17.33	16.70	15.50	14.39	13.35	12.40	11.51	25
26	21.24	20.93	20.77	20.62	20.31	20.01	19.72	19.28	18.58	17.90	17.24	16.01	14.86	13.79	12.80	11.88	26
27	21.90	21.58	21.42	21.26	20.95	20.64	20.33	19.88	19.16	18.46	17.78	16.51	15.32	14.22	13.20	12.26	27
28	22.56	22.22	22.06	21.90	21.57	21.25	20.94	20.48	19.73	19.01	18.31	17.00	15.78	14.65	13.60	12.62	28
29	23.20	22.86	22.69	22.52	22.19	21.86	21.54	21.06	20.29	19.55	18.84	17.49	16.23	15.07	13.99	12.98	29
30	23.84	23.49	23.31	23.14	22.80	22.46	22.13	21.64	20.85	20.09	19.35	17.96	16.68	15.48	14.37	13.34	30
31	24.46	24.10	23.92	23.75	23.39	23.05	22.71	22.21	21.40	20.61	19.86	18.44	17.11	15.89	14.75	13.69	31
32	25.08	24.71	24.53	24.34	23.98	23.63	23.28	22.77	21.93	21.13	20.36	18.90	17.54	16.29	15.12	14.03	32
33	25.69	25.31	25.12	24.93	24.56	24.20	23.84	23.32	22.47	21.64	20.85	19.36	17.97	16.68	15.48	14.37	33
34	26.29	25.90	25.70	25.51	25.14	24.77	24.40	23.86	22.99	22.15	21.34	19.81	18.39	17.07	15.84	14.71	34
35	26.87	26.48	26.28	26.09	25.70	25.32	24.95	24.40	23.50	22.65	21.82	20.25	18.80	17.45	16.20	15.04	35
36	27.46	27.05	26.85	26.65	26.26	25.87	25.49	24.92	24.01	23.14	22.29	20.69	19.21	17.83	16.55	15.36	36
37	28.03	27.61	27.41	27.21	26.80	26.41	26.02	25.44	24.51	23.62	22.75	21.12	19.61	18.20	16.89	15.68	37
38	28.59	28.17	27.96	27.75	27.34	26.94	26.54	25.95	25.01	24.09	23.21	21.55	20.00	18.57	17.23	16.00	38
39	29.15	28.72	28.50	28.29	27.87	27.46	27.06	26.46	25.49	24.56	23.66	21.97	20.39	18.93	17.57	16.31	39
40	29.69	29.26	29.04	28.82	28.40	27.98	27.56	26.95	25.97	25.02	24.11	22.38	20.77	19.28	17.90	16.61	40
41	30.23	29.79	29.57	29.35	28.91	28.49	28.06	27.44	26.44	25.48	24.54	22.78	21.15	19.63	18.22	16.92	41
42	30.76	30.31	30.08	29.86	29.42	28.99	28.56	27.93	26.91	25.92	24.98	23.18	21.52	19.98	18.54	17.21	42
43	31.29	30.83	30.60	30.37	29.92	29.48	29.04	28.40	27.36	26.36	25.40	23.58	21.89	20.32	18.86	17.51	43
44	31.80	31.33	31.10	30.87	30.41	29.96	29.52	28.87	27.81	26.80	25.82	23.97	22.25	20.65	19.17	17.79	44
45	32.31	31.83	31.60	31.36	30.90	30.44	29.99	29.33	28.26	27.23	26.23	24.35	22.60	20.98	19.48	18.08	45
Years of loss	1	2	2.5	3	4	5	6	7.5	10	12.5	15	20	25	30	35	40	Years of loss

Combination grid (Discount rate 2%)

Years of loss	Years before loss starts to run																Years of loss
	1	2	2.5	3	4	5	6	7.5	10	12.5	15	20	25	30	35	40	
1	0.97	0.95	0.94	0.93	0.91	0.90	0.88	0.85	0.81	0.77	0.74	0.67	0.60	0.55	0.50	0.45	1
2	1.92	1.88	1.87	1.85	1.81	1.78	1.74	1.69	1.61	1.53	1.46	1.32	1.20	1.08	0.98	0.89	2
3	2.86	2.80	2.77	2.74	2.69	2.64	2.59	2.51	2.39	2.27	2.16	1.96	1.78	1.61	1.46	1.32	3
4	3.77	3.70	3.66	3.62	3.55	3.48	3.41	3.31	3.15	3.00	2.86	2.59	2.34	2.12	1.92	1.74	4
5	4.67	4.58	4.53	4.49	4.40	4.31	4.23	4.10	3.91	3.72	3.54	3.20	2.90	2.63	2.38	2.16	5
6	5.55	5.44	5.38	5.33	5.23	5.12	5.02	4.88	4.64	4.42	4.20	3.81	3.45	3.12	2.83	2.56	6
7	6.41	6.28	6.22	6.16	6.04	5.92	5.80	5.63	5.36	5.10	4.86	4.40	3.98	3.61	3.27	2.96	7
8	7.25	7.11	7.04	6.97	6.83	6.70	6.57	6.38	6.07	5.78	5.50	4.98	4.51	4.08	3.70	3.35	8
9	8.08	7.92	7.85	7.77	7.62	7.47	7.32	7.11	6.76	6.44	6.13	5.55	5.02	4.55	4.12	3.73	9
10	8.89	8.72	8.63	8.55	8.38	8.22	8.06	7.82	7.44	7.08	6.74	6.11	5.53	5.01	4.54	4.11	10
11	9.69	9.50	9.41	9.31	9.13	8.95	8.78	8.52	8.11	7.72	7.34	6.65	6.02	5.46	4.94	4.48	11
12	10.47	10.27	10.16	10.06	9.87	9.67	9.48	9.21	8.76	8.34	7.94	7.19	6.51	5.90	5.34	4.84	12
13	11.24	11.02	10.91	10.80	10.59	10.38	10.18	9.88	9.40	8.95	8.52	7.71	6.99	6.33	5.73	5.19	13
14	11.99	11.75	11.64	11.52	11.30	11.07	10.86	10.54	10.03	9.55	9.08	8.23	7.45	6.75	6.11	5.54	14
15	12.72	12.47	12.35	12.23	11.99	11.75	11.52	11.19	10.65	10.13	9.64	8.73	7.91	7.16	6.49	5.88	15
16	13.44	13.18	13.05	12.92	12.67	12.42	12.18	11.82	11.25	10.71	10.19	9.23	8.36	7.57	6.86	6.21	16
17	14.15	13.87	13.74	13.60	13.33	13.07	12.82	12.44	11.84	11.27	10.72	9.71	8.80	7.97	7.22	6.54	17
18	14.84	14.55	14.41	14.27	13.99	13.71	13.44	13.05	12.42	11.82	11.25	10.19	9.23	8.36	7.57	6.86	18
19	15.52	15.22	15.07	14.92	14.63	14.34	14.06	13.65	12.99	12.36	11.77	10.66	9.65	8.74	7.92	7.17	19
20	16.19	15.87	15.72	15.56	15.26	14.96	14.66	14.23	13.55	12.89	12.27	11.11	10.07	9.12	8.26	7.48	20
21	16.84	16.51	16.35	16.19	15.87	15.56	15.26	14.81	14.09	13.41	12.77	11.56	10.47	9.48	8.59	7.78	21
22	17.48	17.14	16.97	16.81	16.48	16.15	15.84	15.37	14.63	13.92	13.25	12.00	10.87	9.85	8.92	8.08	22
23	18.11	17.76	17.58	17.41	17.07	16.73	16.40	15.92	15.16	14.42	13.73	12.43	11.26	10.20	9.24	8.37	23
24	18.73	18.36	18.18	18.00	17.65	17.30	16.96	16.47	15.67	14.91	14.19	12.86	11.64	10.55	9.55	8.65	24
25	19.33	18.95	18.77	18.58	18.22	17.86	17.51	17.00	16.18	15.39	14.65	13.27	12.02	10.89	9.86	8.93	25
26	19.92	19.53	19.34	19.15	18.77	18.41	18.04	17.52	16.67	15.87	15.10	13.68	12.39	11.22	10.16	9.20	26
27	20.50	20.10	19.90	19.71	19.32	18.94	18.57	18.03	17.16	16.33	15.54	14.07	12.75	11.55	10.46	9.47	27
28	21.07	20.66	20.45	20.25	19.86	19.47	19.09	18.53	17.63	16.78	15.97	14.46	13.10	11.87	10.75	9.73	28
29	21.63	21.21	21.00	20.79	20.38	19.98	19.59	19.02	18.10	17.22	16.39	14.85	13.45	12.18	11.03	9.99	29
30	22.18	21.74	21.53	21.31	20.90	20.49	20.09	19.50	18.56	17.66	16.81	15.22	13.79	12.49	11.31	10.24	30
31	22.71	22.27	22.05	21.83	21.40	20.98	20.57	19.97	19.00	18.09	17.21	15.59	14.12	12.79	11.58	10.49	31
32	23.24	22.78	22.56	22.33	21.90	21.47	21.05	20.43	19.44	18.50	17.61	15.95	14.45	13.09	11.85	10.73	32
33	23.75	23.29	23.06	22.83	22.38	21.94	21.51	20.88	19.87	18.91	18.00	16.30	14.77	13.38	12.11	10.97	33
34	24.26	23.78	23.55	23.32	22.86	22.41	21.97	21.33	20.30	19.32	18.38	16.65	15.08	13.66	12.37	11.21	34
35	24.75	24.27	24.03	23.79	23.32	22.87	22.42	21.76	20.71	19.71	18.76	16.99	15.39	13.94	12.62	11.43	35
36	25.24	24.74	24.50	24.26	23.78	23.32	22.86	22.19	21.12	20.10	19.13	17.32	15.69	14.21	12.87	11.66	36
37	25.71	25.21	24.96	24.72	24.23	23.76	23.29	22.61	21.52	20.48	19.49	17.65	15.99	14.48	13.11	11.88	37
38	26.18	25.67	25.41	25.16	24.67	24.19	23.71	23.02	21.91	20.85	19.84	17.97	16.28	14.74	13.35	12.09	38
39	26.64	26.12	25.86	25.60	25.10	24.61	24.13	23.42	22.29	21.21	20.19	18.28	16.56	15.00	13.59	12.31	39
40	27.09	26.55	26.29	26.03	25.52	25.02	24.53	23.81	22.66	21.57	20.53	18.59	16.84	15.25	13.81	12.51	40
41	27.53	26.99	26.72	26.46	25.94	25.43	24.93	24.20	23.03	21.92	20.86	18.89	17.11	15.50	14.04	12.72	41
42	27.96	27.41	27.14	26.87	26.34	25.83	25.32	24.58	23.39	22.26	21.19	19.19	17.38	15.74	14.26	12.91	42
43	28.38	27.82	27.55	27.28	26.74	26.22	25.70	24.95	23.75	22.60	21.51	19.48	17.64	15.98	14.47	13.11	43
44	28.79	28.23	27.95	27.68	27.13	26.60	26.08	25.32	24.09	22.93	21.82	19.76	17.90	16.21	14.69	13.30	44
45	29.20	28.63	28.35	28.07	27.52	26.98	26.45	25.67	24.43	23.25	22.13	20.04	18.15	16.44	14.89	13.49	45
Years of loss	1	2	2.5	3	4	5	6	7.5	10	12.5	15	20	25	30	35	40	Years of loss

B6: Multipliers applied by the Criminal Injuries Compensation Authority

Introductory notes:

1. The 1996 Criminal Injuries Compensation Scheme introduced a tariff system for assessing quantum. Paragraph 32 provided that:

   (32) The compensation payable in respect of [future losses] will be a lump sum which is the product of [the appropriate] multiplicand and an appropriate multiplier. The summary table given in note 3 illustrates the multipliers applicable to various periods of future loss to allow for the accelerated receipt of compensation. In selecting the multiplier the claims officer may refer to the Actuarial Tables for use in Personal Injury and Fatal Accident Cases published by the Government Actuary's Department, and take account of any factors and contingencies which appear relevant.

2. Paragraphs 32 and 33 of the 2001 Scheme expand the 1996 provisions:

   (32) The claims officer *will* assess a multiplier, discount factor, or life expectancy by reference to the tables in note 3, and *may* make such adjustments as he considers appropriate to take account of any factors and contingencies which appear to him to be relevant [our emphases]. The tables in note 3 set out the multipliers and (where applicable) discounts and life expectancies to be applied. Table A is to be applied to various periods of future loss to allow for the accelerated receipt of compensation. Table B sets out the discount factor, by which the lump sum is to be multiplied, when the loss does not start until various periods in the future. Table C is a life expectancy table, and in the absence of other factors affecting life expectancy, the table sets out the age to be applied when assessing a multiplier based on a pecuniary loss for life.

   (33) Where a claims officer considers that the approach in the preceding paragraph is impracticable, the compensation payable in respect of continuing loss of earnings and/or earning capacity will be such other lump sum as he may determine.

3. The 1996 Scheme applies to applications for compensation made between April 1, 1996 and March 31, 2001. The 2001 Scheme applies to applications made from April 1, 2001.

4. The tables which follow are from the 2001 Scheme. The 1996 table of multipliers goes up to 40 years rather than 50, but the figures are otherwise the same. The 1996 Scheme did not have Tables B and C.

5. The CICA figures correspond to an annual discount rate of about 4.5 per cent.

2001 Scheme, para.32, note 3, Table A

This converts an annual loss over a period of years into a lump sum payable at the beginning of that period.

Years of loss	Multiplier	Years of loss	Multiplier	Years of loss	Multiplier	Years of loss	Multiplier
5	5	11	8.5	16	11	25	15
6	5.5	12	9	17	11.5	30	16
7	6	13	9.5	18	12	35	17
8	7	14	10	19	12.5	40	18
9	7.5	15	10.5	20	13	50	20
10	8						

2001 Scheme, para.32, note 3, Table B

This is the figure by which the cost of a single item of future expense (e.g. an operation or a wheelchair) must be multiplied, according to the number of years before the claimant will incur the expense.

Years of loss	Multiplier	Years of loss	Multiplier	Years of loss	Multiplier	Years of loss	Multiplier
5	0.80	11	0.62	16	0.50	25	0.34
6	0.77	12	0.59	17	0.48	30	0.27
7	0.74	13	0.57	18	0.46	35	0.22
8	0.71	14	0.54	19	0.44	40	0.18
9	0.68	15	0.52	20	0.42	50	0.12
10	0.65						

2001 Scheme, para.32, note 3, Table C

Life expectancy table.

Age at date of assessment	Age to which expected to live for purposes of calculation		Age at date of assessment	Age to which expected to live for purposes of calculation	
	Males	Females		Males	Females
0–25	80 years of age	84 years of age	81	88	89
26–50	81	84	82	88	90
51–60	81	85	83	89	90
61–65	82	85	84–85	90	91
66–70	83	86	86	91	92
71–73	84	87	87–88	92	93
74–76	85	87	89	93	94
77–78	86	88	90	94	95
79–80	87	89			

Group C
Earnings

C

C1: National minimum wage

Introductory notes

1. The National Minimum Wage became law on April 1, 1999.

2. The National Minimum Wage is the minimum amount of pay to which workers over a specified age are entitled. Up to September 30, 2004, the minimum age was 18. Since October 1, 2004 a new rate has been available to workers aged 16 and 17.

3. Most adult workers who are resident in the UK, who have a written, oral or implied contract and who are not genuinely self-employed, are entitled to the National Minimum Wage.

4. The National Minimum Wage is enforced by the Inland Revenue.

5. There are three levels of National Minimum Wage: a development rate for those aged between 18 and 21; a main rate for workers aged 22 or over; and, from October 1, 2004, a new rate for workers aged 16 and 17.

6. The development rate can also apply, subject to various conditions, to workers aged 22 or over who start a new job with a new employer and do accredited training, being a course approved by the UK government to obtain a vocational qualification. The accredited training rate can only be paid for the first six months of the new job, after which the National Minimum Wage main rate applies.

7. The increased rates shown as applicable from October 1, 2006 are subject to confirmation by the Low Pay Commission in February 2006 that the economic conditions continue to make increases appropriate.

Rates

New rate for workers aged 16 and 17 (note 2)
Pay reference periods

starting on or after:	1/4/99	1/6/00	1/10/01	1/10/02	1/10/03	1/10/04
	£ per hour	£ per hour	£ per hour	£ per hour	£ per hour	£ per hour
Hourly rate	–	–	–	–	–	3.00

Development rate for workers aged 18 to 21 years (note 5)
Pay reference periods

starting on or after:	1/4/99	1/6/00	1/10/01	1/10/02	1/10/03	1/10/04	1/10/05	1/10/06
	£ per hour	£ per hour	£ per hour	£ per hour	£ per hour	£ per hour	£ per hour	£ per hour
Hourly rate	3.00	3.20	3.50	3.60	3.80	4.10	4.25	4.45

Main rate for workers aged 22 or over (note 5)
Pay reference periods

starting on or after:	1/4/99	1/10/00	1/10/01	1/10/02	1/10/03	1/10/04	1/10/05	1/10/06
	£ per hour	£ per hour	£ per hour	£ per hour	£ per hour	£ per hour	£ per hour	£ per hour
Hourly rate	3.60	3.70	4.10	4.20	4.50	4.85	5.05	5.35

Development rate for workers aged 22 years or over doing accredited training (note 6)
Pay reference periods

starting on or after:	1/4/99		1/10/01	1/10/02	1/10/03	1/10/04	1/01/05	1/10/06
	£ per hour		£ per hour	£ per hour	£ per hour	£ per hour	£ per hour	£ per hour
Hourly rate	3.20		3.50	3.60	3.80	4.10	4.25	4.45

C2: Regional unemployment statistics

The following tables show the average duration of claims for benefits, terminating the quarter ending January 2005. They are taken from the April 2005 edition of Labour Market Trends, whose source is the Benefits Agency. They should be used with caution: they can only give the broadest of indications of what is actually happening in any region, and their interpretation is a matter for experts.

Generally, unemployment is falling, with one or two exceptions. Against this, however, the number of "long term unemployed" is rising. The pattern appears to be that those in work who lose a job, while experiencing some time on the labour market, return to work quickly. Those who become "long term unemployed" (*i.e.* those who have been without work for 52 weeks or more) are experiencing greater difficulty in finding work. Those who have had an accident or injury might typically fall into the latter category, which is another reason for approaching these statistics with caution.

Using the "Summary Regional Labour Market Unemployment Statistics" as well, a good picture can be built up for the overall economic climate of an area, and whether there are exceptional difficulties, particularly for the hardcore or long-term unemployed.

United Kingdom

Average duration of benefits claims in weeks

	Mean		Median	
Age	Female	Male	Female	Male
16–17	9	8	6	6
18–19	13	12	8	7
20–24	13	13	8	8
25–29	15	18	8	10
30–34	17	21	9	11
35–39	18	23	10	11
40–44	19	23	10	11
45–49	19	24	9	10
50–54	20	26	9	10
55–59	27	30	11	10
60+	n/a	36	n/a	10
All ages	16	19	9	9

North East

Average duration of benefits claims in weeks

	Mean		Median	
	Female	Male	Female	Male
16–17	7	7	6	5
18–19	12	13	8	7
20–24	12	13	8	8
25–29	14	17	8	9
30–34	18	20	9	9
35–39	20	20	9	9
40–44	19	21	9	9
45–49	17	19	8	8
50–54	22	25	9	7
55–59	29	32	12	8
60+	n/a	39	n/a	8
All ages	16	18	8	8

North West

Average duration of benefits claims in weeks

	Mean		Median	
	Female	Male	Female	Male
16–17	9	8	6	5
18–12	13	12	8	7
20–24	12	13	8	8
25–29	14	17	8	9
30–34	15	21	9	10
35–39	18	22	9	11
40–44	18	23	8	11
45–49	18	24	8	10
50–54	18	25	9	9
55–59	25	29	10	10
60+	n/a	35	n/a	8
All ages	15	18	8	9

Yorkshire and the Humber

Average duration of benefits claims in weeks

	Mean		Median	
Age	Female	Male	Female	Male
16–17	7	6	5	4
18–19	12	11	8	7
20–24	12	12	8	8
25–29	14	16	8	10
30–34	16	19	9	10
35–39	17	21	10	10
40–44	18	22	9	10
45–49	17	21	9	10
50–54	19	24	9	9
55–59	26	31	11	9
60+	n/a	31	n/a	9
All ages	15	17	8	9

East Midlands

Average duration of benefits claims in weeks

	Mean		Median	
Age	Female	Male	Female	Male
16–17	8	8	6	6
18–19	12	11	8	7
20–24	13	13	8	8
25–29	15	18	9	10
30–34	17	20	9	10
35–39	16	22	9	11
40–44	18	22	10	10
45–49	17	22	9	10
50–54	17	26	8	9
55–59	23	27	11	9
60+	n/a	26	n/a	9
All ages	15	19	8	9

West Midlands

Average duration of benefits claims in weeks

	Mean		Median	
Age	Female	Male	Female	Male
16–17	9	8	7	6
18–19	13	12	8	7
20–24	14	14	9	9
25–29	16	19	8	11
30–34	17	22	9	12
35–39	19	25	10	12
40–44	19	25	9	11
45–49	19	25	9	10
50–54	21	27	10	11
55–59	30	33	12	12
60+	n/a	35	n/a	11
All ages	17	20	9	10

East

Average duration of benefits claims in weeks

	Mean		Median	
Age	Female	Male	Female	Male
16–17	9	9	7	7
18–19	12	11	8	7
20–24	12	12	7	8
25–29	14	15	7	8
30–34	14	18	8	9
35–39	16	19	10	9
40–44	15	19	9	9
45–49	15	22	8	10
50–54	16	21	8	10
55–59	21	24	8	10
60+	n/a	24	n/a	10
All ages	14	17	8	8

London

Average duration of benefits claims in weeks

	Mean		Median	
Age	Female	Male	Female	Male
16–17	11	11	8	8
18–19	15	15	11	10
20–24	16	17	11	11
25–29	18	22	10	13
30–34	21	27	11	16
35–39	24	29	14	17
40–44	26	31	14	18
45–49	27	33	15	17
50–54	27	35	14	17
55–59	40	40	17	17
60+	n/a	53	n/a	21
All ages	21	25	12	14

South East

Average duration of benefits claims in weeks

	Mean		Median	
Age	Female	Male	Female	Male
16–17	9	8	6	6
18–19	12	11	8	7
20–24	12	12	8	8
25–29	13	16	8	9
30–34	15	19	8	10
35–39	18	20	10	11
40–44	18	20	10	11
45–49	17	21	9	11
50–54	18	24	9	11
55–59	24	29	10	11
60+	n/a	28	n/a	11
All ages	15	18	8	9

South West

Average duration of benefits claims in weeks

Age	Mean Female	Mean Male	Median Female	Median Male
16–17	8	8	6	6
18–19	10	9	7	6
20–24	10	11	6	7
25–29	12	13	7	7
30–34	13	15	7	8
35–39	14	17	8	8
40–44	14	17	7	8
45–49	14	18	7	8
50–54	14	20	7	9
55–59	19	19	8	8
60+	n/a	25	n/a	6
All ages	13	15	7	7

England

Average duration of benefits claims in weeks

Age	Mean Female	Mean Male	Median Female	Median Male
16–17	8	8	6	6
18–19	13	12	8	7
20–24	13	13	8	8
25–29	15	18	8	10
30–34	17	21	9	11
35–39	19	23	10	11
40–44	19	23	10	11
45–49	19	24	9	11
50–54	20	26	9	10
55–59	27	30	11	11
60+	n/a	33	n/a	10
All ages	16	19	9	9

Wales

Average duration of benefits claims in weeks

Age	Mean Female	Mean Male	Median Female	Median Male
16–17	6	6	5	4
18–19	11	11	7	6
20–24	11	11	7	7
25–29	12	16	7	8
30–34	14	19	8	9
35–39	14	20	8	10
40–44	17	20	8	9
45–49	17	22	8	8
50–54	17	25	8	9
55–59	23	27	9	8
60+	n/a	27	n/a	9
All ages	13	17	7	8

Regional labour market summary 1

	Total aged 16 & over	Economically active				LFS Employment						ILO Unemployment					
	All	All		Male	Female	All		Male		Female		All		Male		Female	
Government Office Regions	Level	Level	Rate (%)	Level	Level	Level	Rate (%)	Level	Rate (%)	Level	Rate (%)	Level	Rate (%)	Level	Rate (%)	Level	Rate (%)
	1	2	3	4	5	6	7	8	9	10	11	12	13	14	15	16	17
North East	2,031	1,187	74.8	634	554	1,122	70.6	593	73.1	529	67.9	66	5.5	40	6.4	25	4.6
North West	5,414	3,342	77.1	1,782	1,560	3,182	73.3	1,690	76.8	1,492	69.7	160	4.8	92	5.2	68	4.3
Yorkshire & the Humber	3,994	2,470	78.0	1,331	1,139	2,366	74.6	1,267	78.6	1,098	70.3	104	4.2	64	4.8	40	3.5
East Midlands	3,413	2,170	79.8	1,185	984	2,077	76.3	1,130	80.8	946	71.4	93	4.3	55	4.6	38	3.9
West Midlands	4,210	2,631	78.4	1,444	1,186	2,508	74.7	1,370	79.6	1,138	69.4	122	4.6	74	5.1	48	4.1
East	4,359	2,845	82.0	1,558	1,287	2,735	78.8	1,494	83.8	1,241	73.4	110	3.9	63	4.1	46	3.6
London	5,909	3,805	75.2	2,116	1,688	3,550	70.0	1,965	76.1	1,585	63.6	255	6.7	151	7.1	103	6.1
South East	6,428	4,230	82.0	2,300	1,930	4,075	78.9	2,216	84.1	1,860	73.3	155	3.7	84	3.7	71	3.7
South West	4,034	2,552	81.8	1,380	1,172	2,462	78.8	1,328	83.0	1,134	74.3	90	3.5	53	3.8	38	3.2
England	39,792	25,231	78.9	13,730	11,501	24,077	75.2	13,053	79.8	11,023	70.2	1,155	4.6	677	4.9	478	4.2
Wales	2,361	1,387	75.1	736	661	1,325	71.6	700	74.5	625	68.6	62	4.5	37	5.0	25	3.9
Scotland	4,076	2,597	80.0	1,371	1,226	2,453	75.4	1,286	78.5	1,167	72.3	144	5.5	85	6.2	59	4.8
Great Britain	46,228	29,215	78.8	15,838	13,377	27,855	75.0	15,040	79.5	12,815	70.3	1,360	4.7	798	5.0	562	4.2
N Ireland	1,310	780	72.3	432	348	743	68.7	406	74.1	336	63.0	37	4.7	26	5.9	11	3.3
United Kingdom	47,538	30,005	78.6	16,276	13,729	28,608	74.9	15,453	79.3	13,155	70.1	1,396	4.7	823	5.1	573	4.2

Labour Force Survey (January to March 2005)

Figures in thousands.

Claimant Count v ILO Unemployment

Along with a large number of other countries, the United Kingdom publishes two defined measures of unemployment that complement each other.

One comes from a monthly count of those claiming unemployment-related benefits. This administrative measure is known as the *Claimant Count.*

The other comes from a quarterly survey of households, the Labour Force Survey. This survey measure is accepted as an international standard because it is based on methods recommended by the International Labour Organisation. It is known as the *p* and is used by the European Union (EU) and the Organisation for Economic Co-operation and Development (OECD).

Both measures have their advantages and disadvantages.

The advantage of the claimant count is that it is available quickly and monthly and because it is a 100 per cent count, it also provides precise information on very small areas.

The ILO measure on the other hand as well as being internationally standard, springs from a data source (the Labour Force Survey) which allows unemployment to be analysed in the context of other labour market information and a variety of demographic characteristics.

A disadvantage of the Claimant Count is that it can be affected if there are changes to the benefit system from which it is derived.

Although changes in the benefit system may also affect the labour market behaviour of respondents to the LFS, the ILO definition itself is entirely independent of the benefit system. Comparatively the LFS results, based on the ILO measure, are not reliable for areas smaller than counties or the larger local authority districts, because of sample size restrictions. Estimates of less than 10,000 persons unemployed (after grossing up) are not shown in published tables because they are subject to unacceptably high sampling error and are, therefore, unreliable.

This said, government statistics apply recognised statistical procedures in order to minimise these disadvantages and maintain the relevance of both measures as accurate labour market indicators.

Claimant count rates

Area	1992	1993	1994	1995	1996	1997	1998	1999	2000	2001	2002	2003	2004	2005
United Kingdom	9.2	9.7	8.8	7.6	7.0	5.3	4.5	4.2	3.6	3.2	3.2	3.1	2.7	2.7
North East	11.3	12.1	11.7	10.8	10.0	8.1	7.2	7.0	6.3	5.7	5.1	4.9	4.0	3.9
North West	9.8	10.0	9.3	8.1	7.5	5.9	5.1	4.6	4.1	3.7	3.6	3.4	2.9	2.8
Yorkshire and the Humber	9.4	9.7	9.1	8.1	7.6	6.1	5.4	5.0	4.4	4.0	3.7	3.5	2.9	2.9
East Midlands	8.6	9.0	8.3	7.1	6.5	4.7	4.0	3.7	3.5	3.1	2.9	2.9	2.5	2.5
West Midlands	9.8	10.3	9.4	7.7	6.9	5.3	4.6	4.5	4.0	3.7	3.5	3.6	3.3	3.3
East	8.1	8.8	7.6	6.2	5.7	4.0	3.2	2.9	2.5	2.1	2.1	2.2	2.0	2.0
London	9.9	10.9	10.1	8.9	8.2	6.2	5.0	4.5	3.8	3.3	3.6	3.7	3.5	3.5
South East	7.4	8.1	6.9	5.6	4.9	3.3	2.6	2.3	1.9	1.6	1.7	1.8	1.6	1.6
South West	8.7	9.0	7.7	6.5	5.9	4.2	3.4	3.1	2.5	2.1	2.0	1.9	1.6	1.6
England	9.1	9.7	8.7	7.5	6.8	5.1	4.3	3.9	3.4	3.0	3.0	3.0	2.6	2.6
Wales	9.5	9.8	8.9	8.1	7.7	6.2	5.4	5.0	4.4	4.0	3.6	3.5	3.0	3.0
Scotland	8.9	9.2	8.7	7.5	7.3	6.2	5.5	5.1	4.6	4.0	4.2	3.8	3.5	3.3
Northern Ireland	13.7	13.6	12.6	11.2	10.7	8.1	7.3	6.4	5.3	4.9	4.8	4.3	3.6	3.4

Seasonally adjusted annual averages – percentages

ILO Unemployment Rates

Area	1992	1993	1994	1995	1996	1997	1998	1999	2000	2001	2002	2003	2004	2005
United Kingdom	9.7	10.3	9.6	8.6	8.2	7.1	6.1	6.0	5.6	4.8	5.1	5.1	4.8	4.7
North East	11.8	12.0	12.5	11.4	10.8	9.8	8.2	10.1	9.2	7.4	7.5	6.5	6.3	5.5
North West	9.1	9.8	9.5	8.3	7.3	6.3	5.6	5.5	5.4	5.1	5.2	4.5	4.9	4.8
Yorkshire and the Humber	10.1	10.0	9.9	8.7	8.1	8.1	7.0	6.6	6.1	4.9	5.2	4.6	5.0	4.2
East Midlands	8.8	9.1	9.1	7.5	7.4	6.3	4.9	5.2	5.2	4.9	4.2	4.3	4.5	4.3
West Midlands	10.7	11.8	11.8	9.0	9.2	6.8	6.3	6.8	6.3	5.0	5.5	5.6	5.5	4.6
East	7.7	9.2	9.2	7.5	6.2	5.9	5.0	4.2	3.6	3.6	3.8	4.1	3.3	3.9
London	12.0	13.2	13.2	11.5	11.3	9.1	8.1	7.5	7.1	5.8	7.0	6.6	6.9	6.7
South East	7.8	8.0	8.0	6.4	6.0	5.2	4.3	3.6	3.4	3.0	3.4	3.8	3.8	3.7
South West	9.1	9.2	9.2	7.8	6.3	5.2	4.5	4.7	4.2	3.5	3.7	3.7	2.8	3.5
England	9.7	10.3	10.3	8.6	8.1	6.9	6.0	5.8	5.3	4.6	4.9	5.0	4.7	4.6
Wales	8.9	9.6	9.6	8.8	8.3	8.4	6.7	7.1	6.2	5.7	5.4	4.8	4.9	4.5
Scotland	9.5	10.2	10.2	8.3	8.7	8.5	7.4	7.4	7.7	5.8	6.8	5.7	5.7	5.5
Northern Ireland	12.3	12.5	12.5	11.0	9.7	7.5	7.3	7.2	7.2	6.2	6.3	5.5	5.6	4.7

Percentages, Spring each year, seasonally adjusted

C3: Average earnings index

Average earnings index
All employees: main industrial sectors (not seasonally adjusted)

Area	1996	1997	1998	1999	2000	2001	2002	2003	2004	2005
Jan	81.2	84.9	89.0	93.0	99.0	103.4	106.4	109.9	118.2	123.3
Feb	83.2	86.2	90.8	95.4	100.8	107.7	110.8	113.8	118.1	124.9
Mar	84.8	89.1	93.8	98.5	103.9	108.4	111.6	116.8	122.2	127.5
Apr	82.9	86.0	91.0	94.4	98.5	103.3	107.2	110.0	115.0	
May	82.3	85.7	91.0	94.7	98.4	102.7	106.5	110.0	114.8	
Jun	83.1	86.3	90.8	95.7	99.2	104.0	107.8	111.2	116.1	
Jul	83.9	87.2	92.0	95.9	99.4	103.7	107.6	111.8	115.4	
Aug	82.4	86.1	90.2	94.5	98.5	102.8	106.3	110.2	114.8	
Sep	82.9	86.3	90.5	94.5	98.3	102.6	106.3	110.4	114.9	
Oct	82.7	86.3	90.4	95.0	98.7	103.0	107.3	110.9	115.7	
Nov	83.6	87.4	91.3	95.8	99.7	103.4	108.1	111.2	116.2	
Dec	86.3	90.6	94.5	100.4	105.6	107.8	111.3	114.7	119.5	
Yearly Average	83.3	86.8	91.3	95.7	100.0	104.4	108.1	111.7	116.7	

Index 2000 = 100

"Average Earnings Index", National statistics © Crown Copyright 2003
Reproduced here with the kind permission of the Controller of HMSO and the Office for National Statistics

C4: Average weekly earnings

These figures are the average gross weekly earnings of full-time employees on adult rates whose pay was not affected by absence.

	Men	Women
	£	£
1985	192.40	126.40
1986	207.50	137.20
1987	224.00	148.10
1988	245.80	164.20
1989	269.50	182.30
1990	295.60	201.50
1991	318.90	222.40
1992	340.10	241.10
1993	353.50	252.60
1994	362.10	261.50
1995	374.60	269.80
1996	391.60	283.00
1997	408.70	297.20
1998	427.10	309.60
1999	442.40	326.50
2000	453.30	337.60
2001	490.50	366.80
2002	513.80	383.20
2003	525.00	396.00
2004	556.80	420.20

These figures are taken from The New Earnings Surveys published by HMSO.

C5: Average earnings statistics

Analyses of earnings by occupation

Introductory notes:

1. It will usually be possible to obtain agreement, or a direction, that the earnings shown in the New Earnings Survey may be adduced in evidence without formal proof but occasionally it is necessary to adduce formal proof. This is done by calling a witness from the New Earnings Survey, Earnings and Employment Division, Office for National Statistics, Room 249, East Lane House, PO Box 12, East Lane, Runcorn, WA7 2DN (Tel: 01928 792077 and 792078).

2. These tables have been compiled from the Department of Employment's New Earnings Survey, by kind permission of the Controller of Her Majesty's Stationery Office. Due to the re-classification of occupations in the 2003 survey (using SOC 2000), only the 2003 figures are shown in this table.

3. The average gross weekly earnings shown are for employees whose pay for the survey pay-period was not affected by absence.

4. Average gross annual earnings have only been published since April 2000.
   Annual earnings figures are only provided for those employees who have been in the same job for at least 12 months, regardless of whether or not their pay was affected by absence.

5. Results are generally given only for those occupations represented by at least 30 persons in the same sample and which have a standard error of 5 per cent or less.

6. n.e.c. stands for "not elsewhere classified".

7. m denotes "manual occupation", where it appears alongside certain occupations listed under non-manual groups 6 and 7.

Full-Time Males on Adult Rates (where pay was not affected by absence) (notes on p.136)

	Average Gross Weekly Pay (in April)	Average Gross Annual Earnings (in April)
	2004	2004
Occupation SOC 2000	£	£
Managers and Senior Officials	825.0	47,520
Corporate Managers	856.3	49,495
Corporate Managers and Senior Officials	1797.1	131,345
Directors and chief executives of major organisations	2132.9	165,232
Production Managers	745.1	39,769
Production, works and maintenance managers	760.9	40,263
Managers in construction	670.5	36,594
Functional Managers	989.3	58,496
Financial managers and chartered secretaries	1230.6	81,989
Marketing and sales managers	938.3	53,447
Purchasing managers	773.1	41,162
Personnel, training and industrial relations managers	905.3	51,537
Information and communication technology managers	928.3	50,937
Quality and Customer Care Managers	709.3	39,090
Quality assurance managers	696.3	37,117
Customer care managers	716.1	40,347
Financial Institution and Office Managers	785.7	44,232
Financial institution managers	813.0	48,409
Office managers	770.2	42,000
Managers in Distribution, Storage and Retailing	540.0	29,393
Transport and distribution managers	624.5	33,839
Storage and warehouse managers	541.9	29,327
Retail and wholesale managers	505.5	27,557
Protective Service Officers	775.0	41,204
Police officers (inspectors and above)	903.3	47,767
Senior officers in fire, ambulance, prison and related services	745.4	38,845
Health and Social Services Managers	690.0	35,431
Residential and day care managers	500.0	24,917
Managers and proprietors in agriculture and services	654.5	37,024
Managers in Farming, Horticulture, Forestry and Fishing	522.1	28,117
Farm Managers	441.3	24,012
Managers and Proprietors In Hospitality and Leisure Services	481.2	26,315
Restaurant and catering managers	469.8	24,671
Publicans and managers of licensed premises	366.3	21,071
Managers and Proprietors In Other Service Industries	734.4	41,391
Property, housing and land managers	722.6	40,472
Shopkeepers and wholesale/retail dealers	552.5	30,896
Managers and proprietors in other services n.e.c.	792.2	45,098

Full-Time Males on Adult Rates (where pay was not affected by absence) (notes on p.136)

Occupation SOC 2000	Average Gross Weekly Pay (in April) 2004 £	Average Gross Annual Earnings (in April) 2004 £
Professional Occupations	715.3	37,444
Science and Technology Professionals	668.4	34,803
Science Professionals	645.5	35,060
Biological scientists and biochemists	640.6	34,047
Engineering Professionals	645.8	33,084
Civil engineers	608.7	31,323
Mechanical engineers	675.9	34,196
Electrical engineers	680.2	34,492
Design and development engineers	647.3	33,691
Production and process engineers	635.5	33,167
Planning and quality control engineers	574.9	29,741
Engineering professionals n.e.c.	658.3	32,767
Information and Communication Technology Professionals	701.1	36,958
IT strategy and planning professionals	867.8	47,397
Software professionals	662.9	34,714
Health Professionals	1198.3	66,539
Medical Practitioners	1284.7	73,184
Teaching and Research Professionals	652.7	33,660
Teaching Professionals	668.4	34,224
Higher education teaching professionals	785.4	40,236
Further education teaching professionals	591.8	30,452
Secondary education teaching professionals	657.6	33,618
Primary and nursery education teaching professionals	635.9	32,617
Special needs education teaching professionals	637.4	32,602
Research Professionals	534.2	29,017
Scientific researchers	591.3	30,826
Social science researchers	436.2	29,246
Business and Public Service Professionals	743.2	40,337
Legal Professionals	972.3	51,573
Solicitors and lawyers, judges and coroners	989.1	53,463
Business and Statistical Professionals	855.0	48,158
Chartered and certified accountants	766.2	41,299
Management consultants, actuaries, economists and statisticians	974.5	57,965
Architects, Town Planners, Surveyors	653.7	35,516
Architects	692.6	39,126
Town Planners	627.0	34,641
Quantity surveyors	602.6	32,511
Chartered surveyors (not quantity surveyors)	675.5	36,097
Public Service Professionals	476.9	24,445
Social workers	485.8	25,189
Clergy	386.4	19,770

Full-Time Males on Adult Rates (where pay was not affected by absence) (notes on p.136)

Occupation SOC 2000	Average Gross Weekly Pay (in April) 2004 £	Average Gross Annual Earnings (in April) 2004 £
Librarians and Related Professionals	487.6	25,356
Associate Professional and Technical Occupations	583.7	31,077
Science and Technology Associate Professionals	510.8	26,796
Science and Engineering Technicians	482.2	24,560
Laboratory technicians	441.8	22,453
Electrical/electronics technicians	476.0	24,374
Engineering techinicians	559.4	27,933
Science and engineering technicians n.e.c.	437.9	22,461
Draughtspersons and Building Inspectors	490.5	25,025
Architectural technologists and town planning technicians	510.3	26,588
Draughtspersons	479.3	24,345
IT Service Delivery Occupations	563.2	31,164
IT operations technicians	595.6	32,742
IT users support technicians	495.8	27,261
Health and Social Welfare Associate Professionals	475.4	24,613
Health Associate Professionals	498.1	25,734
Nurses	505.2	25,960
Paramedics	497.6	24,818
Medical and dental technicians	436.6	23,393
Social Welfare Associate Professionals	434.2	22,802
Youth and community workers	412.3	21,360
Housing and welfare officers	447.8	22,895
Protective Service Occupations	579.4	29,716
Police officers (sergeant and below)	638.6	32,228
Fire service officers (leading fire officer and below)	479.7	25,046
Prison service officers (below principal officer)	466.3	25,297
Protective service associate professionals n.e.c.	507.1	28,196
Graphic designers	490.0	26,442
Media Associate Professionals	649.6	33,527
Journalists, newspaper and periodical editors	608.9	32,729
Photographers and audio-visual equipment operators	497.7	24,751
Business and Public Service Associate Professionals	631.2	34,871
Transport Associate Professionals	768.3	39,493
Train drivers	634.7	33,371

Full-Time Males on Adult Rates (where pay was not affected by absence) (notes on p.136)

	Average Gross Weekly Pay (in April)	Average Gross Annual Earnings (in April)
	2004	2004
Occupation SOC 2000	£	£
Business and Finance Associate Professionals	763.9	44,383
Estimators, valuers and assessors	555.9	29,886
Business and related associate professionals n.e.c.	552.4	29,960
Sales and Related Associate Professionals	554.8	30,179
Buyers and purchasing officers	550.1	29,154
Sales representatives	557.4	29,731
Conservation Associate Professionals	459.6	24,328
Countryside and park rangers	355.2	—
Public Service and Other Associate Professionals	573.1	30,663
Public service associate professionals	706.5	36,498
Vocational and industrial trainers and instructors	458.2	24,137
Careers advisers and vocational guidance specialists	449.5	22,394
Occupational hygienists and safety officers	585.0	31,087
Administrative and Secretarial Occupations	386.9	20,324
Administrative Occupations	383.7	20,100
Administrative Occupations: Government and Related Organisations	382.8	19,759
Civil Service executive officers	453.5	23,645
Civil Service administrative officers and assistants	304.0	15,824
Local government clerical officers and assistants	420.8	21,125
Administrative Occupations: Finance	397.3	20,974
Accounts and wages clerks, book-keepers, other financial clerks	418.7	22,038
Counter clerks	370.1	19,714
Administrative Occupations: Records	391.8	20,502
Filing and other records assistants/clerks	385.4	20,337
Pensions and insurance clerks	412.9	22,055
Stock control clerks	389.5	19,818
Database assistants/clerks	362.5	20,707
Administrative Occupations: Communications	381.9	20,314
Communications operators	413.0	21,334
Administrative Occupations: General	362.1	19,068
General office assistants/clerks	362.1	19,068
Receptionists	301.8	15,991
Skilled Trades Occupations	433.1	22,162
Skilled Agricultural Trades	311.7	16,011
Agricultural Trades	311.7	16,011
Farmers	—	—
Gardeners and groundsmen/groundswomen	309.3	15,844

Full-Time Males on Adult Rates (where pay was not affected by absence) (notes on p.136)

Occupation SOC 2000	Average Gross Weekly Pay (in April) 2004 £	Average Gross Annual Earnings (in April) 2004 £
Skilled Metal and Electrical Trades	467.7	23,757
Metal Forming, Welding and Related Trades	433.5	21,422
Metal plate workers, shipwrights, riveters	456.0	23,539
Metal Machining, Fitting and Instrument Making Trades	477.7	24,287
Metal machining setters and setter-operators	428.9	—
Metal working production and maintenance fitters	493.8	25,255
Precision instrument makers and repairers	426.8	21,924
Vehicle Trades	412.8	20,788
Motor mechanics, auto engineers	407.2	20,623
Vehicle body builders and repairers	424.5	21,066
Vehicle spray painters	425.4	21,166
Electrical Trades	495.4	25,397
Electricians, electrical fitters	498.7	25,714
Telecommunications engineers	524.0	25,970
Lines repairers and cable jointers	534.2	27,916
TV, video and audio engineers	—	—
Computer engineers, installation and maintenace	481.7	24,999
Electrical/electronics engineers n.e.c.	486.6	24,279
Skilled Construction and Building Trades	422.1	21,338
Construction Trades	427.1	21,635
Building Trades	398.7	19,927
Floorers and wall tilers	—	21,568
Painters and decorators	387.7	19,435
Textiles, Printing and Other Skilled Trades	356.5	18,678
Textiles and Garments Trades	371.4	18,652
Weavers and knitters	347.2	17,444
Printing Trades	433.5	22,104
Printers	476.0	25,471
Bookbinders and print finishers	406.1	20,289
Food Preparation Trades	313.0	16,547
Butchers, meat cutters	319.6	16,859
Bakers, flour confectioners	313.1	16,532
Fishmongers, poultry dressers	289.9	15,490
Chefs, cooks	312.9	16,532
Skilled Trades n.e.c.	386.1	19,344
Glass and ceramics makers, decorators and finishers	391.9	20,159
Furniture makers, other craft woodworkers	—	—
Hand craft occupations n.e.c.	419.8	18,479
Personal Service Occupations	323.2	16,958
Caring Personal Service Occupations	317.7	—

Full-Time Males on Adult Rates (where pay was not affected by absence) (notes on p.136)

Occupation SOC 2000	Average Gross Weekly Pay (in April) 2004 £	Average Gross Annual Earnings (in April) 2004 £
Healthcare and Related Personal Services	324.2	16,647
Nursing auxiliaries and assistants	317.5	15,968
Ambulance staff (excluding paramedics)	414.6	20,996
Care assistants and home carers	300.6	15,381
Childcare and Related Personal Services	273.5	14,925
Leisure and Other Personal Service Occupations	328.1	17,335
Leisure and Travel Service Occupations	352.6	18,639
Sport and leisure assistants	295.1	15,563
Air travel assistants	394.7	21,241
Rail travel assistants	415.4	22,120
Housekeeping Occupations	304.1	16,111
Caretakers	305.0	16,079
Personal Services Occupations n.e.c.	330.0	17,039
Sales and Customer Service Occupations	323.1	16,987
Sales Occupations	328.6	17,237
Sales Assistants and Retail Cashiers	298.6	15,339
Sales and retail assistants	298.9	15,328
Retail cashiers and check-out operators	219.7	11,279
Telephone salespersons	365.4	18,862
Sales Related Occupations	435.6	23,183
Debt, rent and other cash collectors	358.1	17,592
Roundsmen/women and van salespersons	—	18,397
Sales related occupations n.e.c.	502.0	28,371
Customer Service Occupations	305.1	15,899
Customer Service Occupations	305.1	15,899
Call centre agents/operators	296.5	15,604
Customer care occupations	306.8	15,952
Process, Plant and Machine Operatives etc.	395.2	20,259
Process, Plant and Machine Operatives	402.4	20,728
Process Operatives	390.9	20,468
Food, drink and tobacco process operatives	357.5	18,631
Textile process operatives	316.2	16,383
Chemical and related process operatives	474.8	25,019
Rubber process operatives	396.9	20,235
Plastics process operatives	363.7	18,525
Metal making and treating process operatives	438.7	22,640
Process operatives n.e.c.	417.7	21,921
Plant and Machine Operatives	404.4	20,825
Paper and wood machine operatives	378.7	19,419
Metal working machine operatives	387.2	19,718
Water and sewerage plant operatives	466.9	24,837
Plant and machine operatives n.e.c.	407.2	20,043

Full-Time Males on Adult Rates (where pay was not affected by absence) (notes on p.136)

Occupation SOC 2000	Average Gross Weekly Pay (in April)	Average Gross Annual Earnings (in April)
	2004	2004
	£	£
Assemblers and Routine Operatives	385.5	19,596
Assemblers (electrical products)	332.2	17,119
Assemblers (vehicles and metal goods)	456.1	22,666
Routine inspectors and testers	419.9	21,135
Weighers, graders, sorters	357.3	17,919
Tyre, exhaust and windscreen fitters	—	16,099
Clothing cutters	311.4	15,354
Construction Operatives	468.7	24,094
Road construction operatives	—	20,972
Construction operatives n.e.c.	481.7	24,422
Transport and Mobile Machine Drivers And Operatives	386.2	19,604
Transport Drivers and Operatives	384.1	19,458
Heavy goods vehicle drivers	425.9	21,035
Van drivers	336.9	17,175
Bus and coach drivers	359.2	18,610
Taxi, cab drivers and chauffeurs	323.2	16,249
Rail transport operatives	554.8	27,568
Transport operatives n.e.c.	392.9	19,806
Mobile Machine Drivers and Operatives	400.0	20,553
Fork-lift truck drivers	356.8	18,834
Mobile machine drivers and operatives n.e.c.	423.5	21,095
Elementary Occupations	326.9	16,898
Elementary Trades, Plant and Storage Related Occupations	331.4	17,069
Elementary Agricultural Occupations	311.9	15,624
Farm workers	324.9	16,124
Fishing and agriculture related occupations n.e.c.	275.9	13,859
Elementary Construction Occupations	342.8	17,875
Elementary Process Plant Occupations	326.4	17,214
Printing machine minders and assistants	437.1	22,787
Packers, bottlers, canners, fillers	296.8	15,696
Labourers inprocess and plant operations n.e.c.	321.9	16,734
Elementary Goods Storage Occupations	333.3	16,952
Stevedores, dockers and slingers	452.0	—
Other goods handling and storage occupations n.e.c.	331.2	16,839
Elementary Administration and Service Occupations	321.2	16,677
Elementary Administration Occupations	382.6	19,204
Postal workers, mail sorters, messengers, couriers	389.9	19,374
Elementary Personal Services Occupations	244.3	12,518
Hospital porters	282.0	14,666
Hotel porters	246.8	12,391
Kitchen and catering assistants	241.7	12,043
Waiters, Waitresses	238.7	12,666
Bar staff	236.4	11,947

Full-Time Males on Adult Rates (where pay was not affected by absence) (notes on p.136)

Occupation SOC 2000	Average Gross Weekly Pay (in April)	Average Gross Annual Earnings (in April)
	2004	2004
	£	£
Elementary Cleaning Occupations	284.7	14,609
Road sweepers	326.6	16,284
Cleaners, domestics	268.7	13,869
Elementary Security Occupations	347.0	17,789
Security guards and related occupations	350.4	18,002
Car park attendants	274.8	13,196
Elementary Sales Occupations	256.6	13,374
Shelf fillers	247.0	12,555
ALL OCCUPATIONS	**556.8**	**30,131**

Full-Time Females on Adult Rates (where pay was not affected by absence) (notes on p.136)

	Average Gross Weekly Pay (in April)	Average Gross Annual Earnings (in April)
	2004	2004
Occupation SOC 2000	£	£
Managers and Senior Officials	593.8	31,987
Corporate Managers	616.9	33,238
Production Managers	612.0	31,837
Production, works and maintenance managers	609.7	31,815
Functional Managers	740.7	40,541
Marketing and sales managers	720.2	38,205
Advertising and public relations managers	677.4	35,926
Personnel, training and industrial relations managers	728.9	39,993
Information and communication technology managers	743.3	40,935
Quality and Customer Care Managers	581.8	31,713
Customer care managers	554.3	31,220
Financial Institution and Office Managers	560.7	29,617
Financial institution managers	602.2	33,888
Office managers	546.6	28,168
Managers In Distribution, Storage and Retailing	374.4	18,830
Storage and warehouse managers	437.2	22,887
Retail and wholesale mangers	354.1	17,569
Health and Social Services Managers	555.1	27,743
Hospital and health service managers	671.3	34,311
Healthcare practice managers	457.5	23,270
Social services managers	567.4	28,773
Residential and day care managers	483.4	23,876
Managers and proprietors in agriculture and services	484.5	26,075
Managers and Proprietors In Hospitality and Leisure Services	398.6	21,208
Hotel and accomodation managers	382.2	19,439
Restaurant and catering managers	394.0	20,547
Publicans and managers of licensed premises	331.9	18,861
Managers and Proprietors In Other Service Industries	556.2	30,105
Property, housing and land managers	563.3	31,045
Shopkeepers and wholesale/retail dealers	385.5	21,307
Managers and proprietors in other services n.e.c.	589.0	31,894
Professional Occupations	603.1	30,620
Science and Technology Professionals	587.6	30,629
Science Professionals	570.2	28,760
Biological scientists and biochemists	553.6	28,876
Engineering Professionals	548.0	28,129
Information and Communication Technology Professionals	615.9	32,947
Software professionals	578.2	30,385

Full-Time Females on Adult Rates (where pay was not affected by absence) (notes on p.136)

Occupation SOC 2000	Average Gross Weekly Pay (in April)	Average Gross Annual Earnings (in April)
	2004	2004
	£	£
Health Professionals	884.2	45,920
Health Professionals	884.2	45,920
Medical Professionals	1054.5	56,124
Pharmacists/pharmacologists	629.7	31,781
Teaching and Research Professionals	570.5	28,875
Teaching Professionals	574.2	28,966
Higher education teaching professionals	657.3	32,811
Further education teaching professionals	539.2	27,199
Secondary education teaching professionals	581.5	29,739
Primary and nursery education teaching professionals	562.8	28,013
Special needs education teaching professionals	601.7	30,211
Research Professionals	504.0	26,896
Scientific researchers	553.5	28,421
Researchers n.e.c.	491.2	26,574
Business and Public Service Professionals	617.6	32,030
Legal Professionals	836.8	44,900
Solicitors and lawyers, judges and coroners	850.8	45,746
Business and Statistical Professionals	656.6	34,135
Chartered and certified accountants	651.9	33,502
Management accountants	590.7	31,312
Management consultants, actuaries, economists and statisticians	683.2	35,974
Architects, Town Planners, Surveyors	588.5	29,835
Public Service Professionals	492.5	24,750
Social workers	497.7	25,122
Librarians and Related Professionals	439.0	22,363
Librarians	437.8	22,315
Associate Professional and Technical Occupations	473.9	24,673
Science and Technology Associate Professionals	420.0	21,823
Science and Engineering Technicians	381.2	19,627
Laboratory technicians	381.8	19,610
Science and engineering technicians n.e.c.	377.7	19,687
Draughtspersons and Building Inspectors	415.9	20,512
IT Service Delivery Occupations	471.3	24,762
IT operations technicians	493.7	26,291
IT user support technicians	420.6	21,161
Health and Social Welfare Associate Professionals	463.6	23,669
Health Associate Professionals	476.6	24,129
Nurses	477.7	24,157
Midwives	573.0	28,647
Medical radiographers	567.5	30,096
Medical and dental technicians	401.7	19,790

Full-Time Females on Adult Rates (where pay was not affected by absence) (notes on p.136)

Occupation SOC 2000	Average Gross Weekly Pay (in April)	Average Gross Annual Earnings (in April)
	2004	2004
	£	£
Therapists	487.5	25,659
Physiotherapists	473.6	24,912
Occupational therapists	465.7	23,956
Therapists n.e.c.	519.5	27,618
Social Welfare Associate Professionals	406.5	21,918
Youth and community workers	390.1	20,845
Housing and welfare officers	413.5	21,320
Protective Service Occupations	519.4	26,687
Protective Service Occupations	519.4	26,687
Police officers (sergeant and below)	560.6	28,172
Prison service officers (below principal officer)	413.6	22,964
Culture, Media and Sports Occupations	526.8	27,357
Design Associate Professionals	513.1	24,996
Graphic designers	485.3	24,099
Product, clothing and related designers	547.1	26,007
Media Associate Professionals	587.7	30,930
Business and Public Service Associate Professionals	483.5	25,959
Legal Associate Professionals	486.4	25,788
Legal associate professionals	486.4	25,788
Business and Finance Associate Professionals	562.5	30,790
Business and related associate professionals n.e.c.	465.6	25,092
Sales and Related Associate Professionals	446.1	23,401
Buyers and purchasing officers	489.4	24,864
Sales representatives	442.9	23,171
Marketing associate professionals	441.7	23,397
Conservation Associate Professionals	470.6	26,007
Conservation and environmental protection officers	506.7	27,151
Public Service and Other Associate Professionals	468.5	25,007
Public service associate professionals	590.6	31,346
Personnel and industrial relations officers	458.9	24,387
Vocational and industrial trainers and instructors	393.6	20,559
Careers advisers and vocational guidance specialists	434.3	23,039
Administrative and Secretarial Occupations	333.6	17,183
Administrative Occupations	330.6	16,958
Administrative Occupations: Government and Related Organisations	336.3	17,363
Civil Service executive officers	413.2	21,637
Civil Service administrative officers and assistants	289.6	15,204
Local government clerical officers,	348.8	17,661

Full-Time Females on Adult Rates (where pay was not affected by absence) (notes on p.136)

Occupation SOC 2000	Average Gross Weekly Pay (in April) 2004 £	Average Gross Annual Earnings (in April) 2004 £
Administrative Occupations: Finance	343.3	17,659
Credit controllers	338.1	17,172
Accounts and wages clerks, book-keepers, other financial clerks	351.4	17,850
Counter clerks	331.4	17,426
Administrative Occupations: Records	315.2	16,083
Filing and other records assistants/clerks	315.1	16,213
Pensions and insurance clerks	329.5	16,966
Stock control clerks	317.0	15,786
Transport and distribution clerks	351.5	17,636
Library assistants/clerks	301.7	15,360
Database assistants/clerks	290.0	14,747
Administrative Occupations: Communications	383.2	18,146
Telephonists	313.7	15,835
Communication operators	485.3	21,891
Administrative Occupations: General	320.3	16,356
General office assistants/clerks	320.3	16,356
Secretarial and Related Occupations	344.3	17,979
Secretarial and Related Occupations	344.3	17,979
Medical secretaries	—	—
Legal secretaries	357.0	18,718
School secretaries	292.4	14,980
Company secretaries	472.0	25,690
Personal assistants and other secretaries	381.4	19,769
Receptionists	261.5	13,174
Skilled Trade Occupations	306.7	15,266
Skilled Agricultural Trades	284.9	14,040
Agricultural Trades	284.9	14,040
Skilled Metal and Electrical Trades	390.2	19,254
Electrical Trades	416.6	20,548
Textiles, Printing and Other Skilled Trades	269.1	13,482
Printing Trades	299.9	—
Food Preparation Trades	259.5	13,094
Chefs, cooks	262.8	13,294
Skilled Trades n.e.c.	245.8	12,344
Personal Service Occupations	278.2	13,770
Caring Personal Service Occupations	277.1	13,695
Healthcare and Related Personal Services	285.4	14,081
Nursing auxiliaries and assistants	284.4	14,147
Ambulance staff (excluding paramedics)	392.3	19,662
Houseparents and residential wardens	337.6	16,597
Care assistants and home carers	280.1	13,661

Full-Time Females on Adult Rates (where pay was not affected by absence) (notes on p.136)

	Average Gross Weekly Pay (in April)	Average Gross Annual Earnings (in April)
	2004	2004
Occupation SOC 2000	£	£
Childcare and Related Personal Services	257.7	12,786
Nursery nurses	257.7	12,927
Childminders and related occupations	251.7	12,384
Educational assistants	257.2	12,640
Animal Care Services	266.3	13,465
Leisure and Other Personal Service Occupations	283.5	14,130
Leisure and Travel Service Occupations	307.3	15,491
Sport and leisure assistants	267.3	12,721
Travel agents	294.5	14,609
Air travel assistants	334.8	17,571
Hairdressers and Related Occupations	251.8	12,066
Hairdressers, barbers	241.3	11,248
Housekeeping Occupations	258.6	12,866
Housekeepers and related occupations	248.1	12,486
Caretakers	274.7	13,632
Sales and Customer Service Occupations	268.1	13,358
Sales Occupations	258.6	12,903
Sales Assistants and Retail Cashiers	245.4	12,140
Sales and retail assistants	240.6	11,919
Retail cashiers and check-out operators	212.0	10,417
Telephone salespersons	319.0	15,940
Sales Related Occupations	370.8	19,257
Debt, rent and other cash collectors	322.5	16,692
Sales related occupations n.e.c.	388.0	19,366
Customer Service Occupations	292.3	14,890
Customer Service Occupations	292.3	14,890
Call centre agents/operators	288.8	15,068
Customer care occupations	293.1	14,860
Process, Plant and Machine Operatives etc.	286.0	14,142
Process, Plant and Machine Operatives	283.8	14,005
Process Operatives	299.0	14,940
Food, drink and tobacco process operatives	299.0	14,786
Textile process operatives	238.8	11,918
Plant and Machine Operatives	276.6	13,536
Metal working machine operatives	267.7	12,766
Assemblers and Routine Operatives	276.5	13,602
Assemblers (electrical products)	276.9	13,541
Assemblers (vehicle and metal goods)	294.4	15,434
Routine inspectors and testers	309.5	14,973
Sewing machinists	248.2	11,837
Routine laboratory testers	280.6	13,953
Assemblers and routine operatives n.e.c.	278.7	13,915
Transport And Mobile Machine Drivers and Operatives	307.9	15,770

Full-Time Females on Adult Rates (where pay was not affected by absence) (notes on p.136)

Occupation SOC 2000	Average Gross Weekly Pay (in April) 2004 £	Average Gross Annual Earnings (in April) 2004 £
Transport Drivers and Operatives	302.1	15,259
Elementary Occupations	250.7	12,516
Elementary Trades, Plant and Storage Related Occupations	267.2	13,493
Elementary Process Plant Occupations	262.1	13,397
Packers, bottles, canners, fillers	264.6	13,230
Labourers in process and plant operations n.e.c.	251.2	13,441
Elementary Goods Storage Occupations	276.3	13,623
Other goods handling and storage occupations n.e.c.	276.3	13,623
Elementary Administration and Service Occupations	243.5	12,048
Elementary Administration Occupations	316.3	16,173
Postal workers, mail sorters, messengers. couriers	348.2	17,094
Elementary Personal Services Occupations	223.9	10,872
Kitchen and catering assistants	228.9	11,112
Waiters, Waitresses	219.6	10,409
Bar staff	214.3	10,151
Elementary Cleaning Occupations	227.9	11,151
Cleaners, domestics	230.3	11,249
Launderers, dry cleaners, pressers	205.9	10,301
Elementary Security Occupations	317.9	16,115
Security guards and related occupations	348.1	17,854
Elementary Sales Occupations	228.3	11,328
Shelf fillers	228.3	11,444
ALL OCCUPATIONS	**396.0**	**20,314**

C6: Comparable earnings

The gross income equivalent of net figures

Net (£)	Gross equivalent (£)	Comparable gross salaries
6,000	6,483	
7,000	7,866	
8,000	9,375	
9,000	10,885	
10,000	12,394	Army Private (B) £13,866, Healthcare Assistant £14,833
12,000	15,413	Nurse (newly qualified) £17,610
14,000	18,431	*Female (M) £18,531*, Teacher Grade 1 (B) £19,023, Anglican Clergy (A) £19,420
16,000	21,449	Nurse Grade F £23,675
18,000	24,468	*Male (M) £24,236*, Army Private (T) £25,043, Junior doctor (B) £25,324
20,000	27,486	Sergeant (B) £25,973, Archdeacon £28,490, Sister Grade G (T) £28,975
22,500	31,259	Teacher (Upper pay scale, B) £30,120, Sergeant (T) £31,956, Captain (B) £32,810
25,000	34,776	Bishop £34,950, Junior doctor (T) £35,511, Head Teacher (B) £37,344
27,500	38,125	Captain (T) £39,019, Major (B) £41,330
30,000	42,397	
32,500	46,767	Major (T) £49,497, Teacher (Advanced skills, T) £49,872
35,000	51,138	Bishop of London £52,620, Civil Service Band 1 (B) £54,788
37,500	55,509	Archbishop of York £56,410, NHS Consultant (B) £57,370
40,000	59,879	Lieutenant Colonel (B) £58,006, M.P. £59,095, Lieutenant Colonel (T) £64,123
42,500	64,250	Archbishop of Canterbury £64,400, Colonel (B) £67,174
45,000	68,620	
47,500	72,991	NHS Consultant (T) £74,658
50,000	77,362	Brigadier (B) £80,574
52,500	81,732	Brigadier (T) £84,008
55,000	86,103	Major General (B) £87,559
57,500	90,474	Head Teacher (T) £92,619, Civil Service Band 3 (B) £93,139
60,000	94,844	District Judge (PRFD) £97,483, Minister of State £97,940, Major General (T) £98,515
62,500	99,215	Lieutenant General (B) £103,084
65,000	103,586	
67,500	107,956	Regional Immigration Adjudicator, & VAT Tribunal Chairman £112,116
70,000	112,327	Civil Service Band 1 (T) £115,616, Circuit Judge £116,515
72,500	116,697	Lieutenant General (T) £117,783
75,000	121,068	
77,500	125,439	Senior Circuit Judge £125,803
80,000	129,809	Permanent Secretary (B) £130,350, General (B) £132,084, Cabinet Minister £133,997
82,500	134,180	
85,000	138,551	
87,500	142,921	General (T) £145,831
90,000	147,292	
92,500	151,662	High Court Judge £155,404
95,000	156,033	
97,500	160,404	
100,000	164,774	
105,000	173,516	Lord Justice of Appeal £175,671
110,000	182,257	Prime Minister £183,932, Lord of Appeal, & President £184,814, Master of the Rolls £191,276
115,000	190,998	Chief of Defence Staff (B) £193,327, Civil Service Band 3 (T) £198,197
120,000	199,739	Chief of Defence Staff (T) £205,160, Lord Chief Justice £211,399
125,000	208,480	Permanent Secretary (T) £264,250

2005–06 tax rates are applied.
Assumptions for the grossed-up equivalent: 3% contributory pension; contracted out of SERPS for Class 1 NIC.
Most salary levels are effective from April 2005. All are subject to diverse terms and conditions.
Entries in italics derive from the ONS Annual Survey of Hours and Earnings 2004 (© Crown Copyright 2005), and relate to (fe)male average earnings in April 2004. Further information from Helpline ☎ 01633 819024.
(B), (M) and (T) indicate bottom, median and top of range or seniority for post rank.

Group D
Interest Rates

D

D1: Interest base rates

Introductory notes:

This table shows the dates of change in the base rate of the four largest London Clearing Banks (Barclays, Lloyds, Midland/HSBC and National Westminster) at close of business on the respective days.

An asterisk denotes that for this period, there was a spread not exceeding ± 0.5 per cent.

Date	New rate (%)	Date	New rate (%)	Date	New rate (%)
1980		**1986**		**1994**	
July 4	16.00	January 9	12.50	February 8	5.25
November 25	14.00	March 19	11.50	September 12	5.75
		April 8	11.25*	December 7	6.25
1981		April 9	11.00		
March 11	12.00	April 24	10.50	**1995**	
September 16	14.00	May 27	10.00	February 2	6.75
October 1	16.00	October 14	11.00	December 13	6.50
October 14	15.50				
November 9	15.00	**1987**		**1996**	
December 3	14.50	March 10	10.50	January 18	6.25
		March 19	10.00	March 8	6.00
1982		April 29	9.50	June 6	5.75
January 12	14.00	May 11	9.00	October 30	6.00
February 25	13.50	August 7	10.00		
March 12	13.00	October 26	9.50	**1997**	
June 8	12.50	November 5	9.00	May 7	6.25
July 13	12.00	December	8.50	June 9	6.50
August 2	11.50			July 11	6.75
August 18	11.00	**1988**		August 8	7.00
August 31	10.50	February 2	9.00	November 7	7.25
October 7	10.00	March 17	8.50		
October 14	9.50	April 11	8.00	**1998**	
November 4	9.00	May 18	7.50	June 5	7.50
November 26	10.125*	June 3	8.00	October 9	7.25
		June 6	8.25*	November 6	6.75
1983		June 7	8.50	December 1	6.25
January 12	11.00	June 22	9.00		
March 15	10.50	June 29	9.50	**1999**	
April 15	10.00	July 5	10.00	January 8	6.00
June 15	9.50	July 19	10.50	February 5	5.50
October 4	9.00	August 8	10.75*	April 8	5.25
		August 9	11.00	June 10	5.00
1984		August 25	11.50	September 8	5.25
March 7	8.875*	August 26	12.00	November 4	5.50
March 15	8.625*	November 25	13.00		
May 10	9.125*			**2000**	
June 27	9.25	**1989**		January 13	5.75
July 9	10.00	May 24	14.00	February 10	6.00
July 11	11.00*	October 5	15.00		
July 12	12.00			**2001**	
August 9	11.50	**1990**		February 8	5.75
August 10	11.00	October 8	14.00	April 5	5.50
August 20	10.50			May 10	5.25
November 7	10.00	**1991**		August 2	5.00
November 20	9.875*	February 13	13.50	September 18	4.75
November 23	9.625*	February 27	13.00	October 4	4.50
		March 25	12.50	November 8	4.00
1985		April 12	12.00		
January 11	10.50	May 24	11.50	**2003**	
January 14	12.00	July 12	11.00	February 7	3.75
January 28	14.00	September 4	10.50	July 10	3.50
March 20	13.75*			November 6	3.75
March 21	13.50	**1992**			
March 29	13.25*	May 5	10.00	**2004**	
April 2	13.125*	September 16	12.00	February 5	4.00
April 12	12.875*	September 17	10.00	May 6	4.25
April 19	12.675*	September 22	9.00	June 10	4.50
June 12	12.50	October 16	8.00	August 5	4.75
July 7	12.25*	November 13	7.00		
July 16	12.00				
July 29	11.75*	**1993**			
July 30	11.50	January 26	6.00		
		November 23	5.50		

D2: Real and nominal interest rates and price inflation

Introductory notes

1. Price inflation is calculated as the rate of change of the Retail Price Index

2. The nominal interest rate is based on the rate on 20 year British Government Securities

3. Data taken from Economic Trends Annual Supplement

4. No account has been taken of tax in these figures

	Price Inflation %	Nominal Interest Rate %	Real Interest Rate %
1970	6.52	9.21	2.69
1971	9.18	8.85	(0.33)
1972	7.48	8.90	1.42
1973	9.13	10.71	1.58
1974	15.94	14.77	(1.17)
1975	24.05	14.39	(9.66)
1976	16.62	14.43	(2.19)
1977	15.91	12.73	(3.18)
1978	8.20	12.47	4.27
1979	13.45	12.99	(0.46)
1980	18.03	13.78	(4.25)
1981	11.88	14.74	2.86
1982	8.70	12.88	4.18
1983	4.44	10.80	6.36
1984	5.01	10.69	5.68
1985	6.04	10.62	4.58
1986	3.40	9.87	6.47
1987	4.16	9.47	5.31
1988	4.92	9.36	4.44
1989	7.79	9.58	1.79
1990	9.44	11.08	1.64
1991	5.91	9.92	4.01
1992	3.73	9.12	5.39
1993	1.57	7.87	6.30
1994	2.48	8.05	5.57
1995	3.41	8.25	4.84
1996	2.44	8.19	5.75
1997	3.12	7.06	3.94
1998	3.42	5.36	1.94
1999	1.56	4.55	2.99
2000	2.93	4.41	1.48
2001	1.84	4.67	2.83
2002	1.62	4.73	3.11
2003	2.91	4.63	1.72
2004	2.96	4.69	1.73
Averages:			
1970–79	12.65	11.95	(0.70)
1980–90	7.62	11.17	3.55
1991–2004	2.85	6.54	3.69
1970–2004	7.15	9.54	2.39

Real interest rates 1970–2003

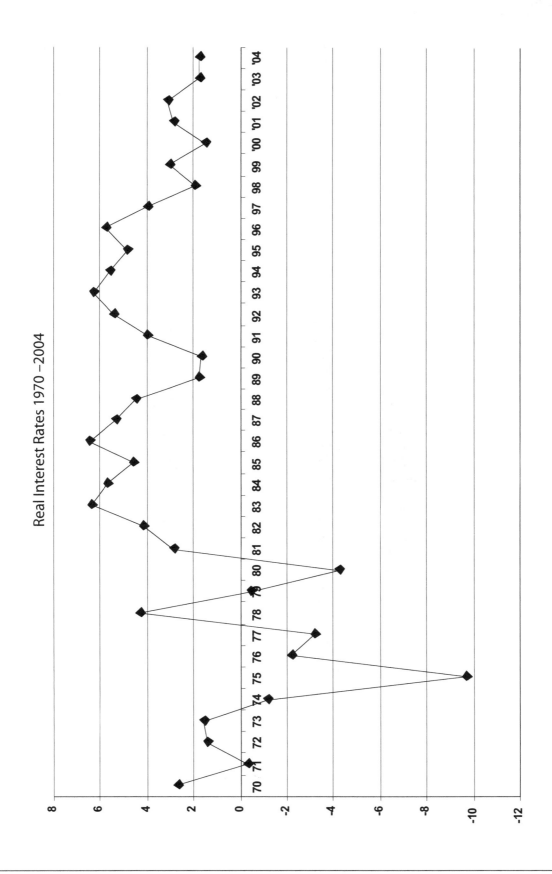

D3: Special investment account rates

Introductory notes:

This is a composite table including both the Short Term Investment Account rate and the succeeding High Court Special Investment Account rate.

The manner of crediting interest is set out in Court Fund Rules 1987, r.27. Interest accruing to a special investment account is credited without the deduction of income tax.

From:		%
October 1	1965	5.0
September 1	1966	5.5
March 1	1968	6.0
March 1	1969	6.5
March 1	1970	7.0
April 1	1971	7.5
March 1	1973	8.0
March 1	1974	9.0
February 1	1977	10.0
March 1	1979	12.5
January 1	1980	15.0
January 1	1981	12.5
December 1	1981	15.0
March 1	1982	14.0
July 1	1982	13.0
April 1	1983	12.5
April 1	1984	12.0
August 1	1986	11.5
January 1	1987	12.25
April 1	1987	11.75
November 1	1987	11.25
December 1	1987	11.0
May 1	1988	9.5
August 1	1988	11.0
November 1	1988	12.25
January 1	1989	13.0
November 1	1989	14.25
April 1	1991	12.0
October 1	1991	10.25
February 1	1993	8.0
August 1	1999	7.0
February 1	2002	6.0

D4: Special and general damage interest

Introductory notes:

Special damages

The appropriate rate of interest for special damages is the rate, over the period for which the interest is awarded, which is payable on the court special account. This rate was reduced to 6 per cent on February 1, 2002. Interest since June 1987 has been paid daily on a 1/365th basis, even in a leap year such as 2004.

In cases of continuing special damages, half the appropriate rate from the date of injury to the date of trial is awarded. In cases where the special damages have ceased and are thus limited to a finite period, there are conflicting Court of Appeal decisions as to whether the award should be half the appropriate rate from injury to trial (*Dexter v Courtaulds*[1]) or the full special account rate from the date within the period to which the special damages are limited (*Prokop v DHSS*[2]).

The relevant rates since 1965 are set out in Table D3.

The table (overleaf) records the total of these rates from January 1980. In the left hand column is shown the month from the first day of which interest is assumed to run. The right hand column shows the percentage interest accumulated from the first day of each month to July 1, 2005.

Continued use may be made of this table by adding to the figures in it 1/365th of the special account rate for each day from July 1, 2005 onwards, using Table D6 which records the number of days between two dates in a two-year period.

Suppose that interest runs from January 1, 1997 to October 13, 2005. The total to July 1, 2005 is 58.68 per cent. (From Table D6, July 1 to October 13 is 286—182 days.) If the rate remains at 6 per cent p.a., the appropriate addition will be 6 per cent $\times$ 104/365 = 1.71 per cent. Thus the grand total from January 1, 1997 to October 13, 2005 will be 58.68 + 1.71 = 60.39 per cent.

General damages

In personal injury cases, the normal rate of interest on general damages for pain, suffering and loss of amenity was, by convention 2 per cent per annum. In *Lawrence v Chief Constable of Staffordshire*[3] the Court of Appeal held that in spite of *Wells v Wells,*[4] the rate should remain at 2 per cent. Interest runs from the date of service of proceedings.

---

[1] [1984] 1 All E.R. 70.

[2] [1985] C.L.Y. 103.7

[3] CA, transcript June 29, 2000.

[4] [1999] A.C. 345.

Table of cumulative interest at the special account rate from the first day of each month to July 1, 2005.

	1980	1981	1982	1983	1984	1985	1986	1987	1988
January	253.28	238.28	225.56	211.91	199.28	187.16	175.16	163.37	151.60
February	252.00	237.22	224.29	210.80	198.22	186.14	174.14	162.33	150.67
March	250.85	236.26	223.14	209.81	197.36	185.22	173.22	161.39	149.79
April	249.58	235.19	221.95	208.70	196.20	184.20	172.20	160.35	148.86
May	248.35	234.17	220.80	207.67	195.22	183.22	171.22	159.38	147.96
June	247.07	233.11	219.61	206.61	194.20	182.20	170.20	158.39	147.15
July	245.84	232.08	218.46	205.57	193.21	181.21	169.21	157.42	146.37
August	244.56	231.02	217.36	204.52	192.19	180.19	168.19	156.42	145.56
September	243.29	229.96	216.25	203.46	191.17	179.17	167.21	155.42	144.63
October	242.06	228.93	215.18	202.43	190.19	178.19	166.27	154.46	143.72
November	240.78	227.87	214.08	201.37	189.17	177.17	165.29	153.46	142.79
December	239.55	226.84	213.01	200.35	188.18	176.18	164.35	152.54	141.78

	1989	1990	1991	1992	1993	1994	1995	1996	1997
January	140.74	127.53	113.28	101.28	90.89	82.70	74.70	66.70	58.68
February	139.64	126.32	112.07	100.30	90.02	82.02	74.02	66.02	58.00
March	138.64	125.22	110.97	99.48	89.40	81.40	73.40	65.38	57.38
April	137.54	124.02	109.77	98.61	88.72	80.72	72.72	64.70	56.70
May	136.47	122.85	108.78	97.77	88.07	80.07	72.07	64.05	56.05
June	135.36	121.65	107.76	96.90	87.39	79.39	71.39	63.37	55.37
July	134.29	120.47	106.78	96.06	86.73	78.73	70.73	62.71	54.71
August	133.19	119.25	105.76	95.18	86.05	78.05	70.05	62.03	54.03
September	132.09	118.04	104.74	94.31	85.37	77.37	69.37	61.35	53.35
October	131.02	116.87	103.75	93.47	84.71	76.71	68.71	60.69	52.69
November	129.91	115.66	102.88	92.60	84.03	76.03	68.03	60.01	52.01
December	128.74	114.49	102.04	91.76	83.38	75.38	67.38	59.36	51.36

	1998	1999	2000	2001	2002	2003	2004	2005	
January	50.68	42.68	35.10	28.08	21.08	14.99	8.99	2.98	
February	50.00	42.00	34.51	27.48	20.48	14.48	8.48	2.47	
March	49.38	41.38	33.95	27.02	20.02	14.02	8.01	2.01	
April	48.70	40.70	33.36	26.51	19.51	13.51	7.50	1.50	
May	48.05	40.05	32.78	26.02	19.02	13.02	7.00	1.00	
June	47.37	39.37	32.19	25.51	18.51	12.51	6.49	0.49	
July	46.71	38.71	31.61	25.02	18.02	12.02	6.00		
August	46.03	38.03	31.02	24.51	17.51	11.51	5.49		
September	45.35	37.44	30.42	24.00	17.00	11.00	4.98		
October	44.69	36.86	29.85	23.50	16.50	10.50	4.49		
November	44.01	36.27	29.25	22.99	15.99	9.99	3.98		
December	43.36	35.69	28.68	22.50	15.50	9.50	3.48		

If the rate remains at 6 per cent, interest up to the first day of successive later months can be found by adding the following figures.

	2005		2006		2006
		January	3.02	July	6.00
August	0.51	February	3.53		
September	1.02	March	3.99		
October	1.51	April	4.50		
November	2.02	May	5.00		
December	2.52	June	5.51		

D5: Base rate + 10 per cent

Introductory notes:

1. Under the Civil Procedure Rules 1998, rule 36.21, where the judgment against a defendant is more advantageous to the claimant than the proposals in a claimant's Part 36 offer, the court may order interest on the sum awarded and on the costs, for some or all of the period starting with the latest date on which the defendant could have accepted the Part 36 offer without needing the permission of the court, at a rate not exceeding 10 per cent above base rate. In *All-in-One Design & Build Ltd v Motcomb Estates Ltd, The Times*, April 4, 2000, it was held that rule 36.21 is not *ultra vires*.

2. Rule 36.21(4) provides that where the rule applies, the court will make those orders unless it considers it unjust to do so; sub-rule (5) sets out the factors to be considered in deciding whether it would be unjust.

3. Since 1998 base rates have been as follows:

		Rate	Rate + 10%			Rate	Rate + 10%
1997	November 7	7.25%	17.25%	**2001**	February 8	5.75%	15.75%
1998	June 4	7.50%	17.50%		April 5	5.50%	15.50%
	October 8	7.25%	17.25%		May 10	5.25%	15.25%
	November 5	6.75%	16.75%		August 2	5.00%	15.00%
	December 10	6.25%	16.25%		September 18	4.75%	14.75%
1999	January 7	6.00%	16.00%		October 4	4.50%	14.50%
	February 4	5.50%	15.50%		November 8	4.00%	14.00%
	April 8	5.25%	15.25%	**2003**	February 6	3.75%	13.75%
	June 10	5.00%	15.00%		July 10	3.50%	13.50%
	September 8	5.25%	15.25%		November 6	3.75%	13.75%
	November 4	5.50%	15.50%	**2004**	February 5	4.00%	14.00%
2000	January 13	5.75%	15.75%		May 6	4.25%	14.25%
	February 10	6.00%	16.00%		June 10	4.50%	14.50%
					August 5	4.75%	14.75%

The following table shows cumulative interest at 10 per cent above base rate from the first day of each month until July 1, 2005. Interest for parts of a month can be found by following the method in the notes to table D4.

	1998 (%)	1999 (%)	2000 (%)	2001 (%)	2002 (%)	2003 (%)	2004 (%)	2005 (%)
January	113.13	95.90	80.56	64.55	49.43	35.43	21.74	7.31
February	111.66	94.54	79.23	63.19	48.24	34.24	20.57	6.06
March	110.34	93.34	77.96	61.97	47.17	33.18	19.46	4.93
April	108.88	92.03	76.60	60.64	45.98	32.01	18.27	3.68
May	107.46	90.77	75.29	59.36	44.83	30.88	17.12	2.47
June	105.99	89.47	73.93	58.06	43.64	29.72	15.91	1.21
July	104.56	88.24	72.61	56.81	42.49	28.59	14.73	
August	103.07	86.96	71.25	55.51	41.30	27.43	13.49	
September	101.58	85.69	69.90	54.24	40.11	26.29	12.24	
October	100.15	84.44	68.58	53.01	38.96	25.18	11.03	
November	98.68	83.14	67.22	51.78	37.77	24.03	9.78	
December	97.29	81.87	65.91	50.62	36.62	22.90	8.57	

If there are no further changes of rate in the meanwhile, interest up to the first day of successive later months can be found by adding the figures from the following table:

	2005 (%)		2006 (%)		2006 (%)
July		**January**	7.44	**July**	14.75
August	1.25	**February**	8.69		
September	2.51	**March**	9.82		
October	3.72	**April**	11.07		
November	4.97	**May**	12.28		
December	6.18	**June**	13.54		

D6: Number of days between two dates

Introductory notes:

Deduct the number of the opening date from the number of the closing date (where necessary adding a day for February 29).
Example: October 14th–March 19th is 443 − 287 = 156 days.

Day numbers

Day of month	Jan	Feb	Mar	Apr	May	Jun	Jul	Aug	Sep	Oct	Nov	Dec	Jan	Feb	Mar	Apr	May	Jun	Jul	Aug	Sep	Oct	Nov	Dec	Day of month
1	1	32	60	91	121	152	182	213	244	274	305	335	366	397	425	456	486	517	547	578	609	639	670	700	1
2	2	33	61	92	122	153	183	214	245	275	306	336	367	398	426	457	487	518	548	579	610	640	671	701	2
3	3	34	62	93	123	154	184	215	246	276	307	337	368	399	427	458	488	519	549	580	611	641	672	702	3
4	4	35	63	94	124	155	185	216	247	277	308	338	369	400	428	459	489	520	550	581	612	642	673	703	4
5	5	36	64	95	125	156	186	217	248	278	309	339	370	401	429	460	490	521	551	582	613	643	674	704	5
6	6	37	65	96	126	157	187	218	249	279	310	340	371	402	430	461	491	522	552	583	614	644	675	705	6
7	7	38	66	97	127	158	188	219	250	280	311	341	372	403	431	462	492	523	553	584	615	645	676	706	7
8	8	39	67	98	128	159	189	220	251	281	312	342	373	404	432	463	493	524	554	585	616	646	677	707	8
9	9	40	68	99	129	160	190	221	252	282	313	343	374	405	433	464	494	525	555	586	617	647	678	708	9
10	10	41	69	100	130	161	191	222	253	283	314	344	375	406	434	465	495	526	556	587	618	648	679	709	10
11	11	42	70	101	131	162	192	223	254	284	315	345	376	407	435	466	496	527	557	588	619	649	680	710	11
12	12	43	71	102	132	163	193	224	255	285	316	346	377	408	436	467	497	528	558	589	620	650	681	711	12
13	13	44	72	103	133	164	194	225	256	286	317	347	378	409	437	468	498	529	559	590	621	651	682	712	13
14	14	45	73	104	134	165	195	226	257	287	318	348	379	410	438	469	499	530	560	591	622	652	683	713	14
15	15	46	74	105	135	166	196	227	258	288	319	349	380	411	439	470	500	531	561	592	623	653	684	714	15
16	16	47	75	106	136	167	197	228	259	289	320	350	381	412	440	471	501	532	562	593	624	654	685	715	16
17	17	48	76	107	137	168	198	229	260	290	321	351	382	413	441	472	502	533	563	594	625	655	686	716	17
18	18	49	77	108	138	169	199	230	261	291	322	352	383	414	442	473	503	534	564	595	626	656	687	717	18
19	19	50	78	109	139	170	200	231	262	292	323	353	384	415	443	474	504	535	565	596	627	657	688	718	19
20	20	51	79	110	140	171	201	232	263	293	324	354	385	416	444	475	505	536	566	597	628	658	689	719	20
21	21	52	80	111	141	172	202	233	264	294	325	355	386	417	445	476	506	537	567	598	629	659	690	720	21
22	22	53	81	112	142	173	203	234	265	295	326	356	387	418	446	477	507	538	568	599	630	660	691	721	22
23	23	54	82	113	143	174	204	235	266	296	327	357	388	419	447	478	508	539	569	600	631	661	692	722	23
24	24	55	83	114	144	175	205	236	267	297	328	358	389	420	448	479	509	540	570	601	632	662	693	723	24
25	25	56	84	115	145	176	206	237	268	298	329	359	390	421	449	480	510	541	571	602	633	663	694	724	25
26	26	57	85	116	146	177	207	238	269	299	330	360	391	422	450	481	511	542	572	603	634	664	695	725	26
27	27	58	86	117	147	178	208	239	270	300	331	361	392	423	451	482	512	543	573	604	635	665	696	726	27
28	28	59	87	118	148	179	209	240	271	301	332	362	393	424	452	483	513	544	574	605	636	666	697	727	28
29	29		88	119	149	180	210	241	272	302	333	363	394		453	484	514	545	575	606	637	667	698	728	29
30	30		89	120	150	181	211	242	273	303	334	364	395		454	485	515	546	576	607	638	668	699	729	30
31	31		90		151		212	243		304		365	396		455		516		577	608		669		730	31

D7: Decimal years

An alternative way of calculating interest is with a table expressing intervals as decimals of a year. Of the two tables below the upper table gives the period between corresponding days of two months, with the later month at the top and the earlier month at the side. (From April 1 to September 1, 2004 is 0.419 years; from September 1, 2003 to April 1, 2004 is 0.581 years.) The lower table gives days and weeks as decimals of a year.

Thus from September 3, 2003 to April 15, 2004 is:

3.9.02–3.4.03		from upper table	0.581
3–15.4.03	12 days	from lower table	0.033
Total	3.9.02–15.4.03	=	0.614 years

Some may find this more complicated than the Number of Days Table but it is in two respects simpler to use: most people find it easier to add than to subtract and it avoids the need to divide by 365.

Intervals between corresponding days of months as decimals of a year

Later month

		Jan	Feb	Mar	Apr	May	Jun	Jul	Aug	Sept	Oct	Nov	Dec
	Jan	**1.000**	0.085	0.162	0.247	0.329	0.414	0.496	0.581	0.666	0.748	0.833	0.915
	Feb	0.915	**1.000**	0.077	0.162	0.244	0.329	0.411	0.496	0.581	0.663	0.748	0.830
	Mar	0.838	0.923	**1.000**	0.085	0.167	0.252	0.334	0.419	0.504	0.586	0.671	0.753
Earlier	Apr	0.753	0.838	0.915	**1.000**	0.082	0.167	0.249	0.334	0.419	0.501	0.58	0.668
month	May	0.671	0.756	0.833	0.918	**1.000**	0.085	0.167	0.252	0.337	0.419	0.504	0.586
	Jun	0.586	0.671	0.748	0.833	0.915	**1.000**	0.082	0.167	0.252	0.334	0.419	0.501
	Jul	0.504	0.589	0.666	0.751	0.833	0.918	**1.000**	0.085	0.170	0.252	0.337	0.419
	Aug	0.419	0.504	0.581	0.666	0.748	0.833	0.915	**1.000**	0.085	0.167	0.252	0.334
	Sept	0.334	0.419	0.496	0.581	0.663	0.748	0.830	0.915	**1.000**	0.082	0.167	0.249
	Oct	0.252	0.337	0.414	0.499	0.581	0.666	0.748	0.833	0.918	**1.000**	0.085	0.167
	Nov	0.167	0.252	0.329	0.414	0.496	0.581	0.663	0.748	0.833	0.915	**1.000**	0.082
	Dec	0.085	0.170	0.247	0.332	0.414	0.499	0.581	0.666	0.751	0.833	0.918	**1.000**

Days and weeks as decimals of a year

Days	1	2	3	4	5	6	7	8	9	10
1 to 10	0.003	0.005	0.008	0.011	0.014	0.016	0.019	0.022	0.025	0.027
11 to 20	0.030	0.033	0.036	0.038	0.041	0.044	0.047	0.049	0.052	0.055
21 to 30	0.058	0.060	0.063	0.066	0.068	0.071	0.074	0.077	0.079	0.082
Weeks	0.019	0.038	0.058	0.077	0.096	0.115	0.134	0.153	0.173	0.192

D8: Judgment debt interest rates (England and Wales)

Introductory notes:

Interest rates under the Judgments Act 1838, s.17.

This table sets out the interest rates as determined by the Judgment Debts (Rate of Interest) Orders. Such orders are made under the Administration of Justice Act 1970, s.44.

By virtue of The County Courts (Interest on Judgment Debts) Order 1991, the general rule is that every judgment debt of not less than £5,000 carries interest from the date on which it was given, at the same rate as that payable on High Court judgments.

From	At %	Order
April 20, 1971	7.5	SI 1971/491
March 1, 1977	10	SI 1977/141
December 3, 1979	12.5	SI 1979/1382
June 9, 1980	15	SI 1980/672
June 8, 1982	14	SI 1982/696
November 10, 1982	12	SI 1982/1427
April 16, 1985	15	SI 1985/437
April 1, 1993 to date	8	SI 1993/564

D9: Judicial rates of interest (Scotland)

From	At %	Act of Sederunt
May 4, 1965 – January 5, 1970	5	SI 1965/321
January 6, 1970 – January 6, 1975	7	SI 1969/1819
January 7, 1975 – April 4, 1983	11	SI 1974/2090
April 5, 1983 – August 15, 1985	12	SI 1983/398
August 16, 1985 – March 31, 1993	15	SI 1985/1178
April 1, 1993 to date	8	SI 1993/770 and SI 1994/1443

Group E
Prices

E

E1: Retail price index

Year	Jan	Feb	Mar	Apr	May	June	July	Aug	Sept	Oct	Nov	Dec	Year
2005	188.90	189.60	190.50	191.60	192.00								2005
2004	183.10	183.80	184.60	185.70	186.50	186.80	181.30	181.60	182.50	182.60	182.70	183.50	2004
2003	178.40	179.30	179.90	181.20	181.50	176.20	175.90	176.40	177.90	177.90	178.20	178.50	2003
2002	173.30	173.80	174.50	175.70	176.20	174.40	173.30	174.00	174.60	174.30	173.60	173.40	2002
2001	171.10	172.00	172.20	173.10	174.20	171.10	170.50	170.50	171.70	171.60	172.10	172.20	2001
2000	166.60	167.50	168.40	170.10	170.70	181.30	181.30	187.40	188.10	188.60	189.00	189.90	2000
1999	163.40	163.70	164.10	165.20	165.60	165.60	165.10	165.50	166.20	166.50	166.70	167.30	1999
1998	159.50	160.30	160.80	162.60	163.50	163.40	163.00	163.70	164.40	164.50	164.40	164.40	1998
1997	154.40	155.00	155.40	156.30	156.90	157.50	157.50	158.50	159.30	159.50	159.60	160.00	1997
1996	150.20	150.90	151.50	152.60	152.90	153.00	152.40	153.10	153.80	153.80	153.90	154.40	1996
1995	146.00	146.90	147.50	149.00	149.60	149.80	149.10	149.90	150.60	149.80	149.80	150.70	1995
1994	141.30	142.10	142.50	144.20	144.70	144.70	144.00	144.70	145.00	145.20	145.30	146.00	1994
1993	137.90	138.80	139.30	140.60	141.10	141.00	140.70	141.30	141.90	141.80	141.60	141.90	1993
1992	135.60	136.30	136.70	138.80	139.30	139.30	138.80	138.90	139.40	139.90	139.70	139.20	1992
1991	130.20	130.90	131.40	133.10	133.50	134.10	133.80	134.10	134.60	135.10	135.60	135.70	1991
1990	119.50	120.20	121.40	125.10	126.20	126.70	126.80	128.10	129.30	130.30	130.00	129.90	1990
1989	111.00	111.80	112.30	114.30	115.00	115.40	115.50	115.80	116.60	117.50	118.50	118.80	1989
1988	103.30	103.70	104.10	105.80	106.20	106.60	106.70	107.90	108.40	109.50	110.00	110.30	1988
1987	100.00	100.40	100.60	101.80	101.90	101.90	101.80	102.10	102.40	102.90	103.40	103.30	1987
1986	96.25	96.60	96.73	97.67	97.85	97.79	97.52	97.82	98.30	98.45	99.29	99.62	1986
1985	91.20	91.94	92.80	94.78	95.21	95.41	95.23	95.49	95.44	95.59	95.92	96.05	1985
1984	86.84	87.20	87.48	88.64	88.97	89.20	89.10	89.94	90.11	90.67	90.95	90.87	1984
1983	82.61	82.97	83.12	84.28	84.64	84.84	85.30	85.68	86.06	86.36	86.67	86.89	1983
1982	78.73	78.76	79.44	81.04	81.62	81.85	81.88	81.90	81.85	82.26	82.66	82.51	1982
1981	70.29	70.93	71.99	74.07	74.55	74.98	75.31	75.87	76.30	76.98	77.79	78.28	1981
1980	62.18	63.07	63.93	66.11	66.72	67.35	67.91	68.06	68.49	68.92	69.48	69.86	1980
1979	52.52	52.95	53.38	54.30	54.73	55.67	58.07	58.53	59.11	59.72	60.25	60.68	1979
1978	48.04	48.31	48.62	49.33	49.61	49.99	50.22	50.54	50.75	50.98	51.33	51.76	1978
1977	43.70	44.13	44.56	45.70	46.06	46.54	46.59	46.82	47.07	47.28	47.50	47.76	1977
1976	37.49	37.97	38.17	38.91	39.34	39.54	39.62	40.18	40.71	41.44	42.03	42.59	1976
1975	30.39	30.90	31.51	32.72	34.09	34.75	35.11	35.31	35.61	36.12	36.55	37.01	1975
1974	25.35	25.78	26.01	26.89	27.28	27.55	27.81	27.83	28.14	28.69	29.20	29.63	1974
1973	22.64	22.78	22.92	23.35	23.52	23.64	23.75	23.82	24.03	24.50	24.69	24.87	1973
1972	21.01	21.12	21.19	21.38	21.49	21.63	21.70	21.87	21.99	22.30	22.37	22.49	1972
1971	19.43	19.53	19.69	20.11	20.25	20.39	20.51	20.52	20.55	20.67	20.79	20.89	1971
Year	Jan	Feb	Mar	Apr	May	June	July	Aug	Sept	Oct	Nov	Dec	Year

Year	Jan	Feb	Mar	Apr	May	June	July	Aug	Sept	Oct	Nov	Dec
1970	17.91	18.00	18.11	18.38	18.44	18.49	18.62	18.61	18.70	18.90	19.03	19.16
1969	17.06	17.15	17.22	17.41	17.38	17.46	17.46	17.42	17.47	17.60	17.64	17.76
1968	16.07	16.15	16.20	16.49	16.51	16.57	16.59	16.61	16.63	16.71	16.74	16.97
1967	15.66	15.67	15.67	15.79	15.78	15.85	15.75	15.71	15.70	15.82	15.91	16.02
1966	15.11	15.12	15.15	15.33	15.44	15.48	15.41	15.50	15.48	15.52	15.61	15.63
1965	14.47	14.47	14.52	14.80	14.85	14.89	14.89	14.92	14.93	14.95	15.01	15.08
1964	13.84	13.85	13.90	14.02	14.14	14.19	14.19	14.25	14.25	14.26	14.38	14.43
1963	13.57	13.69	13.71	13.74	13.73	13.73	13.65	13.61	13.65	13.71	13.74	13.77
1962	13.22	13.23	13.28	13.47	13.51	13.60	13.55	13.43	13.41	13.40	13.45	13.52
1961	12.63	12.63	12.68	12.74	12.78	12.89	12.89	13.01	12.99	13.01	13.15	13.17
1960	12.36	12.36	12.34	12.41	12.41	12.47	12.50	12.42	12.43	12.53	12.59	12.62
1959	12.42	12.41	12.41	12.32	12.27	12.29	12.26	12.29	12.23	12.28	12.37	12.40
1958	12.16	12.10	12.19	12.33	12.28	12.40	12.20	12.18	12.19	12.31	12.35	12.40
1957	11.74	11.73	11.71	11.75	11.77	11.89	11.99	11.97	11.93	12.05	12.11	12.17
1956	11.25	11.25	11.39	11.55	11.53	11.52	11.47	11.51	11.48	11.55	11.60	11.63
1955	10.70	10.70	10.70	10.76	10.74	10.97	11.00	10.93	11.00	11.11	11.29	11.29
1954	10.28	10.26	10.35	10.39	10.36	10.42	10.60	10.53	10.51	10.56	10.61	10.66
1953	10.14	10.17	10.24	10.33	10.30	10.35	10.35	10.29	10.27	10.27	10.30	10.26
1952	9.71	9.72	9.77	9.93	9.93	10.09	10.08	10.02	10.00	10.09	10.08	10.15
1951	8.60	8.68	8.74	8.88	9.10	9.13	9.27	9.31	9.38	9.44	9.48	9.54
1950	8.28	8.30	8.32	8.35	8.37	8.33	8.33	8.30	8.35	8.44	8.47	8.52
1949	–	8.01	7.98	7.96	8.11	8.14	8.15	8.16	8.19	8.23	8.23	8.25
1948	7.64	7.78	7.80	7.91	7.90	8.04	7.92	7.92	7.93	7.95	7.97	7.98
1947	–	–	–	–	–	7.33	7.38	7.34	7.37	7.43	7.58	7.60

Note:

To calculate the equivalent value of a lump sum, divide by the RPI at the time and multiply the result by the current RPI. Thus £460.00 in June 1981 would be calculated as:

$$\left(\frac{460}{74.98}\right) \times \text{current RPI}$$

to show the relative value of that amount in 'today's money'.

E2: Inflation table

Introductory notes:

Showing the value of £ at various dates.

In the left-hand column of this table is the year and in the right-hand column the multiplier which should be applied to the £ in January of that year to show its value in terms of the £ in January 2005.

This table has been calculated from the Official Retail Prices Index, the value of the £ being taken from the figures published in January of each year, ending with January 2005.

Year	Multiplier	Year	Multiplier
1948	22.79	1981	2.68
1949	21.85	1982	2.40
1950	21.11	1983	2.29
		1984	2.18
1951	20.42	1985	2.07
1952	18.63		
1953	18.04	1986	1.96
1954	17.79	1987	1.89
1955	17.29	1988	1.83
		1989	1.70
1956	16.53	1990	1.58
1957	16.31		
1958	15.39	1991	1.45
1959	15.11	1992	1.39
1960	15.11	1993	1.37
		1994	1.34
1961	14.94	1995	1.29
1962	14.30		
1963	13.93	1996	1.26
1964	13.67	1997	1.23
1965	13.05	1998	1.19
		1999	1.16
1966	12.50	2000	1.13
1967	12.06		
1968	11.75	2001	1.10
1969	11.07	2002	1.09
1970	10.55	2003	1.06
		2004	1.03
1971	9.73	2005	1.00
1972	8.99		
1973	8.35		
1974	7.45		
1975	6.21		
1976	5.03		
1977	4.32		
1978	3.93		
1979	3.60		
1980	3.03		

E3: House price indices

Introductory notes:

1. There are eight house price indices available in April 2005. These are the Halifax, Nationwide, the Financial Times, the Royal Institute of Chartered Surveyors, Hometrack, Rightmove, the Government Index and the Land Registry index.

2. The editors of "Facts and Figures" have used the Halifax table in previous editions and continue to do so. In certain circumstances, the data offered by other indices may be useful. For example the Land Registry figures are broken down regionally and contain information about the numbers of first time buyers. However, they exclude cash purchases which account for about a quarter of all transactions. Each table has strengths and weaknesses of this sort.

3. None of the indices should be treated as definitive. They can only be used as guides to the movement of prices over longer periods of time. Readers should be cautious about over-interpreting the analysis of short-term price changes.

All Houses

Year	U.K. Index	%	Average Price £	North Index	%	Yorks/Humb Index	%	N. West Index	%
87	149.9	15.4	46,315	122.0	6.5	130.5	9.1	127.9	7.6
88	184.8	23.3	57,087	136.7	12.1	155.0	18.8	149.0	16.5
89	223.1	20.8	68,946	182.8	33.7	222.7	43.6	202.0	35.5
90	223.2	0.0	68,950	207.7	13.6	237.5	6.6	227.4	12.6
91	220.5	−1.2	68,130	213.5	2.8	240.4	1.2	236.3	3.9
92	208.1	−5.6	64,309	210.1	−1.6	231.9	−3.6	226.1	−4.3
93	202.1	−2.9	62,455	206.3	−1.8	228.3	−1.6	219.3	−3.0
94	203.1	0.5	62,750	203.6	−1.3	226.3	−0.9	215.8	−1.6
95	199.6	−1.7	61,666	195.9	−3.8	219.2	−3.1	207.8	−3.7
96	208.6	4.5	64,441	201.9	3.1	224.5	2.4	210.7	1.4
97	221.7	6.3	68,504	206.5	2.3	228.5	1.8	216.7	2.9
98	233.7	5.4	72,196	211.2	2.3	229.8	0.5	220.4	1.7
99	250.5	7.2	77,405	220.1	4.2	236.5	2.9	231.0	4.8
00	275.1	9.8	85,005	221.9	0.8	243.9	3.2	242.6	5.0
01	298.6	8.5	92,256	234.0	5.5	257.5	5.6	255.7	5.4
02	350.6	17.4	108,342	271.4	16.0	297.7	15.6	292.8	14.5
03	429.1	22.4	132,589	370.6	36.5	395.6	32.9	366.3	25.1
04	507.6	18.3	156,831	490.3	32.3	495.0	25.1	472.8	29.1

Year	E. Midlands Index	%	W. Midlands Index	%	E. Anglia Index	%	S. West Index	%	S. East Index	%
87	145.2	14.6	136.9	14.6	174.1	25.3	158.1	20.2	181.0	25.4
88	187.0	28.8	185.8	35.7	248.9	43.0	217.6	37.6	232.4	28.4
89	243.2	30.0	240.7	29.6	255.5	2.6	242.7	11.5	244.3	5.1
90	234.4	−3.6	238.0	−1.1	225.8	−12.0	221.8	−8.6	224.5	−8.1
91	227.9	−2.8	240.4	1.0	214.4	−5.0	210.4	−5.1	210.8	−6.1
92	214.4	−5.9	229.4	−4.6	198.5	−7.4	193.9	−7.8	192.8	−8.5
93	208.3	−2.8	219.1	−4.5	193.2	−2.7	185.9	−4.1	186.4	−3.3
94	209.1	0.4	218.3	−0.4	195.8	1.3	186.6	1.5	189.8	1.8
95	203.9	−2.5	215.6	−1.2	193.5	−1.1	186.1	−1.3	190.3	0.3
96	209.4	2.7	224.6	4.2	197.7	2.1	195.1	4.8	199.9	5.0
97	221.5	5.8	237.3	5.6	211.0	6.7	209.7	7.5	221.2	10.7
98	229.9	3.8	250.0	5.4	224.4	6.4	226.4	8.0	244.2	10.4
99	244.8	6.5	254.7	1.9	241.1	7.5	248.8	9.9	271.2	11.0
00	265.0	8.2	282.2	10.8	279.7	16.0	291.0	17.0	318.3	17.4
01	287.3	8.4	301.5	6.8	322.6	15.4	327.8	12.6	354.7	11.4
02	361.7	25.9	363.7	20.7	386.0	19.6	403.4	23.0	413.7	16.6
03	457.5	26.5	460.7	26.7	465.0	20.5	477.7	18.4	483.8	17.0
04	541.4	18.3	540.5	17.3	522.3	12.3	545.4	14.2	528.8	9.3

Year	Gr. London Index	%	Wales Index	%	Scotland Index	%	N. Ireland Index	%
87	200.6	25.7	130.4	10.2	126.8	5.8	121.5	0.1
88	245.3	22.3	162.3	24.5	139.7	10.2	126.7	4.2
89	251.1	2.3	215.5	32.8	165.0	18.1	130.6	3.1
90	236.6	−5.8	219.6	1.9	182.1	10.4	132.1	1.1
91	222.9	−5.8	217.1	−1.1	192.8	5.9	146.9	11.2
92	202.0	−9.4	207.7	−4.3	193.2	0.2	145.5	−1.0
93	192.0	−4.9	204.5	−1.6	196.4	1.6	151.7	4.3
94	195.5	1.8	201.9	−1.2	199.4	1.6	162.1	6.9
95	194.9	−0.4	194.2	−3.8	199.4	0.0	172.8	6.6
96	212.4	9.0	205.5	5.9	204.9	2.8	204.5	18.3
97	246.3	16.0	212.0	3.1	204.7	−0.1	210.6	3.0
98	272.3	10.5	220.2	3.8	209.8	2.5	235.6	11.9
99	317.9	16.8	232.3	5.5	212.8	1.4	248.8	5.6
00	373.6	17.5	245.0	5.5	214.2	0.7	264.4	6.3
01	428.3	14.7	263.8	7.7	220.0	2.7	296.8	12.2
02	499.4	16.6	299.8	13.6	238.5	8.4	307.4	3.6
03	563.3	12.8	397.2	32.5	274.5	15.1	340.3	10.7
04	608.5	8.0	516.3	30.0	330.6	20.4	397.9	16.9

New Houses

Year	U.K. Index	%	Average Price £	North Index	%	Yorks/Humb Index	%	N. West Index	%
87	141.9	12.1	49,384	120.0	6.9	125.7	7.5	119.4	4.4
88	175.4	23.6	61,020	136.6	13.8	145.8	16.1	138.1	15.7
89	206.2	17.6	71,733	172.3	26.1	196.9	35.0	177.6	28.7
90	207.8	0.8	72,290	192.5	11.7	210.4	6.9	198.3	11.5
91	204.0	−1.8	70,987	198.3	3.1	214.0	1.7	206.5	4.2
92	197.8	−3.3	68,634	200.6	1.1	210.1	−1.8	199.7	−3.3
93	195.0	−1.1	67,856	200.6	0.0	210.6	0.3	195.3	−2.2
94	195.5	0.3	68,032	196.8	−1.9	208.7	−0.9	189.1	−3.2
95	196.0	0.2	68,183	199.4	1.3	206.5	−1.0	185.3	−2.0
96	199.6	1.9	69,453	195.5	−1.9	216.1	4.6	187.7	1.3
97	204.8	2.6	71,248	197.4	1.0	211.8	−2.0	191.1	1.8
98	217.9	6.4	75,806	212.7	7.7	220.2	4.0	203.5	6.5
99	228.1	4.7	79,384	221.2	4.0	238.0	8.0	202.7	−0.4
00	257.8	13.0	89,709	215.5	−2.6	274.1	15.2	232.5	14.7
01	276.6	7.3	96,252	228.2	5.9	291.4	6.3	237.5	2.2
02	318.5	15.1	110,832	260.1	14.0	302.9	3.9	270.2	13.8
03	380.5	19.4	132,383	316.3	21.6	392.2	29.5	311.2	15.2
04	443.3	16.5	154,235	382.4	20.9	450.3	14.8	441.1	41.8

Year	E. Midlands Index	%	W. Midlands Index	%	E. Anglia Index	%	S. West Index	%	S. East Index	%
87	137.4	10.2	129.9	8.9	167.0	21.0	151.4	19.0	172.3	21.4
88	177.6	29.2	170.4	31.2	237.0	41.9	207.3	36.9	224.8	30.6
89	226.7	27.7	220.0	29.1	243.1	2.6	231.5	11.7	236.3	5.1
90	216.8	−4.3	215.3	−2.1	225.2	−7.4	220.5	−4.7	223.6	−5.4
91	213.5	−1.6	214.4	−0.4	210.1	−6.7	209.4	−5.1	209.9	−6.1
92	204.3	−4.3	213.0	−0.6	199.8	−4.9	194.8	−7.0	194.3	−7.4
93	204.3	0.0	213.7	0.3	196.0	−1.9	191.2	−1.8	190.1	−2.1
94	201.5	−1.3	214.5	0.4	198.8	1.4	189.4	−0.9	194.8	2.4
95	205.9	2.2	210.0	−2.1	202.7	1.9	187.5	−1.0	192.1	−1.3
96	210.7	2.4	220.4	5.0	196.8	−2.9	190.3	1.5	200.0	4.1
97	221.3	5.0	228.5	3.7	211.3	7.4	207.2	8.8	215.5	7.8
98	232.2	4.9	243.6	6.6	219.7	4.0	217.2	4.8	235.8	9.4
99	243.7	4.9	239.8	−1.6	232.7	5.9	229.5	5.7	257.4	9.2
00	253.4	4.0	279.3	16.5	279.6	20.2	260.9	13.7	295.9	15.0
01	266.6	5.2	314.8	12.7	315.3	12.8	293.9	12.7	318.9	7.8
02	346.0	29.8	343.5	9.1	383.6	21.7	345.9	17.7	377.1	18.3
03	417.5	20.7	414.9	20.8	414.6	8.1	408.6	18.1	452.5	20.0
04	501.0	20.0	500.6	20.6	460.3	11.0	460.6	12.7	486.5	7.5

Year	Gr. London Index	%	Wales Index	%	Scotland Index	%	N. Ireland Index	%
87	179.0	18.5	130.6	11.0	129.0	7.2	123.5	1.7
88	224.4	25.3	161.1	23.4	138.6	7.4	133.3	7.9
89	231.5	3.2	207.5	28.8	154.5	11.5	138.9	4.2
90	223.9	−3.3	209.1	0.8	168.3	9.0	146.5	5.4
91	209.4	−6.4	203.2	−2.8	179.9	6.8	156.7	7.0
92	198.2	−5.4	201.0	−1.1	185.8	3.3	158.3	1.0
93	194.4	−1.9	198.7	−1.2	188.5	1.5	160.2	1.2
94	190.0	−2.3	200.1	0.7	191.7	1.7	172.2	7.5
95	188.1	−1.0	200.2	0.0	194.0	1.2	187.8	9.1
96	194.2	3.3	203.4	1.6	190.2	−2.0	208.5	11.0
97	202.2	4.1	205.4	1.0	190.0	−0.1	216.4	3.8
98	221.6	9.6	220.0	7.1	210.9	11.0	244.8	13.1
99	240.4	8.5	221.3	0.6	212.7	0.8	238.5	−2.6
00	302.6	25.9	243.6	10.1	214.2	0.7	269.4	13.0
01	364.1	20.3	253.8	4.2	218.4	2.0	267.3	−0.7
02	394.9	8.4	279.9	10.3	240.8	10.2	231.4	−13.0
03	480.3	21.6	366.1	30.8	270.4	12.3	324.2	40.1
04	492.5	2.6	471.4	28.8	324.4	20.0	384.8	18.7

Existing Houses

Year	U.K. Index	U.K. %	U.K. Average Price £	North Index	North %	Yorks/Humb Index	Yorks/Humb %	N. West Index	N. West %
87	151.6	16.0	46,001	123.1	6.8	131.4	9.4	129.9	8.5
88	186.7	23.2	56,658	137.4	11.6	156.4	19.0	151.8	16.8
89	226.5	21.3	68,732	185.0	34.7	226.4	44.8	207.1	36.4
90	225.8	−0.3	68,537	212.1	14.6	240.8	6.4	233.2	12.6
91	223.1	−1.2	67,717	217.0	2.3	243.3	1.0	241.1	3.4
92	210.2	−5.8	63,797	212.1	−2.3	234.5	−3.6	230.2	−4.5
93	204.0	−3.0	61,911	208.5	−1.7	230.0	−1.9	222.8	−3.2
94	205.1	0.5	62,250	205.6	−1.4	227.9	−0.9	219.5	−1.5
95	201.3	−1.8	61,099	197.1	−4.1	220.0	−3.5	211.1	−3.8
96	211.0	4.8	64,044	204.1	3.5	225.7	2.6	214.1	1.5
97	225.2	6.7	68,334	209.4	2.6	230.3	2.0	220.9	3.2
98	237.3	5.4	72,030	212.6	1.5	231.1	0.3	224.5	1.6
99	255.0	7.5	77,396	222.7	4.8	237.6	2.8	235.5	4.9
00	280.3	9.9	85,061	226.5	1.7	246.8	3.9	245.1	4.1
01	305.8	9.1	92,795	240.2	6.1	259.9	5.3	261.3	6.6
02	360.1	17.8	109,274	278.9	16.1	303.4	16.8	299.5	14.6
03	440.9	22.5	133,808	383.4	37.5	402.6	32.7	377.0	25.8
04	521.0	18.2	158,111	508.5	32.6	505.5	25.6	483.8	28.4

Year	E. Midlands Index	E. Midlands %	W. Midlands Index	W. Midlands %	E. Anglia Index	E. Anglia %	S. West Index	S. West %	S. East Index	S. East %
87	147.2	15.6	139.4	16.0	175.9	26.4	159.9	20.5	183.0	26.2
88	189.7	28.9	189.8	36.2	252.0	43.3	220.2	37.7	234.0	27.9
89	248.0	30.7	246.1	29.7	258.5	2.6	246.0	11.7	245.8	5.0
90	237.6	−4.2	243.1	−1.2	225.6	−13.0	222.3	−9.6	223.8	−8.9
91	230.7	−2.9	244.9	0.7	215.4	−4.5	210.4	−5.4	210.8	−5.8
92	216.3	−6.2	232.0	−5.3	198.9	−7.7	194.2	−7.7	192.7	−8.6
93	210.2	−2.8	220.6	−4.9	193.6	−2.6	186.1	−4.2	186.2	−3.4
94	210.7	0.2	220.8	0.1	197.1	1.8	189.5	1.8	189.9	2.0
95	205.1	−2.6	217.9	−1.3	193.6	−1.8	187.1	−1.3	190.7	0.4
96	211.4	3.0	227.8	4.6	198.7	2.6	197.1	5.3	200.9	5.3
97	223.6	5.8	240.9	5.7	212.5	7.0	212.6	7.9	223.8	11.4
98	232.0	3.7	252.8	4.9	226.5	6.6	230.3	8.3	247.8	10.7
99	246.6	6.3	259.1	2.5	244.1	7.7	254.5	10.5	274.8	10.9
00	267.0	8.2	285.7	10.3	283.4	16.1	298.6	17.3	324.4	18.1
01	294.3	10.3	308.9	8.1	331.7	17.1	336.7	12.8	361.9	11.6
02	371.5	26.2	377.0	22.0	398.2	20.1	413.1	22.7	422.2	16.7
03	468.8	26.2	475.0	26.0	481.5	20.9	492.0	19.1	489.9	16.0
04	553.0	18.0	552.7	16.3	540.8	12.3	561.1	14.0	535.3	9.3

Year	Gr. London Index	Gr. London %	Wales Index	Wales %	Scotland Index	Scotland %	N. Ireland Index	N. Ireland %
87	201.9	26.1	130.8	10.1	126.6	5.4	120.9	−1.0
88	246.3	22.0	163.2	24.8	139.7	10.4	124.6	3.0
89	251.5	2.1	218.3	33.8	167.1	19.6	128.9	3.5
90	236.7	−5.9	222.7	2.0	186.5	11.6	129.6	0.5
91	223.6	−5.6	220.0	−1.2	197.1	5.7	144.9	11.8
92	202.7	−9.4	208.8	−5.1	197.6	0.2	144.2	−0.4
93	192.6	−5.0	206.2	−1.3	199.4	0.9	152.6	5.8
94	196.5	2.0	203.3	−1.4	201.8	1.2	162.6	6.6
95	195.3	−0.6	195.0	−4.1	201.5	−0.1	173.8	6.9
96	213.0	9.1	207.5	6.4	208.6	3.5	206.4	18.7
97	248.6	16.7	214.8	3.5	208.0	−0.3	214.0	3.7
98	274.8	10.5	223.0	3.8	214.1	2.9	240.8	12.5
99	319.7	16.3	235.8	5.7	216.7	1.2	256.7	6.6
00	377.9	18.2	247.7	5.1	219.2	1.1	275.3	7.2
01	433.2	14.6	269.6	8.8	228.8	4.4	310.5	12.8
02	507.2	17.1	307.9	14.2	249.3	9.0	322.7	3.9
03	569.8	12.4	408.5	32.7	289.2	16.0	349.2	8.2
04	614.1	7.8	534.0	30.7	347.4	20.1	409.3	17.2

Reproduced here with the kind permission of Halifax plc.

E4: Average semi-detached house prices by region 2005

Region	£
UK	160,234
North	130,283
North West	147,661
West Midlands	146,494
South East	214,457
Greater London	330,091
Yorkshire & Humberside	128,618
East Midlands	128,055
East Anglia	156,789
South West	183,505
Scotland	120,746
Wales	130,838
Northern Ireland	110,708

Group F
Investment

F

F1: Share price indices

F2: Barclays Equity Index

F3: Index-linked stock

F1: Share price indices

FTSE® A   All-share index (on last day of month)

	1983	1984	1985	1986	1987	1988	1989	1990
January	395.02	501.36	614.62	696.41	903.29	915.84	1054.97	1167.15
February	399.35	493.12	508.28	750.83	983.12	908.08	1042.60	1122.26
March	411.94	542.20	616.26	810.48	1000.04	896.75	1076.15	1114.94
April	439.29	534.83	622.11	816.40	1023.58	928.19	1090.04	1043.16
May	437.63	477.21	634.16	788.92	1097.29	923.52	1091.06	1154.24
June	458.91	487.74	595.54	815.70	1153.12	963.01	1101.67	1171.28
July	445.91	474.83	603.46	771.80	1202.19	965.18	1173.25	1147.05
August	450.36	520.47	646.26	817.06	1146.69	911.17	1207.45	1051.08
September	445.53	535.86	626.24	768.79	1208.89	946.27	1169.55	962.18
October	437.38	543.48	670.64	807.27	887.33	965.54	1080.79	992.67
November	461.87	560.26	696.53	815.34	796.31	933.45	1138.67	1032.11
December	470.50	592.94	682.94	835.48	870.22	926.59	1204.70	1032.25

	1991	1992	1993	1994	1995	1996	1997	1998
January	1036.24	1227.63	1364.33	1745.97	1480.56	1841.96	2087.61	2536.68
February	1150.01	1229.84	1396.53	1675.59	1487.00	1840.77	2107.86	2683.40
March	1193.33	1171.71	1408.07	1561.97	1538.64	1843.44	2099.70	2781.66
April	1202.75	1282.75	1388.88	1580.44	1578.67	1914.61	2135.31	2788.99
May	1201.85	1311.79	1403.42	1501.22	1632.56	1885.78	2200.91	2802.18
June	1161.19	1216.62	1432.31	1463.35	1632.51	1856.33	2184.52	2743.46
July	1235.89	1143.14	1448.76	1545.74	1703.02	1835.44	2295.18	2734.72
August	1268.62	1096.99	1537.21	1626.64	1719.44	1915.98	2276.72	2440.84
September	1265.96	1206.16	1506.55	1510.97	1733.73	1945.00	2255.02	2344.82
October	1238.63	1256.67	1565.37	1536.31	1734.14	1956.90	2293.87	2504.85
November	1168.95	1313.02	1556.45	1528.12	1788.60	1985.17	2288.64	2626.86
December	1187.70	1363.79	1682.17	1421.44	1803.09	2013.66	2411.00	2673.92

	1999	2000	2001	2002	2003	2004	2005	
January	2695.94	2975.87	3018.96	2496.00	1722.28	2187.10	2441.22	
February	2825.39	2989.43	2857.92	2467.00	1759.08	2243.41	2495.46	
March	2894.79	3101.59	2705.94	2557.40	1735.72	2196.97	2457.73	
April	3028.40	2994.08	2869.04	2512.04	1891.50	2237.30	2397.10	
May	2889.65	3009.50	2811.22	2475.57	1968.83	2201.80	2483.40	
June	2946.17	3018.58	2728.12	2263.11	1971.26	2228.70	2560.20	
July	2925.14	3050.85	2664.00	2050.81	2045.82	2192.22		
August	2939.11	3192.10	2590.20	2046.21	2064.74	2214.19		
September	2826.11	3013.02	2340.50	1801.48	2027.72	2271.67		
October	2904.38	3066.39	2413.50	1938.71	2125.37	2297.66		
November	3086.90	2936.20	2514.10	2002.97	2146.72	2345.21		
December	3242.06	2976.20	2523.90	1893.73	2207.38	2410.75		

F2: Barclays Equity Index

Year	Equity Price Index December %		Equity Income Index December %		Income Yield %	Equity Price Index Adjusted for Cost of Living %		Equity Income Index Adjusted for Cost of Living %	
1952	144	−5.9	128	+6.3	6.1	46	−11.5	42	−0.0
1953	170	+17.8	134	+4.3	5.4	54	+16.6	44	+3.2
1954	242	+42.4	155	+16.0	4.4	74	+36.9	49	+11.6
1955	256	+5.8	179	+15.4	4.8	74	−0.0	53	+9.1
1956	220	−13.9	183	+2.2	5.7	62	−16.5	53	−0.8
1957	205	−7.0	188	+2.8	6.3	55	−11.1	52	−1.7
1958	289	+41.1	202	+7.5	4.8	76	+38.5	55	+5.5
1959	432	+49.5	227	+12.1	3.6	113	+49.5	61	+12.1
1960	421	−2.6	276	+21.7	4.5	108	−4.4	73	+19.5
1961	409	−3.0	286	+3.5	4.8	101	−7.0	73	−0.8
1962	391	−4.4	285	−0.4	5.0	94	−6.9	71	−3.0
1963	450	+15.2	266	−6.5	4.1	106	+13.1	65	−8.2
1964	405	−10.0	303	+13.7	5.1	91	−14.2	70	+8.5
1965	428	+5.9	326	+7.7	5.2	92	+1.3	73	+3.1
1966	389	−9.3	328	+0.5	5.8	81	−12.5	70	−3.1
1967	500	+28.7	319	−2.5	4.4	101	+25.6	67	−4.8
1968	718	+43.5	339	+6.1	3.2	137	+35.4	67	+0.2
1969	609	−15.2	342	+0.8	3.9	111	−19.0	65	−3.7
1970	563	−7.5	360	+5.5	4.4	95	−14.3	63	−2.3
1971	799	+41.9	379	+5.1	3.3	124	+30.2	61	−3.6
1972	901	+12.8	414	+9.3	3.2	130	+4.8	62	+1.6
1973	619	−31.4	430	+3.9	4.8	81	−37.9	58	−6.0
1974	276	−55.3	472	+9.6	11.7	30	−62.5	53	−8.0
1975	653	+136.3	521	+10.4	5.5	57	+89.2	47	−11.6
1976	628	−3.9	588	+12.8	6.4	48	−16.5	46	−2.0
1977	886	+41.2	682	+16.1	5.3	60	+25.9	48	+3.5
1978	910	+2.7	768	+12.6	5.8	57	−5.3	50	+3.9
1979	949	+4.3	951	+23.8	6.9	51	−11.0	53	+5.6
1980	1206	+27.1	1073	+12.8	6.1	56	+10.4	52	−2.0
1981	1294	+7.2	1111	+3.5	5.9	54	−4.3	48	−7.6
1982	1579	+22.1	1211	+9.0	5.3	62	+15.8	49	+3.4
1983	1944	+23.1	1309	+8.1	4.6	73	+16.9	51	+2.7
1984	2450	+26.0	1578	+20.6	4.4	88	+20.5	58	+15.3
1985	2822	+15.2	1781	+12.8	4.3	95	+9.0	62	+6.8
1986	3452	+22.3	2033	+14.1	4.0	112	+17.9	68	+10.0
1987	3596	+4.2	2264	+11.4	4.3	113	+0.4	74	+7.4
1988	3829	+6.5	2628	+16.1	4.7	113	−0.3	80	+8.7
1989	4978	+30.0	3076	+17.0	4.2	136	+20.7	87	+8.7
1990	4265	−14.3	3401	+10.5	5.5	107	−21.6	88	+1.1
1991	4907	+15.1	3591	+5.6	5.0	117	+10.1	89	+1.1
1992	5635	+14.8	3573	−0.5	4.4	131	+11.9	86	−3.0
1993	6951	+23.3	3414	−4.4	3.4	159	+21.0	81	−6.2
1994	6286	−9.6	3684	+7.9	4.0	140	−12.1	85	+4.9
1995	7450	+18.5	4127	+12.0	3.8	161	+14.8	92	+8.5
1996	8320	+11.7	4536	+9.9	3.7	175	+9.0	99	+7.3
1997	9962	+19.7	4690	+3.4	3.2	202	+15.5	98	−0.2
1998	11048	+10.9	4026	−14.2	2.5	218	+7.9	82	−16.5
1999	13396	+21.2	4140	+2.8	2.1	260	+19.1	83	+1.0
2000	12329	−8.0	4007	−3.2	2.2	233	−10.6	78	−5.9
2001	10428	−15.4	3998	−0.2	2.6	195	−16.0	77	−0.9
2002	7825	−25.0	4049	+1.3	3.6	142	−27.1	76	−1.6
2003	9121	+16.6	4121	+1.8	3.1	161	+13.4	75	−1.0
2004	88508	+12.5	3418	+8.8	+7.2	154	+3.6	192	+1.1

Note: original investment of £100 December 1945, gross income reinvested.
Reproduced here with the kind permission of Barclays Capital.

F3: Index-linked stock

Return on index-linked government securities

	1996		1997		1998		1999		2000	
	Gross %	Net %	Gross %	Net %	Gross %	Net %	Gross %	Net %	Gross %	Net %
January	3.58	3.04	3.55	3.02	3.06	2.60	1.88	1.60	2.05	1.74
February	3.77	3.20	3.43	2.92	2.98	2.53	1.88	1.60	1.91	1.62
March	3.77	3.20	3.60	3.06	2.85	2.42	1.76	1.50	1.87	1.59
April	3.71	3.15	3.58	3.04	2.82	2.40	1.85	1.57	1.88	1.60
May	3.87	3.29	3.68	3.13	2.68	2.28	1.86	1.58	1.94	1.65
June	3.82	3.25	3.63	3.09	2.65	2.25	1.90	1.62	1.83	1.56
July	3.79	3.22	3.53	3.00	2.57	2.18	1.95	1.66	1.98	1.68
August	3.72	3.16	3.56	3.00	2.40	2.04	2.15	1.83	2.01	1.71
September	3.62	3.08	3.32	2.82	2.47	2.10	2.13	1.81	2.02	1.72
October	3.60	3.06	3.10	2.64	2.43	2.07	2.01	1.71	2.03	1.73
November	3.46	2.94	3.08	2.62	2.22	1.89	1.84	1.56	1.87	1.59
December	3.53	3.00	3.02	2.87	1.94	1.65	1.80	1.53	1.92	1.63

	2001		2002		2003		2004		2005	
	Gross %	Net %	Gross %	Net %	Gross %	Net %	Gross %	Net %	Gross %	Net %
January	1.90	1.62	2.28	1.94	1.90	1.62	1.88	1.60	1.61	1.37
February	1.93	1.64	2.26	1.92	1.78	1.51	1.75	1.49	1.60	1.36
March	2.24	1.90	2.28	1.94	1.85	1.57	1.67	1.42	1.61	1.37
April	2.51	2.13	2.30	1.95	1.91	1.62	1.82	1.55	1.56	1.33
May	2.47	2.10	2.26	1.92	1.73	1.47	1.90	1.61	1.54	1.31
June	2.41	2.05	2.14	1.82	1.76	1.50	1.87	1.59		
July	2.32	1.97	2.32	1.97	1.97	1.67	1.91	1.62		
August	2.12	1.80	2.03	1.73	1.93	1.64	1.75	1.49		
September	2.37	2.01	2.01	1.71	1.84	1.56	1.71	1.45		
October	2.12	1.80	2.13	1.81	2.09	1.78	1.69	1.44		
November	2.17	1.84	2.26	1.92	2.09	1.78	1.62	1.38		
December	2.30	1.95	2.02	1.72	1.83	1.56	1.54	1.31		

Notes:

1. The index used to compile the above table is the month end FTSE Actuaries Government Securities Index for index-linked stock with over five years to maturity assuming 5 per cent inflation. It is not the index created by the UK Government Debt Management Office for the Lord Chancellor when, on June 25, 2001, he prescribed a rate under s.1(1) of the Damages Act 1996.

2. The net percentage yield is stated after deduction of tax at an assumed average rate of 15 per cent: see *Wells v Wells*.[1] The actual average rate of tax will vary from case to case depending on the amount of taxable income. This will be affected both by the size of the award and the fact that only the interest element of the total return is taxable, with any capital loss or gain on redemption being exempt from tax.

[1] [1999] A.C. 345.

Index-linked stock (January 1993 – February 2005)

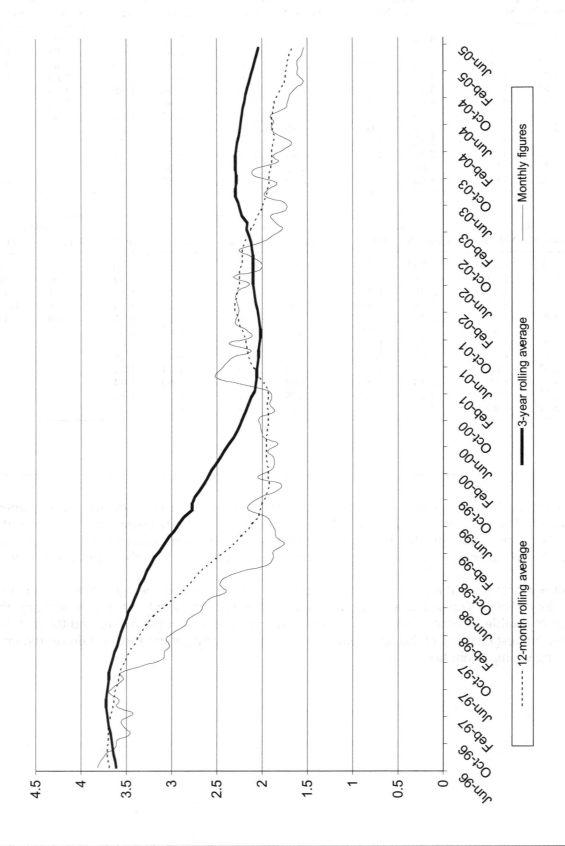

Group G
Tax and National Insurance

G

G1: Net equivalents to a range of gross annual income figures

Gross income £pa	1995/96 Net equivalent income				1996/97 Net equivalent income			
	Employed		Self-employed		Employed		Self-employed	
	Single person £pa	Married man £pa	Single person £pa	Married man £pa	Single person £pa	Married man £pa	Single person £pa	Married man £pa
1,000	1,000	1,000	1,000	1,000	1,000	1,000	1,000	1,000
2,000	2,000	2,000	2,000	2,000	2,000	2,000	2,000	2,000
3,000	3,000	3,000	3,000	3,000	3,000	3,000	3,000	3,000
4,000	3,746	3,841	3,606	3,701	3,807	3,854	3,638	3,685
5,000	4,446	4,704	4,406	4,664	4,507	4,754	4,438	4,685
6,000	5,146	5,404	5,206	5,464	5,207	5,475	5,238	5,507
7,000	5,832	6,090	5,969	6,227	5,907	6,175	6,030	6,299
8,000	6,483	6,741	6,655	6,913	6,593	6,862	6,757	7,025
9,000	7,133	7,391	7,341	7,599	7,253	7,522	7,457	7,725
10,000	7,783	8,041	8,028	8,286	7,913	8,182	8,157	8,425
11,000	8,433	8,691	8,714	8,972	8,573	8,842	8,857	9,125
12,000	9,083	9,341	9,400	9,658	9,233	9,502	9,557	9,825
13,000	9,733	9,991	10,086	10,344	9,893	10,162	10,257	10,525
14,000	10,383	10,641	10,772	11,030	10,553	10,822	10,957	11,225
15,000	11,033	11,291	11,458	11,716	11,213	11,482	11,657	11,925
16,000	11,683	11,941	12,144	12,402	11,873	12,142	12,357	12,625
17,000	12,333	12,591	12,830	13,088	12,533	12,802	13,057	13,325
18,000	12,983	13,241	13,517	13,775	13,193	13,462	13,757	14,025
19,000	13,633	13,891	14,202	14,460	13,853	14,122	14,457	14,725
20,000	14,283	14,541	14,889	15,147	14,513	14,782	15,157	15,425
21,000	14,933	15,191	15,575	15,833	15,173	15,442	15,857	16,125
22,000	15,583	15,841	16,261	16,519	15,833	16,102	16,557	16,825
23,000	16,245	16,503	16,955	17,213	16,493	16,762	17,257	17,525
24,000	16,995	17,253	17,705	17,963	17,187	17,456	17,977	18,246
25,000	17,745	18,003	18,455	18,713	17,947	18,216	18,737	19,005
26,000	18,495	18,753	19,205	19,463	18,707	18,976	19,497	19,765
27,000	19,245	19,503	19,955	20,213	19,467	19,736	20,257	20,525
28,000	19,968	20,226	20,705	20,963	20,227	20,496	21,017	21,285
29,000	20,568	20,826	21,368	21,626	20,987	21,256	21,777	22,045
30,000	21,168	21,426	21,968	22,226	21,630	21,898	22,419	22,687
31,000	21,768	22,026	22,568	22,826	22,230	22,498	23,019	23,287
32,000	22,368	22,626	23,168	23,426	22,830	23,098	23,619	23,887
33,000	22,968	23,226	23,768	24,026	23,430	23,698	24,219	24,487
34,000	23,568	23,826	24,368	24,626	24,030	24,298	24,819	25,087
35,000	24,168	24,426	24,968	25,226	24,630	24,898	25,419	25,687
40,000	27,168	27,426	27,968	28,226	27,630	27,898	28,419	28,687
45,000	30,168	30,426	30,968	31,226	30,630	30,898	31,419	31,687
50,000	33,168	33,426	33,968	34,226	33,630	33,898	34,419	34,687
55,000	36,168	36,426	36,968	37,226	36,630	36,898	37,419	37,687
60,000	39,168	39,426	39,968	40,226	39,630	39,898	40,419	40,687
65,000	42,168	42,426	42,968	43,226	42,630	42,898	43,419	43,687
70,000	45,168	45,426	45,968	46,226	45,630	45,898	46,419	46,687
75,000	48,168	48,426	48,968	49,226	48,630	48,898	49,419	49,687
80,000	51,168	51,426	51,968	52,226	51,630	51,898	52,419	52,687
85,000	54,168	54,426	54,968	55,226	54,630	54,898	55,419	55,687
90,000	57,168	57,426	57,968	58,226	57,630	57,898	58,419	58,687
95,000	60,168	60,426	60,968	61,226	60,630	60,898	61,419	61,687
100,000	63,168	63,426	63,968	64,226	63,630	63,898	64,419	64,687
150,000	93,168	93,426	93,968	94,226	93,630	93,898	94,419	94,687
200,000	123,168	123,426	123,968	124,226	123,630	123,898	124,419	124,687
250,000	153,168	153,426	153,968	154,226	153,630	153,898	154,419	154,687
300,000	183,168	183,426	183,968	184,226	183,630	183,898	184,419	184,687

G1: Net equivalents to a range of gross annual income figures

Gross income £pa	1997/98 Net equivalent income				1998/99 Net equivalent income			
	Employed		Self-employed		Employed		Self-employed	
	Single person £pa	Married man £pa	Single person £pa	Married man £pa	Single person £pa	Married man £pa	Single person £pa	Married man £pa
1,000	1,000	1,000	1,000	1,000	1,000	1,000	1,000	1,000
2,000	2,000	2,000	2,000	2,000	2,000	2,000	2,000	2,000
3,000	3,000	3,000	3,000	3,000	3,000	3,000	3,000	3,000
4,000	3,858	3,858	3,680	3,680	3,866	3,866	3,670	3,670
5,000	4,567	4,758	4,489	4,680	4,605	4,766	4,509	4,670
6,000	5,267	5,541	5,289	5,564	5,305	5,590	5,309	5,594
7,000	5,967	6,241	6,089	6,364	6,005	6,290	6,109	6,394
8,000	6,667	6,941	6,830	7,104	6,705	6,990	6,867	7,152
9,000	7,341	7,615	7,544	7,819	7,390	7,675	7,592	7,877
10,000	8,011	8,286	8,254	8,529	8,060	8,345	8,302	8,587
11,000	8,681	8,956	8,964	9,239	8,730	9,015	9,012	9,297
12,000	9,351	9,626	9,674	9,949	9,400	9,685	9,722	10,007
13,000	10,021	10,296	10,384	10,659	10,070	10,355	10,432	10,717
14,000	10,691	10,966	11,094	11,369	10,740	11,025	11,142	11,427
15,000	11,361	11,636	11,804	12,079	11,410	11,695	11,852	12,137
16,000	12,031	12,306	12,514	12,789	12,080	12,365	12,562	12,847
17,000	12,701	12,976	13,224	13,499	12,750	13,035	13,272	13,557
18,000	13,371	13,646	13,934	14,209	13,420	13,705	13,982	14,267
19,000	14,041	14,316	14,644	14,919	14,090	14,375	14,692	14,977
20,000	14,711	14,986	15,354	15,629	14,760	15,045	15,402	15,687
21,000	15,381	15,656	16,064	16,339	15,430	15,715	16,112	16,397
22,000	16,051	16,326	16,774	17,049	16,100	16,385	16,822	17,107
23,000	16,721	16,996	17,484	17,759	16,770	17,055	17,532	17,817
24,000	17,391	17,666	18,194	18,469	17,440	17,725	18,242	18,527
25,000	18,143	18,418	18,953	19,228	18,110	18,395	18,952	19,237
26,000	18,913	19,188	19,723	19,998	18,858	19,143	19,709	19,994
27,000	19,683	19,958	20,493	20,768	19,628	19,913	20,479	20,764
28,000	20,453	20,728	21,263	21,538	20,398	20,683	21,249	21,534
29,000	21,223	21,498	22,033	22,308	21,168	21,453	22,019	22,304
30,000	21,993	22,268	22,803	23,078	21,938	22,223	22,789	23,074
31,000	22,618	22,893	23,428	23,703	22,708	22,993	23,559	23,844
32,000	23,218	23,493	24,028	24,303	23,358	23,643	24,209	24,494
33,000	23,818	24,093	24,628	24,903	23,958	24,243	24,809	25,094
34,000	24,418	24,693	25,228	25,503	24,558	24,843	25,409	25,694
35,000	25,018	25,293	25,828	26,103	25,158	25,443	26,009	26,294
40,000	28,018	28,293	28,828	29,103	28,158	28,443	29,009	29,294
45,000	31,018	31,293	31,828	32,103	31,158	31,443	32,009	32,294
50,000	34,018	34,293	34,828	35,103	34,158	34,443	35,009	35,294
55,000	37,018	37,293	37,828	38,103	37,158	37,443	38,009	38,294
60,000	40,018	40,293	40,828	41,103	40,158	40,443	41,009	41,294
65,000	43,018	43,293	43,828	44,103	43,158	43,443	44,009	44,294
70,000	46,018	46,293	46,828	47,103	46,158	46,443	47,009	47,294
75,000	49,018	49,293	49,828	50,103	49,158	49,443	50,009	50,294
80,000	52,018	52,293	52,828	53,103	52,158	52,443	53,009	53,294
85,000	55,018	55,293	55,828	56,103	55,158	55,443	56,009	56,294
90,000	58,018	58,293	58,828	59,103	58,158	58,443	59,009	59,294
95,000	61,018	61,293	61,828	62,103	61,158	61,443	62,009	62,294
100,000	64,018	64,293	64,828	65,103	64,158	64,443	65,009	65,294
150,000	94,018	94,293	94,828	95,103	94,158	94,443	95,009	95,294
200,000	124,018	124,293	124,828	125,103	124,158	124,443	125,009	125,294
250,000	154,018	154,293	154,828	155,103	154,158	154,443	155,009	155,294
300,000	184,018	184,293	184,828	185,103	184,158	184,443	185,009	185,294

| Gross income £pa | 1999/2000 Net equivalent income | | | | 2000/01 Net equivalent income | | 2001/02 Net equivalent icnome | |
| | Employed | | Self-employed | | Employed | Self-employed | Employed | Self-employed |
	Single person £pa	Married man £pa	Single person £pa	Married man £pa	£pa	£pa	£pa	£pa
1,000	1,000	1,000	1,000	1,000	1,000	1,000	1,000	1,000
2,000	2,000	2,000	2,000	2,000	2,000	2,000	2,000	2,000
3,000	3,000	3,000	3,000	3,000	3,000	3,000	3,000	3,000
4,000	3,943	3,943	3,659	3,659	3,995	3,896	4,000	3,896
5,000	4,776	4,843	4,592	4,659	4,834	4,791	4,906	4,817
6,000	5,555	5,743	5,471	5,659	5,622	5,610	5,706	5,647
7,000	6,225	6,422	6,241	6,438	6,302	6,320	6,436	6,407
8,000	6,895	7,092	6,983	7,180	6,982	7,030	7,116	7,117
9,000	7,565	7,762	7,693	7,890	7,662	7,740	7,796	7,827
10,000	8,235	8,432	8,551	8,748	8,342	8,450	8,476	8,537
11,000	8,905	9,102	9,113	9,310	9,022	9,160	9,156	9,247
12,000	9,575	9,772	9,823	10,020	9,702	9,870	9,836	9,957
13,000	10,245	10,442	10,533	10,730	10,382	10,580	10,516	10,667
14,000	10,915	11,112	11,243	11,440	11,062	11,290	11,196	11,377
15,000	11,585	11,782	11,953	12,150	11,742	12,000	11,876	12,087
16,000	12,255	12,451	12,663	12,860	12,422	12,710	12,556	12,797
17,000	12,925	13,122	13,373	13,570	13,102	13,420	13,236	13,507
18,000	13,595	13,792	14,083	14,280	13,782	14,130	13,916	14,217
19,000	14,265	14,462	14,793	14,990	14,462	14,840	14,596	14,927
20,000	14,935	15,132	15,503	15,700	15,142	15,550	15,276	15,637
21,000	15,605	15,802	16,213	16,410	15,822	16,260	15,956	16,347
22,000	16,275	16,472	16,923	17,120	16,502	16,970	16,636	17,057
23,000	16,945	17,142	17,633	17,830	17,182	17,680	17,316	17,767
24,000	17,615	17,812	18,343	18,540	17,862	18,390	17,996	18,477
25,000	18,285	18,482	19,053	19,250	18,542	19,100	18,676	19,187
26,000	18,955	19,152	19,763	19,960	19,222	19,810	19,356	19,897
27,000	19,725	19,922	20,533	20,730	19,902	20,520	20,036	20,607
28,000	20,495	20,692	21,303	21,500	20,600	21,243	20,716	21,317
29,000	21,265	21,462	22,073	22,270	21,380	22,023	21,396	22,027
30,000	22,035	22,232	22,843	23,040	22,160	22,803	22,086	22,744
31,000	22,805	23,002	23,613	23,810	22,940	23,583	22,866	23,524
32,000	23,575	23,772	24,383	24,580	23,720	24,363	23,646	24,304
33,000	24,232	24,429	25,040	25,237	24,461	25,104	24,426	25,084
34,000	24,832	25,029	25,640	25,837	25,061	25,704	25,194	25,852
35,000	25,432	25,629	26,240	26,437	25,661	26,304	25,794	26,452
40,000	28,432	28,629	29,240	29,437	28,661	29,304	28,794	29,452
45,000	31,432	31,629	32,240	32,437	31,661	32,304	31,794	32,452
50,000	34,432	34,629	35,240	35,437	34,661	35,304	34,794	35,452
55,000	37,432	37,629	38,240	38,437	37,661	38,304	37,794	38,452
60,000	40,432	40,629	41,240	41,437	40,661	41,304	40,794	41,452
65,000	43,432	43,629	44,240	44,437	43,661	44,304	43,794	44,452
70,000	46,432	46,629	47,240	47,437	46,661	47,304	46,794	47,452
75,000	49,432	49,629	50,240	50,437	49,661	50,304	49,794	50,452
80,000	52,432	52,629	53,240	53,437	52,661	53,304	52,794	53,452
85,000	55,432	55,629	56,240	56,437	55,661	56,304	55,794	56,452
90,000	58,432	58,629	59,240	59,437	58,661	59,304	58,794	59,452
95,000	61,432	61,629	62,240	62,437	61,661	62,304	61,794	62,452
100,000	64,432	64,629	65,240	65,437	64,661	65,304	64,794	65,452
150,000	94,432	94,629	95,240	95,437	94,661	95,304	94,794	95,452
200,000	124,432	124,629	125,240	125,437	124,661	125,304	124,794	125,452
250,000	154,432	154,629	155,240	155,437	154,661	155,304	154,794	155,452
300,000	184,432	184,629	185,240	185,437	184,661	185,304	184,794	185,452

From 2000–2001 onwards there is no difference between single and married people for tax purposes.

G1: Net equivalents to a range of gross annual income figures

Gross income £pa	2002/03 Net equivalent income		2003/04 Net equivalent income		2004/05 Net equivalent income		2005/06 Net equivalent income	
	Employed	Self-employed	Employed	Self-employed	Employed	Self-employed	Employed	Self-employed
£pa	£pa	£pa	£pa	£pa	£pa	£pa	£pa	£pa
1,000	1,000	1,000	1,000	1,000	1,000	1,000	1,000	1,000
2,000	2,000	2,000	2,000	2,000	2,000	2,000	2,000	2,000
3,000	3,000	3,000	3,000	3,000	3,000	3,000	3,000	3,000
4,000	4,000	4,000	4,000	4,000	4,000	4,000	4,000	4,000
5,000	4,924	4,830	4,919	4,827	4,946	4,847	4,977	4,872
6,000	5,724	5,660	5,709	5,647	5,736	5,667	5,767	5,692
7,000	6,469	6,435	6,448	6,416	6,498	6,459	6,556	6,511
8,000	7,149	7,145	7,118	7,116	7,168	7,159	7,226	7,211
9,000	7,829	7,855	7,788	7,816	7,838	7,859	7,896	7,911
10,000	8,509	8,565	8,458	8,516	8,508	8,559	8,566	8,611
11,000	9,189	9,275	9,128	9,216	9,178	9,259	9,236	9,311
12,000	9,869	9,985	9,798	9,916	9,848	9,959	9,906	10,011
13,000	10,549	10,695	10,468	10,616	10,518	10,659	10,576	10,711
14,000	11,229	11,405	11,138	11,316	11,188	11,359	11,246	11,411
15,000	11,909	12,115	11,808	12,016	11,858	12,059	11,916	12,111
16,000	12,589	12,825	12,478	12,716	12,528	12,759	12,586	12,811
17,000	13,269	13,535	13,148	13,416	13,198	13,459	13,256	13,511
18,000	13,949	14,245	13,818	14,116	13,868	14,159	13,926	14,211
19,000	14,629	14,955	14,488	14,816	14,538	14,859	14,596	14,911
20,000	15,309	15,665	15,158	15,516	15,208	15,559	15,266	15,611
21,000	15,989	16,375	15,828	16,216	15,878	16,259	15,936	16,311
22,000	16,669	17,085	16,498	16,916	16,548	16,959	16,606	17,011
23,000	17,349	17,795	17,168	17,616	17,218	17,659	17,276	17,711
24,000	18,029	18,505	17,838	18,316	17,888	18,359	17,946	18,411
25,000	18,709	19,215	18,508	19,016	18,558	19,059	18,616	19,111
26,000	19,389	19,925	19,178	19,716	19,228	19,759	19,286	19,811
27,000	20,069	20,635	19,848	20,416	19,898	20,459	19,956	20,511
28,000	20,749	21,345	20,518	21,116	20,568	21,159	20,626	21,211
29,000	21,429	22,055	21,188	22,816	21,238	21,859	21,296	21,911
30,000	22,109	22,765	22,858	22,516	21,908	22,559	21,966	22,611
31,000	22,847	23,516	22,534	23,220	22,578	23,259	22,636	23,311
32,000	23,627	24,296	23,304	23,990	23,276	23,979	23,306	24,011
33,000	24,407	25,076	24,074	24,760	24,046	24,749	23,976	24,728
34,000	25,187	25,856	24,844	25,530	24,816	25,519	24,646	25,498
35,000	25,879	26,548	25,614	26,300	25,586	26,289	25,316	26,268
40,000	28,879	29,548	28,585	29,271	28,742	29,445	28,904	29,631
45,000	31,879	32,548	31,535	32,221	31,692	32,395	31,854	32,581
50,000	34,879	35,548	34,485	35,171	34,642	35,345	34,804	35,531
55,000	37,879	38,548	37,435	38,121	37,592	38,295	37,754	38,481
60,000	40,879	41,548	40,385	41,071	40,542	41,245	40,704	41,431
65,000	43,879	44,548	43,335	44,021	43,492	44,195	43,654	44,381
70,000	46,879	47,548	46,285	46,971	46,442	47,145	46,604	47,331
75,000	49,879	50,548	49,235	49,921	49,392	50,095	49,554	50,281
80,000	52,879	53,548	52,185	52,871	52,342	53,045	52,504	53,231
85,000	55,879	56,548	55,135	55,821	55,292	55,995	55,454	56,181
90,000	58,879	59,548	58,085	58,771	58,242	58,945	58,404	59,131
95,000	61,879	62,548	61,035	61,721	61,192	61,895	61,354	62,081
100,000	64,879	65,548	63,985	64,671	64,142	64,845	64,304	65,031
150,000	94,879	95,548	93,485	94,171	93,642	94,345	93,804	94,531
200,000	124,879	125,548	122,985	123,671	123,142	123,845	123,304	124,031
250,000	154,879	155,548	152,485	153,171	152,642	153,345	152,804	153,531
300,000	184,879	185,548	181,985	182,671	182,142	182,845	182,304	183,031

From 2000–2001 onwards there is no difference between single and married people for tax purposes.

G2: Illustrative net earnings calculations

Person under 65 at 2003/04 tax rates

			Employed person				Self-employed person		
		£pa	£pa	£pa	£pa	£pa	£pa	£pa	£pa
Gross income	[a]	15,000	25,000	30,000	40,000	15,000	25,000	30,000	40,000
Income Tax									
Gross		15,000	25,000	30,000	40,000	15,000	25,000	30,000	40,000
Personal allowance		(4,615)	(4,615)	(4,615)	(4,615)	(4,615)	(4,615)	(4,615)	(4,615)
Taxable		10,385	20,385	25,385	35,385	10,385	20,385	25,385	35,385
Tax payable									
– At 10%		196	196	196	196	196	196	196	196
– At 22%		1,854	4,054	5,154	6,278	1,854	4,054	5,154	6,278
– At 40%		–	–	–	1,954	–	–	–	1,954
	[b]	2,050	4,250	5,350	8,428	2,050	4,250	5,350	8,428
National Insurance									
Class 1									
– At 11%		1,142	2,242	2,792	2,896				
– At 1%					91				
Class 2						104	104	104	104
Class 4									
– At 8%						830	1,630	2,030	2,106
– At 1%									91
	[c]	1,142	2,242	2,792	2,987	934	1,734	2,134	2,301
Net Income	[a-b-c]	11,808	18,508	21,858	28,585	12,016	19,016	22,516	29,271
Net % of gross		78.7%	74.0%	72.9%	71.5%	80.1%	76.1%	75.1%	73.2%

Person under 65 at 2004/05 tax rates

		Employed person				Self-employed person		
		£pa	£pa	£pa	£pa	£pa	£pa	£pa	£pa
Gross income	[a]	15,000	25,000	30,000	40,000	15,000	25,000	30,000	40,000
Income Tax									
Gross		15,000	25,000	30,000	40,000	15,000	25,000	30,000	40,000
Personal allowance		(4,745)	(4,745)	(4,745)	(4,745)	(4,745)	(4,745)	(4,745)	(4,745)
Taxable		10,255	20,255	25,255	35,255	10,255	20,255	25,255	35,255
Tax payable									
– At 10%		202	202	202	202	202	202	202	202
– At 22%		1,812	4,012	5,112	6,464	1,812	4,012	5,112	6,464
– At 40%		–	–	–	1,542	–	–	–	1,542
	[b]	2,014	4,214	5,314	8,208	2,014	4,214	5,314	8,208
National Insurance									
Class 1									
– At 11%		1,128	2,228	2,778	2,967				
– At 1%					83				
Class 2						107	107	107	107
Class 4									
– At 8%						820	1,620	2,020	2,158
– At 1%									82
	[c]	1,128	2,228	2,778	3,050	927	1,727	2,127	2,347
Net Income	[a-b-c]	11,858	18,558	21,908	28,742	12,059	19,059	22,559	29,445
Net % of gross		79.1%	74.2%	73.1%	71.9%	80.4%	76.2%	75.2%	73.6%

Person under 65 at 2005/06 tax rates

		Employed person				Self-employed person			
		£pa	£pa	£pa	£pa	£pa	£pa	£pa	£pa
Gross income	[a]	15,000	25,000	35,000	40,000	15,000	25,000	35,000	40,000
Income Tax									
Gross		15,000	25,000	35,000	40,000	15,000	25,000	35,000	40,000
Personal allowance		(4,895)	(4,895)	(4,895)	(4,895)	(4,895)	(4,895)	(4,895)	(4,895)
Taxable		10,105	20,105	30,105	35,105	10,105	20,105	30,105	35,105
Tax payable									
– At 10%		209	209	209	209	209	209	209	209
– At 22%		1,763	3,963	6,163	6,668	1,763	3,963	6,163	6,668
– At 40%		–	–	–	1,082	–	–	–	1,082
	[b]	1,972	4,172	6,372	7,959	1,972	4,172	6,372	7,959
National Insurance									
Class 1									
– At 11%		1,112	2,212	3,065	3,065				
– At 1%				22	72				
Class 2						109	109	109	109
Class 4									
– At 8%						808	1,608	2,229	2,229
– At 1%								22	72
	[c]	1,112	2,212	3,087	3,137	917	1,717	2,360	2,410
Net Income	[a-b-c]	11,916	18,616	25,541	28,904	12,111	19,111	26,268	29,631
Net % of gross		79.4%	74.4%	73.0%	72.2%	80.7%	76.4%	75.1%	74.1%

G3: Income tax reliefs and rates

Introductory notes

Personal allowance
Every taxpayer resident in the UK (as well as certain non-UK residents) is entitled to a personal allowance.

Age-related personal allowance
Higher personal allowances are available to taxpayers who are 65 or more in the tax year, subject to an income limit—£19,500 for 2005/06.

Where total income exceeds the prescribed income limit, the higher personal allowance is reduced by 50 per cent of the excess, although the allowance cannot be reduced below the ordinary personal allowance.

For 2005/06, the higher personal allowances available are:

Age 65 to 74 (at any time during the year)	£7,090
Age 75 and above	£7,220

Married couple's allowance
Relief in respect of the married couple's allowance, given at the taxpayer's marginal rate in years up to and including 1993/94, was restricted in subsequent years as follows:

Tax year 1994/95	20% of allowance
Tax years 1995/96 to 1998/99	15% of allowance
Tax year 1999/00	10% of allowance

Married couple's allowance was abolished with effect from 2000/01 onwards, except for couples at least one member of which was born before April 6, 1935. To reflect the abolition of the married couple's allowance (with the exception specified), the net equivalent incomes from 2000/01 onwards for a single person and a married person are identical in table G1.

A Children's Tax Credit was introduced from 2001/02 to replace the married couple's allowance [see below].

This in turn was replaced by Child Tax Credit from 2003/04 [see below].

Age-related married couple's allowance
As noted above, from 2000/01 onwards, married couple's allowance is only available where either spouse was born before April 6, 1935. Subject to this, higher married couple's allowances are available to taxpayers who are 65 or over at the end of the fiscal year, subject to the same income limit as the age-related personal allowance—£19,500 for 2005/06.

For 2005/06, the higher married couple's allowances available are:

Age 65 to 74 (at any time during the year)	£5,905
Age 75 and above	£5,975

Where the husband's income exceeds the prescribed income limit, the higher married couple's allowance is reduced by 50 per cent of the excess less any reduction of the personal allowance (as above), until the allowance is equal to the ordinary married couple's allowance for years up to and including 1999/00, and the following amounts for subsequent years:

Tax year 2000/01	Minimum allowance £2,000
Tax year 2001/02	Minimum allowance £2,070
Tax year 2002/03	Minimum allowance £2,110
Tax year 2003/04	Minimum allowance £2,150
Tax year 2004/05	Minimum allowance £2,210
Tax year 2005/06	Minimum allowance £2,280

The level of the wife's income does not restrict the allowance available.

Children's Tax Credit

For 2001/02 and 2002/03, a Children's Tax Credit was available to parents who had at least one child under sixteen living with them. The credit was given through PAYE codes or tax calculations.

In 2002/03 the credit was £5,290 and the rate of relief 10 per cent, such that the value of the credit was £529. This was reduced if the main earner in the family was a higher rate taxpayer, by £2 for every £3 of taxable income above £29,900. No credit was therefore received when the total income reached £42,450.

For 2002/03 there was an increased Children's Tax Credit available for a child born in that year, for one year only—the baby rate. The increased credit was £10,490 and the rate of relief 10 per cent such that the value of the credit was £1,049. The baby rate was subject to the same reduction as the main rate. No credit was therefore available when the total income reached £50,250.

Child Tax Credit

Child Tax Credit replaced Children's Tax Credit, as well as the child elements of Working Families' Tax Credit and Disabled Person's Tax Credit, with effect from April 6, 2003.

Child Tax Credit is a means-tested benefit paid directly into the bank account of the main carer of the child(ren), on a weekly or 4-weekly basis.

Child Tax Credit neither is affected by, nor affects, Child Benefit, which continues to be paid in the usual way.

From 2004/05 onwards, Child Tax Credit is based initially on the income of the previous tax year.

For 2003/04 only, however, the initial claim was based on the income for the last tax year but one, 2001/02.

In all cases, the claim is corrected to actual income basis in due course.

Families (including single parents) with income up to £58,175 qualify for Child Tax Credit. If, however, the family has a child under one in the tax year, the income limit is increased to £66,350.

Taxation of savings income

Savings income is subdivided into dividends and other savings income, with dividends treated as the top slice of savings income.

From 1996/97 to 1998/99, the savings income of lower and basic rate taxpayers was taxed at 20 per cent at source. Higher rate taxpayers had to account for the 20 per cent difference between the 20 per cent deduction at source and their 40 per cent marginal rate.

From 1999/00 onwards, tax is payable on dividend income at the Schedule F ordinary rate of 10 per cent up to the basic rate limit, and at the Schedule F upper rate of 32½ per cent thereafter. Tax is payable on other savings income at 10 per cent on income in the starting rate band, at 20 per cent on income in the basic rate band, and at 40 per cent thereafter.

1994/95 to 2004/06

Fiscal year:	1994/95	1995/96	1996/97	1997/98	1998/99	1999/00	2000/01	2001/02	2002/03	2003/04	2004/05	2005/06
	£	£	£	£	£	£	£	£	£	£	£	£
Income tax reliefs												
Personal allowance	3,445	3,525	3,765	4,045	4,195	4,335	4,385	4,535	4,615	4,615	4,745	4,895
Married couple's allowance	1,720	1,720	1,790	1,830	1,900	1,970	–	–	–	–	–	–
Self-employed only: Class 4 national insurance contributions	50%	50%	–	–	–	–	–	–	–	–	–	–
Income tax rates												
Starting rate band – Payable at 10%	–	–	–	–	–	1,500	1,520	1,880	1,920	1,960	2,020	2,090
Lower rate band – Payable at 20%	3,000	3,200	3,900	4,100	4,300	–	–	–	–	–	–	–
Basic rate band – Payable at 22%	–	–	–	–	–	–	26,880	27,520	27,980	28,540	29,380	30,310
Basic rate band – Payable at 23%	–	–	–	22,000	22,800	26,500	–	–	–	–	–	–
Basic rate band – Payable at 24%	–	–	21,600	–	–	–	–	–	–	–	–	–
Basic rate band – Payable at 25%	20,700	21,100	–	–	–	–	–	–	–	–	–	–
Higher rate band – Payable at 40%	Balance	Balance	Balance	Balance	Balance	Balance	Balance	Balance	Balance	Balance	Balance	Balance

G4: National Insurance contributions

Introductory notes

1. Married women and widows may elect to pay a reduced contribution as follows:

   - 3.85% on earnings between lower earnings limit and upper earnings limit up to 1999/00

   - 3.85% on earnings between primary threshold and upper earnings limit in 2000/01 to 2002/03

   - 4.85% on earnings between primary threshold and upper earnings limit, and 1% on earnings above upper earnings limit in 2003/04, 2004/05 and 2005/06.

2. Until April 5, 1996, special rates of contribution were payable by members of the Armed Forces.

3. Class 1 employee contributions and Class 2 contributions cease to be payable when a man has reached 65 and a woman 60.

4. Class 4 contributions are not payable in respect of any fiscal year that starts after pensionable age has been reached.

5. Class 3 contributions are voluntary at a flat weekly rate (£7.35 pw in 2005/06).

1994/95 to 1999/00

Fiscal year:	1994/95 £	1995/96 £	1996/97 £	1997/98 £	1998/99 £	1999/00 £
Class 1 contributions (Employees)						
Lower earnings limit (LEL) (pa)	2,964	3,016	3,172	3,224	3,328	3,432
Primary threshold (PT) (pa)	N/A	N/A	N/A	N/A	N/A	N/A
Upper earnings limit (UEL) (pa)	22,360	22,880	23,660	24,180	25,220	26,000
Standard rate						
If earnings below LEL:	Nil	Nil	Nil	Nil	Nil	Nil
If earnings at or above LEL: – Contribution rate on earnings up to LEL	2%	2%	2%	2%	2%	Nil
– Contribution rate on earnings between LEL and UEL	10%	10%	10%	10%	10%	10%
Maximum contribution (pa)	1,999	2,047	2,112	2,160	2,256	2,257
Contracted out rate						
As standard rate except – Contribution rate on earnings between LEL and UEL	8.2%	8.2%	8.2%	8.4%	8.4%	8.4%
Maximum contribution (pa)	1,650	1,689	1,743	1,825	1,905	1,896
Class 2 contributions (Self-employed)						
Small earnings exception limit	3,200	3,310	3,430	3,480	3,590	3,770
Fixed weekly contributions (pw)	5.65	5.75	6.05	6.15	6.35	6.55
Class 4 contributions (Self-employed)						
Lower profits limit (pa)	6,490	6,640	6,860	7,010	7,310	7,530
Upper profits limit (pa)	22,360	22,880	23,660	24,180	25,220	26,000
Contribution rate	7.3%	7.3%	6.0%	6.0%	6.0%	6.0%
Maximum contribution (pa)	1,159	1,186	1,008	1,030	1,075	1,108

2000/01 to 2005/06

Fiscal year:	2000/01 £	2001/02 £	2002/03 £	2003/04 £	2004/05 £	2005/06 £
Class 1 contributions (Employees)						
Lower earnings limit (LEL) (pa)	3,484	3,744	3,900	4,004	4,108	4,264
Primary threshold (PT) (pa)	3,952	4,535	4,615	4,615	4,745	4,895
Upper earnings limit (UEL) (pa)	27,820	29,900	30,420	30,940	31,720	32,760
Standard rate						
If earnings below LEL:	Nil	Nil	Nil	Nil	Nil	Nil
If earnings at or above LEL: – Contribution rate on earnings up to PT	Nil	Nil	Nil	Nil	Nil	Nil
– Contribution rate on earnings between PT and UEL	10%	10%	10%	11%	11%	11%
– Contribution rate on earnings above UEL	Nil	Nil	Nil	1%	1%	1%
Maximum contribution (pa)	2,387	2,537	2,581	2,896 +1% of excess over UEL	2,967 +1% of excess over UEL	3,065 +1% of excess over UEL
Contracted out rate						
As standard rate except – Contribution rate on earnings between PT and UEL	8.4%	8.4%	8.4%	9.4%	9.4%	9.4%
Maximum contribution (pa)	2,005	2,132	2,167	2,475 +1% of excess over UEL	2,536 + 1% of excess over UEL	2,619 + 1% of excess over UEL
Class 2 contributions (Self-employed)						
Small earnings exception limit	3,825	3,955	4,025	4,095	4,215	4,345
Fixed weekly contributions (pw)	2.00	2.00	2.00	2.00	2.05	2.10
Class 4 contributions (Self-employed)						
Lower profits limit (LPL) (pa)	4,385	4,535	4,615	4,615	4,745	4,895
Upper profits limit (UPL) (pa)	27,820	29,900	30,420	30,940	31,720	32,760
Contribution rate on profits between LPL and UPL	7.0%	7.0%	7.0%	8.0%	8.0%	8.0%
Contribution rate on profits above UPL	Nil	Nil	Nil	1.0%	1.0%	1.0%
Maximum contribution (pa)	1,640	1,775	1,806	2,106 + 1% of excess over UPL	2,158 + 1% of excess over UPL	2,229 + 1% of excess over UPL

G5: Net equivalents to a range of gross annual pension figures

Introductory notes

1. The following table sets out the net equivalents to a range of annual pension figures in 2005/06, distinguishing between:

   — a single person aged under 65;
   — a single person aged 65 to 74 at any time during the tax year;
   — a single person aged 75 or over at any time during the tax year;
   — a married person aged under 65;
   — a married person aged 65 to 74 at any time during the tax year; and
   — a married person aged 75 or over at any time during the tax year.

2. The table is followed by illustrative net pension calculations for each marital status and age category, at income levels of £15,000, £20,000, £30,000 and £40,000 per annum.

3. The age ranges selected reflect the availability of age-related personal and married couple's allowances, as detailed in G3.

4. Since pensions are not subject to national insurance contributions, the net equivalent figures represent the gross pension less income tax. Given that liability to primary Class 1 national insurance contributions falls away when the earner has reached pensionable age [note 3 of G4], it follows that the net equivalent figures for those aged 65 and over apply equally to earnings from employment and pensions.

   Similarly, given that Class 4 contributions are not payable in respect of any fiscal year that starts after pensionable age has been reached [note 3 of G4], it follows that the net equivalent figures for those aged 65 and over apply also to earnings from self-employment where pensionable age has been reached in a prior fiscal year.

Gross pension	2005/06 Net equivalent pension					
	Single			Married		
	Aged under 65	Aged 65–74	Aged 75 or over	Aged under 65	Aged 65–74*	Aged 75 or over*
£pa	£pa	£pa	£pa	£pa	£pa	£pa
1,000	1,000	1,000	1,000	1,000	1,000	1,000
2,000	2,000	2,000	2,000	2,000	2,000	2,000
3,000	3,000	3,000	3,000	3,000	3,000	3,000
4,000	4,000	4,000	4,000	4,000	4,000	4,000
5,000	4,989	5,000	5,000	4,989	5,000	5,000
6,000	5,889	6,000	6,000	5,889	6,000	6,000
7,000	6,788	7,000	7,000	6,788	7,000	7,000
8,000	7,568	7,909	7,922	7,568	8,000	8,000
9,000	8,348	8,809	8,822	8,348	9,000	9,000
10,000	9,128	9,611	9,639	9,128	10,000	10,000
11,000	9,908	10,391	10,419	9,908	11,000	11,000
12,000	10,688	11,171	11,199	10,688	11,762	11,797
13,000	11,468	11,951	11,979	11,468	12,542	12,577
14,000	12,248	12,731	12,759	12,248	13,322	13,357
15,000	13,028	13,511	13,539	13,028	14,102	14,137
16,000	13,808	14,291	14,319	13,808	14,882	14,917
17,000	14,588	15,071	15,099	14,588	15,662	15,697
18,000	15,368	15,851	15,879	15,368	16,442	16,477
19,000	16,148	16,631	16,659	16,148	17,222	17,257
20,000	16,928	17,367	17,384	16,928	17,947	17,982
21,000	17,708	18,026	18,054	17,708	18,617	18,652
22,000	18,488	18,696	18,724	18,488	19,287	19,322
23,000	19,268	19,366	19,394	19,268	19,957	19,992
24,000	20,048	20,048	20,048	20,048	20,633	20,662
25,000	20,828	20,828	20,828	20,828	21,363	21,383
26,000	21,608	21,608	21,608	21,608	22,093	22,113
27,000	22,388	22,388	22,388	22,388	22,823	22,843
28,000	23,168	23,168	23,168	23,168	23,553	23,573
29,000	23,948	23,948	23,948	23,948	24,283	24,303
30,000	24,728	24,728	24,728	24,728	25,013	25,033
31,000	25,508	25,508	25,508	25,508	25,743	25,763
32,000	26,288	26,288	26,288	26,288	26,516	26,516
33,000	27,068	27,068	27,068	27,068	27,296	27,296
34,000	27,848	27,848	27,848	27,848	28,076	28,076
35,000	28,628	28,628	28,628	28,628	28,856	28,856
40,000	32,041	32,041	32,041	32,041	32,269	32,269
45,000	35,041	35,041	35,041	35,041	35,269	35,269
50,000	38,041	38,041	38,041	38,041	38,269	38,269
55,000	41,041	41,041	41,041	41,041	41,269	41,269
60,000	44,041	44,041	44,041	44,041	44,269	44,269
65,000	47,041	47,041	47,041	47,041	47,269	47,269
70,000	50,041	50,041	50,041	50,041	50,269	50,269
75,000	53,041	53,041	53,041	53,041	53,269	53,269
80,000	56,041	56,041	56,041	56,041	56,269	56,269
85,000	59,041	59,041	59,041	59,041	59,269	59,269
90,000	62,041	62,041	62,041	62,041	62,269	62,269
95,000	65,041	65,041	65,041	65,041	65,269	65,269
100,000	68,041	68,041	68,041	68,041	68,269	68,269

*These figures depend on the availability of the married couple's allowance, which is only available where either spouse was born before April 6, 1935.

Illustrative net pension calculations

Single person aged under 65 at 2005/06 rates

		£pa	£pa	£pa	£pa
Gross pension	[a]	15,000	20,000	30,000	40,000
Income tax					
Gross		15,000	20,000	30,000	40,000
Personal allowance		(4,895)	(4,895)	(4,895)	(4,895)
Taxable		10,105	15,105	25,105	35,105
Tax payable					
– At 10%		209	209	209	209
– At 22%		1,763	2,863	5,063	6,464
– At 40%		–	–	–	1,082
	[b]	1,972	3,072	5,272	7,959
Net income	[a–b]	13,028	16,928	24,728	32,041
Net % of gross		86.6%	84.6%	82.4%	80.1%

Single person aged between 65 and 74 at 2005/06 rates

		£pa	£pa	£pa	£pa
Gross pension	[a]	15,000	20,000	30,000	40,000
Income tax					
Gross		15,000	20,000	30,000	40,000
Personal allowance (note 1)		(7,090)	(6,840)	(4,895)	(4,895)
Taxable		7,910	13,160	25,105	35,105
Tax payable					
– At 10%		209	209	209	209
– At 22%		1,280	2,424	5,063	6,668
– At 40%		–	–	–	1,082
	[b]	1,489	2,633	5,272	7,959
Net income	[a–b]	13,511	17,367	24,728	32,041
Net % of gross		90.1%	86.8%	82.4%	80.1%

Note 1: personal allowance

Allowance for age 65 to 74	7,090	7,090	7,090	7,090
Restriction for excess of income over limit*	–	(250)	(2,195)	(2,195)
Net allowance	7,090	6,840	4,895	4,895

*If gross pension does not exceed £19,500,
no restriction.
If gross pension does exceed £19,500,
restriction is the lower of:
(a) (gross pension—£19,500)/2; and
(b) £7,090–4,895=£2,195

Single person aged 75 or over at 2005/06 rates

		£pa	£pa	£pa	£pa
Gross pension	[a]	15,000	20,000	30,000	40,000
Income tax					
Gross		15,000	20,000	30,000	40,000
Personal allowance (note 1)		(7,220)	(6,970)	(4,895)	(4,895)
Taxable		7,780	13,030	25,105	35,105
Tax payable					
– At 10%		209	209	209	209
– At 22%		1,252	2,407	5,063	6,668
– At 40%		–	–	–	1,082
	[b]	1,461	2,616	5,272	7,959
Net income	[a–b]	13,539	17,384	24,728	32,041
Net % of gross		90.2%	86.9%	82.4%	80.1%

Note 1: personal allowance

	£pa	£pa	£pa	£pa
Allowance for age 65 to 84	7,220	7,220	7,220	7,220
Restriction for excess of income over limit*	–	(250)	(2,325)	(2,325)
Net allowance	7,220	6,970	4,895	4,895

*If gross pension does not exceed £19,500,
no restriction.
If gross pension does exceed £19,500,
restriction is the lower of:
(a) (gross pension—£19,500; and
(b) £7,220–4,895=£2,325

Married person aged under 65 at 2005/06 rates

		£pa	£pa	£pa	£pa
Gross pension	[a]	15,000	20,000	30,000	40,000
Income tax					
Gross		15,000	20,000	30,000	40,000
Personal allowance		(4,895)	(4,895)	(4,895)	(4,895)
Taxable		10,105	15,105	25,105	35,105
Tax payable					
– At 10%		209	209	209	209
– At 22%		1,763	2,863	5,063	6,668
– At 40%		–	–	–	1,082
	[b]	1,972	3,072	5,272	7,959
Net income	[a–b]	13,028	16,928	24,728	32,041
Net % of gross		86.9%	84.6%	82.4%	80.1%

Married person aged between 65 and 74 at 2005/06 rates

		£pa	£pa	£pa	£pa
Gross pension	[a]	15,000	20,000	30,000	40,000
Income tax					
Gross		15,000	20,000	30,000	40,000
Personal allowance (note 1)		(7,090)	(6,840)	(4,895)	(4,895)
Taxable		7,910	13,160	25,105	35,105
Tax payable					
– At 10%		209	209	209	209
– At 22%		1,280	2,435	5,063	6,668
– At 40%		–	–	–	1,082
		1,489	2,644	5,272	7,959
Relief for married couple's allowance (note 2)		(591)	(591)	(285)	(228)
	[b]	898	2,053	4,987	7,731
Net income	[a–b]	14,102	17,947	25,013	32,269
Net % of gross		94.0%	89.7%	83.4%	80.7%

Note 1: personal allowance

	£pa	£pa	£pa	£pa
Personal allowance for age 65 to 74	7,090	7,090	7,090	7,090
Restriction for excess of income over limit*	–	(250)	(2,195)	(2,195)
Net allowance	7,090	6,840	4,895	4,895

*If gross pension does not exceed £19,500,
no restriction.
If gross pension does exceed £19,500,
restriction is the lower of:
(a) (gross pension—£19,500)/2; and
(b) £7,090−4,895=£2,195

Note 2: married couple's allowance

Assumptions:
1 at least one spouse born before April 6, 1935; and
2 full married couple's allowance allocated to pensioner.

	£pa	£pa	£pa	£pa
Married couple's allowance for age 65 to 74	5,905	5,905	5,905	5,905
Restriction for excess of income over limit*	–	–	(3,055)	(3,625)
Net allowance	5,905	5,905	2,850	2,280
Relief at 10%	591	591	285	228

*If gross pension does not exceed £19,500,
no restriction.
If gross pension does exceed £19,500,
restriction is the lower of:
(a) (gross pension—£19,500)/2 **less**
    restriction of personal allowance; and
(b) £5,905−2,280=£3,625

Married person aged 75 or over at 2005/06 rates

		£pa	£pa	£pa	£pa
Gross pension	[a]	15,000	20,000	30,000	40,000
Income tax					
Gross		15,000	20,000	30,000	40,000
Personal allowance (note 1)		(7,220)	(6,970)	(4,895)	(4,895)
Taxable		7,780	13,030	25,105	35,105
Tax payable					
– At 10%		209	209	209	209
– At 22%		1,252	2,407	5,063	6,668
– At 40%		–	–	–	1,082
		1,461	2,616	5,272	7,959
Relief for married couple's allowance (note 2)		(598)	(598)	(305)	(228)
	[b]	863	2,018	4,967	7,731
Net income	[a–b]	14,137	17,982	25,033	32,269
Net % of gross		94.2%	89.9%	83.4%	80.7%

Note 1: personal allowance

	7,220	7,220	7,220	7,220
Personal allowance for age 75 and over	7,220	7,220	7,220	7,220
Restriction for excess of income over limit*	–	(250)	(2,325)	(2,325)
Net allowance	7,220	6,970	4,895	4,895

*If gross pension does not exceed £19,500,
no restriction.
If gross pension does exceed £19,500,
restriction is the lower of:
(a) (gross pension—£19,500)/2; and
(b) £7,220–4,895=£2,325

Note 2: married couple's allowance

Assumption:
1 at least one spouse born before April 6,
  1935 and
2 full married couple's allowance allocated
  to pensioner.

Married couple's allowance for age 65 to 74	5,975	5,975	5,975	5,975
Restriction for excess of income over limit*	–	–	(2,925)	(3,695)
Net allowance	5,975	5,975	3,050	2,280
Relief at 10%	598	598	305	228

*If gross pension does not exceed £19,500,
no restriction.
If gross pension does exceed £19,500,
restriction is the lower of:
(a) (gross pension—£19,500)/2 **less**
    restriction of personal allowance; and
(b) £5,975–£2,280=£3,695

G6: Note on pension losses

1 Purpose of note

The purpose of this note is to provide some basic guidance to practitioners who need to consider whether a pension loss is likely to arise in any specific case.

2 Final Salary "or Money Purchase" scheme?

Ascertain which type of scheme was being contributed to.

Final Salary schemes (also known as Deferred Benefit schemes)

- benefits are defined in advance, usually in terms of:
    - final salary
    - number of years of service
    - a factor (often $1/60^{th}$ or $1/80^{th}$ for each year of service)
- the financial risk (of ensuring that benefits are paid) lies with the employer.

Money Purchase schemes (also known as Personal Pensions and/or Defined Contribution schemes)

- benefits depend on a combination of:
    - the amounts paid in by the member
    - any amounts paid in by the employer (if there is one)
    - the investment returns achieved up to retirement
    - the annuity rates available on retirement
- the financial risk lies with the member

By definition, a self-employed person will have no employer contributions.

3 Is there likely to be a loss?

Start by assuming that there will be a loss to be evaluated, if:

- The claimant was contributing to a pension scheme; and

- There is a claim for loss of earnings; and

- There was an employer contribution.

4 Final Salary scheme member

Potential pension:

- Obtain a copy of the member's guide (which will often be in simple terms).

- Obtain a copy of the most recent statement of the individual member's scheme benefits (an estimate of pension at normal retirement age based on current salary).

- With these documents, and the projection of final salary being used for evaluating loss of earnings, it should be possible to calculate the expected pension at retirement date (at its present day value).

Actual pension:

- Establish the actual (reduced) pension that will be payable at normal retirement date (at its present day value).

Proceed by:

- Applying *Auty* principles. Table A9 refers.

- Calculating loss of annual pension (after tax). Table G5 will assist.

- Applying an appropriate multiplier drawn from the Ogden tables. Tables A1 and B2 refer.

Calculations incorporating a loss of lump sum benefit can be complex and will only be possible if the effect that taking the lump sum has on the annual pension can be ascertained with reasonable certainty. (Public pension schemes usually provide separately for lump sum and annual pension benefits, so the figures are generally straightforward to ascertain.)

5   Money Purchase scheme member

A forensic accountant will often approach evaluation of loss along the following lines:

Potential pension:

- Ascertain current value of pension fund

- Calculate contributions foregone (payable by member and by employer if applicable)

- Calculate value of potential pension fund at retirement, based on contributions foregone and an assumed rate of investment return within the fund

- Calculate in turn
    - the lump sum benefit available on retirement (discounted to present day value)
    - the gross annual pension (based on annuity tables)

Actual pension:

- Calculate value of actual pension fund at retirement, based on any future contributions to the scheme and the assumed rate of investment return within the fund

- Calculate in turn
    - the lump sum benefit available (discounted to present day value)
    - the gross annual pension

Proceed by:

- Calculating the loss of lump sum (at present day value)

- Calculating the loss of annual pension (after tax). Table G5 will assist.

- Applying an appropriate multiplier drawn from the Ogden tables.

- Consider whether any further adjustments should be applied, of the sort discussed at Table A9.

6   Important cases

Have regard to:

- *Parry v Cleaver (1970)*

    briefly: pension loss only runs from anticipated retirement age

    so that: no credit need be given against earnings losses for an early/ill health pension

- *Longden v British Coal Corporation (1998)*

  briefly: explains how to apportion an actual tax-free lump sum received ahead of expected retirement age between pre- and post-retirement periods

  so that: treatment of the actual lump sum is brought into line with *Parry v Cleaver* principles

- *Aboul-Hosn v Trustees of the Italian Hospital (1987)*

  briefly: allows a simple calculation by which pension loss is based simply on the tax relief foregone on the claimant's potential personal pension contributions.

  (This would only be appropriate in a case where there are no employer contributions foregone.)

7 Further points

- Do not rely on quotations from pension providers; they invariably incorporate inflation and are not therefore compatible with conventional multipliers.

- Keep in mind the reality of life expectancy. If life expectancy is impaired, pension loss will be reduced.

- That said, do not overlook the possibility of a "lost years" claim in respect of pension losses between the end of the post-accident life expectancy and the end of the pre-accident life expectancy.

- Do not assume, without careful thought, that males necessarily retire at 65 and females at 60.

  Bear in mind that, between April 2010 and April 2020, the state pension age for women will gradually increase from 60 to 65.

- Claims for loss of state pension may arise, particularly in relation to the State Second Pension (S2P).

- Smaller pension losses may sometimes not be worth pursuing, given the safety net of the State Pension Credit. See Table H2.

Group H
Benefits, Allowances, Charges

H1: Social security benefits (non means-tested)

How they work

Generally, all these benefits may be claimed independently of each other. However, there are overlapping benefit rules which prevent more than one income replacement benefit being payable. If the claimant is entitled to more than one, then the amount of the highest will be payable.

Many benefits are contributory, entitlement being dependent on satisfying conditions as to amount of national insurance contributions paid.

Until April 2003, increases were payable for many benefits for dependent children, subject to an earnings limit. The increases have now been replaced by child tax credit (see section H2) but people in receipt of the increases on April 5, 2003 have transitional protection.

Entitlement to non means-tested benefits is frequently affected if claimants are in hospital or in full-time care. Claims for all benefits must be made in writing. Claims can be backdated only to a limited extent (varying according to the type of benefit).

1. RETIREMENT

Retirement Pension	04–05	05–06
Claimant (Category A)	£79.60	£82.05
Spouse/adult dependant	£47.65	£49.15

For all categories of RP, claimant must be over pensionable age (60 for woman,* 65 for man). All categories of RP are taxable. Increases available for adult and child dependants (except category D). Overlapping benefit rules apply.

Category A: contribution conditions must be satisfied by claimant himself.

Category B: available for:

— married women whose husbands satisfy contribution conditions and are entitled to category A RP

— widows whose husbands satisfied contribution conditions or who died from industrial accident or disease

— widowers whose wives satisfied contribution conditions and who died when both over pensionable age.

Category D: available for claimants aged 80 or over, resident in Great Britain on 80th birthday and for 10 years out of any 20 year period prior to that time, and not entitled to RP of greater than category D amount.

* Note: For women born before April 6, 1950, state pension age is 60.
For women born after April 6, 1955, state pension age is 65.

For women born between April 6, 1950 and April 6, 1955, state pension age reduces in steps—by one month every two months (on the 6th of that month).
For example:
Date of birth 6.4.50 to 5.5.50: state pension date 6.5.10
Date of birth 6.3.53 to 5.4.53: state pension date 6.3.16
Date of birth 6.3.55 to 5.4.55: state pension date 6.3.20

2. ILL HEALTH

i Statutory Sick Pay	04–05	05–06
Standard rate	£66.15	£68.20

Payable by employer for up to 168 days where employee is incapable of doing job for at least four days and is earning at least lower earnings limit (currently £79 per week). Taxable. Non-contributory. Overlapping benefit rules do not apply.

ii Incapacity Benefit		04–05	05–06
Short-term (under pension age)			
Lower rate		£55.90	£57.65
Higher rate		£66.15	£68.20
Adult dependant — extra		£34.60	£35.65
Short-term (over pension age)			
Lower rate		£71.15	£73.35
Higher rate		£74.15	£76.45
Adult dependant — extra		£42.65	£43.95
Long term		£74.15	£76.45
Increase for age	Higher rate	£15.55	£16.05
	Lower rate	£7.80	£8.05
Adult dependant — extra		£44.35	£45.70

Short-term ICB is payable at the lower rate for first 28 weeks and at higher rate for next 24 weeks. Thereafter long-term ICB is payable. Increases payable if incapacity commenced before age 35 (higher rate) or age 45 (lower rate).
Short-term ICB requires that claimant is incapable of their usual job. Long-term ICB requires the claimant to pass the personal capability assessment (certain categories are exempt). The PCA awards points under descriptors of physical and mental disability. To qualify, claimant must score 15 points on physical descriptors, 10 on mental descriptors or 15 on both.
Claimants actually working while on ICB may be disqualified depending on circumstances.
Taxable save for short-term ICB in first 28 weeks and part of ICB paid to certain elderly claimants in continuous receipt since 1995. Contributory save for those incapacitated between 16 and 20 (sometimes 25). Increases payable for adult and child dependants. Overlapping benefit rules apply.

iii Industrial Injuries Benefits	04–05	05–06
Industrial injuries Disablement Benefit		
Under 18: 20% disabled (see below)	£14.71	£15.17
Under 18: 100% disabled	£73.55	£75.85
Over 18: 20% disabled	£24.02	£24.76
Over 18: 100% disabled	£120.02	£123.80

Entitlement to contributory benefits depends on payment of National Insurance Contributions. Amounts are per week.

Increases:

— Constant attendance allowance (higher)	£96.20	£99.20
— Constant attendance allowance (lower)	£48.10	£49.60
— Exceptionally severe disablement allowance	£48.10	£49.60
Reduced Earnings Allowance		see below
Retirement allowance		see below

Claimants may receive Industrial Injuries Benefits if they suffer personal injury in an industrial accident or suffer from prescribed industrial diseases.

The injury must occur in the course of employment as an employed earner, and must have caused the claimant to suffer from disablement which is assessed as a percentage. Some percentages are prescribed by regulations (*e.g.* for loss of limbs) and others will be assessed by doctors. Assessments may be made for a limited period or for life.

The main industrial injuries benefit is Industrial Injuries Disablement Benefit. IIDB is payable on a sliding scale depending on the percentage of disablement. The claimant must be at least 14% disabled, save for certain industrial diseases.

Increases to IIDB are available. Constant attendance allowance is payable if claimant is 100% disabled and needs constant attendance (high rate) or attendance for a prolonged period (lower rate). Exceptionally severe disablement allowance is payable if claimant is getting CAA and will do so permanently.

Reduced Earnings Allowance is payable in respect of industrial accidents prior to October 1st 1990 where claimant cannot perform his regular job and cannot earn as much (or anything) following the accident. The amount payable is the difference in earnings, up to a maximum (currently £49.52 per week). A lesser amount, retirement allowance, becomes payable on reaching pensionable age (currently £14.01 per week or 25% of REA previously payable). Non-taxable and non-contributory. Overlapping benefit rules apply.

iv Severe Disablement

Allowance	04–05	05–06
Claimant	£44.80	£46.20
Age-related additions		
Higher	£15.55	£16.05
Middle	£10.00	£10.30
Lower	£5.00	£5.15

Abolished from April 6 2001, save for existing recipients.

Paid if 80% disabled and unfit for work on the personal capability assessment.

Non-contributory and non-taxable. Overlapping benefit rules apply.

3. Unemployment — Jobseeker's Allowance (JSA)

i Contribution-based JSA		04–05	05–06
Claimant	18–24	£44.05	£44.05
	25 and over	£55.65	£56.20

ii Income-based JSA		04–05	05–06
Claimant	18–24	£44.05	£44.50
	25 and over	£55.65	£56.20
Couple. One or both over 18		£87.30	£88.15
Dependent children			
Till Sept after 16th birthday		£42.37	£43.88
From Sept after 16th birthday		£42.37	£43.88

Neither claimant nor partner must be in full-time work (16 hours per week for claimant, 24 hours per week for partner). Claimant must be below pensionable age (65 for men, 60 for women), capable of work, not be a full-time student (save for limited exceptions), be available for and actively seeking work, and have a current "jobseeker's agreement".

Claimant may be "sanctioned" and disqualified from benefit for misconduct.

Taxable. Contributory. Overlapping benefit rules apply.

4. Parenthood

i Statutory Maternity Pay	04–05	05–06
Higher rate		90% of average weekly wage
Lower rate	£102.80*	£106.00

* or 90% of woman's weekly average earnings if that sum less.

Payable by employer, from 11 weeks prior to birth. Notice must be given to employer. Must earn at least lower earnings limit (currently £82 per week). Claimant must have been employed for at least 26 weeks prior to 15 weeks before birth. Higher rate payable for 6 weeks. Lower rate payable for 20 weeks.

Taxable. Non-contributory. Overlapping benefit rules do not apply.

ii Statutory Paternity Pay	04–05	05–06
Standard rate (or 90% of earnings if less)	£102.80	£106.00

Payable by employer. Conditions as for SMP, and in addition claimant must have responsibility for child and intend to provide support for child. Can be claimed for birth of child or for adoption.

Taxable. Non-contributory. Overlapping benefit rules do not apply.

iii Statutory Adoption Pay	04–05	05–06
Standard rate (or 90% of earnings if less)	£102.80	£106.00

Payable by employer from 2 weeks prior to adoption for up to 26 weeks. Conditions as for SMP, and in addi-

Entitlement to contributory benefits depends on payment of National Insurance Contributions. Amounts are per week.

tion claimant or partner must be jointly adopting child. Only one partner may claim SAP.
Taxable. Non-contributory. Overlapping benefit rules do not apply.

iv Maternity Allowance	04–05	05–06
Standard rate	£102.80	£106.00
Adult dependant extra	£34.60	£35.65
Maternity Allowance Threshold	£30.00	£30.00

Payable by Benefits Agency. May be claimed from 11 weeks prior to birth. Claimant must have worked (employed or self-employed) for 26 weeks out of 66 weeks prior to birth, must have earned at least threshold amount, must not be working, and must not be entitled to SMP.
Non-taxable. Contributory. Overlapping benefit rules do not apply.

5. BEREAVEMENT

i Bereavement Benefit
Lump sum of £2,000 payable on spouse's death, unless claimant was cohabiting with another partner at time of death.
Non-taxable. Contributory (save for certain cases of death following industrial injury or disease). Overlapping benefit rules do not apply.

ii Widowed Parent's Allowance	04–05	05–06
Widowed Parent's Allowance	£79.60	£82.05

Payable where claimant is receiving child benefit for a dependent child (living with claimant or for whom claimant is providing maintenance). Not payable if claimant is cohabiting.
Taxable. Contributory (save for certain cases of death following industrial injury or disease). Overlapping benefit rules apply.

iii Bereavement Allowance	04–05	05–06
Bereavement Allowance	£23.88–	£24.62–
	£79.60	£76.31

Payable where claimant was aged over 45 at death of spouse, is under pensionable age (65 for man, 60 for woman). Not payable if claimant is cohabiting.
Taxable. Contributory (save for certain cases of death following industrial injury or disease). Overlapping benefit rules apply.

6. DISABILITY

i Disability Living Allowance		04–05	05–06
Care Component	Higher	£58.80	£60.60
	Middle	£39.35	£40.55
	Lower	£15.55	£16.05
Mobility Component	Higher	£41.05	£42.30
	Lower	£15.55	£16.05

Claimant must be aged under 65 and for mobility component (MC) over 3 (higher rate) or 5 (lower rate). Claimant must have been satisfied conditions for 3 months prior to claim and for 6 months or more afterwards (unless terminally ill). Severe restrictions on entitlement if claimant in hospital or care home (care component only). Child claimants must show lack of ability over and beyond that normal for a child. MC requires that enhanced ability to move will be of benefit.
For higher rate MC, claimant must show he is unable to walk, virtually unable to walk, is deaf and blind, has no feet or is severely mentally impaired.
For lower rate MC, claimant must show that disability means that guidance or supervision is required when walking in unfamiliar places.
For highest rate CC, claimant must satisfy both "night" and "day" conditions or be terminally ill. Night condition is that prolonged or repeated attention is required at night in connection with bodily functions, or prolonged watching to avoid danger. Day condition is that frequent attention is required repeatedly throughout day in connection with bodily functions, or continual supervision to prevent danger.
For middle rate CC, claimant must satisfy either "night" or "day" condition.
For lower rate CC, claimant must either be unable to cook a meal or need attention for significant portion of day in connection with bodily functions.
Non-taxable. Non-contributory. Overlapping benefit rules do not apply.

ii Attendance Allowance	04–05	05–06
Higher rate	£58.80	£60.60
Lower rate	£39.35	£40.55

Identical to DLA highest and middle rate CC for the over 65s.
Non-contributory and non-taxable.

7. CHILDREN

i Child Benefit	04–05	05–06
Only/elder/eldest child	£16.50	£17.00
Only/elder/eldest child of lone parent with protected rights	£17.55	£17.55
Each subsequent child	£11.05	£11.40

A child must be under 16, or under 19 and in full-time secondary education.
Non-contributory and non-taxable.

ii Guardian's Allowance	04–05	05–06
Each child	£11.85	£11.35

Non-contributory and non-taxable.

Entitlement to contributory benefits depends on payment of National Insurance Contributions. Amounts are per week except for lump sum widow's payment.

H2: Social security benefits and tax credits (means-tested)

How they work

The main means-tested benefits are income support (IS), income-based jobseeker's allowance (IBJSA), state pension credit (SPC), housing benefit (HB), and council tax benefit (CTB). The means-tested tax credits are working tax credit (WTC) and child tax credit (CTC).

These rules are not applicable to payments under the social fund.

The means-tested benefits and credits operate in broadly the same way. An amount is worked out based on the circumstances of the claimant's family by adding various amounts together. That amount is then fed into a calculation along with the claimant's weekly income in order to work out the level of benefit to which the claimant is entitled.

Capital possessed by a claimant's partner is treated as the claimant's; capital possessed by a child may mean that no personal allowance can be received for that child.

Capital possessed by a claimant is subjected to two limits. Above the lower limit, it is treated as generating tariff income: a weekly amount of income for each block of capital (or part thereof) in excess of the lower limit. For example, a claimant in a care home claiming IS with capital of £12,400 will be treated as having £10 income per week (£1 per £250, or part thereof over £10,000).

Above the upper capital limit, the claimant is disqualified from benefit altogether. The capital limits, and the tariff income rates, are set out under each benefit in a table.

Some income and capital is ignored altogether, other income and capital may be ignored in part or for a limited period. In certain situations, such as where there is deprivation of income or capital in order to qualify for benefit, a claimant may be treated as having an equivalent amount of income or capital (notional capital).

Means-tested benefits are all non-contributory.

Income support

		04–05	05–06
			pounds per week
Personal Allowances		£	£
Single person	18–24	44.05	44.50
	25 or over	55.65	56.20
Lone Parent			
Under 18	Usual rate	33.50	33.85
	Higher rate	44.05	44.50
Over 18		55.65	56.20
Couple	Both over 18	87.30	88.15
Dependent children	Until Sept after 16th birthday	42.27	43.886
	From Sept after 16th birthday until day before 19th	42.37	43.88
Premiums			
Family		15.95	16.10
Family (lone parent addition)		15.95	16.10
Disabled child		42.49	43.89
Carer		25.55	25.80

		04–05	05–06
		pounds per week	
Disability	Single	23.70	23.95
	Couple	33.85	34.20
Enhanced disability	Single	11.60	11.70
	Child	17.08	17.71
	Couple	16.75	16.90
Severe Disability	Single	44.15	45.50
	Couple (both qualifying)	88.30	91.00
Bereavement		23.95	25.85

Only the highest of the following premiums which is applicable to the family is received: family (lone parent addition), disability, any of the pensioner premiums, bereavement.

Capital limits

Type of claimant	Lower limit	Tariff income rate	Upper limit
Under age 60	£3,000	£1 per £250	£6,000
Over age 60	£6,000	£1 per £250	£12,000
Care home resident	£10,000	£1 per £250	£16,000

Income Support is for specified groups not required to make themselves available for work and claim IBJSA (see below). Main groups are: single parents, long-term sick and disabled, carers and certain students. Elderly claim SPC instead from October 2003 (see below). Administered by the Benefits Agency. Not ordinarily taxable.

"Applicable amount" is calculated by taking the relevant personal allowance, adding amounts for dependent children and then adding any premiums that are relevant to the circumstances of the family and any housing costs.

Amount of IS is: applicable amount minus relevant income.

Housing costs are mainly interest payable on mortgages, plus certain types of loans for essential repairs. Interest is only paid on first £100,000 of loan. Severe restrictions on increases to loans while claimant is on IS, and during first 39 weeks of claim.

Claimant disqualified from IS if he works more than 16 hours per week, or partner works more than 24 hours per week.

Income-Based Jobseeker's Allowance

IBJSA is the means-tested benefit for the unemployed. For the main conditions of entitlement, see the entry for contribution-based jobseeker's allowance in section H1 (save that it is not necessary to satisfy the contribution conditions). Personal allowances, premiums and capital limits are the same as for IS. Joint-claim jobseeker's allowance is a form of IBJSA paid to couples who are both out of work. Administered by the Benefits Agency. Taxable.

State Pension Credit

	04–05	05–06
	pounds per week	
Standard minimum guarantee		
Single person	105.45	109.45
Couple	160.95	167.05
Additional amounts		
Severe disability: single	44.15	45.50
Severe disability: couple	88.30	91.00
Carer: each person who qualifies	25.55	25.80
Savings credit threshold		
Single person	79.60	82.05
Couple	127.25	131.20
Maximum savings credit		
Single person	15.51*	16.44
Couple	20.22*	21.51

* note: this is 60% of difference between standard minimum guarantee and savings credit threshold

Capital limits

Type of claimant	Lower limit	Tariff income rate	Upper limit
Normal	£6,000	£1 per £500	none
Care home resident	£10,000	£1 per £500	none

SPC was brought into existence from October 2003. Two elements: the guarantee credit (GC) and savings credit (SC). Either may be received separately. Rules for calculation and disregarding of income are different, and there is no upper capital limit. No restriction on the hours of work a person may do. Administered by Pensions Service. Not taxable.

GC replaces IS for those aged over 60. The "appropriate minimum guarantee" (AMG) is the equivalent of the IS or IBJSA applicable amount: calculated by adding up the standard minimum guarantee (SMG), any additional amounts and any housing costs.

Amount of GC is: standard minimum guarantee minus income.

SC is designed to benefit those who have made savings for retirement. "Qualifying income" is any income other than certain benefits or maintenance. Only the amount of income between the savings credit threshold and the SMG counts (*e.g.* for single people in 2005–6, a maximum of £27.40).

Amount of SC is: 60% of qualifying income (where total income less than AMG).

Or amount of SC is: 60% of qualifying income minus 40% of difference between total income and AMG (where total income is more than AMG).

Working Tax Credit (WTC) 05–06

	p.w	p.a
First income threshold	£100.38	£5,220
First withdrawal rate	37%	
Second Income threshold	£961.53	£50,000
Second withdrawal rate	6.67%	
Basic Credit	£31.15	£1,620
Additional couple's/ lone parent element	£30.67	£1,595
30 hours element	£12.69	£660
Disabled worker element	£41.63	£2,165
Enhanced disabled adult element	£17.69	£920
50+ return to work payment:		
16–29 hours	£21.35	£1,110
30+ hours	£31.92	£1,660

Childcare element

Maximum eligible cost	£300.00
Maximum eligible cost for one child	£175.00
Percentage of eligible costs covered	70%

Based on gross annual income, in-work support for families with child/young person where adult works 16 hours per week or single/couple claimants over 25 where adult works 30 hours p.w. 16 hour condition also for those 50+ or with disability. Awards in effect provisional until end of year notice identifies under/overpayments. Administered by the Inland Revenue. Not taxable.

Elements are cumulative except for the 50+ return to work elements.

Assessment on annual incomes, joint incomes for couples. Tapers as income rises. Up to first threshold, claimants receive the maximum. Above first threshold, the reduction applies last to the childcare element.

Child Tax Credit (CTC) 05–06

	p.w	p.a
First income threshold for those entitled to CTC only	£267.50	£13,910
First withdrawal rate	37%	
Second Income threshold	£963.53	£50,000
Second withdrawal rate	6.67%	
Family element	£10.45	£545
Family element, baby addition	£10.45	£545
Child element	£32.50	£1,690
Disabled child additional element	£43.94	£2,285
Enhanced disabled child additional element	£17.69	£920

Based on gross annual income, support for families with children. Tapers as income rises, but Working Tax Credit is abated first. The per child element is reduced for income above £13,910. The family element is reduced for incomes above £50,000. Replaces most benefit additions for children and earlier tax credits. Administered by the Inland Revenue. Not taxable.

Only one family element per family. The per child elements are cumulative; the baby element is for the first year of a child's life. Paid to nominated main carer.

Those on Income Support or Income-Based Jobseeker's Allowance will receive the maximum but not usually until April 2005.

Housing Benefit and Council Tax Benefit

		04–05 £	05–06 £
Claimant	16–24	44.05	44.50
	25 or over	55.65	56.20
Lone Parent	Under 18	44.05	44.50
	18 or over	55.65	56.20
Couple	Both under 18	66.50	67.15
	One or both over 18	87.30	88.15
Dependent children	Until Sept after 16th birthday	42.27	43.88
	From Sept after 16th birthday to day before 19th	42.27	43.88

Premiums

As for Income Support except:

	04–05	05–06
Lone parent family premium protected for certain claimants	22.20	22.20
Family premium increased for one or more child(ren) under 1 year	–	10.50

Capital limits

Type of claimant	Lower limit	Tariff income rate	Upper limit
Under age 60	£3,000	£1 per £250	£16,000
Over age 60	£6,000	£1 per £250	£16,000
Care home resident	£10,000	£1 per £250	£16,000

Housing Benefit
HB assists non-owners with housing costs. Administered by local authorities. Not taxable.

Claimants must be liable to make payments for their home and must be ordinarily resident there, subject to certain exceptions. Payments must qualify for HB purposes: broadly rent, certain service charges and analogous payments. Amount of rent eligible for HB may be restricted by Rent Officer if higher than market rent. Further reductions may be made for non-dependants living in the household to give "maximum HB".

Applicable amount is calculated as for IS but amounts are different. Income and capital rules are very similar. Claimant on IS or IBJSA has all income and capital ignored and qualifies for full HB. Rules are substantially modified for those on SPC.

Amount of HB is: maximum HB minus 60% of amount (if any) by which total income exceeds applicable amount.

Discretionary housing payments can be made by local authorities to cover shortfall in liabilities.

Council Tax Benefit
CTB assists with payment of council tax. Administered by local authorities, claimed along with HB. Not taxable.

Personal allowances, premiums and capital limits are the same as for HB.

Two types of CTB. Local authority will assess both if applicable and pay whichever is higher.

"Main CTB" has very similar rules to HB. "Maximum CTB" is amount of council tax payable weekly after reductions for non-dependants living in the home and restrictions for homes in band F or higher.

Amount of main CTB is: maximum CTB minus 20% of amount (if any) by which total income exceeds applicable amount.

"Second adult rebate" is payable regardless of income of claimant, where there is a "second adult" jointly liable for council tax on the home. The following cannot be "second adults": persons under 18, people paying the claimant rent, people eligible for council tax discount, the claimant's partner. If the "second adult" (or all of them if more than one) have income of less than £177 per week, a reduction of up to 15% is applied to the claimant's bill.

The Social Fund

The Social Fund is administered by the DWP and is designed to meet one-off payments for those on low income.

Maternity grants
£500 is payable in respect of each child if the claimant is on IS, IBJSA, SPC, WTC or CTC and receives advice from a health professional.

Funeral expenses

Funeral expenses are payable if the claimant is on any income-related benefit and the deceased is the claimant's partner, a child for whom the claimant was responsible or a close relative or friend and it was reasonable for the claimant to accept responsibility for the costs. The burial must be in the UK or an EEA country.

Amounts are payable in respect of purchasing a burial plot, cremation fees, costs of documentation, some transport costs and up to £700 for other costs. Certain capital assets or sums due to the claimant or deceased will be deducted.

Funeral expenses payments may be recovered from the deceased's estate.

Cold Weather and Winter Fuel Payments

Lump sums are payable to those in receipt of IS, IBJSA or SPC during a period of cold weather lasting at least a week.

Sums are payable to those aged over 60 (£200) or those aged over 80 (£300) in respect of winter fuel costs. The rates are halved for those in residential care.

H3: Effect of social security benefits and tax credits on damages

The Compensation Recovery Scheme

The DWP is entitled to recover certain "listed benefits" from a defendant liable to pay damages to a claimant, where the claimant has received social security benefits. The defendant is entitled to offset some of its liabilities against the claimant's damages awards. The financial consequences for parties can be profound and an awareness of the working of the scheme is essential.

The relevant legislation is the Social Security (Recovery of Benefits) Act 1997 and the Social Security (Recovery of Benefits) Regulations 1997. References to sections ("s.", "ss.", "reg.", or "regs") are to the corresponding parts of the 1997 Act and Regulations respectively. References commencing "CCR", "CSCR" and "R(CR)" are to decisions of Social Security Commissioners. They are available on the web at: *http://www.osscsc.gov.uk/pages/des.htm*

The liability of the defendant

The scheme applies to damages for "accident, injury or disease": s.1(1). Claims brought by parents for wrongful birth have been said not to come within that phrase: *Rand v E Dorset HA*.[1] The scheme applies to payments made on settlement or under a court order: s.1(3). It applies to the MIB: s.1(2)(b). It does not apply to certain categories of exempt payments: s.1(2)(b), Sch. 1, reg. 2.

Before making a compensation payment, a defendant must apply for a certificate of recoverable benefits ("CRB"): s.4, reg. 7. The CRB specifies the benefits that are recoverable: s.5. The Secretary of State must provide clarification if required: s.5(6). If the Secretary of State fails to provide a certificate within a month of a request being made with the requisite information, then the liability to pay the benefits will not arise: s.21.

The Secretary of State has powers to require information to be provided by a compensator, claimant and the claimant's employer: s.23, regs 3–6.

The liability to pay arises on the making of the compensation payment (or the first of them, if more than one): s.6(2). Failing to apply for a CRB does not prevent the liability arising: s.7(1), (2). There are powers to enforce the liability through the County Court: s.7(4).

For cases where there is more than one defendant, see s.19 and reg. 9. For modifications to the scheme in respect of structured settlements, see reg. 10.

What benefits are recoverable?

The benefits recoverable are those which are "listed benefits" paid during the "relevant period" and which were paid "in respect of" the accident, etc: s.1(1)(a).

"Listed benefits" are those listed in Sch. 2: s.29. The table from Sch. 2 is reproduced below.

In the case of accidents or injuries, the "relevant period" is five years from the date of accident or injury: s.3(2). In the case of disease, the five year period runs from the date of the first claim for benefit on the basis of the disease: s.3(3). The relevant period may be brought to an end sooner by a payment being made in *final* discharge of a claim, or an agreement that an earlier payment is made in *final* discharge: s.3(4). Thus interim payments do not stop the relevant period running, and neither do payments into court: reg.8(1). The "relevant period" is not restricted by the length of period of the claimant's loss of earnings claim: *CCR/8023/1995*.

The words "in respect of" make it clear that there must be a link between the accident etc and the payment of the benefit. The accident etc need not be the sole cause of the payment of benefit. For example, if the claimant is incapable of work and receiving incapacity benefit, then the following rules apply:

---

[1] [2001] P.I.Q.R. Q1.

— the fact that the claimant was receiving incapacity benefit before the accident etc does not of itself mean that the benefit is not paid "in respect of" the accident: *Hassall v Secretary of State for Social Security*.[1] If a claimant's pre-existing benefits become recoverable as a result of the accident, a special damages claim may be made for the amount of benefit thereby lost: *Hassall*; *Neal v Bingle*.[2]

— if the claimant is permanently incapable of work as a result of accident and then gets an unrelated ailment which would have rendered him incapable, the benefits remain recoverable from that date: *CCR/5336/1995*.

— if neither the accident etc nor unrelated ailment individually render the claimant incapable of work but cumulatively they do so, the benefits are recoverable: *CCR/5336/1995*. That is so even if the unrelated ailment is the dominant cause: *CSCR/1/1995*.

— if the claimant's accident would not itself incapacitate the claimant but the unrelated ailment does, the accident is not an effective cause of the incapacity and the benefits are not recoverable: *CCR/4/1993*; *CCR/5336/1995*.

— in an "exacerbation" or "acceleration" case, where the evidence is that the accident only contributed to the claimant's symptoms for a limited period and thereafter the symptoms were attributable to some underlying disability, only benefits payable during the limited period are recoverable: *R(CR) 1/01*.

— it may be necessary to ascertain precisely what ailment the claim for damages relates to and in relation to what ailment benefit was awarded. The mere fact that both a disease forming the basis of the claim and one forming the basis of the award of benefit were related to asbestos exposure is insufficient to make benefit recoverable: *R(CR) 3/03*.

Generally, it is not possible to reduce the amount of benefit recoverable on the ground that part of it would have been paid anyway: *CCR/4/1993*. Nor can the amount payable be reduced where the claimant is contributorily negligent: *Williams v Devon CC*.[3] However, if a claimant would only have been paid industrial injuries disablement benefit as someone 20 per cent disabled following the accident and an unrelated accident increases disability to 50 per cent, and hence the amount of IIDB, the additional IIDB will not be recoverable: *R(CR) 1/03*.

Benefits which should not have been paid at all are not paid "in respect of" the accident etc: *R(CR) 1/02*; *R(CR) 2/02*. So if benefit is paid as a result of fraud, or a mistake by the DWP, a compensator can challenge the CRB.

The defendant's right to offset the liability
The scheme attempts to strike a fair balance between the interests of the public purse, the claimant and the defendant by allowing a defendant to deduct recoverable benefits from heads of loss which those benefits are, broadly speaking, supposed to compensate: s.8.

A table specifies the heads of loss and the recoverable benefits that may be deducted from it: Sch.2, which is reproduced below.

---

[1] [1995] 1 W.L.R. 812.
[2] [1998] Q.B. 466.
[3] [2003] P.I.Q.R. Q4.

Calculation of compensation payment

Head of compensation	Benefit
1. Compensation for earnings lost during the relevant period	[. . .][1] Disablement pension payable under section 103 of the 1992 Act Incapacity benefit Income support Invalidity pension allowance Jobseeker's allowance Reduced earnings allowance Severe diablement allowance Sickness benefit Statutory sick pay Unemployment supplement Unemployment benefit
2. Compensation for cost of care incurred during the relevant period	Attendance allowance Care component of disability living allowance Disablement pension increase payable under section 104 or 105 of the 1992 Act
3. Compensation for loss of mobility during the relevant period	Mobility allowance Mobility component of disability living allowance

[1] words omitted by Tax Credits Act (1999 c.10), Sch.6, para.1.

Notes

1. (1) References to incapacity benefit, invalidity pension and allowance, severe disablement allowance, sickness benefit and unemployment benefit also include any income support paid with each of those benefits on the same instrument of payment or paid concurrently with each of those benefits by means of an instrument for benefit payment.
   (2) For the purpose of this Note, income support includes personal expenses addition, special transitional additions and transitional addition as defined in the Income Support (Transitional) Regulations 1987.
2. Any reference to statutory sick pay—
   (a) includes only 80 per cent of payments made between 6th April 1991 and 5th April 1994, and
   (b) does not include payments made on or after 6th April 1994
3. In this Schedule "the 1992 Act" means the Social Security Contributions and Benefits Act 1992.

It is to be noted that offsets may be made only against damages in so far as the claims are made in relation to the "relevant period". So there can be no offsetting against future losses.

"Compensation" in Sch.2 includes interest, so that an offset may be made against any interest payable on a head of loss in column 1 in addition to the damages: *Griffiths v British Coal Corporation*.[1]

"Compensation for loss of earnings" includes damages to compensate for loss of receipts as a self-employed individual running a business and not merely profit: *Chatwin v Lowther*.[2]

"Compensation for cost of care" includes claims for gratuitous care provided by relatives: *Griffiths*, not following *McManus v Babcock Energy Ltd*.[3]

[1] [2001] 1 W.L.R. 1493.
[2] [2003] P.I.Q.R. Q5.
[3] 1999 S.C. 569.

On the other hand, "compensation for loss of mobility" applies only to financial losses and not to any element of the general damages award which is attributable to loss of mobility: *Mitchell v Laing*.[1] This principle must also apply to the other heads of loss in column 1.

If, however, no claim is made for a certain head of loss, the defendant must still repay the benefit even if such a claim should have been made, and may not deduct the benefit from any other head of loss: *CCR/3396/2000*.

It is unclear whether the deduction under s.8 is to be applied before or after a reduction for contributory negligence, or whether a compensator is entitled to deduct benefits paid over a different period to that over which the head of loss is claimed. In *CCR/427/2003*, a Commissioner suggested, *obiter*, that s.8 had to be applied before the reduction, and that if a loss of earnings claim was limited to eighteen months then the compensator may only deduct benefits paid during that period under s.8.

Interest is awarded on the full amount of special damages before any deductions under s.8: *Wisely v John Fulton (Plumbers) Ltd*.[2]

Offers to settle

The 1997 Act causes complications in relation to offers to settle and defendants need to ensure that Part 36 offers are correctly drawn. If CPR 36.23 and PD 36 para. 10 are not complied with, the offer will not usually be capable of being relied upon when the court considers costs.

Williams v Devon CC[3] gives detailed guidance on the proper operation of these provisions and confirms that if the defendant does not take into account the proper operation of s.8, the Pt 36 offer will not be effective.

Challenging certificates

The DWP may review a certificate and issue a fresh one: s.10. However, it is not possible to increase the amount recoverable on a review unless the DWP was misled: s.10(3).

A compensator has a right to appeal to an Appeal Tribunal to challenge different types of error alleged to have been made in a CRB: s.11(1). An appeal may be made only once the claim has been finally settled and the payment due under the CRB made: s.11(3). A claimant may also appeal if his compensation has been reduced (see below).

Tribunals are administered by the Appeals Service and consist of a legally qualified chairman and a medical practitioner member. A Tribunal must take into account, but is not bound by, a court decision on similar issues such as the extent of the claimant's injury: s.12(3). The Tribunal may confirm the certificate, specify variations or order that it be revoked: s.12(4).

Most appeals will revolve around questions as to whether benefits were paid "in respect of" the accident etc. Opinions expressed in DWP medical reports are not binding: *CCR/12532/1996*; *R(CR) 1/04*. Such practitioners are often entirely unaware of a claimant's medical history or of unrelated ailments and Tribunals tend to regard full reports from consultants with sight of medical records as being of greater weight. For this reason, practitioners should ensure that medical experts are asked to express opinions on whether the conditions of entitlement for a particular benefit were met or whether the benefit was, or should have been, paid in respect of the accident etc. Where an expert changes his opinion at trial, a Tribunal will still be entitled to rely upon his original evidence in his reports if it finds it appropriate to do so: *CCR/2046/2002*.

Further appeals lie to a Social Security Commissioner on a point of law: s.13.

---

[1] 1998 S.C. 342.
[2] [2000] 1 W.L.R. 820.
[3] [2003] P.I.Q.R. Q4.

If a CRB is altered on review or appeal, then there are provisions for the amount payable by the defendant to the Secretary of State and the deduction under s.8 to be recalculated: s.12(4), reg.11. The Tribunals and Commissioners have no jurisdiction over such a question: *CCR/427/2003*. If a defendant fails or refuses to pay over a balance following a successful appeal, a claimant may either sue for it or make an application in the personal injury proceedings, even if the proceedings were settled by agreement: *Bruce v Genesis Fast Food Ltd.*[1]

Benefits Outside the Compensation Recovery Scheme

Many categories of benefit are not been listed in Sch.2. The question therefore arises as to whether those benefits can be offset by a defendant. They can be divided into two categories. Cases under the Law Reform (Miscellaneous Provisions) Act 1948 provide assistance.

Benefits specified in Schedule 2

In *Jackman v Corbett*,[2] it was held that since Parliament had set out a detailed statutory scheme in the 1948 Act specifically limiting the defendant's right to deduct benefits received to a period of five years, there was no right to offset benefits paid after that period.

There is as yet no authoritative decision, but there is County Court authority that in respect of those benefits specified in Sch. 2, the defendant's right to offset the benefits payable is exclusively that provided for in the 1997 Act: *Easton v Ellis*.[3] So it was not possible to deduct future entitlements to mobility allowance (or the mobility component of disability living allowance) from an award for the future cost of a wheelchair. It is suggested that the approach in *Jackman* should apply to benefits mentioned in the 1997 Act.

Benefits not mentioned in the 1997 Act

In *Hodgson v Trapp*[4] it was confirmed that where benefits were not dealt with in the 1948 Act, they should be deducted in full from a damages award if the claimant would otherwise receive dual compensation. There were only two recognised exceptions: payments received under insurance policies and charitable payments. This decision has now been applied in post–1997 cases.

Compensation under the Pneumoconiosis (Workers Compensation) Act 1979 is deductible in full from an award of damages: *Ballantine v Newalls Insulation Co Ltd.*[5]

Housing benefit administered by local authorities may be deducted in full from an award of damages if the claimant would not have received HB in the absence of being injured: *Clenshaw v Tanner.*[6] It is suggested that the same conclusion will follow in respect of council tax benefit. It is less clear whether it will follow in respect of other benefits administered by the DWP.

[1] [2004] P.I.Q.R. P9.
[2] [1988] Q.B. 154.
[3] [1999] 1 C.L.Y. 1525.
[4] [1989] A.C. 807.
[5] [2001] I.C.R. 25.
[6] [2002] EWCA Civ. 1848.

H4: Damages and publicly-funded care

In cases involving severely-injured claimants, the largest element of a damages award may be the cost of future provision of accommodation and care to meet their needs. The amount awarded to such claimants may be radically affected by the question of whether such needs will be met privately or publicly.

Practitioners therefore need to consider the following issues in such cases:

— What public assistance is available to people to meet the claimant's needs?

— What public assistance has the claimant been receiving and will be entitled to receive in the future?

— Can the provider charge for past services provided to the claimant when an award of damages is received?

— How will an award of damages affect entitlement to the forms of public assistance to which a claimant would otherwise be entitled?

For a more detailed treatment of this topic, see Kemp & Kemp, *The Quantum of Damages* Ch.5.

Social security benefits
See sections H1 and H2 for the benefits that are available and the rules of entitlement. See section H3 for details of when benefits paid in the past may be recouped.

Non means-tested benefits will be unaffected by a damages award. A damages award will usually be treated as a capital sum for the purpose of means-tested benefits. However, the sum will be disregarded if it is held in trust, by the High Court, by the Court of Protection or is in the form of an annuity (as with structured settlements). To preserve entitlement to one of those benefits after an award is made, it will have to be held in one of those forms.

Consideration also needs to be given to the effect of use of monies held in one of those forms. The following rules apply:

— Monies paid to the claimant will ordinarily be treated as income or capital in the normal way. However, monies paid out of the High Court or the Court of Protection will either be treated as capital payments or will be ignored altogether.

— Monies paid direct to third parties will only be taken into account as income or capital to the extent that they are used for necessities.

Health and social care
A table showing the different forms of public-funded health and social care that are available may be found at the end of this section.

NHS bodies and local social services authorities are under statutory duties to co–operate. Claimants with complex needs may be having health care needs met by NHS bodies and other needs met by social services authorities. It is always essential to establish from the outset who is paying for what under the claimant's current provision. If a claimant is charged for past or future services, then the claimant will be entitled to claim those charges from a defendant.

There are a number of different charging provisions, as set out in the table:

— National Assistance Act 1948, s.22: no charge for past services, detailed means-test for future services very similar to that for means-tested benefits (see section H2). Upper capital limit: £20,000. Lower capital limit: £12,250.

— Health and Social Services and Social Security Adjudications Act 1983 s.17: general discretion to charge but may not do so if the claimant cannot afford the charge. Local authority must normally act in accordance with guidance: *Fairer Charging Policies for Home Care and other non-residential Social Services* (September 2003 revision, available on the Department of Health website). Charge may be levied for past services if reasonable: *Avon CC v Hooper.*[1] Charge may also be made for future services if within legislation and guidance, and reasonable to do so.

— Children Act 1989, s.29, Sch.2: only children aged over 16 can be charged, under that age only parents can be charged. Charges must not be more than someone can reasonably be expected to pay. Local authority must clearly demonstrate that statutory basis for charging is applicable: *Kidd v Plymouth HA.*[2]

— Supporting People: there are powers to charge only in limited circumstances and depends on local policies. No charge for past services, charge for future services only if within statutory powers and policy.

— Independent Living Fund: powers to charge largely discretionary.

There may be considerable uncertainty as to whether a charge will be levied once a damages award is finalised. In those circumstances, the court has no power to order a defendant to provide an indemnity against future costs: *Firth v Geo Ackroyd Junior Ltd*[3]; *Howarth v Whittaker.*[4] Neither can damages be awarded on the basis of a chance of such charges being levied if the chance is speculative: *Firth.* However, the parties may agree for the provision of such an indemnity by way of a Tomlin Order.

---

[1] [1997] 1 W.L.R. 1605.
[2] [2001] Lloyd's Rep Med 165.
[3] [2000] Lloyd's Rep. Med. 312.
[4] [2003] Lloyd's Rep. Med. 235.

Summary of Sources of Publicly-Funded Care

Type of Service	Legal Sources of Powers	Provider	Client Group	Power or Duty	Description of Services	Charging Power
Health care	National Health Service Act 1977	GPs, Primary Care Trusts	All	Duty	Primary health care including hospital treatment, general practitioner services, provision of drugs and appliances, nursing care.	None
Residential care	National Assistance Act 1948, s.21 LAC (93) 10 App 1	Local social services authority	Adults	Duty	Residential accommodation for those adults who require it due to "age, illness, disability or any other circumstances", plus ancillary care.	NAA 1948, s.22
Domiciliary care (i.e. provided in the service user's own home)	National Assistance Act 1948, s.29 LAC (93) 10 App 2	Local social services authority	Disabled adults	Duty	Social work services, advice and support, rehabilitation and adjustment to a person's disability, occupational, social, cultural and recreational activities, workshop and associated hostel services.	Health and Social Services and Social Security Adjudications Act 1983, s.17
				Power	Holiday homes, travel, assistance in finding accommodation, warden services and the provision of general information	LAC (2001) 32
	Health Services and Public Health Act 1968, s.45 Circular 19/71	Local social services authority	Old adults	Power	Meals and recreation in the home or elsewhere, travel assistance, assistance with finding boarding accommodation, home help, home adaptations, warden services and information	HASSASSA 1983, s.17
	Chronically Sick and Disabled Persons Act 1970, s.2	Local social services authority	Disabled	Power	Practical assistance in the home, provision of radio, television, library or similar facilities, provision of recreational facilities outside the home, travel outside the home, adaptations to the home, facilitation of holidays, provision of meals, provision of a telephone.	HASSASSA 1993, s.17: see R v Powys DC ex p Hambidge (1998) 1 C.C.L.R. 458.
	National Health Service Act 1977, Sch. 8 LAC (93) 10 App 3	Local social services authority	Ill, aged, disabled	Duty	Centres and facilities for training and occupation, and a variety of social work support to alleviate mental disorder. Home helps.	HASSASSA 1983, s.17
				Power	Centres and facilities for training and occupation, meals, social services support, night-sitter services, recuperative holidays, facilities for social and recreational activities, and services for alcoholic and drug addicts, all to alleviate illness. Laundry service.	
	Independent Living Funds Guidance Notes	Independent Living Fund trustees	Disabled adults (not old)	Power	Supplementary funds to pay for domiciliary care packages, up to £375 per week where local social services authority is paying at least £200 per week. www.ilf.org.uk	Means test in Guidance Notes.

Type of Service	Legal Sources of Powers	Provider	Client Group	Power or Duty	Description of Services	Charging Power
Counselling and support	Local Government Act 2000, s.93 Supporting People Directions and Guidance	Private and voluntary sector provider (LA funded)	People requiring support	Power	Housing-related support services which develop or sustain a person's capacity to live independently in accommodation, and other services ancillary to those services. *www.spkweb.org.uk*	Local Authorities (Charge for Specified Welfare Schemes) Regulations 2003, in some cases; Local Government Act 2003, s.94(1) (when in force).
Combined provision	Mental Health Act 1983, s.117	Local social services authority	Formerly detained mental patients	Duty	Any services that individual may require: may include accommodation, care, counselling, support, and domiciliary services of whatever nature.	None.
	Children Act 1989, s.17	Local social services authority	Children "in need".	Duty	"A range and level of services appropriate to those children's needs" in respect of any child in need. Can include accommodation, care, counselling, support and domiciliary services of whatever nature. Note: services within CSDPA 1970, s.2 are treated as being provided under that legislation: *R v Bexley LBC ex p B* (1995) 3 C.C.L.R. 15.	CA 1989, s.29, Sch. 2 paras 21–23 (general services); Sch. 2, para. 21 (accommodation).

1. Personal injury damages, income support and care funding

This notice deals with the question whether income from an award of damages for personal injury held on trust must be taken into account for the purpose of eligibility for income support and for the purpose of assessment of resources by the local authority in relation to the funding of residential care. It replaces an earlier website notice with the same title, which is now out of date.

The law has recently been changed in the following respects:

- The treatment of income from personal injury damages held on trust
- The treatment of annuities where there is a structured settlement.

There has been **no change** in respect of:

- The treatment of the capital of a trust fund deriving from personal injury damages
- The treatment of personal injury damages held in the Court of Protection.

I will refer to the last two matters simply by way of a reminder.

INCOME SUPPORT
Treatment of capital
The income support regulations provide that the *capital* is not taken into account for income support purposes so long as the money is either held on trust or administered by the Court of Protection (*e.g.* held on Special Account). This has not changed.

Treatment of interest accruing to personal injury damages in court and payments out
Where the funds are in court, the Income Support regulations **treat the income accruing to the capital as capital.** In a case which came before Commissioner Powell on July 28, 2000 (CIS/4037/1999), it was decided that **payments out to the receiver were also to be treated as capital**. That case involved personal injury damages held in Court, where a monthly payment of £625 was made to the receiver. The result of the Commissioner's decision was that the applicant qualified for income support. Although the money withdrawn is treated as capital, it is no longer treated as disregarded capital when it leaves the Court. The effect of this is that the applicant will remain eligible for income support unless ruled out by the amounts of capital held *outside* the Court of Protection.

Commissioner Powell's decision is not affected by the recent change in the law, nor has it been affected by any subsequent decision of the courts. Another Commissioner made a similar decision in 2001 (CIS/929/00), and in November 2002 Commissioner Henty (CIS/2211/2002) held that monthly payments from a damages award held in court counted as capital, ie could not be disregarded, and, so far as the payments exceeded the income support capital threshold, they were subject to the "tariff income" rule. This made the claimant ineligible for income support.

Annuity payments under structured settlements
Prior to the recent change in the law, such payments ranked as income, with the result that the beneficiary would not be eligible for income support. This was confirmed by the Court of Appeal in *Beattie v Secretary of State for Social Security.*[1] **This decision has been reversed by an amendment to the Income Support Regulations**, as explained below.

Income from personal injury damages held on trust
Prior to the recent change in the law, income from such a trust ranked as income for the purposes of income support, so that the beneficiary would not normally be eligible. The rules differed from those applicable to personal injury damages held in court, although it was not easy to see why this should be so. However, the rules applicable to income from trusts have now been changed.

---

[1] [2001] 1 W.L.R. 1404.

The new rules

The Income Support Regulations have been amended as from 28 October 2002 by the Social Security Amendment (Personal Injury Payments) Regulations 2002 (No.2442). [This makes similar amendments to the regulations on housing benefit, council tax and jobseeker's allowance, but the details of those will not be given here].

The changes are as follows:

- Periodical payments received under an agreement (including an out of court settlement) or a court order to make personal injury payments are treated as income
- Payments under an annuity purchased with funds deriving from personal injury payments are **disregarded income** to the extent described below
- Payments received under an agreement or court order to make personal injury payments are **disregarded income** to the extent described below
- Payments of income from trusts whose funds derive from personal injury payments are **disregarded income** to the extent described below.

The new rule does not provided that these payments of income are automatically disregarded. **They are disregarded entirely when used for items other than everyday living expenses. If used for everyday living expenses, the first £20 is disregarded.** This means that the trustees will normally be able to ensure that the income is used in such a way that the beneficiary does not lose eligibility for income support.

ASSESSMENT OF RESOURCES FOR THE PURPOSE OF RESIDENTIAL CARE FUNDING

This is governed by the National Assistance (Assessment of Resources) Regulations 1992. The rules on the treatment of personal injury damages are the same as for income support, both as to capital and income. The changes described above come into operation in England on 28 October 2002 in relation to care funding, under the National Assistance (Assessment of Resources) (Amendment) (No.2) (England) Regulations 2002. Local Authorities have been advised of the changes by Local Authority Circular LAC (2002) 15, which may be accessed on the DOH website (www.doh.gov.uk/publications/coinh.html). Hard copies of the Circular may be obtained from Department of Health, PO Box 777, London SE1 6XH.

Similar changes to the care funding rules in Wales have been made by the National Assistance (Assessment of Resources) (Amendment) (Wales) Regulations 2003, with effect from April 7, 2003.

Jill Martin
Legal Adviser to the Public Guardianship Office
October 18, 2002 (updated April 2003)

2. Editor's Note on the Court of Protection

1. **When the jurisdiction of the Court of Protection applies.** A 'patient' is defined by the Mental Health Act 1983,(see below). If the claimant is a child or patient and certainly if the claimant is likely to be both, then an application should be made to the Court of Protection the moment that it is likely that any funds are going to be received on behalf of the child or patient. The one exception to that statement is where the claimant is a child and the sum of money is regarded as small. The word "small" in this context has not been defined, but a sum of less than £20,000 can be left in the Special Investment Account, subject to the supervision of the local District Judges or the Queen's Bench Masters. The Court of Protection appears to have jurisdiction in respect of infants, who are not Patients, partly stemming from the inherent jurisdiction, which the Court has over all infants, and also from its own previous practice: *Stringman v McArdle*.[1]

2. **Who is a Patient.** The decision as to who is a "patient" is defined by two separate criteria. Firstly, the patient must comply with the terms of the Mental Health Act 1983, section 1. Section 1(2) defines four separate categories of "mental disorder" from which the patient must be suffering. They are: "mental disorder", "severe mental impairment", "mental impairment" and "psychopathic disorder". The second is the question of incapacity. There must be a causal nexus between the incapacity and the disorder: section 94, Mental Health Act 1983. The second criteria requires that the patient has to be adjudged incapable of managing his/her own affairs. There are two authorities on this, *White v Fell*[2] and *Masterman-Lister v Brutton & Co and Anr.,* (Nos 1and 2).[3] This latter decision was upheld by the Court of Appeal, on appeal, Kennedy, Potter and Chadwick L.J.J., December 19, 2002.[4] As this second criterion would probably apply to a considerable proportion of the population, (including barristers), on one level this test can be satisfied without great problems. Any doubt in difficult cases should be resolved by the instruction of a neuro-psychiatrist, and/or of a neuro-psychologist. The Court of Protection will accept a medical report, (the medical certificate, CP3), from any registered medical practitioner. A doctor reporting on this aspect, ought not only to consider the effect of the judgments in *Masterman-Lister v Brutton & Co*, but also will find assistance in *"Assessment of Mental Capacity—Guidance for Doctors and Lawyers"*, published by the British Medical Association, 2003. A Report from a neuro-psychologist is not sufficient for a medical report under the requirements of CP3, as it is rare that a neuro-psychologist is a qualified medical practitioner. The position of the patient and management of his/her own affairs has been more recently considered in *Russell Mitchell v Ryan Alasia*[5] and *A v The Archbishop of Birmingham*.[6]

3. **Court of Protection Fees.** These are, as a general rule claimable, as are the fees of a professional receiver and associated solicitors' costs. They need detailed and careful calculation. There are a number of special factors to be taken into account in the calculation of the claimable fees. In Table H5 ss.3 and 4 some assistance will be found to help in calculating these figures.

4. **Suspicion that a Claimant may be a "Patient".** Once a solicitor has any reason to suspect that a claimant maybe a patient, then he should not accept or handle any money or property on behalf of the claimant without leave of the Court of Protection. A solicitor would be personally liable for all sums passing through his accounts to a patient without authorisation of the Court of Protection.

---

[1] [1994] 1 W.L.R. 1653 at 1656.
[2] (1987), QBD, Boreham J., (unreported).
[3] [March 15, 2002], QBD, Wright J.,[2002] Lloyd's Rep. Med. 239.
[4] [2002] EWCA Civ 1889, [2003] 1 W.L.R. 1511, [2003] 3 All E.R. 162.
[5] [2005] EWHC 11 (QB), Laura Cox J.
[6] [2005] EWHC 1363 (QB), Christopher Clarke J.

---

5. **The Court of Protection and the Public Guardianship Office.** The Public Guardianship Office has well over 600 staff and is, effectively, the secretariat for the Court of Protection. It is a separate Government Agency. For those who need to contact the Court of Protection, the Public Guardianship Office is the front office for those who wish to have any contact with the Court of Protection at the outset. The Court and its officials are user friendly. The Court is capable of acting very quickly in the case of urgent applications, but the normal method is for the claimant's solicitors to write in and complete the Forms and The First General Order will be made if the application is supported by proper evidence. Any solicitor or counsel may make an appointment to see the Master or his assistants. In cases of real urgency, such as replacing a litigation friend immediately before a hearing, then the Master is prepared to act with great speed, but the trial judge would also have to have an application made to him about such a transaction.

6. **Settlements.** No settlements, in the sense of a compromise or agreement in a personal injury action, should take place, as a general rule, without authorisation from the Court of Protection. It is a parallel authority to that given to a High Court Judge under CPR Pt 21. The Master has power to make orders and give directions for the conduct of the legal proceedings in the name of the patient: s.96(1)(i) Mental Health Act 1983. Further, the Master (for settlement purposes only) will accept an email from Counsel, including the Advice, and provide an email response very swiftly indicating his approval. Plainly, that email facility is not for correspondence with him or for any other purpose. [The email address for settlement purposes is: *Denzil.Lush@guardianship.gsi.gov.uk*].

7. **Management of Funds.** There are four ways in which a patient's funds may be managed. Three are common and the fourth is relatively unusual. They are as follows:

    a.   The receiver is the Public Trustee.
    b.   The receiver is a professional receiver.
    c.   The receiver is a private individual.
    d.   A private trust with professional or private trustees: this will need the specific approval of the Master.

8. As a matter of practice, it is to be preferred that a Panel Receiver should be appointed rather than the Public Trustee. The Panel Receivers are Receivers who have been placed upon a Public Guardianship Office Panel. They are those who are to receive work of last resort for those for whom there is no easily appointed Receiver available, and who have satisfied the Public Guardianship Office of their expertise. There is a list of Panel Receivers. Cases are allocated on a geographical and speciality basis.

9. The fourth, (d), is that the Court, if properly satisfied that it is in the best interests of the patient, may permit private or professional trustees to manage the patient's affairs completely, bypassing the normal control and charges of the Court of Protection. It can be a valuable solution but would depend on the particular circumstances and it needs the leave of the Court, either by the Master or a Judge of the Supreme Court or both, for such an arrangement to take effect. The Official Solicitor may intervene in Private Trusts, both as to their creation and as to their powers, and given that the costs of running a Private Trust seem to be, generally, no cheaper than the normal Receivership, this is an area that needs to be approached with caution. The Trust Deed may require specialist advice, because of the statutory benefits' problems. The circumstances need to be unusual and justified for this route to be followed.

10. **Role of the Receiver.** Being a receiver is an onerous responsibility. There is valuable guidance to be found in the Receiver's Handbook, which is now available on the Public Guardianship Office's website. One set of accounts needs to be sent to the Court during the year. It is usual that

the Patient would have a bank account in the receiver's name. An Income Tax Return needs to be made to the Inland Revenue every year. A receiver has to complete a Receiver's Declaration. This includes the fact that the Receiver promises to visit the Patient regularly. The usual professional receiver is a solicitor. It is not a role exclusive to solicitors. It may be a task which is handled by a partner responsible for tax, trustee and probate work in the practice. Some firms carry out a considerable amount of business for private clients, trustees and for those authorised under the enduring powers of attorney.

11. There is now a Panel of Professional Receivers. The Public Guardianship Office considers their own provision of receivership to be a matter of last resort, there being no one else available or suitable or both. (*cf.* The Public Guardianship Office's Annual Report and Accounts 2002/03, which can be easily downloaded from the website: *www.guardianship.gov.gsi*).

12. **Charges for professional receivers.** A professional receiver is allowed to charge fees for his work and this should be claimed for in the action. A multiplier is applied to the annual rate, dependent on the patient's expectation of life. The requirements and needs of a patient, who is subject to the Court of Protection as the result of a personal injury tort, are different from those who are normal private clients. The work varies, but often the initial work of setting up the regime is more intensive, in comparison to the regular, routine running of the receivership. Some, but not all, of the costs are dealt with below and on the following pages. The sum of £2,650 pa was awarded for the professional receiver's services in *Cassel v Riverside Health Authority*.[1] In argument in *Eagle v Chambers*,[2] in the Court of Appeal, it was suggested by the Court that it was improper for the Receiver, if he is directly concerned in the litigation, to argue for his own fees. See also: para.[85] of the judgement, where evidence from the Master of the Court of Protection was given to the Court. The evidence was that the costs of a professional receiver, if there is no family member willing to act as receiver or there is no appropriate person, subject to detailed assessment if not agreed, are likely to exceed £3,500 a year (plus VAT).

13. **A Statutory Will.** At or after the age of 18 a child, who reaches the age of majority, who is also a patient, may have a statutory will made, to reflect the situation in which the receiver, manager, parent or other person concerned deals with the estate of the child, now adult. A sum is allowable and claimable for this and should be put in the Schedule. It does not seem unreasonable that such a will should be reviewed, say every ten years, and a claim could be made for this activity. There are some contested wills. The costs for this can be substantial, as the Official Solicitor will be appointed to represent the interests of the patient. There are other complexities, upon which specialist advice should be taken, such as the provision of Trusts with testamentary capacity. The whole area is replete with difficulties, as, for example, a Patient may have testamentary capacity, but still be a Patient for the purpose of the Mental Health Act 1983, in respect of the capacity of managing his/her own affairs.

14. **Surety Bonds.** The Court of Protection now requires a professional receiver to give a surety bond in every new application and reference to a Table of premium rates will be found later in this book. A claim is maintainable for the costs of such a bond.

15. **The Court of Protection Rules.** These are to be found set out in Statutory Instruments, SI 2001/824, amended by SI 2001/2977 and SI 2002/833. These contain the procedural code in respect of the powers, duties and operation of the Court of Protection. They can be downloaded from the web and are available from the Public Guardianship Office website: *www.guardianship.gov.gsi.*

---

[1] [1992] P.I.Q.R. Q168.
[2] (No.2) EWCA Civ 1033.

16. **Learning and Textbooks.** There is no single source which will aid the practitioner on the range and powers of the Court of Protection and its practice. *Kemp & Kemp: Quantum of Damages* covers some of the problems, (and has been carefully rewritten); *Andrews & Lee on Catastrophic Injuries*, Sweet & Maxwell, 1997, covers some aspects not found in *Kemp & Kemp*. Further information on the Court of Protection can be found in Ch.28 of *Kemp and Kemp.* This will be of great assistance to anyone with a practical difficulty on the Court of Protection Practice and Procedure. Other resources include the Law Commission Paper, *Damages for Personal Injury: Medical, Nursing and other Expenses, A Consultation Paper* (Law Commission 1996, No.144) and the Recommendation Paper (Law Commission 1999, No. 262). There is an interesting document obtainable on the Parliament website, in which a Joint Committee of the House of Lords and the House of Commons considered after open hearings the Draft Mental Incapacity Bill, (HL Paper 189–1, HC 1083–1). A Mental Capacity Bill is before Parliament as is a Mental Health Bill. There is a large quantity of information on both the Department of Health and the Department of Constitutional Affairs web sites. Heywood & Massey, *Court of Protection Practice*, Sweet & Maxwell, 2002, was never written for the common lawyer. It should incorporate a common lawyer in the editorial team, who has to face the matters discussed above. It is the bible for those dealing with the Court of Protection. The Court of Protection, through the Public Guardianship Office, supplies a series of pamphlets explaining what it does and how it works. These can be obtained on application to the Court and from the website.

July 6, 2005

3. Court of Protection Solicitors' Fixed Costs 2005
Notice published on the Court of Protection's website

Fees and Charges

This page explains the fees charged by the Public Guardianship Office (PGO). Some of our fees changed on 1 April 2005. Fees apply to all new applications to the Court of Protection, and in some instances, apply to cases already under the jurisdiction of the Court.

This information is also available for download in an *easy to understand format* for people with a learning disability.

Commencement Fee
This fee is payable when submitting the first application for the appointment of a receiver or other initial application for a Court direction or Order. From 1 April 2005, this fee is **£240**. **Please note that this is not the fee for** *registering an EPA*.

Appointment Fee
The appointment fee is payable when the Court appoints a receiver for the first time. A fee of **£315** applies to all orders appointing a receiver made on or after the 1 April 2005.

Administration Fee
From 1 April 2005, there will be two types of administration fee. For cases where the Court makes a short order, the fee will be **£190 (new fee)**, payable on the anniversary of the short order. Where the Court appoints a receiver, the fee will be **£240**, due annually on the anniversary date of the appointment. There are occasions when we will charge part of the fee for other periods. The administration fees apply to all anniversary dates falling on or after 1 April 2005.

Account Fee
This fee covers the cost of collecting and passing receivership accounts and from 1 April 2005 is **£100**. The fee is payable 28 days after the last day of the period covered by the account and will apply to all accounts ending on or after the 1 April 2005.

Transaction Fee
These are fees payable at the time of application in cases where it is necessary for the Court of Protection to approve or authorise a service, action or activity, which falls outside the usual administration fee. A separate transaction fee applies to *Enduring Power of Attorney applications*.

From 1 April 2005 these fees are as follows:

For the settlement or gift of property under section 96(1)(d) of the Mental Health Act 1983.	**£100** (for transactions with a value of up to £10,000) **£360** (for transactions with a value over £10,000)
For the carrying out of contract under section 96(1)(h) of the Mental Health Act 1983.	
Under section 1(3) of the Variation of Trusts Act 1958.	**£500** (payable on the court fixing a date for an attended hearing to consider the application)
For vesting stock in a curator outside England & Wales under section 100 of the Mental Health Act 1983.	**£60**
For the exercise of powers under section 96(1)(k) of the Mental Health Act 1983.	**£130**
Pursuant to section 54 of Trustee Act 1925 (concurrent jurisdiction with High Court over trusts).	**£130**
For authorisation of person to act as trustee under section 20 of the Trusts of Land and Appointment of Trustees Act 1996.	**£130**
Appointing a Trustee pursuant to section 36(9) of the Trustee Act 1925.	**£130**

For the execution of a Will under section 96(1)(e) of the Mental Health Act 1983.	**£540**
For the sale or purchase of land under section 96(1)(b) of the Mental Health Act 1983.	**£170**
On an application under section 96(1)(a) or (b) of the Mental Health Act 1983 authorising managing and letting of property.	**£170 (new fee)**
On making an application for the appointment of a new Receiver.	**£190**
On approval of an estate account where the client has an absolute interest or a life interest.	**£100 (new fee)**

Winding up Fee

This fee covers work connected with winding up our involvement in the client's finances. From 1 April 2005, this fee is **£290**, payable on the death of a client where a receiver has been appointed. From 1 April 2005, an additional winding up fee of **£150 (new fee)** is payable on each anniversary of the death of the client, until the Court passes the final receiver's account or directs it be dispensed with.

Enduring Power of Attorney Fees

Enduring Power of Attorney Registration Fees

A fee of £120 is payable when an application is made to register an enduring power of attorney (EPA). We cannot refund this fee if the power is not registered.

Enduring Power of Attorney Transaction Fee

EPA transaction fees apply in certain cases where it is necessary for the Court to approve or authorise a service or action or activity, which is outside the normal powers of the attorney.

From 1 April 2005 the fee is as follows:

On making an application or making a direction under section 8(2)(d) or (e) of the Enduring Powers of Attorney Act 1985.	**£100** (for transactions with a value of up to £10,000)
	£360 (for transactions with a value over £10,000)
	£500 (payable on the court fixing a date for an attended hearing to consider the application)

Enduring Power of Attorney Account Fee

The EPA account fee of **£100** is payable if the Court directs that an Attorney should submit accounts. The fee is due when the Court passes the account and applies to all accounts passed by the Court after 1 April 1005.

Enduring Power of Attorney Search Fee

There is a **£20** fee payable to search the Register to see if an EPA has been registered.

Fees where PGO acts as receiver

Separate fees apply where the Public Guardianship Office acts as receiver. If you would like details you can download our *Receivership Fees Leaflet*.

HOW TO PAY

Fee Remissions

The Court has discretion to remit (i.e. waive or postpone collection) all or part of any fee if payment would cause hardship to the client, to his or her dependants, or if there are other exceptional circumstances. If you would like more information on remission of fees, please see our *Fee Remissions Guidance*.

Paying Fees

Please pay by cheque, made payable to "The Public Guardianship Office". Please send this to the *Public Guardianship Office, Archway Tower, 2 Junction Road, London N19 5SZ*. To help us deal with your application quickly, please quote your case reference number, if you have one, and return any paperwork we have requested.

Published April 2005

1. The Public Guardianship Office does not provide legal advice to receivers or any other persons, and recommends that you consider seeking your own independent legal advice.

2. While the information contained in this publication is believed to be correct at the time of publication, the Public Guardianship Office does not accept liability for any error it may contain.

---

4. Court of Protection and Receiver's Fees

Draft Schedule of Calculations

1. Court of Protection Fees:
    a. Commencement fee: £240
    b. Appointment fee: £315
    c. Annual administration fee: £190 or £240 (where Court appoints a Receiver) × multiplier:
    d. Account fee: £100
    e. Transaction fees, say £100 pa × multiplier:
    f. Past receivership expenses (when appropriate):
        i. Initial costs of order:
        ii. Disbursements (doctor's fees, process server, etc.)[1]:
        iii. Total past costs to date of trial:
    g. Statutory will fees: £540
    h. Review of Statutory Will (say every 10 years): £540
    i. On the death of the client (winding up fee): £290
2. Receivership Fees and Costs:
    a. Professional Receiver's fees at £ xx per hour for 25 hours pa + VAT = yy × multiplier:
    b. Alternatively, the employment of a book keeper at £ zz per hour at ww hours per year × multiplier:
    c. Preparation of Accounts: £500.00 pa (including VAT) × multiplier:
    d. Appointment of new Receiver: say 5 receivers (depending upon life expectation) + contingency balancing out discount for accelerated receipt at £300 per appointment:
    e. Trustee Act 1925 directions: allow £500 for fees:
    f. Security Bond premium; qq pa × multiplier[2]:
    g. Costs and expenses for statutory will: £750
    h. Cost and Expenses for review of Statutory Will (say every 10 years): £750
    i. Past Receiver's fees to date of trial.

For rates see previous pages, pp.230–232 and the website *www.guardianship.gov.gsi.*

Note:

It would be valuable to have the benefit of details from those who have successfully claimed fees under either of these headings. These items are too easily neglected, but it should be noted that the Court of Protection even charges fees for the death of the patient. Such fees are clearly claimable, for though all of us die, not all of us will have the need to have the Court of Protection clear up our estates.

Panel Brokers are not claimable: *cf. Eagle v Chambers (No. 2)* Buxton L.J.[3]

---

[1] BMA Professional Fees Committee recommendation as to Court of Protection.
[2] Court of Protection Amendment Rules 2001 (S.I. 2001/824 r.56).
[3] [2004] EWCA Civ 1033, dissenting.

5. Special Needs Trusts

1. The Special Needs Trust is a device for protecting a claimant from losing his income support, housing benefit, council tax benefit or any other form of means tested benefit, including long term care and care at home, when he receives damages for personal injuries. These means tested benefits may be of importance to a claimant who receives less than a full award, for whatever reason, such as contributory negligence. They are also important in the general sense of prudent asset management.

2. With most means tested benefits, the ownership of capital sums will often disqualify a recipient from receiving these benefits, either in whole or in part.

3. Other varieties of capital are commonly disregarded for means tested benefit purposes, such as the value of the house in which the claimant lives or in which a specified relative lives.

4. The relevant Regulations are complex. There are various factors which will determine the entitlement to benefits, for example age (usually 60), and whether the claimant is living in residential care.

5. The Regulations can be used to a claimant's advantage. Schedule 10 of the Income support (General) Regulations 1987 provides for those to whom payment is made in consequence of any personal injury.

6. Capital sums are to be disregarded under two circumstances, so long as the funds are:

   a. held in trust for the claimant: Income Support (General) Regulations 1987, Sch.10, para.12; or

   b. administered by the court on the claimant's behalf; Income Support (General) Regulations 1987, Sch.10, para.44(a) and 45(a).

   Both 6(a) and 6(b) are incorporated into other benefits' rules by reference and that includes council tax and housing benefits and, importantly, by the National Assistance (Assessment of Resources) Regulations 1992 (as amended), which applies to long term care and (indirectly) to care at home.

7. These capital disregards were extended by the Social Security Amendment (Personal Injury Payments) Regulations 2002 (SI 2002/2442), which came into force on October 28, 2002. Regulation 3 provides that compensation related income will, in most circumstances, be disregarded for the purposes of assessing entitlement to council tax benefit, income support and job seeker's allowance. The circumstances include payments from a trust or periodical payments whose funds are derived from a payment made in consequence of any personal injury to the claimant. So long as the income is not used for the claimant's normal expenses of daily living (met by benefits), it will be ignored in assessments.

8. A further Statutory Instrument, the National Assistance (Assessment of Resources) (Amendment No.2) (England) Regulations (SI 2002/2531) deals with the mirror changes to the regulations governing local authority provision. The effect is that income received from trusts whose funds derive from personal injury payments to a resident, from an annuity purchased with such funds and those received by virtue of any agreement or court order to make personal injury payments to the resident in local authority accommodation (and, also, arguably for those cared for at home), are now treated in the same way. All are disregarded in their entirety, when intended and used for any item which was not taken into account when the "contract rate" or "standard rate" was fixed for the accommodation provided. The "intention" aspect is not regulatory. It derives from the Guidance attached to the Statutory Instrument. It appears to apply to the intention "in use" not intention relating to the award itself.

9. It is advisable to have a trust deed in place well before the settlement takes place. A copy should be supplied to the relevant benefit agency, if they ask for it when being notified.

10. Any money received by way of damages should ideally not pass through the claimant's hands. It should pass into the trust, previously created, without being controlled by the claimant. Money in a solicitor's client account is not in a trust, unless cost related issues prohibit its payment to the claimant. Receipt will trigger a relevant change in circumstances and benefits will be lost. But trusts can be set up late as the notional capital rules do not apply to such trusts. In the meantime, however, there will be a benefits hiatus.

11. Money from the trust for capital amounts should ideally pass from the trust directly to a third party, for example when it is being used to purchase a car for the claimant. But the money, if allocated to a specific use by the trustees, the payments themselves, may still not amount to "available" and thus "assessable capital" of the recipient if mistakes are made.

12. Payments to the claimant should never amount to more than £3,000, when combined with other capital held by the claimant or members of their "claimant unit".

13. A Special Needs' Trust is viable when the level of benefits being retained outweighs the costs of setting up and running the trust. As one commentator has shrewdly observed, it has nothing to do with the size of the award. The adviser should always be aware of the possibility of the cost of long term care.

14. Failure to advise a claimant about this scheme could be negligent. However, many claimants prefer to have control of their own money, despite the loss of benefits, and this must be a matter of personal choice. It is an option for this reason.

15. The learning on this topic is not extensive, but some accountants and others do understand the maze that is the various benefits schemes. *"Special needs trusts—How to ensure your personal injury clients retain their means tested benefits post-settlement"*, John Frenkel, the barrister. October 1, 2001; *"Money Management"*, Master Denzil Lush, Trusts and Estates Law Journal; March 2001, p.4. Also see David Coldrick's *"Personal Injury Trusts: a solicitor's guide to founding a compensation service"*; 2002, intended primarily for private client work, but relevant for any personal injury lawyer. Also, see: *"Structured Settlements, Report of the Master of the Rolls Working Party"*, Chairman: Brian Langstaff, QC, October 2002. See, also, on the Public Guardianship Office website: (1) *"Are you acting in the best interest of your clients?"*; Pauline Thompson, Age Concern, England; (2) Note by Jill Martin, Legal Adviser to the PGO, entitled *"Local Authority Funding of Domiciliary Care and Personal Injury Damages"*, dated April 29, 2004; and (3) an interesting article by Nicholas Davies, barrister, in Quantum, July 8, 2004, Issue 4/2004, pp.4 & 5: *"Housing Benefit and the Special Needs Trust"*. David Coldrick and Wrigleys, solicitors, of 3rd Floor, Fountain Precinct, Balm Green, Sheffield, South Yorkshire S1 2JA, run a *"Compensation Protection Unit"*, which is a virtual private client service on this area provided to many specialist personal injury firms.

6. Personal Injury Trusts

1. **Introduction.** The "Personal Injury Trust" is not only relevant when there is a claimant in receipt of benefits, it may be appropriate for a range of other situations. It could be relevant for a claimant who may need benefits later, and even long term care provision may also be, essentially, a means-tested benefit. There may be other advantages, ranging from tax, reluctance to control money, or otherwise in the case of older claimants or those who are potentially vulnerable. The vulnerable could include those who may become "patients" or need to operate their affairs under an enduring power of attorney at another stage in their lives.

2. **Purpose of a Trust.** There may be one or more different reasons for such a trust as follows:

   a. **Tax:** there are not usually any tax advantages as the trust is a "settlor interested" in this case. Specialist advice should be taken. Beware placing large awards in a discretionary trust as this can trigger an unexpected inheritance tax bill. This would be negligent.

   b. **To avoid loss of means-tested benefits:** the classic example is to secure means-tested benefits, for which it is usually necessary to have less than £3,000 in capital to achieve the maximum award of benefits. There is a separate article on them under the heading of "Special Needs Trusts".

   c. **Control:** not everyone wishes to be personally responsible for managing and controlling a fund of money. They may feel more comfortable with someone else, namely professionals, running such money as they have, without the additional burden of being directly concerned themselves.

   d. **Court of Protection approved private trust:** there may be good reasons for the Court of Protection to approve a private trust. If such approval is given, the management of the fund is placed in the hands of professional trustees and funds can be dealt with outside the court brokers' system.

   e. **Minors who are not mentally incapable:** they can have funds paid into a trust under CPR 21.11. This avoids problems of continuity at age 18 when they are, perhaps, too young to obtain a large sum outright. Only bare trusts can be founded under CPR 21.11.

3. **Timing and Planning.** The moment that it seems likely that a settlement is likely to take place, then that is the time when such a trust should be set up. The benefits of a "personal injury trust" should always be considered.

4. **Notification.** When means-tested benefits are involved, it is probably good practice to inform the relevant agency and supply them with a copy of the trust deed, upon request, and an explanation, in plain language, of the purpose of the trust.

5. **Statutory Authority.** Reference should be made to paras 5 to 8 of the Note on Special Needs Trust.

6. **Conclusion.** There may be very good and practical reasons for the claimant to arrange his affairs so that a "personal injury trust" is set up. Often, it should be remembered, claimants wish to control their own money. The fact that the advantages and disadvantages of a "personal injury trust" have been considered and explained to a claimant, is an important step in giving a claimant a complete professional service.

7. **Further Reading.** There is a valuable article on this subject by David Coldrick of Wrigley, Solicitors of Sheffield in the December 2001 issue of Personal Injury Law Journal. Also see David Coldrick's "Personal Injury Trusts: a solicitor's guide to founding a compensation service"; 2002, intended primarily for private client work, but relevant for any personal injury lawyer.

H6: Foster care allowances

Introductory notes:

Every April the Fostering Network publishes the cost of bringing up a child in its own home for the next 12 months. Contact Fostering Network Publications, 87 Blackfriars Road, London SE1 8HA (tel: 020 7620 6400; www.fostering.net.).

The Fostering Network publishes Foster Care Finance, with recommended minimum weekly allowances for fostering in the UK and a full survey of allowances paid by each local authority. The Fostering Network's recommended minimum allowance depends on the age of the child and whether or not the placement is in London. The allowances do not include any form of reward for carers themselves. The Fostering Network recommends four extra weeks' payment, to cover the cost of birthdays, holidays and a religious festival. It encourages local authorities to pay allowances to all carers at least in line with its recommended rates. Despite such encouragement the majority of local authorities give foster carers less than the Fostering Network's recommended minimum allowances for spending on the care of fostered children. From a survey published by the Fostering Network in September 2003, 53 per cent of local authorities in England and 87 per cent of local authorities in Wales paid *below* the Fostering Network's recommended minimum allowance.

Fostering Network recommended costs of bringing up a child in its own home for the year beginning April 1, 2005

Age of child (years)	National (£ per week)	London (£ per week)
0–4	80.46	94.43
5–10	91.65	107.65
11–15	114.10	134.05
16+	138.77	162.80

The cost of fostering services is not an appropriate measure for the value of the loss of a (deceased) mother's services (*Spittle v Bunney*[1]).

---

[1] [1988] 1 W.L.R. 847.

Group I
Other Material

I

I1: British Nursing Association rates

Introductory notes

1. These figures represent the British Nursing Association's rates for Central London, Cardiff and Newcastle: rates vary throughout London and the rest of the country. Contact BNA Care Assessment Services, The Colonnades, Beaconsfield Close, Hatfield, Herts AL10 8TD for rates elsewhere.

2. There are a range of other rates both for nursing and other carers. The highest of these are usually the Whitley scale rates which are used by the NHS and local authorities; the lowest, in some areas, are the "Crossroads: Caring for Carers" rates, based on another body which produces the "National Joint Council Rates".[1] Other scales are provided by private nursing homes and other nursing and care agencies, which vary according to location.

3. The figures are appropriate for use when third parties have provided gratuitous help.

4. The range of care can be extensive, so:
   - (a) Short Visit;
   - (b) Care by the Hour;
   - (c) Night Sleeper;
   - (d) Night Sitter;
   - (e) Residential Live-In.

   All of the above can be carried out by a Home Care Assistant, Qualified Nurse and NNEB (Nursery Nurse).

5. "Case Manager" is a specialist job. A definition of case management is: "A collaborative process which assesses, plans, implements, co-ordinates, monitors and evaluates the options and services required to meet an individual's health, care, educational and employment needs, using communication and available resources to promote quality cost effective outcomes." A full Case Manager will plan the care, organise, hire and pay staff, supervise, organise or provide training and act as the first point of contact in a complex case. There are now two Associations of Case Managers. The first and oldest is BABICM, which is the source of the concept, from the treatment of the acute problems in looking after brain injured patients. There is also, now, the Case Management Society UK (CMSUK – www.cmsuk.org). Plainly, an expert Report is required in supporting the need for a Case Manager. The appropriate rate for a Case Manager would be as much as £75 per hour plus travelling time. A Case Manager would have a case load consisting of a number of different clients and there is a physical limit as to the number that can be properly managed.

   The status of a claimant's clinical case manager in the context of contested litigation is considered in an interesting case in the Court of Appeal in the judgment of Brooke L.J. in *Wright v Sullivan*.[2] "It seems inevitable to me that the clinical case manager should owe her duties to her patient alone" para.26. "The role of a clinical case manager, if she is called to give evidence at the trial, will clearly be one of a witness of fact, as the BABICM guidelines suggest. She is there to give evidence of what she did and why she decided to do it" para.33.

6. **The Manual Handling Operations Regulations 1992**, implementing the EEC Directive on Health and Safety at Work, require the provision of appropriate equipment for manual handling of disabled people. This makes it a requirement to have hoist type equipment available whenever a disabled person is moved by another and that person doing the moving falls into the category of being employed by someone to do this work.

---

[1] This is the national agreement between the Employers Organisation (whose parent body is the Local Government Association) and the relevant unions. The rates are based on a spinal scale from 4 to 69. There is no national grading system. The local authorities agree local rates individually, depending on the circumstances of their area.

[2] [2005] EWCA Civ 656.

7. Recent legislation and case law have required considerable changes in the quality of service provided.

Night Sleeper and "On Call" rates

8. Night Sleeper "On Call" rates will have to be increased as a result of the Employment Appeal Tribunal decisions of *Scottbridge Construction Ltd v James Wright*, Lord Johnston and ors; unreported; and *British Nursing Association v Inland Revenue*;[1] Judge Altman and ors.

9. The basis for the decisions was that at times when the employees were awake and "on call" or asleep on the premises where they were required to be, they were engaged in "time work" within the meaning of reg.15(1) of the National Minimum Wages Regulation 1999, made under the National Minimum Wage Act 1998. Both decisions appear to flow from the European Court of Justice decision of *SIMAP V Conselaria de Sanidad v Consump de la Generalidad Valenciana*.[2]

10. These decisions will increase the costs of sleeper rates.

Care Standards Act 2000

11. The draft National Minimum Standards for Domiciliary Agencies envisage a change in July 2002, when the regulations implementing the National Minimum Standards and the required provisions of the Care Standards Act 2000 come into force.

12. There is a requirement that before employment, checks and satisfactory results shall have been obtained. It applies to temporary staff, both agency and bank staff. All must be provided with written contracts specifying the terms and conditions which must also comply with the Code of Conduct of the General Social Care Council.

13. There is also a requirement for an Induction process for all new care and support staff. Further, the employer is required to have a staff development and training programme in place, which is reviewed and updated annually.

14. It is thought that it may now be necessary to provide an extra week per year for the purpose of complying with these new requirements. They will, also, increase the cost of care staff of all categories.

Gratuitous Care

15. *Evans v Pontypridd Roofing*[3] is the first time that the question of gratuitous care has been carefully examined since the classic decision *of Housecroft v Burnett* [1986].[4] It expressly declines to lay down any general rules or guidance, but by the comments made, it does in fact do so. May L.J., in a careful judgment, explains the jurisprudential basis for such awards and then echoes the statement in *Hunt v Severs*,[5] where Lord Bridge stated that what has to be quantified is the amount "to enable the voluntary carer to receive proper recompense for his and her services".

16. This May L.J. stated, is in substance the same as O'Connor L.J.'s statement when he referred to "a capital sum . . . sufficient . . . to make recompense to the relative" in *Housecroft v Burnett*. He then says that: "On this basis, it seems to me that the guidance given as to quantification in *Housecroft v Burnett* remains helpful". (para.24.)

17. May L.J. then says at para.25, that: "In my judgement, this court should avoid putting first instance judges into too restrictive a straight-jacket, such as might happen if it was said that the means of assessing a proper recompense for services provided gratuitously by a family carer had to be assessed in a particular way or ways. Circumstances vary enormously and what is appropriate and just in one case may not be so in another . . . .".

---

[1] [2001] I.R.L.R. 659.
[2] [2000] I.R.L.R. 845.
[3] [2001] EWCA Civ 1657; [2002] P.I.Q.R. Q5.
[4] 1 All E.R. 322, CA.
[5] [1994] 2 A.C. 350 at 363A.

18. He states that the first task is to determine the extent of the services and then decide the discount, which he suggested in the instant case should be 25 per cent but the reasons for the discount should be considered. He also states that: "there is no scientific basis for a strictly mathematical answer to this question. The assessment has to be a broad one, and what in the end is required is a single broad assessment to achieve a fair result in the particular case." He then says that: "But I do not consider that one possible element of a single broad assessment should be required to be a conventional figure. On the contrary it seems to me that first instance judges should have latitude to achieve a fair result." (para.37.) This has been followed by another division of the Court of Appeal in *Newman v Folkes & Anr*[1] where Ward, Sedley L.JJ., and Sumner J. followed the decision of May L.J. in *Evans v Pontypridd Roofing*.

19. On that basis, the previously cited cases of first instance judges continue to be set out, as indicating a range of approaches.

   (a) Damages can be awarded to compensate a relative for nursing care, even if the carer has not lost wages of his/her own, but such an award will only be justified where that care has been well beyond the call of duty: *Mills v British Rail Engineering Ltd*;[2] Brook L.J. in *Giambrone v Sunworld Holidays Ltd*[3] expressly stated that he rejected the contention that *Mills* presents any binding authority for the proposition that such awards are reserved for "very serious cases".

   (b) The extra care and its extent should be such as results from the disability and which, but for that disability, would not be provided by the parents: *McDaid v Howletts & Port Lympne Estates Ltd*;[4]

   (c) To determine the monetary value which should be placed on such care has resulted in a normal practice of awarding gratuitous family care at about 75 per cent. (*Lamey v Wirral Health Authority*) September 22, 1993, Morland J., unreported *Kemp & Kemp* A4-120.

   (d) The market rate is merely a guide and provides a ceiling but the Court may consider it unnecessary to discount that commercial rate. It has to do its best to translate into money something which, in truth, was freely given out of natural affection and duty: *McDaid v Howletts* etc. (above).

   (e) "I next have to consider the appropriate reduction for tax, National Insurance and the fact that this is non-commercial care. The range of percentages normally deducted are between 20 and 33 per cent. Mr Justice Connell adopted 20 per cent for *Burns v Davies*, August 7, 1998, having regard to the high quality of care provided and the basic rate of tax at the present time. Both points apply here. I adopt a deduction of 20 per cent." McKinnon J. in *Sparks v Royal Hospitals NHS Trust*.[5]

   (f) "The care regime can be designed to put [the child] in a position where he can benefit from that normal attention from his parents; so that the parents' attention to him should not itself be viewed as part of that care regime. . . . that the care programme proposed by the plaintiff and endorsed by Mrs Sargent and Dr Smith is a reasonable arrangement in the light of [the child's] needs and difficulties, in particular his handicaps with communication, movement and self-care. It is such as the court can and should adopt as a proper means of putting [the child] as nearly as possible in the position he would have been in had the tort not been committed." *per* Buxton J., *Stephens v Doncaster Health Authority*.[6]

   (g) The principle of *restitutio in integrum* applies and may be stated as "*What may be regarded as necessary or reasonable to place the claimant in a position that will approximate most closely to his/her pre-accident state*". "A point to which Mr Davies returned on several occasions during the trial was that there would be times virtually every day when the services of such a carer

---

[1] [2001] EWCA Civ 591 (May 3, 2002).

[2] [1992] P.I.Q.R Q130, CA.

[3] [2004] EWCA Civ 158, [2004] P.I.Q.R. Q4 at Q46.

[4] May 17, 1996, QBD, Collins J., unreported.

[5] December 21, 1998, QBD.

[6] [1996] 7 Med. L.R. 357 at 366.

would be voluntarily dispensed with by the Plaintiff, because he might well prefer to have the necessary tasks carried out by Ms Godding, his parents or friends. I am sure that is so, but it does not seem to me to affect the principle of what may be regarded as necessary or reasonable to place the plaintiff in a position that will approximate most closely to his pre-accident state" Eady J. in *Biescheuvel v Birrell*.[1]

(h) Also see *Newman v Folkes Anr*,[2] where Ward, Sedley L.JJ. and Sumner J. allowed gratuitous care without discount. The facts are unusual. N, as a result of the accident, was obsessive and potentially violent and could demand attention at any time of day and night. The trial judge, Garland J. had not exercised his discretion wrongly and the whole matter had to be looked at in the round.

(i) *Giambrone v Sunworld Holidays Ltd*[3] is an interesting case where the Court of Appeal, upholding an award by Judge MacDuff QC, sitting as a High Court Judge, who had relied upon the judgement of May L.J. in *Evans v Pontypridd Roofing Ltd*,[4] The Court of Appeal agreed with Judge MacDuff by deciding that awards for gratuitous care are not limited to "very serious cases" or cases in which the care provided is "well beyond the ordinary call of duty", and the Court of Appeal awarded £50 per week in respect of care provided to claimants with gastro-enteritis contracted on holiday with the unhappy supplier in Majorca.

(j) *A v The Archbishop of Birmingham*[5] gives an example of the application of the Giambrone decision in respect of care provided by A's family (para.111).

20. Gardeners and handymen are untrained people with experience in maintaining their own and other people's homes and gardens. The hourly rates are for labour only: tools and equipment must be provided.

21. DIY—loss of capacity to perform. See below I3.

---

[1] [1999] P.I.Q.R. Q68.
[2] [2000] EWCA Civ 591, (May 3, 2002).
[3] [2004] EWCA Civ 158 [2004] P.I.Q.R. Q4.
[4] [2001] EWCA Civ 1157; [2002] P.I.Q.R. Q5.
[5] [2005] EWHC 1361 (QB), Christopher Clarke J.

Notes to the Tables

The figures that follow are taken from BNA's network of 128 branches throughout the U.K. The cost of care staff varies across the country, reflecting local employment environments, although the pricing structure generally falls into six bands. Three representative areas have been chosen: high (Central London – Marble Arch), medium (Cardiff) and low (Newcastle). For further information, contact BNA Care Assessment Services, The Colonnades, Beaconsfield house, Hatfield, Herts AL10 8YD (01707 255658).

There are other rates of pay for nurses and other carers. The Whitley Scale usually gives the highest rates: these are used by the NHS and local authorities. The lowest rates are usually the Crossroads Rates.

There are many different sorts of care régime—*e.g.* home helps, short visits, care by the hour, night sleepers, night sitters, residential carers and case managers. Some of the regimes call for skilled and trained carers, others will only need unskilled care. "Case manager" is a specialised job: the case manager will plan the care, organise, hire and pay staff, and supervise and provide the first point of contact in a complex case.

"Input Rate"

"Input Rate" refers to a provision made in the cost for holiday pay, in accordance with European legislation. Carers accrue an hour's pay for every thirteen worked. This holiday pay can be taken at any time, provided that the carer is not also working at the same time. Thus, the "Members' Pay" does not represent the true cost of care, as the carer is accruing holiday pay as each work hour passes. In order to cost past care accurately, the "Input Rate" needs to be used alongside the "Members' Pay" rate.

The Commercial Rate

The *Commercial Rate* (the rate charged per hour to the client) represents the cost of commissioning care from an agency. It should not be used when the care is to be provided gratuitously. Its cost is higher than the "Input Rate", because it includes the Agency's charge for finding and managing the agency staff, as well as the carer's pay. The "inclusive cost to clients" is the same as the "commercial rate".

Short Visits

The Agency may charge a minimum fee for a visit of less than four hours. Branches usually have a minimum charge of two hours per visit.

Travel Costs

If the client lives in an area where the carer's return journey is more than ten miles, there will be a charge of 20p. per mile (which includes Employer's National Insurance Contribution at 10.95%). Additional travel costs (*e.g.* tolls, local ferries, etc.) will be charged at cost (plus Employer's National Insurance Contribution).

Sleep-in Service

The care assistant will help with evening and morning routines, and will be on call during the night. Rates for sleep-in services are subject to negotiation according to assessed needs and the level of dependency. If the care arrangement does not provide for appropriate rest periods for the carer it is likely to be in breach of Working Time Directives. If the gross pay for the work period, divided by the total time available to provide care or be on-call, is less than the Minimum Wage level, it will fall foul of the minimum wage legislation.

Live-in Service

The carer will be available over a 24-hour cycle to help with personal care during the day, and to be on-call during the night. Rates for live-in services are subject to negotiation according to assessed needs and the level of dependency. Again, the European Working Time Directives and Minimum Wage legislation apply (see above).

Future Care Costs—inflation

When costing future care, it is helpful to note that between 1992 and 2002 the cost of agency care increased by an average of 4.8 per cent a year, during which time the Retail Price Index rose by 2.8 per cent a year and the Average Earnings Index rose by 4.9 per cent a year. (See pp.141 and 169).

General notes

1. Costs are inclusive of VAT, where applicable.
2. Night rates apply from 6 pm.
3. Public holiday rates apply on all statutory public holidays, from midnight to midnight.
4. For visits less than four hours a minimum charge may be repayable, as advised by your local branch.
5. Please give as much notice of cancellation as possible, as a fee is applicable for all confirmed bookings cancelled with 24 hours' notice or less.
6. If a BNA carer is directly employed by a patient within 12 months of the end of an assignment, BNA will charge an introduction fee.

CARERS

Hourly gross rates of pay (rates to March 24, 2002 are for central London)

Past Rates: April 1, 1994 – August 11, 2002

	Weekday	Weekend	Public holiday
April 1, 1994 – January 29, 1995	5.05	5.56	10.10
January 30, 1995 – January 27, 1996	5.20	5.72	10.40
January 28, 1996 – February 23, 1997	5.36	5.90	10.72
February 24, 1997 – February 1, 1998	5.55	6.66	11.10
February 2, 1998 – March 31, 1999	6.05	7.26	12.10
April 1, 1999 – November 22, 1999	6.73	8.08	13.46
November 23, 1999 – March 26, 2000	6.86	8.23	13.71
March 27, 2000 – February 25, 2001	7.10	8.52	14.19
February 26, 2001 – November 4, 2001	7.46	8.95	14.91
November 5, 2001 – March 24, 2002	7.61	9.13	15.22

March 25, 2002 – August 11, 2002		Weekday		Weekend		Public holiday	
		Input Rate (£)	Inclusive Cost to Client (£)	Input Rate (£)	Inclusive Cost to Client (£)	Input Rate (£)	Inclusive Cost to Client (£)
Marble Arch	per hour/day	7.84	12.32	9.40	14.79	15.68	24.66
	per hour/night	8.62	13.56	10.34	15.96	17.24	27.12
Cardiff	per hour/day	5.82	9.14	6.41	10.07	11.64	18.30
	per hour/night	6.41	10.07	7.05	11.08	12.80	20.13
Newcastle	per hour/day	5.41	8.51	5.95	9.36	10.82	17.00
	per hour/night	5.95	9.36	9.36	10.29	11.90	18.71

August 12, 2002 – April 1, 2004		Weekday		Weekend		Public holiday	
		Input Rate (£)	Inclusive Cost to Client (£)	Input Rate (£)	Inclusive Cost to Client (£)	Input Rate (£)	Inclusive Cost to Client (£)
Marble Arch	per hour/day	7.84	12.70	9.40	15.24	15.68	25.41
	per hour/night	8.62	13.98	10.34	16.78	17.24	27.94
Cardiff	per hour/day	6.23	10.11	6.86	11.11	12.46	20.19
	per hour/night	6.86	11.11	7.55	12.22	13.71	22.21
Newcastle	per hour/day	5.41	8.77	5.95	9.65	10.82	17.53
	per hour/night	5.95	9.65	6.55	10.60	11.90	19.28

April 1, 2004 →*		Weekday		Weekend		Public holiday	
		Input Rate (£)	Inclusive Cost to Client (£)	Input Rate (£)	Inclusive Cost to Client (£)	Input Rate (£)	Inclusive Cost to Client (£)
Marble Arch	per hour/day	8.14	13.94	9.75	16.71	16.28	27.88
	per hour/night	8.95	15.34	10.72	18.36	17.90	30.66
Cardiff	per hour/day	6.47	10.86	7.12	11.94	12.93	21.69
	per hour/night	7.12	11.94	7.83	13.13	14.22	23.84
Newcastle	per hour/day	5.62	9.46	6.17	10.38	11.23	18.89
	per hour/night	6.17	10.38	6.79	11.42	12.36	20.79

* We have been unable to obtain rates after April 1, 2004.

HOME HELPS AND COMPANIONS

Hourly gross rates of pay

Past Rates: April 1, 1994 – March 24, 2002

	Weekday	Weekend	Public holiday
April 1 1994 – January 29, 1995	4.55	5.01	9.10
January 30, 1995 – January 28, 1996	4.70	5.17	9.40
January 29, 1996 – February 23, 1997	4.86	5.35	9.72
February 24, 1997 – February 1, 1998	5.05	6.06	10.10
February 2, 1998 – September 30, 1998	5.55	6.66	11.10
October 1, 1998 – March 31, 1999	5.91	7.09	11.82
April 1, 1999 – November 22, 1999	6.23	7.48	12.46
November 23, 1999 – March 26, 2000	6.36	7.63	12.71
March 27, 2000 – February 25, 2001	6.55	7.86	13.09
February 26, 2001 – November 4, 2001	6.55	7.86	13.10
November 5, 2001 – March 24, 2002	6.88	8.02	13.36

March 25, 2002 – August 11, 2002		Weekday		Weekend		Public holiday	
		Input Rate (£)	Inclusive Cost to Client (£)	Input Rate (£)	Inclusive Cost to Client (£)	Input Rate (£)	Inclusive Cost to Client (£)
Marble Arch	per hour/day	6.88	12.49	8.26	14.99	13.76	24.98
	per hour/night	7.57	13.74	9.08	16.47	15.14	27.48
Newcastle	per hour/day	5.13	9.31	5.64	10.25	10.26	18.62
	per hour/night	5.64	10.25	6.21	11.27	11.29	20.49

August 12, 2002 – April 1, 2004		Weekday		Weekend		Public holiday	
		Input Rate (£)	Inclusive Cost to Client (£)	Input Rate (£)	Inclusive Cost to Client (£)	Input Rate (£)	Inclusive Cost to Client (£)
Marble Arch	per hour/day	6.88	12.88	8.26	15.45	13.76	25.73
	per hour/night	7.57	14.15	9.08	16.98	15.14	28.33
Newcastle	per hour/day	5.13	9.60	5.64	10.56	10.26	19.20
	per hour/night	5.64	10.56	6.21	11.61	11.29	21.11

April 1, 2004 →*		Weekday		Weekend		Public holiday	
		Input Rate (£)	Inclusive Cost to Client (£)	Input Rate (£)	Inclusive Cost to Client (£)	Input Rate (£)	Inclusive Cost to Client (£)
Marble Arch	per hour/day	8.14	13.94	9.75	16.71	16.28	27.88
	per hour/night	8.95	15.34	10.72	18.36	17.90	30.66
Cardiff	per hour/day	6.47	10.86	7.12	11.94	12.93	21.69
	per hour/night	7.12	11.94	7.83	13.13	13.22	23.84
Newcastle	per hour/day	5.56	10.18	6.41	11.74	10.45	19.14
	per hour/night	6.41	11.74	6.41	11.74	10.45	19.14

* We have been unable to obtain rates after April 1, 2004.

QUALIFIED NURSE – PERSONAL CARE

Past hourly gross rates of pay: April 1, 1994 – November 4, 2001

	Weekday	Weekend	Public holiday
April 1 1994 – January 29, 1995	7.13	7.84	14.26
January 30, 1995 – January 28, 1996	7.20	7.92	14.40
January 29, 1996 – February 23, 1997	7.42	8.16	14.84
February 24, 1997 – February 1, 1998	7.80	9.36	15.60
February 2, 1998 – September 30, 1998	8.47	10.16	16.94
October 1, 1998 – March 31, 1999	8.98	10.78	17.96
April 1, 1999 – November 22, 1999	10.33	12.39	20.66
November 23, 1999 – March 26, 2000	10.52	12.63	21.04
March 27, 2000 – February 25, 2001	11.10	13.32	22.20
February 26, 2001 – November 4, 2001	11.67	14.00	23.33

From November 5, 2001 – March 24, 2002		Weekday		Weekend		Public holiday	
		Input Rate (£)	Inclusive Cost to Client (£)	Input Rate (£)	Inclusive Cost to Client (£)	Input Rate (£)	Inclusive Cost to Client (£)
Marble Arch	per hour/day	11.90	16.23	14.28	19.47	23.80	35.45
	per hour/night	13.09	17.85	15.71	21.41	26.18	35.70
Cardiff	per hour/day	9.46	12.89	10.88	14.82	18.92	25.78
	per hour/night	10.41	14.18	11.97	16.31	20.81	28.36
Newcastle	per hour/day	8.37	11.41	12.56	17.12	16.74	22.82
	per hour/night	9.21	12.56	13.82	18.83	18.41	25.11

From March 25, 2002 – August 11, 2002		Weekday		Weekend		Public holiday	
		Input Rate (£)	Inclusive Cost to Client (£)	Input Rate (£)	Inclusive Cost to Client (£)	Input Rate (£)	Inclusive Cost to Client (£)
Marble Arch	per hour/day	12.26	16.88	14.71	20.25	24.51	33.75
	per hour/night	13.48	18.56	16.18	22.27	26.97	37.13
Cardiff	per hour/day	9.74	13.41	11.21	15.41	19.49	26.81
	per hour/night	10.72	14.75	12.33	16.96	21.43	29.49
Newcastle	per hour/day	8.62	11.87	12.94	17.80	17.24	23.73
	per hour/night	9.49	13.06	14.23	19.58	18.96	26.11

August 12, 2002 – April 1, 2004		Weekday		Weekend		Public holiday	
		Input Rate (£)	Inclusive Cost to Client (£)	Input Rate (£)	Inclusive Cost to Client (£)	Input Rate (£)	Inclusive Cost to Client (£)
Marble Arch	per hour/day	12.26	17.30	14.71	20.76	24.51	34.59
	per hour/night	13.48	19.02	16.18	22.83	26.97	38.06
Cardiff	per hour/day	10.50	14.81	11.55	16.28	20.99	29.60
	per hour/night	11.55	16.28	12.70	17.91	23.09	32.56
Newcastle	per hour/day	8.62	12.17	12.94	18.25	17.24	24.32
	per hour/night	9.49	13.39	14.23	20.07	18.96	26.76

April 1, 2004 →*		Weekday		Weekend		Public holiday	
		Input Rate (£)	Inclusive Cost to Client (£)	Input Rate (£)	Inclusive Cost to Client (£)	Input Rate (£)	Inclusive Cost to Client (£)
Marble Arch	per hour/day	12.75	18.59	15.30	22.32	25.49	37.17
	per hour/night	14.02	20.45	16.82	24.52	28.05	40.91
Cardiff	per hour/day	10.13	14.78	11.66	17.01	20.28	29.58
	per hour/night	11.16	16.27	12.44	18.14	22.28	32.50
Newcastle	per hour/day	9.50	13.86	14.26	20.81	19.01	27.72
	per hour/night	10.45	15.24	15.69	22.89	20.91	30.50

* We have been unable to obtain rates after April 1, 2004.

I2: Nannies, cleaners and school fees

The death or incapacity of a spouse frequently involves incurring the costs of a nanny, a cleaner or of sending a child to boarding school so that the surviving parent can continue working. Also, with some employments, typically when they involve overseas postings or frequent moves, school fees are part of the remuneration and will be lost if the employee dies or is disabled from that particular employment.

Nannies

The following table is for weekly wages for nannies in 2005.

	Daily		Live-in	
	Gross wage	Cost to client	Gross wage	Cost to client
Central London	£421.15	£581.19	£303.65	£419.04
Outer London/Home Counties	£339.42	£468.40	£251.10	£346.51
Other cities/towns	£285.77	£394.36	£215.29	£297.10
Rural areas	£267.21	£368.75	£204.88	£282.74

The figures are derived from the BBC website and from table G1. It is necessary to pay for holidays, employer's national insurance contribution, agency fees and so on. The inclusive cost to the client has been calculated on the same basis as in the BNA figures for nurses in table I1.

Cleaners

The services of cleaners in London are currently (April 2005) advertised at the following rates. These are for three or more hours a week; one-off visits usually cost more.

Anyclean	£8.00 per hour
MK Londyn	£8.00 per hour
Amycleaners	£8.47 per hour (decreasing to £7.27 depending on the number of hours)

Note: Table I1 contains BNA figures for home helps.

School fees

Typical annual school fees for a three-term year in 2004/5 are as follows.

	Public school	Private school (average)	Private school (range)
Boarders (Upper school)	£21,948	£12,525	£8,100–£14,500
Day pupils (Upper school)	£15,204	£ 6,399	£5,100–£ 7,200
Day pupils (Under school or preparatory school)	£10,563	£ 4,956	£4,100–£10,200

Notes
1. Fees for pupils entering in the sixth form may be higher.
2. Fees for weekly as opposed to full-time boarders may be lower.

The information has been obtained from Professional Nanny Survey and the websites of the BBC, Anyclean, MK Londyn, Amycleaners, money.msn and Westminster School.

13: DIY, Gardening and Housekeeping

1. Claimants are entitled to damages for the loss of the ability to do these tasks. Anyone who is responsible for the running of a house knows that there is a real cost in bringing in an electrician, tiler, carpenter, joiner, plumber or other skilled tradesmen to carry out tasks that they themselves cannot do. "The loss of ability to do work in the home is a recoverable head of damages and includes 'services' such as general housekeeping, gardening and maintenance".[1]

2. The same principle applies to loss of housekeeping skills. Claimants can be compensated for their inability to carry out the tasks which occur in most households—*e.g.* cleaning, shopping, laundry, ironing, cooking and washing up. Even sewing on buttons, cleaning the windows, and performing the mundane routines of daily existence, such as putting out the bins and dealing with the milkman, all have to be carried out by someone, though it is too easy to forget them.

3. The loss can be valued commercially, In *Phipps v Brooks Dry Cleaning Services*[2] Stuart-Smith LJ says that such skills have "a real money value", and Brandon J. in *Daly v General Steam Navigation Co. Ltd*[3] says "The loss occurred and the cost of employing someone else is no more than a way of measuring it".

4. The difficulty is always in finding an appropriate rate and working out a number of hours every week which such housekeeping tasks take to perform. Whether as a "jury award" or by using a multiplier/multiplicand approach, a judge is perfectly able to assess the evidence and make an award which reflects the reality of the loss to the claimant or the dependents. The courts have made a wide range of awards, which are analysed in Kemp & Kemp, 2004, Vol.1, Ch.17, where Simon Levene sets out such awards ranging, in 2004 values, from £21,948 downwards. In *Lawrence v Osborn*,[4] the defendant insurers accepted an annual rate of £750 pa as the standard figure for inability to perform DIY functions. In *Wells v Wells*,[5] the Court of Appeal accepted an award under this head of £1,000 pa. In *Dixon v Wene*,[6] Gross J. awarded £15,000 (a global sum), for loss of services: gardening and DIY.

5. Plainly, evidence is needed to support such a claim, photographs being an excellent addition to witness statement evidence. A report from a local surveyor and/or an independent agency can also strengthen this claim.

6. It should be borne in mind that often, as people get older, their appetite and energy for such tasks diminishes. This is not true for all, however; some 70 and 80 year olds seem to have an undiminished enthusiasm for these activities.

7. A Claimant need not prove an actual intention to employ replacement services (paid or unpaid). It is worth remembering the words of Bridge LJ in *Daly v General Steam Navigation Co*:[7] "It has been energetically argued by Mr. Bennett, for the defendants, that before future loss of capacity to undertake housekeeping duties can properly be assessed at the estimated cost of employing some third person to come in and do that which the plaintiff is unable to do for herself, the plaintiff has to satisfy the court that she has a firm intention in any event that such a person shall be employed. For my part, I am quite unable to see why that should be so. Once the judge had concluded, as this judge did, that, to put the plaintiff, so far as money could do so, in the position in which she would have been if she had never been injured, she was going to need, in the future,

[1] Damages for Personal Injury: Medical, Nursing and Other Expenses; Law Commission, Law Com No 262 (1999), para 2.34.
[2] [1996] PIQR Q 100.
[3] [1979] 1 Lloyds Rep. 257.
[4] (November 7, 1997), Anthony May J., QBD (unreported).
[5] [1997] 1 W.L.R. 652.
[6] [2004] EWHC 2273 (QB).
[7] [1981] WLR 120, 127.

domestic assistance for eight hours a week, it seems to me that it was entirely reasonable and entirely in accordance with principle in assessing damages, to say that the estimated cost of employing labour for that time, for an appropriate number of years having regard to the plaintiff's expectation of life, was the proper measure of her damages under this heading. It is really quite immaterial, in my judgment, whether having received those damages, the plaintiff chooses to alleviate her own housekeeping burden, which is an excessively heavy one, having regard to her considerable disability to undertake housekeeping tasks, by employing the labour which has been taken as the basis of the estimate on which damages have been awarded, or whether she chooses to continue to struggle with the housekeeping on her own and to spend the damages which have been awarded to her on other luxuries which she would otherwise be unable to afford".

14: BUPA hospital self pay (uninsured) charges

The following figures are inclusive of hospital charges and surgeons/anaesthetists fees. The charges are approximate, as certain factors affecting cost, such as length of stay or prosthesis used, vary from patient to patient.

Treatment	Cost
Arthrodesis	from £3,500
Arthroscopy	£1,700–£2,500
Hernia treatment	£1,500–£2,000
Investigation — CT — single system	from £578
Investigation — MRI — single investigation	from £706
Investigation — X-ray	from £75
Replacement — hip	£7,200–£9,000
Replacement — knee	£8,850–£10,200
Scar revision	£450–£2,000
Spine — discectomy — lumbar (including fusion)	from £4,880
Therapy — physiotherapy (hourly rate)	from £104
Outpatient consultation (consultant charge)	£130–£150

The following rates are approximate only, because the amounts allowable by private healthcare insurers can vary from hospital to hospital and from policy to policy. Further, doctors' own charges may vary. Nevertheless, the rates reflect a representative range of insurers, doctor and hospitals.

I5: NHS charges

NHS prescriptions (from April 1, 2005)

Charge per prescribed item	£6.50
Support stockings	£6.50 (each)
Support tights *available from hospitals only*	£13.00 (per pair)
Prescription prepayment certificate: 4 months	£33.90
12 months	£93.20

For items dispensed in combination (duo) packs, there is a charge for each different drug in the pack.

Sight tests (from April 1, 2005)

NHS sight test	£18.39
NHS sight test at home	£50.77
Private sight test	*ask your optician*
Private sight test at home	*ask your optician*
Hospital Eye Department sight test	*free*

NHS dental treatment (from April 1, 2005)

Those unable to claim free treatment or help with the cost pay 80 per cent of the cost of the treatment, up to a maximum of £360.

Basic examination	£5.84
Extensive clinical examination	£8.72
Simple scale and polish	from £9.20
Two small X-rays and one small filling	from £11.96
One large filling	from £18.24
A precious metal crown	from £92.28
A full set of plastic dentures	from £126.48
An upper or lower metal denture	from £111.44

NHS wigs and fabric supports

Stock modacrylic wig	£53.90
Partial wig — human hair	£142.30
Full bespoke wig — human hair	£208.10
Abdominal support	£33.00
Spinal support	£33.00
Surgical brassière	£21.80

I6: AA motoring costs (2005)

Petrol cars

	New car purchase price				
	Up to £10,000	£10,000 to £13,000	£13,000 to £20,000	£20,000 to £30,000	Over £30,000
Standing charges per annum (£)					
(a) Road tax	110.00	138.00	165.00	165.00	165.00
(b) Insurance	343.00	356.00	459.00	646.00	880.00
(c) Cost of capital	251.00	358.00	486.00	719.00	1,153.00
(d) Depreciation	1,050.00	1,570.00	2,133.00	3,095.00	5,218.00
(e) Breakdown cover	40.00	40.00	40.00	40.00	40.00
Total (£)	1,794.00	2,462.00	3,283.00	4,665.00	7,456.00
Standing charges per mile (in pence)					
5,000	35.54	48.82	65.02	92.24	147.52
10,000	17.94	24.62	32.83	46.65	74.56
15,000	12.23	16.84	22.49	32.06	51.15
20,000	9.44	13.00	17.38	24.90	39.68
25,000	7.66	10.57	14.16	20.32	32.34
30,000	6.41	8.85	11.85	17.04	27.11
Running costs per mile (in pence)					
(f) Petrol*	8.25	9.09	11.54	13.46	15.34
(g) Tyres	0.76	0.95	1.09	1.31	1.79
(h) Servicing labour costs	2.83	2.74	2.79	3.24	3.64
(i) Replacement parts	1.60	2.03	2.45	2.94	4.31
(j) Parking and Tolls	1.80	1.80	1.80	1.80	1.80
Total pence	15.24	16.61	19.67	22.75	26.88
* Unleaded petrol at 82.0 p/litre. For every penny more or less, add or subtract:	0.10	0.11	0.14	0.16	0.19

Total of standing and running costs (in pence) based on annual mileage of:

	Cost new (£)				
	Up to £10,000	£10,000 to £13,000	£13,000 to £20,000	£20,000 to £30,000	Over £30,000
5,000 miles	50.78	65.43	84.69	114.99	174.40
10,000 miles	33.18	41.23	52.50	69.40	101.44
15,000 miles	27.47	33.45	42.16	54.81	78.03
20,000 miles	24.67	29.61	37.05	47.65	66.56
25,000 miles	22.90	27.18	33.83	43.07	59.22
30,000 miles	21.65	25.46	31.52	39.79	53.99

Please see the associated notes for more detail. These figures are typical but do not represent all types of vehicle and conditions of use. The figures change from time to time.

Diesel cars

Standing charges per annum (£)	New car purchase price				
	Up to £10,000	£10,000 to £13,000	£13,000 to £20,000	£20,000 to £30,000	Over £30,000
(a) Road tax	165.00	165.00	165.00	165.00	165.00
(b) Insurance	343.00	356.00	459.00	646.00	880.00
(c) Cost of capital	268.00	345.00	475.00	728.00	1009.00
(d) Depreciation	1144.00	1647.00	2312.00	2929.00	4178.00
(e) Breakdown cover	40.00	40.00	40.00	40.00	40.00
Total (£)	1960.00	2553.00	3451.00	4508.00	6272.00
Standing charges per mile (in pence)					
5,000	38.78	50.62	68.38	88.92	124.06
10,000	19.60	25.53	34.51	45.08	62.72
15,000	13.36	17.37	23.60	31.27	43.17
20,000	10.30	13.34	18.18	24.44	33.46
25,000	8.37	10.82	14.76	20.00	27.25
30,000	7.01	9.05	12.34	16.78	22.82
Running costs per mile (in pence)					
(f) Diesel*	8.07	8.41	7.87	10.36	13.21
(g) Tyres	0.85	0.92	1.03	1.20	1.47
(h) Servicing labour costs	2.69	2.77	2.99	3.36	3.79
(i) Replacement parts	1.67	2.08	2.46	2.95	3.93
(j) Parking and Tolls	1.80	1.80	1.80	1.80	1.80
Total pence	15.08	15.98	16.15	19.67	24.20

* Diesel fuel at 82.8 p/litre.
For every penny more or less,

add or subtract:	0.09	0.10	0.09	0.12	0.15

Total of standing and running costs (in pence) based on annual mileage of:

	Cost new (£)				
	Up to £10,000	£10,000 to £13,000	£13,000 to £20,000	£20,000 to £30,000	Over £30,000
5,000 miles	53.86	66.60	84.53	108.59	148.26
10,000 miles	34.68	41.51	50.66	64.75	86.92
15,000 miles	28.44	33.35	39.75	50.94	67.37
20,000 miles	25.38	29.32	34.33	44.11	57.66
25,000 miles	23.44	26.80	30.91	39.67	51.45
30,000 miles	22.08	25.03	28.50	36.45	47.02

Road Tax Note:

Subtract £55 if the car was registered before March 2001 and the engine is less than 1549cc. This equals a saving of 1.1 pence per mile at 5,000 miles per year reducing down to 0.18 pence per mile at 30,000.

Notes to the AA tables:

The AA tables are published annually as a guide to the likely cost to the average private user to run a car. (In previous years tables were also produced for motorcycles and scooters). The figures given can only be a guide, as individual vehicles will vary: for instance fuel consumption will depend on traffic conditions and the type of journey, and repairs can be very unpredictable. The aim is to show a representative cost that reflects all the important items, so that the motorist can see how it all adds up. This should help make the most suitable choice of economical and environmentally less damaging transport.

Standing Charges   The basic costs you have to pay whether you use the car or not. They include the Road Tax (annual VED), insurance, the cost of the capital used for the vehicle, the loss of value of the vehicle or depreciation, and AA breakdown cover. They also include depreciation, which is affected by mileage. (The figure for depreciation in £ is based on 10,000 miles a year.)

Running Costs   The actual costs of using the car include petrol, oil, tyres, routine servicing and repairs and replacements. The effects of warranties are also taken into account.

Vehicle Groups   Cars are put into groups depending on the new car price, as this is a better guide to what it costs to run than for instance the engine size. Take the new car list price when it was first sold (including the main options supplied with the car) not the current list price. If in doubt, used car price-guides will give the original list prices.

Claiming Mileage   How much an employer pays for mileage is a matter for negotiation between them and the employees, as circumstances will vary. The Inland Revenue operates the Approved Mileage Allowance Payment (AMAP) system (in our Table I6)—further details from your local tax office or:
www.inlandrevenue.gov.uk/cars/using_own.htm and
www.inlandrevenue.gov.uk/cars/fuel_company_cars.htm
The figures given in our tables are VAT inclusive.

The AA Website   The Motoring Costs tables are also on the AA website at *www.theaa.com*
Here some of the data will be updated throughout the year, and there's an interactive version that can tailor the costs to an individual car model and, for instance, the actual insurance premium paid.

Road Tax   For cars registered after March 1, 2001 the rate of Vehicle Excise Duty depends on their fuel type and their emissions of carbon dioxide in the legislated Type Approval tests. Older cars will have one of two rates; the lower rate for cars with an engine capacity of less than 1549cc (in 2005–06, £110), the higher for larger engines (in 2005–06, £170). In the tables, averages for the price groups are used for the VED rate.

Insurance   The UK average cost for a comprehensive policy with a 60 per cent no-claims discount.

Cost of capital   This represents the loss of income from the owner's having money tied up in a vehicle, which could otherwise be earning interest in a deposit account, calculated at 3.75 per cent of the average value for the car cost group. Charges for loans or hire-purchase finance will be extra.

Depreciation   Cars lose value at different rates, depending on make, age, mileage and condition and even colour. Older cars will in general depreciate at a slower rate. These are broad averages for typical models, but there may be significant variations.

AA breakdown cover   For "Option 100" for an individual not paying by continuous payment.

Fuel cost   Based on the average UK price, but can be adjusted as required using the factors given. The fuel consumption figures taken are typical for each of the car bands listed.

Tyres   Based on a tyre life of 20,000 miles, varying with price band. Actual tyre life will vary with individual driving style.

Labour costs   Average cost for each price band of routine servicing as recommended by the manufacturer, taking a labour rate of £56 per hour (including VAT). Older cars may cost more.

Replacement parts   Routine repairs and replacements likely to be needed because of normal wear and tear. It is unrealistic to allow for major repairs due to unexpected electrical or mechanical failure.

Parking   Running costs include an allowance for parking and road tolls based on a national average. However, the sums paid could vary substantially according to patterns of use.

Editors' note:

1. The AA notes have been rearranged by us, with the AA's permission, in the interests of space.
2. Figures for the taxation of car and fuel benefits are at Table I6.
3. The Vehicle Excise Duty bands are as follows:

Band	CO_2 Emission (g/km)	Diesel Car £	Petrol Car £	Alternative Fuel Car £
Band A	Up to 100	75.00	65.00	55.00
Band B	101 to 120	85.00	75.00	65.00
Band C	121–150	115.00	105.00	95.00
Band D	151–165	135.00	125.00	115.00
Band E	166–185	160.00	150.00	140.00
Band F	Over 185	170.00	165.00	160.00

The CO_2 emission of a particular vehicle can be found at a website provided by the Vehicle Certification Agency (VCA): *www.vcacarfueldata.org.uk//ved_calculator.asp.*

I7: Taxation of car and fuel benefits

Car benefit 1990/91 to 1993/94

Year	Car (Manufacturer's list price and engine capacity)		Age of car at end of tax year	
			Under 4 years	4 years +
1990/91	Original market value up to £19,250	1,400cc or less 1,401cc–2,000cc More than 2,000cc	£1,700 2,200 3,550	£1,150 1,500 2,350
	Original market value up to £19,250; no cylinder capacity	Up to £5,999 £6,000–£8,499 £8,500–£19,249	1,700 2,200 3,550	1,150 1,500 2,350
	Original market value over £19,250	£19,250–£28,999 £29,000+	4,600 7,400	3,100 4,900
1991/92	Original market value up to £19,250	1,400cc or less 1,401cc–2,000cc More than 2,000cc	2,050 2,650 4,250	1,400 1,800 2,850
	Original market value up to £19,250; no cylinder capacity	Up to £5,999 £6,000–£8,499 £8,500–£19,249	2,050 2,650 4,250	1,400 1,800 2,850
	Original market value over £19,250	£19,250–£28,999 £29,000+	5,500 8,900	3,700 5,900
1992/93	Original market value up to £19,250	1,400cc or less 1,401cc–2,000cc More than 2,000cc	2,140 2,770 4,440	1,460 1,880 2,980
	Original market value up to £19,250; no cylinder capacity	Up to £5,999 £6,000–£8,499 £8,500–£19,249	2,140 2,770 4,440	1,460 1,880 2,980
	Original market value over £19,250	£19,250–£28,999 £29,000+	5,750 9,300	3,870 6,170
1993/94	Original market value up to £19,250	1,400cc or less 1,401cc–2,000cc More than 2,000cc	2,310 2,990 4,800	1,580 2,030 3,220
	Original market value up to £19,250; no cylinder capacity	Up to £5,999 £6,000–£8,499 £8,500–£19,249	2,310 2,990 4,800	1,580 2,030 3,220
	Original market value over £19,250	£19,250–£28,999 £29,000+	6,210 10,040	4,180 6,660

Notes: 1 If the business use is **less than 2,500 miles per annum**, multiply the figures by 1.5
2 If the business use is **more than 18,000 miles per annum**, divide the figures by 2

Car benefit 1994/95 to 2001/02

	Age of car at end of tax year	Business use of car (miles p.a.)					
		0–2,500		2,500–17,199		18,000+	
		One car	More than one car	One car	More than one car	One car	More than one car
1994/5 to 1998/9	Under 4 years old	35	35	23.33	35	11.67	23.33
	4 years or more	23.33	23.33	15.55	23.33	7.78	15.55
1999/00 to 2001/02	Under 4 years old	35	35	25	35	15	25
	4 years or more	26.25	26.25	18.75	26.25	11.25	18.75

Car benefit 2002/03 to 2005/06

CO$_2$ emissions (g/km)				Percentage of car's price taxed if car does not run solely on diesel (%)	Percentage of car's price taxed if car does run solely on diesel (%)
2002/03	2003/04	2004/05	2005/06		
165	155	145	140	15	18
170	160	150	145	16	19
175	165	155	150	17	20
180	170	160	155	18	21
185	175	165	160	19	22
190	180	170	165	20	23
195	185	175	170	21	24
200	190	180	175	22	25
205	195	185	180	23	26
210	200	190	185	24	27
215	205	195	190	25	28
220	210	200	195	26	29
225	215	205	200	27	30
230	220	210	205	28	31
235	225	215	210	29	32
240	230	220	215	30	33
245	235	225	220	31	34
250	240	230	225	32	35
255	245	235	230	33	35
260	250	240	235	34	35
265	255	245	240	35	35

Notes

1. From April 6, 2002, although the benefit of a company car is still to be calculated as a percentage of the price of the car (normally list price), the percentage is graduated according to carbon dioxide (CO$_2$) emissions and adjustments for business mileage and older cars no longer apply.
2. There are discounts for certain cleaner alternatively-propelled cars, which may reduce the minimum charge to below 15 per cent.
3. The diesel supplement and the discounts for cleaner alternatives apply only to cars first registered on January 1, 1998 or later.
4. Cars without an approved CO$_2$ emissions figure are taxed according to engine size. This will include all cars registered before 1998 but only a tiny proportion of those registered 1998 and later.
5. The exact CO$_2$ figure is rounded down to the nearest 5 grams per kilometre when using the above table.

Car fuel benefit – petrol – cash equivalent 1987/88 to 2002/03

| Year | Cylinder Capacity cc | | | | Year | Cylinder Capacity cc | | |
	0–1400	1401–2000	2001+			0–1400	1401–2000	2001+
1987/88–1991/92	480	600	900		1997/98	800	1,010	1,490
1992/93	500	630	940		1998/99	1,010	1,280	1,890
1993/94	600	760	1,130		1999/00	1,210	1,540	2,270
1994/95	640	810	1,200		2000/01	1,700	2,170	3,200
1995/96	670	850	1,260		2001/02	1,930	2,460	3,620
1996/97	710	890	1,320		2002/03	2,240	2,850	4,200

Notes

1. From 1987/88 to 1993/94, where there is no cylinder capacity,
   cars whose original market value is   Up to £5,999   £6,000–£8,499   £8,500+
   are treated as having a capacity of   0–1400   1401–2000   2001+
   respectively.
2. The original market value means the manufacturer's list price.
   The editors do not claim to understand how a car with an engine can have no engine capacity.

Car fuel benefit – diesel – cash equivalent 1991/92 and earlier to 2002/03

| Year | Cylinder Capacity cc | | | Year | Cylinder Capacity cc | |
	0–2,000	2,001+			0–2,000	2,001+
1991/92 and earlier	As petrol	As petrol		1997/98	740	940
1992/93	460	590		1998/99	1,280	1,890
1993/94	550	710		1999/00	1,540	2,270
1994/95	580	750		2000/01	2,170	3,200
1995/96	605	780		2001/02	2,460	3,620
1996/97	640	820		2002/03	2,850	4,200

(For the years up to and including 1992/93, divide the cash equivalent by 2 if the taxpayer drove more than 18,000 miles pa on business.)

Car fuel benefit – petrol and diesel – cash equivalent 2003/04 to 2005/06

Notes

1. From April 6, 2003, the car fuel benefit is, like the car benefit, linked directly to the CO_2 emissions of the company car.
2. There are the same diesel supplement and discounts for cleaner alternatively-propelled cars as there are in calculating the car benefit.
3. To calculate the car fuel benefit the percentage in the table used for calculating car benefit is multiplied against a set figure for the year. For 2003/04, 2004/05 and 2005/06 the set figure is £14,400. Thus, if the car benefit percentage is 23%, the fuel benefit would be £14,400 × 23% = £3,312.
4. For cars registered before January 1, 1998 and cars with no approved CO_2 emissions figure, the percentage to be applied is the same as that used to calculate the car benefit.

Fixed Profit Car Scheme – tax free rates in pence per mile 1990/91 to 2001/02

This applied when employers paid employees an allowance for using their own cars. The scheme was abolished with effect from April 6, 2002 and replaced by a system of mileage allowance payments applying equally for all cars. The tax-free mileage rates under the Fixed Profit Car Scheme are set out below.

Annual mileage cylinder capacity cc Year	Up to 4,000				4,0001 +			
	0–1000	1001–1500	1501–2000	2001+	0–1000	1001–1500	1501–2000	2001+
1990/91	24.5	30.0	34.0	43.0	9.5	11.5	13.5	16.5
1991/92	24.5	30.0	34.0	45.0	11.0	13.0	16.0	20.5
1992/93	25.0	30.0	38.0	51.0	14.0	17.0	21.0	27.0
1993/94	26.0	32.0	40.0	54.0	15.0	18.0	22.0	30.0
1994/95	27.0	33.0	41.0	56.0	15.0	19.0	23.0	31.0
1995/96	27.0	34.0	43.0	60.0	15.0	19.0	23.0	32.0
1996/97	27.0	34.0	43.0	61.0	16.0	19.0	23.0	33.0
1997/98	28.0	35.0	45.0	63.0	17.0	20.0	25.0	36.0
1998/99	28.0	35.0	45.0	63.0	17.0	20.0	25.0	36.0
1999/00	28.0	35.0	45.0	63.0	17.0	20.0	25.0	36.0
2000/01	28.0	35.0	45.0	63.0	17.0	20.0	25.0	36.0
2001/02	40.0	40.0	45.0	63.0	25.0	25.0	25.0	36.0

Authorised mileage allowance payments – tax-free rates in pence per mile 2002/03 to 2005/06

Annual mileage	Pence per mile
Up to 10,000	40p
10,001 +	25p

18: The Motability Scheme

Disabled people who need a motor vehicle may obtain one by utilising most if not all of the Higher Rate component of the Disability Living Allowance or the War Pensioner's Mobility Supplement. Motability is only available to those in receipt of either of these benefits who assign them to the Scheme for the duration of the contract. Because of the very wide range of physical and mental disabilities of those in receipt of them the Scheme does not require the person seeking to use it to be a driver: anyone in receipt of either allowance who is over three is entitled to use it. Under the Scheme there are three available options:

1. A new car can be obtained on a three-year hire lease contract.
2. A new, or used, car can be taken on hire purchase over two to five years.
3. A quadricycle can be obtained on a five-year lease (a quadricycle is a light steering three door vehicle that can be driven on a motorcycle licence).

A national network of some 3,500 dealers provides a wide range of suitably adapted new and used cars. In the case of option (1) (three-year contract hire), the Scheme requires a capital sum and a monthly payment which is provided for by the assignment of the relevant state benefit to the Scheme. As well as the adapted vehicle all maintenance is provided to include the cost of tyres, as is insurance for two named drivers who are over 25 and roadside recovery. Fuel, oil and other incidentals are the responsibility of the driver. There is a 45,000 mile limit on use over three years of the contract. Any mileage over that limit attracts a penalty of 10p per mile. At the end of the contract period the car reverts to the Scheme. In the case of option (2) (hire purchase) the Scheme provides only for the hire purchase of the vehicle, with any necessary adaptation, in return for a capital payment and the assignment of the relevant state benefit. It does not provide for maintenance, roadside recovery or insurance. There is no mileage restriction. At the end of the period the car belongs to the disabled person.

When costing care must be taken to distinguish between the three elements of any claim:

(i)   the capital cost of both purchase and adaptation which recur every three years;
(ii) the monthly running costs covered by the Motability Scheme;
(iii) the running costs not covered by the Scheme such as oil, petrol and car washes.

Not all cars are available and advice must be obtained as to whether what is available adequately meets the needs of the disabled person. When experts have recommended that a car be obtained under the Scheme practitioners should ensure that they are clear which option is being recommended and ensure that they compare like for like.

The condition precedent for using the Motability Scheme is that the beneficiary is in receipt of a state benefit which falls within the second Schedule of the Social Security (Recovery of Benefits) Act 1997. It is now clear, following *Eagle v Chambers (No.2)*,[1] that s.17 of the Act precludes a court from insisting that the mobility component of the Disabled Living Allowance should be used by any recipient to mitigate her loss. Henceforth no Defendant, can insist that a Claimant use the mobility allowance to participate in the Motability Scheme.

Further reading and assistance in specific cases can be obtained at:
www.motabilityonline.co.uk and Customer Services (0845) 456 4566.

---

[1] [2004] EWCA Civ 1033.

I9: Calculations involving motor cars

There are a number of commonly encountered calculations involving the cost of motor cars. This section contains tables and examples of calculations dealing with the following and should be read along with the table of AA motoring costs in section I5:

1. New car prices
2. Cost of future replacements
3. Cost of more frequent replacement
4. Cost of automatic cars
5. Cost of additional mileage

We have categorised cars as follows:

Mini:	Most cars under 1.1 litre, such as VW Lupo 1.0, Nissan Micra 1.0 etc.
Super mini:	Similar cars between 1.1 and 1.4, VW Polo 1.2, Fiesta 1.3
Small:	Cars of the smaller Ford Focus, VW Golf type, mostly 1.3–1.6
Medium:	The Ford Mondeo, VW Passat type, mostly cars from 1.6–1.9
Executive:	The larger Mondeo, Volvo S80 type, mostly 2.0–2.8 litre
Prestige:	The BMW 330i, Vauxhall Vectra 3.2, mostly 2.9–3.5 litre
Luxury:	The Jaguar XJ8 4.0, Audi S8 4.2, mostly over 3.5 litre and expensive
Estate, etc:	Self-explanatory

Notes:

1. The first table is intended to convey in broad terms the purchase costs of motor cars across a range of models. The material is taken from the May 2005 editions of *Parker's Car Price Guide* and *Parker's Car Chooser* with the kind permission of the publishers.

    The "New Price" is the recommended retail price (including VAT) according to the latest manufacturer's price list: all prices stated are "on the road" and include delivery charges, 12 months' road fund licence, number plates and £25 registration tax. "VED band" is the vehicle excise duty band.

2. Depreciation: Different cars, even produced by the same manufacturer, depreciate at different rates. As a model of car may change after a few years even if the same name is retained, losses over a long period cannot be calculated for individual models but only by reference to the general position.

3. Automatics: The comparison of manual and automatic cars is similarly a generalisation. The calculation for depreciation assumes that the new price of the automatic is *higher* than for the manual model. There is considerable variation, even among cars of similar type with similar new prices, in the rate at which the premium for the automatic version is eroded. With some cars the gap disappears very quickly: with some the premium for the automatic version is actually greater for used cars than for new ones.

4. Where the current new price of the manual and automatic versions is the same, which is often the case with expensive cars, the used automatic tends to retain its value *better* than the manual model. It may nevertheless have a higher fuel consumption but whether it will be more expensive overall may depend on the mileage.

1. New Car Prices

	New Price (£)		VED	Mileage
Mini	Manual	Automatic	band	adjustment
Citroën C2 1.1 L 3d	7,995	-	C	A
Nissan Micra 1.0 E 3d	7,895	-	C	A
Suzuki Alto 1.1 GL 5d	6,032	+ 700	C	A
Toyota Yaris 1.0 T2 3d	7,295	+ 500	C	A
Vauxhall Corsa 1.0i Expression 3d	6,995	+2,020	C	A
Volkswagen Lupo 1.0 E 3d	7,880	-	C	A
Super Mini				
Citroën C2 1.4i Furio 3d	9,495	+ 100	C	B
Ford Fiesta 1.5 Finesse 3d	8,595	-	C	A
Nissan Micra 1.4 SE 3d	9,650	+ 900	D	B
Rover 25 1.4iE (84PS) 3d	8,795	-	D	A
Suzuki Ignis 1.3 GL 3dr	7,546	+1,220	C	A
Vauxhall Corsa 1.2i Design 3d	10,300	+ 150	C	A
Volkswagen Polo 1.2 S 65 3d	9,755		C	B
Small				
Citroën Xsara Picasso 1.6i Desire 5d	14,295	-	D	B
Ford Focus 1.6i Zetec 5d	13,695	+ 320	D	C
Honda Civic 1.4i SE 5d	12,600	+ 880	D	C
Nissan Almera 1.5 SE 5d	11,600	-	D	C
Renault Megane 1.4 16v Dyn 5d	12,730	-	D	C
Rover 25 1.6 SEi 5d	12,795	+ 100	D	B
Vauxhall Astra 1.6i Club 16v 5d	13,795	+ 450	E	B
Volkswagen Golf 1.6 S FSI 5d	14,360	+1,150	D	D
Medium				
BMW 320i 4d	22,750	+ 100	E	G
Citroën C5 2.0i VTR 16v 5d	16,495	+3,300	F	C
Ford Mondeo 1.8 LX 4d	15,585	-	E	D
Nissan Primera 1.8i S 5d	14,850	+ 940	E	C
Renault Laguna 1.8 16v Dyn 5d	16,475	+ 990	E	D
Rover 75 1.8i Classic 4d	16,395	+1,200	E	C
Vauxhall Vectra 1.8 Elite 5d	20,020	+ 730	D	E
Volkswagen Passat 1.8T SE 4d	17,285	+ 80	F	E
Volvo S40 1.6 S Classic 4d	15,298	-	E	D
Executive				
BMW 520i SE 4d	26,100	+1,350	F	G, H
Honda Accord 2.0i VTEC Executive 4d	19,100	+ 90	E	H
Rover 75 2.5 V6 Connoisseur SE 4d	23,895	+1,200	F	D
Saab 9-3 2.0t 4d Linear	20,830	+ 100	F	F
Volkswagen Passat 2.5 V6 TDi 4d	22,230	+ 820	F	G
Volvo S80 2.4 S (170 bhp) 4d	22,913	+1,100	F	F
Prestige				
Audi Quattro A4 3.0 TDi 4d	26,670	+1,400	F	H
BMW 330i SE 4d	28,250	+1,150	F	G
Jaguar X 3.0 V6 SE 4d	29,140	+1,250	F	G
Mercedes-Benz E320 Elegance Auto 4d	-	35,110	F	H
Saab 9-5 3.0t V6 Vector Auto 4d	25,705	-	F	H
Vauxhall Vectra 3.2 V6 Elite 4d	22,120	+1,300	F	E
Volvo S80 2.9 SE 4d	-	28,593	F	G

Luxury	New Price (£)		VED band	Mileage adjustment
	Manual	Automatic		
Audi Quattro A8 4.2 Tip Auto 4d	-	55,975	F	H
BMW 545I SE 4d	42,350	+ 910	F	H
Jaguar S 4.2 V8 SE Auto 4d	-	37,495	F	H
Mercedes-Benz E500 Elegance 4d	-	45,220	F	H
Estate				
Citroën C5 1.8i 16v LX 5d	16,095	-	F	D
Ford Mondeo Estate 2.0 V6 Ghia X	21,480	+1,000	F	F
Honda HR-V 1.6i 4WD 5d	15,100	+ 400	F	E
Nissan Primera 1.8 S 5d	17,100	-	E	D
Saab 9-5 2.0t Linear 5d	21,830	+1,300	F	G
Vauxhall Vectra 2.2 Elite 5d	21,620	+1,300	F	-
Volkswagen Passat 2.5 V6 5d	23,445	+ 560	F	G
4 × 4				
Isuzu Trooper 3.0 Duty 5d	21,772	+1,250	F	F
Land Rover Freelander 1.8 SE St/Wagon 5d	20,995	-	F	F
Nissan Patrol 3.0 Di S 5d	24,850	+6,900	F	G
Volkswagen Touareg 2.5 V6 Tdi	30,325	+1,440	F	-
People carriers				
Chrysler Grand Voyager 3.3 LE Auto 5d	-	30,460	F	H
Fiat Ulysse 2.0 Dynamic 5d	17,595	+3,000	F	E
Ford Galaxy 2.3 Ghia 7-seat 5d	22,615	+1,200	F	F
Land Rover Discovery 4.4 V8i S 5d	-	37,995	F	-
Mitsubishi Grandis 2.4 Equippe MIVEC 5d	20,499	+1,000	F	-
Renault Espace 2.0t 16v Expr 5d	22,445	+1,500	F	F
Toyota Landcruiser 3.0 D-4D LC3 5d	28,495	+ 560	F	H
Vauxhall Zafira 2.0 DTi Energy 5d	17,345	-	?	C?D

2. Cost of future replacements

Table 1 below has representative trade-in values of used *manual* cars expressed as a proportion of the *current* new price (calculated from material in *Parker's Car Price Guide*). Automatic cars may depreciate faster. Where the new price of an automatic car is *higher* than that of the corresponding manual car, there is a tendency for the automatic to depreciate by about 1 per cent more (altogether, not per year).

Table 1 Trade-in values of used manual cars

Age of car	Residual value	Loss of value	Equivalent annual depreciation
1	0.64	0.36	0.360
2	0.50	0.50	0.256
3	0.41	0.59	0.204
4	0.36	0.64	0.168
5	0.33	0.67	0.143
Adjustment for automatics	− 0.01	+ 0.01	

The table can be used to calculate the future net costs of replacements where replacements will be second hand as well as where they will be new.

Example 1: The claimant is 54 and needs a people carrier such as a Chrysler Grand Voyager 3.3 LE 7-seat Auto 5d, automatic version. He will need to replace it every 4 years, the final replacement being when he is 70. He would not otherwise have had a car (or the car is additional to whatever vehicle would have been bought in any event).

Initial price of people carrier (from Table 18, above)		30,460.00
Proportion of price lost at each replacement (Table 1 above, + 0.01)	0.65	
Cost of each replacement	0.65 × 30,460 = 19,799.00	
Multiplier for 16 years (Table A3, 2.5%, 4-yearly)	3.14	
Cost of future replacements	3.14 × 19,799.00 =	62,168.86
Total		£92,628.86

Example 2: The same claimant currently runs a manual Volvo S80 2.4 S (£22,913) and will replace it with the Chrysler people carrier. The additional cost is the future cost of the Chryslers *minus* the corresponding figure saved on Volvos. (If either both cars are manual or both automatic the calculation is simpler.)

Initial price of Volvo saved (from Table 18, above)		22,913.00
Proportion of price saved at each replacement (Table 1 above, manual)	0.64	
Cost of each replacement	0.64 × 22,913 = 14,662.32	
Multiplier for 16 years (Table A3, 2.5%, 4-yearly)	3.14	
Cost of future replacements saved	3.14 × 14,662.32 =	46,019.68
Total saved		68,932.68
Net future cost of Chryslers instead of Volvos (92,628.86 − 68,932.68)		= £23,696.18

3. Cost of more frequent replacement

A claimant is sometimes advised that because of his condition he needs a more reliable car and should therefore replace it more often than he needed to do before his injury. Table 2, which is derived from Table 1, shows the additional annual cost, expressed as a proportion of the new price. Find the row corresponding to the new interval in years and the column corresponding to the old interval.

Note that the table expresses the multiplier as an *annual* cost, not the cost *on each exchange*. Thus in row 2, column 4, the figure 0.088 means that the additional expense of replacing a car every two years, instead of every four years, is 8.8 per cent of the price of the car per year for however long the claimant continues to drive.

Table 2 Multipliers for additional annual cost of replacing car more frequently

		Old interval in years				
		1	2	3	4	5
	1	0	0.104	0.156	0.192	0.217
New	2		0	0.052	0.088	0.113
interval	3			0	0.036	0.061
in	4				0	0.025
years	5					0

Example: The claimant is 40 and drives a car currently costing £11,995 new. She has just bought one. She can continue to drive a similar car, with modifications. She has been advised that because of her disability she should now change it every 3 years rather than every 5 as she has until now. She should stop driving at about 73, so the last change will be at about age 70.

Multiplier for additional annual cost from table above		
– new frequency 3 years, old frequency 5 years	0.061	
Multiplier for woman of 40 until age 70 (Ogden table 28, at 2.5%)	20.55	
Multiplier for additional cost of more frequent replacement	0.061 × 20.55 = 1.25	
Current cost of car	11,995.00	
Additional cost of replacing car more frequently until age 70	<u>14,993.75</u>	

4. Cost of automatic cars

A claimant's injuries sometimes make it necessary for him to have an automatic car which he would not otherwise have needed. Generally this involves additional costs in three respects: the automatic car is more expensive to buy, is more expensive to run; and it tends to depreciate faster than the corresponding manual model (but see the notes in the introduction).

Table 3 Added cost of automatic cars

	Mini and Super mini	Small	Medium and Executive	Prestige and Luxury	Estate, 4 × 4 and MPV
Added cost of new car (in £)	850	1,075	1,145	1,275	1,245

Table 4 Added cost of petrol

	Mini and Super mini	Small	Medium and Executive	Prestige and Luxury
(in pence per mile) Petrol at 79.0p/litre	2.03	1.04	0.86	0.29
For every penny more or less add or subtract	0.030	0.015	0.012	0.004

Greater depreciation

Where the new price of an automatic model of a car is *higher* than that of the corresponding manual car, there is a tendency for the automatic to depreciate by about 1 per cent more (altogether, not per year) — see Table 1 above. Thus:

New manual model	£11,000	3 year old manual	11,000 × 0.41 = £4,510
New automatic	£12,000	3 year old automatic	12,000 × 0.40 = £4,800

Example: The claimant drives a manual car of medium type whose price new is about £16,000. He drives about 10,000 miles a year and changes his car every 3 years. Because of his injury he now needs an automatic. He is likely to stop driving in about 30 years.

Extra cost of automatic car:
On first purchase (from Table 3 column 3 above):   £1,145.00

Cost at each replacement of automatic (Table 1 row 3): £17,145 × 0.60 = 10,293.00
less cost at each replacement of manual £16,000 × 0.59   = 9,440.00
Additional cost at each replacement   853.00
Multiplier for replacements (Table A3 at 2.5%, 27 years, 3-yearly)   6.33   5,399.49

Extra cost per mile, petrol at 78 p/litre = 0.86 − (1.0 × 0.012) =   0.85
Extra running cost 10,000 miles pa   85.00
Multiplier for running costs (Table A3 at 2.5%, 30 yrs continuous)   21.19   1,801.15
Total extra cost: £8,345.64

5. Cost of additional mileage

The AA figures for *running* costs at Table I5 do not include depreciation. Mileage reduces the value of a car by a factor which varies with the type of car and its age on resale. Age on resale is not necessarily the length of time the claimant had the car. The categories A, B, C etc are derived from *Parker's Car Price Guide*.

Table 5 Adjustment for depreciation for extra mileage

Age on resale	PETROL			Depreciation in pence per mile				
	A	B	C	D	E	F	G	H
2	2.56	3.06	4.06	4.56	5.56	6.56	7.63	10.63
3	2.06	2.56	3.13	4.06	4.63	5.63	6.63	9.63
4	1.56	2.06	2.56	3.13	3.63	4.63	5.63	7.75
5	1.06	1.56	2.06	2.56	3.06	3.63	4.63	6.63
6	1.00	1.06	1.56	2.06	2.56	3.06	3.63	5.63

Example: The claimant would have had a car anyway. His mileage is increased by 4,000 miles a year because of his injury. He buys a one year old and changes at three years old costing about £14,000 in category B in the mileage adjustment table. Petrol costs 81 pence per litre.

Running cost per mile from AA figures (Table I5)   19.67 pence
Adjustment for petrol price from table I5 (−1.0 × 0.14)   −0.14
Adjustment for mileage (small, 3 years old)   2.56
Total per mile   22.09 pence
Total annual cost (4,000 × 22.09)   £883.60

Based on figures in *Parker's Car Price Guide* and *Parker's Car Chooser* and from the websites of the *Vehicle Certification Agency* and the *United States Department of Transportation*.

I10: The Rehabilitation Code

(Code of Best Practice on Rehabilitation, Early Intervention and Medical Treatment in Personal Injury Claims)

The main aim of this Code, first introduced in 1999, is to promote the use of rehabilitation and early intervention in the claims process so that the injured person makes the best and quickest possible medical, social and psychological recovery. This objective applies whatever the severity of the injury sustained by the claimant. The Code provides a framework supported by all the main associations for insurers and personal injury lawyers in the UK, but is neither compulsory nor the only way to approach rehabilitation. The objectives of the Rehabilitation Code will be met whenever the parties co-operate to assess and then provide for the claimant's rehabilitation needs.

1. INTRODUCTION

1.1 It is recognised that, in many claims for damages for personal injuries, the claimant's current medical situation, and/or the long-term prognosis, may be improved by appropriate medical treatment, including surgery (referred to in this document as "medical treatment"), being given at the earliest practicable opportunity, rather than after the claim has been settled. Similarly, claims may involve a need for non-medical treatment, such as physiotherapy, counselling, occupational therapy, speech therapy and so forth ("rehabilitation"): again, there is a benefit in these services being provided as early as practicable.

1.2 It is also recognised that (predominantly in cases of serious injury) the claimant's quality of life can be immediately improved by undertaking some basic home adaptations and/or by the provision of aids and equipment and/or appropriate medical treatment as soon as these are needed ("early intervention"), rather than when the claim is finally settled.

1.3 It is further recognised that, where these medical or other issues have been dealt with, there may be employment issues that can be addressed for the benefit of the claimant, to enable the claimant to keep his/her existing job, to obtain alternative suitable employment with the same employer or to retrain for new employment. Again, if these needs are addressed at the proper time, the claimant's quality of life and long-term prospects may be greatly improved.

1.4 Solicitors acting for claimants understand that, taking all these matters into account, they can achieve more for the claimant—by making rehabilitation available—than just the payment of compensation. The insurance industry realises that great benefit may be had in considering making funds available for these purposes.

1.5 The aim of this Rehabilitation Code is therefore to ensure that the claimant's solicitor and the insurer (and the insurer's solicitor or handling agent) both actively consider the use of rehabilitation services and the benefits of an early assessment of the claimant's needs. The further aim is that both should treat the possibility of improving the claimant's quality of life and their present and long-term physical and mental well-being as issues equally as important as the payment of just, full and proper compensation.

1.6 The report mentioned in s.6 of the Code focuses on the early assessment of the claimant's needs in terms of treatment and/or rehabilitation. The assessment report is not intended to determine the claimant's long-term needs for care or medical treatment, other than by way of general indication and comment.

2. THE CLAIMANT'S SOLICITOR'S DUTY

2.1 It shall be the duty of every claimant's solicitor to consider, from the earliest practicable stage, and in consultation with the claimant and/or the claimant's family, whether it is likely or possible that early intervention, rehabilitation or medical treatment would improve their present and/or long-term physical or mental well-being. This duty is ongoing throughout the life of the case but is of most importance in the early stages.

2.2 It shall be the duty of a claimant's solicitor to consider, with the claimant and/or the claimant's family, whether there is an immediate need for aids, adaptations or other matters that would seek to alleviate problems caused by disability, and then to communicate with the insurer as soon as practicable about any rehabilitation needs, with a view to putting this Code into effect.

2.3 It shall not be the responsibility of the solicitor to decide on the need for treatment or rehabilitation or to arrange such matters without appropriate medical consultation. Such medical consultation should involve the claimant and/or the claimant's family, the claimant's primary care physician and, where appropriate, any other medical practitioner currently treating the claimant.

2.4 Nothing in this Code of Practice shall in any way affect the obligations placed on a claimant's solicitor by the Personal Injury Pre Action Protocol. However, it must be appreciated that very early communication with the insurer will enable the matters dealt with here to be addressed more effectively.

2.5 It must be recognised that the insurer will need to receive from the claimant's solicitor sufficient information for the insurer to make a proper decision about the need for intervention, rehabilitation or treatment. To this extent, the claimant's solicitor must comply with the requirements of the Pre Action Protocol to provide the insurer with full and adequate details of the injuries sustained by the claimant, the nature and extent of any, or any likely, continuing disability and any suggestions that may already have been made concerning rehabilitation and/or early intervention. There is no requirement under the Pre Action Protocol, or this Code, for the claimant's solicitor to have obtained a full medical report. It is recognised that many cases will be identified for consideration under this Code before medical evidence has actually been commissioned.

3. THE INSURER

3.1 It shall be the duty of the insurer to consider, from the earliest practicable stage in any appropriate case, whether it is likely that the claimant will benefit in the immediate, medium or longer term from further medical treatment, rehabilitation or early intervention. This duty is ongoing throughout the life of the case but is of most importance in the early stages.

3.2 If the insurer considers that a particular claim might be suitable for intervention, rehabilitation or treatment, the insurer will communicate this to the claimant's solicitor as soon as practicable.

3.3 On receipt of such communication, the claimant's solicitor will immediately discuss these issues with the claimant and/or the claimant's family pursuant to his duty as set out above and, where appropriate, will seek advice from the claimant's treating physicians/surgeons.

3.4 Nothing in this or any other Code of Practice shall in any way modify the obligations of the insurer under the Pre Action Protocol to investigate claims rapidly and in any event within three months (except where time is extended by the claimant's solicitor) from the date of the formal claim letter. It is recognised that, although the rehabilitation assessment can be done even where liability investigations are outstanding, it is essential that such investigations proceed with the appropriate speed.

4. ASSESSMENT

4.1 Unless the need for intervention, rehabilitation or treatment has already been identified and disclosed by medical reports obtained by either side, the need for and extent of such intervention, rehabilitation or treatment will be considered by means of an independent assessment.

4.2 "Independent assessment" in this context means that the assessment will be carried out neither:

a.   by one or more/Some or all of the treating physicians/surgeons; or
b.   by an agency suitably qualified and/or experienced in such matters, which is financially and managerially independent of the claimant's solicitor's firm and the insurers dealing with the claim.

4.3 It is essential that the process of assessment and recommendation be carried out by appropriately qualified specialists/experts (including physiotherapists, occupational therapists, psychologists and psychotherapists). It would be inappropriate for assessments to be done by someone who does not have a medical or other appropriate qualification. Those doing the assessments should not only have an appropriate qualification but should have experience in treating the type of disability from which the individual claimant suffers.

5. THE ASSESSMENT PROCESS

5.1 Where possible, the agency to be instructed to provide the assessment should be agreed between the claimant's solicitor and the insurer. The instruction letter will be sent by the claimant's solicitor to the medical agency and a copy of the instruction letter will be sent to the insurer.

5.2 The medical agency will be asked to interview the claimant at home (or in hospital, if the claimant is still hospitalised, with a subsequent visit to the claimant's home) and will be asked to produce a report, which covers the following issues:

1.   The injuries sustained by the claimant
2.   The claimant's present medical condition (medical conditions that do not arise from the accident should also be noted where relevant to the overall picture of the claimant's needs)
3.   The claimant's domestic circumstances (including mobility, accommodation and employment), where relevant
4.   The injuries/disability in respect of which early intervention or early rehabilitation is suggested
5.   The type of intervention or treatment envisaged
6.   The likely cost
7.   The likely short/medium-term benefit to the claimant.

5.3 The report will not deal with diagnostic criteria, causation issues or long-term care requirements.

6. THE ASSESSMENT REPORT

6.1 The reporting agency will, on completion of the report, send a copy of the report to both the instructing solicitor and the insurer simultaneously. Both parties will have the right to raise queries on the report, disclosing such correspondence to the other party.

6.2 It is recognised that for this independent assessment report to be of benefit to the parties, it should be prepared and used wholly outside the litigation process. Neither side can therefore rely on its contents in any subsequent litigation. With that strict proviso, to be confirmed in writing by the individual solicitor and insurer if required, the report shall be disclosed to both parties.

6.3 The report, any correspondence relating to it and any notes created by the assessing agency will be covered by legal privilege and will not under any circumstances be disclosed in any legal proceedings. Any notes or documents created in connection with the assessment process will not be disclosed in any litigation, and any person involved in the preparation of the report or involved in the assessment process shall not be a compellable witness at court.

6.4 The provision in para.6.3 above as to treating the report, etc. as outside the litigation process is limited to the assessment report and any notes relating to it. Once the parties have agreed, following an assessment report, that a regime of rehabilitation or treatment should be put in place, the case management of that regime falls outside this Code and para.6.3 does not therefore apply. Any notes and reports created during the subsequent case management will be governed by the usual principles relating to disclosure of documents and medical records relating to the claimant.

6.5 The insurer will pay for the report within 28 days of receipt.

6.6 The need for any further or subsequent assessment shall be agreed between the claimant's solicitor and the insurer. The provisions of this Code shall apply to such assessments.

7. RECOMMENDATIONS

7.1 When the assessment report is disclosed to the insurer, the insurer will be under a duty to consider the recommendations made and the extent to which funds will be made available to implement all or some of the recommendations. The insurer will not be required to pay for intervention or treatment that is unreasonable in nature, content or cost. The claimant will be under no obligation to undergo intervention, medical investigation or treatment that is unreasonable in all the circumstances of the case.

7.2 Any funds made available shall be treated as an interim payment on account of damages. However, if the funds are provided to enable specific intervention, rehabilitation or treatment to occur, the insurers warrant that they will not, in any legal proceedings connected with the claim, dispute the reasonableness of that treatment nor the agreed cost, provided of course that the claimant has had the recommended treatment.

8. UPDATING THE GUIDE TO REHABILITATION

8.1 In the previous bodily injury study, we published a simple Guide, mainly for the benefit of claims practitioners and personal injury lawyers. It outlines the main specialist skills that may be needed in the rehabilitation process, why and when they should be used, and an indication of likely cost.

8.2 The Guide does not provide a list of care providers. The organisation that created the Guide, the Bodily Injury Claims Management Association (BICMA), plans to put such a list on its website (*www.bicma.org.uk*) later in 2003.

8.3 BICMA has been a pioneer of immediate needs assessment and rehabilitation since 1995. Its members include insurance and reinsurance representatives, and claimant and defence lawyers. It was instrumental in the setting up of the Case Management Society of the UK.

8.4 Like the Code, the Guide has been reviewed in the light of experience. Although it has stood the test of time, there has been a series of minor modifications to bring the document up-to-date and into line with new developments. the main difference in the updated Guide is the greater recognition given to Case Management and the Case Management Society of the UK.

8.5 The Guide takes the reader from the start of the process and an immediate needs assessment, through many of the stages that are likely to be appropriate. It includes:

- Assessing the personal circumstances and needs of the claimant and his/her family;
- The use of case managers;
- Monitoring medical rehabilitation and, if necessary, providing multi-disciplinary assessment;
- Liaising with the Department of Social Security and claiming appropriate benefits;
- Liaising with the local authority and obtaining interim support prior to an assessment under the Community Care Act, reviewing such assessment and negotiating the provision of services and financial assistance from the local authority;
- Arranging for therapies;
- Monitoring the needs of the claimant's family and arranging for respite care, if necessary;
- Training the claimant and his/her family in the employment of carers, and assisting in the provision of carers;
- Facilitating employment rehabilitation.

8.6 The Guide has been drawn up by experienced practitioners, who have given generously and freely of their time. Nonetheless, it does not seek to create hard and fast rules. How a case is handled is ultimately the responsibility of the individuals concerned.

I11: Rehabilitation: a Practitioner's Guide

Compiled by the Bodily Injury Claims Management Association

Norman W Cottington The Injury Care Clinics (President)
David Blofeld, past Claims Manager, Hart Re
Christopher Crook, Solicitor, Edwards Duthie
Tony Goff, Solicitor, George Ide Phillips
Graham Plumb, Claims Manager, AXA Insurance
Keith O. Popperwell, Solicitor Silverbeck Rymer
Bernard Rowe, Solicitor, Lyons Davidson (Treasurer)
Martin Saunders, Alliance Cornhill Insurance
Martin Staples, Solicitor, Vizards
Janet Tilley, Solicitor, Colemans CTTS (Secretary)
Ian Walker, Solicitor, Russell Jones and Walker (Vice President)

CONTENTS

1. CASE MANAGEMENT

One of the first decisions to make is who will manage the rehabilitative process. The various specialist disciplines are outlined below. The task of organising so many disciplines may seem daunting, but help can be found.

One way is to use a case manager to act as case co-ordinator.

The appointment of a case manager at an early stage in the claim will need to be discussed and preferably agreed with the claimant and the insurer. A case manager must have close contact with the claimant and his/her family.

A case manager must have the time available to deal with the claimant and preferably be based close to the claimant.

Case managers can come from a variety of disciplines, but look for someone trained and committed to the standards laid down by the Case Management Society of the UK (CMSUK).

There are a number of specialist case management organisations in the UK, although the number of claimants is likely to outweigh the availability of specialists for some time to come.

A case manager will co-ordinate all of the available services and should be required as appropriate to:

- Assess the personal circumstances and needs of the claimant and his/her family;
- Monitor medical rehabilitation and, if necessary, provide for multi-disciplinary assessment;
- Liaise with the DSS and claim appropriate benefits;

- Liaise with the local authority for interim support prior to a statutory assessment (currently Community Care Act 1990); review such assessment and negotiate the provision of services and financial assistance from the local authority;
- Arrange for therapies;
- Monitor the needs of the claimant's family and arrange for respite care, if necessary;
- Assist the claimant in obtaining training and monitoring carers;
- Facilitate employment rehabilitation;
- Arrange appropriate accommodation;
- Review personal transport arrangements;
- Consider mobility issues;
- Consider funding arrangements for rehabilitation.

Cost

Following an initial assessment, case management will normally be charged on an hourly basis (expect to pay between £65 and £85 per hour). Input by a case manager should reduce once rehabilitation needs have been addressed.

2. IMMEDIATE NEEDS ASSESSMENT

Why?

Rehabilitation in the long term will be difficult, if not impossible, if short-term needs are overlooked. "First Aid" support is essential to overcome the immediate aftermath of an injury and to provide a platform on which to build long-term rehabilitation.

At What Level?

As a rule of thumb, an immediate needs assessment is applicable to claimants who have sustained injuries likely to cause incapacity for several months or longer.

When?

The assessment should be done as soon as possible, even before discharge from hospital, with a view to ensuring the home environment to which the claimant will be discharged is suitable at least for the basic needs of the claimant and his/her family. However, an assessment undertaken years after the event of the injury can still help.

What to Expect

The report should provide preliminary background information about the claimant's circumstances, including the following:

a. The nature and extent of the injury;
b. Any relevant medical background;
c. Family circumstances;
d. Immediate home adaptation needs;
e. Steps to improve the claimant's quality of life and support for family carers;
f. How, and at what cost, recommendations can be implemented.

Relatively simple and inexpensive measures can make a big difference, for example, stair handrails, ramps for wheelchair access, raised toilet seats, widened doorways, lowered light switches or doorknobs.

Recommendations should be capable of being put into immediate effect and at proportionate, reasonable cost.

Do not confuse an immediate needs assessment with long-term care needs and costs, which will be addressed by appropriate experts in the claim.

By Whom?

A case manager trained and committed to the standards laid down by the Case Management Society of the UK (CMSUK) is the most obvious choice.

An occupational therapist or anyone with a social care background, for example, a community care nurse, a social worker or a general practitioner, may similarly be able to conduct the assessment.

Cost

The Code requires that the insurer be responsible for the cost.

The charge will depend upon the complexity of the report and travel expenses, but expect to pay between £750 and £1,750.

The defendant's insurer should usually fund reasonable recommendations by way of an interim payment (see section 7 of the Code).

Liability

Only a complete denial of liability should prevent a defendant's insurer from considering an immediate needs assessment (but also consider an assessment via Social Services).

If the dispute is confined to contributory negligence, the comparatively low cost of an assessment will be justified.

3. EMOTIONAL AND PSYCHOLOGICAL CARE

Why?

Anyone who has suffered a serious injury has experienced a major life event. The injured person, his/her family and close friends will be totally unprepared for either the injury or what follows.

Those who have suffered a serious injury will need to come to terms with what has happened to them. There may also be psychological disorders triggered by the accident, which must be recognised and dealt with. Failure to do so may prevent other treatments from being effective and may hinder a return to work.

Emotional, and in many cases psychological, support needs to be given to help the claimant and those upon whom he/she depends.

When?

Support should be offered as soon as possible. Often this will be determined by the willingness of the injured claimant and/or his/her family to accept outside help. Many people are frightened by their feelings or by the idea of sharing them with someone. Proper counselling can also be of great assistance to relatives acting as carers.

An early assessment can in itself help identify problems or potential problems in time to prevent prolonged post-traumatic stress disorder.

An assessment and, where needed, counselling or psychological treatment are best considered soon after the injury and/or return home from hospital (*i.e.* within the first three months of injury). The need for emotional and psychological support may last much longer than the medical treatment.

By Whom?

Clinical psychologists should normally carry out an initial assessment. If there is any suggestion of brain injury, then a neuropsychologist should be used.

It is useful to check first whether the claimant's hospital team has already involved a psychologist to help with rehabilitation or whether there is a facility within the GP's practice.

Arrangements should be made with a clinical psychologist close to the claimant's home. Where necessary, appointments can be arranged at the claimant's home, which is important if the claimant is distressed by travel.

There are a number of agencies that have panels of psychologists available or you can contact the British Psychological Society at St. Andrew's House, 48 Princess Road East, Leicester LE1 7DR or by telephone on 0116 254 9568.

What to Expect

Most assessments involve some psychological testing. This is necessary to determine what help is needed. Better insight and understanding by the claimant and/or his/her family of what to expect of themselves and their feelings will help to achieve maximum recovery.

Cost

A clinical psychologist's assessment and recommendations will cost between £200 and £500.

A neuropsychologist's assessment will cost between £750 and £1,750.

Psychological therapy costs between £75 and £150 per session.

4. PHYSIOTHERAPY, OSTEOPATHY AND CHIROPRACTIC

Why?

Early mobilisation following injury is now widely recognised as an important part of treatment and needs to be encouraged, provided that it is consistent with medical advice. Damaged tissue needs careful handling. Injury victims need to be shown how to regain movement and function as soon as possible. Whilst treatment methods vary amongst the different professions, these all work towards maximising useful function and can help prevent an injury from becoming a permanent disability.

When?

In the case of serious injuries, this type of treatment is normally determined by the hospital medical team. After discharge from hospital, it is all too easy to overlook the benefit to be gained from continuing physiotherapy and other treatments. Treatment is not just about relieving pain, but equally about achieving the best possible recovery of movement, strength and function. In the case of soft tissue injuries, treatment should be assessed as soon as possible, i.e. within a few weeks, not months, of the injury. In more serious cases, initial treatment should be considered as part of the overall medical management of the patient. After discharge, treatment should be considered as part of the overall nursing plan or by direct referral to a practitioner.

By Whom?

This type of treatment is provided by chartered physiotherapists, osteopaths or chiropractors. Increasingly, it is possible to find that two or more of these disciplines are offered at the same clinic. There are a number of specialist agencies that will provide and co-ordinate treatment. Details of local practitioners can also be found in the Yellow Pages. Alternatively, information is available from:

- Chartered Society of Physiotherapists   0207 306 6666
- General Council of Osteopaths   0207 357 6655
- British Association of Chiropractic   0118 950 5950

What to Expect

Make sure the practitioner is a member of a relevant professional body and that there are well-equipped treatment rooms. All practitioners will want to assess the patient before offering treatment. The assessment may involve x-rays as well as a physical examination.

If treatment is offered, a treatment plan should be prepared that identifies the number of treatments and when they are to be given. Often a patient will be taught exercises to help speed up the recovery process.

Cost

The cost will vary from clinic to clinic. Average costs for an assessment will be in the order of £40 to £60. Treatment is likely to cost in the order of £30 to £45 per session depending upon locality.

5. ACCOMMODATION

Why?

A secure, comfortable and accessible home is likely to be a prerequisite for any home-based rehabilitation plan. Accommodation that was suitable for a claimant before an injury may be unsuitable after injury.

When?

Assessment of accommodation needs should be undertaken as soon as possible. For many patients, the only obstacle to being discharged from hospital is their inability to access their own home.

The need for substantial adaptations to accommodation or even a purpose-built property is normally a long-term consideration. Permanent arrangements are best dealt with when it is reasonably clear what the long-term requirements will be.

Physical needs will be identified in medical, occupational therapist and nursing reports.

Short-term needs are as important a consideration as long-term needs. Short term may, in fact, mean several months or even longer. Immediate needs may have been dealt with under an immediate needs report, but this will need to be updated.

By Whom?

A case manager or occupational therapist may be able to advise upon minor alterations that are needed until permanent needs become clear. Once these needs have been identified, a good local builder will be able to carry out minor works such as installing rails, ramps and widening doorways.

If major alterations are needed, a report will be required from an accommodation expert, usually a surveyor or architect, and preferably one with experience of designing accommodation for use by people with disabilities. Whoever carries out the assessment should be familiar with and liaise with the local authority, from which grants may be available. This is particularly relevant in cases where damages may be reduced as a result of an apportionment of liability.

What to Expect

A visit to the claimant's home or proposed home, after consideration of the medical and other reports. This will lead to a report detailing the physical requirements of the property that are necessary in order for the claimant to maximise his/her potential for independent living. In addition, it will take into account the possibility that a carer might need accommodation.

The report should detail the work needed, together with costs, including likely maintenance and/or replacement costs.

Cost

The cost of this report will vary from case to case. Hourly charge-out rates will be in the order of £100 to £150 per hour. A detailed report is likely to cost £1,000 or more.

6. NURSING, CARE AND EQUIPMENT

Why?

The objective will be to establish the most beneficial regime, aimed at ensuring the health and welfare of the injured person, and optimising independence and self-esteem by the most cost-effective means.

When?

It is important to establish in advance what arrangements will be beneficial at each stage of the recovery process, and not address each stage as it occurs. At each stage, it is vital that the case manager, or those reporting, are fully aware of the current medical prognosis, including any anticipated changes.

By Whom?

The appointed case manager is likely to be the best choice, as they often possess all the relevant experience. The person chosen must have an understanding of the medical and physical needs of the claimant, and how to provide for them. Not all nursing/care experts may deal with aids and equipment. Separate advice may be needed from an occupational therapist.

What to Expect

The expert will need to see all existing reports and it may be beneficial for the different disciplines to confer.

The expert will need to speak to the claimant and his/her family and carers as well as those responsible for medical treatment. The report should address:

- The injured person's capacity for coping with the challenges of his/her injury and impairment;
- Existing care, by whom and in what environment;
- External features impacting on the situation, e.g. accommodation, social contact, locality and family dynamics;
- The level of nursing care required;
- Vulnerabilities—health and safety issues for the claimant and his/her carers at present and in the future;
- The need for an enabler;
- The need for domestic assistance;
- Details of equipment needed;
- Detailed cost of recommendations and suggested providers;
- Objectives and their timescales.

Cost

This will depend upon the circumstances and the complexity of each case. Reports will cost from £1,000. Hourly charging rates are likely to range from £65 to £90 per hour, but could possibly be higher.

7. SOCIAL SERVICES

Social services are provided pursuant to the National Health Service Community Care Act 1990 by local authorities' Social Services departments, which are entitled to call upon:

- Health Authorities; and
- Housing Departments

The trigger for support is an assessment by the local authority pursuant to Section 47 of the NHS and Community Care Act 1990. The right to an assessment is absolute.

Once an assessment has been carried out, a written copy must be provided to the Social Services department. A complaints and review procedure is available if the assessment is considered unsatisfactory.

Following assessment, the local authority will make a decision about whether to provide services and the type of services to be provided.

Social services available include:

- Home helps or carers;
- Respite breaks for carers;
- Laundry service;
- Therapies;
- Odd job scheme;
- Rehabilitation;
- Carer support;
- Residential care;
- Transport;
- Housing adaptation;
- Provision of accommodation suitable to the claimant's needs.

The provision of services may be dependent upon the resources of the local authority. Each local authority publishes eligibility criteria. Certain services must be provided under a legal duty. Other services may be provided on a discretionary basis, but there is no duty to do so.

Section 2 of the Chronically Sick and Disabled Persons Act sets out services that must be supplied as a legal duty:

- Home help;
- Provision of radio, television, library or residential services;
- Home adaptations for greater safety, comfort or convenience;
- Holidays;
- Meals;
- Telephone.

The local authority will formulate a case plan, which will be administered by a case manager. This will specify all needs, including those that cannot be met due to budge restraints.

Local authorities are empowered to make direct cash payments to disabled persons so that they can purchase care services for themselves (Community Care (Direct Payments) Act 1996). In addition, cash payments are available from Independent Living Funds and from the DSS.

If the claimant needs suitable accommodation, the local authority has a duty to provide this pursuant to Section 21 of the National Assistance Act.

Residential care can be arranged by both local authorities and health authorities. Provision of residential care by a health authority is free, but DSS benefits are treated as if the claimant were in hospital. Local authority residential care is subject to means testing. Residential care includes the provision of basic accommodation.

A claimant can choose his/her preferred accommodation and can ask a third party (e.g. an insurer or tortfeasor) to meet any shortfall if the cost is more than the local authority would normally pay.

If a local authority provides services free of charge, a claimant cannot make a claim against the insurer in respect of such services.

A local authority has discretion to charge for services other than residential care.

The right to charge for services is subject to a two-stage test:

1.   Whether it is reasonable in all the circumstances;
2.   Whether the claimant has sufficient means to pay for the services.

Where residential accommodation is provided by a local authority, there is a duty to charge, subject to means testing.

However, such charges can be avoided by the creation of a trust or if the damages are administered by the court (see Preservation of Benefits below).

8. SOCIAL SECURITY BENEFITS

Aim
To maximise benefits and to preserve the right to means-tested benefits.

Non Means-Tested Benefits
There are four main groups of non means-tested benefits that are payable as a consequence of disability:

1.   Incapacity for Work
     Incapacity Benefit
     Severe Disablement Allowance

2.   Care and Supervision
     Disability Living Allowance
     Care Component
     Constant Attendance Allowance

3.   Mobility
     DLA Mobility Component

4.   Degree of Disablement
     Severe Disablement Allowance
     Industrial Disablement Benefit

Income Support
This is paid to the claimant if he/she is incapable of working, and to a carer if regularly and substantially engaged in caring for another person.

If the claimant has capital in excess of £8,000.00 (or £16,000.00 if in residential care), he/she does not qualify for income support.

Disability Working Allowance
This is intended to encourage people with disabilities to return to work. It is paid to people who work 16 hours or more per week. If a claimant (or his/her partner) has capital of more than £16,000, the claimant does not qualify for this allowance.

Disability Living Allowance
The DLA is not means-tested.

This allowance comprises a care component and a mobility component. The care component is for personal care needs and is paid at three different rates. The mobility component is paid at two different rates.

Tests are administered by an Adjudication Officer.

Receipt of the DLA acts as a gateway to the following benefits:

- Disability Premium;
- Severe Disability Premium;
- Independent Living Funds;
- Motability Scheme.

Industrial Injuries Benefit

This benefit is paid to those who are disabled by a loss of physical and mental capacity caused by an industrial accident or disease.

It is paid in addition to any other non means-tested benefit.

Incapacity Benefit

This is paid to those who are unable to work due to disability. It is non means-tested, but it is only payable if sufficient national insurance contributions (NIC) have been made.

Severe Disablement Allowance

This allowance is paid for 28 weeks to those who are incapable of working but have made insufficient NIC to qualify for the incapacity benefit.

How to Claim

Benefit is generally paid from the date a claim is received by a DSS Office.

There is discretion to accept anything in writing "as sufficient" in the circumstances of a particular case.

The DLA is paid from the date a claim form is requested, so long as the claim form is returned within six weeks.

Income support is paid from the date of notifying the DSS, so long as the claim form is returned within one month. There is discretion to extend time limits in some cases.

Claims should be made to a local DSS Office or by telephoning the Benefit Enquiry Line on 0800 882200.

Appeals are made to the local DSS Office. An appeal can be made within three months of any decision. There is some discretion to extend the time limit up to six years, but it is difficult to make a late appeal.

The Effect of Receipt of Damages on Income-Related Benefits

Lump sum payments of compensation are treated as capital and are added to any other capital that the claimant may have. The effect is that:

- A claimant or partner may have up to £8,000.00 (£16,000.00 if in residential care) in capital and benefit will not be affected;
- Deductions are made on a sliding scale in Income Support, DLA, Housing Benefit and Council Tax Benefit, depending on the amount of capital;
- Income support is not payable where there is capital in excess of £8,000.00 (or £16,000 if in residential care);
- No Housing Benefit, Council Tax Benefit or DLA is payable if capital exceeds £16,000.

Preservation of Benefits

Benefits paid to a claimant can be managed by creating a trust or ensuring the damages fund is administered by the court.

Trusts

The trust may be set up by the claimant or someone acting on behalf of the claimant. If a trust is created:

- The capital value of the trust fund is wholly disregarded;
- Payments from the trust fund to the claimant or on his/her behalf will be treated as income or capital, depending on frequency of payment and the terms of the trust;
- Regular discretionary payments will be disregarded, provided they are used for needs other than those intended to be covered by benefits.

Funds Administered by the Court

A decision of the Social Security Commissioner (1996 3J.S.S.L.D. 136) makes it clear that money in the Court of Protection should not be taken into account for entitlement to Income Support under the terms of Paragraph 12 to Schedule 120 of the Income Support (General) Regulations (as amended).

9. MOBILITY

Why?

Restricted mobility emphasises impairment and threatens independence. Mobility contributes toward independence.

When?

Immediate thought should be given to mobility within the home, which is often effectively achieved by simple steps such as providing ramps and widening doorways for wheelchair users.

Longer-term projects, such as specialised wheelchairs or appropriate motor vehicles, may have to await medical recovery.

What to Expect?

A driving assessment can identify and address any barriers to independent driving ability, and can identify aids, adaptations or controls required to overcome those barriers.

The Disability Living centres identify and cost aids and equipment to mobility and dexterity.

By Whom?

Personal mobility can be assessed by an occupational therapist.

Disability Living centres exhibit and assist in identifying appropriate aids, including wheelchairs, vehicles and prosthetic appliances.

Driving Assessment centres can assist in determining the right choice of vehicle and wheelchair.

The claimant or his/her family can apply to the DSS for a Mobility Allowance and/or payment under the Motability Scheme to defray the cost of a vehicle.

Disabled living experts, usually architects, can advise on property alterations to ensure ease of access.

Cost

A driving assessment is unlikely to cost £50 to £100 or more, at a mobility centre.

The Disability Living centres provide their services at no cost, although the equipment they recommend can cost anything from a few pounds for a wide-handled toothbrush to more than £1,000 for a suitable wheelchair.

10. VOCATIONAL

Why?

A return to work is more likely to raise a claimant's self-esteem than anything else. It provides independence and self-respect.

When?

A claimant should be helped to return to work, if appropriate, as soon as possible.

It is vital to:

a. Take early steps to consider, with the involvement of the employer, the preservation of the claimant's pre-accident job, by adapting the workplace or duties in accordance with the Disability Discrimination Act 1997;

b. If remaining with the pre-accident employer is not possible, then consider all alternative avenues.

Insurers may be willing to fund the necessary steps to achieve these goals.

By Whom?

A vocational or employment rehabilitation expert should assess the claimant's suitability to return to work and his/her requirements.

A vocational report should not be confused with the reports commonly commissioned from employment consultants. The latter are generally designed to assist in the quantification of loss, whereas the former is intended to identify the injured person's potential and motivation for employment, and to recommend how to achieve a return to suitable work. The expert should know the local area and sympathetic employers, whilst having a good working relationship with the Disability Employment Advisor.

What to Expect

A detailed interview should be undertaken to identify the claimant's former work experience abilities and qualifications, his/her aspirations, and a general assessment of his/her current physical and mental ability.

The next stage should, ideally, be a meeting between the vocational assessor and the previous employer with a view to identifying whether re-employment is possible, either in full or reduced capacity; whether other placements may be available; and/or whether adaptations to the work place may be necessary to facilitate such employment.

If employment with the pre-accident employer is not possible for whatever reason, then consideration will be given to other suitable local job opportunities.

If no such opportunities exist, a more detailed vocational assessment, carried out over a period of one week, may be recommended.

There are numerous facilities nationwide where such assessments can take place either on a day or residential basis. Assessments take place in a working environment and measure dexterity, co-ordination, ability, communication skills, confidence and motivation. Speed, ability and quality of work is recorded, assessed and reported upon.

Following assessment, recommendations may include finding a work placement properly suited to the claimant's skills and abilities or sending the claimant on a training scheme to learn new skills. Another possibility is for the claimant to be supported by a trainer or friend, who would work alongside him/her in a work placement until confidence is gained in employment skills.

A return to some form of remunerative employment is the most effective way an injured person can regain his/her self-esteem and achieve an improved quality of life.

Cost

This will vary depending upon the type of assessment and the time it takes. Expect charges of £750 to £1,500 for a vocational interview and report. More detailed assessments will cost more. A residential five-day assessment is likely to cost £2,000 or more.

Case Management—the early days

As health care options, delivery methods and financing mechanisms became more complex, with inconsistent incentives and accountability, the need for assistance in obtaining timely and appropriate care to achieve recovery and optimal functioning has become increasingly evident.

The first Case Management Society was established in America in 1990 (CMSA) after recognition of the need for a supportive body for this rapidly expanding profession. In 1996, the Case Management Society International was established to provide an umbrella for global affiliation. Canada, Australia, South Africa and a number of European countries already have their own case management societies.

In response to this growth in case management, an informal group of care professionals involved in case management practice started meeting during 2000 to explore the possibility of a national, non-profit, professional membership association for case managers.

About CMSUK

The overall goals and ambitions are to:

- Advise on the development of a professional case management qualification;
- Develop and encourage consistent professional standards of best practice, competence, service and conduct of case managers;
- Provide comprehensive continuing education programmes;
- Provide support for its members;
- Instil confidence for purchasers when employing the services of a CMSUK member;
- Development of case managers within existing public/private health and social environment;
- One of our main aims is to be affiliated with and accredited by the main professional bodies that currently register practising case managers.

With evolving care structures, CMSUK will play an integral part in setting and upholding standards to ensure that cost-effective and timely outcomes are achieved.

If you would like to know more about CMSUK, please write to: CMSUK 100 Fetter Lane London EC4A 1BN Email *cmsukltd@yahoo.co.uk*

I12: Conversion formulae

	To convert	Multiply by
Area	Square inches to square centimetres	6.452
	Square centimetres to square inches	0.1555
	Square metres to square feet	10.7638
	Square feet to square metres	0.0929
	Square yards to square metres	0.8361
	Square metres to square yards	1.196
	Square miles to square kilometres	2.590
	Square kilometres to square miles	0.3861
	Acres to hectares	0.4047
	Hectares to acres	2.471
Length	Inches to centimetres	2.540
	Centimetres to inches	0.3937
	Feet to metres	0.3048
	Metres to feet	3.281
	Yards to metres	0.9144
	Metres to yards	1.094
	Miles to kilometres	1.609
	Kilometres to miles	0.6214
Temperature	Centigrade to Fahrenheit	$\times 9 \div 5 + 32$
	Fahrenheit to Centigrade	$-32 \times 5 \div 9$
Volume	Cubic inches to cubic centimetres	16.39
	Cubic centimetres to cubic inches	0.06102
	Cubic feet to cubic metres	0.02832
	Cubic metres to cubic feet	35.31
	Cubic yards to cubic metres	0.7646
	Cubic metres to cubic yards	1.308
	Cubic inches to litres	0.01639
	Litres to cubic inches	61.024
	Gallon to litres	4.545
	Litres to gallons	0.22

	To convert		Multiply by
Weight	Grains to grams		0.0647
	Grams to grains		15.43
	Ounces to grams		28.35
	Grams to ounces		0.03527
	Pounds to grams		453.592
	Grams to pounds		0.0022
	Pounds to kilograms		0.4536
	Kilograms to pounds		2.2046
	Tons to kilograms		1016.05
	Kilograms to tons		0.0009842
Speed	Miles per hour to kilometres per hour		1.6093
	Kilometres per hour to miles per hour		0.6214
Fuel cost	Pence per litre to pounds per gallon		0.045
	Pounds per gallon to pence per litre		22.00
USA measures	Dry	USA pint to UK pint	0.9689
		UK pint to USA pint	1.1032
		USA pint to litres	0.5506
		Litres to USA pint	1.816
		USA bushel to UK bushel	0.9689
		UK bushel to USA bushel	1.032
		USA bushel to litres	35.238
		Litres to USA bushel	0.0283
	Liquid	USA pint (16 fl oz) to UK pint	0.8327
		UK pint to USA pint	1.2
		USA pint to litres	0.4732
		Litres to USA pint	2.113
		USA gallon to UK gallon	0.8327
		UK gallon to USA gallon	1.2
		USA gallon to litres	3.7853
		Litres to USA gallons	0.2641

Clothing

Shirts

UK/USA	14	$14\frac{1}{2}$	15	$15\frac{1}{2}$	16	$16\frac{1}{2}$	17	$17\frac{1}{2}$
Europe	36	37	38	39	40	41	42	43

Ladies clothes

UK

Size code	10	12	14	16	18	20	22
Bust/hip inches	32/34	34/36	36/38	38/40	40/42	42/44	44/46
Bust/hip cm	84/89	88/93	92/97	97/102	102/107	107/112	112/117

USA

Size code	10	12	14	16	18	20	22
Bust/hip inches	33/35	$34\frac{1}{2}/36\frac{1}{2}$	$37\frac{1}{2}/39\frac{1}{2}$	$37\frac{1}{2}/39\frac{1}{2}$	39/41	41/43	44/45

European sizes vary from country to country

Footwear – Men

British	6	7	8	9	10	11	12
American	$6\frac{1}{2}$	$7\frac{1}{2}$	$8\frac{1}{2}$	$9\frac{1}{2}$	$10\frac{1}{2}$	$11\frac{1}{2}$	$12\frac{1}{2}$
Continental	40	41	42	43	44	45	46

Footwear – Women

British	3	4	5	6	7	8	9
American	$4\frac{1}{2}$	$5\frac{1}{2}$	$6\frac{1}{2}$	$7\frac{1}{2}$	$8\frac{1}{2}$	$9\frac{1}{2}$	$10\frac{1}{2}$
Continental	36	37	38	39	40	41	41

Children's clothes

UK

Age	1	2	3	4	5	6	7	8	9	10	11	12
Height/inches	32	36	38	40	43	45	48	50	53	55	58	60
Height/cm	80	92	98	104	110	116	122	128	134	140	146	152

USA

Boys' size code	1	2	3	4	5	6	8		10		12	
Girls' size code	2	3	4	5	6	6x	7	8	10		12	

Europe

Height/cm	80	92	98	104	110	116	122	128	134	140	146	152

Table of speeds and distances

Speeds				Distances in yards																			
mph	km/h	yd/sec	m/sec	5	10	15	20	25	30	40	50	60	75	100	125	150	175	200	225	250	300	400	500
5	8.0	2.44	2.24	2.0	4.1	6.1	8.2	10.2	12.3	16.4	20.5	24.5	30.7	4.09	51.1	61.4	71.6	81.8	92.0	102.3	122.7	163.6	204.5
10	16.1	4.89	4.47	1.0	2.0	3.1	4.1	5.1	6.1	8.2	10.2	12.3	15.3	20.5	25.6	30.7	35.8	40.9	46.0	51.1	61.4	81.8	102.3
15	24.1	7.33	6.71	0.7	1.4	2.0	2.7	3.4	4.1	5.5	6.8	8.2	10.2	13.6	17.0	20.5	23.9	27.3	30.7	34.1	40.9	54.5	68.2
20	32.2	9.78	8.94	0.5	1.0	1.5	2.0	2.6	3.1	4.1	5.1	6.1	7.7	10.2	12.8	15.3	17.9	20.5	23.0	25.6	30.7	40.9	51.1
25	40.2	12.22	11.18	0.4	0.8	1.2	1.6	2.0	2.5	3.3	4.1	4.9	6.1	8.2	10.2	12.3	14.3	16.4	18.4	20.5	24.5	32.7	40.9
30	48.3	14.67	13.41	0.3	0.7	1.0	1.4	1.7	2.0	2.7	3.4	4.1	5.1	6.8	8.5	10.2	11.9	13.6	15.3	17.0	20.5	27.3	34.1
35	56.3	17.11	15.65	0.3	0.6	0.9	1.2	1.5	1.8	2.3	2.9	3.5	4.4	5.8	7.3	8.8	10.2	11.7	13.1	14.6	17.5	23.4	29.2
40	64.4	19.56	17.88	0.3	0.5	0.8	1.0	1.3	1.5	2.0	2.6	3.1	3.8	5.1	6.4	7.7	8.9	10.2	11.5	12.8	15.3	20.5	25.6
45	72.4	22.00	20.12	0.2	0.5	0.7	0.9	1.1	1.4	1.8	2.3	2.7	3.4	4.5	5.7	6.8	8.0	9.1	10.2	11.4	13.6	18.2	22.7
50	80.5	24.44	22.35	0.2	0.4	0.6	0.8	1.0	1.2	1.6	2.0	2.5	3.1	4.1	5.1	6.1	7.2	8.2	9.2	10.2	12.3	16.4	20.5
60	96.6	29.33	26.82	0.2	0.3	0.5	0.7	0.9	1.0	1.4	1.7	2.0	2.6	3.4	4.3	5.1	6.0	6.8	7.7	8.5	10.2	13.6	17.0
70	112.7	34.22	31.29	0.1	0.3	0.4	0.6	0.7	0.9	1.2	1.5	1.8	2.2	2.9	3.7	4.4	5.1	5.8	6.6	7.3	8.8	11.7	14.6
80	128.7	39.11	35.76	0.1	0.3	0.4	0.5	0.6	0.8	1.0	1.3	1.5	1.9	2.6	3.2	3.8	4.5	5.1	5.8	6.4	7.7	10.2	12.8
90	144.8	44.00	40.23	0.1	0.2	0.3	0.5	0.6	0.7	0.9	1.1	1.4	1.7	2.3	2.8	3.4	4.0	4.5	5.1	5.7	6.8	9.1	11.4
100	160.9	48.89	44.70	0.1	0.2	0.3	0.4	0.5	0.6	0.8	1.0	1.2	1.5	2.0	2.6	3.1	3.6	4.1	4.6	5.1	6.1	8.2	10.2

Seconds

Notes:

1. The table shows the time taken to cover a given distance at a given speed, to the nearest $\frac{1}{10}$ second.

2. The table can also be used to ascertain the approximate speed of a vehicle, if the time and distance are known.

3. As an example, to find how long it would take to cover 125 yards at 35 mph, follow the vertical column down from the figure 125 and follow the horizontal row across from the figure 35: they meet at the figure 7.3, which is the number of seconds taken to cover the distance.

4. A speed of z miles per hour approximately equals [0.5z] yards per second.

5. The general formula for the number of seconds to cover a given distance at a given speed is approximately:

$$\frac{\text{distance in yards} \times 2.04545}{\text{speed in miles per hour}}$$

Typical Stopping Distances (average car length = 4 metres)

Speed (mph)	Thinking Distance (metres)	Braking Distance (metres)	Total Stopping Distance (metres)	(car lengths)
20	6	6	12	3
30	9	14	23	6
40	12	24	36	9
50	15	38	53	13
60	18	55	73	18
70	21	75	96	24

Extracted from The Highway Code, published by the Stationery Office.

I13: Perpetual calendar

The number opposite each of the years in the list below indicates which of the calendars on the following pages is the one for that year. Thus the number opposite 2000 is 14, so calendar 14 can be used as a 2000 calendar.

Leap years

Years divisible by four without remainder are leap years with 366 days instead of 365 (29 days in February instead of 28). However the last year of the century is not a leap year except when divisible by 400.

Easter Sunday

These dates apply unless there is a change to a fixed Easter.

Year	Date	Year	Date	Year	Date
1990	15 April	1997	30 March	2004	11 April
1991	31 March	1998	12 April	2005	27 March
1992	19 April	1999	4 April	2006	16 April
1993	11 April	2000	23 April	2007	8 April
1994	3 April	2001	15 April	2008	23 March
1995	16 April	2002	31 March	2009	12 April
1996	7 April	2003	20 April	2010	4 April

Year	Calendar	Year	Calendar	Year	Calendar	Year	Calendar	Year	Calendar	Year	Calendar
1980	10	1992	11	2004	12	2016	13	2028	14	2040	8
1981	5	1993	6	2005	7	2017	1	2029	2	2041	3
1982	6	1994	7	2006	1	2018	2	2030	3	2042	4
1983	7	1995	1	2007	2	2019	3	2031	4	2043	5
1984	8	1996	9	2008	10	2020	11	2032	12	2044	13
1985	3	1997	4	2009	5	2021	6	2033	7	2045	1
1986	4	1998	5	2010	6	2022	7	2034	1	2046	2
1987	5	1999	6	2011	7	2023	1	2035	2	2047	3
1988	13	2000	14	2012	8	2024	9	2036	10	2048	11
1989	1	2001	2	2013	3	2025	4	2037	5	2049	6
1990	2	2002	3	2014	4	2026	5	2038	6	2050	7
1991	3	2003	4	2015	5	2027	6	2039	7		

1

	January	February	March	April
M	2 9 16 23 30	6 13 20 27	6 13 20 27	3 10 17 24
T	3 10 17 24 31	7 14 21 28	7 14 21 28	4 11 18 25
W	4 11 18 25	1 8 15 22	1 8 15 22 29	5 12 19 26
T	5 12 19 26	2 9 16 23	2 9 16 23 30	6 13 20 27
F	6 13 20 27	3 10 17 24	3 10 17 24 31	7 14 21 28
S	7 14 21 28	4 11 18 25	4 11 18 25	1 8 15 22 29
S	1 8 15 22 29	5 12 19 26	5 12 19 26	2 9 16 23 30

	May	June	July	August
M	1 8 15 22 29	5 12 19 26	3 10 17 24 31	7 14 21 28
T	2 9 16 23 30	6 13 20 27	4 11 18 25	1 8 15 22 29
W	3 10 17 24 31	7 14 21 28	5 12 19 26	2 9 16 23 30
T	4 11 18 25	1 8 15 22 29	6 13 20 27	3 10 17 24 31
F	5 12 19 26	2 9 16 23 30	7 14 21 28	4 11 18 25
S	6 13 20 27	3 10 17 24	1 8 15 22 29	5 12 19 26
S	7 14 21 28	4 11 18 25	2 9 16 23 30	6 13 20 27

	September	October	November	December
M	4 11 18 25	2 9 16 23 30	6 13 20 27	4 11 18 25
T	5 12 19 26	3 10 17 24 31	7 14 21 28	5 12 19 26
W	6 13 20 27	4 11 18 25	1 8 15 22 29	6 13 20 27
T	7 14 21 28	5 12 19 26	2 9 16 23 30	7 14 21 28
F	1 8 15 22 29	6 13 20 27	3 10 17 24	1 8 15 22 29
S	2 9 16 23 30	7 14 21 28	4 11 18 25	2 9 16 23 30
S	3 10 17 24	1 8 15 22 29	5 12 19 26	3 10 17 24 31

2

	January	February	March	April
M	1 8 15 22 29	5 12 19 26	5 12 19 26	2 9 16 23 30
T	2 9 16 23 30	6 13 20 27	6 13 20 27	3 10 17 24
W	3 10 17 24 31	7 14 21 28	7 14 21 28	4 11 18 25
T	4 11 18 25	1 8 15 22	1 8 15 22 29	5 12 19 26
F	5 12 19 26	2 9 16 23	2 9 16 23 30	6 13 20 27
S	6 13 20 27	3 10 17 24	3 10 17 24 31	7 14 21 28
S	7 14 21 28	4 11 18 25	4 11 18 25	1 8 15 22 29

	May	June	July	August
M	7 14 21 28	4 11 18 25	2 9 16 23 30	6 13 20 27
T	1 8 15 22 29	5 12 19 26	3 10 17 24 31	7 14 21 28
W	2 9 16 23 30	6 13 20 27	4 11 18 25	1 8 15 22 29
T	3 10 17 24 31	7 14 21 28	5 12 19 26	2 9 16 23 30
F	4 11 18 25	1 8 15 22 29	6 13 20 27	3 10 17 24 31
S	5 12 19 26	2 9 16 23 30	7 14 21 28	4 11 18 25
S	6 13 20 27	3 10 17 24	1 8 15 22 29	5 12 19 26

	September	October	November	December
M	3 10 17 24	1 8 15 22 29	5 12 19 26	3 10 17 24 31
T	4 11 18 25	2 9 16 23 30	6 13 20 27	4 11 18 25
W	5 12 19 26	3 10 17 24 31	7 14 21 28	5 12 19 26
T	6 13 20 27	4 11 18 25	1 8 15 22 29	6 13 20 27
F	7 14 21 28	5 12 19 26	2 9 16 23 30	7 14 21 28
S	1 8 15 22 29	6 13 20 27	3 10 17 24	1 8 15 22 29
S	2 9 16 23 30	7 14 21 28	4 11 18 25	2 9 16 23 30

I13: Perpetual calendar

3

```
        January          February           March             April
M    7 14 21 28       4 11 18 25         4 11 18 25       1  8 15 22 29
T  1 8 15 22 29       5 12 19 26         5 12 19 26       2  9 16 23 30
W  2 9 16 23 30       6 13 20 27         6 13 20 27       3 10 17 24
T  3 10 17 24 31      7 14 21 28         7 14 21 28       4 11 18 25
F  4 11 18 25       1 8 15 22          1 8 15 22 29       5 12 19 26
S  5 12 19 26       2 9 16 23          2 9 16 23 30       6 13 20 27
S  6 13 20 27       3 10 17 24         3 10 17 24 31      7 14 21 28

          May             June              July             August
M    6 13 20 27       3 10 17 24         1  8 15 22 29      5 12 19 26
T    7 14 21 28       4 11 18 25         2  9 16 23 30      6 13 20 27
W  1 8 15 22 29       5 12 19 26         3 10 17 24 31      7 14 21 28
T  2 9 16 23 30       6 13 20 27         4 11 18 25       1 8 15 22 29
F  3 10 17 24 31      7 14 21 28         5 12 19 26       2 9 16 23 30
S  4 11 18 25       1 8 15 22 29         6 13 20 27       3 10 17 24 31
S  5 12 19 26       2 9 16 23 30         7 14 21 28       4 11 18 25

        September         October          November          December
M    2 9 16 23 30      7 14 21 28         4 11 18 25       2 9 16 23 30
T    3 10 17 24      1 8 15 22 29         5 12 19 26       3 10 17 24 31
W    4 11 18 25      2 9 16 23 30         6 13 20 27       4 11 18 25
T    5 12 19 26      3 10 17 24 31        7 14 21 28       5 12 19 26
F    6 13 20 27      4 11 18 25        1 8 15 22 29        6 13 20 27
S    7 14 21 28      5 12 19 26        2 9 16 23 30        7 14 21 28
S  1 8 15 22 29      6 13 20 27        3 10 17 24        1 8 15 22 29
```

4

```
        January          February           March             April
M    6 13 20 27       3 10 17 24         3 10 17 24 31      7 14 21 28
T    7 14 21 28       4 11 18 25         4 11 18 25       1 8 15 22 29
W  1 8 15 22 29       5 12 19 26         5 12 19 26       2 9 16 23 30
T  2 9 16 23 30       6 13 20 27         6 13 20 27       3 10 17 24
F  3 10 17 24 31      7 14 21 28         7 14 21 28       4 11 18 25
S  4 11 18 25       1 8 15 22         1 8 15 22 29        5 12 19 26
S  5 12 19 26       2 9 16 23         2 9 16 23 30        6 13 20 27

          May             June              July             August
M    5 12 19 26       2 9 16 23 30        7 14 21 28       4 11 18 25
T    6 13 20 27       3 10 17 24       1 8 15 22 29        5 12 19 26
W    7 14 21 28       4 11 18 25       2 9 16 23 30        6 13 20 27
T  1 8 15 22 29       5 12 19 26       3 10 17 24 31       7 14 21 28
F  2 9 16 23 30       6 13 20 27       4 11 18 25        1 8 15 22 29
S  3 10 17 24 31      7 14 21 28       5 12 19 26        2 9 16 23 30
S  4 11 18 25       1 8 15 22 29       6 13 20 27        3 10 17 24 31

        September         October          November          December
M  1 8 15 22 29        6 13 20 27         3 10 17 24       1 8 15 22 29
T  2 9 16 23 30        7 14 21 28         4 11 18 25       2 9 16 23 30
W  3 10 17 24        1 8 15 22 29         5 12 19 26       3 10 17 24 31
T  4 11 18 25        2 9 16 23 30         6 13 20 27       4 11 18 25
F  5 12 19 26        3 10 17 24 31        7 14 21 28       5 12 19 26
S  6 13 20 27        4 11 18 25        1 8 15 22 29        6 13 20 27
S  7 14 21 28        5 12 19 26        2 9 16 23 30        7 14 21 28
```

5

```
        January          February           March             April
M    5 12 19 26       2 9 16 23          2 9 16 23 30       6 13 20 27
T    6 13 20 27       3 10 17 24         3 10 17 24 31      7 14 21 28
W    7 14 21 28       4 11 18 25         4 11 18 25       1 8 15 22 29
T  1 8 15 22 29       5 12 19 26         5 12 19 26       2 9 16 23 30
F  2 9 16 23 30       6 13 20 27         6 13 20 27       3 10 17 24
S  3 10 17 24 31      7 14 21 28         7 14 21 28       4 11 18 25
S  4 11 18 25       1 8 15 22         1 8 15 22 29        5 12 19 26

          May             June              July             August
M    4 11 18 25     1 8 15 22 29         6 13 20 27         3 10 17 24 31
T    5 12 19 26     2 9 16 23 30         7 14 21 28         4 11 18 25
W    6 13 20 27     3 10 17 24        1 8 15 22 29          5 12 19 26
T    7 14 21 28     4 11 18 25        2 9 16 23 30          6 13 20 27
F  1 8 15 22 29     5 12 19 26        3 10 17 24 31         7 14 21 28
S  2 9 16 23 30     6 13 20 27        4 11 18 25          1 8 15 22 29
S  3 10 17 24 31    7 14 21 28        5 12 19 26          2 9 16 23 30

        September         October          November          December
M    7 14 21 28       5 12 19 26         2 9 16 23 30        7 14 21 28
T  1 8 15 22 29       6 13 20 27         3 10 17 24       1 8 15 22 29
W  2 9 16 23 30       7 14 21 28         4 11 18 25       2 9 16 23 30
T  3 10 17 24       1 8 15 22 29         5 12 19 26       3 10 17 24 31
F  4 11 18 25       2 9 16 23 30         6 13 20 27       4 11 18 25
S  5 12 19 26       3 10 17 24 31        7 14 21 28       5 12 19 26
S  6 13 20 27       4 11 18 25        1 8 15 22 29        6 13 20 27
```

6

```
        January          February           March             April
M    4 11 18 25     1 8 15 22          1 8 15 22 29         5 12 19 26
T    5 12 19 26     2 9 16 23          2 9 16 23 30         6 13 20 27
W    6 13 20 27     3 10 17 24         3 10 17 24 31        7 14 21 28
T    7 14 21 28     4 11 18 25         4 11 18 25        1 8 15 22 29
F  1 8 15 22 29     5 12 19 26         5 12 19 26        2 9 16 23 30
S  2 9 16 23 30     6 13 20 27         6 13 20 27        3 10 17 24
S  3 10 17 24 31    7 14 21 28         7 14 21 28        4 11 18 25

          May             June              July             August
M    3 10 17 24 31     7 14 21 28         5 12 19 26       2 9 16 23 30
T    4 11 18 25     1 8 15 22 29         6 13 20 27        3 10 17 24 31
W    5 12 19 26     2 9 16 23 30         7 14 21 28        4 11 18 25
T    6 13 20 27     3 10 17 24        1 8 15 22 29         5 12 19 26
F    7 14 21 28     4 11 18 25        2 9 16 23 30         6 13 20 27
S  1 8 15 22 29     5 12 19 26        3 10 17 24 31        7 14 21 28
S  2 9 16 23 30     6 13 20 27        4 11 18 25         1 8 15 22 29

        September         October          November          December
M    6 13 20 27       4 11 18 25       1 8 15 22 29         6 13 20 27
T    7 14 21 28       5 12 19 26       2 9 16 23 30         7 14 21 28
W  1 8 15 22 29       6 13 20 27       3 10 17 24         1 8 15 22 29
T  2 9 16 23 30       7 14 21 28       4 11 18 25         2 9 16 23 30
F  3 10 17 24       1 8 15 22 29       5 12 19 26         3 10 17 24 31
S  4 11 18 25       2 9 16 23 30       6 13 20 27         4 11 18 25
S  5 12 19 26       3 10 17 24 31      7 14 21 28         5 12 19 26
```

7

```
        January          February           March             April
M    3 10 17 24 31     7 14 21 28         7 14 21 28       4 11 18 25
T    4 11 18 25     1 8 15 22          1 8 15 22 29        5 12 19 26
W    5 12 19 26     2 9 16 23          2 9 16 23 30        6 13 20 27
T    6 13 20 27     3 10 17 24         3 10 17 24 31       7 14 21 28
F    7 14 21 28     4 11 18 25         4 11 18 25        1 8 15 22 29
S  1 8 15 22 29     5 12 19 26         5 12 19 26        2 9 16 23 30
S  2 9 16 23 30     6 13 20 27         6 13 20 27        3 10 17 24

          May             June              July             August
M    2 9 16 23 30     6 13 20 27         4 11 18 25       1 8 15 22 29
T    3 10 17 24 31    7 14 21 28         5 12 19 26       2 9 16 23 30
W    4 11 18 25     1 8 15 22 29         6 13 20 27       3 10 17 24 31
T    5 12 19 26     2 9 16 23 30         7 14 21 28       4 11 18 25
F    6 13 20 27     3 10 17 24        1 8 15 22 29        5 12 19 26
S    7 14 21 28     4 11 18 25        2 9 16 23 30        6 13 20 27
S  1 8 15 22 29     5 12 19 26        3 10 17 24 31       7 14 21 28

        September         October          November          December
M    5 12 19 26       3 10 17 24 31        7 14 21 28       5 12 19 26
T    6 13 20 27       4 11 18 25       1 8 15 22 29         6 13 20 27
W    7 14 21 28       5 12 19 26       2 9 16 23 30         7 14 21 28
T  1 8 15 22 29       6 13 20 27       3 10 17 24         1 8 15 22 29
F  2 9 16 23 30       7 14 21 28       4 11 18 25         2 9 16 23 30
S  3 10 17 24       1 8 15 22 29       5 12 19 26         3 10 17 24 31
S  4 11 18 25       2 9 16 23 30       6 13 20 27         4 11 18 25
```

8

```
        January          February           March             April
M    2 9 16 23 30      6 13 20 27         5 12 19 26       2 9 16 23 30
T    3 10 17 24 31     7 14 21 28         6 13 20 27       3 10 17 24
W    4 11 18 25     1 8 15 22 29          7 14 21 28       4 11 18 25
T    5 12 19 26     2 9 16 23          1 8 15 22 29        5 12 19 26
F    6 13 20 27     3 10 17 24          2 9 16 23 30       6 13 20 27
S    7 14 21 28     4 11 18 25          3 10 17 24 31      7 14 21 28
S  1 8 15 22 29     5 12 19 26          4 11 18 25       1 8 15 22 29

          May             June              July             August
M    7 14 21 28       4 11 18 25         2 9 16 23 30       6 13 20 27
T  1 8 15 22 29       5 12 19 26         3 10 17 24 31      7 14 21 28
W  2 9 16 23 30       6 13 20 27         4 11 18 25       1 8 15 22 29
T  3 10 17 24 31      7 14 21 28         5 12 19 26       2 9 16 23 30
F  4 11 18 25       1 8 15 22 29         6 13 20 27       3 10 17 24 31
S  5 12 19 26       2 9 16 23 30         7 14 21 28       4 11 18 25
S  6 13 20 27       3 10 17 24        1 8 15 22 29        5 12 19 26

        September         October          November          December
M    3 10 17 24      1 8 15 22 29         5 12 19 26       3 10 17 24 31
T    4 11 18 25      2 9 16 23 30         6 13 20 27       4 11 18 25
W    5 12 19 26      3 10 17 24 31        7 14 21 28       5 12 19 26
T    6 13 20 27      4 11 18 25        1 8 15 22 29        6 13 20 27
F    7 14 21 28      5 12 19 26        2 9 16 23 30        7 14 21 28
S  1 8 15 22 29      6 13 20 27        3 10 17 24        1 8 15 22 29
S  2 9 16 23 30      7 14 21 28        4 11 18 25        2 9 16 23 30
```

9

	January	February	March	April
M	1 8 15 22 29	5 12 19 26	4 11 18 25	1 8 15 22 29
T	2 9 16 23 30	6 13 20 27	5 12 19 26	2 9 16 23 30
W	3 10 17 24 31	7 14 21 28	6 13 20 27	3 10 17 24
T	4 11 18 25	1 8 15 22 29	7 14 21 28	4 11 18 25
F	5 12 19 26	2 9 16 23	1 8 15 22 29	5 12 19 26
S	6 13 20 27	3 10 17 24	2 9 16 23 30	6 13 20 27
S	7 14 21 28	4 11 18 25	3 10 17 24 31	7 14 21 28

	May	June	July	August
M	6 13 20 27	3 10 17 24	1 8 15 22 29	5 12 19 26
T	7 14 21 28	4 11 18 25	2 9 16 23 30	6 13 20 27
W	1 8 15 22 29	5 12 19 26	3 10 17 24 31	7 14 21 28
T	2 9 16 23 30	6 13 20 27	4 11 18 25	1 8 15 22 29
F	3 10 17 24 31	7 14 21 28	5 12 19 26	2 9 16 23 30
S	4 11 18 25	1 8 15 22 29	6 13 20 27	3 10 17 24 31
S	5 12 19 26	2 9 16 23 30	7 14 21 28	4 11 18 25

	September	October	November	December
M	2 9 16 23 30	7 14 21 28	4 11 18 25	2 9 16 23 30
T	3 10 17 24	1 8 15 22 29	5 12 19 26	3 10 17 24 31
W	4 11 18 25	2 9 16 23 30	6 13 20 27	4 11 18 25
T	5 12 19 26	3 10 17 24 31	7 14 21 28	5 12 19 26
F	6 13 20 27	4 11 18 25	1 8 15 22 29	6 13 20 27
S	7 14 21 28	5 12 19 26	2 9 16 23 30	7 14 21 28
S	1 8 15 22 29	6 13 20 27	3 10 17 24	1 8 15 22 29

10

	January	February	March	April
M	7 14 21 28	4 11 18 25	3 10 17 24 31	7 14 21 28
T	1 8 15 22 29	5 12 19 26	4 11 18 25	1 8 15 22 29
W	2 9 16 23 30	6 13 20 27	5 12 19 26	2 9 16 23 30
T	3 10 17 24 31	7 14 21 28	6 13 20 27	3 10 17 24
F	4 11 18 25	1 8 15 22 29	7 14 21 28	4 11 18 25
S	5 12 19 26	2 9 16 23	1 8 15 22 29	5 12 19 26
S	6 13 20 27	3 10 17 24	2 9 16 23 30	6 13 20 27

	May	June	July	August
M	5 12 19 26	2 9 16 23 30	7 14 21 28	4 11 18 25
T	6 13 20 27	3 10 17 24	1 8 15 22 29	5 12 19 26
W	7 14 21 28	4 11 18 25	2 9 16 23 30	6 13 20 27
T	1 8 15 22 29	5 12 19 26	3 10 17 24 31	7 14 21 28
F	2 9 16 23 30	6 13 20 27	4 11 18 25	1 8 15 22 29
S	3 10 17 24 31	7 14 21 28	5 12 19 26	2 9 16 23 30
S	4 11 18 25	1 8 15 22 29	6 13 20 27	3 10 17 24 31

	September	October	November	December
M	1 8 15 22 29	6 13 20 27	3 10 17 24	1 8 15 22 29
T	2 9 16 23 30	7 14 21 28	4 11 18 25	2 9 16 23 30
W	3 10 17 24	1 8 15 22 29	5 12 19 26	3 10 17 24 31
T	4 11 18 25	2 9 16 23 30	6 13 20 27	4 11 18 25
F	5 12 19 26	3 10 17 24 31	7 14 21 28	5 12 19 26
S	6 13 20 27	4 11 18 25	1 8 15 22 29	6 13 20 27
S	7 14 21 28	5 12 19 26	2 9 16 23 30	7 14 21 28

11

	January	February	March	April
M	6 13 20 27	3 10 17 24	2 9 16 23 30	6 13 20 27
T	7 14 21 28	4 11 18 25	3 10 17 24 31	7 14 21 28
W	1 8 15 22 29	5 12 19 26	4 11 18 25	1 8 15 22 29
T	2 9 16 23 30	6 13 20 27	5 12 19 26	2 9 16 23 30
F	3 10 17 24 31	7 14 21 28	6 13 20 27	3 10 17 24
S	4 11 18 25	1 8 15 22 29	7 14 21 28	4 11 18 25
S	5 12 19 26	2 9 16 23	1 8 15 22 29	5 12 19 26

	May	June	July	August
M	4 11 18 25	1 8 15 22 29	6 13 20 27	3 10 17 24 31
T	5 12 19 26	2 9 16 23 30	7 14 21 28	4 11 18 25
W	6 13 20 27	3 10 17 24	1 8 15 22 29	5 12 19 26
T	7 14 21 28	4 11 18 25	2 9 16 23 30	6 13 20 27
F	1 8 15 22 29	5 12 19 26	3 10 17 24 31	7 14 21 28
S	2 9 16 23 30	6 13 20 27	4 11 18 25	1 8 15 22 29
S	3 10 17 24 31	7 14 21 28	5 12 19 26	2 9 16 23 30

	September	October	November	December
M	7 14 21 28	5 12 19 26	2 9 16 23 30	7 14 21 28
T	1 8 15 22 29	6 13 20 27	3 10 17 24	1 8 15 22 29
W	2 9 16 23 30	7 14 21 28	4 11 18 25	2 9 16 23 30
T	3 10 17 24	1 8 15 22 29	5 12 19 26	3 10 17 24 31
F	4 11 18 25	2 9 16 23 30	6 13 20 27	4 11 18 25
S	5 12 19 26	3 10 17 24 31	7 14 21 28	5 12 19 26
S	6 13 20 27	4 11 18 25	1 8 15 22 29	6 13 20 27

12

	January	February	March	April
M	5 12 19 26	2 9 16 23	1 8 15 22 29	5 12 19 26
T	6 13 20 27	3 10 17 24	2 9 16 23 30	6 13 20 27
W	7 14 21 28	4 11 18 25	3 10 17 24 31	7 14 21 28
T	1 8 15 22 29	5 12 19 26	4 11 18 25	1 8 15 22 29
F	2 9 16 23 30	6 13 20 27	5 12 19 26	2 9 16 23 30
S	3 10 17 24 31	7 14 21 28	6 13 20 27	3 10 17 24
S	4 11 18 25	1 8 15 22 29	7 14 21 28	4 11 18 25

	May	June	July	August
M	3 10 17 24 31	7 14 21 28	5 12 19 26	2 9 16 23 30
T	4 11 18 25	1 8 15 22 29	6 13 20 27	3 10 17 24 31
W	5 12 19 26	2 9 16 23 30	7 14 21 28	4 11 18 25
T	6 13 20 27	3 10 17 24	1 8 15 22 29	5 12 19 26
F	7 14 21 28	4 11 18 25	2 9 16 23 30	6 13 20 27
S	1 8 15 22 29	5 12 19 26	3 10 17 24 31	7 14 21 28
S	2 9 16 23 30	6 13 20 27	4 11 18 25	1 8 15 22 29

	September	October	November	December
M	6 13 20 27	4 11 18 25	1 8 15 22 29	6 13 20 27
T	7 14 21 28	5 12 19 26	2 9 16 23 30	7 14 21 28
W	1 8 15 22 29	6 13 20 27	3 10 17 24	1 8 15 22 29
T	2 9 16 23 30	7 14 21 28	4 11 18 25	2 9 16 23 30
F	3 10 17 24	1 8 15 22 29	5 12 19 26	3 10 17 24 31
S	4 11 18 25	2 9 16 23 30	6 13 20 27	4 11 18 25
S	5 12 19 26	3 10 17 24 31	7 14 21 28	5 12 19 26

13

	January	February	March	April
M	4 11 18 25	1 8 15 22 29	7 14 21 28	4 11 18 25
T	5 12 19 26	2 9 16 23	1 8 15 22 29	5 12 19 26
W	6 13 20 27	3 10 17 24	2 9 16 23 30	6 13 20 27
T	7 14 21 28	4 11 18 25	3 10 17 24 31	7 14 21 28
F	1 8 15 22 29	5 12 19 26	4 11 18 25	1 8 15 22 29
S	2 9 16 23 30	6 13 20 27	5 12 19 26	2 9 16 23 30
S	3 10 17 24 31	7 14 21 28	6 13 20 27	3 10 17 24

	May	June	July	August
M	2 9 16 23 30	6 13 20 27	4 11 18 25	1 8 15 22 29
T	3 10 17 24 31	7 14 21 28	5 12 19 26	2 9 16 23 30
W	4 11 18 25	1 8 15 22 29	6 13 20 27	3 10 17 24 31
T	5 12 19 26	2 9 16 23 30	7 14 21 28	4 11 18 25
F	6 13 20 27	3 10 17 24	1 8 15 22 29	5 12 19 26
S	7 14 21 28	4 11 18 25	2 9 16 23 30	6 13 20 27
S	1 8 15 22 29	5 12 19 26	3 10 17 24 31	7 14 21 28

	September	October	November	December
M	5 12 19 26	3 10 17 24 31	7 14 21 28	5 12 19 26
T	6 13 20 27	4 11 18 25	1 8 15 22 29	6 13 20 27
W	7 14 21 28	5 12 19 26	2 9 16 23 30	7 14 21 28
T	1 8 15 22 29	6 13 20 27	3 10 17 24	1 8 15 22 29
F	2 9 16 23 30	7 14 21 28	4 11 18 25	2 9 16 23 30
S	3 10 17 24	1 8 15 22 29	5 12 19 26	3 10 17 24 31
S	4 11 18 25	2 9 16 23 30	6 13 20 27	4 11 18 25

14

	January	February	March	April
M	3 10 17 24 31	7 14 21 28	6 13 20 27	3 10 17 24
T	4 11 18 25	1 8 15 22 29	7 14 21 28	4 11 18 25
W	5 12 19 26	2 9 16 23	1 8 15 22 29	5 12 19 26
T	6 13 20 27	3 10 17 24	2 9 16 23 30	6 13 20 27
F	7 14 21 28	4 11 18 25	3 10 17 24 31	7 14 21 28
S	1 8 15 22 29	5 12 19 26	4 11 18 25	1 8 15 22 29
S	2 9 16 23 30	6 13 20 27	5 12 19 26	2 9 16 23 30

	May	June	July	August
M	1 8 15 22 29	5 12 19 26	3 10 17 24 31	7 14 21 28
T	2 9 16 23 30	6 13 20 27	4 11 18 25	1 8 15 22 29
W	3 10 17 24 31	7 14 21 28	5 12 19 26	2 9 16 23 30
T	4 11 18 25	1 8 15 22 29	6 13 20 27	3 10 17 24 31
F	5 12 19 26	2 9 16 23 30	7 14 21 28	4 11 18 25
S	6 13 20 27	3 10 17 24	1 8 15 22 29	5 12 19 26
S	7 14 21 28	4 11 18 25	2 9 16 23 30	6 13 20 27

	September	October	November	December
M	4 11 18 25	2 9 16 23 30	6 13 20 27	4 11 18 25
T	5 12 19 26	3 10 17 24 31	7 14 21 28	5 12 19 26
W	6 13 20 27	4 11 18 25	1 8 15 22 29	6 13 20 27
T	7 14 21 28	5 12 19 26	2 9 16 23 30	7 14 21 28
F	1 8 15 22 29	6 13 20 27	3 10 17 24	1 8 15 22 29
S	2 9 16 23 30	7 14 21 28	4 11 18 25	2 9 16 23 30
S	3 10 17 24	1 8 15 22 29	5 12 19 26	3 10 17 24 31

I14: Table of Religious Festivals

2005		
P	Birthday of Guru Gobind Singh	January 5
☾	Eid al-Adha	January 10
✝	Ash Wednesday	February 9
☾	New Year	February 10
ॐ	Holi	March 25
✝	Good Friday	March 25
✝	Easter Sunday	March 27
✝	Easter Monday	March 28
✡	Purim	March 25
P	Hola Mohalla	March 26
P	Baisakhi Day	April 13
☾	Mawlid	April 21
✡	Passover	April 24
✝	Ascension Day	May 5
✝	Pentecost	May 15
✡	Shavuot	June 13
✡	Rosh Hashanah	October 4
☾	Ramadan begins	October 5
ॐ	Dasarah	October 12
✡	Yom Kippur	October 13
✡	Succot	October 18
ॐ	Diwali	November 1
☾	Eid al-Fitr	November 4
P	Birthday of Guru Nanak	November 15
✝	Christmas Day	December 25
✡	Chanukah	December 26

2006		
P	Birthday of Guru Gobind Singh	January 5
☾	New Year	January 31
✝	Ash Wednesday	March 1
✡	Purim	March 14
ॐ	Holi	March 14
P	Hola Mohalla	March 15
☾	Mawlid	April 11
P	Baisakhi Day	April 13
✡	Passover	April 13
✝	Good Friday	April 14
✝	Easter Sunday	April 16
✝	Easter Monday	April 17
✝	Ascension Day	May 25
✡	Shavuot	June 2
✝	Pentecost	June 4
✡	Rosh Hashanah	September 23
☾	Ramadan begins	September 24
ॐ	Dasarah	October 2
✡	Yom Kippur	October 2
✡	Succot	October 7
ॐ	Diwali	October 21
☾	Eid al-Fitr	October 24
P	Birthday of Guru Nanak	November 5
✡	Chanukah	December 16
✝	Christmas Day	December 25
☾	Eid al-Adha	December 31

2007		
P	Birthday of Guru Gobind Singh	January 5
☾	New Year	January 20
✝	Ash Wednesday	February 21
ॐ	Holi	February 25
✡	Purim	March 4
P	Hola Mohalla	March 4
☾	Mawlid	March 31
✡	Passover	April 3
✝	Good Friday	April 6
✝	Easter Sunday	April 8
✝	Easter Monday	April 9
P	Baisakhi Day	April 13
✝	Ascension Day	May 17
✡	Shavuot	May 23
✝	Pentecost	May 27
☾	Ramadan begins	September 13
✡	Rosh Hashanah	September 13
✡	Yom Kippur	September 22
✡	Succot	October 4
☾	Eid al-Fitr	October 13
ॐ	Dasarah	October 21
ॐ	Diwali	November 9
P	Birthday of Guru Nanak	November 24
✡	Chanukah	December 5
☾	Eid al-Adha	December 20
✝	Christmas Day	December 25

✝ Christian
ॐ Hindu
✡ Jewish
☾ Muslim
P Sikh

Note: all Islamic and Jewish holidays begin at sundown on the preceding day.

115: Medical reference intervals and scales

Haematology – reference intervals

Measurement	Reference interval
White cell count	$4.0–11.0 \times 10^9/l$
Red cell count – Male:	$4.5–6.5 \times 10^{12}/l$
Female:	$3.9–5.6 \times 10^{12}/l$
Haemoglobin – Male:	13.5–18.0g/dl
Female:	11.5–16.0g/dl
Platelet count	$150.0–400.0 \times 10^9/l$
Erythrocyte sedimentation rate (ESR) – Male:	Up to age in years divided by 2.
Female:	Up to (age in years plus 10) divided by 2.
Prothrombin time (factors II, VII, X)	10–14 seconds
Activated partial thromboplastin time (VIII, IX, XI, XII)	35–45 seconds

Proposed therapeutic ranges for prothrombin time (British Society for Haematology guidelines on oral anticoagulants, 1984)

British ratio (INR)	Clinical state
2.0–2.5	Prophylaxis of deep vein thrombosis including high risk surgery (e.g. for fractured femur).
2.5–3.0	Treatment of deep vein thrombosis, pulmonary embolism, transient ischaemic attacks.
3.0–4.5	Recurrent deep vein thrombosis and pulmonary embolism; arterial disease including myocardial infarction; arterial grafts; cardiac prosthetic valves and grafts.

Cerebrospinal fluid – reference intervals

Opening pressure (mmCSF)	Infants: < 80; children: < 90; adults: < 210

Substance	Reference interval
Glucose	3.3–4.4 mmol/l or $\geq$ 2/3 of plasma glucose
Chloride	122–128 mmol/l
Lactate	< 2.8 mmol/l

Biochemistry – reference intervals

Substance	Specimen	Reference Interval
Albumin	P	*35–50 g/l
α-amylase	P	0–180 Somogyi U/dl
Bicarbonate	P	*24–30 mmol/l
Calcium (ionised)	P	1.0–1.25 mmol/l
Calcium (total)	P	*2.12–2.65 mmol/l
Chloride	P	95–105 mmol/l
Cholesterol	P	3.9–7.8 mmol/l
Creatinine	P	*70–150 mmol/l
Glucose (fasting)	P	3.5–5.5 mmol/l
Glycosylated haemoglobin	B	5–8%
Phosphate	P	0.8–1.45 mmol/l
Potassium	P	3.5–5.0 mmol/l
Protein (total)	P	60–80 g/l
Sodium	P	*135–145 mmol/l
Urea	P	*2.5–6.7 mmol/l

Key: P = plasma; B = whole blood

*Reference intervals for these substances differ in pregnancy. Reference intervals in pregnancy are not reproduced here.

Arterial blood gases – reference intervals

pH:	7.35–7.45
PaO_2:	> 10.6 kPa
$PaCO_2$:	4.7–6.0 kPa
Base excess	± 2 mmol/l

NB: 7.6 mmHg = 1 kPa (atmospheric pressure = 100 kPa)

Apgar scoring chart

A baby's condition is assessed at 1 and 5 minutes after birth by means of the Apgar score. This system observes five signs. A score of nought, one or two is awarded for each sign.

Sign	0	1	2
Heart rate	Absent	Slow (below 100)	Over 100
Respiratory effort	Absent	Weak cry, hypoventilation	Good cry
Muscle tone	Limp	Some flexion of extremities	Well flexed
Reflex irritability	No response	Some motion	Cry
Colour	Blue, pale	Body pink, extremities blue	Completely pink

NB: An Apgar score of 10 represents optimal condition. A score of 3 or less indicates a markedly asphyxiated infant.

Glasgow coma scale

Three types of response are assessed:

	Score	
Best motor response	6	Obeys commands
	5	Localises to pain
	4	Flexion/withdrawal to pain
	3	Abnormal flexion
	2	Abnormal extension
	1	None
Best verbal response	5	Oriented
	4	Confused
	3	Inappropriate words
	2	Incomprehensible sounds
	1	None
Eye opening	4	Spontaneously
	3	To speech
	2	To pain
	1	None

The overall score is the sum of the scores in each area, *e.g.* no response to pain + no verbal response + no eye opening = 3.

In severe injury the score is 8 or under.
In moderate injury the score is 9–12.
In minor injury the score is 13–15.

I16: Web Sites

Useful web sites

Site	Address
Acts of Parliament	www.opsi.gov.uk/acts.htm
American Academy of Matrimonial Lawyers	www.aaml.org
Australasian Legal Information Institute	www.austlii.edu.au
Bank of England	www.bankofengland.co.uk
Bar Council	www.barcouncil.org.uk
British and Irish Legal Information Institute	www.bailii.org
CGT Indexation Allowance	www.number7.demon.co.uk/cgt/allow.htm
Child Support Agency	www.csa.gov.uk
Child Support Commissioners' Decisions	www.hywels.clara.co.uk/commrs/decns.htm
Companies House	www.companies-house.gov.uk
Court of Justice of the European Communities	www.europa.eu.int/cj/en/index.htm
Court Service	www.courtservice.gov.uk
Crossroads Caring for Carers	www.crossroads-wirral.org.uk
Service Legal Information Portal	www.courtservice.gov.uk/lexicon/
Delia Venables Legal Resources	www.venables.co.uk
Department for Constitutional Affairs	www.dca.gov.uk
DCA Human Rights site	www.dca.gov.uk/hract/hramenu.htm
Department of Social Security (Press Releases)	www.gov.im/dhss/
Electronic Share Information (iii)	www.iii.co.uk
European Court of Human Rights	www.echr.coe.int
Financial Times	www.ft.com
Government Actuary's Department	www.gad.gov.uk
Government Information Service	www.direct.gov.uk
Hague Conference on Private International Law	www.hcch.net/index_en.php
Hague Convention on Child Abduction	www.hcch.e-vision.nl/index_en.php?act=text.display&tid=21
Hansard: House of Commons Debates	www.publications.parliament.uk/pa/cm/cmhansrd.htm
House of Lords Debates	www.parliament.the-stationery-office.co.uk/pa/ld/ldhansrd.htm
H.M. Land Registry	www.landreg.gov.uk
H.M.S.O.	www.hmso.gov.uk
Home Office Human Rights Unit	www.homeoffice.gov.uk/inside/org/dob/direct/dcou.html
House of Commons	www.parliament.uk/about_commons/about_commons.CFM
House of Lords	www.parliament.uk/about-lords/about-lords.cfm
Judgments	www.privy-council.org.uk/output/Page31.asp
House Price Indices (Halifax)	www.halifax.co.uk
Information for Lawyers	www.infolaw.co.uk
Inland Revenue	www.inlandrevenue.gov.uk
International Academy of Matrimonial Lawyers	www.iaml.org
Judge Overend's homepage (CPR and Human Rights)	www.beagle.org.uk
Laurie West-Knight's homepage	www.lawonline.cc
Law Society	www.lawsociety.org.uk
Legal Services Commission	www.legalservices.gov.uk/
Life Assurance quotations	www.royalsunalliance.co.uk
National Savings	www.nationalsavings.co.uk
Official Solicitor	www.offsol.demon.co.uk
Pension annuity quotes	www.annuity-bureau.co.uk
RPI (full table)	www.devon-cc.gov.uk/dris/economic/retprice.html
Smith Bernal (transcripts of judgments)	www.smithbernal.com
Solicitors' Family Law Association	www.sfla.org.uk
Statutory Instruments	www.legislation.hmso.gov.uk/stat.htm
Sweet & Maxwell	www.sweetandmaxwell.co.uk
The Times	www.timesonline.co.uk
UK Parliament	www.parliament.uk
Upmystreet (regional data)	www.upmystreet.com

I17: Addresses of useful organisations

Part 1 – Medical

British Medical Association

BMA House
Tavistock Square
London WC1H 9JP
Tel: 020 7387 4499
Fax: 020 7383 6400
Email: info.web@bma.org.uk

General Dental Council

37 Wimpole Street
London W1G 8DQ
Tel: 020 7887 3800
Fax: 020 7224 3294
Email: information@gdc-uk.org

Accident and emergency

British Association for Accident and
Emergency Medicine
The Royal College of Surgeons of England
35–43 Lincoln's Inn Fields
London WC2A 3PN
Tel: 020 7831 9405
Fax: 020 7405 0318
Email: baem1@compuserve.com

Accidents

Royal Society for the Prevention of
Accidents (RoSPA)
Edgbaston Park
353 Bristol Road
Edgbaston
Birmingham B5 7ST
Tel: 0121 248 2000
Fax: 0121 248 2001
Email: help@rospa.co.uk

Alcoholism

Medical Council on Alcohol
3 St. Andrew's Place
Regent's Park
London NW1 4LB
Tel: 020 7487 4445
Fax: 020 7935 4479
Email: mca@medicouncilalcol.demon.co.uk

General Medical Council

Regent's Place
350 Euston Road
London NW1 3JN
Tel: 020 7580 7642
Fax: 020 7915 3641
Email: webmaster@gmc-uk.org

General Optical Council

41 Harley Street
London W1G 8DJ
Tel: 020 7580 3898
Fax: 020 7436 3525
Email: goc@optical.org

Alzheimer's disease

Alzheimer's Disease Society
Gordon House
10 Greencoat Place
London SW1P 1PH
Tel: 020 7306 0606
Fax: 020 7306 0808
Email: info@alzheimers.org.uk

Anaesthetics

Obstetric Anaesthetists' Association
PO Box 3219
London SW13 9XR
Tel: 020 8741 1311
Fax: 020 8741 0611
Email: secretariat@oaa-anaes.ac.uk

Asthma

National Asthma Campaign
Providence House
Providence Place
London N1 0NT
Tel: 020 7226 2260
Fax: 020 7704 0740
Email: enquiries@asthma.org.uk

Bereavement

Child Bereavement Trust
Aston House
High Streeet
West Wycombe
High Wycombe
Buckinghamshire HP14 3AG
Tel: 01494 446 648
Fax: 01494 440 057
Email: enquiries@childbereavement.org.uk

The Compassionate Friends
(counselling for bereaved parents)
National Office
53 North Street
Bristol BS3 1EN
Tel: 08451 203785
Fax: 08451 203786
Email: info@tcf.org.uk

Biochemistry

Biochemical Society
Third Floor, Eagle Society
16 Procter Street
London WC1V 6NX
Tel: 020 7580 5530
Fax: 020 7637 3626
Email: genadmin@biochemistry.org

Blindness

Royal National Institute of the Blind
105 Judd Street
London WC1H 9NE
Tel: 020 7388 1266
Fax: 020 7388 2034
Email: helpline@rnib.org.uk

Brain

Brain Research Trust
15 Southampton Place
London
WC1A 2AJ
Tel: 020 7404 9982
Fax: 020 7404 9983
Email: info@brt.org.uk

British Association of Brain Injury Case
Managers (BABICAM)
PO Box 1800
Salisbury
Wiltshire
SP1 2XH
Tel: 0700 2222 426

Centre for Brain Injury, Rehabilitation and
Development (BIRD)
131 Main Road
Broughton
Chester
CH4 0NR
Tel: 01244 532 047
Fax: 01244 538 723
Email: admin@b-i-r-d.org.uk

Brittle bone disease

Brittle Bone Society
30 Guthrie Street
Dundee
Tayside DD1 5BS
Tel: 01382 204 446
Fax: 01382 206 771
Email: bbs@brittlebone.org

Cancer

British Association of Cancer United Patients
(BACUP)
3 Bath Place
Rivington Street
London EC2A 3DR
Tel: 020 7696 9003
Fax: 020 7696 9002

BASO – The Association for Cancer Surgery
Royal College of Surgeons
35–43 Lincoln's Inn Fields
London WC2A 3PE
Tel: 020 7405 5612
Fax: 020 7404 6574

CancerLink
11–21 North Down Street
London N1 9BN
Tel: 020 7833 2818
Fax: 020 7833 4963
Email: cancerlink@cancerlink.org.uk

Macmillan Cancer Relief
89 Albert Embankment
London SE1 7UQ
Tel: 020 7840 7840
Fax: 020 7840 7841

Cancer Research UK
P.O. Box 123
Lincoln's Inn Fields
London WC2A 3PX
Tel: 020 7242 0200
Fax: 020 7269 3100

Marie Curie Cancer Care
89 Albert Embankment
London SE1 7TP
Tel: 020 7599 7777
Fax: 020 7599 7708
Email: info@mariecurie.org.uk

Cardiology

British Cardiac Society
9 Fitzroy Square
London W1T 5HW
Tel: 020 7383 3887
Fax: 020 7388 0903
Email: enquiries@bcs.com

British Heart Foundation
14 Fitzhardinge Street
London W1H 6DH
Tel: 020 7935 0185
Fax: 020 7486 5820
Email: internet@bhfs.org.uk

Society of Cardiothoracic Surgeons of Great
Britain & Northern Ireland
The Royal College of Surgeons
35–43 Lincoln's Inn Fields
London WC2A 3PE
Tel: 020 7869 6893
Fax: 020 7869 6890
Email: sctsadmin@scts.org

Childbirth

The Association for Post-Natal Illness
145 Dawes Road
London SW6 7EB
Tel: 020 7386 0868
Fax: 020 7386 8885
Email: info@apni.org

The National Childbirth Trust
Alexandra House
Oldham Terrace
London W3 6NH
Tel: 0870 770 3236
Fax: 0870 770 3237
Email: enquiries@national-childbirth-trust.co.uk

Royal College of Midwives
15 Mansfield Street
London W1G 9NH
Tel: 020 7312 3535
Fax: 020 7312 3536
Email: info@rcm.org.uk

Stillbirth and Neonatal Death Society (SANDS)
28 Portland Place
London W1N 4DE
Tel: 020 7436 5881
Fax: 020 7436 3715
Email: support@UK-sands.org

Children

The National Association for Children with
Lower Limb Abnormalities (STEPS)

Lymm Court
11 Eagle Brow
Lymm
Cheshire WA13 OLP
Tel/Fax: 0871 717 0045
Email: info@steps-charity.org.uk

Barnado's
Tanner's Lane
Barkingside
Ilford
Essex IG6 1QG
Tel: 020 8550 8822
Fax: 020 8551 6870
Website: barnados.org.uk

Baby Life Support Systems (Bliss)
2nd Floor, 89 Albert Embankment
London SE1 7TP
Tel: 0870 770 0337
Fax: 0870 770 0338
Email: information@bliss.org.uk

Child Accident Prevention Trust
4th Floor
Clerks Court
18–20 Farringdon Lane
London EC1R 3HA
Tel: 020 7608 3828
Fax: 020 7608 3674
Email: safe@capt.org.uk

Child Poverty Action Group (CPAG)
94 White Lion Street
London N1 9PF
Tel: 020 7837 7979
Fax: 020 7837 6414
Email: staff@cpag.demon.co.uk

(see also **Paediatric**)

Chiropody

Institute of Chiropodists & Podiatrics
27 Wright Street
Southport
Merseyside PR9 OTL
Tel: 01704 546 141
Fax: 01704 500 477
Email: secretary@inst-chiropodist.org.uk

Society of Chiropodists & Podiatrists
1 Fellmongers Pass
Tower Bridge Road
London SE1 3LY
Tel: 020 7234 8620
Fax: 020 7234 8621
Website: feetforlife.org

Colostomy

British Colostomy Association
15 Station Road
Reading RG1 1LG
Tel: 0118 939 1537
Fax: 0118 956 9095
Email: sue@bcass.org.uk

Counselling

British Association for Counselling and
Psychotherapy
BACP House
35–37 Albert Street
Rugby
Warwickshire CV21 2SG
Tel: 0870 443 5252
Email: bacp@bacp.co.uk

Cystic fibrosis

Cystic Fibrosis Trust
11 London Road
Bromley
Kent BR1 1BY
Tel: 020 8464 7211
Fax: 020 8313 0472

Day surgery

British Association of Day Surgery
The Royal College of Surgeons
35–43 Lincoln's Inn Fields
London WC2A 3PN
Tel: 020 7973 0308
Fax: 020 7973 0314
Email: bads@bads.co.uk

Deafness

Royal Association in Aid of Deaf People
Walsingham Road
Colchester CO2 7BP
Tel: 01206 509 509
Fax: 01206 769 755
Email: info@royaldeaf.org.uk

Royal National Institute for Deaf People
19–23 Featherstone Street
London EC1Y 8SL
Tel: 020 7296 8000
Minicom: 020 7296 8001
Fax: 020 7296 8199
Email: informationline@rnid.org.uk

Dentists

British Dental Association
64 Wimpole Street
London W1G 8YS
Tel: 020 7935 0875
Fax: 020 7487 5232
Email: enquiries@bda.org

Dermatology

British Association of Dermatologists
19 Fitzroy Square
London W1T 6EH
Tel: 020 7383 0266
Fax: 020 7388 5263
Email: admin@bad.org.uk

Development

British Association for Developmental
Disabilities
5 Handsworth Drive
Great Barr
Birmingham B43 6ED
Tel/Fax: 0121 360 2027

Diabetes

Diabetes UK Central Office
Macleod House
10 Parkway
London NW1 7AA
Tel: 020 7424 1000
Fax: 020 7424 1001
Email: info@diabetes.org.uk

Diagnostics

Cellmark Diagnostics
PO Box 265
Abingdon
OX14 1YX
Tel: 01235 528 000
Fax: 01235 528 141
Email: cellmark@orchid.co.uk

University Diagnostics Ltd
Queens Road
Teddington
Middx TW11 0NJ
Tel: 020 8943 8400
Email: udl@lgc.co.uk

Dietetics

British Dietetic Association
5th Floor Charles House
148–9 Great Charles Street

Queensway
Birmingham B3 3HT
Tel: 0121 200 8080
Fax: 0121 200 8081
Email: info@bda.uk.com

British Nutrition Foundation
High Holborn House
52–54 High Holborn
London WC1V 6RQ
Tel: 020 7404 6504
Fax: 020 7404 6747
Email: postbox@nutrition.org.uk

Digestion

Digestive Disorders Foundation
3 Saint Andrew's Place
London NW1 4LB
Tel: 020 7486 0341
Fax: 020 7224 2012
Email: ddf@digestivedisorders.org.uk

Disability

Disabled Living Foundation
380–384 Harrow Road
London W9 2HU
Tel: 020 7289 6111
Fax: 020 7226 2922 [111]
Email: info@dlf.org.uk

Royal Association for Disability and
Rehabilitation (RADAR)
12 City Forum
250 City Road
London
EC1V 8AF
Tel: 020 72503222
Fax: 020 72500212
Email: radar@radar.org.uk

Changing Faces

(Charity for Facially Disfigured People)
The Squire Centre
33–37 University Street
London WC1E 6JN
Tel: 0845 4500 275
Fax: 0845 4500 276

Down's Syndrome

Down's Syndrome Association (DSA)
Langdon Down Centre
2a Langdon Park
Teddington TW11 9PS
Tel: 020 8682 4001
Fax: 020 8682 4012
Email: info@downs-syndrome.org.uk

Drugs

Committee on Safety of Medicines (for
adverse reaction reports)
1 Nine Elms Lane
London SW8 5NQ
Tel: 020 7273 0451
Fax: 020 7273 0453

Narcotics Abusers' Register
Chief Medical Officer
Home Office Drugs Branch
Queen Anne's Gate
London SW1H 9AT
Tel: 020 7273 3302

Dyslexia

Dyslexia Institute
Park House
Wick Road
Egham
Surrey TW20 0HH
Tel: 01784 463 851
Fax: 01784 460 747
Email: info@dyslexia-inst.org.uk

Ear, nose and throat

British Association of Otorhinolaryngologists
The Royal College of Surgeons
35–43 Lincoln's Inn Fields
London WC2A 3PE
Tel: 020 7404 8373
Fax: 020 7404 4200
Email: orl@bao-hns.demon.co.uk

(see also **Deafness**)

Elderly

British Geriatrics Society
31 St John's Square
London EC1M 4DN
Tel: 020 7608 1369
Fax: 020 7608 1041
Email: info@bgs.org.uk

British Association for Service to the Elderly
119 Hassell Street
Newcastle under Lyme
Staffordshire ST5 1AX
Tel/Fax: 01782 661 033

Endocrinology

Society for Endocrinology
22 Apex Court
Woodlands
Bradley Stoke
Bristol BS32 4JT
Tel: 01454 642 200
Fax: 01454 642 222
Email: info@endocrinology.org

Epilepsy

British Epilepsy Association
New Anstey House
Gate Way Drive
Yeadon
Leeds LS19 7XY
Tel: 0113 210 8800
Fax: 0113 391 0300
Email: epilepsy@bea.org.uk

Forensic science

British Academy of Forensic Sciences
Anaesthetic Unit
London Hospital Medical Unit
London E1 1BB
Tel: 020 7377 9201

Gastroenterology

British Society of Gastroenterology
3 Saint Andrew's Place
Regent's Park
London NW1 4LB
Tel: 020 7387 3534
Fax: 020 7487 3734
Email: bsg@mailbox.ulcc.ac.uk

Glaucoma

International Glaucoma Association
108c Warner Road
Camberwell
London SE5 9HQ
Tel: 020 7737 3265
Fax: 020 7346 5929
Email: info@iga.org.uk

General information

Health Information (will provide a wide
range of health information for both
doctors and their patients)
The Mapels
Level 2
The Lister Hospital
Coreys Mill Lane
Stevenage
Hertfordshire SG1 4AB
Tel: 0800 665544

Haematology

British Society for Haematology
2 Carlton House Terrace
London SW1Y 5AF
Tel: 020 8643 7305
Fax: 020 8770 0933
Email: Janice@bsh8ya.demon.co.uk

Haemophilia

British Society for Haemophilia
96–100 White Lion Street
London N1 9PF
Tel: 020 7380 0600
Fax: 020 7387 8220
Email: info@haemophilia.org.uk

Hand surgery

British Society of Surgery of the Hand
Royal College of Surgeons
37–43 Lincoln's Inn Fields
London WC2A 3PL
Tel: 020 7831 5162
Fax: 020 7831 4041
Email: secretariat@bssh.ac.uk

Head injuries

Headway (National Head Injuries Association)
200 Mansfield Road
Nottingham
NG1 3HX
Tel: 0115 924 0800
Email: enquiries@headway.org

Health visitors

Community Practitioners' Health Visitors
Association
40 Bermondsey Street
London SE1 3UD
Tel: 020 7939 7000
Fax: 020 7403 2964
website: msfcphva.org

Hysterectomy

Hysterectomy Association
60 Redwood House
Charlton Down
Dorchester
Dorset DT2 9UH
Tel: 0871 7811141
Email: info@hysterectomy-association.org.uk

Injury

(See **Rehabilitation**)

Kidneys

National Kidney Federation
6 Stanley Street
Worksop
Nottinghamshire S81 7HU
Tel: 01909 487 795
Email: webmaster@kidney.org.uk

The National Kidney Research Fund
Kings Chambers
Priestgate
Peterborough PE1 1FG
Tel: 01733 704670
Fax: 01733 704692
Email: enquiries@nfrf.org.uk

Lungs

(See **Thoracic**)

Lupus

Lupus U.K.
103 Lee Moor Road
Stanley
Wakefield
West Yorkshire WF3 4EQ
Tel: 01708 731 251
Fax: 01708 731 252

Maxillofacial surgery

(See **Oral**)

M.E.

Myalgic Encephalomyelitis Association
4 Top Angel
Buckingham MK18 1TH
Tel: 01375 361013
Email: enquiries@meassociation.org.uk

Medicine

Committee on Safety of Medicines
Market Towers
1 Nine Elms Lane
London SW8 5NQ
Tel: 020 7273 0451
Fax: 020 7273 0493
Email: leslie.whitbread@mca.gov.uk

Medical Society of London
Lettsom House
11 Chandos Street
London W1G 9EB
Tel: 020 7580 1043
Fax: 020 7580 5793

Medicines Commission
1 Nine Elms Lane
London SW8 5NQ
Fax: 020 7218 3093
Email: info@mhra.gsi.gov.uk

The Royal Society of Medicine
1 Wimpole Street
London W1G 0AE
Tel: 020 7290 2900

Meningitis

The National Meningitis Trust
Fern House
Bath Road
Stroud
Gloucestershire GLS 3TJ
Tel: 01453 768 000
Fax: 01453 768 001
Email: support@meningitis-trust.org.uk

Menopause (Premature)

The Amarant Trust
18 Chiswick Staithe
London WH4 3TB
Tel: 01293 413 000 (Advice Line)
Website: www.amarantmenopausetrust.org.uk

Mental health

National Association for Mental Health
(MIND)
Granta House
15/19 Broadway
London E15 4BQ
Tel: 020 8519 2122
Fax: 020 8522 1725
Email: contact@mind.org.uk

Royal Society for Mentally Handicapped
Children and Adults (MENCAP)
Mencap National Centre
123 Golden Lane
London EC1Y 0RT
Tel: 020 7454 0454
Email: information@mencap.org.uk

Midwives

(See **Childbirth**)

Migraine

Migraine Trust
55–56 Russell Square
London WC1B 4HP
Tel: 020 7831 4818
Fax: 020 7831 5174
Email: info@migrainenetrust.org

Motor Neurone Disease

Motor Neurone Disease Association
PO Box 246
Northampton NN1 2PR
Tel: 01604 250505
Tel: 0345 626262 (helpline)
Fax: 01604 638289/624726
Email: enquiries@mndassociation.org

Multiple Sclerosis

Multiple Sclerosis Society of Great Britain &
Northern Ireland
372 Edgware Road
London NW2 6ND
Tel: 020 8438 0700
Fax: 020 8430 0701
Email: info@mssociety.org.uk

Muscular Dystrophy

Muscular Dystrophy Group
7–11 Prescott Place
London SW4 6BS
Tel: 020 7720 8055
Fax: 020 7498 0670
Email: info@muscular-dystrophy.org

Narcolepsy

The Narcolepsy Association (U.K.)
Cherry Orchard Cottage,
50–52 Culver Street
Newent
Gloucestershire GL18 1DA
Tel: 020 7721 8904
Fax: 01322 863 056 (020 7721 8009)
Email: narcolepsy@btinternet.com

Neurology

Association of British Neurologists
27 Boswell Street
London WC1W 3JZ
Tel: 020 7405 4060
Fax: 020 7405 4070
Email: info@theabn.org

Neurosurgery

Society of British Neurological Surgeons
Dept. of Neurosurgery
Manchester Royal Infirmary
Oxford Road
Manchester M13 9WL
Tel: 0161 276 4567
Fax: 0161 276 4681

Nursing

Royal College of Nursing of the United
Kingdom
20 Cavendish Square
London W1M 0AB
Tel: 020 7409 3333
Fax: 020 7647 3435
Website: rcn.org.uk

BNA Care Assessment Services
The Colonnades
Beaconsfield Close
Hatfield
Hertfordshire AL10 8YD
Tel: 01707 255 658
Fax: 01707 255 660
Website: care.assessment.bna.co.uk

Crossroads Caring for Carers

10 Regent Place
Rugby
Warwickshire CU21 2PN
Tel: 0845 450 0350
Fax: 01788 565 498
Email: communications@crossroads.org.uk

Occupational medicine

Society of Occupational Medicine
6 Saint Andrew's Place
Regent's Park
London NW1 4LB
Tel: 020 7486 2641
Fax: 020 7486 0028
Email: som@sococcmed.demon.co.uk

Occupational therapy

British Association of Occupational Therapists/
College of Occupational Therapists
106–114 Borough High Street
Southwark
London SE1 1LB
Tel: 020 7357 6480
Website: cot.co.uk

Oncology

(See **Cancer**)

Oral

British Association of Oral & Maxillofacial
Surgeons
Royal College of Surgeons
35–43 Lincoln's Inn Fields
London WC2A 3PN
Tel: 020 7405 8074
Fax: 020 7430 9997
Email: baoms@netcomuk.co.uk

British Society for Oral Medicine
Dr David Felix
Glasgow Dental Hospital
378 Sauchiehall Street
Glasgow G2 3GZ
Tel: 0141 211 9654
Fax: 0141 353 2899
Email: d.h.felix@doctors.org.uk

Orthopaedic

British Orthopaedic Association
Royal College of Surgeons
35–43 Lincoln's Inn Fields
London WC2A 3PN
Tel: 020 7405 6507
Fax: 020 7831 2676
Email: secretary@boa.ac.uk

Osteoporosis

National Osteoporosis Society
Camerton
Bath BA2 OPJ
Tel: 01761 471 771
Fax: 01761 471 104
Website: nos.org.uk
Email: info@nos.org.uk

Pain

The Pain Society
21 Portland Place
London W1B 1PY
Tel: 020 7631 8870
Fax: 020 7323 2015
Email: info@painsociety.org

National Back Pain Association
16 Elmtree Road
Teddington
Middlesex TW11 8ST
Tel: 020 8977 5474
Fax: 020 8943 5318
Email: back-pain@compuserve.com

Bamstead Mobility Centre
Damson Way
Orchard Hill
Queen Mary's Avenue
Carshalton
Surrey SM5 4NR
Tel: 020 8770 1151
Fax: 020 8770 1211
Email: info@mobility-ge.com

Parkinson's disease

Parkinson's Disease Society of the United
Kingdom Ltd
215 Vauxhall Bridge Road
London SW1V 1EJ
Tel: 020 7931 8080
Fax: 020 7233 9908
Email: enquiries@parkinsons.org.uk

Pathology

Pathological Society of Great Britain &
Ireland
2 Carlton House Terrace
London SW1Y 5AF
Tel: 020 7976 1260
Fax: 020 7976 1267
Email: admin@pathsoc.org.uk

Royal College of Pathologists
2 Carlton House Terrace
London SW1Y 5AF
Tel: 020 7451 6700
      7451 6701
Fax: 020 9767 1267
Email: admin@pathsoc.org.uk

Patients

Patients Association
PO Box 935
Harrow HA1 3YJ
Tel: 020 8423 9119

Physiotherapy

Chartered Society of Physiotherapy
14 Bedford Row
London WC1R 4ED
Tel: 020 7306 6666
Fax: 020 7306 6611
Email: csp@csphysio.org.uk

Plastic surgery

British Association of Plastic Surgeons
The Royal College of Surgeons
35–43 Lincoln's Inn Fields
London WC2A 3PN
Tel: 020 7831 5161/2
Fax: 020 7831 4041
Email: secretariat@bat.co.uk

Polio

British Polio Fellowship
Ground Floor
Unit A
Eagle Office Centre
The Runway
South Ruislip
Middlesex HA4 6SE
Tel: 020 8842 4999
Fax: 020 8842 0555
Email: info@britishpolio.org

Post-natal illness

(See **Childbirth**)

Psoriasis

Psoriasis Association
7 Milton Street
Northampton NN2 7JG
Tel: 01604 711129
Fax: 01604 792894
Email:psoriasis.demon.co.uk

Psychiatry

Royal College of Psychiatrists
17 Belgrave Square
London SW1X 8PG
Tel: 020 7235 2351
Fax: 020 7245 1231
Email: rcpsyche@rcpsych.ac.uk

Psychology

British Psychological Society
Saint Andrew's House
48 Princess Road East
Leicester LE1 7DR
Tel: 0116 2529 520
Fax: 0116 2470 787
Email: mail@bps.org.uk

David McGlown
Clinical Psychologist Public Trust Office
Stewart House
24 Kingsway
London WC2B 6JX
Tel: 020 7269 7085

Psychotherapy

British Association of Psychotherapists
37 Mapesbury Road
London NW2 4HJ
Tel: 020 8452 9823
Fax: 020 8452 5182
Email: mail@bap-psychotherapy.org

Radiography and Radiology

Society and College of Radiographers
207 Providence Square
Mill Street
London SE1 2EW
Tel: 020 7740 7200
Fax: 020 7740 7233
Email: info@sor.org

Royal College of Radiologists
38 Portland Place
London W1N 4JQ
Tel: 020 7636 4432
Fax: 020 7323 3100
Email: enquiries@rcr.ac.uk

Rehabilitation

British Society of Rehabilitation Medicine
c/o Royal College of Physicians
11 Saint Andrew's Place
London NW1 4LE
Tel/Fax: 01992 638 865
Email: admin@bsm.co.uk

REMEDI (Rehabilitation and Medical
Research Trust for Relief of Disability)
14 Crondace Road
London SW6 4BB
Tel: 01761 470 662
Fax: 01761 470 662
Email: g.coles-remedi@btinternet.com

The Injury Care Clinics Ltd
The Hollies
Dog Lane
Nether Whitcare
Birmingham
West Midlands B46 2DT
Tel: 0239 283 6780
Fax: 0239 221 9522
Email: info@ticcs.co.uk

Research

Medical Research Society
3 Littleton Road
Harrow
Middlesex HA1 3SY
Tel: 020 8743 2030
Fax: 020 8846 7447

Rheumatology

British Society for Rheumatology
41 Eagle Street
London WC1R 4TL
Tel: 020 7242 3313
Fax: 020 7242 3277
Email: bsr@rheumatology.org.uk

Schizophrenia

National Schizophrenia Fellowship
28 Castle Street
Kingston-upon-Thames
Surrey KT1 1SS
Tel: 020 8547 3937 (General Enquiries)
Tel: 020 8974 8614
Fax: 020 8547 3862

SCOPE

Scope (formerly The Spastics Society)
Flat 6
12 Market Square
London N7 9PW
Tel: 020 7619 7100
  0808 800333 (Helpline: 11am–9pm
  Mon–Fri, 2–6pm weekend)
Fax: 020 7619 7399

Speech

Royal College of Speech & Language
Therapists
2/3 White Hart Yard
London SE1 1NX
Tel: 020 7378 1200
Fax: 020 7403 7254
Email: postmaster@rcslt.org

Association for all Speech-Impaired
Children (AFASIC)
2nd Floor
50–52 Great Sutton Street
London EC1V 0DJ
Tel: 020 7236 3632
Fax: 020 7236 8115

Spinal injuries

Spinal Injuries Association
Acorn House
387–391 Midsummer Boulevard
Milton Keynes MK9 3HP
Tel: 01908 608 492
Email: sia@spinal.co.uk

(See also **Back pain** under **Pain**)

Stroke

The Stroke Association
Stroke House
240 City Road
London EC1V 2PR
Tel: 020 7566 0300
Fax: 020 7490 2686
Email: stroke@stroke.org.uk

Torture

Medical Foundation for the Care of Victims
of Torture
111 Isledon Road
London NW7 7JW
Tel: 020 769 77762
Fax: 020 769 77739

Thoracic

British Thoracic Society
17 Doughty Street
London WC1N 2PL
Tel: 020 7831 8778
Fax: 020 7831 8766
Email: admin1@brit-thoracic.org.uk

British Lung Foundation
Lung Foundation House
73–75 Goswell Road
London EC1V 7ER
Tel: 020 7688 5555
Email: blf@britishlungfoundation.com

Society of Cardiothoracic Surgeons of Great
Britain & Ireland
35–43 Lincoln's Inn Fields
London WC2A 3PE
Tel: 020 7869 6893
Fax: 020 7869 6890
Email: sctsadmin@scts.org

(See also **Asthma**)

Transplants

U.K. Transplant
Foxden Road
Stoke Gifford BS34 8RR
Tel: 0117 975 7574
Fax: 0117 975 7577
Email: infoexec@ukfsa-info.demon.co.uk

Tropical Medicine

Liverpool School of Tropical Medicine
Pembroke Place
Liverpool L3 5QA
Tel: 0151 708 9393
Fax: 0151 708 8733

London School of Hygiene and Tropical
Medicine
Keppel Street
London WC1E 7HT
Tel: 020 7636 8636
Fax: 020 7436 5389

Malaria Reference Laboratory (for advice
on prophylaxis)
Tel: 020 7636 7921
Website: www.malaria-reference.co.uk

Urology

British Association of Urological Surgeons
Royal College of Surgeons
35–43 Lincoln's Inn Fields
London WC2A 3PE
Tel: 020 7869 6950
Fax: 020 7404 5048
Email: admin@baus.org.uk

Part 2 – Litigation

Action Against Medical Accidents (AVMA)

44 High St
Croydon
Surrey CR0 17B
Tel: 020 8688 9555
Fax: 020 8667 9065
Website: www.avma.org.uk

Association of Personal Injury Lawyers (APIL)

11 Castle Quay
Nottingham NG7 1FW
Tel: 0115 958 0585
Fax: 0115 958 0595
Email: mail@apil.com

Association of Trial Lawyers of America

PO Box 3717
Washington DC 20007
USA
Tel: 001 202 965 3500
Email: help@atlahq.org

Clinical Disputes Forum

Chairman: Dr Alastair Scotland
Medical Director and Chief Officer
National Clinical Assessment Authority
9th Floor, Market Towers
London SW8 5NQ
Tel: 020 7273 0850

Secretary: Sarah Leigh
c/o Margaret Dangoor
3 Clydesdale Gardens
Richmond
Surrey TW10 5EG
Tel: 020 8408 1012

Compensation Recovery Unit (CRU)

Compensation Recovery Unit
Durham House
Washington
Tyne & Wear NE38 7SF
Tel: 0191 225 2005
Fax: 0191 225 2048
Email: cru-customer-services@mso2.dss.gsi.gov.uk

Disability Law Service

(free advice for the disabled on legal matters, benefits and grants)
39–45 Cavell Street
London E1 2BP
Tel: 020 7791 9824
Fax: 020 7791 9802

General Council of the Bar

3 Bedford Row
London WC1R 4DB
Tel: 020 7242 0082
Fax: 020 7831 9217
Email: generaloffice@barcouncil.org.uk

Incorporated Council of Law Reporting for England and Wales

Megarry House
119 Chancery Lane
London WC2A 1PP
Tel: 020 7242 6471
Fax: 020 7831 5247
Email: postmaster@iclr.co.uk

Inquest

89–93 Fronthill Road
London N4 3JH
Tel: 020 7263 1111
Email: inquest@inquest.org.uk

Law Society

113 Chancery Lane
London WC2A 1PL
Tel: 020 7242 1222
Fax: 020 7831 0344

Legal Services Commisson

Legal Services Commission Head Office
85 Gray's Inn Road
London WC1X 8TX
Tel: 020 7759 0000
Website: legalservices.gov.uk

Legal Services Commission London/South
Eastern Group Area Offices (Area No. 1)
29–37 Red Lion Street
London WC1R 4PP
Tel: 020 7813 5300

Legal Services Commission (Area No. 2)
Invicta House
Trafalgar Place
Cheapside
Brighton BN1 4FR
Tel: 01273 878800

Legal Services Commission (Area No. 3)
80 Kings Road
Reading RG1 4LT
Tel: 0117 921 4801

Legal Services Commission Wales and the
West Group Area Offices (Area No. 4)
33–35 Queen Square
Bristol BS1 4LU
Tel: 0117 302 3000

Legal Services Commission (Area No. 5)
Marland House
Central Square
Cardiff CF1 1PF
Tel: 02920 647 100

Legal Services Commission Midlands Group
Area Offices (Area No. 6)
Centre-City Podium
5 Hill Street
Birmingham B5 4UD
Tel: 0121 665 4700

Legal Services Commission (Area No. 7)
2nd Floor Lee House
90 Great Bridewater Street
Manchester M1 5JW
Tel: 0161 244 5000

Legal Services Commission (Area No. 8)
Eagle Star House
Fenkle Street
Newcastle NE1 5RU
Tel: 0191 232 3461

Legal Services Commission (Area No. 9)
Harcourt House
Chanceller House
21 The Calls
Leeds LS2 7EH
Tel: 0113 390 7300

Legal Services Commission (Area No. 10)
1st Floor
Fothergill House
16 King Street
Nottingham NG1 2AS
Tel: 0115 908 4200

Legal Services Commission (Area No. 11)
62–68 Hills Road
Cambridge CB2 1LA
Tel: 01223 366 511

Legal Services Commission North Western
Group Area Offices (Area No. 12)
2nd Floor
Pepper House
Pepper Row
Chester CH1 1DW
Tel: 01244 3154 55

Legal Services Commission (Area No. 15)
Cavern Court
8 Matthew Street
Liverpool L2 6RE
Tel: 0151 242 5200

Medical Defence Union

230 Blackfriars Road
London SE1 8PG
Tel: 020 7202 1500
Fax: 020 7202 1666
Website: v-mdu.com

The Medical Protection Society Ltd

33 Cavendish Square
London W1G OPS
Tel: 0845 605 4000
Fax: 020 7399 1301
Email: info@mps.org.uk

Medico-Legal Society

Dr Jill Crombie
20 Embankment Place
London WC2N 6NN
Tel: 020 839 0278
Email: jlc@hempsons.co.uk

Motor Insurers Bureau

6–12 Capital Drive
Milton Keynes MK14 6XT
Tel: 01908 830 001
Fax: 01908 671 681
Website: www.mib.org.uk

National Association of Guardians ad Litem and Reporting Officers (NAGLRO)

PO Box 264
Esher
Surrey KT10 0WA
Tel: 01372 818504

Official Solicitor to the Supreme Court

81 Chancery Lane
London WC2A 1DD
Tel: 020 7911 7127
Fax: 020 7911 7105
Email: enquiries@offsol.gsi.gov.uk

The Patients' Association

PO Box 935
Harrow HA1 3YJ
Tel: 020 8423 9111
Fax: 020 8423 9119
Email: mailbox@patients-association.com

Personal Injury Bar Association (PIBA)

Richard Methuen QC
12 Kings Bench Walk
Temple
London EC4Y 7EL
Tel: 020 7353 5892
Email: clerk@oldsquarechambers.co.uk

Professional Negligence Bar Association (PNBA)

Andrew Goodman
No. 1 Serjeants Inn
London EC4Y 1LH
Tel: 020 7415 6666 (Enquiries)
Email: agoodman@no1serjeantsinn.com

Prevention of Professional Abuse Network

Delta House
175–177 Borough High Street
London SE1 1HR
Tel: 020 7939 9920
Email: popau@easynet.co.uk

Smith Bernal Reporting Ltd

(Court of Appeal Transcribers)
190 Fleet Street
London EC4A 2AG
Tel: 020 7404 1400
Fax: 020 7404 1424
Email: mail@smithbernal.com

Part 3 – Government

Commission for Local Administration in England

(Local Government Ombudsman)
10th Floor, Millbank Tower
Millbank
London SW1P 4QP
Tel: 020 7217 4620
Fax: 020 7217 4621

Department of Health

Richmond House
79 Whitehall
London SW1A 2NS
Tel: 020 7210 4850
Email: dhmail@doh.gov.uk

Department of Work and Pensions

Correspondence Unit
Room 112 The Adelphi
1–11 Adam Street
London WC2N 6HT
Tel: 020 7712 2171
Fax: 020 7712 2386
Website: www.dwp.gov.uk

Department of Health Social Care Group

Richmond House
79 Whitehall
London SW1A 2NS
Tel: 020 7210 4850

Health & Safety Executive

Bootle Information Centre
Health & Safety Executive
Magdalen House
Trinity Road
Bootle, Merseyside L20 3QZ
Tel: 01787 881 165
Fax: 01787 313 995
Email: hse.books@prolog.uk.com

HSE Information Centre

Caerphilly Business Park
Caerphilly CF83 3GG
Tel: 08701 345 500
Fax: 02920 859 260
Email: hse.books@prolog.uk.com

Health and Safety Executive – Health Policy Division

Rose Court
2 Southwark Bridge
London SE1 9HS
Tel: 020 7717 6000 (Head Office)
Fax: 020 7717 6717

Home Office

Home Office Direct Communications Unit
2 Marsham Street
London SW1P 4DF
Tel: 0870 000 1585
Email: public.enquiries@homeoffice.gsi.gov.uk

HM Inspector of Anatomy

Dept. of Health
Rm 311 Wellington House
133–155 Waterloo Road
London SE1 8UG
Tel: 020 7972 4551
Fax: 020 7972 4791
Email: khuscrof@doh.gov.uk

Lord Chancellor's Department

Selbourne House
54–60 Victoria Street
London SW1E 6QW
Tel: 020 7210 8614
Email: dcaweb.comments@dca.gsi.gov.uk

Mental Health Act Commission

Maid Marian House
56 Houndsgate
Nottingham NG1 6BG
Tel: 0115 943 7100
Fax: 0115 943 7101
Email: chiefexec@mhac.trent.mhs.uk

Mental Welfare Commission for Scotland

K Floor, Argyle House
3 Lady Lawson Street
Edinburgh EH3 9SH
Tel: 0131 222 6111
Fax: 0131 222 6112
Email: enquiries@mwcscot.org.uk

Ministry of Defence Medical Services Directorate

Lacon House
Theobalds Road
London WC1X 8RY

National Blood Authority

Oak House
Reeds Crescent
Watford WD24 4QN
Tel: 01923 486 800
Fax: 01923 486 801
Website: blooddonor.org.uk

Scottish Office Home and Health Department

1 Melville Crescent
Edinburgh EH3 7HW
Tel: 0131 244 9010
Fax: 0131 244 7059
Email: sharon.nicol@scotland.gov.uk

London Office: Dover House
Whitehall
London SW1A 2AU
Tel: 020 7270 6754
Fax: 020 7270 6812
Email: scottish.secretary@scotland.gsi.gov.uk

Scottish National Blood Transfusion Service

21 Ellen's Glen Road
Edinburgh EH17 7QT
Tel: 0131 536 5700
Fax: 0131 536 5781

United Kingdom Central Council for Nursing, Midwifery and Health Visiting

23 Portland Place
London W1N 3AF
Tel: 020 7637 7181
Website: ukcc.org.uk

Part 4 – Courts and Tribunals

Judicial Office of the House of Lords

London SW1A 0PW
Tel: 020 7219 3000

Court of Appeal

Civil Division
Room E330
Royal Courts of Justice
Strand
London WC2A 2LL
Tel: 020 7947 6000 (Listings Office)

High Court of Justice

Royal Courts of Justice
Strand
London WC2A 2LL
Tel: 020 7947 6000 (General Office)

Court of Protection

Archway Tower
2 Junction Road
London N19 5SZ
Tel: 020 7664 7178
Fax: 020 7664 7705
Website: publictrust.gov.uk

Criminal Injuries Compensation Authority (CICA)

Tay House
300 Bath Street
Glasgow G2 4LN
Tel: 0141 331 2726
Fax: 0141 331 2287

Part 5 – Other

Child Action Poverty Group

94 White Lion Street
London N1 9PF
Tel: 020 7837 7979
Fax: 020 7837 6414

Fostering Network

87 Blackfriars Road
London SE1 8HA
Tel: 020 7620 6400
Fax: 020 7620 6401

Leonard Cheshire Foundation

26-29 Maunsel House
London SW1P 2QN
Tel: 020 7828 1822
Email: info@k-uk.org

The Bank of England

Threadneedle Street
London EC2R 8AH
Tel: 020 7601 4444